DESKTOP PUBLISHING

BY DESIGN

▲▲▲▲▲▲▲▲▲▲▲▲▲▲▲▲▲▲▲▲▲

DESKTOP PUBLISHING
BY DESIGN

▲▲▲▲▲▲▲▲▲▲▲▲▲▲▲▲▲▲▲

Blueprints for Page Layout
Using
Aldus® PageMaker®
on IBM® and
Apple® Macintosh®
Computers.
Includes
Hands-On
Projects.

Ronnie Shushan
and
Don Wright

PUBLISHED BY
Microsoft Press
A Division of Microsoft Corporation
16011 NE 36th Way, Box 97017, Redmond, Washington 98073-9717

Library of Congress Cataloging in Publication Data
Shushan, Ronnie.
Desktop publishing by design.
Includes index.
1. Desktop publishing.   2. PageMaker (Computer program)
3. IBM Personal Computer—Programming.   4. Macintosh (Computer)—Programming.
5. Printing, Practical—Layout—Data Processing.   I. Wright, Don, date.
II. Title.
Z286.D47S59   1989   686.2'2   88-27367
ISBN 1-55615-134-9

Printed and bound in the United States of America.

1 2 3 4 5 6 7 8 9   MLML   3 2 1 0 9

Distributed to the book trade in the United States
by Harper & Row.

Distributed to the book trade in Canada by General
Publishing Company, Ltd.

Distributed to the book trade outside the United States
and Canada by Penguin Books Ltd.

Penguin Books Ltd., Harmondsworth, Middlesex, England
Penguin Books Australia Ltd., Ringwood, Victoria, Australia
Penguin Books N.Z. Ltd., 182–190 Wairau Road, Auckland 10, New Zealand

British Cataloging in Publication Data available

Editor: Rebecca Pepper   Production Editor: Mary Ann Jones

To all the pioneers

scientists and artists
engineers and designers
programmers and publishers

who have shown the way

▶▶▶ CONTENTS ◀◀◀

Acknowledgments

No advances in technology will ever replace the information and experience shared by colleagues or the support and contribution of publishing professionals throughout the development, production, and marketing of a book such as this. Our thanks to:

All of the designers who took the time to send us their work and talk with us about their experiences.

Vicki Farmer at Aldus Corporation and David Doty, editor and publisher of *ThePage*, for putting us on to many of those designers.

John Odam, who provided answers and inspiration.

David Pope, for encouraging us to make the leap.

The technical support crew at Aldus, whose help with everything from naive questions to near catastrophes was invaluable.

The technical support staff at Jasmine Technologies, who were always willing to answer questions that extended beyond matters concerning their hard disks.

All of the manufacturers and publishers who sent books and software for evaluation. Thanks especially to Henry Niles and John Taylor at Moniterm and to James McNaul at DataCopy, for equipment loans that dramatically increased our production efficiency.

Richard DiLorenzo and Jim Lawton at Microcomputer Publishing, for technical assistance in producing the type samples in Chapter 2.

Rebecca Pepper and Mary Ann Jones, our editors at Microsoft Press, for their careful and thoughtful comments and for their patience with the unorthodox, circular fashion in which the book developed. (To the degree that desktop publishing increases the flexibility of authors, it complicates the work of editors.)

Larry Anderson, who coaxed even the most ornery pages through Microsoft's L300.

Darcie Furlan, who coordinated the traditional art production that turned electronic files and printed samples into this book.

Min Yee, for introducing us to Microsoft Press and for his well-timed enthusiasm.

Our other friends and colleagues at Microsoft, for their patience and support.

And special thanks to our assistant, Megan Denver, who juggled more tasks than we could mention.

INTRODUCTION

T his book is about two dramatically different and wonderfully complementary tools of communication: graphic design and electronic page assembly. The first is a tradition as old as recorded history, the second a technology unimaginable to most of us even five years ago. In addition to changing the way we produce documents and publications of every kind, the combination of these tools is introducing more people than ever before to the art and technology of publishing.

Technology has always had an impact on visual communication, which is essentially what graphic design is. At every stage of the evolution of the communication arts—from prehistoric cave paintings to Guttenberg's movable type to today's computerized typesetting and imaging systems—technology has increased the potential for communication with audiences that are both broader and more specialized.

The computer is by all odds the most extraordinary of the technological clothing ever devised by man, since it is an extension of our central nervous system. Beside it the wheel is a mere hula-hoop.
—Marshall McLuhan

In the past, especially in the last half century or so during which graphic design as a commercial art has flourished, people entered the field through formal training in art schools and apprenticeships with experienced designers. The almost overnight proliferation of desktop publishing technology has attracted and, through management expectations, forced many people with no training in the visual arts to take responsibility for a wide range of printed material. Increased access to publishing tools has motivated many businesses to produce in-house publications that were previously done, in whole or in part, by outside contractors. At the same time, the promise and the inevitable hype surrounding desktop publishing has raised expectations about internal and external communications of all kinds.

While expanding the number of people involved in printed communication, desktop typesetting and electronic page assembly are also dramatically changing the day-to-day operations of an increasing number of publishers, design studios, corporate art departments, and independent freelancers. Writers and editors who cannot draw a straight line find themselves assembling pages in electronic templates. Designers used to specifying type on manuscripts are setting and manipulating it themselves. Production managers used to trafficking hard copy from one department to another are wrestling with the management of electronic files. And pasteup artists with T-squares and ruling pens are, quite simply, an endangered species.

Although they approach desktop publishing from different perspectives, people within both the business community and the publishing industry share a need for two different kinds of training. This book focuses on that need. It is not a general overview of desktop publishing. It assumes that you already appreciate the potential benefits the technology offers: the ability to integrate text and graphics electronically, to see and alter on-screen what the printed page will look like, and to print that page on a variety of different printers depending upon the quality you require. The book does not try to convince you of the ways in which desktop publishing can save you time or money, enhance the creative process, or give you more control over the pages you produce. It assumes you're already convinced. Instead, it reviews the fundamental elements of graphic design for the many people without any training or experience in the visual arts who are suddenly responsible for producing—or who want to learn to produce—business publications. And it provides hands-on tutorials for using Aldus Page-Maker, the most popular electronic page layout program for both Macintosh and IBM-compatible computers.

There are many techniques that can be applied in the search for visual solutions. Here are some of the most often used and easily identified:

Contrast	Harmony
Instability	Balance
Asymmetry	Symmetry
Irregularity	Regularity
Complexity	Simplicity
Fragmentation	Unity
Intricacy	Economy
Exaggeration	Understatement
Spontaneity	Predictability
Activeness	Stasis
Boldness	Subtlety
Accent	Neutrality
Transparency	Opacity
Variation	Consistency
Distortion	Accuracy
Depth	Flatness
Juxtaposition	Singularity
Randomness	Sequentiality
Sharpness	Diffusion
Episodicity	Repetition

—Donis A. Dondis,
A Primer of Visual Literacy

There are very few rules in graphic design. A relatively subjective craft, it requires the designer to make one judgment after another based on such intangible criteria as "look" and "feel." Even if you have no inkling of the formal traditions and techniques taught in design schools, you have some personal experience with the elements designers work with—words, lines, colors, pictures.

On the other hand, there are hundreds and hundreds of rules for using Aldus PageMaker. Even with its user-friendly mouse, pull-down menus, and familiar drawing-board metaphor, PageMaker is not—for most people—a program you just jump into and start producing pages with. It requires learning which commands to use and how to respond to dialog boxes and how the same commands in different sequences produce different results. Sometimes the program appears to have a mind of its own. It can display your headline in one style when you know you specified another. It can refuse to place your graphic. It can appear to eat your text. It can tell you there's a bad hole record index detected by the line walker. (A bad what?)

One important quality common to designing printed pages and assembling them in PageMaker is that both tasks become intuitive as you gain experience. The variety of typefaces that intimidates a novice designer, for example, becomes a rich resource once you gain a feeling for the often subtle distinctions between them. The apparent mysteries of layout grids become time-saving production tools when you understand the simple principles that govern their use. Similarly, the endless rules that slow down the PageMaker rookie provide control and flexibility to the experienced user.

Think of buying a computer as like buying a car. A car just moves your body; your computer, though, is the chariot of your mind, carrying it through the whole universe. How much is your mind worth to you?
—Ted Nelson,
Computer Lib

In a sense, this book tries to simulate experience both in graphic design and in using PageMaker. Section 1, "The Elements of Design," is a sort of primer of visual literacy as it relates to the printed page. It provides a working vocabulary of graphic design in the context of desktop technology.

Section 2, "A PageMaker Portfolio" (and the chapter on Creating a Grid in Section 1) show sample pages from more than a hundred documents along with notes about design elements such as grid structure, type treatment, and use of art. Although these documents can't replace personal experience, they can provide the novice designer with a sense of the many different solutions to common design problems, and they can help you develop an eye for effective combinations. All of the publications were created using PageMaker (along with other applications for word processing and graphics), so these samples also illustrate both simple and complex applications of this program.

The third section, "Hands-On Projects," provides actual experience. Here you'll find six different tutorials, each with step-by-step instructions for creating a particular publication. The purpose is to help you learn and become more confident with PageMaker's tools and techniques by applying them to actual documents. PageMaker operates almost identically on Macintosh and IBM-compatibles, so you can do the projects on either type of computer. (Keystroke combinations are given for both types.)

The book was conceived to be used as a resource, rather than to be read from start to finish. If you want to start right in working with Page-Maker, begin in Section 3. If you want to review publications of a particular kind, flip through Section 2. And if you want some grounding in design basics, start with Section 1. Even within each section, the chapters are organized so that you can begin at whatever point suits your needs and experience. If you stumble across an unfamiliar term, refer to the glossary at the back of the book.

Visual communication of any kind, whether persuasive or informative, from billboards to birth announcements, should be seen as the embodiment of form and function: the integration of the beautiful and the useful.

—Paul Rand,
Thoughts on Design

Throughout this book, we emphasize that the computer is only a tool. Design is not one of its default settings. PageMaker can enable you to draw a straight line, but it can't tell you how heavy to make it or where to put it on the page. It makes it possible to place text in perfectly aligned columns, but it doesn't tell you how wide the columns should be or when to place text as one long file and when to divide it into several smaller ones. It offers hundreds of typefaces but requires your visual judgment to select and size the one that's right for your publication. It's a wonderful, powerful tool, getting better and more sophisticated and easier to use every day. But it's still only a tool.

We hope this book will help you gain some of the skill, experience, and visual discrimination needed to use it well.

THE ELEMENTS OF DESIGN

CHAPTER 1

EFFECTIVE COMMUNICATION IN AN INFORMATION ENVIRONMENT

Past	Present	Future
Data	Information	Knowledge
Control	Access	Exploration
Calculation	Presentation	Communication

—Stuart Greene,
Apple viewpoints

The electronic age has given us an almost magical ability to store, retrieve, and analyze data. Whether you're making travel plans, checking the status of an insurance policy, or changing an assumption in a five-year plan, the computer can provide almost instantaneous answers to questions that only a decade ago might have remained unanswered for a day, a week, or even a month.

But the electronic age has not given us a paperless office. In fact, in a single year computers are said to churn out some 1200 pages of print for every man, woman, and child in the United States. Although they help us manage individual pieces of data, computers have increased our information overload.

In the midst of this overload, desktop publishing reaffirms the fundamental power of print. Print is tangible; it has a life of its own. You can read it when you want, at your own pace, and keep it for future reference. And now, with desktop publishing, the newest darling of the electronic age, you can produce more pages faster and cheaper than ever before.

But can you produce effective pages?

In the information environment, competition for the ever-shrinking attention span is fierce. We are saturated both as senders (too much to say, too little space) and as receivers (too much to read, too little time). The result is often information that is confusing, that you can't find when you need it, or that simply sits unread in a rotating stack of other communications that failed to deliver their messages. The cumulative result is an enormous amount of wasted effort. The hidden costs, whether in sales or productivity or corporate image, are difficult to calculate.

The elements that make up a successful document—careful writing, thoughtful organization, effective design—grow out of an understanding of your message, your audience, and your resources. The publication checklist below can help guide you toward that understanding. The questions it raises force you to think through a great many variables and even some unpleasant realities. Some of the answers may raise more questions. The purpose of the checklist is to help you define your communication problem so that you can use graphic design as a way of solving it. We'll briefly consider each item on the checklist after a look at a few diverse examples of effective communication.

An erroneous conception of the graphic designer's function is to imagine that in order to produce a "good layout" all he need do is make a pleasing arrangement of miscellaneous elements. What is implied is that this may be accomplished simply by pushing these elements around until something happens. At best, this procedure involves the time-consuming uncertainties of trial and error, and at worst, an indifference to plan, order, or discipline.
—Paul Rand
Thoughts on Design

PUBLICATION CHECKLIST

- What is the purpose of your publication?

- Why is it needed?

- Who is the intended audience?

- What kind of information will your publication include?

- What kind of image do you want to project?

- Does the publication need to fit into a larger program or conform to a corporate style?

- What is the overall format?

- What kinds of art and photography—and how much—will be needed?

- What are the printing specifications?

- What will you use for camera-ready pages?

- How will the publication be reproduced?

- How will it be distributed?

- When is it needed?

- What is the budget?

The dramatically different documents reproduced on this and the following two pages illustrate the rich range of visual form that effective communication can take. Each of the four samples successfully solves a very different design problem, and their contrasting styles say a great deal about the different purpose and audience of each message.

A poster is one of the simplest and most direct forms of communication. It delivers a message that is as brief as it is bold. Although many posters rely heavily on graphics, this one is a reminder of the power of words.

The street language is well suited to the young audience; the rhythm of the words is in their own vernacular.

The typography follows the cadence of the words, so that the visual rhythm literally echoes the verbal message. Reverse type on a red background supports the jazzy rhythm and the serious message.

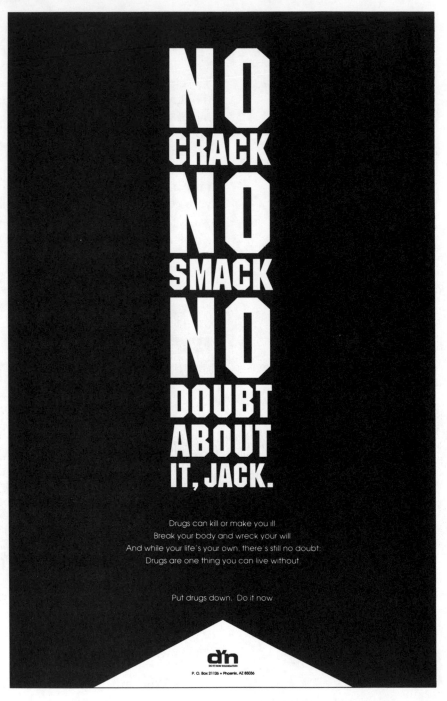

Design: Jim Parker (Phoenix, AZ)
Poster produced by the Do It Now Foundation.
Trim size: 12 by 19

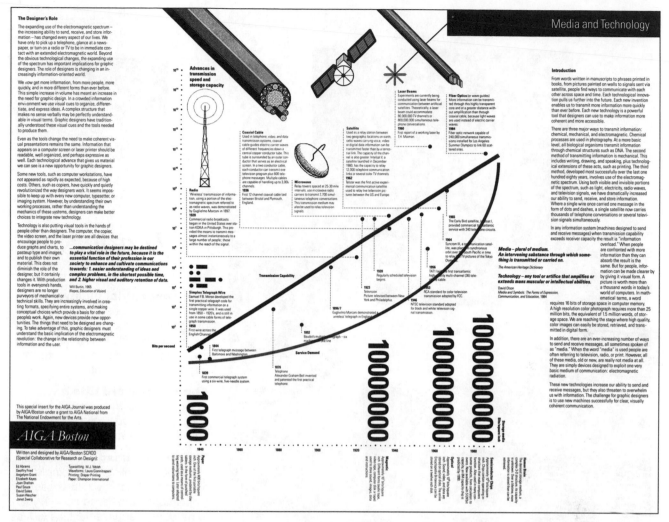

The carefully organized collection of information above is at the opposite end of the communications spectrum from the poster. The subject is media and technology; the audience is sophisticated (the document was designed as an insert for a graphic arts journal) and so is the delivery of information.

The chart encapsulates advances in transmission speed and storage capacity of media in the context of a time line. In addition to providing a great deal of information in a very small space, it cuts through the stereotypical image of charts as bland and linear.

Quotations inset between the running text and the chart provide a point of easy access in this complex page as well as another layer of historical context:

…communication designers may be destined to play a vital role in the future, because it is the essential function of their profession in our society to enhance and cultivate communications towards: 1. easier understanding of ideas and complex problems, in the shortest possible time, and 2. higher visual and auditory retention of data.
—Will Burtin, 1965

Design: Paul Souza, Ed Abrams, and Susan Wascher (Boston, MA)

Insert for the American Institute of Graphic Arts journal produced by AIGA/ Boston.
Trim size: 22 by 17

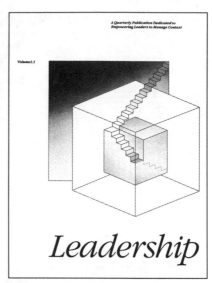

The conceptual illustration on the cover of this quarterly publication brings to bear the personal and subjective vision of the artist. It invites the reader to participate and engages the imagination.

The single-word title is very focused. It succinctly states the subject but leaves you curious as to how it will be addressed.

The overall image of the cover combines a feeling of accomplishment and success with the need for innovation and a sense of work yet to be done. Each element, as well as the whole, echoes the nature of leadership itself.

The dramatic photo composition on the cover of this PBS-series program guide has an emotional content that touches the reader in a way that straight typography cannot. The juxtaposition of a mushroom cloud against the outstretched hands of Gorbachev and Reagan evokes the terror and hope, the despair and optimism of our time. The photos also suggest the mix of historical and contemporary components in the series.

The title over the photos suggests that the series will be comprehensive. The wording is restrained and sets a tone that encourages the viewer to suspend moral judgments temporarily .

Design: Alison Kennedy (Boston, MA)

Program guide produced by WGBH and Central Independent Television.

Trim size: 8-1/2 by 11

Design: Weisz Yang Dunkelberger Inc. (Westport, CT)

Periodical published by Lefkoe & Associates, a management consulting and training organization.

Trim size: 9 by 12

What is the purpose of your publication?

Desktop publishing can be used to produce documents as diverse as calling cards and novels. This book is concerned primarily with business documents, which usually fall into several categories. Identifying the category to which your document belongs (it may be more than one) can help you develop the right approach for the purpose.

Information technology was supposed to let us taper off paper.... From 1959 to 1986 America's consumption of writing and printing paper increased from 6.83 million to 21.99 million tons, or 320 percent, while the real [GNP] rose 280 percent.

—Edward Tenner, Harvard Magazine, cited in The Computer Desk Reference & Appointment Calendar 1989

Documents that persuade
Advertisements
Invitations
Fund raisers
Posters
Press releases
Promotional flyers
Prospectuses
Sales brochures

Documents that identify
Business cards
Certificates
Labels
Stationery

Documents that inform
Brochures
Bulletins
Curriculum listings
Fact sheets
Marketing plans
Product lists
Programs
Rate cards
Specification sheets

Periodicals that inform
Magazines
Newsletters
Newspapers
Reports

Documents that elicit response
Applications
Order forms
Surveys

Documents that provide reference
Calendars
Directories
Lists
Parts lists
Schedules
Timetables

Documents that give how-to information
Curriculum guides
Instruction manuals
Training guides

Why is your publication needed?

One of the most important questions to ask yourself is why the reader needs or wants the information in your document. If you can zero in on that need, you can use it in your headlines and art to get the reader's attention. Keeping the reader's needs in mind also helps focus your writing.

Desktop publishers get carried away with their tools. They...spend more time on the aesthetics of a document than the content of it.
—Boeing's DTP product manager, in an article in MacWEEK

In many cases the reader is at best indifferent and at worst resistant to the information you want to convey. If you acknowledge that indifference, you can try to devise some way of overcoming it. In the face of audience resistance, you might want to put extra effort and money into the cover. Or consider printing a strong opening sentence or two in large type on the cover to lure readers in. Puzzles, quizzes, and other involvement techniques can sometimes draw readers to a subject they might otherwise ignore. A headline that poses a bold question is a simpler version of this same approach and can work if your audience is likely to want to know the answer. (Readers can often be hooked by a question even if it's one they think they can answer.) Humor, where appropriate, can also cajole the audience into reading on. The technique depends on the publication, the audience, and the budget. But do try something. If you ignore audience indifference when you write and design a document, you can guarantee that it won't be read.

Who is your audience?

Unless you write like Stephen King or address a subject as important to your reader as his or her bank balance, you can't assume that your intended reader will actually read your document. You may have a target audience or even a captive audience, but you don't have a reader until you've involved that person through words or pictures or an overall impression. Identifying your audience helps you choose the techniques that engage readers. Are they colleagues? Customers? Potential investors? Clients? What style is appropriate? How much do they know about your subject? How much time are they likely to spend with your publication? What other information do they have on the subject? Is this their only source?

The business of reaching the audience is no different than before.
—*Ben Bagdikian,*
in a New York Times *interview about desktop publishing*

Think in terms of interaction rather than one-way communication. It doesn't hurt to think of yourself as an entertainer or a sales person anticipating your audience's reaction. Consider readers' responses so that you can adjust your approach.

As you develop your publication, put yourself in the readers' position:

- How quickly can they pick out the highlights? Most readers scan. They want a sense of what you have to say before they make a commitment to read on. They want the highlights before the details.

- Can they find the items that are relevant to their particular concerns? Many publications have a mix of information, with different subjects, themes, or types of material. In a company newsletter, for example, one employee may be interested in educational assistance while another is concerned with after-hours security. Understanding your readers' special interests helps you organize the material.

- How quickly can they read the text? Remember the problem of information overload. Your text should be clear and lean. Less is more in print.

- Can your readers understand the information? Have you assumed knowledge they don't have?

Instruction manuals and reference books require careful organization and graphic devices that help the reader to find what he or she needs. One study of computer documentation revealed that of all the questions phoned in to the technical support staff, 80 percent were covered in the manual; the users either couldn't find the answers quickly enough or didn't understand them.

What kind of information will be included?

Different kinds of publications have different elements. A brochure for a professional conference may require a program, a workshop schedule, brief biographies of the speakers, and a map. An advertisement may consist entirely of slogans, tag lines, and little pieces of information such as prices or an address. A press release needs the name of a person to contact for more information. A technical manual needs a glossary. Review the different kinds of information—text and visual—early on so that you'll have space for all the pieces and avoid oversights.

An awareness of the elements needed in your document also affects your format and pacing. For a newsletter with several short articles and small photographs, you might choose a four-column format, whereas a newsletter with one major article and a number of short, newsy items might work best in two unequal columns. You can't possibly make an intelligent decision about format until you have a fix on the kinds of information you'll be formatting.

What kind of image do you want to project?

The layout of the circus under canvas is more like the plan of the Acropolis than anything else; it is a beautiful organic arrangement established by the boss canvas man and the lot boss.... The concept of "appropriateness," this "how-it-should-be-ness," has equal value in the circus, in the making of a work of art, and in science.

—Charles Eames

Everything about a publication, from the style of the prose to the quality of the paper it's printed on, contributes to the image it conveys about the sender. And the single most important guideline in fashioning that image is appropriateness. The elements you select and the way you assemble and reproduce them become a matter not so much of good or bad design as of design that is appropriate for your purpose and audience. Even the crammed-full, poorly printed advertisements for discount department stores cannot be dismissed as "bad" design when put to the tests of appropriate and effective communication.

If you are promoting a financial service, you want prose that is well informed and authoritative and design and printing that is prosperous without being indulgent. A company that has had a bad year, on the other hand, wants to appear careful and restrained without creating concern about quality. And you want an entrepreneurial business plan to appear energetic, bold, and thorough all at the same time.

A travel brochure for a Caribbean cruise might use color photos to suggest escape, adventure, and celebration, and an ad for a new restaurant in the theater or art district might use words and decorative motifs to project a similar experience close to home.

As you consider the elements and design of your publication, write down a list of impressions you want to make. Formal. Informal. Friendly. Playful. Elegant. Stylish. Trendy. Classic. Adventurous. Conservative. Scholarly. Provocative. Diverse. Spirited. Generous. Concerned. How do you want your audience to perceive you?

Must your publication fit into a program or conform to a corporate style?

For a new program that requires continuity—say a series of health seminars, each with a promotional mailing before the event, a seminar program distributed at the event, and a follow-up questionnaire after the event—you'll want to develop a design that establishes an identity for the series and that can be followed for each event.

The issue of corporate identity has emerged as some companies have discovered that desktop publishing encourages more creativity than their image can handle. The logo begins appearing in different sizes and positions on the page. Documents from one department have a streamlined, stylized look, whereas documents from another use Victorian clip art. The corporate response is to establish formats and design standards so that different kinds of documents—order forms, product sheets, newsletters, reports, and so on—all have a consistent look. You may feel that having to adhere to these standards puts a damper on your style, but in fact it will probably free you to concentrate on the clarity and effectiveness of the elements within the established format.

What is the overall format?

Format includes everything from the organization of material to the page size to the underlying structure, or grid, of your layout. You rarely start a publication with an idea of what the format should be; rather, the format evolves out of the material and often changes as your understanding of the publication changes.

In developing your format, consider first the common elements in the publication. How many levels of headlines will you need? How will you separate items that appear on the same page?

Readers want what is important to be clearly laid out; they will not read anything that is troublesome to read.
—Jan Tschichold,
writing in 1935, cited in
Thirty Centuries of Graphic Design

Look at the formats of other publications, keep a file of what you like, and adapt those techniques to fit your needs. Professional designers do this all the time. Don't limit your file to the kinds of publications you will produce. You may never create an accordion-fold brochure, but some aspect of the format may help you solve a problem in your own publication.

Keep in mind that readers scan printed matter, and consider techniques to facilitate this:

- A strong visual framework will separate one item from another and indicate relative importance.

- Several short stories are almost always more accessible and inviting than one long one.

- Use sidebars or boxed copy to break the text into accessible chunks.

- Every headline and caption is a hook, a potential entry point for busy readers.

- Pay attention to the pacing: Balance text with visuals and offset "quick reads" with more demanding material.

- Use graphic devices to move the reader's eye from one place on the page to another, especially to key points or to little bits of information that you think are particularly interesting.

- Keep in mind also that many readers scan from back to front; can you get their attention in the middle of a story?

For magazines, newsletters, and other periodicals, develop your format with great care so that you can maintain a consistent style from one issue to the next. What departments and features will be included in every issue? Where will they appear?

What kinds of art or photography will be included?

We learn language by applying words to visual experiences, and we create visual images to illustrate verbal ideas. This interaction of word and image is the background for contemporary communication.
—Allen Hurlburt,
The Design Concept

You can produce professional, attractive documents without any art, but pictures unquestionably draw readers in more easily than words, and illustrations can greatly enhance your message. Art and photography can illustrate the text, provide additional information, create a mood, provoke questions in the reader's mind, and set the overall tone of a publication. Charts and graphs can squeeze a lot of facts into a small amount of space and be visually interesting at the same time. Even abstract geometric shapes can intrigue and invite and add movement to the page. Graphic devices such as borders, boxes, and tinted areas, along with icons such as arrows, bullets, and ballot boxes, all help create a strong sense of organization and move the reader from one part of the page to another. Consider these devices as ways to break up the text and make your pages more interesting, more accessible, and more informative. Keep in mind that you don't necessarily need a lot of art; often one or two strong images are more effective than half a dozen mediocre ones.

You will need to consider the amount and type of art to be used early on, because it will affect your format and will also generate loose odds and ends of text. Will you have captions? Numbers to identify figures? Sources for charts? Where will the art credits appear?

The art will affect the schedule, too. Will the printer make halftones from your black-and-white photos, or will you need to have that done? How long will it take to have color separations made? Desktop publishing is expanding into color work and scanned black-and-white photographs, but most publications created with computers still treat photos and four-color art the way they've always been treated, as a process handled by the printer.

What are the printing specifications?

Specifications— including page size, number of pages, type of binding, paper stock, quantity to be printed, and use of color, if any—are inextricably related to the overall format. Changing one often affects the other. Review your options early on with any outside vendors you plan to use (commercial printers, color separators, full-service copy centers); your specifications must be consistent with their capabilities and requirements.

If you've come to desktop publishing without any experience in working with printed materials, you'll encounter a new set of jargon as you move into printing and binding. It's just trade talk, and you'll pick it up in time. If your printer can print in four- and eight-page signatures as well as in sixteens, that might affect the number of pages you produce. If you can get a good price on an odd-size paper that works for your needs, you might want to adjust your page size. The binding you select may affect your page margins. See the Resources section in the back of this book for production guides that will help you understand the fundamentals of commercial printing.

What will you use for camera-ready pages?

For many documents, the 300-dots-per-inch output from a laser printer is sufficient for camera-ready pages. For others, you may want the higher resolution provided by an imagesetter such as the Linotronic. Again, your decision here will affect your schedule and your budget.

When you plan to use Linotronic output, be sure to run test pages of your format early on. Rules, shades, and type weight are lighter at higher resolutions, and you may want to adjust your specs when you see the early tests. You'll want to work with the service center that will provide your Linotronic output just as you do with your printer. Find out what kind of compatibility the service center requires in order to print your files—what versions of programs they use, which fonts they have, what backup you must provide, whether they use screen fonts for boldface and italic styles or require that you apply these from the Type style menu. Knowledgeable personnel at good service centers are a valuable resource and can help you troubleshoot problems early on.

How will your document be reproduced?

For any but those jobs you consider routine, talk with the printer as early in the planning as possible.... Describe your needs and ask whether your piece can be printed practically. Consider suggestions about alternate papers, design changes, and other ideas about how to save time and money.... [But] remember that they want your business. By suggesting changes which take advantage of particular presses or papers, a printer may be shaping your job to fit that shop. Keep in mind that you are getting consultation and may not be ready to write specifications.

—Mark Beach,
Getting It Printed

As is the case with many aspects of publishing, the new technology has expanded the ways in which documents are reproduced. Will you use the office photocopy machine? A full-service copy center? A quick printer with offset presses and binderies? Or a commercial printer for higher-quality reproduction? Your printing needs will be determined by the number of copies, the quality desired, and your budget.

If you will be using commercial printers on a regular basis and you are new to publishing, try to develop a working relationship with local printers and learn more about that end of the business. Printing is a fine art but an inconsistent one; even highly experienced professionals fear the nasty surprises that can happen on press. Poor communication between publisher and printer can result in poor quality. Let your printer know what you expect. If you're not satisfied with the quality, follow up after you receive printed copies to find out what the problem was. Often the printer will blame it on the paper (which is rarely as good as you'd like it to be) or on the size of the run (it is difficult to maintain certain standards in large press runs, but the printer is supposed to have quality-control mechanisms to catch problems as they come up), or on some other plausible factors. But sometimes the problem could have been avoided. Perhaps your photograph was cut off because you didn't leave enough space between your art and the trim; next time you'll know to determine the tolerance and adjust your margins accordingly. By asking, you'll let the printer know you care about quality, and you may learn something.

How will it be distributed?

Whether your document is distributed through interoffice mail, given away in stores, or sent through the mail or some other delivery service, you want the purpose to be easily discernible. What is the reader's first impression? Is a person as likely to see the back cover first as the front? If the publication is folded, will the pacing of the words and images keep the recipients moving through the folds? If a flyer is to be tacked on a bulletin board, can the headline be read from a distance?

If your document will be mailed, it must conform to postal regulations for the appropriate mailing class. This may affect the size, the way the publication is folded, the placement of the mailing label, and the amount of space for the address if the publication is a self-mailer.

An early understanding of the restrictions and requirements of your distribution method can save you time and money and can affect certain decisions about your format as well.

When is it needed?

Regardless of your experience and that of your staff, expect productivity to drop in the beginning, as everyone learns the new system.... It will probably take at least three production cycles before you can get all the kinks out.... Many organizations continue to use traditional production methods in parallel with their new desktop systems, phasing in the new methods gradually. This means you won't see your cost savings right away, but you're not putting all your eggs in one new and untested basket.
—Janet Millenson,
writing in Publish! *magazine*

Schedules are a blessing and a curse. On the one hand there is the feeling that there's not enough time to do the job the way you'd like, but on the other hand everyone knows that any project will expand to fill the time available. Scheduling is especially sensitive when you are working with new technology. Desktop publishing is supposed to shave days off of a project that would have taken a week, and weeks off of one that would have taken a month. That can happen, but not the first week you have your system. You need time to learn, time to find out what you can and can't do with your particular configuration.

Most schedules are determined backwards, starting with when you want the document in your reader's hands. You then figure in the time required for distribution, printing, and other outside services, and finally you determine not how long you *need* to create the publication, but how long you *have*.

Schedules are a reality factor. The tighter the schedule, the simpler your format should be.

What is the budget?

Money is also a reality factor. It so affects everything about a publication that it's often the first consideration. We've put it last on the checklist, not out of disregard for its importance, but out of a belief that first you should think about what you want to do, and then you should look at what you can do. It's the nature of dreams to make us reach, and even when we can't grab hold of what we want, dreams often produce good ideas that can be scaled down to fit a budget. Take your budget and your schedule seriously, but don't let them be ever-present blinders.

CHAPTER 2

THE PRINCIPLES OF TYPOGRAPHY

Typographic arrangement should achieve for the reader what voice tone conveys to the listener.
　　　　　　　　　—El Lissitzky

The ability to set type, to modify it on-screen, to compose it in pages, and then print the result in camera-ready form is the foundation of desktop publishing. Suddenly, the fundamental building block of graphic design is in the hands of anyone with a few thousand dollars. What are we to make of this access to such a rich tradition, one developed over 500 years of practice?

The answer, of course, varies widely. Typography at its most basic is simply the selection and arrangement of typefaces, sizes, and spacing on the printed page. But faced with the raw material for a page that isn't printed, how do you style the elements so that the page is inviting and easy to read, so that the eye can distinguish the relative importance of items and pick out the ones of interest, so that the overall appearance is both varied and unified?

In addition to the utilitarian functions implied in those questions, typography also gives a page a certain personality (formal or informal, modern or classic, ornate or sturdy) and an overall feeling (dense or open, light or dramatic). How do you choose from among the many typefaces available to project the desired image and to give your publication a distinctive and recognizable personality?

As much as in any other area of graphic design, the answers come largely from experience. Some of that experience we all have as readers. A great deal more can be gained by looking carefully at how type is styled in the whole range of printed materials. And finally, the computer makes it possible to discover the nuances of type through hands-on experimentation.

Computers have given us an invaluable control over typography, but they have also made possible a counterproductive versatility. In desktop publishing we have so many typefaces available and so many special effects, we can change so readily from one size and style to another, that undisciplined typography can as easily fragment the message as help hold it together. Use the control to experiment, to find the right face and size and spacing for your purpose, but don't use the versatility to pack your pages with a half dozen or more styles that confuse more than they communicate.

The power to control typography from the desktop is all the more miraculous when you review the history of typesetting and see the

72 dots per inch (screen image)

300 dpi

1270 dpi

2540 dpi

There is a story, no doubt apocryphal, that a fifteenth-century scribe, upon examining one of Gutenberg's press sheets, exclaimed, "It's nice, but it's not calligraphy."

progression from a craftsman's handling of each individual letter to a computer operator's ability to send electrical impulses around the world. In the fifteenth century, Johann Gutenberg liberated the printed word from the painstaking craft of handscripting with what now seems the almost equally painstaking craft of individually setting each metal character. With the introduction of linotype machines in the 1880s, keyboard operators could type in the text and the machine would cast an entire line in a single slug of hot metal. Phototypesetting eliminated the actual type altogether and produced text by projecting the images of characters on light-sensitive film or paper. Today's computer-driven laser printers have turned letters into patterns of dots and computer owners and operators into typographers.

This most recent "democratization" of typography has created something of a holy war between the traditionalists and the new breed of desktop publishers. The traditionalists—designers of typefaces and graphic designers who have worked with commercial type throughout their careers—lament the distortion of letterforms in standard faces, the uneven spacing between letters and words, and the lower resolution in the type created on desktop systems. The desktop publishers see savings in time and money and, in some documents, a quality that is far superior to the previous typewritten and mimeographed forms.

The real miracle, which it is the nature of holy wars to overlook, is choice. The laser printer resolution of 300 dots per inch (dpi) is perfectly adequate as well as cost effective for many newsletters, reports, bulletins, price sheets, and a great many other documents. The higher resolution of a Linotronic 100 or 300 (1270 and 2540 dots per inch respectively) is appropriate for many brochures, books, catalogs, technical manuals, magazines, and annual reports; in these situations the desktop computer serves as the front end for commercial typesetting and still gives the user greater control and considerable savings of time and money over traditional typesetting. High-quality, commercial typesetting is still available for advertising agencies, design studios, and publishers of fine books and magazines whose products require, and can afford, the cleanest, sharpest, most beautifully proportioned type. It's a matter of choosing the quality of type appropriate for your needs and budget, and then using that type as well as you possibly can.

This chapter is about the many ways of using type. The main purpose is not to put forth rules you must remember but to suggest ways of looking at type on the printed page. As Sumner Stone, the director of typography at Adobe Systems, said in a *Publish* Magazine roundtable discussion on typography, "It's like learning how to appreciate different flavors of wine." Drink up.

A VISUAL GLOSSARY OF TYPOGRAPHY

The terminology used to describe type and its appearance on the printed page is a colorful and useful jargon. As with any specialized language, it enables people to communicate unambiguously, so that the instruction "align baseline of flush right caption with bottom of art" means the same thing to everyone involved in a job. But the language of typography also describes the subtlety and diversity among letterforms. This glossary is intended to display some of that richness in the process of setting forth basic definitions.

TYPEFACE

The name of a typeface refers to an entire family of letters of a particular design. (Historically, face referred to the surface of the metal type piece that received the ink and came into contact with the printing surface.) The faces shown on this spread are resident on most Post-Script printers. Hundreds of faces are available for desktop production today; by the end of 1990, the number will be in the thousands.

Avant Garde

ABCDEFGHIJKLMNOPQRSTUVWXYZ
abcdefghijklmnopqrstuvwxyz
1234567890!$,""?
ABCDEFGHIJKLMNOPQRSTUVWXYZ
abcdefghijklmnopqrstuvwxyz
1234567890!$,""?

Bookman

ABCDEFGHIJKLMNOPQRSTUVWXYZ
abcdefghijklmnopqrstuvwxyz
1234567890!$,""?
ABCDEFGHIJKLMNOPQRSTUVWXYZ
abcdefghijklmnopqrstuvwxyz
1234567890!$,""?

Courier

ABCDEFGHIJKLMNOPQRSTUVWXYZ
abcdefghijklmnopqrstuvwxyz
1234567890!$,""?
ABCDEFGHIJKLMNOPQRSTUVWXYZ
abcdefghijklmnopqrstuvwxyz
1234567890!$,""?

Helvetica

ABCDEFGHIJKLMNOPQRSTUVWXYZ
abcdefghijklmnopqrstuvwxyz
1234567890!$,""?
ABCDEFGHIJKLMNOPQRSTUVWXYZ
abcdefghijklmnopqrstuvwxyz
1234567890!$,""?

New Century
Schoolbook

ABCDEFGHIJKLMNOPQRSTUVWXYZ
abcdefghijklmnopqrstuvwxyz
1234567890!$,""?
ABCDEFGHIJKLMNOPQRSTUVWXYZ
abcdefghijklmnopqrstuvwxyz
1234567890!$,""?

Palatino

ABCDEFGHIJKLMNOPQRSTUVWXYZ
abcdefghijklmnopqrstuvwxyz
1234567890!$,""?
ABCDEFGHIJKLMNOPQRSTUVWXYZ
abcdefghijklmnopqrstuvwxyz
1234567890!$,""?

Times Roman

ABCDEFGHIJKLMNOPQRSTUVWXYZ
abcdefghijklmnopqrstuvwxyz
1234567890!$,""?
ABCDEFGHIJKLMNOPQRSTUVWXYZ
abcdefghijklmnopqrstuvwxyz
1234567890!$,""?

Zapf Chancery

ABCDEFGHIJKLMNOPQRSTUVWXYZ
abcdefghijklmnopqrstuvwxyz
1234567890!$,""?
ABCDEFGHIJKLMNOPQRSTUVWXYZ
abcdefghijklmnopqrstuvwxyz
1234567890!$,""?

For all of the variety found across thousands of typefaces, most of them can be grouped into three basic styles—serif, sans serif, and script. The samples shown on these two pages suggest the variation available in each style. These samples (and the ones throughout this chapter) are PostScript fonts from Adobe Systems.

Some legibility studies have found that serif typefaces are easier to read, the theory being that the serifs help move the eye from one letter to the next without the letters blurring together. On the other hand, sans serif typefaces are generally thought to be easier to read at very large and especially at very small sizes. It's difficult to make any hard-and-fast rules because legibility is affected not only by typeface but also by size, length of line, amount of leading, amount of white space on the page, and even by the quality of the paper.

SANS SERIF

Sans serif typefaces do not have finishing strokes at the end of the letterforms. The name comes from the French *sans*, meaning "without." Sans serif faces are also referred to as Gothic.

Helvetica   Futura   Univers

Avant Garde   Franklin Gothic

Eurostile   News Gothic   Optima

SCRIPT

Script faces simulate handwriting, with one letter connected to another visually if not physically.

Freestyle Script   Zapf Chancery

SERIF

Serifs are lines or curves projecting from the end of a letterform. Type-faces with these additional strokes are called serif faces. They are also referred to as Roman faces because the serifs derived from the marks made chiseling letters into Roman monuments. (Note that when de-scribing serif faces, the word Roman is capitalized; when describing vertical letters as distinguished from italic ones, roman is lowercase.)

Palatino   Times Roman   Garamond

New Century Schoolbook   Caslon

Bookman   Century Old Style

Goudy Old Style   Glypha

Bodoni   American Typewriter

Trump Mediæval   Galliard

Lubalin Graph   New Baskerville

SIZE

Type is measured by its vertical height, from the top of the capital letter or ascender (whichever is higher) to the bottom of the descender. That height, or size, is expressed in points. There are 12 points to a pica and approximately 6 picas to an inch.

HeightHeightHeightHeightHeightHeight Height Height

6 pt 8 pt 10 pt   12 pt   14 point   18 point   36 point   72 point

WEIGHT

Weight refers to the density of letters, to the lightness or heaviness of the strokes. It is described as a continuum: light, regular, book, demi, bold, heavy, black, extra bold. Not all typefaces are available for all weights, and the continuum varies in some faces.

HELVETICA LIGHT   HELVETICA REGULAR
HELVETICA BOLD   HELVETICA BLACK

WIDTH

The horizontal measure of the letters is described as condensed, normal, or expanded. The commonly used faces—Times, Helvetica, New Century Schoolbook— are normal. Quite a few condensed faces are available in desktop publishing. And drawing programs such as Illustrator and Freehand enable you to condense or expand type in any face and then import it into PageMaker, a technique which is very fashionable in type design today.

CONDENSED   NORMAL   EXPANDED

SLANT

Slant is the angle of a type character, either vertical or inclined. Vertical type is called roman (in PageMaker it is called Normal, and in some word-processing programs, Plain). Inclined type is called italic or oblique.

roman & *italic*

STYLE

In desktop publishing, style refers to weight, slant, and certain special effects such as outline or shadow. The samples shown here are the styles available in PageMaker. In a more general sense, style refers to the broad characteristics of a typeface (such as serif or sans serif) and to its distinctive personality as well (such as elegant or friendly).

STYLE   **STYLE**   *STYLE*   STYLE

~~STYLE~~   STYLE   STYLE   STYLE

FAMILY

All of the variations of a single typeface—the different weights, widths, slants, and styles—constitute a type family. Some families have more styles than others, providing for considerable type contrast within a document without the need to change typefaces. In addition to the Helvetica styles shown below, the family includes Compressed, Thin, Ultra Light, and Heavy variations. Some other families with many variations are Bodoni, Futura, Univers, and Stone.

Helvetica
Helvetica Italic
Helvetica Bold
Helvetica Bold Italic
Helvetica Condensed Light
Helvetica Condensed Light Oblique
Helvetica Condensed
Helvetica Condensed Oblique
Helvetica Condensed Bold
Helvetica Condensed Bold Oblique
Helvetica Condensed Black
Helvetica Condensed Black Oblique
Helvetica Light
Helvetica Light Oblique
Helvetica Black
Helvetica Black Oblique

ANATOMY

In designing, measuring, and identifying type, a precise vocabulary is essential. Here are the basics:

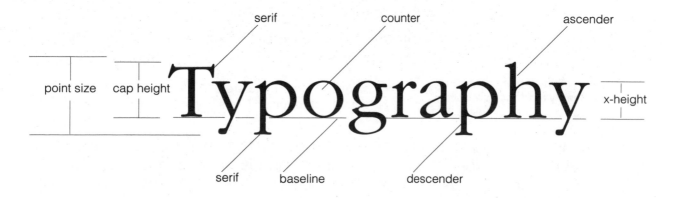

LEADING

The vertical space between lines of type is called leading (pronounced "led·ing"). It is measured in points and is expressed as the sum of the type size and the space between two lines. For example, 10 point type with 2 points between the lines is described as 10-point type on 12-point leading. It is written 10/12 and spoken "10 on 12." The term was originally used to describe the narrow metal strips inserted between lines of hand-set type.

Type with a generous amount of space between lines is said to have open leading; type with relatively little space between lines is said to be set tight. Type without any space between lines (such as the 10/10 and the 30/30 samples below) is said to be set solid. Leading that is less than the point size, as in the 30/26 sample, is called negative, or minus, leading; it is used primarily for large type sizes set in all caps.

10/10 Times Roman

These three type samples are all set in 10-point Times Roman. The first is set solid (10/10), the second is set tight (10/11), and the third (10/12) is set with PageMaker's automatic leading (120% of the point size).

10/11 Times Roman

These three type samples are all set in 10-point Times Roman. The first is set solid (10/10), the second is set tight (10/11), and the third (10/12) is set with PageMaker's automatic leading (120% of the point size).

10/12 Times Roman

These three type samples are all set in 10-point Times Roman. The first is set solid (10/10), the second is set tight (10/11), and the third (10/12) is set with PageMaker's automatic leading (120% of the point size).

30/26 Helvetica Condensed Black

THIS DISPLAY TYPE IS SET MINUS

30/30 Helvetica Condensed Black

THIS DISPLAY TYPE IS SET SOLID

30/34 Helvetica Condensed Black

THIS DISPLAY TYPE IS SET OPEN

LINE LENGTH

The length of a line of type is called the measure and is traditionally specified in picas. Fractions of picas are expressed as points (there are 12 points to a pica) not as decimals. So a column that is 10 and one-quarter picas wide is 10 picas 3 points, or 10p3.

Generally, the longer the line length the larger the type should be.

This is set to a 12p6 measure and can be easily read with a relatively small type size. This sample is 9/11.

This is set to a 21p9 measure and needs a larger type size for ease of reading. This sample is 10/12.

This is set to a 39p measure and needs a larger type size to be easily read. This measure is too wide for most running text and is best used for subheads, blurbs, and other short display type. This sample is set 13/15.

ALIGNMENT

Alignment refers to the shape of the type block relative to the margins. The common settings are flush left, centered, flush right, and justified. Body text is generally set flush left or justified, but with the controls available in PageMaker, flush left produces much better results.

Flush left

The lines of text are even on the left edge (flush with the left margin) and uneven, or ragged, on the right. Flush left is the recommended alignment for body text in desktop publishing. It is easy to read and allows even word spacing.

Centered

Each line is centered;
thus, both left and right margins
are ragged.
Centered text is often used
for headlines and
other display type,
as well as for formal invitations
and announcements.

Flush right

The lines of text are even on the right and uneven on the left. This alignment is sometimes used for captions, headlines, and advertising copy but is not recommended for body text. We are used to reading from left to right; if the left edge of the text is not well-defined, the eye falters, and the text is more difficult to read.

Justified

The type is flush, or even, on both the right and the left margins. Because the normal space between letters and words is altered in order to justify text, justification sometimes results in uneven spacing, with "rivers" of white space running through the type. The narrower the measure, the more uneven the spacing is likely to be, as you can see by comparing these side-by-side examples.

Justified

The type is flush, or even, on both the right and the left margins. Because the normal space between letters and words is altered in order to justify text, justification sometimes results in uneven spacing, with "rivers" of white space running through the type. The narrower the measure, the more uneven the spacing is likely to be, as you can see by comparing these side-by-side examples.

Rag left and right

A less common setting is rag left and rag right.
This is sometimes used for small amounts of display type.
It gives the page a poetic feeling without being formal.
This setting cannot be achieved automatically:
You must specify the indent for each individual line.

RULES

Rules are also typographic elements and are measured in points. You can select the weight of rules in PageMaker's Lines menu. Additional weights and styles are available by importing rules from drawing programs.

TYPE SPECIMEN SHEETS

Designers have traditionally relied on specimen sheets to select and specify type in their publications. "Spec" sheets, as they are known, simply display typefaces in various sizes, weights, and styles so that you can judge the appropriateness of a particular face for the publication you're about to design, as well as the readability, color, and overall look of frequently used sizes. Spec sheets are also useful when you want to identify a typeface that you see and like in another publication.

Commercial typesetters generally supply spec sheets to their customers as a sort of catalog of what is available. You can also buy books of spec sheets, and some are now available specifically for desktop publishing. (See the Resources section in the back of this book.)

Type is the first impression you have of what you're about to read. Each typeface, like a human face, has a subtle character all its own. Depending on which face you choose, the same word can have many different shades of meaning. And since you must have type in order to have words, why not make sure those words are presented in the most elegant, or the most powerful, or the softest way possible.
—Roger Black
from an interview in Font & Function

You can also make your own spec sheets for the typefaces available on your own system or network. The little time it takes will repay you generously every time you need to design a publication. In addition to providing you with a useful resource, making spec sheets is a good way to begin learning the nuances of type.

The page at right shows one format for a spec sheet. Depending upon the kind of publication work you do, you may want to vary the components, with more or less display type, more or less running text, more or fewer small-size settings for captions, data, and so on. You may also want more variation in line length than our sample shows. Expand it to two pages, include character counts for various settings—in short, do whatever will be most useful to you. Once you have a format worked out and have set up one complete spec sheet as an electronic page, you can simply open a copy of that page for each typeface in your system, change the typeface, and then type over the identifying names for the new typeface. By using the same words and style for each sheet, you'll get a true comparison between the faces that are available to you.

In the sample, we've kerned the name of the typeface at the very top of the page, adding space between letters where needed so that none of the letters butt. You want to be able to see the shape of each letter when you use the spec sheets as an identification aid.

GARAMOND

Garamond Light
Garamond Light Italic
Garamond Bold
Garamond Bold Italic

ABCDEFGHIJKLMNOPQRSTUVWXYZ
abcdefghijklmnopqrstuvwxyz
1234567890!@#$%^&*( )+[ ] , ; " " ?

WALDEN BY HENRY DAVID THOREAU   12/14
WALDEN BY HENRY DAVID THOREAU

WALDEN BY HENRY DAVID THOREAU   caps/sm caps
WALDEN BY HENRY DAVID THOREAU

Walden by Henry David Thoreau
Walden by Henry David Thoreau

14/16

When I wrote the following pages, I lived alone, in the woods, a mile from any neighbor, in a house which I had built myself, on the shore of Walden Pond.

9/11

I lived alone, in the woods, a mile from any neighbor, in a house which I had built myself, on the shore of Walden

I lived alone, in the woods, a mile from any neighbor, in a house which I had built myself, on the shore of

11/13

When I wrote
the following pages,
or rather
the bulk of them,
I lived alone, in the woods,
a mile from any neighbor,
on the shore of Walden Pond.

36

Aa Ee Gg Tt Ww
1 2 3 4 5 6 7 8 9 $? ' '

When I wrote the following pages, or rather the bulk of them, I lived alone, in the woods, a mile from any neighbor, in a house which I had built myself, on the shore of Walden Pond, in Concord, Massachusetts, and earned my living by the labor of my hands only. I lived there two years and two months. At present I am a sojourner in civilized life again.

I should not obtrude my affairs so much on the notice of my readers if very

W 72

hen I wrote the following pages, or rather the bulk of them, I lived alone, in the woods, a mile from any neighbor, in a house which I had built myself, on the shore of Walden Pond, in Concord, Massachusetts, and earned my living by the labor of my hands only. I lived there two years and two months. At present I am a sojourner in civilized life again.

I should not obtrude my affairs so much on the notice of my readers if

When I wrote the following pages, or rather the bulk of them, I lived alone, in the woods, a mile from any neighbor, in a house which I had built myself, on the shore of Walden Pond, in Concord, Massachusetts, and earned my living by the labor of my hands only. I lived there two years and two months. At present I am a sojourner in civilized life again.

I should not obtrude my affairs so much on the notice of my

When I wrote the following pages, or rather the bulk of them, I lived alone, in the woods, a mile from any neighbor, in a house which I had built myself, on the shore of Walden Pond, in Concord, Massachusetts, and earned my living by the labor of my hands only. I lived there two years and two months. At present I am a sojourner in civilized life again.

I should not obtrude my affairs so much on the notice of

Using key letters to identify type

When using spec sheets to identify type from other publications, look for key letters that tend to be distinctive, including the T, g, and M shown here (all 60 point). Numbers and question marks are also good indicators. You quickly learn to look for the shape of the serif (straight, triangular, rounded, or square), whether the bowls of the Ps and Rs and the tails of the g's are open or closed, the contrast between thick and thin parts of the letter, and so on.

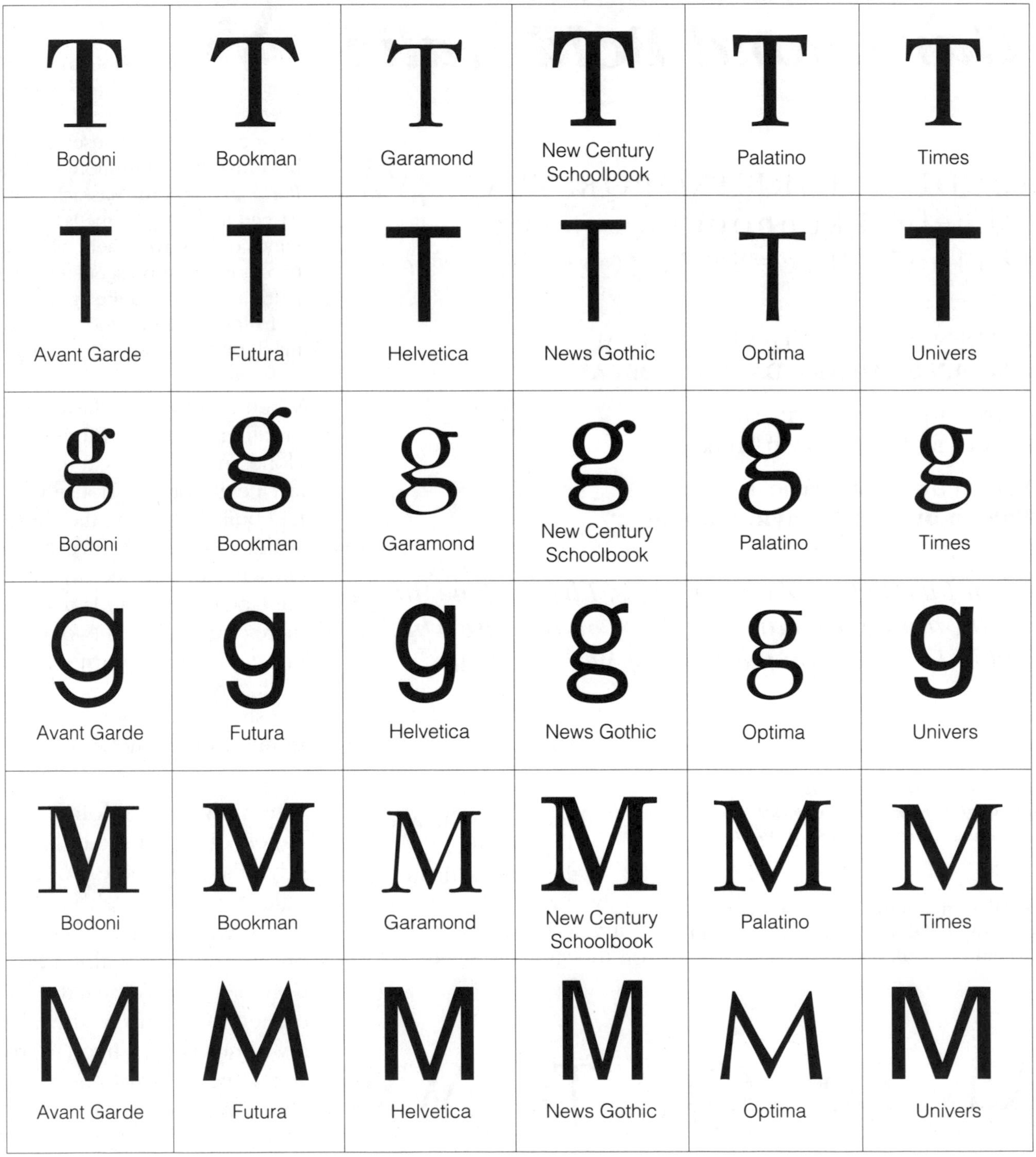

T	T	T	T	T	T
Bodoni	Bookman	Garamond	New Century Schoolbook	Palatino	Times
T	T	T	T	T	T
Avant Garde	Futura	Helvetica	News Gothic	Optima	Univers
g	g	g	g	g	g
Bodoni	Bookman	Garamond	New Century Schoolbook	Palatino	Times
g	g	g	g	g	g
Avant Garde	Futura	Helvetica	News Gothic	Optima	Univers
M	M	M	M	M	M
Bodoni	Bookman	Garamond	New Century Schoolbook	Palatino	Times
M	M	M	M	M	M
Avant Garde	Futura	Helvetica	News Gothic	Optima	Univers

The color of type

The addition of a second (or several) colors can enhance the typographic design of a publication in many ways. But even when printed in black and white, type has a color on the printed page. Color in this sense means the overall tone, or texture, of the type; the lightness or darkness, which varies from one typeface and style to another; and also the eveness of the type as determined by the spacing. Spec sheets provide valuable guides to the color of different typefaces, which, as you can see in the samples below, vary considerably.

A large rose-tree stood near the entrance of the garden: the roses growing on it were white, but there were three gardeners at it, busily painting them red. Alice thought this a very curious thing, and she went nearer to watch....
—Futura Light

A large rose-tree stood near the entrance of the garden: the roses growing on it were white, but there were three gardeners at it, busily painting them red. Alice thought this a very curious thing, and she went nearer to...
—Goudy Old Style

A large rose-tree stood near the entrance of the garden: the roses growing on it were white, but there were three gardeners at it, busily painting them red. Alice thought this a very curious thing, and she went nearer to...
—Optima

A large rose-tree stood near the entrance of the garden: the roses growing on it were white, but there were three gardeners at it, busily painting them red. Alice thought this a very curious thing, and she went nearer...
—Palatino

A large rose-tree stood near the entrance of the garden: the roses growing on it were white, but there were three gardeners at it, busily painting them red. Alice thought this a very curious thing, and she went nearer to...
—Garamond

A large rose-tree stood near the entrance of the garden: the roses growing on it were white, but there were three gardeners at it, busily painting them red. Alice thought this a very curious thing...
—Avant Garde

A large rose-tree stood near the entrance of the garden: the roses growing on it were white, but there were three gardeners at it, busily painting them red. Alice thought this a very curious thing...
—Univers

A large rose-tree stood near the entrance of the garden: the roses growing on it were white, but there were three gardeners at it, busily painting them red. Alice thought this a very curious thing, and she went nearer...
—Franklin Gothic Demi

A large rose-tree stood near the entrance of the garden: the roses growing on it were white, but there were three gardeners at it, busily painting them red. Alice thought this a very curious thing, and she went nearer...
—Helvetica

A large rose-tree stood near the entrance of the garden: the roses growing on it were white, but there were three gardeners at it, busily painting them red. Alice thought this a very curious thing, and she went nearer to watch....
—New Baskerville Bold

A large rose-tree stood near the entrance of the garden: the roses growing on it were white, but there were three gardeners at it, busily painting them red. Alice thought this a very curious thing...
—Souvenir Demi

A large rose-tree stood near the entrance of the garden: the roses growing on it were white, but there were three gardeners at it, busily painting them red. Alice thought this a very curious thing...
—Bookman Demi

A large rose-tree stood near the entrance of the garden: the roses growing on it were white, but there were three gardeners at it, busily painting them red. Alice thought this a very curious thing, and she went nearer to watch....
—Glypha

A large rose-tree stood near the entrance of the garden: the roses growing on it were white, but there were three gardeners at it, busily painting them red. Alice thought this a very curious thing, and she went nearer to watch....
—Century Old Style Bold

A large rose-tree stood near the entrance of the garden: the roses growing on it were white, but there were three gardeners at it, busily painting them red. Alice thought this a very curious thing and she went ...
—Am. Typewriter Bold

A large rose-tree stood near the entrance of the garden: the roses growing on it were white, but there were three gardeners at it, busily painting them red. Alice thought this a very curious...
—Futura Extra Bold

The many personalities of type

Typefaces clothe words. And words clothe ideas and information.... Typefaces can do for words, and through words for ideas and information, what clothes can do for people. It isn't just the hat or tie or suit or dress you wear. It's the way you put it on...and its appropriateness to you and to the occasion that make the difference. And so it is with type. A type library is a kind of wardrobe with garments for many occasions. You use your judgment and taste to choose and combine them to best dress your words and ideas.
— U&lc, June 1980,
cited in an Adobe poster

Every typeface has its own personality, a look that makes it more or less suited for a particular type of publication. Confident, elegant, casual, bold, novel, romantic, friendly, stylish, nostalgic, classic, delicate, modern, crisp...the possibilities are endless. You have only to know the feeling you want, select an appropriate face, and then test it for legibility and effectiveness within your overall design.

The faces shown on these pages merely suggest the range available to today's desktop publisher. Having to choose from the many faces available can be intimidating to new designers. Begin by using a few faces and learning them well: how to achieve contrast through different styles and spacing within those families, which letter pairs require kerning, which counters fill in at small sizes, and so on.

Take note of typefaces you like in other publications and identify them using a type book. Then gradually add new faces to your system, learning their unique subtleties as you did the few faces that you started with. As one designer cautioned in the same *Publish* roundtable on typography quoted earlier in this chapter, "There are only two kinds of typefaces: those you know how to use and those you don't."

GEOMETRY AND PRECISION
WHEN YOU WANT THE CUTTING EDGE

USE AVANT GARDE. IT'S MODERN WITHOUT BEING FORMAL AND GIVES A PAGE A VERY CRISP LOOK. IT SETS BEST IN ALL CAPS AND BENEFITS FROM KERNING SO THAT THE LETTERS SNUGGLE UP TIGHT AGAINST ONE ANOTHER.

A REPORT THAT SUGGESTS
The Writer Has Big Shoulders

would work well in Bookman. It's a sturdy, highly legible typeface, used in many newspapers and often described as a workhorse because it's so versatile. In both its light and bold faces, it has relatively little contrast between the thick and thin strokes.

WHEN YOU WANT TO KNOW THE SCORE

MACHINE IS THERE TO DELIVER IT IN A VERY BOLD WAY. IT IS A FACE WITH NO CURVES, ONLY ANGLES, AND IT SETS VERY CONDENSED. IT SHOULD BE USED FOR SHORT DISPLAY COPY ONLY AND NO SMALLER THAN 18 POINT (WHICH IS WHY THIS 9-POINT DESCRIPTION IS SET IN HELVETICA LIGHT RATHER THAN IN MACHINE). FOR BEST VISUAL RESULTS, MACHINE SHOULD BE KERNED. IN THE SAMPLE ABOVE, WE'VE KERNED TO TIGHTEN UP BOTH THE LETTER AND THE WORD SPACE.

This message demands your immediate attention...

so it is set in American Typewriter, which has the immediacy of a standard typewriter face but is more sophisticated. Type sets more economically, with more words per line, in this face than in true typewriter faces such as Courier.

If the plan is to GET ON THE FAST TRACK

try Lubalin Graph Demi. It's actually a serif version of Avant Garde with a square, Egyptian-style serif that is both modern and utilitarian. (Both Lubalin Graph Demi and Avant Garde were created by renowned designer Herb Lubalin.)

LIGHT AS THE ESSENCE OF SUNSHINE
AND BOLD AS A MOONLESS NIGHT

is the broad personality of Futura. It's a classic typeface: Born of the machine age in the twenties, it continues to be a designer favorite. Its versatility ranges from advertising to editorial, from fashion to technology. It comes in a wide selection of weights and widths. An all-time favorite combination is Futura Light and Extra Bold, shown above. This text is Futura Light Condensed.

If the need is to be DRAMATIC AND SOPHISTICATED AT THE SAME TIME

then look no further than the Bodoni family. It is very urban, with a touch of the theatrical. This is especially true with Bodoni Poster, used above. This text is in Bodoni Bold.

THE ANNUAL MESSAGE FROM THE EXECUTIVE OFFICES

might well be set in Garamond. It's an extremely graceful, refined, and legible face that suggests the confidence that comes from success. The italic face is highly legible (many italic faces are not), as you can see from these few lines set in Garamond Light Italic.

The efficiency of type

The number of characters per line varies from one typeface to another, even when the same size type is specified. A typeface that has a relatively high character count per line is said to set efficiently (or tightly or economically), and is likely to look smaller than a less efficient typeface set in the same size.

Traditional type charts (and some books on typography) provide tables for determining the character count of each typeface in various sizes and line lengths. These may not translate with 100 percent accuracy to your desktop system because there are subtle differences in the same typeface from one manufacturer to another. Still, they can be helpful for determining the relative efficiency of different faces, as well as the approximate character count for your type specifications.

The words in these twelve blocks of text are exactly the same, and each text block is set 10/12. But the length varies from 10 to 15 lines because some typefaces set more economically than others, with more characters per line. Note also that the type in the shortest text block does not look the smallest. A condensed typeface with a large x-height sets tighter than a noncondensed face but still looks larger.

—Times Roman

The words in these twelve blocks of text are exactly the same, and each text block is set 10/12. But the length varies from 10 to 15 lines because some typefaces set more economically than others, with more characters per line. Note also that the type in the shortest text block does not look the smallest. A condensed typeface with a large x-height sets tighter than a noncondensed face but still looks larger.

—Garamond

The words in these twelve blocks of text are exactly the same, and each text block is set 10/12. But the length varies from 10 to 15 lines because some typefaces set more economically than others, with more characters per line. Note also that the type in the shortest text block does not look the smallest. A condensed typeface with a large x-height sets tighter than a noncondensed face but still looks larger.

—New Baskerville

The words in these twelve blocks of text are exactly the same, and each text block is set 10/12. But the length varies from 10 to 15 lines because some typefaces set more economically than others, with more characters per line. Note also that the type in the shortest text block does not look the smallest. A condensed typeface with a large x-height sets tighter than a noncondensed face but still looks larger.

—Helvetica Condensed Light

The words in these twelve blocks of text are exactly the same, and each text block is set 10/12. But the length varies from 10 to 15 lines because some typefaces set more economically than others, with more characters per line. Note also that the type in the shortest text block does not look the smallest. A condensed typeface with a large x-height sets tighter than a noncondensed face but still looks larger.

—Futura

The words in these twelve blocks of text are exactly the same, and each text block is set 10/12. But the length varies from 10 to 15 lines because some typefaces set more economically than others, with more characters per line. Note also that the type in the shortest text block does not look the smallest. A condensed typeface with a large x-height sets tighter than a noncondensed face but still looks larger.

—News Gothic

The samples on these two pages show the relative efficiency of a number of popular faces, with the serif faces across the top and the sans serif faces across the bottom. (All are from Adobe Systems.) In general, the more efficient faces have a smaller x-height; in addition to getting more characters per line, these faces require less lead because there is more built-in white space between the lines. Note the relatively small visual size and open lines of the New Baskerville setting, for example, compared to the larger, visually tighter look of Bookman or Avant Garde.

When efficiency is extremely important, consider using a condensed face with a large x-height. Note that the Helvetica Condensed Light sample looks larger than some of the others even though it sets the most economically.

The words in these twelve blocks of text are exactly the same, and each text block is set 10/12. But the length varies from 10 to 15 lines because some typefaces set more economically than others, with more characters per line. Note also that the type in the shortest text block does not look the smallest. A condensed typeface with a large x-height sets tighter than a noncondensed face but still looks larger.

—Palatino

The words in these twelve blocks of text are exactly the same, and each text block is set 10/12. But the length varies from 10 to 15 lines because some typefaces set more economically than others, with more characters per line. Note also that the type in the shortest text block does not look the smallest. A condensed typeface with a large x-height sets tighter than a noncondensed face but still looks larger.

—New Century Schoolbook

The words in these twelve blocks of text are exactly the same, and each text block is set 10/12. But the length varies from 10 to 15 lines because some typefaces set more economically than others, with more characters per line. Note also that the type in the shortest text block does not look the smallest. A condensed typeface with a large x-height sets tighter than a noncondensed face but still looks larger.

—Bookman

The words in these twelve blocks of text are exactly the same, and each text block is set 10/12. But the length varies from 10 to 15 lines because some typefaces set more economically than others, with more characters per line. Note also that the type in the shortest text block does not look the smallest. A condensed typeface with a large x-height sets tighter than a noncondensed face but still looks larger.

—Helvetica

The words in these twelve blocks of text are exactly the same, and each text block is set 10/12. But the length varies from 10 to 15 lines because some typefaces set more economically than others, with more characters per line. Note also that the type in the shortest text block does not look the smallest. A condensed typeface with a large x-height sets tighter than a noncondensed face but still looks larger.

—Univers

The words in these twelve blocks of text are exactly the same, and each text block is set 10/12. But the length varies from 10 to 15 lines because some typefaces set more economically than others, with more characters per line. Note also that the type in the shortest text block does not look the smallest. A condensed typeface with a large x-height sets tighter than a noncondensed face but still looks larger.

—Avant Garde

STYLING TYPE IN PAGEMAKER

It is very difficult to give general rules for specifying type. The variables are so numerous—the kind of publication, the nature of the audience, the size of the page, the type of reading material, the relationship of text to white space, how the text is broken up, the resolution of the output, the quality of the printing, and on and on and on.

Outside of design school, there are two basic ways to learn about styling type. The first is to examine printed material and note what, to your eye, does and doesn't work. Does the type get your attention? Is it easy to read? Does it help move your eye from one part of the page to another and clarify the relationship between different items? Do special typographic effects further the communication or are they gratuitous? You'll find comments about how type is used in many of the samples reproduced in the next several chapters of this book (and also in some of the books listed in the Resources section). This kind of commentary seems more useful to us than general rules.

The second way to learn about type is to experiment. Desktop publishing facilitates experimentation to an unprecedented degree, which alone is likely to speed the learning curve of anyone coming into the field of graphic design today. Even a seasoned designer may need several settings before getting just the right relationship of display to body text, the desired contrast between captions or sidebars and the main story, and the balance of size, leading, and column width for the amount of text on a page. With commercial typesetting, both the cost and the turnaround time severely limit the ability to test different possibilities; when you work on the desktop, the time is your own (which, to be sure, can be a mixed blessing), and the cost of laser printouts is a few cents each.

You should take advantage of this ability to experiment once you are comfortable with the mechanics of changing and controlling type in PageMaker. (See the Projects section for hands-on practice with the mechanics.) In fact, "playing" with type styles is a good way to learn both the mechanics of the program and the nuances of type. In addition to creating spec sheets as described earlier in this chapter, experimenting with different type settings in the early stages of any particular project is likely to be a good investment of time. Use text in whatever stage it exists, or use a file of dummy type. PageMaker 3.0 comes with a *lorem ipsum* file, a Latin text which designers often use in the early layouts of a project; you'll see it also in many of the sample documents we created for this book. Some designers actually prefer using *lorem ipsum* to real text in the early stages because it encourages people to focus on the format and design, rather than on reading the copy.

When you begin to develop the format for a project, try two or three different typefaces with several settings. If you know you need a

---

TIP

Keyboard shortcuts for formatting text can save you time when you are testing different specifications. Here are some of the most useful:

	Macintosh	PC
One pt larger	Opt-Com-Shft->	F4
One pt smaller	Opt-Com-Shft-<	F3
Align left	Command-Shift-L	Ctrl-L
Align right	Command-Shift-R	Ctrl-R
Justify	Command-Shift-J	Ctrl-J
Center	Command-Shift-C	Ctrl-C
Bold	Command-Shift-B	F6
Italic	Command-Shift-I	F7
Plain text	Com-Shift-Spbar	F5
All caps	Command-Shift-K	N/A
Small caps	Command-Shift-H	N/A
Subscript	Command-Shift--	N/A
Superscript	Command-Shift-+	N/A

relatively small text size, try 9/10, 9/11, 10/11, 10/12. Remember that in PageMaker you can specify leading in increments of 0.5 point; an extra half point may be just what you need to achieve the proper balance. (You must specify type in whole-point sizes.) Vary the margins and the space between columns. Stretch the windowshade handles horizontally to see different line lengths. Try different headline treatments in relation to the body text—different sizes and styles, with different amounts of space between the headline and the text. The size of the headline should be proportional to the column width, the body text size, and the length and importance of the story.

Once you have a text block or a number of different text elements formatted, you can use the Select All command or draw a marquee around them, copy them, paste them on another page, and change the type specs for comparison. No lesson in any book will teach you as much as the comparisons you make of these printouts.

Learn early on to use the Paragraph Specifications dialog box to specify paragraph indents and space between paragraphs or between different text elements, such as headlines and body text. For many new users, the familiar typewriter functions of the space bar and the carriage return

MEASURING TYPE

As mentioned previously, type is measured vertically, in points, and line lengths are measured in picas. Of course you can measure lines and page elements other than type in inches as well, but because type size and line length are so interrelated, it is useful to become comfortable with picas and to be able to visualize in that system of measure. If you have not worked with points and picas before, you will soon appreciate the small unit of measure this system provides:

12 points = 1 pica

6 picas = 1 inch

To measure type in printed samples, you will need a type gauge, a special ruler with several slots running for most of its length and various sizes (usually ranging from 5 or 6 to 15 points) marked along the sides of different slots. You can buy a type gauge in any art supply store; they're very inexpensive. (The most common one is called a Haberule.) When using a type gauge, keep in mind that the conversion from picas to inches is slightly different from that on the computer: 6 picas (72 points) is 0.996 inches on a traditional type ruler; the conversion has been rounded off in most desktop publishing systems, where the 72 dots-per-inch resolution of many monitors converts so easily to 72 points to the inch.

seem easier, but it is virtually impossible to maintain consistency using them, or to remember, when you compare different samples, how much space you inserted. (When several people work on the same job, space bar and carriage return spacing can really wreak havoc.) Learn the keyboard shortcut for displaying the Paragraph Specifications dialog box (Command-m on a Macintosh, Ctrl-m on a PC) and use the

A HANDFUL OF TYPOGRAPHIC CONVENTIONS

If you're a writer or editor used to working on a typewriter or word processor or a designer used to sending manuscripts out to someone else to typeset or new to publishing altogether, you should remember these typographic conventions:

• **Space between sentences** One space after a period at the end of a sentence is sufficient. It's difficult to get used to this if you've spent years pressing a typewriter space bar twice between sentences, but typesetting requires only one space after periods, question marks, exclamation points, and colons.

• **Dash** Type Option-Shift-hyphen (Ctrl-Shift-= on a PC) to get a long dash—also called an em dash—rather than typing two hyphens as you do on a typewriter. (Mac users: If you get a short dash close to the baseline, you've typed Command instead of Option, thus specifying a subscript instead of a dash; select that subscript dash and change the Position option to Normal in the Type Specs dialog box.)

For an en dash, used to indicate continuing or inclusive numbers such as 1988–1991, type Option-hyphen (Ctrl-= on a PC).

• **Quotation Marks and Apostrophe** Type Option-[to open a quotation and Option-Shift-[to close a quotation. (On a PC, type Ctrl-Shift-[to open quotes and Ctrl-Shift-] to close them.) This will give you true "typeset" quotation marks designed for the font you are using instead of straight, "typewriter style" marks. When you place text in Page-Maker from a word-processing program, you can get typeset-style quotation marks automatically by selecting the Convert Quotes option in the Place dialog box, but you will need to use the keyboard sequence for quotation marks that you type in PageMaker.

For single quotation marks, the keyboard sequences are Option-] to open the quote and Option-Shift-] to close the quote. (On a PC, type Ctrl-[to open single quotes and Ctrl-] to close them.)

For an apostrophe, use the Option-Shift-] sequence (Ctrl-] on a PC).

• **Ellipsis** Type Option-semicolon on a Mac to insert three properly spaced dots when you omit words from a quote or want to use this punctuation to suggest a pause. On a PC, the ASCII value for an ellipsis is 201 in some fonts.

TIP

Do not press the space bar numerous times to indent paragraphs, align text or numbers in columns, or create hanging indents. What appears aligned onscreen may not be aligned on the printed page. In addition to the options available through the Paragraph and Indents/Tabs commands, use the following typographic spaces as needed:

Space	Macintosh	PC
em	Command-Shift-M	Ctrl-Shift-M
en	Command-Shift-N	Ctrl-Shift-N
fixed	Option-space bar	n/a
thin	Command-Shift-T	Ctrl-Shift-T

Tab key to move from one value box to another; you'll be amazed at how quickly you can specify indents and spacing. (See Projects 4 and 5 for practice with the Paragraph Specifications box.)

For most people, setting tabs properly is more difficult than specifying indents and line spacing, but if you need tabs, you won't get them right until you learn to use the Indents/Tabs dialog box. (It's called Indents/Tabs because you can also set left, first, and right indents in this dialog box.) Don't even be tempted to use the space bar to set tabs; it simply won't work. (See Projects 3 and 5 for hands-on practice with tabs.)

For complex documents, use the Styles command to specify various type elements. Then open a copy of the test document, change whatever style specifications you want for your next sample, and those styles will automatically be changed throughout the document. (See Projects 4 and 5 for working with style sheets.)

And, as we will say many times throughout this book, get ideas from other publications. If you see headlines or body text that has the feeling you want, use a type book to identify the typeface, measure the size and leading with a type gauge, run out a sample on your computer, and begin building your type design from that base.

TYPOGRAPHIC REFINEMENTS

Part of what distinguishes well-executed typography is the fine-tuning of details that we generally take for granted, such as hyphenation and the space between letters and words. This section will briefly address some of those details.

Hyphenation

You can turn hyphenation on and off through Pagemaker's Paragraph Specifications dialog box. You can also specify a zone of hyphenation through the Spacing dialog box. The smaller the number you specify for the zone, the softer the rag will be in flush left, ragged right text (and the more two- or three-letter word divisions you're likely to get).

Soft rag	Hard rag
The first type sample has a soft rag, with relatively little difference between the short and long lines; hyphenation is used to make every line as long as possible without forcing the text to be justified on the right margin. The second sample has a hard rag, with some of the lines much shorter than others, because hyphenation is not allowed.	The first type sample has a soft rag, with relatively little difference between the short and long lines; hyphenation is used to make every line as long as possible without forcing the text to be justified on the right margin. The second sample has a hard rag, with some of the lines much shorter than others, because hyphenation is not allowed.

TIP

To add a discretionary hyphen, which PageMaker will insert only if a line break occurs at that point, set an insertion point and then type Command-hyphen on a Mac, Ctrl-hyphen on a PC. To delete an undesirable hyphen (such as one that occurs in an already hyphenated word), insert a discretionary hyphen immediately preceding the word to force the word to the next line (or edit the text to pull up all of the word to the line it begins on).

With a very hard rag, you may sometimes want to fill a hole at the end of a short line for a more even appearance, and you can do this by adding a discretionary hyphen. It's called discretionary because Page-Maker inserts it only if the word breaks at that point; if later editing causes the word to fall anywhere other than the end of the line, Page-Maker won't insert the hyphen. See the marginal tip for how to insert a discretionary hyphen.

A few do's and don'ts for end-of-line hyphenation:

- Don't hyphenate words in headlines and other display text.
- Don't hyphenate captions set to a very short measure.
- Don't hyphenate more than two consecutive lines.
- Do observe the proper conventions for word division. Use an unabridged dictionary and a good style manual (see the Resources section at the end of this book).

Pay attention to headlines

Because they are set large, headlines often require some typographic refinement. It's not simply that their size and styling make them such a dominant element on the page but also that larger-size type in general requires special attention.

Editorially, the purpose of a headline is to attract the reader's attention, to make the subject immediately apparent, and to indicate the relative importance of items. Visually, headlines add variety to page design and in the absence of art may be the primary graphic device a designer has to work with in setting a tone and style.

There are many ways to achieve visual emphasis with headlines: type size, typeface, line length, surrounding white space, and use of rules and banners are a few. You will see these and many other techniques in the samples reproduced later in this book. Whichever approach you select, your headlines will almost surely require attention to the spacing between letters, words, and lines. As much as any other aspect of typography, spacing in display type distinguishes amateurs from professionals.

TIP

When you experiment with headline sizes in PageMaker, keyboard shortcuts are real timesavers:
- one point smaller
  Mac: Option-Command-Shift-<
  PC: F3
- one point larger
  Mac: Option-Command-Shift->
  PC: F4
- The next smaller "graphic art" size listed on the Type Size submenu (Mac only)
  Command-Shift-<
- The next larger "graphic art" size
  Command-Shift->

To keep the leading proportional to the larger sizes, set the leading to Auto and, through the Spacing command, reduce the default for Auto leading from 120% to 100%.

In general, large type sizes require proportionately less leading than body text. PageMaker's automatic leading of 120%, which works very well for 10- or 11-point reading text, would result in more than 7 points of lead in a 36-point headline. Especially when headlines are set in all caps, they usually look better set solid or with minus leading so that the lines hold together as a unit.

Large type sizes also generally require kerning, the process of adjusting the space between individual letters for better overall balance. The shape of some letter pairs, such as Wo, Ya, and Tu, makes the space between the letters seem too big. The shape of other letters, such as Mi and Il, makes the letters seem too close together. Mechanically, it is very easy to adjust the space in PageMaker (see the tip on the next page), but how much to add or delete is a subjective visual judgment.

TIP

To remove space between letter pairs in PageMaker, set an insertion point with the text tool, then press Command-Backspace on a Mac, Ctrl-Backspace on a PC. To add space, press Command-Shift-Backspace on a Mac, Ctrl-Shift-Backspace on a PC.

When you kern, the goal is to achieve an overall balance of spacing across the entire headline. One approach is to imagine pouring sand between the letters and then to add or delete space so that there would be a nearly equal volume of sand between each pair. Another approach is to visually isolate three letters to see if the space on both sides of the center one is equal; you can quickly "scan" an entire headline this way.

In the samples below, the top two are set 30/30, the bottom two 20/20. The samples with the tighter leading hold together much better as a unit and are easier to read.

The top two samples have not been kerned. The unkerned Times Roman setting (top left) is better balanced than the unkerned Helvetica Condensed setting to its right; in general, serif typefaces are more forgiving of spacing imbalances because the serifs form a visual connection between the letters. Compare the kerned and unkerned samples in each typeface to see where we've added and removed space. In the Helvetica version of the word DETAIL, for example, we've closed up the ET and the TA and opened up the IL so the word doesn't seem to have a "hole" in it.

HEADLINES WITH ATTENTION TO DETAIL

Spacing is too open

Good spacing

HEADLINES WITH ATTENTION TO DETAIL

HEADLINES WITH ATTENTION TO DETAIL

Spacing is too open

Good spacing

HEADLINES WITH ATTENTION TO DETAIL

Understanding proportional leading

In the early days of typesetting, "leading" described the thin strips of lead inserted between lines of hot metal type. In electronic publishing, leading is measured from baseline to baseline as the total of the type size plus the space between lines.

PageMaker 3.0 uses proportional leading, with two-thirds of the leading above the baseline and one-third below it. So in the example below, which is set 20/24, the leading is calculated with 16 points above the baseline and 8 points below it.

```
                          This type has
24 points lead            proportional        —16 points above baseline
24 points lead                                —8 points below baseline
                          leading
```

Proportional leading ensures consistent line spacing when there is more than one size type in a given line; in such a line, leading is based on the largest leading (which may or may not be assigned to the largest type size) in the line.

In the sample below left with 10/11 body text and a 48-point inital cap, the initial cap is specified as 48/11. In the sample below right with a 14-point word inserted for emphasis in 10-point running text, the entire text block is set with 15 points of lead to accommodate the larger word.

When you have an initial cap, whether it is raised above the text or dropped in it, specify the same leading for the cap as for the body text.

If you insert a larger size text style for emphasis in a text block, specify the leading to accommodate the larger size.

A few words about emphasis

When used for emphasis, boldface, italic, underline, and all caps can sometimes have the reverse effect of what is intended.

Boldface is generally the most effective way to make type stand out. Its usefulness in **headlines** needs little comment. It can also be used to emphasize **keys words, names, or events in running text**, either as a leadin or interspersed throughout the text as it is in this paragraph. (Note, however, that some typefaces, such as the Palatino used here, do not have much contrast between the bold and regular face.) Like anything else, too much can undermine the intended effect; too much boldface also makes the page look uneven and dark. In addition, when used in small sizes, boldface type can fill in the open space in letters such as o, e, and b; this is of particular concern when using a 300 dots-per-inch printer for final output, when using paper that absorbs a lot of ink (such as newsprint), and in poorer-quality printing in general.

Italic type may be the most misused of all forms of emphasis because it is actually softer, not bolder, than roman text. The calligraphic nature of italic text also makes it relatively difficult to read. Used for captions, quotes, display type, marginalia, leadins, and other short items, *italic type can provide a subtle contrast to the main text, but it does not provide emphasis.* As is the case with boldface, some typefaces have more contrast than others between their italic and roman styles; the Palatino used here is one of them.

ALL CAPS works well in headlines but should be avoided for sustained reading. Words set in upper and lower case have distinctive and recognizable shapes. WORDS SET IN ALL CAPS LOOK LIKE RECTANGLES OF DIFFERENT LENGTHS AND ARE MORE DIFFICULT TO READ, ESPECIALLY IN RUNNING TEXT, WHERE THERE ISN'T MUCH WHITE SPACE. It's fine to use all caps sparingly to get attention or emphasize a headline. But don't overdo it.

Underlining is a holdover from typewriters, where it is one of the few means of emphasis available. Even with the many other typographic techniques in electronic publishing, underlining can be useful when there are many different elements, as in the Garamond spec sheet earlier in this chapter, and in the presentation of data and other complex information. The underline style in PageMaker, however, is heavy and sets too close to the body text in many typefaces. If you want to use underlining, draw a hairline rule with the perpendicular line tool. Remember, though, that if you edit the text, you'll have to move the underline manually. And when you use underlining for labels (as we've done for samples in this chapter), use a placeholder to maintain a uniform distance between the baseline of the text and the underline.

> In this type sample, we used the Underline style on Page-Maker's Type menu.
>
> In this type sample, we used a hairline-weight rule to achieve an underline style.

Widows and orphans

Widows and orphans are colloquialisms for words or sentences that are visually isolated. The two terms are defined a little differently in different sources. We define a widow as a short line at the end of a paragraph, or the last line of a paragraph when it is isolated at the top of a column or page. Widows have traditionally been considered bad form because they make the type appear uneven on the page and in some situations interrupt the reader's eye movement. Widows are less of a problem in ragged right text than in justified text, especially when there is space between paragraphs. The widow in this paragraph, for example, is acceptable to us; if it were the last or the first line in a column we would have eliminated it by cutting or adding to the text. In advertising and display typography, widows should always be eliminated.

We define an orphan as the opening line of a paragraph isolated at the bottom of a column or page. Orphans can interrupt the reader's eye movement at the beginning of a new thought and they should be eliminated by editing the text, either to force the orphan to the next column or to pull up additional lines of the paragraph.

SPECIAL CHARACTERS & SYMBOLS

Both the Macintosh and the PC have extended character sets that enable you to incorporate special symbols—copyright and register marks, pound and yen signs, accents used in foreign languages, and so on—into your documents.

On the Macintosh, you can review the special characters by selecting the Key Caps desk accessory from the Apple menu. This displays the Key Caps window, which displays a typewriter keyboard. When this window is active, the usual PageMaker menu bar is replaced by the Key Caps menu bar. Point to the Key Caps menu, hold down the mouse button, and scroll to select the typeface you want. The keyboard in the Key Caps window will correspond to that typeface. With the Key Caps window still visible, press Option and Option-Shift to see the extended characters available for each key in the selected typeface. To insert a special character in your document, close the Key Caps window, set an insertion point with the text tool, check that the correct typeface is selected, and then type the appropriate key combinations.

In PC PageMaker, the situation is more complex because it is less uniform: Different printer fonts have different extended character sets, and there is no on-screen equivalent to the sort of directory provided by the Macintosh Key Caps accessory. Appendix D of the PC Page-Maker *Reference Manual* lists the ANSI character set used in Windows and also the HP Roman 8 character set used by some fonts. It's possible, though, that what you see on the screen will not match what is printed. In that situation, you'll need to keep a list of the characters, the keyboard commands, and the screen characters displayed for each.

Here are few commonly used characters. (A blank means that a special font is required for that character.) PC users note: All numbers in Alt key combinations must be entered on the numeric keypad. Typing Alt + 0 + the subsequent three-digit number instructs PageMaker to remap the standard ASCII code to the ANSI code used in Windows.

Char	Macintosh	PC
®	Option-r	Ctrl-Shift-R
©	Option-g	Ctrl-Shift-C
™	Option-2	
£	Option-3	Alt-0163
¢	Option-4	Alt-0162
¥	Option-y	Alt-0165
§	Option-6	Ctrl-Shift-M
¶	Option-7	Ctrl-Shift-7
•	Option-8	Ctrl-Shift-8
∞	Option-5	
÷	Option-/	
√	Option-v	

Char	Macintosh	PC
´	Option-e then type letter	*Accents not separated from letters; see the PageMaker Reference Manual for list.*
¨	Option-u then type letter	
^	Option-i then type letter	
~	Option-n then type letter	
ç	Option-c	Alt-0231
Ç	Option-Shift-C	Alt-0199
¿	Option-Shift-/	Alt-0191
¡	Option-1	Alt-0161
¼		Alt-0188
½		Alt-0189
⅓		Alt-0190

ZAPF DINGBATS

The Zapf Dingbats typeface provides useful typographic embellishments. It is resident on many PostScript printers and available as a downloadable font from Adobe. The characters are shown below with the key combinations used to produce them. (The Shift and Option keys are abbreviated as "Sh" and "Op," respectively.) PC users: For characters in columns 4, 5, and 6, you must hold down the Alt key and use the numeric keypad to type 0 and the three numbers listed.

Ch	Mac/PC	Ch	Mac/PC
✁	Sh-1	✣	Sh-C
✂	Sh-'	✤	Sh-D
✃	Sh-3	✥	Sh-E
✄	Sh-4	✦	Sh-F
☎	Sh-5	✧	Sh-G
✆	Sh-7	★	Sh-H
✇	'	☆	Sh-I
✈	Sh-9	✪	Sh-J
✉	Sh-0	✫	Sh-K
☛	Sh-8	✬	Sh-L
☞	Sh-=	✭	Sh-M
✌	,	✮	Sh-N
✍	-	✯	Sh-O
✎	.	✰	Sh-P
✏	/	✱	Sh-Q
✐	0	✲	Sh-R
✑	1	✳	Sh-S
✒	2	✴	Sh-T
✓	3	✵	Sh-U
✔	4	✶	Sh-V
✕	5	✷	Sh-W
✖	6	✸	Sh-X
✗	7	✹	Sh-Y
✘	8	✺	Sh-Z
✙	9	✻	[
✚	Sh-;	✼	\
✛	;	✽	]
✜	Sh-,	✾	Sh-6
✝	=	✿	Sh- -
✞	Sh-.	❀	`
✟	Sh-/	❁	a
✠	Sh-2	❂	b
✡	Sh-A	❃	c
✢	Sh-B	❄	d

Ch	Mac/PC
❅	e
❆	f
❇	g
❈	h
❉	i
❊	j
❋	k
●	l
❍	m
■	n
❏	o
❐	p
❑	q
❒	r
▲	s
▼	t
◆	u
❖	v
◗	w
❘	x
❙	y
❚	z
❛	Sh-[
❜	Sh-\
❝	Sh-]
❞	Op-n (Mac only)

Ch	Mac	PC
❡	Sh-Op-8	161
❢	Op-4	162
❣	Op-3	163
❤	Op-6	164
❥	Op-8	165
❦	Op-7	166
❧	Op-s	167
♣	Op-r	168
♦	Op-g	169
♥	Op-2	170
♠	Op-e	171
①	Op-u	172
②	Op-=	173
③	Sh-Op-'	174
④	Sh-Op-O	175
⑤	Op-5	176
⑥	Sh-Op-=	177
⑦	Op-,	178
⑧	Op-.	179
⑨	Op-y	180
⑩	Op-m	181
❶	Op-d	182
❷	Op-w	183
❸	Sh-Op-P	184
❹	Op-p	185
❺	Op-b	186
❻	Op-9	187
❼	Op-0	188
❽	Op-z	189
❾	Op-'	190
❿	Op-o	191

Ch	Mac	PC
➀	Sh-Op-/	192
➁	Op-1	193
➂	Op-l	194
➃	Op-v	195
➄	Op-f	196
➅	Op-x	197
➆	Op-j	198
➇	Op-\	199
➈	Sh-Op-\	200
➉	Op-;	201
➊	Op-spbar	202
➋	(PC only)	203
➌	(PC only)	204
➍	(PC only)	205
➎	Sh-Op-Q	206
➏	Op-q	207
➐	Op- -	208
➑	Sh-Op- -	209
➒	Op-[	210
➓	Sh-Op-[	211
➔	Op-]	212
→	Sh-Op-]	213
↔	Op-/	214
↕	Sh-Op-V	215
➘	(PC only)	216
➙	Sh-Op-	217
➚	Sh-Op-1	218
➛	Sh-Op-2	219
➜	Sh-Op-3	220
➝	Sh-Op-4	221
➞	Sh-Op-5	222

Ch	Mac	PC
➟	Sh-Op-6	223
➠	Sh-Op-7	224
➡	Sh-Op-9	225
➢	Sh-Op-0	226
➣	Sh-Op-W	227
➤	Sh-Op-E	228
➥	Sh-Op-R	229
➦	Sh-Op-T	230
➧	Sh-Op-Y	231
➨	Sh-Op-U	232
➩	Sh-Op-I	233
➪	Sh-Op-S	234
➫	Sh-Op-D	235
➬	Sh-Op-F	236
➭	Sh-Op-G	237
➮	Sh-Op-H	238
➯	Sh-Op-J	239
➱	Sh-Op-L	241
➲	Sh-Op-;	242
➳	Sh-Op-Z	243
➴	Sh-Op-X	244
➵	Sh-Op-B	245
➶	Sh-Op-N	246
➷	Sh-Op-M	247
➸	Sh-Op-,	248
➹	Sh-Op-.	249
➺	Op-H	250
➻	Op-K	251
➼	(PC only)	252
➽	(PC only)	253
➾	(PC only)	254

CHAPTER 3

CREATING A GRID: THE UNDERLYING STRUCTURE OF PAGE COMPOSITION

There is nothing mysterious about a grid. It is simply an underlying structure that defines where to put things on the page. A letter typed on an old manual typewriter uses a grid; so does a handwritten list on a sheet of paper in which you note the names of items on the left and the costs on the right. Although grids used in publication design can be considerably more complex than that, they can also be that simple.

The grid itself is a series of nonprinting vertical and horizontal lines that divide the page. This technique has been the dominant approach to publication design for at least twenty years, primarily because it provides such an effective way of organizing the page and speeds up layout time considerably. A well-constructed grid can make a lot of decisions for you—where to place the headlines, text, and art and how to handle the many details that inevitably turn up. A grid gives a publication a planned, cohesive look and helps ensure consistency from one page to the next. It also sets visual ground rules that everyone involved in a publication can follow.

A major virtue of the grid system is the discipline it imposes on the untrained designer. As a teacher of publication design, I have found that it is only when the student divides and analyzes the space he is working with that he is able to achieve a cohesive design solution.
—Allen Hurlburt, The Grid

The grid system is perfectly matched to designing on computers, where the basic unit is a square pixel. It works on the same principle as modular furniture, storage units, and old-fashioned wooden building blocks. In fact, constructing and using a grid has the same tactile tidiness and infinite variety as playing with blocks.

Of course, not all graphic designers use the grid system in their work. Some use other formal techniques, such as perspective, and some use a more intuitive, more purely aesthetic approach to page design. In general, however, designers find it far easier to introduce diversity and visual interest to a formal grid than to impose order and balance on a free-form approach.

This chapter looks at the grids found in a wide variety of publications, some of them real, some of them hypothetical documents created for this book. (The real publications carry a credit identifying the designer and the purpose of the document; the hypothetical publications, which generally use a Latin *lorem ipsum* file for running text, do not carry that credit.) The chapter begins with simple one-column grids and proceeds to increasingly complex formats. By following the progression from simple to complex, you should get a good feel for how grids work and how to use them in your publications.

Because grids provide the underlying structure of the page, we've used them as a sort of lens for looking at the other elements of page composition—typography and art. Type size and leading are inextricably related to column width, as are the size and position of graphic elements. So although the organizing principle of this chapter is grids, you will also find information about styling type and working with art. Terms that may be unfamiliar to some readers, whether having to do with graphic design or electronic page assembly, are defined in the glossary.

Throughout the chapter there are blueprints for grids that you can adapt for your own needs. Each blueprint is based on one of the hypothetical documents; your own documents may have different elements. If you use a different typeface, it might look better a little smaller or a little larger than the one in the document on which the blueprint was based. If your headline is longer than the one in the sample, you might need to adjust the space between the head and the text. The blueprints are only guidelines; as you change one element, be sure to reevaluate the others to see if additional changes are needed.

Before moving on to the structure of the page, we'll look at the shape of the page and the elements that are often found on it.

THE ANATOMY OF A PAGE

Designing and assembling pages, whether by hand or on a computer, is more than a mechanical or electronic task. It's a way of looking at a page as having a certain size, shape, and proportion.

Look through the printed material around you and you'll see that most of the pages are 8.5 by 11 inches, the same size as the letters we read and the memos we send. It's the most efficient cut of paper, it stacks up in newsstand racks with other printed material, and it fits nicely in files. But it's the vertical, or portrait shape—more than the size—that feels so familiar.

Although the page itself is usually vertical, in multipage documents the reader sees two facing pages as a horizontal unit with the slight interruption of the gutter down the center. Take advantage of this wider, more expansive unit as you organize your material and design the actual pages. And think of consecutive pages as part of a three-dimensional whole that exists in time as the reader turns the pages.

In addition to its shape, the printed page has a vocabulary that enables editors, designers, layout artists, and printers to communicate unambiguously about a job. Turn the page for a visual glossary of terms you're likely to encounter in this book and elsewhere.

THE ANATOMY OF A PRINTED PAGE

Byline The author's name, which may appear after the headline or at the end of an article.

Overline (also called a kicker or eyebrow) A brief tag over the headline that categorizes the story.

Headline The title of an article.

Deck (also called a tag line) A line that gives more information about the story.

Stick-up cap An enlarged initial letter extending above the body text.

Bleed art A photo, drawing, or tint that runs off the edge of the page.

Picture window A rectangle that indicates the position and size of art to be stripped into the page.

Caption The text describing a photograph or illustration.

Body text The main text, also called running text.

Folio The page number.

Running foot A line across the bottom of the page that helps orient the reader within a document. Here it contains the folio and date.

Verso Left-hand page (literally, the reverse, with the right-hand page considered the front).

Alley The space between columns.

Wraparound text Copy that wraps around a graphic.

Subhead A phrase that identifies a subtopic.

Inside margin The space between the binding edge of the page and the text.

THE COMPANY BULLETIN

Cover story

The Headline Goes Here

Optional secondary lines follow the headline to guide the reader into the story.

by John Hamilton

Lorem ipsum dolor sit amet, consectetuer adipiscing elit, sed diam nonummy nibh euismod tincidunt ut laoreet dolore magna aliquam erat volutpat. Ut wisi enim ad minim veniam, quis nostrud exerci tation ullamcorper suscipit lobortis nisl ut aliquip ex ea commodo consequat.

Duis autem vel eum iriure dolor in hendrerit in vulputate velit esse molestie consequat, vel illum dolore eu feugiat nulla facilisis at vero eros et accumsan et iusto odio dignissim qui blandit praesent luptatum zzril delenit augue duis dolore te feugait nulla facilisi. Lorem ipsum dolor sit amet, consectetuer adipiscing elit, sed diam nonummy nibh euismod tincidunt ut laoreet dolore magna aliquam erat volutpat.

Ut wisi enim ad minim veniam, quis nostrud exerci tation ullamcorper suscipit lobortis nisl ut aliquip ex ea commodo consequat. Duis autem vel eum iriure dolor in hendrerit in vulputate velit esse molestie consequat, vel illum dolore eu feugiat nulla facilisis at vero eros et accumsan et iusto odio dignissim qui blandit praesent luptatum zzril delenit augue duis dolore te feugait nulla facilisi.

Nam liber tempor cum soluta nobis eleifend option congue nihil imperdiet doming id quod mazim placerat facer possim assum. Lorem ipsum dolor sit amet, consectetuer adipiscing elit, sed diam nonummy nibh euismod tincidunt ut laoreet dolore magna aliquam erat volutpat. Ut wisi enim ad minim veniam, quis nostrud exerci tation ullamcorper suscipit lobortis nisl ut aliquip ex ea commodo consequat. Duis autem vel eum iriure dolor in hendrerit in vulputate velit esse molestie conse-

The caption helps entice the reader into the text of your story and also provides information about the art and photography.

quat, vel illum dolore eu feugiat nulla facilisis at vero eros et accumsan et iusto odio dignissim qui blandit praesent luptatum zzril delenit augue duis dolore te feugait nulla facilisi. Lorem ipsum dolor sit amet, consectetuer adipiscing elit, sed diam nonummy nibh euismod

Duis autem vel eum iriure

Ttincidunt ut laoreet dolore magna aliquam erat volutpat. Ut wisi enim ad minim veniam, quis nostrud exerci tation ullamcorper suscipit lobortis nisl ut aliquip ex ea commodo consequat. Duis autem vel eum iriure dolor in hendrerit in vulputate velit esse molestie consequat, vel illum dolore eu feugiat nulla facilisis at.

Vero eros et accumsan et iusto odio dignissim qui blandit praesent luptatum zzril delenit augue duis dolore te feugait nulla facilisi. Lorem ipsum dolor sit amet, consectetuer adipiscing elit, sed diam nonummy nibh euismod tincidunt ut laoreet dolore magna aliquam erat volutpat. Ut wisi enim ad minim veniam, quis nostrud exerci tation ullamcorper suscipit lobortis nisl ut aliquip ex ea commodo consequat. Duis autem vel eum iriure dolor in hendrerit in vulputate velit esse molestie consequat, vel illum dolore eu feugiat nulla facilisis at vero eros et accumsan et iusto odio dig- nissim qui blandit prae-

Sidebar A smaller story inside a larger one, boxed with its own headline to set it apart from the main text. (It can be positioned anywhere on the page.)

Breakout (also called a pull quote, blurb, or callout) A sentence or passage excerpted from the body copy and set in large type.

Top margin The distance from the top trim to the top of the text area. Running heads and feet and folios are often positioned in the top or bottom margin.

THE COMPANY BULLETIN

This display type is another technique to grab the reader's attention and pull him or her into the article.

Running head A line of text across the top of the page that helps orient the reader within a document. It might include the document's title, author, chapter, subject of current page, or page number.

Callout A label that identifies part of an illustration.

Sidebar heading is centered over the text in the sidebar

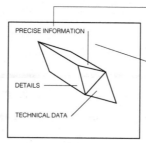

PRECISE INFORMATION

DETAILS

TECHNICAL DATA

The caption helps entice the reader into the text of your story and provides additional information about the art and photography.

◆ ◆ ◆

S equat, vel illum dolore eu feugiat nulla facilisis at vero eros et accumsan et iusto odio dignissim qui blandit praesent luptatum zzril delenit augue duis dolore te feugait nulla facilisi.

Lorem ipsum dolor sit amet, consectetuer adipiscing elit, sed diam nonummy nibh euismod tincidunt ut laoreet dolore magna aliquam erat volutpat. Ut wisi enim ad minim veniam, quis nostrud exerci tation ullamcorper suscipit lobortis nisl ut aliquip ex ea commodo consequat.

Duis autem vel eum iriure dolor in hendrerit in vulputate velit esse molestie consequat, vel illum dolore eu feugiat nulla facilisis at vero eros et accumsan et iusto odio dignissim qui blandit praesent luptatum zzril delenit augue duis dolore te feugait nulla facilisi. Lorem ipsum dolor sit amet, consectetuer adipiscing elit, sed diam.

Nonummy nibh euismod tincidunt ut laoreet dolore magna aliquam erat volutpat. Ut wisi enim ad minim veniam, quis nostrud exerci tation ullamcorper suscipit lobortis nisl ut aliquip ex ea commodo consequat.

sent luptatum zzril delenit augue duis dolore te feugait nul ummy nibh euismod tincidunt ut laoreet dol magna aliquam erat volutpat.

Ut wisi enim ad minim veniam, quis nostrud exerci tation ullamcorper suscipit lobortis nisl ut aliquip ex ea commodo consequat. Duis autem vel eum iriure dolor in hendrerit in vulputate velit esse molestie consequat, vel illum dolore eu feugiat nulla facilisis at vero eros et accumsan et iusto odio dignissim qui blandit praesent luptatum zzril delenit augue duis dolore te feugait nulla facilisi. Lorem ipsum dolor sit amet, consectetuer adipiscing elit, sed diam nonummy nibh euismod tincidunt ut laoreet dolore magna aliquam erat volutpat. Ut wisi enim ad minim veniam, quis nostrud exerci tation ullamcorper suscipit lobortis nisl ut aliquip ex ea

Continued on page 11

JANUARY 1989   9

Leader A rule that moves the eye from a callout to the part of the illustration it describes.

Dingbat A decorative or symbolic device used to separate items on the page or denote items in a list.

Outside margin The space between the outside trim and the text.

Continued line (also called jumpline) A line of text indicating the page on which an article continues. Its counterpart on the continuation page is a carryover line identifying the story that is being continued.

Bottom margin The space between the bottom trim and the baseline of the last line of text.

Drop cap An enlarged initial letter that drops below the first line of body text.

Screen (also called tone) A tint, either a percentage of black or a second color, behind text or art.

Page trim The edge of the page. In commercial printing, the size of the page after it is cut during the binding process.

Gutter The space between two facing pages.

Printing rule A rule that traps a screen or surrounds a text block or a piece of art.

Recto Right-hand page.

ONE-COLUMN GRIDS

The fewer the columns, the easier a grid is to work with. A simple one-column format requires relatively little planning and allows you to place text quickly. When done well, this format has an unstudied, straightforward look in which the hand of the designer is relatively invisible. That lack of "fuss" suggests a serious purpose that is appropriate for business plans, reports, proposals, press releases, announcements, simple manuals, and various forms of internal communications. Even when you use a two-column grid for these types of documents, consider a one-column format for the opening page to create the feeling of a foreword. When you mix grids in this way, be sure to maintain consistent margins throughout.

The generous margins and leading and the frequent subheads make this page very open for a one-column format. The text is 10/16 Helvetica with an 8-pica left margin and a 7-pica right margin.

The sans serif Helvetica face used here has a straightforward look that is well suited to factual or practical information. By comparsion, the serif type in the sample on the facing page suggests a narrative, essay-like writing style.

The 6-point rules at the top and bottom give the page structure. Note that with an anchor such as this you can vary the depth of the text from one page to the next and still maintain continuity of page format.

The justified text balances the overall openness, creating a strong right margin that completes the definition of the image area. The page would not hold together nearly as well with ragged right text.

Charts and diagrams (not shown) run as half or full pages centered left to right.

Design: Wadlin & Erber (New Paltz, NY)

Page from a manual that addresses the subject of radon occurrence in homes for an audience of building inspectors, architects, and contractors.
Trim size: 8-1/2 by 11

REDUCING INDOOR RADON

UNIT I

RADON OCCURRENCE AND HEALTH EFFECTS

Introduction

Radon is a colorless, odorless, and tasteless gas produced by the normal decay of uranium and radium. It is a naturally occuring radioactive gas produced in most soil or rock which surrounds houses. As a result, all houses will have some radon. It is an inert gas, which means it tends to be chemically inactive. Since radon is not chemically bound or attached to other materials, it can move easily through all gas permeable materials.

Radioactive Decay

Radioactive decay is the disintegration of the nucleus of atoms in a radioactive element by spontaneous emission of charged particles, often accompanied by photon (gamma) emission. As these charged particles are released, new elements are formed. The radioactive decay chain for radon begins with **uranium** producing **radium**, which in turn produces **radon.** Each of these elements has a different "half-life" (the time required for half of the atoms of a radioactive element to decay). The "half-life" is important because its length determines the time available for decay products to be dispersed into the environment.

Types of Radiation

The three types of radiation are gamma, beta, and alpha.

Gamma radiation is photon "parcels of energy" which operate at much higher energy levels than visible light. These rays are relatively high in penetrating power. They can travel much more deeply into objects than alpha or beta particles, and can pass through the body.

Beta radiation involves an energized particle emitted from the nucleus of a radioactive atom. It has a negative charge, and has a mass equal to one electron. Beta particles have medium penetrating power, and can penetrate up to about 0.5 centimeter of surface tissue, or about a millimeter of lead.

1

The simpler grids are generally "quiet." They don't allow for as much variety in art and headline treatment as the multicolumn formats, but with the typefaces, rules, and other simple graphic devices available in desktop publishing these pages can be effective and smart-looking.

Keep in mind that longer lines are more difficult to read than shorter ones because the eye has to travel farther from the end of one line to the beginning of the next. One-column pages risk becoming dense, dull, and uninviting. To compensate for this, use generous margins and space between lines and a relatively large typeface (10 to 13 points). Space between paragraphs also helps keep the page open.

The Past, Present and Future of Lotteries
People prefer to play on-line games

Three quarters of all lottery revenues in North America now come from on-line games.

1981
1983
1985
1987

Lottery sales are booming. In North America, the combined annual revenues from state-run lotteries have risen from approximately $3 billion in 1980 to over $15.7 billion in 1987.

Approximately 75 percent of the total revenues generated by North American lotteries is now derived from on-line games. The attraction of the on-line games lies in the daily drawing of the Numbers game and the frequent, multimillion-dollar jackpots of the Lotto games. These huge and enticing Lotto jackpots are the result of the top-prize pot "rolling over." The pot rolls over when all the numbers drawn were not picked by any player, and the unclaimed money rolls back into the pot for the next drawing. Rollovers cause wagering on the game to soar which, in turn, pushes the jackpot even higher until, finally, one or more lucky players win by matching the numbers drawn and the prize money is paid.

Outside of North America, those lottery jurisdictions that have added on-line technology to their operations have experienced great increases in revenues. For example, GTECH provided the first lottery-specific on-line system in Asia for Singapore Pools, Singapore's government-owned lottery company. The accompanying chart demonstrates the impact in sales gained by Singapore Pools after the GTECH network began operation.

In May 1986, Singapore Pools added on-line games. By the end of the year its sales had climbed 1600%, to average $8 million Singapore per week.

$8 million

on-line operations begin

months

The continuous running text in this sample requires a different treatment than the broken blocks of copy on the facing page. The inset art shortens the line length and makes the page more readable than it would be if the text were solid.

The margins are 6 picas top and bottom and 7 picas left and right.

The text is 12/16 Times Roman with a ragged right margin.

The headline treatment borrows editorial and typographic techniques used in magazines, with the contrasting style and size unified by the flush right alignment. The relationship of the two sizes is very nice here: The headline is 24-point Times Roman, and the tag line is 18-point Times Roman italic.

The chart, graph, and angled type were created in Adobe Illustrator. The ability to create dramatic, three-dimensional art for charts and graphs without having to be a technical illustrator is a great asset of desktop technology.

Design: Tom Ahern (Providence, RI)
Page from a capabilities brochure for GTECH, which provides on-line games for lottery networks.
Trim size: 8-1/2 by 11

Wide-margin one-column

A one-column grid with a wide margin is perhaps the most useful of all the designs in this book for internal reports, press releases, proposals, prospectuses, and other documents that have unadorned running text and need to be read fast. You may be tempted, with desktop publishing, to take something you used to distribute as a typewritten page and turn it into a multicolumn format, simply because you can. The danger is that you'll devote time to layout that would be better spent on content. As the hypothetical documents on the next three pages show, this simple one-column format can be smart, authoritative, and well planned. And though the line length is long, the white space provided by the wide margin gives the eye room to rest and makes the copy more inviting to read.

This format is especially well suited for single-sided documents that are either stapled or intended for three-ring binders. Use the left side of the page for the wide margin so that the space will look planned. (If you use the right side, it may look as though you ran out of copy and couldn't fill the page.) Although none are shown in these pages, headlines and subheads could extend into the margin for visual interest. So could short quotes, diagrams, and even small photos. When you want to make extensive use of the margin in this way, consider the "one + one-column" format discussed later in this section.

Extremely open leading facilitates quick scanning of a press release (on facing page), which usually commands less than a minute of the reader's time. The body text here is 11/20 Times Roman. With this much leading you probably would not want space between paragraphs; so you need an indent that is markedly wider than the space between lines. The indent in the sample shown is 3 picas for all paragraphs except the first.

The first paragraph is not indented. With flush left text, you rarely need to indent the opening paragraph or any paragraph that immediately follows a headline or a subhead. An indent would create an unnecessary visual gap at a place where the start of a new paragraph is obvious to the reader. To achieve this in running text where your paragraph indent is specified, for example, as 1 pica, you will need to select the opening paragraph and change its first line indent to 0.

The logo treatment can vary. The symbol could be flush with the left edge of the 6-point rule; a company name or logo could run across the top of the page, replacing the symbol and release line shown. (See the following page for an example.)

The headline should be short and straightforward. This is not the place to be clever.

The names of contacts for more information are positioned on a grid of two equal columns within the single-column format. The type is 9/12 Helvetica for contrast with the body text. If there is only one contact to list, position it in the right column of the two-column grid and move the "for immediate release" line to the left so that it is aligned left with the contact name.

The blueprint for this page appears on the following spread.

XYZ Corporation Announces New Plant Opening

For more information contact:

High Profile Publicity
Ann Millard
5432 Schoolhouse Road
Santa Monica, CA 92131
213-555-4664

XYZ Corporation
Marilyn Ferguson
1104 Beltway Drive
Los Angeles, CA 92111
213-555-3030

SANTA MONICA, CA. APRIL 10, 1989—Lorem ipsum dolor sit amet, consectetuer adipiscing elit, sed diam nonummy nibh euismod tincidunt ut laoreet dolore magna aliquam erat volutpat. Ut wisi enim ad minim veniam, quis nostrud exerci tation ullamcorper suscipit lobortis nisl ut aliquip ex ea commodo consequat. Duis autem vel eum iriure dolor in hendrerit in vulputate velit esse molestie consequat, vel illum dolore eu feugiat nulla facilisis at vero eros et accumsan et iusto odio dignissim qui blandit praesent luptatum zzril delenit augue duis dolore te feugait nulla facilisi. Lorem ipsum dolor sit amet, consectetuer adipiscing elit, sed diam nonummy nibh euismod tincidunt ut laoreet dolore magna aliquam erat volutpat. Ut wisi enim ad minim veniam, quis nostrud exerci tation ullamcorper suscipit lobortis nisl ut aliquip ex ea commodo consequat.

Duis autem vel eum iriure dolor in hendrerit in vulputate velit esse molestie consequat, vel illum dolore eu feugiat nulla facilisis at vero eros et accumsan et iusto odio dignissim qui blandit praesent luptatum zzril delenit augue duis dolore te feugait nulla facilisi. Nam liber tempor cum soluta nobis eleifend option congue nihil imperdiet doming id quod mazim placerat facer possim assum. Lorem ipsum dolor sit amet, consectetuer adipiscing elit, sed diam nonummy nibh euismod tincidunt ut laoreet dolore magna aliquam erat volutpat. Ut wisi enim ad minim veniam, quis nostrud exerci tation ullamcorper suscipit lobortis nisl ut aliquip ex ea commodo consequat. Duis autem vel eum iriure dolor in hendrerit in vulputate velit esse molestie consequat, vel illum

Business Plan for Squeaky Clean Dry Cleaning Co.

Overview
Lorem ipsum dolor sit amet, consectetuer adipiscing elit, sed diam nonummy nibh euismod tincidunt ut laoreet dolore magna aliquam erat volutpat. Ut wisi enim ad minim veniam, quis nostrud exerci tation ullamcorper suscipit lobortis nisl ut aliquip ex ea commodo consequat.

Duis autem vel eum iriure dolor in hendrerit in vulputate velit esse molestie consequat, vel illum dolore eu feugiat nulla facilisis at vero eros et accumsan et iusto odio dignissim qui blandit praesent luptatum zzril delenit augue duis dolore te feugait nulla facilisi. Lorem ipsum dolor sit amet, consectetuer adipiscing elit, sed diam nonummy nibh euismod tincidunt ut laoreet dolore magna aliquam erat volutpat. Ut wisi enim ad minim veniam, quis nostrud exerci tation ullamcorper suscipit lobortis nisl ut aliquip ex ea commodo consequat

Duis autem vel eum iriure dolor in hendrerit in vulputate velit esse molestie consequat, vel illum dolore eu feugiat nulla facilisis at vero eros et accumsan et iusto odio dignissim qui blandit praesent luptatum zzril delenit augue duis dolore te feugait nulla facilisi. Nam liber tempor cum soluta nobis eleifend option congue nihil imperdiet doming id quod mazim placerat facer possim assum.

Recent History
Lorem ipsum dolor sit amet, consectetuer adipiscing elit, sed diam nonummy nibh euismod tincidunt ut laoreet dolore magna aliquam erat volutpat. Ut wisi enim ad minim veniam, quis nostrud exerci tation ullamcorper suscipit lobortis nisl ut aliquip ex ea commodo consequat. Duis autem vel eum iriure dolor in hendrerit in vulputate velit esse molestie consequat, vel illum dolore eu feugiat nulla facilisis at vero eros et accumsan et iusto odio dignissim

Duis autem vel eum iriure dolor in hendrerit in vulputate velit esse molestie consequat, vel illum dolore eu feugiat nulla facilisis at vero eros et accumsan et iusto odio dignissim qui blandit praesent luptatum zzril delenit augue duis dolore te feugait nulla facilisi. Lorem ipsum dolor sit amet, consectetuer adipiscing elit, sed diam nonummy nibh euismod tincidunt ut laoreet dolore magna aliquam erat volutpat. Ut wisi enim ad minim veniam, quis nostrud exerci tation ullamcorper suscipit lobortis nisl ut aliquip ex ea commodo consequat Nam liber tempor cum soluta nobis eleifend option congue nihil imperdiet doming id quod mazim placerat facer possim assum.

Page 1

Business Plan for Squeaky Clean Dry Cleaning Co.

Lorem ipsum dolor sit amet, consectetuer adipiscing elit, sed diam nonummy nibh euismod tincidunt ut laoreet dolore magna aliquam erat volutpat. Ut wisi enim ad minim veniam, quis nostrud exerci tation ullamcorper suscipit lobortis nisl ut aliquip ex ea commodo consequat.

Duis autem vel eum iriure dolor in hendrerit in vulputate velit esse molestie consequat, vel illum dolore eu feugiat nulla facilisis at vero eros et accumsan et iusto odio dignissim qui blandit praesent luptatum zzril delenit augue duis dolore te feugait nulla facilisi. Lorem ipsum dolor sit amet, consectetuer adipiscing elit, sed diam nonummy nibh euismod tincidunt ut laoreet dolore magna aliquam erat volutpat. Ut wisi enim ad minim veniam, quis nostrud exerci tation ullamcorper suscipit lobortis nisl ut aliquip ex ea commodo consequat

Duis autem vel eum iriure dolor in hendrerit in vulputate velit esse molestie consequat, vel illum dolore eu feugiat nulla facilisis at vero eros et accumsan et iusto odio dignissim qui blandit praesent luptatum zzril delenit augue duis dolore te feugait nulla facilisi. Nam liber tempor cum soluta nobis eleifend option congue nihil imperdiet doming id quod mazim placerat facer possim assum.Lorem ipsum dolor sit amet, consectetuer adipiscing elit, sed diam nonummy nibh euismod tincidunt ut laoreet dolore magna aliquam erat volutpat. Ut wisi enim ad minim veniam, quis nostrud exerci tation ullamcorper suscipit lobortis nisl ut aliquip ex ea commodo consequat. Duis autem vel eum iriure dolor in hendrerit in vulputate velit esse molestie consequat, vel illum dolore eu feugiat nulla facilisis at vero eros et accumsan et iusto odio

Duis autem vel eum iriure dolor in hendrerit in vulputate velit esse molestie consequat, vel illum dolore eu feugiat nulla facilisis at vero eros et accumsan et iusto odio dignissim qui blandit praesent luptatum zzril delenit augue duis dolore te feugait nulla facilisi. Lorem ipsum dolor sit amet, consectetuer adipiscing elit, sed diam nonummy nibh euismod tincidunt ut

Duis autem vel eum iriure dolor in hendrerit in vulputate velit esse molestie consequat, vel illum dolore eu

Vulputate velit esse molestie consequat

Page 3

The following is the descriptive commentary.

The basic grid for the documents on this page is the same as the one used for the press release. Tighter leading here (11/15 Times Roman) is balanced with a full line space (15 points) between paragraphs.

The business plan above has 6 picas between the left trim and the rule. The text block is 12 picas from the top trim.

Boldface subheads are the same size as the body text. Omitting paragraph space after the subheads visually connects each subhead to its respective text block.

The company name is 14-point Times Roman bold italic.

The caption is inset in the box around the art (a style commonly found in reports and business plans) and set in 10/12 Times Roman italic.

In the proposal at right, the art is the full column width with the caption (10/13 Times Roman italic) in the margin. Note the alignment of the date, folio, rules at the top and bottom of the page, and left margin of the caption. This alignment is important: It creates an implied border that gives structure to the page.

XYZ

Prospectus for merger with ABC Corporation

January 1989

Lorem ipsum dolor sit amet, consectetuer adipiscing elit, sed diam nonummy nibh euismod tincidunt ut laoreet dolore magna aliquam erat volutpat. Ut wisi enim ad minim veniam, quis nostrud exerci tation ullamcorper suscipit lobortis nisl ut aliquip ex ea commodo consequat.

Duis autem vel eum iriure dolor in hendrerit in vulputate velit esse molestie consequat, vel illum dolore eu feugiat nulla facilisis at vero eros et accumsan et iusto odio dignissim qui blandit praesent luptatum zzril delenit augue duis dolore te feugait nulla facilisi. Lorem ipsum dolor sit amet, consectetuer adipiscing elit, sed diam nonummy nibh euismod tincidunt ut laoreet dolore magna aliquam erat volutpat. Ut wisi enim ad minim veniam, quis nostrud exerci tation ullamcorper suscipit lobortis nisl ut aliquip ex ea commodo consequat

Duis autem vel eum iriure dolor in hendrerit in vulputate velit esse molestie consequat, vel illum dolore eu feugiat nulla facilisis at vero eros et accumsan et iusto odio dignissim qui blandit praesent luptatum zzril delenit augue duis dolore te feugait nulla facilisi. Nam liber tempor cum soluta nobis eleifend option congue nihil imperdiet doming id quod mazim placerat facer possim assum.

Duis autem vel eum iriure dolor in hendrerit in vulputate velit esse molestie consequat, vel illum dolore eu feugiat nulla facilisis at vero eros et accumsan et

Duis autem vel

Dolor in hendrerit in

Page 14

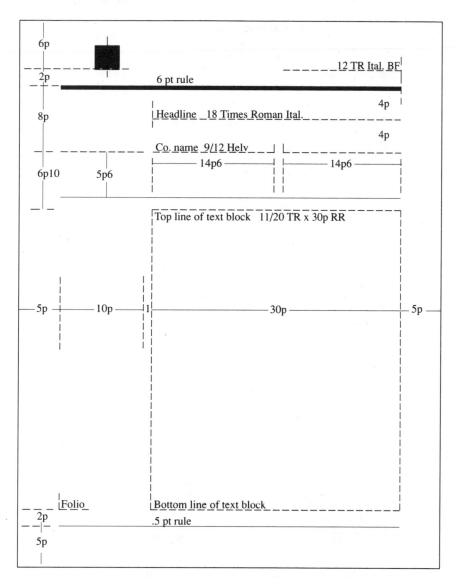

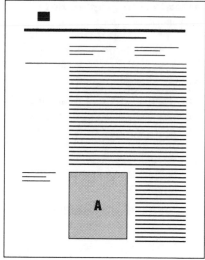

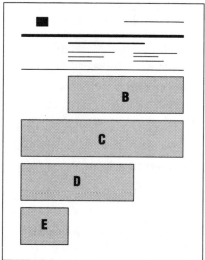

This blueprint shows the grid and type specifications for the press release on the preceding spread. The documents on the facing page use the same grid (except as noted in the annotations) but, for the most part, different type sizes.

A mixed grid structure is useful even in this simple format. Divide the text column into two equal units with a 1-pica space between. This creates two additional grid lines for placing small text and sizing art.

Blueprint measurements throughout the book are given in picas unless otherwise noted. The notation "x 30p" describes the measure, or length, of a text line. "RR" denotes a ragged right margin.

Guidelines for placing art on this grid

- Size all art to one of the following widths:
  A: 14p6—half the width of the text column with 1p between the art and the wraparound text
  B: 30 picas—the full width of the text column
  C: 41 picas—from the left edge of the 6-point rule to the right margin
  D: 25 picas—from the left edge of the 6-point rule to a point 1 pica short of the midpoint of the text column
  E: 10 picas—in the wide margin (if you have small mug shots)

- Avoid placing half-column art in the text column. Small charts and illustrations should be boxed with a 0.5- or 1-point rule to the sizes suggested.

- Placement is best at the bottom of the page, as shown in the examples at left. The top of the page is acceptable; the middle is not.

- For art that extends the full width of the column, the space between the text and the art should be equal to or greater than the leading.

- Place captions in the margin or inset them in a box around the art, as shown. Captions generally should be set one size smaller than the body text with tighter leading. Italic or a contrasting typeface is often used.

Attention to graphic detail makes the designer's hand more apparent in these documents than in the ones on the preceding pages. Both use a strong organization identity for external communication.

The large vertical headline fills the wide margin and establishes a distinctive style for a series of information sheets. Vertical type should always read upward unless the words themselves suggest downward motion.

The underlined headlines and bullets (which are gray) add variety to the simple page design.

Bulleted paragraphs with hanging indents are very effective when a message can be broken down into small chunks of information. The text immediately following the bullet should align exactly with subsequent lines.

The typeface is Palatino throughout.

IMAGESET :
First in Digital Graphic Design and
Desktop Publishing

GRAPHIC DESIGN SERVICES

■ ImageSet provides professional graphic design services for creating state-of-the-art computer graphics and page layouts for a variety of businesses, firms, and publications.

■ Brochures, newsletters, magazine covers, advertisements, menus, logos, annual reports, and corporate identity programs can be designed from start to finish by our graphic design department. If there is a special design problem, ImageSet will find a solution.

■ ImageSet offers electronic design templates that can be purchased and modified for a client's use. Design templates are preformatted designs that can be quickly adapted to just about any publication task (newsletters, flyers, price lists, etc.).

■ ImageSet offers graphic design consultation for companies and individuals using desktop publishing technology. ImageSet can provide graphic design consultancy to assist the client in designing templates for newsletters, brochures, logos, or even help develop a coherent corporate identity program which can be utilized for all the client's desktop publishing applications.

■ Should the need arise, ImageSet offers individual and group instruction on computer graphics and page layout programs.

DESKTOP PUBLISHING SERVICES

■ ImageSet offers an output service of high resolution print for individuals and organizations whose publishing tasks demand higher quality typeset than laser printer (300 dpi) resolution. To implement this service, ImageSet utilizes a Mergenthaler Linotype L100 commercial laser phototypesetting device.

*Design:
Mark Beale,
ImageSet Design
(Portland, OR)*

*One of a series of information sheets in the promotional literature for ImageSet Associates.
Size: 8-1/2 by 11*

A distinctive logo gives this simple page a unique personality. The descriptive line explains the otherwise cryptic name.

The black and gray border echoes the logo style and gives structure to what would otherwise have been an overly loose composition. Borders provide a very simple and effective way to add graphic interest and importance to a page. To create a gray border in Page-Maker, such as the one used here, create a white rectangle inside a gray one. The technique is similar to that used for the coupon in Project 5 later in this book.

Initial caps add variety to the text and help draw the reader into the page. Like the bullets in the sample above, the initial caps facilitate the "quick scan" nature of information presented in short paragraphs.

The typeface, Galliard throughout, has a calligraphic feeling that is more friendly than formal.

Stick Your Neck Out

*Thanks for re-enlisting
in the Giraffe Campaign*

To show you how much we appreciate that, we've enclosed our official H.W.C.S.F.F.* telling the world that your membership in the Giraffe Project is in good standing and that you're entitled to all the rights and privileges thereof.

You'll also find an updated membership card, an *Instant Giraffe Citation* and a new campaign button — we're assuming that you, like so many other members, have been hit up for your old button by a friend or one of your kids.

People's faces do light up when they see Giraffe stuff — instead of letting them take yours, you can use the enclosed order form to get them their own buttons, mugs, shirts — and memberships. And don't forget to order more *Instant Giraffe Citations* yourself. Members who use these report maximum satisfaction in being able to cite a Giraffe on-the-spot for meritorious action.

There will be exciting New Ideas and new "giraffenalia" in your upcoming year's worth of *Giraffe Gazettes.* We think you'll be surprised and delighted.

Keep scouting for new Giraffes and reporting your sightings to Giraffe Headquarters. We couldn't do the job without you.

And thanks again for your renewed vote of confidence in Giraffeness.

* Handsome Wall Certificate Suitable For Framing

*Design:
Scot Louis Gaznier
(Langley, WA)*

*Page acknowledging membership in the Giraffe Project, an organization that encourages people to "stick their neck out for the common good."
Size: 8-1/2 by 11*

Centering text inside a border creates a more formal image. The style of the border subtly changes the look of a page; experiment with the borders in PageMaker and clip art files to find a style appropriate for your needs.

The justified text and centered headline add to the formality. Positioning the border slightly off center keeps the design from being quite so rigid.

On subsequent pages the border would be repeated and the position of the first line of text would remain constant, leaving the space occupied by the headline open.

The 33-pica line length is the widest of the one-column formats shown in this section. The density of the running text (11/15 New Century Schoolbook) is maximum for a readable page, and you should avoid paragraphs longer than the last one shown here (11 lines).

The inset text helps relieve the density of the long text lines. Use this device on as many pages as possible in a document with this wide a column.

This blueprint defines the guidelines for the proposal above.

Charts, graphs, financials, and other art should be centered horizontally within the text block, inset at least 2 picas from the left and right margins. Graphics of various sizes can be accommodated, as shown in the schematics at far right. If you have data or art on several consecutive pages, placing them in the same vertical position on the page suggests care and planning. (It also takes a little more time.)

Southside Coolant Incorporated

**A Proposal for Temperature Control
in the Mesa School District**

Lorem ipsum dolor sit amet, consectetuer adipiscing elit, sed diam nonummy nibh euismod tincidunt ut laoreet dolore magna aliquam erat volutpat. Ut wisi enim ad minim veniam, quis nostrud exerci tation ullamcorper suscipit lobortis nisl ut aliquip ex ea commodo consequat. Duis autem vel eum iriure dolor in hendrerit in vulputate velit esse molestie consequat, vel illum dolore eu feugiat nulla facilisis at vero eros et accumsan et iusto odio dignissim qui blandit

Praesent luptatum zzril delenit augue duis dolore te feugait nulla facilisi. Lorem ipsum dolor sit amet, consectetuer adipiscing elit, Sed diam nonummy nibh euismod tincidunt ut laoreet dolore magna aliquam erat volutpat. Ut wisi enim ad minim veniam, quis nostrud exerci tation ullamcorper suscipit lobortis nisl ut aliquip ex ea commodo consequat.Duis autem vel eum iriure dolor in hendrerit in vulputate velit esse molestie consequat, vel illum dolore eu feugiat nulla facilisis at vero eros et accumsan et iusto odio dignissim qui blandit praesent luptatum zzril delenit augue duis dolore te feugait

Nulla facilisi. Nam liber tempor cum soluta nobis eleifend option congue nihil imperdiet doming id quod mazim placerat facer possim assum. Lorem ipsum dolor sit amet, consectetuer adipiscing elit, sed diam nonummy nibh euismod tincidunt ut laoreet dolore magnaAliquam erat volutpat. Ut wisi enim ad minim veniam, quis nostrud exerci tation ullamcorper suscipit lobortis nisl ut aliquip ex ea commodo consequat. Duis autem vel eum iriure dolor in hendrerit in vulputate velit esse molestie

Consequat, vel illum dolore eu feugiat nulla facilisis at vero eros et accumsan et iusto odio dignissim qui blandit praesent luptatum zzril delenit augue duis dolore te feugait . Lorem ipsum dolor sit amet, consectetuer adipiscing elit, sed diam nonummy nibh euismod tincidunt ut laoreet dolore magna aliquam erat volutpat.Ut wisi enim ad minim veniam, quis nostrud exerci tation ullamcorper suscipit lobortis nisl ut aliquip ex ea Commodo consequat. Duis autem vel eum iriure Dolor in hendrerit in vulputate velit esse molestie consequat, vel illum dolore eu feugiat nulla facilisis at vero eros et accumsan et iusto odio dignissim qui blandit praesent luptatum zzril delenit augue duis dolore te feugait nulla facilisi. Lorem ipsum dolor sit amet, consectetuer adipiscing elit, sed diam nonummy nibh euismod tincidunt ut laoreet dolore magna aliquam erat

3

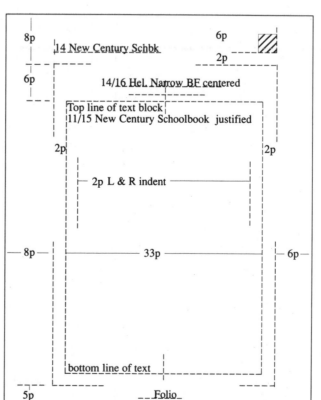

8p   14 New Century Schbk   6p
2p
6p   14/16 Hel. Narrow BF centered
Top line of text block
11/15 New Century Schoolbook justified
2p   2p
— 2p L & R indent —
8p—   33p   —6p—
bottom line of text
5p   __ Folio __

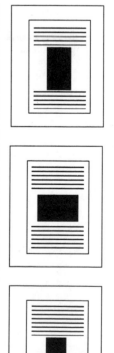

One-column grid with display heads

Many complex reports and proposals contain straight running text separated by subheads that recur throughout the document. The wide, one-column measure is ideal for the running text, and when the subheads are set fairly large and given plenty of white space and structural rules, the effect is well organized and easy to scan.

The highly structured report shown below contains a single topic on each page, with two recurring subheads placed in the same position on every page. You can adapt this format for a less structured document, placing the topic headline anywhere on the page with running text continuing from one page to the next as needed.

Bulleted text is used here to summarize the contents of each page. This technique works particularly well in long documents: The reader can make a horizontal pass through the pages for the highlights and then drop vertically into the running text for details. The ballot boxes are 11-point Zapf Dingbats.

The rules and generous white space (3 to 4 picas above each 0.5-point rule) provide a strong horizontal grid that facilitates scanning.

Art can be centered in the text column or inset on one side with the text wrapped around it, as shown in the schematics below.

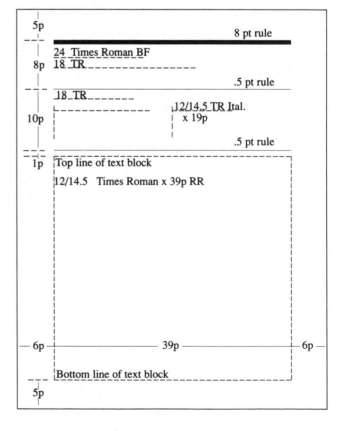

Tax Appeals
Providing Fair Hearings on Tax Disputes

Guiding Principles

■ *Lorem ipsum dolor sit amet, consectetuer adipiscing elit, sed diam nonummy nibh euismod tincidunt ut laoreet dolore magna al.*

■ *Ut wisi enim ad minim veniam, quis nostrud exerci tation ullamcorper suscipit lobortis nisl ut aliquip ex ea commodo consequat.*

Highlights of the Commission's Proposals

■ **Duis autem vel eum iriure dolor in hendrerit in vulputate velit esse molestie consequat, vel illum dolore eu feugiat nulla facilisis at vero eros.**

Lorem ipsum dolor sit amet, consectetuer adipiscing elit, sed diam nonummy nibh euismod tincidunt ut laoreet dolore magna aliquam erat volutpat. Ut wisi enim ad minim veniam, quis nostrud exerci tation ullamcorper suscipit lobortis nisl ut aliquip ex ea commodo consequat. Duis autem vel eum iriure dolor in hendrerit in vulputate velit esse molestie consequat, vel illum dolore eu feugiat nulla facilisis at vero eros et accumsan et iusto odio dignissim qui blandit praesent luptatum zzril delenit augue duis dolore te feugait nulla facilisi.
　　　Lorem ipsum dolor sit amet, consectetuer adipiscing elit, sed diam nonummy nibh euismod tincidunt ut laoreet dolore magna aliquam erat volutpat. Ut wisi enim ad minim veniam, quis nostrud exerci tation ullamcorper suscipit lobortis nisl ut aliquip ex ea commodo consequat.
　　　Duis autem vel eum iriure dolor in vulputate velit esse molestie consequat, vel illum dolore eu feugiat nulla facilisis at vero eros et accumsan et iusto odio dignissim qui blandit praesent luptatum zzril delenit augue duis dolore te feugait nulla facilisi. Nam liber tempor cum soluta nobis eleifend option congue nihil imperdiet doming id quod mazim placerat facer possim assum. Lorem ipsum dolor sit amet, consectetuer adipiscing elit, sed diam nonummy nibh euismod tincidunt ut laoreet dolore magna aliquam erat volutpat.

■ **Lorem ipsum dolor sit amet, consectetuer adipiscing elit, sed diam nonummy nibh euismd.**

Ut wisi enim ad minim veniam, quis nostrud exerci tation ullamcorper suscipit lobortis nisl ut aliquip ex ea commodo consequat. Duis autem vel eum iriure dolor in hendrerit in vulputate velit esse molestie consequat, vel illum dolore eu feugiat nulla facilisis at vero eros et accumsan et iusto odio dignissim qui blandit praesent luptatum zzril delenit augue duis dolore te feugait nulla facilisi. Lorem ipsum dolor sit amet, consectetuer adipiscing elit, sed diam nonummy nibh euismod tincidunt ut laoreet dolore magna aliquam erat volutpat.
　　　Ut wisi enim ad minim veniam, quis nostrud exerci tation ullamcorper suscipit lobortis nisl ut aliquip ex ea commodo consequat. Duis autem vel eum iriure dolor in hendrerit in vulpu.

5p

8 pt rule

24　Times Roman BF

8p　18　TR

.5 pt rule

18　TR

12/14.5 TR Ital.
x 19p

10p

.5 pt rule

1p　Top line of text block

12/14.5　Times Roman x 39p RR

6p　　　　　　　39p　　　　　　6p

Bottom line of text block

5p

One + one-column grid

The combination of one narrow and one wide column might be considered either a one- or a two-column grid. The narrow column isn't a true text column, but it is wide enough to use for different kinds of text, graphics, and display type without crowding.

Whether you set up this format as one or two columns on the screen may well depend on the length of the document: In a long document with a great deal of running text, setting up as one column enables you to "autoflow" the text; in a short document, setting up as two columns eliminates the need to "drag place" the text in the narrow column.

Whatever you call it and however you set it up, keep this format in mind. It's extremely useful for a wide variety of reports, newsletters, bulletins, and data sheets.

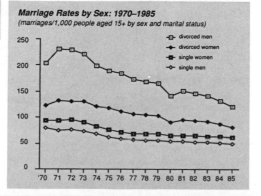

THE NUMBERS NEWS
6

A Publication of American Demographics
Martha Farnsworth Riche, Editor   Diane Crispell, Associate Editor

June 1988   Volume 8 Number

Will fewer couples tie the knot this June?

inside:

■ **How are population projections tracking?** (page 6)

■ **Regions shift in per capita income** (page 2)

■ **Women's labor force patterns approach men's** (page 3)

Divorced people are still more likely to marry than single people, but the gap is narrowing

Businesses that depend on married couples for a market need some hard rethinking: **the marriage rate continues to decline, the number of unmarried couples continues to increase, and divorced people are waiting longer to remarry.**

Final marriage statistics for 1985, produced by the National Center for Health Statistics, all point downward. Barbara Foley Wilson, who wrote the report ("Advance Report of Final Marriage Statistics, 1985"), said it was depressing to write: **Marriages dropped substantially in every region, almost every month, in most states, and for every marital status group.** To put these figures in context, remember that preliminary figures for 1986 and 1987 show the drop in the marriage rate continuing (*Numbers News*, Vol. 8, No. 5).

About two-thirds of the newly married were marrying for the first time; most of the rest had been divorced. However, as the chart shows, marriage rates are far higher for divorced persons: divorced men have higher marriage rates than divorced women, and single women have higher marriage rates than single men. **Marriage rates have declined for all these groups since the early 1970s, falling by about one-third for single people to nearly one-half for divorced men.**

Most people are now aware that young people are waiting longer to marry: the mean age at first marriage was 24.0 for women in 1985 and

Marriage Rates by Sex: 1970–1985
(marriages/1,000 people aged 15+ by sex and marital status)

□	divorced men
◆	divorced women
■	single women
◇	single men

250
200
150
100
50
0
'70 71 72 73 74 75 76 77 78 79 80 81 82 83 84 85

This newsletter uses the narrow column on the cover for headlines, contents listings, and story highlights. On inside pages the use is even more versatile, accommodating charts, graphs, news items, product notes, and conference listings.

The narrow column is 11p6, the wide column is 29 picas, and the space in between is 1 pica. The inside margins are 4p6, wide enough to accommodate the holes for a three-ring binder.

The tinted boxes run the full column measure without rules. Once you adopt this style, you should maintain it throughout. Text inside the boxes is indented 1 pica at both the left and right margins.

The logo uses the currently popular technique of enlarging the initial caps in an all cap name. Here the caps drop below the other letters, and tie in with the large issue number, a good device for quick reference and continuity.

The 2-point rules at the bottom of the page enclose publishing and masthead information. This type can be as small as 5 or 6 points.

Design: Carol Terrizzi (Ithaca, NY)

The Numbers News *is published monthly by American Demographics.*
Trim size: 8-1/2 by 11

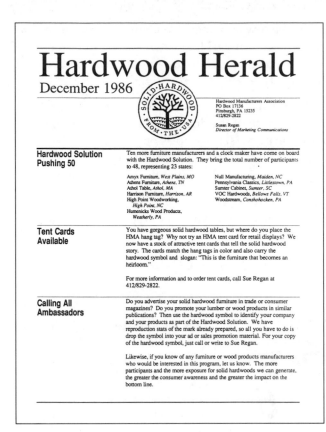

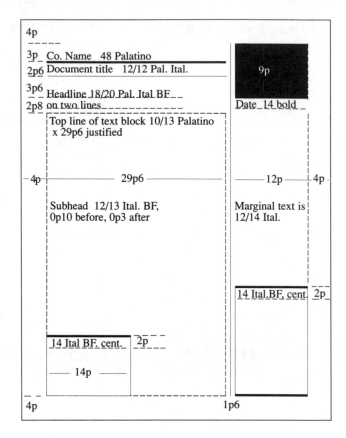

A deep space at the top of the page for the company identification, a narrow column for headlines and overhanging rules, and a wide column for information add up to a very simple, very effective use of desktop publishing.

The text column is divided into two equal columns for listings. The address above the text area follows this grid line.

The main headline and running text are Times Roman; the marginal heads are Helvetica Narrow. Keep in mind that Helvetica Narrow, while very useful when a laser printer is used for final output, is not a PostScript font and should not be used for Linotronic output.

The text column is 29 picas. The outside margins are 3 picas, and the top and bottom margins are 4 picas.

Design: Agnew Moyer Smith (Pittsburgh, PA)

The Hardwood Herald is published by the Hardwood Manufacturer's Association. Trim size: 8-1/2 by 11

This blueprint matches the monthly report on the facing page. You can adapt the grid for either of the other publications shown in this section by reversing the narrow and wide columns and adjusting the margins.

The text is Palatino throughout.

The bold rules are 4 point, the lighter ones are 0.5 point.

The sales highlights box in the lower left has a 1-pica standoff for the text wraparound. The type in the sample is 12/14, with 1p3 left and right indents. The tab is set at 7p.

The type in the contents box is 10/11.5 italic with 1p3 left and right indents, a leadered tab at 9 picas, and 6 points after each listing.

The screens in both of the boxes are 10%.

The maple leaf logo was created from clip art (DrawArt from Desktop Graphics) in MacDraw.

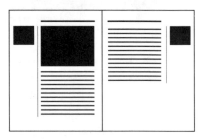

You can use four art sizes, as shown above. Another approach is to hang the art from a horizon line, as in the second schematic.

Instructions for producing a newsletter or report using a one + one-column format can be found in Project 3 later in the book.

University Press

The Monthly Report on Sales, Promotion, and Product Development

March 1990

Political History and Economics Titles Continue to Boost Overseas Sales

Lorem ipsum dolor sit amet, consectetuer adipiscing elit, sed diam nonummy nibh euismod tincidunt ut laoreet dolore magna aliquam erat volutpat. Ut wisi enim ad minim veniam, quis nostrud exerci tation ullamcorper suscipit lobortis nisl ut aliquip ex ea commodo consequat. Duis autem vel eum iriure dolor in hendrerit in vulputate velit esse molestie consequat, vel illum dolore eu feugiat nulla facilisis at vero eros et accumsan et iusto odio dignissim qui blandit.

Praesent luptatum zzril delenit augue duis dolore te feugait nulla facilisi. Lorem ipsum dolor sit amet, consectetuer adipiscing elit, sed diam nonummy nibh euismod tincidunt ut laoreet dolore magna aliquam erat volutpat. Ut wisi enim ad minim veniam, quis nostrud exerci tation ullamcorper suscipit lobortis nisl ut aliquip ex ea commodo consequat.

Duis autem vel eum iriure dolor in hendrerit in vulputate velit esse molestie consequat, vel illum dolore eu feugiat nulla facilisis at vero eros et accumsan et iusto odio dignissim qui blandit praesent luptatum zzril delenit augue duis dolore te feugait nulla facilisi. Nam liber tempor cum soluta nobis eleifend option congue nihil imperdiet doming id quod mazim placerat facer possim assum. Lorem ipsum dolor sit amet, consectetuer adipiscing elit, sed diam nonummy nibh euismod tincidunt ut laoreet dolore magna aliquam erat volutpat.

London office to open this summer

Ut wisi enim ad minim veniam, quis nostrud exerci tation ullamcorper suscipit lobortis nisl ut aliquip ex ea commodo consequat. Duis autem vel eum iriure dolor in hendrerit in vulputate velit esse molestie consequat, vel illum dolore eu feugiat nulla facilisis at vero eros et accumsan et iusto odio dignissim qui blandit praesent luptatum zzril delenit augue duis dolore te feugait nulla facilisi. Lorem ipsum dolor sit amet, consectetuer adipiscing elit, sed diam nonummy nibh euismod tincidunt ut laoreet dolore magna aliquam erat volutpat.

Ut wisi enim ad minim veniam, quis nostrud exerci tation ullamcorper suscipit lobortis nisl ut aliquip ex ea commodo consequat. Duis autem vel eum iriure dolor in hendrerit in vulputate velit esse molestie consequat, vel illum dolore eu feugiat nulla facilisis at vero eros et accumsan et iusto odio dignissim qui blandit praesent luptatum zzril delenit augue duis dolore te feugait nulla facilisi. Lorem ipsum lobortis nisl ut aliquip ex ea commodo consequat. Duis autem vel eum iriure dolor elit, sed diam nonummy nibh euismod tincidunt ut laoreet dolore magna aliquam erat volutpat. Ut wisi enim ad minim veniam, quis nostrud exerci tation ullamcorper suscipit lobortis nisl ut aliquip ex ea commodo consequat.

Duis autem vel eum iriure dolor in hendrerit in vulputate velit esse molestie consequat, vel illum dolore eu feugiat nulla facilisis at vero eros et accumsan et

University Press authors Jonathan Pritchard and Michelle Colibier are honored by the United States Library of Congress; see page 6.

Overseas Sales

FY 85	16, 365
FY 86	25,347
FY 87	36,897
FY 88	47,356
FY 89	59,000

TWO-COLUMN GRIDS

Two-column grids have a more designed and polished look than the one-column formats, yet they don't require a great deal of planning and can be assembled fairly quickly in PageMaker. They're useful for a wide variety of publications, including newsletters, brochures, annual reports, bulletins, menus, fact sheets, and catalog listings. When done well, they can range from honest simplicity to punchy straightforward- ness. When done poorly, they can be boring or heavy-handed.

With two equal columns, the line length in an 8.5- by 11-inch page is usually between 16 and 21 picas, depending on the margins and the space between the columns. The type can drop down to 10/12 and still be quite readable. These factors make this format very economical in that you can fit quite a lot of text on a page. The greatest danger of the

Each editorial topic is contained on a single page, giving this brief annual report a simple, consistent, accessible style. The text does not have to fill out to the bottom margin. When your message can be broken down into one and two page units, this is a very effective format that is quite simple to produce.

The narrow margins (3 picas on the outside and bottom, 5 picas on the inside) work here because of the undersized page, the simple design, the open leading, and the white space at the top of the page. You wouldn't want margins any narrower than this, and without the compen- sating factors just mentioned wider margins would be essential.

The inset photos with wrap- around text keep the running text from being too symmetrical. The depth of the photos varies according to the picture and the amount of text on the page. Photos can also run the full column width or extend halfway into the second column.

The body text is 10/14 Times Roman with 36-point initial caps. The headlines are 22 point.

PATIENT SERVICES

A kidney patient faces hardships that most healthy people never encounter. The Kidney Foundation of Mary- land attempts to help these patients by providing an exten- sive array of patient programs and services.

The second annual Kids Having Fun Camp for pediatric renal patients was held during the weekend of August 23 at the pastoral YMCA Camp Letts in Edgewater, Maryland. This year's camp attracted 13 young renal patients from a three-state area. Smiles were abundant as the youngsters enjoyed a care- free weekend away from the all- too-familiar medical environment. Exciting activities such as horseback riding and boating, as well as the more traditional sports of tennis, softball and volleyball, thrilled the campers and volunteers alike. The camp also provided a respite from the constant demands imposed by kidney disease on the patients' parents.

December is an unlikely time to have a pic- nic. The Kidney Foundation, however, chose to beat summer's heat and hold a " Picnic in Decem- ber" for its annual patient party for the second consecutive year. The University of Maryland Medical School Teaching Facility was the site for the party attended by special guests Mr. and Mrs. Santa, who presented gifts donated by Santa Claus Anonymous, to over 40 children. Volun- teers from Maryland Casualty Company portrayed the visitors from the North Pole, as well as a snowman and other storybook characters. The Boys Latin Magicians' Guild provided entertain- ment that delighted the entire audience.

The Patient Emergency Assistance Program provided one-time grants to kidney patients in need of financial help. Patients were awarded nearly $2,000 in emergency grants.

The Medication Discount Program allowed dialysis, transplant, and chronic kidney disease patients to purchase medication at the lowest pos- sible cost. Patients were regis- tered for the program by their physicians. Under this pro- gram, all prescription drugs related to the patient's kidney condition can be purchased at wholesale price through the Kidney Foundation, which pays the pharmacist's fees and handling costs.

Transplant and dialysis patients also re- ceived free medical identification jewelry. This jewelry alerts medical personnel to the patient's kidney condition and is especially valuable in emergency situations.

Young kidney patients from Maryland and Washington, D.C. had an opportunity to show off their creativity in the Foundation's "Gift of Life" poster contest, held on November 15 at the Top of the World Trade Center in Baltimore. The youngsters' artwork was displayed and judged by such celebrities as Ken Matz of WMAR- TV and Bob MacAvan of the Baltimore Blast.

Eight-year-old Mario Velez, of Baltimore, won third prize in his category and was awarded a trip for his entire family to the Six Flags Power Plant in Baltimore. First prize winners in each category advanced to the National "Gift of Life" poster contest in Washington, D.C.

PUBLIC EDUCATION

K idney disease is an intricate and complex subject. One of the Kidney Foun- dation's primary responsi- bilities is to educate the public about kidney disease and the benefits of organ donation.

Over 78,000 Americans die each year of kidney dis- ease. Many of these patients die because a suitable organ donor cannot be found. As a result, the Kidney Foundation has expanded its efforts to promote voluntary organ donation through its "Give the Gift of Life" campaign.

In December and January the Maryland affil- iate participated in a nationwide campaign based on the theme, "Sign an organ donor card....It's one New Year's resolution that's easy to keep." The Foundation distributed public service an- nouncements to the major Baltimore TV stations and to radio stations across the state. Public ser- vice ads and fact sheets were also provided to area newspapers.

Public information efforts were intensified during Organ Donation Awareness Week in April. NKF-Maryland held an organ donor sign-in at Johns Hopkins Hospital, and area radio stations gave frequent air play to public service announce- ments about organ donation. Although April marked the height of the organ donor campaign, "Gift of Life" materials were used extensively by the media throughout the year.

Health fairs provided an excellent opportunity for Foundation representatives to personally

speak with the public about kidney disease and organ donation. During the year Kidney Foundation staff and volunteers were on hand at many health fairs throughout the area. The KF newsletter, refreshed with a new format, continued to inform thousands of readers with interesting information about kidney disease issues and the many activities of the Foundation. Educational brochures, on topics ranging from "Transplantation" to "Nutritional Considerations for the Patient on Dialysis," were available to the public free of charge.

The KF Membership Drive held in the spring featured an effective plea for funds by WMAR- TV anchorman Ken Matz and kidney patient Jason Ogle. The drive culminated in May, with a three-night phone-a-thon from the offices of the Baltimore Gas and Electric Company. Friends of the Foundation generously responded to the drive, contributing a total of nearly $10,000 to the fight against kidney disease.

Since organ donation is a key step in solving the problem of kidney disease, the Foundation strongly supported the efforts of Delegate Paula Hollinger to pass a state law regarding the "routine inquiry" issue. The law now states that parents of a deceased minor must be approached by a hospital medical staff member concerning post-mortem organ donation.

Design: Carl A. Schuetz, Foxglove Communications (Baltimore, MD)

Pages from the annual report of the National Kidney Foundation of Maryland.

Trim size: 7-1/2 by 10

two-column grid, however, is that you will try to fit in too much text and create pages that are dense and difficult to read. When in doubt, add an extra pica to the margins rather than to the text block.

With two columns you have more options in both the size and placement of headlines. You need to be careful, however, of the position of the heads—they shouldn't be too close to the top or the bottom of a column. (The very top of a column is, of course, okay). Also, take care that headlines in adjoining columns do not align with one another.

The off-center page created by a wide outer margin adds variety and sophistication to a two-column grid. This format is especially well suited to house organs.

A tight grid structure and well-defined image area is established by the extension of visual elements into the side and top margins and by the strong graphic treatment of the folios at the bottom of the page.

The graphic style of the breakout, folios, and logo and the contemporary headline treatment with bracket-style rules give the format a personal signature, as well as a consistency of visual style from one page to the next. The overall feeling is restrained without being bland.

Photos can be sized as shown here or, in the case of mug shots, used in half-column width with wrap-

around text filling out the other half column. The rules around the photos crisp up the otherwise soft edges.

The text is Palatino throughout.

Design: Michael Waitsman, Synthesis Concepts (Chicago, IL)

The Wildman Herald *is the national newsletter of Wildman, Harrold, Allen & Dixon, a law firm.*
Trim size: 8-1/2 by 11

THE
WILDMAN
HERALD

March 1988

Judge Turner and his wife Kay (right) enjoy themselves at the Federal Bar Association reception following the swearing-in ceremony.

In 1967 Turner hired on with the firm of Canada, Russell & Turner (Memphis predecessor of Wildman, Harrold), where his father Cooper Turner had helped establish a thriving practice. He became a partner in 1974, the year of his father's death.

In 20 years of private practice with the firm, Turner earned a reputation as one of the Mid South area's top civil litigators. Working in state and federal courts throughout the region, he ran the gamut — commercial and corporate cases, products liability, banking, insurance defense, you name it. His most recent success was the recovery of a summary judgment in favor of Richards Medical Company, requiring that

The ABA declared him "well qualified," a rating not often given, and the nomination sailed through the Judiciary Committee and the full Senate.

Richards' parent company turn over $13 million in pension plan assets to Richards. (The parent has appealed.)

Over the years Turner has also found time for various civic endeavors. He worked in the successful campaigns of Rep. Don Sundquist, a Memphis-area congressman, and he has filled numerous offices and

committee positions with the local bar, which he now serves as president.

With this kind of background, Turner was as ready as one can be for the intricate and sometimes intensive process of becoming a federal judge. "There was a form for Department of Justice, a form for the FBI, a form for the ABA, a form for the Federal Bar Association..." the nominee recounted with a weary sigh. Scores of friends and family members were interviewed by men in dark suits. Detailed financial disclosure forms had to be completed.

After being put through the washer and dryer, though, he emerged clean — and more. The ABA declared him "well qualified," a rating not often given, and once the Senate finally got past the logjam over the Battle of Bork, the Turner nomination sailed through the Judiciary Committee and the full Senate.

A few days before his swearing in, Turner, along with another large gathering of the legal profession, attended the funeral of Judge Marion Boyd. The father of Memphis partner Boots Boyd, Judge Boyd was the first man to occupy the seat which Judge Turner now occupies. He was known for his honesty, fairness, timeliness, and strictness in sentencing. As the eulogist reviewed Judge Boyd's long career of public service, Turner felt a special kinship with his early predecessor. "I would like to be seen after a number of years as being completely honest, with a good temperament, polite and courteous, as one who knows his law and does his work and comes up with fair results. If I can do all of that I will be a great judge."

Because of his caseload, with 370 civil cases and an unknown number of criminal cases awaiting him when he first arrived, it is difficult to see how Judge Turner will find time for his hobbies, which include tennis, bird hunting, and gardening. But he vows to make time for his family, who have been his biggest boosters throughout the long nominating process: wife Kay Farese Turner, herself a practicing attorney, and five children, Park (18), Alexandra (14), Oliver (13), Christian (12), and Whitney (9).

Looking back on his private practice, Turner noted that leaving the firm was not easy. "I have practiced law with most of the lawyers here longer than I have been with anyone else in my life, and I've liked it. I've liked the firm, and I respect the integrity of the lawyers here. I hope I'll be lucky enough to enjoy my job as judge as much as I have enjoyed practicing law."

Janet Wilson has something special to remember, too. "Can you believe it?" she marvelled. "I put the President on hold!"

Firm Promotes Valuable European Contacts
by Robert Keel

In November, 1987, Tom Smith of the New York office and Bob Keel of the Toronto office visited Rome and London. The visit to Rome was arranged by Keel to introduce Smith to clients of the Toronto office. Moreover, Keel Cottrelle maintains an office in Rome in association with Avvocato Francesco Ruggieri and Avvocato Giovanni Iasilli. The trip therefore, presented an opportunity to introduce this affiliated office to a member of the national management committee. Indeed, Bob and Tom were delighted to discover that there are now two affiliated offices in Italy because Avv. Ruggieri now maintains an office in Milan. Avv. Ruggieri made it clear that both the Rome and Milan offices are available to anyone in the firm, either for business or merely to drop in to get acquainted. The Rome office is in the center of the city at 95 Via Barberini, which is just around the corner from the American Embassy.

While they were in Italy, Keel and Smith devoted a considerable amount of time to client business. Among other things, Bob introduced Tom to a number of multi-national corporate clients. As you might expect, the trip was not all work. The hospitality extended to them by clients and by Avv. Ruggieri and Avv. Iasilli was delightful and occupied a considerable amount of otherwise billable hours. Moreover, Tom's wife Terry, who also made the trip, convinced Tom to take a side trip to Venice.

After Rome, Tom, Terry and Bob flew on to London. This time, it was Smith's turn to show Keel around. Tom visited his business acquaintances at Shell International. Bob and Tom also visited an acquaintance at Hambros Bank. They spent some time with representatives of Network Security Management Limited, which is based in London. Keel managed to squeeze in visits with a number of business acquaintances who are now doing business in London.

With our expanding practice and our shrinking world, our European contacts will assume increasing importance. We should all be aware of the global networks that are in place.

Left to right: Bob Keel, Giovanni Iasilli, Tom Smith, and Francesco Ruggieri.

Four wide-margin, two-column designs

Wide margins are the foundation for an open, two-column format that is very appealing and highly readable. All four documents in this section were designed using the grid in the blueprint on the following spread, but the kind of information, the intended audience, and the style of the publications differ considerably.

The most varied and dynamic of the four designs (facing page) divides the vertical grid into horizontal story areas. This modular format requires more time and planning to execute than the others; you may have to adjust the depth of the text blocks several times to balance all the elements on the page.

The overall busyness of the design elements is appropriate here because it evokes the adventure of travel. You can create a more conservative look with this horizontal format by using a simpler nameplate and more uniform art styles. The format works for all-text documents, too, though to very different effect.

The nameplate at the top of the page uses the multiple headline style commonly found in magazines, including a list of the contents and the "Summer Specials" stamp, which is similar to the diagonal banner on many magazine covers. Deft handling of typography is critical in composing so many elements with varying emphasis into a unified, readable whole.

The pictures use the grid effectively precisely because they break out of it. The mountains seem more expansive because they exceed the margins; the balloon seems to float off the page. The range of art styles, from realistic to schematic, adds to the feeling of adventure that a travel bulletin wants to project. The pictures are all from clip art files. (The stamp and mountains are from WetPaint; the compass and balloon are from The Mac Art Dept.; the plane is from Artware; and the ship is from Images with Impact.)

The type used throughout is Futura. Alternating Light, Extra Bold, and Oblique in the headlines creates a colorful contrast without introducing another typeface. The unity of a single type family balances the complex nameplate treatment and the different styles of art.

Type specifications
Nameplate overline: 16-point Futura Light
Going: 96-point Light
Places: 36-point Futura Extra Bold Oblique
Contents: 14/14 Extra Bold
Lead story headline: 28/29 Light
Second story head: 18/18 Extra Bold
Body text: 10/12p6 Light

Instructions for producing a newsletter that uses a wide-margin, two-column format can be found in Project 4.

SUMMER SPECIALS

GOING PLACES

RIVERBOAT RACES

GRAND TETONS

GREAT BARRIER REEF

AROUND THE WORLD IN SO MANY WAYS

Lorem ipsum dolor sit amet, consectetuer adipiscing elit, sed diam nonummy nibh euismod tincidunt ut laoreet dolore magna aliquam erat volutpat. Ut wisi enim ad minim veniam, quis nostrud exerci tation ullamcorper suscipit lobortis nisl ut aliquip ex ea commodo Consequat. Duis

PLUS THE MANY ADVENTURES THAT AWAIT YOU CLOSE TO HOME

Autem vel velit esse molestie Consequat, vel illum dolore eu feugiat nulla facilisis at vero eros et accumsan et iusto odio dignissim qui blandit praesent luptatum zzril delenit augue duis dolore te feugait nulla facilisi. Lorem ipsum dolor sit amet, consectetuer adipiscing elit, sed diam nonummy nibh euismod tincidunt ut laoreet dolore magna aliquam erat volutpat. Ut wisi enim ad minim veniam, quis nostrud exerci tation ullamcorper suscipit lobortis nisl ut aliquip ex ea commodo consequat.

Duis autem vel eum iriure dolor in hendrerit in vulputate velit esse molestie consequat, vel illum dolore eu feugiat nulla facilisis at vero eros et accumsan et iusto odio dignissim qui blandit

praesent luptatum zzril delenit augue duis dolore te feugait nulla facilisi. Nam liber tempor cum soluta nobis eleifend option congue nihil imperdiet doming id quod mazim placerat facer pos assum.

Lorem ipsum dolor sit amet, consectetuer adipiscing elsed diam nonummy nibh euismod tincidunt ut laoreet magna aliquam erat volutpat. Ut wisi enim ad minveniam, quis nostrud exerci tation ullamcorper suscipit lobortis nisl ut aliquip ex ea com-modo

---

The Symonton Foundation

What We've Accomplished

Lorem ipsum dolor sit amet, consectetuer adipiscing elit, sed diam nonummy nibh euismod tincidunt ut laoreet dolore magna aliquam erat volutpat. Ut wisi ad minim veniam, quis nostrud exerci tation ullamcorper suscipit lobortis nisl ut aliquip ex ea commodo consequa te feugait nulla facilisi.t.

The Centerville Nursing Home
Duis autem vel eum iriure dolor in hendrerit in vulputate velit esse molestie consequat, vel illum dolore eu feugiat nulla facilisis at vero eros et accumsan et iusto odio dignissim qui blandit praesent luptatum zzril delenit augue duis dolore te feugait nulla facilisi. Lorem ipsum dolor sit amet, consectetuer adipiscing elit, sed diam nonummy nibh euismod tin-

cidunt ut laoreet dolore magna aliquam erat volutpat. Ut wisi enim ad minim veniam, quis nostrud exerci tation ullamcorper suscipit lobortis nisl ut aliquip ex ea commodo consequat te feugait nulla

Duis autem vel eum iriure dolor in hendrerit in vulputate velit esse molestie consequat, vel illum dolore eu feugiat nulla facilisis at vero eros et accumsan et iusto odio dignissim qui blandit praesent luptatum zzril delenit augue duis dolore te feugait nulla facilisi. Nam liber tempor cum soluta nobis eleifend option congue nihil imperdiet doming id quod mazim placerat facer possim assum.

Job Training Program for Disadvantaged Youth
Lorem ipsum dolor sit amet, consectetuer adipiscing elit, sed diam nonummy nibh euismod tincidunt ut laoreet dolore magna aliquam erat volutpat. Ut wisi enim ad minim veniam, quis nostrud exerci tation ullamcorper suscipit lobortis nisl ut aliquip ex ea commodo consequat. Duis autem vel eum iriure dolor in hendrerit in vulputate velit esse molestie con- sequat, vel illum dolore eu feugiat nulla facilisis at vero eros et accumsan et iusto odio dignis- sim qui blandit praesent luptatum zzril delenit augue duis dolore te feugait nulla facilisi. Lorem ipsum dolor sit amet, consectetuer adipiscing elit, sed diam nonummy nibh euismod tincidunt ut laoreealiquam erat volut

---

The Symonton Foundation

What We Need to Do

Ut wisi enim ad minim veniam, quis nostrud exerci tation ullamcorper suscipit lobortis nisl ut aliquip ex ea commodo consequat. Duis autem vel eum iriure dolor in hendrerit in vulputate velit esse molestie consequat, vel illum dolore eu feugiat nulla facilisis at vero eros et accumsan et iusto odio dignissim qui blandit praesent luptatum zzril delenit augue duis dolore te feugait nulla facilisi.

Capital Fund
Lorem ipsum dolor sit amet, consectetuer adipiscing elit, sed diam nonummy nibh euismod tincidunt ut laoreet dolore magna aliquam erat volutpat. Ut wisi enim ad minim veniam, quis nostrud exerci tation ullamcorper suscipit lobortis nisl ut aliquip ex ea commodo consequat. Duis autem vel eum iriure dolor in hendrerit in vulputate velit esse molestie con- sequat, vel illum dolore eu feugiat nulla facilisis at vero eros et accumsan et iusto odio dignis- sim qui blandit praesent luptatum zzril delenit augue duis dolore te feugait nulla facilisi.

Lorem ipsum dolor sit amet, consectetuer adipiscing elit, sed diam nonummy nibh euismod tincidunt ut laoraliquam eratorem Lorem ipsum dolor sit amet, consectetuer adipiscing elit, sed diam nonummy nibh euismod tincidunt ut laoreet dolore magna..

ipsum dolor sit amet, consectetuer adipiscing elit, sed diam nonummy nibh euismod tin- cidunt ut laoreet dolore magna aliquam erat volutpat. Ut wisi enim ad minim veniam, quis nostrud exerci tation ullamcorper suscipit lobortis nisl ut aliquip ex ea commodo conse- quat. Duis autem vel eum iriure dolor in hendrerit in vulputate velit esse molestie consequat, vel illum dolore eu feugiat nulla volutpat.orem ipsum dolor sit amet, con- sectetuer adipiscing elit, sed diam nonummy nibh euismod tincidunt ut laoreet dolore magna aliquam erat volutpat. Ut wisi enim ad minim veniam, quis nostrud exerci tation ullamcorper suscipit lobortis nisl ut aliquip ex ea commodo consequat. Duis autem vel eum iriure dolor in hendrerit in vulputate velit esse molestie consequat, vel illum dolore eu feugiat

Staff Expansion
Ut wisi enim ad minim veniam, quis nostrud exerci tation ullamcorper suscipit lobortis nisl ut aliquip ex ea commodo consequat. Duis autem vel eum iriure dolor in hendrerit in vulputate velit esse molestie consequat, vel illum dolore eu feugiat nulla facilisis at vero eros et accumsan et iusto odio dignissim qui blandit praesent luptatum zzril delenit augue duis dolore te feugait nulla facilisi. Lorem ipsum dolor sit amet, consectetuer adipiscing elit, sed diam nonummy nibh euismod tin

duis dolore te feugait nulla facilisi. Nam liber tempor cum soluta nobis eleifend option congue nihil imperdiet doming id quod mazim placerat facer possim assum. Lorem ipsum dolor sit amet, consectetuer adipiscing elit, sed diam nonummy nibh euismod tincidunt ut laoreet dolore magna aliquam erat volutpatillum .

This document shares the dignified simplicity found in the annual report reproduced at the beginning of the two-column grid section. It is designed to accommo- date a subject head over a 0.5-point rule at the top of each page. If you omit that head, leave the rule in place.

The text seems to hang from the rule under the main headline. This strong structure provides consistency from page to page regardless of the column depth. The variable column depth gives you flexibility and speed when you assemble the pages on screen.

The banner, the main headline, and the rule below that headline extend 3 picas past the left text margin shown in the blueprint on the facing page. The banner is 2 picas deep with 14-point Garamond Bold type.

The main headlines are 30-point Bodoni Bold.

The body text is 10/13 Helvetica Light. The subheads are 10/12 Helvetica Black under 0.5-point rules.

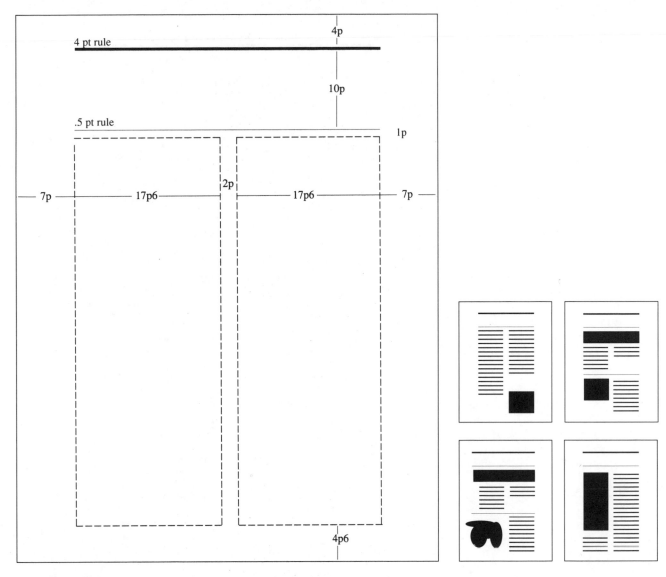

The blueprint above shows the basic grid for the four documents on the previous three and following two pages.

The column width (17p6) is excellent for easy reading.

The generous margins require a generous space between the columns.

The grid is centered on the page. If you shift the grid to one side for an off-center page, the wider margin can be used for annotations, notes, small pieces of art, and other marginalia.

A variation with a more structured nameplate and headline treatment is shown on the next spread.

Art can be placed on the grid as shown in the schematics or as shown in the sample pages.

1989 PROGRAM OF EVENTS

SCHOOL OF PHYSICAL SCIENCES

SOUTHEAST STATE UNIVERSITY
70TH SCIENTIFIC FORUM

MONDAY, MAY 8, 1989   FULTON AUDITORIUM

MORNING PROGRAM

7:45   Registration

Hendrerit in vulputate velit esse molestie
consequat, vel illum dolore eu feugiat.

7:45   Continental Breakfast

Nonummy nibh euismod tincidunt ut
laoreet dolore magna aliquam erat
volutpat. Ut wisi enim ad minim.

9:00   Introduction

Veniam, quis nostrud exerci tation ullamcorper suscipit lobortis nisl ut
aliquip ex ea commodo consequat.
Duis autem vel eum iriure dolor in.

10:00   Break

Hendrerit in vulputate velit esse
molestie consequat, vel illum dolore
eu feugiat nulla facilisis at vero eros et
accumsan et iusto odio dignissim qui.

10:30   Opening Address

Blandit praesent luptatum zzril delenit
augue duis dolore te feugait nulla
facilisi. Lorem ipsum dolor sit amet,
consectetuer adipiscing elit, sed diam.

12:00   Open House and Lunch

Nonummy nibh euismod tincidunt ut
laoreet dolore magna aliquam erat
volutpat. Ut wisi enim ad minim.

AFTERNOON PROGRAM

2:00   Overview of Seminars

Veniam, quis nostrud exerci tation
ullamcorper suscipit lobortis nisl ut
aliquip ex ea commodo consequat.

3:00   Faculty Roundtable

Duis autem vel eum iriure dolor in
hendrerit in vulputate velit esse
molestie consequat, vel illum dolore eu
feugiat nulla facilisis at vero eros et
accumsan et iusto odio dignissim qui
blandit praesent luptatum zzril delenit
augue duis dolore te feugait nulla
facilisi. Nam liber tempor cum soluta.

4:00   The Year in Review

Option congue nihil imperdiet doming
id quod mazim placerat facer possim
assum. Lorem ipsum dolor sit amet.,

4:30   Agenda for the Nineties

Consectetuer adipiscing elit, sed diam
nonummy nibh euismod tincidunt ut
laoreet dolore magna aliquam erat
volutpat. Ut wisi enim ad minim
veniam, quis nostrud exerci tation.

5:00   Discussion Period

UlLamcorper suscipit lobortis nisl ut
aliquip ex ea commodo consequat.
Duis autem vel eum iriure dolor in
hendrerit in vulputate velit esse.

EVENING PROGRAM

6:30   School of Chemistry Buffet

Consequat, vel illum dolore eu
feugiat nulla facilisis at vero eros et.

8:00   Class Reunion

Et iusto odio dignissim qui blandit
praesent luptatum zzril delenit augue
duis dolore te feugait nulla facilisi.
Lorem ipsum dolor sit amet, con.

Programs with many items briefly described, like the one shown here, work very well in this two-column format. The column measure is wide enough to contain the agenda listings on single lines, but short enough so that the indented descriptions run over, creating visual separation between the headings.

A classic, traditional feeling appropriate for an academic program is created by the centered text in the open space at the top of the page and by the use of Garamond, a very refined and graceful typeface.

Nameplate type
1989 Program: 18-point Garamond
Top rule: 4 point
School of…: 12 point
Southeast State…: 18/21
Date and place: 10 point
Bottom rule: 0.5 point

The three subheads (Morning Program, etc.) are 10-point Garamond small caps. The double rules below them are from PageMaker's Lines menu. The hand-placed rules under the agenda listings are 0.5 point, to match the weight of the double rules. You should maintain consistency in line weight throughout a page. The typeface underscore would be too heavy here.

The boldface time for each part of the program adds a different color to the type, which keeps the page from being too monotonous.

The program listings are 10/12 Garamond. The event after the time is tabbed to 3 picas from the left margin; the descriptive copy is set with a 3-pica left indent so that it is flush with the tabbed text.

The space between listings in the sample is specified as 1 pica paragraph space before each event heading and 4 points after it.

A newsletter style is adapted here for a sales department's monthly bulletin. The rules, bold heads with tag lines, and initial caps dress up and give a newsy image to what could be a pedestrian report.

The highly structured nameplate shows another way of using the open space at the top of the grid. (See the blueprint detail below right for specifications.)

The strong headline treatment requires white space around the various elements and makes separation of headlines in adjoining columns essential.

The initial caps are 60-point Helvetica Condensed Black. Often found in the editorial pages of magazines to highlight points of entry on a page, initial caps are generally underused in business publications. They are especially effective in complex pages such as this sample.

The wide, 3-pica paragraph indent is proportional to the initial cap. Be aware that very narrow letters (such as I) and very wide letters (M and W) will not conform to this proportion. The price of a truly professional document is editing to avoid these letters. Really.

The body text is 10/12 Bookman.

The illustration was created with PageMaker's drawing tools. The box around it uses a 2-point rule and a 10% shade. The headline is 10-point Helvetica Black Oblique, and the descriptive lines are 9/9 Helvetica Light with Helvetica Black numbers. The caption is 10/12 Bookman italic, centered.

The centered folio (10-point Helvetica Light) and the flush right continued line (9-point Helvetica Light Oblique) are aligned at their baselines 2 picas below the bottom margin.

THE GREAT OUTDOORS STORE

Month in Review

July 1989

BRISK START FOR CAMPING AND BACKPACKING EQUIPMENT

Fewer travelers abroad spurs sales in do it yourself activities.

orem ipsum dolor sit amet, consectetuer adipiscing elit, sed diam nonummy nibh euismod tincidunt ut laoreet dolore magna aliquam erat volutpat. Ut wisi enim ad minim veniam, quis nostrud exerci tation ullamcorper suscipit lobortis nisl ut aliquip ex ea commodo consequat. Duis autem vel eum iriure dolor in hendrerit in vulputate velit esse molestie consequat, vel illum dolore eu feugiat nulla facilisis at vero eros et accumsan et iusto odio dignissim qui blandit praesent luptatum zzril delenit augue duis dolore te feugait nulla facilisi.

Lorem ipsum dolor sit amet, consectetuer adipiscing elit, sed diam nonummy nibh euismod tincidunt ut laoreet dolore magna aliquam erat volutpat. Ut wisi enim ad minim veniam, quis nostrud exerci tation ullamcorper suscipit lobortis nisl ut aliquip ex ea commodo consequat. Duis autem vel eum iriure dolor in hendrerit in vulputate velit esse molestie consequat, vel illum dolore eu feugiat nulla facilisis at vero eros et accumsan et iusto odio dignissim qui blandit praesent luptatum zzril delenit augue duis dolore te feugait nulla facilisi. Nam liber tempor cum soluta nobis eleifend option congue nihil imperdiet doming id quod mazim placerat facer possim assum.

Lorem ipsum dolor sit amet, consectetuer adipiscing elit, sed diam nonummy nibh euismod tincidunt ut laoreet dolore magna aliquam erat volutpat. Utwisi enim ad minim veniam, quis nostrud wisi enim ad minim veniam, quis nostrud exerci tation ex ea commodo

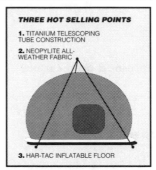

THREE HOT SELLING POINTS

1. TITANIUM TELESCOPING TUBE CONSTRUCTION

2. NEOPYLITE ALL-WEATHER FABRIC

3. HAR-TAC INFLATABLE FLOOR

The newly introduced two-person model X-2000-2 tent

WEATHERMAN PREDICTS ANOTHER HOT SUMMER. EXPECT BOOST IN WATER SPORTS GEAR

Jump in on the action in the new colorful inflatable water toys.

consequat. Duis autem vel eum iriure dolor in hendrerit in vulputate velit esse molestie consequat, vel illum dolore eu feugiat nulla facilisis at vero eros et accumsan et iusto odio dignissim qui blandit praesent luptatum zzril delenit augue duis dolore te feugait nulla facilisi.

Lorem ipsum dolor sit amet, consectetuer adipiscing elit, sed diam nonummy nibh euismod tincidunt ut laoreet dolore magna aliquam erat volut. Lorem ipsum dolor sit amet, consectetuer adipiscing elit, sed diam nonummy nibh euismod tincidunt ut laoreet dolore magna

1

Continued on page 3

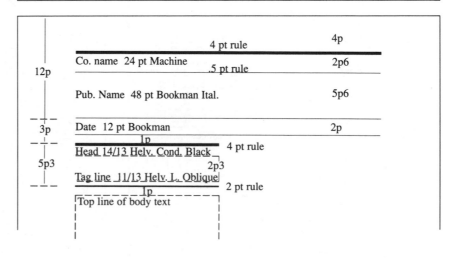

	4 pt rule	4p
Co. name 24 pt Machine	.5 pt rule	2p6
12p		
Pub. Name 48 pt Bookman Ital.		5p6
Date 12 pt Bookman		2p
3p	1p	
Head 14/13 Helv. Cond. Black	4 pt rule	
5p3	2p3	
Tag line 11/13 Helv. L. Oblique	2 pt rule	
	1p	
Top line of body text		

Wide-measure two-column grids

When you need to put a lot of running text or data on a page but still want a fairly simple format, consider a two-column grid with narrow margins and wide columns. You can see from the documents in this section—a newsletter, a catalog, an instruction sheet, and a journal—how adaptable this grid is to many different kinds of publications. Each of the examples uses this format in a completely different way and creates a very different image through typography and art.

A self-contained cover story emphasizes the importance of the topic, in this case a substantial contribution to a small boarding school.

The sidebar inset in the two-column grid is used here to quote the donor. The box is 14 picas wide with a 12p6 column measure. The use of a second color, blue, for the italic type draws the reader's attention to this statement.

Blue is also used in the banner, with reverse type, and for the display text.

The typeface on the cover is Galliard throughout.

A bolder, busier style for an inside story is created by the large headline, the recurrent subheads, and the bold rule around the photo. The banner, headline, and subheads print in blue.

The column width—22 picas—is the absolute maximum for running text on an 8.5- by 11-inch page. With a rule down the center of the page, you don't have to align the text in adjoining columns.

Other pages of the newsletter use a three-column grid, maintaining the banner, page frame, and rules

between columns for continuity. Mixing grids within a publication in this way accommodates a mix of short and long stories and different-size pictures and gives the publication a varied texture.

The body text is Galliard. The headlines are Helvetica Black Oblique.

Design: Scot Louis Gaznier (Langley, WA)

Pages from The Solebury School newsletter. Trim size: 8-1/2 by 11

The two-column grid is used in this book catalog to create an extremely open, well-organized, easily referenced format.

The long line length (maximum measure is 20p6) minimizes runover lines, so it's easy to pick out the title, author, and other details in each listing.

The small type size (8/11 Friz Quadrata) helps contain the lines, but the leading and white space are designed so that readability isn't compromised. This typeface has a good contrast of boldface to light-face that makes the book titles stand out. The use of boldface, roman, italics, and all caps is handled carefully to delineate clearly what could have been a hodgepodge of details.

The hard left edge created by the type and the hairline rules contrasts with the openness of the very uneven right margin. Open at the top and the bottom, the page has a strong sense of verticality, which is emphasized by the weight of the category heads.

The headline type is Aachen Bold. The weight of the headlines is emphasized by the bold rules below. Note that in a two-line head the length of the bold rule is determined by the short second line; the hairline rule above the bold rule extends to the maximum measure.

The faceted sphere, with its mathematical precision and crystalline structure, is appropriate for the scientific line of books being sold. The art was created in Pro3D, using one of the generic solids available in that program, and imported into PageMaker as a PICT file. Because PICT-file tones print differently on LaserWriters and Linotronics (the final output was from an L300), the Pro3D art was kept a little lighter and lower in contrast on-screen than was desired in the printed piece.

Design: John Odam (San Diego, CA)

Catalog from Academic Press, Harcourt Brace Jovanovich, Publishers. Trim size: 24-3/4 by 11 inches, folded twice

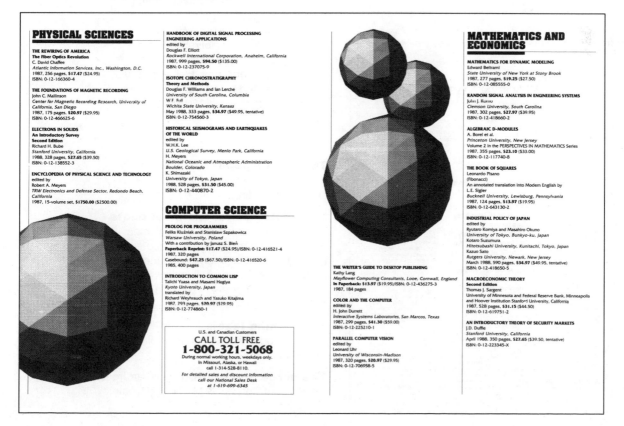

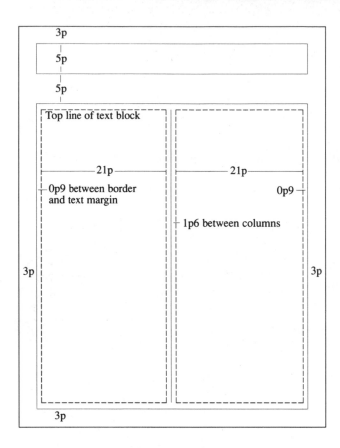

```
                    3p
        ┌─────────────────────────┐
        │          5p             │
        └─────────────────────────┘
                    5p

  ┌─ Top line of text block ──────────────────┐
  │                                            │
  │         ─── 21p ───      ─── 21p ───        │
  │  ─ 0p9 between border                0p9 ─  │
  │    and text margin                         │
  │                                            │
  │           ── 1p6 between columns ──         │
  │                                            │
3p│                                            │3p
  │                                            │
  └────────────────────────────────────────────┘
                    3p
```

This blueprint was used for both documents on these two pages.

Equal margins on all four sides work best in this format. If you vary from that, do it decisively, as in a deep top margin, rather than subtly.

The depth of the panel at the top of the page and the space between the panel and the text block can vary depending on the elements to be included.

Art is best sized to the width of a single column. Small diagrams can be accommodated as shown in the instruction sheet at right. Art can also be inset in the text, like the quote in the page below.

The illustrations in the instruction sheet were scanned with a Datacopy 730 and traced in Aldus Freehand for the purpose of position only. Using a scanner in this way provides an opportunity to test sizes in the layout and to eliminate elements of the art that are unnecessary. The printer strips in the halftones to match the size and position in the layout.

Type specs for instruction sheet
Company name: 18-point Bookman with
    20-point caps
Headline: 16/15 Helvetica Black
Subheads: 12-point Helvetica Black
Text: 10/10 Helvetica Light with 6 points
    between paragraphs, Helvetica Black
    numbers, and a 1p4 hanging indent
Numbers in diagrams: 18-point Helvetica
    Black

The Journal of Contemporary Mythology
WINTER 1990

IN SEARCH OF
THE MODERN MYTH
By Raymond Chavoustier

Lorem ipsum dolor sit amet, consectetuer adipiscing elit, sed diam nonummy nibh euismod tincidunt ut laoreet dolore magna aliquam erat volutpat. Ut wisi enim ad minim veniam, quis nostrud exerci tation ullamcorper suscipit lobortis nisl ut aliquip ex ea commodo consequat hendrerit in velit esse molestie.

Duis autem vel eum iriure dolor in hendrerit in vulputate velit esse molestie consequat, vel illum dolore eu feugiat nulla facilisis at vero eros et accumsan et iusto odio dignissim qui blandit praesent luptatum zzril delenit augue duis dolore te feugait nulla facilisi. Lorem ipsum dolor sit amet, consectetuer adipiscing elit, sed diam nonummy nibh euismod tincidunt ut laoreet dolore magna aliquam erat volutpat. Ut wisi enim ad minim veniam, quis nostrud exerci tation ullamcorper suscipit lobortis nisl ut aliquip ex ea commodo ut aliquip ex ea commodo ut aliquip ex ea commodoseq.

Duis autem vel eum iriure dolor in hendrerit in vulputate velit esse molestie consequat, vel illum dolore eu feugiat nulla facilisis at vero eros et accumsan et iusto odio dignissim qui blandit praesent luptatum zzril delenit augue duis dolore te feugait nulla facilisi. Nam liber tempor cum soluta nobis eleifend option.Ut wisi enim ad minim veniam, quis nostrud exerci

Congue nihil imperdiet doming id quod mazim placerat facer possim assum. Lorem ipsum dolor sit amet, consectetuer adipiscing elit, sed diam nonummy nibh euismod tincidunt ut laoreet dolore magna aliquam erat volutpat. Ut wisi enim ad minim veniam, quis nostrud exerci tation ullamcorper suscipit lobortis nisl ut aliquip ex ea commodo consequat.

Duis autem vel eum iriure dolor in hendrerit in vulputate velit esse molestie consequat, vel illum dolore eu feugiat nulla facilisis at vero eros et accumsan et iusto odio dignissim qui blandit praesent luptatum zzril delenit au-

We have not even to risk
the adventure alone,
for the heroes of all time have
gone before us.
The labyrinth is thoroughly
known. We have only to follow
the thread
of the hero path,
... and where we had thought
to be alone,
we will be with all the world.
—Joseph Campbell

gue duis dolore te feugait nulla facilisi. Lorem ipsum dolor sit amet, consectetuer adipiscing elit, sed diam nonummy nibh euismod tincidunt ut laoreet dolore magna aliquam erat qui blandit praesent luptatumvolutpatquis augue duis dolore tenostrud exerci.

Ut wisi enim ad minim veniam, quis nostrud exerci tation ullamcorper suscipit lobortis nisl ut aliquip ex ea commodo consequat. Duis autem vel eum iriure dolor in hendrerit in vulputate velit esse molestie consequat, vel illum dolore eu feugiat nulla facilisis at vero eros et accumsan et iusto odio dignissim qui blandit praesent luptatum zzril delenit augue duis dolore te feugait nulla facilisis hendrerit in vulputate velit esse molestie.

Lorem ipsum dolor sit amet, consectetuer adipiscing elit, sed diam nonummy nibh euismod tincidunt ut laoreet dolore magna aliquam erat volutpat. Ut wisi enim ad minim veniam, quis nostrud exerci tation ullamcorper suscipit lobortis nisl ut aliquip ex ea commodo consequat. Duis autem vel eum iriure dolor in hendrerit in vulputate velit esse molestie consequat, vel illum dolore eu feugiat nulla facilisis at vero eros et accumsan et iusto odio dignissim qui blandit praesent luptatum zzril delenit augue duis dolore te feugait nulla facilisi.Lorem ipsum dolor sit amet, consectetuer adipiscing elit, sed diam nonummy nibh euismod tincidunt ut laoreet dolore magna aliquam erat volutpat. Ut wisi enim ad minim veniam, quis nostrud exerci tation ullamcorper suscipit lobortis nisl ut aliquip ex ea commodo consequat. Duis autem vel eum iriure dolor in hendrerit in vulputate velit esse molestie consequat.

Vel illum dolore eu feugiat nulla facilisis at vero eros et accumsan et iusto odio dignissim qui blandit praesent luptatum zzril delenit augue duis dolore te feugait nulla facilisi. Lorem ipsum dolor sit amet, consectetuer adipiscing elit, sed diam nonummy nibh euismod tincidunt ut

The journal page at left is obviously designed for an audience predisposed to sustained reading.

The white box for the inset quote is the same width as the text columns. The 12-point rule anchors the quote so that it doesn't float in empty space. The type is 16/18 Helvetica Condensed Bold, centered, and contrasts with the classic feeling of the rest of the page.

The running text is Palatino. The initial cap is 96-point Zapf Chancery followed by a 5p6 indent.

The border decoration is clip art from Desktop Art Borders & Mortices (Dynamic Graphics).

AntarcticA

AUTOMATIC ICE MAKER INSTALLATION KIT FOR TWO-DOOR SIDE-BY-SIDE REFRIGERATOR

IMPORTANT

The refrigerator must be level to ensure proper operation of the ice maker. See your owner's manual.

TOOLS YOU WILL NEED

Phillips head screwdriver
Drill with 1/4" bit
Adjustable open-end wrench
Needlenose pliers

PARTS LIST

1. Harness and fill-tube grommet.
2. Water supply unit with hose nut, rubber washer, water valve, and compression nuts.
3. Rectangular clip (4) for end assembly unit and split grommet (2).
4. Screws and nuts (See screw identification chart on page 3).
5. Fill spout.
6. Plastic fill tube for ice maker harness.

STEPS IN THIS PROCEDURE

Ut wisi enim ad minim veniam, quis nostrud exerci tation ullamcorper suscipit lobortis nisl ut aliquip ex ea commodo consequat. Duis autem vel eum iriure dolor in hendrerit in vulputate velit esse molestie consequat, vel illum dolore eu feugiat nulla facilisis

1. At vero eros et accumsan et iusto odio dignissim qui blandit praesent luptatum zzril delenit augue duis dolore te feugait
2. Nulla facilisihendrerit in vulputate velit esse molestie . Lorem ipsum dolor sit amet, consectetuer adipiscing elit, sed diam nonummy nibh euismod tincidunt ut laoreet dolore magna aliquam erat volutpat.
3. Ut wisi enim ad minim veniam, quis nostrud exerci tation ullamcorper suscipit lobortis nisl ut aliquip ex ea commodo consequat.
4. Duis autem vel eum iriure dolor in hendrerit in vulputate velit esse molestie consequat, vel illum dolore eu feugiat nulla facilisis at vero eros et accumsan et iusto odio dignissim qui blandit praesent luptatum zzril delenit augue
5. Duis dolore te feugait nulla facilisi.Lorem ipsum dolor sit amet, consectetuer adipiscing elit, sed diam nonummy nibh euismod tincidunt ut laoreet dolore magna

1

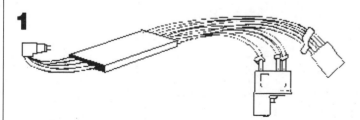

Ut wisi enim ad minim veniam, quis exerci tation

2

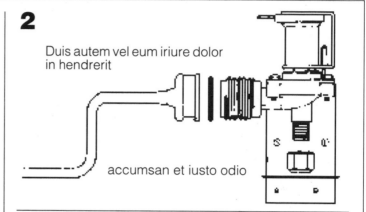

Duis autem vel eum iriure dolor in hendrerit

accumsan et iusto odio

3

Ut wisi enim ad minim veniam, quis exerci tation

4

accumsan et iusto odio

5

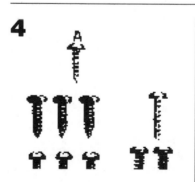

Duis autem vel eum iriure dolor in hendrerit

6

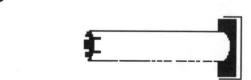

Nulla facilisihendrerit in vulpu

THREE-COLUMN GRIDS

The three-column grid is the most common format in publishing, widely used in magazines, newspapers, newsletters, catalogs, and annual reports. It is popular because it is so flexible, allowing you to place headlines, art, boxed copy, and other elements across any one, two, or even all three columns. This enables you to break the material into small chunks or modules, using various graphic devices to indicate the relative importance of items and relationships between them.

In the short line length, usually 12 to 14 picas, type sets efficiently in relatively small sizes (9- or 10-point type is frequently used for running

This informal, three-column format shows the value of simplicity. With the controls available in desktop publishing, these pages are probably easier to produce than a single-column typewritten document. A stapled, four-page statement of purpose, this was created when the organization first converted to desktop publishing. Three years later, they print the same information in an 11-by-17, three-color folder with computer-drawn art.

The horizontal rules provide a consistent structure that is balanced by open, ragged right type. The two-column heads, the angled, bit-mapped initial caps, and the playful art keep the three-column grid from feeling rigid and also suggest the personality of a foundation trying to reach young people.

The headline type is Bookman (with open spacing in the foundation's name). The running text is Avant Garde, a sans serif face with a large x-height. When generously leaded, as it is here, it is distinctive and inviting.

Lists of names work very well in the three-column format.

D O   I T   N O W   F O U N D A T I O N

Editorial Advisory Board

The process of maintaining the reliability of our information is made

Peter Bourne, M.D.
President,

City College of New York
New York, NY

Eugene Schoenfeld, M.D.
Medical Director,
Steinbeck Treatment
Center
Community Hospital
Salinas, CA

William A. Siler, R.Ph.
President,
Gemini Foundation
Urbana, IL

David E. Smith, M.D.
Founder and Medical
Director,
Haight-Ashbury
Free Medical Clinic
San Francisco, CA

J. Thomas Ungerleider, M.D.
Neuropsychiatric Institute
University of California
at Los Angeles
Los Angeles, CA

Charles V. Wetli, M.D.
Deputy Chief Medical
Examiner,
Dade County
Miami, FL

Norman E. Zinberg, M.D.
Department of Psychiatry
The Cambridge Hospital
Cambridge, MA

D O   I T   N O W   F O U N D A T I O N

History & Philosophy

Do It Now Foundation was established in 1968 by five people concerned with the dramatic increase in amphetamine use among young people in the Los Angeles area.

Among its early services, the Foundation provided one of the first drug abuse hotlines in the United States, a crisis rescue service, street drug analysis, and treatment services.

But it has been as a producer of innovative public information that the Foundation has made its greatest and longest-lasting impact.

D.I.N. information services were developed in response to the need for alternative approaches to substance abuse education and prevention.

As drug use surged across the country in the late 1960s and early 1970s, it became obvious that young people simply were no longer heeding the message of the "establishment." New tools were needed. Do It Now helped create them.

To finance the Foundation's early activities, a long-playing record album titled "First Vibration" was produced and distributed nationwide. Containing selections donated by 15 top performers and groups

(including the Beatles, Jimi Hendrix, Jefferson Airplane and Buffalo Springfield), the record raised more than $50,000 and helped establish Do It Now as a internationally-acclaimed youth-oriented information project.

An activity growing out of early Do It Now fund-raising and education efforts which quickly evolved into a central focus of the Foundation was the production and distribution of print information materials.

Drug Abuse: A Realistic Primer for Parents, True Facts About Sniffing, and Allen Ginsberg Talks About Amphetamines, were among the first publications produced by the Foundation.

Do It Now gained further national prominence in the early 1970s by producing and distributing radio public service announcements and programs carrying the message of the Foundation to rock music listeners in the U.S. and Canada.

Featuring personalities such as Frank Zappa, Steve Stills, Eric Burdon, Grace Slick, and John Sebastian, the Foundation's public service spots promoted the message that speed and other drugs could be deadly, indeed, and featured the tag line:

"Put speed down. Do it now."

The message achieved saturation coverage and, at the campaign's height, was aired by some 1,500 radio stations nationally.

Design: Jim Parker (Phoenix, AZ)

Pages from a statement of purpose by the Do It Now Foundation. Trim size: 8-1/2 by 11

text) that is still easy for readers to scan. The three-column grid also accommodates small pictures and large ones equally well, so that a really terrific photo can be given adequate space while a not-very-good mug shot can be kept appropriately sized to the width of a single column. This range enables you to use contrast in sizing art as a design element.

So why doesn't everyone use a three-column grid? One of the disadvantages of the format is that so many people do, and it can be difficult to devise a style that distinguishes your publication from all the others.

Page frames and column rules create a classic, three-column newsletter format. A second color, used for banners, breakouts, art, and sidebar tints, adds to the appeal.

Note the many devices used to vary the page composition: inset art, two-column tables and breakouts, sidebars that run the full page width in a two-column format rather than a three-column one. Note

also how the horizontal rules turn into the page on one or both sides of the center column; often, the facing page runs the horizontal rule across all three columns for contrast.

The shatter outline of the art (below left) contrasts sharply with the page structure. In general, irregularly shaped art helps keep a tight grid from being too rigid.

The reverse type in the banners is Avant Garde with open letter spacing, which greatly improves the legibility of reverse type. The breakout is Avant Garde italic, the headlines are Helvetica, and the running text is Times Roman.

Design: Jim Parker (Phoenix, AZ)
Pages from Newservice, *published by the Do It Now Foundation.*
Trim size: 8-1/2 by 11

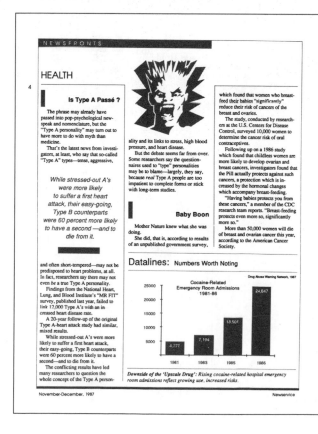

Modular verticals

The easiest way to lay out a three-column page is to run the text continuously in vertical columns. And one of the easiest ways to keep those verticals from being dull is through the use of tones. Whether shades of gray or a second color, tones can be used to separate, isolate, emphasize, or unify. Three different treatments are shown on these two pages.

The tones used in headline banners both unify and separate different elements on the page. The headline banners in this newsletter are 8-point rules (which print 60% black) on top of 20% black boxes, which vary in depth according the length of the headline. The two-line heads are centered in 3p9-deep boxes, the one-line heads in 3p-deep boxes. You can leave a master banner for each headline size on the pasteboard of your document, and then make copies of them as needed.

The caption also prints in a 20% box. A three-line caption fits in the same 3p9 box as a two-line head.

The clip art is from the Metro ImageBase NewsletterMaker.

Nashville, the type used for the publication name, is from Compugraphic, a phototypesetter that is just beginning to release its library to the desktop market. When Nashville is set tightly, its slab-serif style works well, and the word "NewsBeat" has been kerned to bring out that characteristic. The date, set in 9-point Futura, is set with 200% letter space for additional contrast with the type above.

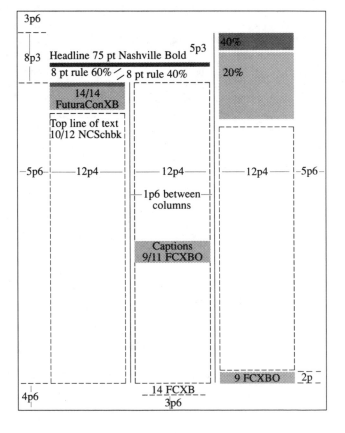

Art, headlines, and color tints are placed loosely in the grid to create a collage-like feeling in the first sample. The effect is casual and gives an inviting sense of the unexpected, which is relatively rare in three-column newsletters.

Color is a strong element in this design. The tone unifying the two related stories under a single headline is orange; it drops out to create a white border around the photos, which print over a blue tint. The two-column headline, initial caps, 8-point rules, and exclamation point also print in orange. The logo prints orange and blue.

The distinctive logo collages small sans serif type, boxed and angled, over the larger Roman-style title. An effective way to integrate the company and newsletter names, this device is relatively easy to execute if you have a good eye for proportioning type.

The Times Roman running text is set in relatively narrow columns surrounded by generous white space. For contrast, the display type is set in a bold Helvetica.

In the bottom sample, the tone is used behind secondary material—the issue highlights on the cover and sidebars on inside pages—rather than behind features.

The structured rules, justified text, and even column bottoms represent a completely different approach to page design than the previous sample. Each sets a style appropriate for its audience.

Design (top): Tom Ahern (Providence, RI)

Dateline *is published quarterly by*
GTECH Lottery.
Size: 8-1/2 by 11

Design (bottom): Kimberly Mancebo,
Robert Bryant Associates (Campbell, CA)

TeleVisual Market Strategies *is published by*
Telecommunications Productivity Center.
Size: 8-1/2 by 11

Introducing the horizontal

A true grid has a precise horizontal structure that is generally determined by the type specifications of the dominant text face, so that a given number of lines will fit in each grid unit. The construction of the grid must also take into account the space between grid units. For example, if your type is 10/12, each grid unit and the space beween two units will be in multiples of 12 points, or 1 pica. If your type is 11/13, then the grid units will be in multiples of 13 points, obviously a less convenient measurement to work with.

Visual elements are sized to fit different combinations of these units, allowing for varied sizes and shapes which, because of their relationship to the underlying structure, are in proportion to one another and to the page as a whole. In some ways, the truly modular grid simplifies layout more than the mostly vertical structures apparent in many of the samples reproduced in this book. But an orthodox grid is also more difficult to construct. If you find the mathematically determined horizontal structure confusing or inhibiting, then adopt a more informal approach to placing the elements vertically on the page. If, on the other hand, you are drawn to the possibilities inherent in the technique introduced on these and the following two pages, you'll find a number of useful books listed in the resource section.

If you want to study an expertly used horizontal grid, see the Pitney Bowes publication toward the beginning of the Brochure section in Chapter 5.

The sample on the facing page is built on an 18-unit grid, with 3 vertical divisions and 6 horizontal ones. This schematic shows the placement of the sample's visual elements on the grid. You can see how the structure facilitates decision making by suggesting both size and placement; note also how the design overrides the grid when needed. Turn the page for additional diagrams, grid specifications, and another, very different design based on the same grid.

Type Specifications
Overline: 10/12 Avant Garde reverse, centered, +200%
    letterspace
Publication name: 48-point Avant Garde, –20% letterspace
Story heads: 24/24 Bodoni Bold Italic
Body text: 10/12 Bodoni
Captions: 11/12 Bodoni Bold Italic

The clip art is from Metro ImageBase NewsletterMaker. The trumpet image was created by silhouetting, in DeskPaint, one of a trio that were all the same size; that silhouette was placed in PageMaker, copied, and resized to produce the trio you see here. The other images were used as is, except for the party scene in which we moved a balloon or two and some confetti (again in DeskPaint) to fit the image area. This sort of manipulation is typical of how clip art is adapted to suit specific layouts.

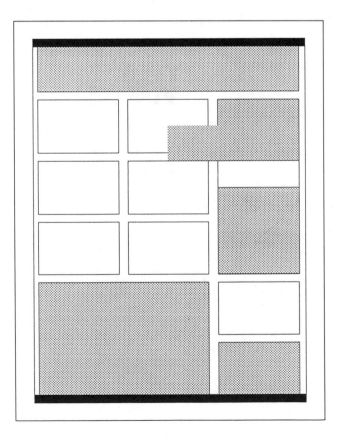

Triangle Hotel Trumpet

EAT, DRINK AND BE MERRY

Lorem ipsum dolor sit amet, consectetuer adipiscing elit, sed diam nonummy nibh euismod tincidunt ut laoreet dolore magna aliquam erat volutpat. Ut wisi enim ad minim veniam, quis nostrud exerci tation ullamcorper suscipit lobortis nisl ut aliquip ex ea commodo consequat.

Duis autem vel eum iriure dolor in hendrerit in vulputate velit esse molestie consequat, vel illum dolore eu feugiat nulla facilisis at vero eros et accumsan et iusto odio dignissim qui blandit praesent luptatum zzril delenit augue duis dolore te feugait nulla facilisi. Lorem ipsum dolor sit amet, consectetuer adipiscing elit, sed diam nonummy nibh euismod tincidunt ut laoreet dolore magna aliquam erat volutpat. Ut wisi enim ad minim veniam, quis nostrud exerci tation ullamcorper suscipit lobortis nisl ut aliquip ex ea commodo consequat.

Duis autem vel eum iriure dolor in hendrerit in vulputate velit esse molestie consequat, vel illum dolore eu feugiat nulla facil at vero eros et

accumsan et iusto etei odio dignissim qui blandit praesent luptatum zzril delenit augue duis dolore te. feugait nulla facilisi. Nam liber tempor

Sunday Jazz Brunch

FROM BIG BAND TO ROCK 'N ROLL

Duis autem vel eum iriure dolor in hendrerit in vulputate velit esse molestie consequat, vel illum dolore eu feugiat nulla facilisis at vero eros et accumsan et iusto odio dignissim qui blandit praesent luptatum zzril delenit augue duis dolore te feugait nulla facilisi.

Lorem ipsum dolor sit amet, consectetuer adipiscing elit, sed diam nonummy nibh euismod tincidunt ut laoreet dolore magna aliquam erat volutpat. Ut wisi enim ad minim veniam, quis nostrud exerci tation

ullamcorper suscipit lobortis nisl ut aliquip ex ea commodo consequat. Duis autem vel eum iriure dolor in hendrerit in vulputate velit esse

All-Night Buffet

molestie consequat. Lorem ipsum dolor sit amet, consectetuer adipiscing elit, sed diam nonummy nibh euismod tincidunt ut

Baoreet dolore magna aliquam erat volutpat. Ut wisi enim ad minim laoreet dolore magna aliquam erat veniam, quis nostrud eu feugiat nulla facilisis at vero eros et accumsan et

New Year's Gala in the Ballroom

Morning- After Room Service

**This is a good place for the placement of
a pull quote from the text**

Lorem ipsum dolor sit amet, consectetuer adipiscing elit, sed diam nonummy nibh euismod tincidunt ut laoreet dolore magna aliquam erat volutpat. Ut wisi enim ad minim veniam, quis nostrud exerci tation ullamcorper suscipit lobortis nisl ut aliquip ex ea commodo consequat. Duis autem vel eum iriure dolor in hendrerit in vulputate velit esse molestie consequat, vel illum dolore eu feugiat nulla facilisis at vero eros et accumsan et iusto odio dignissim qui blandit praesent luptatum zzril delenit augue duis dolore te feugait nulla facilisi. Lorem ipsum dolor sit amet, consectetuer adipiscing elit,

in hendrerit in vulputate velit esse molestie consequat, vel illum dolore eu feugiat nulla facilisis at vero eros et accumsan et iusto odio dignissim qui blandit praesent luptatum zzril delenit augue duis dolore te feugait nulla facilisi. Nam liber tempor cum soluta nobis eleifend option

nostrud exerci tation ullamcorper suscipit lobortis nisl ut aliquip ex ea commodo consequat. Duis autem vel eum iriure dolor in hendrerit in vulputate velit esse molestie consequat, vel illum dolore eu feugiat nulla facilisis at vero eros et accumsan et iusto odio dignissim qui blandit prae-

nostrud exerci tation ul-lamcorper suscipit lobortis nisl ut aliquip ex ea commodo consequat. Duis autem vel eum iriure dolor in hendrerit in vulputate velit esse molestie consequat, vel illum dolore eu

sed diam nonummy nibh euismod tincidunt ut laoreet dolore magna aliquam erat volutpat. Ut wisi enim ad minim veniam, quis nostrud exerci tation ullamcorper suscipit lobortis nisl ut aliquip ex ea commodo consequat. Duis autem vel eum iriure dolor

congue nihil imperdiet doming id quod mazim placerat facer possim assum. Lorem ipsum dolor sit amet, consectetuer adipiscing elit, sed diam nonummy nibh euismod tincidunt ut laoreet dolore magna aliquam erat volutpat. Ut wisi enim ad minim veniam, quis

sent luptatum zzril delenit augue duis dolore te feugait nulla facilisi. Lorem ipsum dolor sit amet, consectetuer adipiscing elit, sed diam nonummy nibh euismod tincidunt ut laoreet dolore magna aliquam erat volutpat. Ut wisi enim ad minim veniam,

1   2   3

4

Page composition within an 18-unit grid such as the one discussed on these four pages can vary considerably. The page at left and schematic 1, above, show picture placement in which the horizontal and vertical structures are balanced. The second schematic shows a strong horizontal arrangement; the third, a strong vertical. In the fourth, one column is used only for headlines, captions, and small photos, creating still another look.

Research Paper

Lorem ipsum dolor sit amet, consectetuer adipiscing elit, sed diam nonummy nibh euismod tincidunt ut laoreet dolore magna aliquam erat volutpat. Ut wisi enim ad minim veniam, quis nostrud exerci tation ullamcorper suscipit lobortis nisl ut aliquip ex ea commodo consequat.

Duis autem vel eum iriure dolor in hendrerit in vulputate velit esse molestie consequat, vel illum dolore eu feugiat nulla facilisis at vero eros et accumsan et iusto odio dignissim qui blandit praesent luptatum zzril delenit augue duis dolore te feugait nulla facilisi.

Lorem ipsum dolor sit amet, consectetuer adipiscing elit, sed diam nonummy nibh euismod tincidunt ut laoreet dolore magna aliquam erat volutpat. Ut wisi enim ad minim veniam, quis nostrud exerci tation ullamcorper suscipit lobortis nisl ut aliquip ex ea commodo consequat.

Duis autem vel eum iriure dolor in hendrerit in vulputate velit esse molestie consequat, vel illum dolore eu feugiat nulla facilisis at vero eros et accumsan et iusto odio dignissim qui blandit praesent luptatum zzril delenit augue duis dolore te feugait nulla facilisi. Nam liber tempor cum soluta nobis eleifend option congue nihil imperdiet doming id quod mazim placerat facer possim assum.

Lorem ipsum dolor sit amet, consectetuer adipiscing elit, sed diam nonummy nibh euismod tincidunt ut laoreet dolore magna ut aliquam ea commodo conse-quat.

Duis autem vel eum iriure dsent luptatum zzril delenit augue duis dolore te feugait nulla

TEST RESULTS	Grp A	Grp B	Control
Uptatum zzril delenit augue	1,745	1,398	1,598
Dolore eu feugiat nulla	4,978	2,467	1,028
Tincidunt ut ladolore wisi enim	3,684	1,746	5,896
Tin vulputate velit esse	2,678	3,986	1,038
Dignissim qui blandit praesent	3,794	1,840	2,096
Uptatum zzril delenit augue	1,493	2,047	3,208
Dolore eu feugiat nulla	2,067	2,067	3,906
Total	17,376	13,982	20,387

NARRATIVE

Amet consectetuer adipiscing elit, suscipit lobortis nisl ut aliquip ex ea commodo consequat. Duis autem vel eum iriure dolor in hendrerit in vulputate velit esse molestie consequat, vel illum dolore eu feugiat nulla facilisis at Vero eros et

sectetuer adipiscing elit, sed diam nonummy nibh euismod tincidunt ut lcommodo consequat. Duis autem aoreet dolore magna aliquam erat volutpat. Ut wisi enim ad minim

continued on following page

FURTHER RESEARCH

Accumsan et iusto odio dignissim qui blandit praesent luptatum zzril delenit augue duis dolore te feugait nulla facilisi.
Lorem ipsum dolor sit amet, consectetuer adipiscing elit, sed

CONCLUSIONS

Diam nonummy nibh euismod tincidunt ut laoreet dolore magna aliquam erat volutpat. Ut wisi enim ad minim veniam, quis nostrud exerci tation ullamcorper suscipit lobortis nisl ut aliquip ex ea com-modo consequat. Duis facilisi.

Lorem ipsum dolor sit amet, tincidunt ut laoreet dolore magna aliquam erat volutpat. Ut wisi enim ad minim veniam, quis.

The sample at left uses the grid on the facing page to create horizontal divisions for text blocks. A text block can run any number of grid units and need not fill the entire unit. But regardless of the depth of the text, rules separating text blocks are placed at the midpoint of the space between two grid units.

The banner runs from the top margin to the midpoint of the space between the first two horizontal grid units. A hairline horizontal rule is placed midway between the last grid unit and the bottom margin.

The headline is 60-point American Typewriter, reversed out of the 60% black banner.

The body text is 10/12 New Century Schoolbook.

Subheads are 12-point Helvetica Black, aligned at top with the top of a grid unit. The running text in these text blocks is 10/12 Helvetica Light. The text in the table is 10/24, creating a full line space between each item so that this text aligns with running text in the adjacent column.

Grid units and type size are designed in relation to one another. The first detail here shows how 10/12 text fits in the grid units used in the samples on these two pages. For the sake of comparison, the second detail shows 10/14 text in the same 10/12 grid; you can see that with the increased leading, the grid no longer works. Both details are shown full size.

When constructing a horizontal grid, you can customize PageMaker's vertical ruler with the leading value specified in points. (Use the Preferences command on the Edit menu.) With Snap to Rulers on, all guidelines, text, and graphics that you place on the page will align with ruler tick marks calibrated to the leading that you specified.

This grid was used for the samples in this section. Although all the units are of equal size, elements placed on the grid need not be. The grid is constructed as follows:

Margins: 3p top and bottom, 4p side
Columns: three, 1p6 space between
Horizontal grid units: 8p9 deep
beginning at top margin, 1p3
between units
Hairline vertical rules from top to
bottom margin: 1p outside left and
right margins and, where appropriate, between columns
Horizontal rules (Triangle Hotel
sample on preceding spread):
1p3 deep; top rule flush with top
grid unit; bottom rule just below last
grid unit.

Note that the grid is slightly asymmetrical along the vertical axis. In the Triangle Hotel sample on the preceding spread, the 1p3-deep horizontal rule fills the space between the bottom grid unit and the bottom margin. In the Research Paper at left, a hairline rule visually fills the space at the bottom of the page. If you were to use this grid without horizontal rules to balance the space, you would probably want to shift the entire grid down 9 points to center it on the page.

Lorem ipsum dolor sit amet, consectetuer adipiscing elit, sed diam nonummy nibh euismod tincidunt ut laoreet dolore magna aliquam erat volutpat. Ut wisi enim ad minim veniam, quis nostrud exerci tation ullamcorper suscipit lobortis nisl ut aliquip ex ea commodo consequat.
Duis autem vel eum iriure dolor in hendrerit in vulputate velit esse molestie consequat, vel illum dolore eu feugiat nulla facilisis at vero eros et accumsan et iusto odio dignissim qui blandit praesent luptatum zzril delenit augue duis dolore te feugait nulla facilisi. Lorem ipsum dolor sit amet, consectetuer adipiscing elit, sed diam nonummy nibh euismod tincidunt ut duis laoreet dolore magna

1

Lorem ipsum dolor sit amet, consectetuer adipiscing elit, sed diam nonummy nibh euismod tincidunt ut laoreet dolore magna aliquam erat volutpat. Ut wisi enim ad minim veniam, quis nostrud exerci tation ullamcorper suscipit lobortis nisl ut aliquip ex ea commodo consequat.
Duis autem vel eum iriure dolor in hendrerit in vulputate velit esse molestie consequat, vel illum dolore eu feugiat nulla facilisis at vero eros et accumsan et iusto odio dignissim qui blandit praesent luptatum zzril delenit augue duis dolore te feugait nulla facilisi. Lorem ipsum dolor sit

2

A mixed grid

Varying the column width within a single page has many uses. It accommodates different kinds of material, allows for a varied page design, and can inspire you to organize the components of your document in a way that strengthens the intrinsic relationships and forms contrasts among them. In the sample shown below, the mixed grid is both functional and dramatic.

Sidebar vignettes set to a 13-pica measure are inset in a single wide column that provides the background narrative in this annual report. The sidebars, which run throughout the report, are human-interest stories. On other pages not shown, some sidebars are styled as two single columns that face each other across the gutter, others as two singles in the outer columns of facing pages.

The two different settings are unified by a single typeface (Goudy Old Style), generously leaded, yet they are styled for considerable contrast: The larger, roman type in the wide measure is justified and prints in warm brown; the smaller, italic type is ragged right and prints in black. The italic caption at the bottom of the page is set to the wide measure and prints in brown.

Design: Tom Lewis (San Diego, CA)
Page from the Medic Alert Annual Report.
Trim size: 8-1/2 by 11

Design (facing page): Edward Hughes, Edward Hughes Design (Evanston, IL)
Pages from the Roosevelt University Annual Report.
Trim Size: 8-1/4 by 11-5/8

REPORT TO THE READER

"My membership is like insurance coverage - the very best protection, and for a reasonable cost. I'm sure all the members feel as I do - grateful there is an organization called Medic Alert."

That's how one member described the secure feeling enjoyed by the more than 2.6 million people worldwide who wear the Medic Alert emblem. For 32 years, Medic Alert has warned health professionals about patients' special medical conditions, saving thousands of lives and sparing needless suffering. "As an EMT," another member wrote, "I know how much Medic Alert helps emergency personnel. If people would only realize how important it is for us to know their medical problems in an emergency maybe more would wear Medic Alert emblems."

In recent years, Medic Alert's emergency medical identification system has substantially improved operations management and product and service quality. The Foundation's quest for excellence is ongoing.

MEDIC ALERT'S NEW SERVICES This year, Medic Alert launched plans to diversify into services that capitalize on the Foundation's ability to manage an accurate, confidential medical data base. In August, in 1987, Medic Alert began

MEDIC ALERT PROTECTS TRANSPLANT RECIPIENT

Eleven years ago, a New Zealand school girl named Ann Crawford became ill with the flu. Unlike many flu victims for whom the malady is a fleeting annoyance, Ann suffered permanent lung damage. She fell prey to a series of infections that strained her breathing and weakened her heart.

In the years that followed, Ann endured a revolving door of hospital treatments. Her doctors experimented with megadose drug therapies to clear her frequent infections, but her lungs continued to worsen. Eight years

after her bout with the flu, Ann's health had become so fragile that few expected her to survive the winter.

Only 19, Ann was not ready to give up. She had read up on the latest advances in thoracic surgery and transplant technology. She wondered, "Why not start all over again with a new heart and lungs?"

Ann's enthusiasm sparked support from the Lions Club in her area, which agreed to help finance the cost of her surgery. She traveled to the United Kingdom for the operation, and returned home with a new heart and lungs. Shortly after, she penned Pumps & Bellows, a detailed account of her illness and transplant operation.

This brave young woman from New Zealand, is breathing easier these days. But she will always require anti-rejection drugs to ensure that her body will not declare war on her new organs. In a medical emergency, responders need to know instantly of her transplant operation and drug regimen to administer proper treatment.

That is why Ann, like many others around the world, wears a Medic Alert emblem. After years of hospital stays and bed rest, the young New Zealander takes every precaution to protect her most treasured gift, a second chance at life.

From Evangeline: Thanks to Medic Alert my husband is alive today. He was in a very bad car accident. The paramedics saw his Medic Alert necklace and found his wallet card. His seat belt and his Medic Alert tag saved his life.

Asymmetrical three-column

Generally, asymmetrical three-column grids have two wide columns and one narrow one. This produces a slightly more interesting and an inherently more variable look than three equal columns, especially when you consider the possibilities that derive from combining two columns, whether two equal columns or one wide and one narrow.

The underlying structure is two 11-pica columns and one 18-pica column. When the wide column is combined with the inside narrow column, the resulting 31-pica measure provides additional flexibility in page composition.

The depth of the photographs remains constant from page to page, although the depth of the captions varies. Good photographs, well-printed, result in the rich blacks and grays evident here.

The captions are styled as display type, reversed out against the gray background.

The uneven bottoms of the three columns helps balance the tight structure created by the strong horizontal line across the top of the page, the strong left edge of the type columns (which is emphasized by the elongated page), and the tabbed folios that bleed off the bottom of the page.

Note that single-digit numbers are indented so that all numbers align right. This typographic refinement is all the more needed here with the hanging indent.

As precise as this format is, the pages are relatively easy to assemble. Having two standardized picture sizes minimizes art decisions, and the uneven bottoms speed up page assembly.

The slightly elongated page, elegant gray paper, and high-quality printing create an image that is both distinctive and consequential. Fine printing on excellent paper stock is essential to provide an even gray background throughout and to hold the crisp detail on the small, reverse-type numbers seen here and in reverse hairline rules used on tables (not shown).

Director **Geraldine Piorkowski** (left) and Associate Director **Rod Esbrook** (right) of Counseling & Testing and Career Planning & Placement Director **Arthur Eckberg** (center) will administer a three-year "Career Analysis & Placement Project" funded by the Irvin Stern Foundation.

Roosevelt University student **Kendy Kloepfer** met some of the requirements for a major in theatre by taking classes at the Lou Conte Dance Studio, home of the Hubbard Street Dance Company. Cooperative agreements with local institutions enable University students to earn degree credits while learning from experts unique to Chicago.

Two narrow outer columns and a wide center column create a somewhat specialized three-column grid. The layout implies that the center item is the most important one. In the pages shown here, the outer columns are used to present contrasting viewpoints on the same subject, an editorial approach that works particularly well in this format. The outer columns could also be used for quotes and other marginalia, for resources related to the main story, brief listings, short profiles or news items, and so on.

The justified text in these pages adds to the formality of the subject matter and to the point-counterpoint approach of the editorial.

The clip art is from Wet Paint, except for the student in the center column on the cover, which is from MacMemories.

The blueprint gives dimensions and type specs for the nameplate on the cover. On subsequent pages, as in the one shown below left, the top of the text block is 9p from the top trim, so that would be the dimension to use for the top margin on the page setup.

The Bodoni and Bookman headlines were set in Freehand, condensed on the horizontal axis, and then placed in PageMaker. The document title was cropped to clip off the bottom of the letters, which makes the type look like it is emerging from behind the rule.

The Avant Garde ID lines on the cover and inside page were set with open letter and word spacing so that the "Educational Advancement" line filled the three-column measure.

The depth of the framed illustrations on both pages is a guideline only. The placement of visuals in the center column is best at the bottom of the page, although the top is also acceptable.

Space between art, captions, rules, and adjacent body text is often a difficult detail in page assembly unless you are working on a very precise grid. The closer any two elements are to each other, the more related they will seem to the reader. In these samples, the caption is closer to the picture frame below it than to the rule above, and the rule is closer to the caption than to the preceding text.

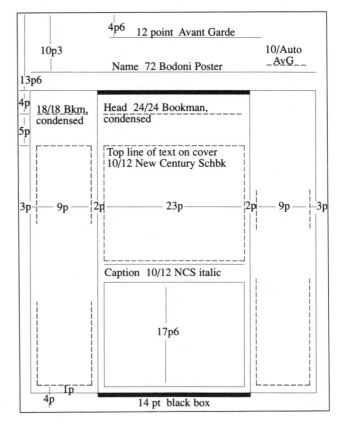

ASSOCIATION

BULLETIN

TEACHERS
ADMINISTRATORS
COUNSELORS

PARENTS
SOCIAL WORKERS
PSYCHOLOGISTS

EDUCATIONAL ADVANCEMENT IN AMERICA

A Case for Gradual Growth in Our Schools

Feugait nulla facilisi. Nam liber tempor cum soluta nobis eleifend option congue nihil imperdiet doming id

quod mazim placerat facer possim assum. Lorem ipsum dolor sit amet, consectetuer adipiscing elit, sed

Diam nonummy nibh euismod tincidunt ut laoreet dolore magna aliquam erat volutpatUt wisi enim ad minim veniam, quis nostrud exerci tation ullamcorper suscipit lobortis nisl ut aliquip ex ea commodo conse

A Primer for School Administrators in the Nineties

Torem ipsum dolor sit amet, consectetuer adipiscing elit, sed diam nonummy nibh euismod tincidunt ut laoreet dolore magna aliquam erat volutpat. Ut wisi enim ad minim veniam, quis nostrud exerci tation ullamcorper suscipit lobortis nisl ut aliquip ex ea commodo consequat.

Duis autem vel eum iriure dolor in hendrerit in vulputate velit esse molestie consequat, vel illum dolore eu feugiat nulla facilisis at vero eros et accumsan et iusto odio dignissim qui blandit praesent luptatum zzril delenit augue duis dolore te feugait nulla facilisi. Lorem ipsum dolor sit amet, consectetuer adipiscing elit, sed diam nonummy nibh euismod tincidunt ut laoreet dolore magna aliquam erat volutpat. Ut wisi enim ad minim veniam, quis nostrud exerci tation ullamcorper suscipit lobortis nisl ut aliquip ex ea commodo consequat.

Duis autem vel eum iriure dolor in hendrerit in vulputate velit esse molestie consequat, vel illum dolore eu feugiat nulla facilisis at vero eros et accumsan et iusto odio dignissim qui blandit praesent luptatum zzril delenit augue duis dolore te

Aliquip ex ea commodo consequat. Duis autem vel eum iriure dolor in hendrerit in vulputate velit esse mo

The Wisdom of Revolutionary Change in Education

Autem vel eum iriure dolor in hendrerit in vulputate velit esse molestie consequat, Vel illum dolore eu feugiat nulla facilisis at vero eros et accumsan et iusto odio dignissim qui blandit praesent luptatum zzril delenit augue duis dolore te feugait nulla facilisi.

Lorem ipsum dolor sit amet, consectetuer adipiscing elit, sed diam nonummy nibh euismod tincidunt ut laoreet dolore magna aliquam erat volutpat.

Narrow outer columns in a three-column grid are useful for publications as diverse as catalogs and technical journals.

In text-heavy publications, such as the one shown below, the narrow outer column can provide much-needed white space when reserved for art, captions, breakouts, and marginalia.

When you wrap ragged right text around a rectangular graphic, you get a much neater appearance if the graphic juts into the flush left margin.

The body text in the sample is 10/12 Galliard. The display type is Futura Condensed Extra Bold, set in 30-, 14-, and 10-point sizes. The captions are 10/12 Futura Heavy.

The clip art is from DeskTop Art Business 1.

A classic catalog format on the facing page uses rules, art, white space, and the edge of text blocks to frame pictures. The art and text requirements dictate the size, the only restraints being the vertical rules (and even those can be violated effectively).

The blueprint shows measurements for the sample below. To set up the format, specify 4p side margins, and 3 columns with 1p6 space between; then drag the column guides to the measurements shown in the blueprint.

The grid for the catalog on the facing page is similar, but the left edge of the text is flush with the column rules, which drop out behind the text. This maintains the structure of the rules while providing maximum measure for copy. To construct this grid, position the vertical rules, including those in the page frames, at these intervals: 3p, 17p, 17p, 11p, 3p.

The type reinforces the impression of variety, with six different faces used. From top to bottom, they are Futura Condensed, Aachen Bold, Avant Garde, Palatino Italic, Franklin Gothic Heavy, and American Typewriter.

The clip art is from WetPaint.

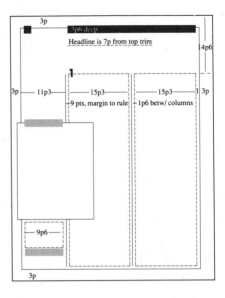

AUDIO DELIVERY SYSTEMS FOR THE 1990S

CD ROM TECHNOLOGY REPORT

The Most Realistic Stuffed Animals You Ever Saw

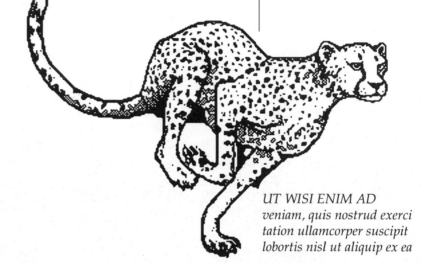

UT WISI ENIM AD veniam, quis nostrud exerci tation ullamcorper suscipit lobortis nisl ut aliquip ex ea

LOREM IPSUM DOLOR SIT AMET, sectetuer adipiscing elit, sed diam nonummy nibh euismod tincidunt ut laoreet dolore magna aliquam erat volutpat. Ut wisi enim ad minim veniam, quis nostrud exerci tation ullamcorper suscipit lobortis nisl ut aliquip ex ea commodo consequat. Duis autem vel eum iriure dolor in hendrerit in vulputate velit esse molestie consequat, vel illum dolore eu feugiat nulla facilisis at vero eros et accumsan et iusto odio dignissim qui blandit praesent luptatum zzril delenit augue duis dolore te feugait nulla facilisi. Lorem ipsum dolor sit amet, consectetuer adipiscing elit, sed diam nonummy nibh euismod tincidunt ut laoreet dolore magna aliquam erat

UT WISI ENIM AD veniam, quis nostrud exerci tation ullamcorper suscipit

LOREM IPSUM DOLO, autem vel eum iriure dolor in hendrerit in vulputate velit esse molestie consequat, vel illum consectetuer adipiscing elit, sed diam

FOUR-COLUMN GRIDS

Four-column grids are even more versatile than three-column formats. They provide an opportunity for varied page design within the same publication and for dramatic contrast among visual elements of different sizes. These grids are used frequently in magazines, newspapers,

Boxed sidebars work extremely well in a four-column setting, and can be sized with considerable variety depending on the number and depth of the columns used.

A half-page sidebar prints against a gray tone, with two narrow columns at the bottom combined to accommodate tables. Note that the box extends beyond the page frame, a technique you see frequently in graphic design today. Here those extra 9 points make it possible for the text set in the four-column format to run at the same 9-pica measure as the unboxed text. (Usually you loose a few points to the box.)

The "At a Glance" headline is used repeatedly over charts and graphs, which, with their captions, are self-contained items. A three-column treatment is shown, although other sizes are used as well.

The Times Roman running text is set 8/10 ragged right. Text this small really requires the narrow 9-pica column measure. Tables, captions, and headlines are set in a sans serif face for contrast.

Repeating headlines are inset between gray rules, with shorter rules on each end providing a spot of red that livens up the mostly text pages. The second color is repeated in charts and rules under initial caps.

Display type at the top of News Briefs pages, like the one shown below right, are tickertape-style previews of the stories on that page.

Design: Kimberly Mancebo, Robert Bryant Associates (Campbell, CA)

Pages from TeleVisual Market Strategies, published ten times per year by Telecommunications Productivity Center. Trim size: 8-1/2 by 11

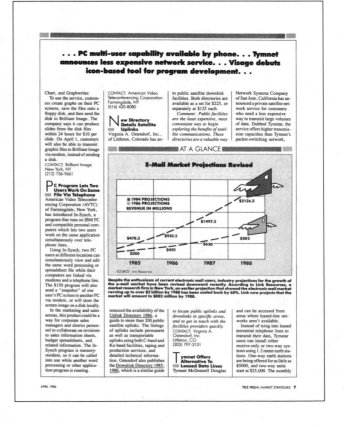

and newsletters. They are also well-suited to reference material, directories, price sheets, and other documents that require collecting many small items on a page.

But four-column grids are also more demanding to work with and require more decisions throughout the design and production process. Inherent in their flexibility, also, is the need for balance, proportion, and a deft handling of detail.

Narrow columns also require special care with typography. The type size should be relatively small, to be in proportion to the column width, and so the face must be chosen for ease of readability. With relatively few words in a line, you need to watch for excessive hyphenation. Generally, you should avoid more than two hyphens in a row. Also, a narrow column accentuates the uneven spacing inherent in justified text, so choose that style with caution.

The ease of combining running text set to a two- and a four-column measure is a definite advantage of the four-column grid. As in the previous sample, serif and sans serif faces are used for contrast.

The bold 2-point rules and unusual folio and publication identification in the upper right corner add to the distinctive and contemporary look of the page.

The graphic combines bit-mapped, graduated-tone, and geometric art. A low-resolution scan of a photo was placed in PageMaker. The same digitized image was imported in Freehand's template layer; the swimsuit was traced over the template in the drawing layer and filled with a graduated tone; the grid was drawn on a layer above that by cloning a square with a 2-point white line and no fill. The Freehand art was saved as an EPS file and placed in PageMaker on top of the bit-mapped image. Using Page-Maker's Text Wrap option, a graphic boundary was defined around the silhouette and the wraparound text was brought to the front layer to ensure that it printed over the white grid.

Design: John Odam (San Diego,CA)

Page from Verbum, *published quarterly.*
Trim size: 8-1/2 by 11

try, are losing a battle to stay alive against foreign clothing manufacturers. "Since 1980, 3,000 apparel/textile companies have closed their doors and 350,000 jobs have been lost. Of the $170 billion trade deficit, $20 billion is in the apparel industry.... In 1974, 80% of the shoes sold in this country were made in this country. Now more than 80% of the shoes are imports and footwear manufacturing in this country is practically dead." VanFossen was vice president of Corporate Information Services at Wolverine Worldwide, makers of Hush Puppies shoes, when he analyzed the company's declining competitiveness in marketplace would only be turned around with a fully automated factory. The design of the footwear in 3-D appeared to be the answer. "If I could design a shoe in 3-D, then I would have the data I needed to drive an automated factory," he concluded. "Everything you needed to know about price of material, what you had to do with it, how you had to stitch it together — I'd have all this information. That was what I was after."

In 1983 VanFossen started Computer Design Inc. in Grand Rapids, MI which was partially financed at that time by Wolverine. CDI installed their first system about five years ago at H.H. Cutler Co. of Grand Rapids, a childrens' wear company. Since then they have installed more than 50 systems in the U.S. and Europe. The CDI system is IBM PC-based, and the software starts at about $25,000. The designer can visualizes garment in 3-D on the screen and the program will automatically create 2-D flat pattern pieces. According to Jerry Johnson, vice president of Marketing at CDI, "On our CAD systems today designers can design fabrics, then wrap those fabrics onto a model to actually see how it would look. Change colors and try it again in minutes, not hours or days as it now takes to repaint or recolor fabric designs. Change necklines, sleeves, add pockets, take pockets away...all of these functions can be performed on our computer. These functions can greatly reduce product development time."

INTUITION AND INFORMATION IN FASHION DESIGN

Jackie Shapiro became one of the first fashion designers in the United States to explore the application of the computer with fashion design when she picked up her first Macintosh in 1984. She first used the computer to help develop her own line called "GARB", or Global Apparel Resource Bank, and even then she claimed that the computer was a vital part of her design process. "GARB has taken available technology and applied it...for designing clothing. To experiment and explore an infinite number of design solutions. To visualize...garments before making them. To coordinate one silhouette with another. To create, store and retrieve frequently used images: bodies, basics, prints, parts, stuff (garment treatments). To scale for measurements for pattern specification detail. To design labels, logos, illustrate...and to write this."

But using a computer alone does not make one a great de-

CUSTOMERS LIKE TO DESIGN IT THEMSELVES

One Southern California store blends fashion design with a novel marketing approach. The store's name is Softwear Swimwear and they sell custom swimsuits "designed" on a computer.

Liz Norling and Gary Leeds opened a swimwear boutique which featured an unusual gimmick of allowing customers create their own sportswear. "Not necessarily a gimmick but a new twist." Liz corrected me. "In order to succeed in this day and age in retail, one needs a unique idea." The customer's image in a swimsuit would be scanned into a color computer program, and the customer could then select from 300 fabric patterns which can be projected on the scanned image of the sportswear on the computer monitor. That way the customer would know exactly what the swimsuit would look like before it's made.

Fashion trends change quickly, and this is one way for the customer to keep up with the fashion...or start his or her own trend.

"There are problems created by using the computer," acknowledged Norling. "We are working on a solution to the two dimensional look of the person on the screen. There is also a problem of confusing the customer with so many possibilities of color and fabric that it's hard for them to make a decision on which suit they want. We also tend to get into trouble by taking colors from the screen...and then finding out that we do not have the color in stock."

The customer can see three suits on the screen at one time to compare and evaluate which one looks best. The customer's image can also be saved in the computer and pulled up at a later time for design another suit. "This is a good feature" Norling says, "as the store's sales volume can be larger. If they like all three swimsuits they may buy all three! Overall, I think the addition of the computer system to our retail store is a great one as many customers are highly excited about designing their own clothing."

13

VERBUM 2.2

The flexible size of art in a four-column grid is used to good advantage in this signage manual, where similarities and contrasts in visual details are the heart of the message. In the pages shown, note the possibilities for grouping photos as well as the variety of sizes.

Strong perspective lines in many of the photos lead your eye back into the distance. This depth illusion separates the photographs from the surface of the page. The severity of the grid structure, with the bolder-than-usual column rules, in turn enhances the perception of depth in the photos.

The vertical rules also delineate sections, as seen in the top page.

The text is Times Roman throughout, with italic captions set on a narrower measure with open leading for contrast to the running text. The white space makes it possible to run headlines the same size as body text so that they do not compete with typographic elements in the art.

Design:
Denise Saulnier,
Communication
Design Group
Limited
(Halifax, Nova
Scotia)

Pages from A
Guide to Better
Signs *published
by the City of
Halifax.
Size: 8-1/2 by 11*

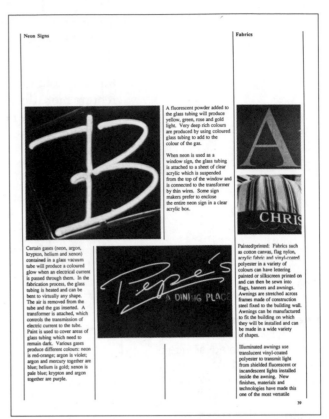

Neon Signs

Certain gases (neon, argon, krypton, helium and xenon) contained in a glass vacuum tube will produce a coloured glow when an electrical current is passed through them. In the fabrication process, the glass tubing is heated and can be bent to virtually any shape. The air is removed from the tube and the gas inserted. A transformer is attached, which controls the transmission of electric current to the tube. Paint is used to cover areas of glass tubing which need to remain dark. Various gases produce different colours: neon is red-orange; argon is violet; argon and mercury together are blue; helium is gold; xenon is pale blue; krypton and argon together are purple.

A fluorescent powder added to the glass tubing will produce yellow, green, rose and gold light. Very deep rich colours are produced by using coloured glass tubing to add to the colour of the gas.

When neon is used as a window sign, the glass tubing is attached to a sheet of clear acrylic which is suspended from the top of the window and is connected to the transformer by thin wires. Some sign makers prefer to enclose the entire neon sign in a clear acrylic box.

Fabrics

Painted/printed: Fabrics such as cotton canvas, flag nylon, acrylic fabric and vinyl-coated polyester in a variety of colours can have lettering painted or silkscreen printed on and can then be sewn into flags, banners and awnings. Awnings are stretched across frames made of construction steel fixed to the building wall. Awnings can be manufactured to fit the building on which they will be installed and can be made in a wide variety of shapes.

Illuminated awnings use translucent vinyl-coated polyester to transmit light from shielded fluorescent or incandescent lights installed inside the awning. New finishes, materials and technologies have made this one of the most versatile

39

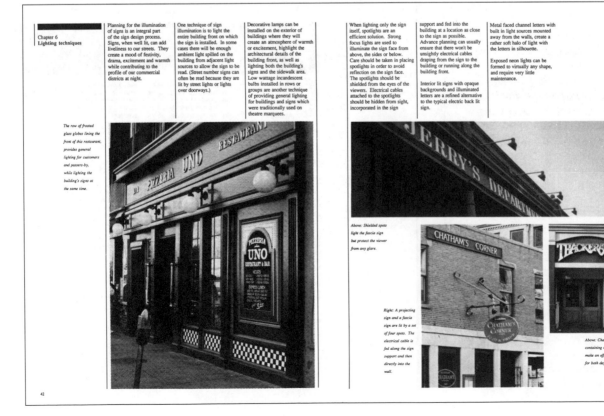

Chapter 6
Lighting techniques

Planning for the illumination of signs is an integral part of the sign design process. Signs, when well lit, can add liveliness to our streets. They create a mood of festivity, drama, excitement and warmth while contributing to the profile of our commercial districts at night.

One technique of sign illumination is to light the entire building front on which the sign is installed. In some cases there will be enough ambient light spilled on the building from adjacent light sources to allow the sign to be read. (Street number signs can often be read because they are lit by street lights or lights over doorways.)

Decorative lamps can be installed on the exterior of buildings where they will create an atmosphere of warmth or excitement, highlight the architectural details of the building front, as well as lighting both the building's signs and the sidewalk area. Low wattage incandescent bulbs installed in rows or groups are another technique of providing general lighting for buildings and signs which were traditionally used on theatre marquees.

When lighting only the sign itself, spotlights are an efficient solution. Strong focus lights are used to illuminate the sign face from above, the sides or below. Care should be taken in placing spotlights in order to avoid reflection on the sign face. The spotlights should be shielded from the eyes of the viewers. Electrical cables attached to the spotlights should be hidden from sight, incorporated in the sign

support and fed into the building at a location as close to the sign as possible. Advance planning can usually ensure that there won't be unsightly electrical cables draping from the sign to the building or running along the building front.

Interior lit signs with opaque backgrounds and illuminated letters are a refined alternative to the typical electric back lit sign.

Metal faced channel letters with built in light sources mounted away from the walls, create a rather soft halo of light with the letters in silhouette.

Exposed neon lights can be formed to virtually any shape, and require very little maintenance.

The row of frosted glass globes lining the front of this restaurant, provides general lighting for customers and passers-by, while lighting the building's signs at the same time.

Above: Shielded spots light the fascia sign but protect the viewer from any glare.

Right: A projecting sign and a fascia sign are lit by a set of four spots. The electrical cable is fed along the sign support and then directly into the wall.

Above: Channel letters containing neon tubing make an effective sign for both day and night.

42

43

The need to accommodate different kinds of editorial material often suggests the use of a four-column grid. The pages shown demonstrate the ease of combining two- and four-column settings.

The contents pages use the narrow measure for the short program descriptions on the left-hand page, and the wider measure for a tidy listing of the publication contents on the right. Contrasting column widths provide an immediate visual clue to the reader that these are different kinds of material. Art is sized to both column widths for variety and visual contrast, and the silhouetted dancing figures break the grid and float above it.

Note the implied horizon line that runs across all four pages, 11 picas from the top trim.

The short listings in the Program Highlights work especially well in narrow columns. The boldface dates are Helvetica Black, the listings are Garamond with boldface heads. Garamond is used for the contents page and running text in feature stories as well.

The music headline is Futura Condensed Extra Bold; the Program headline on the facing page is Futura Bold. Display typefaces with a variety of styles enable you to create subtle contrasts within the same type family.

Optical character recognition software (OCR) is a key component in the production cycle. The designer uses a DEST scanner with Publish Pac OCR software to capture text from typewritten copy that is provided by the client. They experience only about a 3 percent error, which the designer attributes to their using clean, double-spaced copy typed in a big, round face (they use Pica) and output on an impact printer. (With smaller faces and dot matrix output, the counters of letters tend to fill in, resulting in error rates as high as 20 percent.) The text is checked for spelling and typesetting conventions (single space after periods, and so on) in Microsoft Word and then formatted in PageMaker.

Design: Tom Suzuki (Falls Church, VA)

Pages from Worldnet *magazine, published bimonthly by the United States Information Agency.*
Trim size: 8-1/4 by 10-3/4

PROGRAM HIGHLIGHTS

Monday, August 1

CinemAttractions
Hosts Steve March and Pat Kelley preview the hottest scenes from the hottest American theaters

Tuesday, August 9

National Gallery of Art
David Smith, one of the most prolific American sculptors of this century, was a pioneer of free-standing, open metal forms. His life is lyrics, old photo-ed the massive, movable forms he called "mobiles," created his last great sculpture for the East Building of the National Gallery. The program traces the evolution of this signature work.   11.30 GMT

Wednesday, August 17

Jazz at the Smithsonian
Sidney

Thursday, August 25

Wild America
Every summer when Pacific salmon make their massive spawning run, up to a hundred brown bears—the largest carnivores in North America—line up along the McNeil River in Alaska to feast on the fish.   11.00 GMT

MUSIC MUSIC MUSIC

The Forum Presents
Fridays, Hour

Sing along Coolidge, Judy Collins, Flack and more. Forum Presents and exciting shows top entertaining the old favorite new hits sung by the stars who the music family Filmed in p each Forum has one entertaining an uninterrupted of song: sweet such as "Kill and "Send in gospel hym "Amazing in the Servi and sagas City of Ne "American Each brings ba all from house—

6 WO

WORLDNET   VOLUME II, ISSUE 5   AUGUST/SEPTEMBER 1988

CONGRESS: WE, THE PEOPLE
Meet the men and women, senators and congressional representatives elected by their fellow citizens to serve in Congress, the legislative branch of the United States government.

ADAM SMITH'S MONEY WORLD
Adam Smith, that is to say, George J. W. Goodman, knows his business—which is wisely and wittily explaining the ins and outs of high finance. Goodman's credo is: "Economics is boring; money is fascinating."

JAZZ AT THE SMITHSONIAN
The golden age of jazz, the improvisational music rooted in blues, band music and ragtime, is recreated in special concerts by talented performers such as Art Farmer, Red Norvo, Mel Lewis and Alberta Hunter.

GEORGE MICHAEL'S SPORTS MACHINE
George goes out to the ball games—the opening of the 1988 football season and baseball's championship World Series. George also gets the inside scoop on every fall sport.

Alexander Calder's "Mobile" (detail on front cover) is the focal point of The National Gallery of Art East's atrium.

CONTENTS

The cover and an inside flap show the contrasting but unified look in a folder that uses the four-column grid to combine two- and four-column settings.

The GTE logo on the cover is aligned left with the type. The underlying grid will almost always suggest an appropriate placement for loose items on the page.

The large, Palatino italic type on the cover shows off the calligraphic nature of this typeface.

The text in the narrow columns hugs the column rules, creating a very crisp left edge that emphasizes the verticality of the page. The loose ragged right margin makes the left edge seem stronger still in comparison.

The horizontal lines running through the map contrast with the strong verticality of the text above. Note the implied vertical edge of the map, aligned left with the second column of text. The map and rules print gray on the inside flap, with different colored dots denoting the locations listed. The cover map, surrounded by graduated tones of color that suggest the dimensionality of the earth, prints as green lines against white, with the background rules in gray.

Design: Weisz Yang Dunkelberger Inc. (Westport, CT)

Pages from The World of GTE, Year-End Highlights.
Trim size: 11 by 33-3/4, double gatefold

The World of GTE

GTE is one of the major corporations in the world, with annual sales and revenues exceeding $15.1 billion and assets of $27.4 billion. It has operations in 48 states and 33 countries. These facilities employ 160,000 people who work in three core businesses: telecommunications, lighting products and precision materials.

GTE

Argentina
Buenos Aires *Lighting, P*

Australia
Gosford *Lighting, P*
Queensland *Lighting, P*
Victoria *Precision Materials, P*

Austria
Grossenzerdorf *Lighting, M*

Belgium
Tienen *Lighting, P*
Tienen *Precision Materials, P*

Brazil
Santa Amaro *Precision Materials, P*
Sao Paulo *Lighting, P*
Vinhedo *Lighting, P*

Canada
Brockville, Ont. *Microtel Ltd., P**
Burnaby, B.C. *Microtel Ltd., P(2),L**
Drummondville, Que. *Lighting, P*
Montreal, Que. *Lighting, P*
Toronto, Ont. *Lighting, P*
Vancouver, B.C. *Microtel Ltd., P**
Windsor, Ont. *Precision Materials, P(5)*

Colombia
Bogota *Lighting, P*

Costa Rica
San Jose *Lighting, P*

Denmark
Hvidovre *Lighting, M*

Ecuador
Quito *Lighting, M*

France
Andrezieux-Boutheon *Precision Materials, P*
Barentin *Precision Materials, P*
La Fouilllouse *Lighting, P*
Lyon *Lighting, P*
Nantes *Lighting, P*
Reims *Lighting, P*
St. Marcellin *Lighting, P*

Germany
Erlangen *Lighting, P*
Precision Materials, P
Sinsheim *Precision Materials, P(3)*

Greece
Athens *Lighting, M*

Haiti
Port au Prince *Precision Materials, P*

Hong Kong
Lighting, M
Precision Materials, M

Italy
Pero *Lighting, M*
Milan *Precision Materials, P*

Japan
Kahoku *Lighting, P*
Tokyo *Precision Materials, P*

Mexico
Juarez *Lighting, P*
Monterrey *Precision Materials, P*

Netherlands
Breda *Lighting, M*
Haarlem *Lighting, P*

Norway
Vestvollvn *Lighting, M*

Peru
Lima *Lighting, M*

Portugal
Lisbon *Lighting, M*

Singapore
Lighting, M

Spain
Madrid *Lighting, M*

Sweden
Stockholm *Lighting, M*

Switzerland
Geneva *Lighting, M*
Precision Materials, M

Taiwan
Taipei *Lighting, M*

Thailand
Bangkok *Lighting, M*

Trinidad
Mount Hope *Lighting, M*

United Kingdom
Charlestown *Lighting, P*
London *Lighting, M*
Malmesburg *Lighting, P*
Newhaven *Lighting, P*
Swansea *Precision Materials, P*

Total GTE Employment by Country

Argentina, 340
Australia, 210
Austria, 16
Belgium, 870
Brazil, 1,260
Canada, 19,285
Colombia, 230
Costa Rica, 730
Denmark, 13
Dominican Republic, 2,765
Ecuador, 14
France, 1,525
Germany, 1,180
Greece, 6
Haiti, 950
Hong Kong, 270
Italy, 180
Japan, 385
Mexico, 345
Netherlands, 18
Norway, 11
Panama, 67
Peru, 12
Philippines, 150
Portugal, 10
Singapore, 6
Spain, 80
Sweden, 23
Switzerland, 75
Taiwan, 260
Thailand, 10
Trinidad, 5
United Kingdom, 1,460

Total: 32,761

*Telecommunications plants operated by Microtel Ltd., a part of British Columbia Telephone Company.

One narrow + three wide columns for oversize pages

In a tabloid publication, the four-column grid provides a relatively wide measure for reading text, especially when one column is narrow as in the page shown here.

The body text is 10/13 New Baskerville, a graceful face with a light weight. It makes this oversize, mostly text page inviting and easy to read. The generous use of boldface in the running text emphasizes the "people" focus of the publication and facilitates scanning.

The display type is Helvetica Condensed Black.

The rules for the page frame and columns are a little bolder than is usually found, and the inside rules for the narrow columns run all the way to the page frame. The rigidity of that structure is balanced by white space and appropriately sized type. Note also how the initial caps interrupt the column rule.

The distinctive large folio reverses out of a box, which prints in a second color used also for the page frames, the initial caps in the headlines, and the ballot boxes signalling the end of each piece.

The bold, silhouette-style illustration, used throughout the publication, helps small images hold up on the oversize pages.

Design: Kate Dore, Dore Davis Design (Sacramento, CA)

Page from Communique, *published by Sacramento Association of Business Communicators.*
Trim size: 11 by 17

2

IABC Board

President
Robert L. Deen
Deen & Black
444-8014

First Vice President
Tracy Thompson
Carlson Associates
973-0600

Vice President/Programs
Tamra Weber
Deen & Black
444-8014

Vice President/ Professional Development
Mary Closson
The Packard Group
484-8709

Vice President/ Membership
Terri Lowe
Crocker Art Museum
449-8709

Vice President/ Communications
Pat Macht
AmeriGas/Cal Gas
686-3553

Vice President/ Academic Affairs
Jeff Aran
Sacramento Board of Realtors
922-7711

Treasurer
Diana Russell
Pacific Legal Foundation
444-0154

SYNERGY Chair
Della Gilleran
Della Gilleran Design
446-4616

Past President
Betsy Stone
Sutter Health
927-5211

Staff Secretary
Barbara Davis
Creative Consulting
424-8400

Delegates At Large:
Cindy Simonsen
Hanson Simonsen
451-2270

Rick Cabral
Connolly Development, Inc.
454-1416

Colleen Sotomura
The Sierra Foundation
635-4755

Newsletter Editors
Marisa Alcalay
Mercy San Juan Hospital
537-5245
Mary C. Towne
California Veterinary Medical Association
344-4905

Newsletter Design & Layout
Kate Dore
Dore Davis Design
920-3448

IABC Communiqué
January/February 1988

About Sacramento Communicators

Jolaine Collins, past president of the IABC Denver chapter and a recent addition to IABC Sacramento, will represent District 6 on the IABC Professionalism Committee. **Jan Emerson** has moved from Foundation Health Plan to a new position with the publications department at Sutter Health. **Dan Brown,** Group Director of Public Affairs for Aerojet General, will be the 1988 President of the new Sacramento chapter of the Public Relations Society of America.

IABC 1988 president **Robert Deen** and **Christi Black** have formed the partnership of Deen & Black, Communications and Public Affairs. Christi is the former executive director of the American River Parkway Foundation. They will be joined by IABC member **Tamra Weber,** former Communications Director for United Way, who will be an associate, and **Colleen Jang,** a recent CSU Chico communication graduate and member of the student IABC chapter. The new firm is located in an office building at 2212 K Street recently purchased by fellow IABC member **Della Gilleran** (who will chair SYNERGY in 1988).

Terri Lowe of the Crocker Art Museum is interested in volunteers to assist with Crocker's 1988 Bike-a-Thon fundraiser, scheduled for June. **Robert Deen** will chair the overall event, with IABC'ers **Jolaine Collins** and **Janice White.** Terri's number is 449-8709.

Stacey Eachus, former IABC Sacramento member who went to San Diego in June for a position with the National Cash Register Company, has returned to Sacramento in a public relations position with the California Association of Health Facilities.

The **CSU Chico student chapter** has expressed an interest in repeating the successful exchange program in which students were matched for a day with IABC Sacramento members

to observe a typical work day.

The Sacramento Communications Council has been restructured as a quarterly meeting of the presidents of the dozen professional communications organizations involved, and will be chaired by the IABC president.

The IABC's annual international conference will finally be closer to home in 1988 — Anaheim. It should be an interesting one as the proposed IABC/PRSA merger comes to a head.

Mark your calendars now for upcoming **IABC Sacramento luncheons,** held the first Thursday of each month: Feb. 4, March 3, April 7, and May 5. ■

(Have something to contribute? Send information to Communicator Column, c/o editor, IABC Sacramento, P.O. Box 160481, Sacramento, Ca. 95816.)

Chapter Business

Meet the 1988 IABC Board of Directors

The IABC Sacramento Board of Directors serves on a calendar year basis. Being involved is an important part of the IABC experience, and members are encouraged to contact board members to find out more about the areas of activity outlined below.

Immediate Past President Betsy C. Stone will represent IABC Sacramento at the District level, and as circumstances dictate will speak for the chapter on the proposed IABC/PRSA merger. She is also responsible for organizing the District 6 conference for 1990 which Sacramento will host.

Robert L. Deen, the chapter president is responsible for group's overall direction and functioning.

1st Vice President Tracy Thompson oversees administrative matters and special projects at the president's direction.

Treasurer Diana Russell is responsible for the chapter's finances, including coordinating with the SYNERGY management team.

Vice President, Communications, Pat Macht is responsible for the chapter newsletter, all media relations (meeting notices, awards, etc.), and for any and all activities which relate to the chapter's image and visibility.

Vice President, Membership, Terri Lowe, directs membership recruiting efforts, including correspondence, planning, renewal program, roster, and special efforts as required.

Vice President, Programs, Tamra Weber, surveys the membership for their interests and selects luncheon speakers accordingly, coordinates arrangements, and ensures that monthly meeting notices go out in a timely manner.

Vice President, Academic Affairs, Jeff Aran serves as a liaison to local universities and coordinates with the IABC student chapter at CSU Chico.

Vice President, Professional Development, Mary Closson, develops seminars and programs to enhance members' professional skills and abilities, and conducts the annual membership survey.

Della Gilleran, 1988 SYNERGY Chair, is responsible for the overall direction and management of SYNERGY, Sacramento's coalition-based special event for the communications profession.

Delegates at Large: Rick Cabral, Cindy Simonsen, and Colleen Sotomura serve as at-large members of the board and take responsibility for special assignments as needed.

The board is responsible for the functioning and direction of the Chapter. Members are encouraged to discuss concerns or make suggestions to any board member at any time. ■

Plan On Being Active in 1988

The best way to meet new people, learn new skills and become a part of new groups is through active volunteerism.

Working together on projects gives you a chance to get to know people and for them to get to know you and your skills, capabilities and interests.

IABC/Sacramento encourages members to be involved in both IABC activities and general community activities. Consider your options:

The IABC chapter conducts ongoing efforts such as the scholarship and communications (including the newsletter). The board members responsible for these areas are listed in each issue of the newsletter, with their phone number, and all are interested in hearing from those who want to help.

Community involvement — IABC/Sacramento encourages members to accept leadership positions in community organizations such as United Way, KVIE, March of Dimes, etc. These members deserve and need the support of fellow chapter communicators and the chapter is often approached directly by organizations in need of volunteers.

To help you get involved, the chapter needs to know about your interest. Contact the appropriate board member directly, or let Chapter President Robert Deen know.

Make being an active volunteer part of your plan for self improvement in 1988! ■

Using the center columns

In this four-column grid, photos are enlarged to a two-column measure. The text in the narrow outer columns frames the pictures, and the generous white space provides an opportunity to dramatize the shape of the photos against the structure of the page.

The digitized photos, which are reproduced from a laser printout, need a layout in which the overall composition has more impact than the individual parts. Sizes and placements were chosen for dramatic contrast, with a passive close-up against an active middle shot on the cover and a dancing full-figure long shot against a close-up on the inside page.

The logotype gives the name *FLASH* a strong identity and emphasizes the action and boldness implied by in the name. The typeface, Bodoni Poster, doesn't come with a true italic, so FLASH was typed in Adobe Illustrator and shifted on a horizontal axis with the shear tool to create an oblique. The word was given a white fill with no stroke, imported into PageMaker, and placed over the black panel to create the reverse type. Note that the serifs of the F and the H bleed off the left and right edges of the banner, which themselves have been stretched beyond the text margins.

Futura, used in the story headline and names of the models, is forever stylish. It has graced the cover of virtually every fashion magazine at one time or another. Each text unit was created and rotated in Illustrator and then imported into PageMaker. Placing the type on a 15-degree angle creates an additional dimension, a layer that seems to float above the rectilinear grid of the logo, text columns, rules, and photos. Keeping all the names and the headline on the same angle creates organized spontaneity rather than random movement.

MANNER continued from page 1

we can send them right away to clients here that are willing to use brand new people. That starts the ball rolling, and if things start to click right away, they stay in New York. If things don't happen immediately, we ask them to go to Europe and develop a strong book, learn how to really model, and then come back to New York. We deal with several agencies in Milan, Paris and Germany and we try to send models to the appropriate agency. Each individual model is different of course, and how much time each one would stay in Europe varies. It can take a couple of months or even a couple of years to get started. The truth of the matter is, if you are a real good model, you don't need a strong book, you need to have a look that works in New York. If you are a brand new model, and you have that look, you can start to work immediately. We are very lucky to have models like that.

If any men are interested in being with our agency

they should send a couple a pictures in the mail. Don't spend alot of money on pictures - snapshots will do - put your stats on the back, and send them in. You'll get an answer quickly, usually within a week after we receive them. We answer all mail that we get, but a warning, more than 99% of the people who send in pictures receive a "no."

If you are interested in modeling in New York, you should just take a deep breath, swallow, and come. You can go on and on wonder and worry, but if you want to model you should come here and see everybody and find out what your chances are. But don't kid yourself. If the answer is "no" the answer is "no". Don't get the attitude of "Well, I'll show them!" The business is much too rough for that kind of attitude. Chances are you won't show them, they'll show you.

MANNER is located at 874 Broadway New York, NY 10003 (212) 475-5001

9

Bodoni, used for the running text, is hard to beat for typographic elegance. Its alternating thicks and thins give this newsletter a distinctive look—fashionable but not trendy. The type just feels like Fred Astaire dancing. Bodoni needs open leading (10/13 was used) to take advantage of its tall ascenders and descenders without sacrificing legibility.

The logo treatment is adapted as a visual "prop" throughout the publication. On the page above, for example, it becomes a stage on which one of the models dances. The stylized lightening bolt from the logo provides an additional motif that can be used decoratively.

The photographs were scanned and then retouched in ImageStudio. In the Charles Winslow photo, for example, the background was removed to create a silhouette, and the neck area was lightened. Billy Haire's feet were given some tone (they were white in the original).

The images were balanced both for contrast and for light and dark using PageMaker's Image Control feature. The goal was to get enough contrast to be dramatic without letting the technique steal the show from the models themselves. Because laser printer proofs tend to print very heavy blacks, the darkness had to be carefully controlled.

The blueprint on the next page provides the basic grid structure for this and the following design, which conveys a very different image than the one shown here. For type specs for this design, refer to the commentary on these two pages, rather than the ones in the blueprint. Note also that the cover banner here has been stretched 2 picas beyond the side margins defined in the blueprint.

Design: Don Wright (Woodstock, NY)

Pages from Flash, *a bimonthly newsletter for models published by Nautilus Books, designed as a "Page Makeover" for* Publish! *magazine.*
Trim size: 8-1/2 by 11

The business report at right and on the facing page uses the same four-column grid as the fashion newsletter on the previous spread but to very different effect.

The report title in the nameplate is spaced to fill the banner. In Page-Maker, you can insert a fixed space (which varies from one font to another) by pressing Option-space bar. In the sample, we inserted five spaces. The slash is a hairline rule drawn with the perpendicular tool.

On page 2, the banner is 2p6 deep, with the same fonts and letter-spacing as the nameplate type but dropped down to 14 point. The top of the text block is 5 picas from the top of the banner.

The charts and graphs were created in PageMaker with 10-point Futura Light type.

The clip art, from Metro Image-Base ReportMaker, was silhouetted in DeskPaint and placed in Page-Maker as a TIFF compressed file.

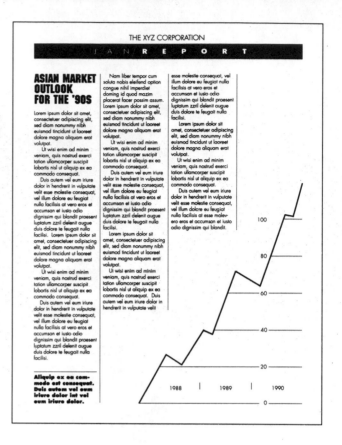

The blueprint shows the details for the sample on the facing page. The same column structure is used for the newsletter on the preceding page.

The basic column width is 10p3. In addition to combining the center columns for art as shown on these samples, you could combine any two or three columns for variable art sizes and self-contained sidebar material.

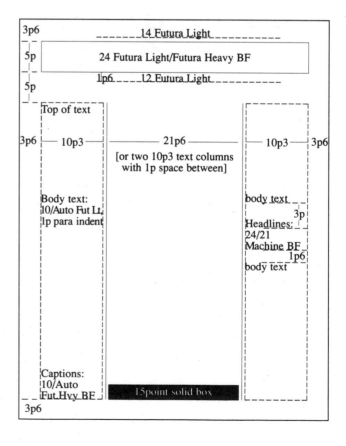

PRODUCTION LANDMARK FOR THE XYZ MACHINE: 100,000 UNITS

Lorem ipsum dolor sit amet, consectetuer adipiscing elit, sed diam nonummy nibh euismod tincidunt ut laoreet dolore magna aliquam erat volutpat. Ut wisi enim ad minim veniam, quis nostrud exerci tation ullamcorper suscipit lobortis nisl ut aliquip ex ea commodo consequat.

Duis autem vel eum iriure dolor in hendrerit in vulputate velit esse molestie consequat, vel illum dolore eu feugiat nulla facilisis at vero eros et accumsan et iusto odio dignissim qui blandit praesent luptatum zzril delenit augue duis dolore te feugait nulla facilisi.

Lorem ipsum dolor sit amet, consectetuer adipiscing elit, sed diam nonummy nibh euismod tincidunt ut laoreet dolore magna aliquam erat volutpat. Ut wisi enim ad minim veniam, quis nostrud exerci tation ullamcorper suscipit lobortis nisl ut aliquip ex ea commodo consequat. Duis autem vel eum iriure dolor in hendrerit in vulputate velit esse molestie consequat, vel illum dolore eu feugiat

---

Aliquip ex ea comi-modo es consequat. Duis vel ex eat com modovel eumet.

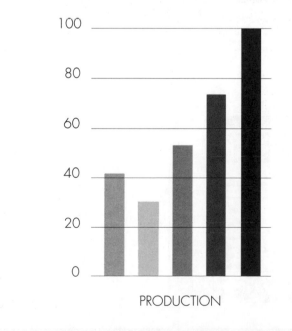

PRODUCTION

Aliquip ex ea com-modo est consequat. Duis autem vel eum iriure dolor int vel eum iriure dolor.

---

nulla facilisis at vero eros et accumsan et iusto odio dignissim qui blandit praesent luptatum zzril delenit augue duis dolore te feugait nulla facilisi. Nam liber tempor cum soluta nobis eleifend option congue nihil imperdiet doming id quod mazim placerat facer possim assum.

DO YOU KNOW YOUR CUSTOMER?

Lorem ipsum dolor sit amet. Consectetuer adipiscing elitt. Sed diam nonummy nibh euismod tincidunt ut laoreet dolore magna aliquam erat volutpat. Ut wisi enim ad minim veniam, quis nostrud exerci tation ullamcorper suscipit lobortis nisl ut aliquip ex ea commodo consequat. Duis autem vel eum iriure dolor in hendrerit in

Vulputate velit esse molestie consequat, vel illum dolore eu feugiat nulla facilisis at vero eros et accumsan et iusto odio dignissim qui blandit praesent luptatum zzril delenit augue duis dolore te feugait nulla facilisi. Lorem ipsum dolor sit amet, consectetuer adipiscing elit, sed diam nonummy nibh euismod suscipit lobortis nisltincidunt ut laoreet dolore magna aliquam erat volutpat.

Within the four-column format you can balance strong vertical and horizontal material, as in the sample on the facing page.The image area for visuals in the first three horizontal units is almost square (9 by 9p3), a nice proportion in this grid, although other sizes are possible.

The layout in the Safety Tips page could be used as an expanded contents page, with the cover story in the text column and four different stories, briefly described with art from each, in the outer two columns. When using this technique, which is very effective, the cover art can be repeated inside or can be a detail from a piece of art that runs with the story.

The word "Safety" is 18-point Bookman italic. In order to inset it in the T of "Tips," we created a T with an elongated bar across the top by drawing a black box over the top of an I. In doing this, we encountered WYSIWYG problems: the manually-created T aligned with the I on-screen but not in the printed page. We went through several trial-and-error adjust-

ments before an incorrect on-screen image produced a correct printed page.

Events listings are well suited to the narrow measure, as shown in the sample flyer below left. And short introductory copy is still quite readable in one wide column.

The clip art was altered to allow for text in the upper right corner of the image area: We merely erased that part of the image in DeskPaint. The image is from the Metro Image-Base Newsletter Maker package.

The column specifications for the listings use the same measurements as the four-column format in

the blueprint. The headline and listing specifications are shown in the details below.

The blueprint specifications are for the Safety Tips sample. You can divide the space in other ways to balance the vertical and horizontal divisions; the schematic below shows another possible arrangement. Don't forget white space as an element in the grid.

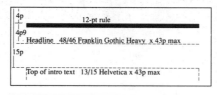

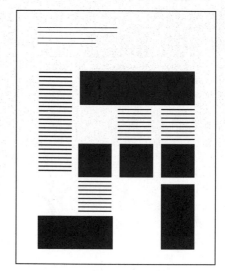

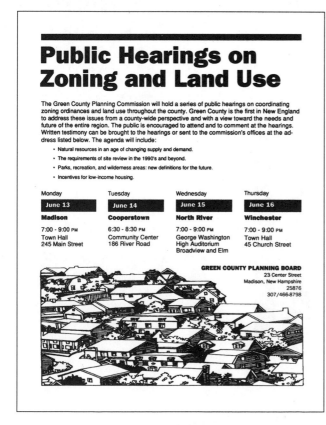

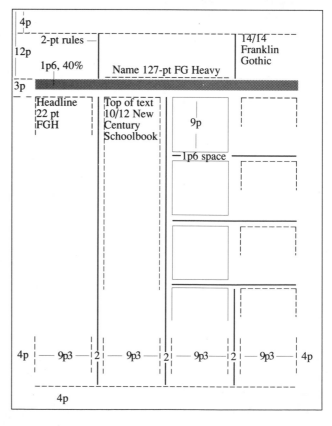

Safety TIPS

from Timberline Power & Light Co.

Tools and Hazards of the Trade

Lsectetuer sed adipiscing elite in sed utm diam nonummy nibh euismod tincidunt ut laoreet dolore magna aliquam erat volutpat. Ut wisi enim ad minim veniam, quis nostrud exerci tation dolor in ullamcorper suscipit lobortis nisl ut aliquip ex ea commodo feugiat consequat. Duis autem vel eum iriure dolor in hendrerit in vulputate velit esse molestie vero consequat, vel illum dolore eu feugiat nulla facilisis at vero eros et accumsan et iusto odio dignissim qui blandit.

Praesent luptatum zzril delenit augue duis dolore te feugait nulla facilisi. Lorem ipsum dolor sit amet,et zzril delenit consectetuer adipiscing elit, urt sed diam nonummy nibh euismod tincidunt ut laoreet dolore magna aliquam erat volutpat.

Ut wisi enim ad minim veniam, quis nostrud exerci tation ad minim ullamcorper suscipit lobortis nisl ut aliquip ex ea facilisi. Lorem ipsum commodo Duis autem vel eum iriure dolor iscingin hendrerit in vulputate velit esse molestie consequat, vel illum dolore eu feugiat nulla facilisis at vero eros et

Consequat duis aute vel eum iriure dolor in hendrerit in vulputate velit esse

Molestie consequal illum dolore eu feugiat nulla facilisis at vero eros et accumsan et iusto odio dignissim qui blandit praesent

Tatum zzril delenit augue duis dolore te feugait nulla facilisi. Nam liber tempor cum

Lorem ipsum dolor sit amet, consectetuer adipiscing elit, sed diam nonummy nibh euismod tincidunt ut laoreet dolore magna aliquam erat volutpat.

Ut wisi enim ad minim veniam, quis nostrud exerci tation ullamcorper suscipit

MIXED GRIDS

Grids with multiple and variable column widths can handle the widest range of elements, partly because the columns combine to produce so many different page arrangements. These grids allow for several different widths of text, which in turn allow for more contrast in type sizes and faces to distinguish components from one another. And of course the possibilities for picture placement are even more varied in size and scale than those of the text.

This type of grid is particularly useful in publications such as catalogs, which have many different kinds of elements that need to be distinguished from one another. The format also encourages browsing, with numerous headlines and art providing multiple entry points for busy readers.

Constructing this sort of grid requries a careful analysis of the material to determine the format. And executing the design requires a good eye for balance. This is "breaking the rules" territory and can backfire if you don't know what you're doing.

This five-column grid accommodates newsletter-style essays alongside catalog listings, with short quotes and 19th-century engravings adding verbal and visual personality to the pages. The result is lively, inviting, and well-organized.

The variable column width is the key to the diverse page composition. From rule to rule, the narrow outer columns are 7 picas, the wider inner columns are 10p6. With 6-point margins between the text and rules, this creates four different measures for use in this publication:

- 6p (a single narrow column used for quotes)
- 9p6 (a single wider column used for product listings and for the continuation of essays from a previous page)
- 20p (two wide columns used for essays and product listings)
- 16p6 (one narrow and one wide column, used for listings).

In fact, additional combinations are available by combining three wide columns, one narrow and three wide, and, of course, all five columns.

Note the contrast in typeface among the different kinds of text. The essays are Palatino for both body text and headlines (which print blue), with Bodoni initial caps (also blue). The product listings are various weights of Futura . The category heads reverse out of 15-point blue banners; product titles, numbers, and prices also print blue.

The engravings are traditional clip art, photostatted and pasted onto camera-ready pages. Matching 19-century thematic art with contemporary subject matter provides a subtle visual humor, reinforced by placement which invariably breaks the grid.

The short quotes in the narrow columns include humor, anonymous aphorisms, and testimonials from satisfied customers.

Design: Barbara Lee,
Folio Consulting (Englewood, NJ)

Pages from the SuperLearning
Newsletter/Catalog.
Trim size: 8-1/2 by 11

Self-Hypnosis

Self-hypnosis can be the royal road to self-mastery. A good man to learn with is Lee Pulos, Ph.D., professor, psychologist, past president of the Canadian Society of Clinical Hypnosis.

Learn the classical approach on Side A. Then on Side B, experience Pulos' original double induction – two voices weaving in and out, in counterpoint, to help you understand the power of indirect suggestion.

Creative Thinking & Problem Solving
Get your creative juices flowing with hypnotic imagery, suggestion, dream programming. Create solutions instead of problems.
TAPE 401 $12.95

Sports Excellence
Weekend sport or competitive athlete – you can sharpen performance with the same training Pulos used to coach Team Canada.
TAPE 403 $12.95

Recover Quickly and Stay Well
Accelerate your body's natural healing processes. How to team up with your subconscious to maintain and improve all-round health.
TAPE 404 $12.95

Sleep & Dream Enhancement
Insomnia? Sink into a whole new level of deep, comfortable sleep. Enjoy more pleasant, positive dreams. You owe it to yourself to try this drugless way to good quality sleep.
TAPE 405 $12.95

Subtle Seducer, Procrastination
Banish the wiles of procrastination. Instead of kicking yourself, get a kick out of accomplishment. Don't procrastinate! Order this one today!
TAPE 406 $12.95

Self-Talk

Positive self-talk is a secret that life's winners have always known. What you say to yourself and what you believe is what you achieve.

Let Dr. Pulos turn your self talk into a powerful, positive route to achievement. Affirmations are in a 3D Holosonic surround of Superlearning-type music. SideA: guided relaxation with active participation. Side B: positive self-talk statements you can listen to anywhere.

Improving Self-Esteem and Self-Image
Strengthen self-esteem, build a good self image to help you succeed in any endeavor and enjoy life to the fullest.
TAPE 413 $12.95

Successful Selling
Learn how to meet challenges head on with a positive attitude, prepare yourself fully for each situation and make it easy for people to say YES! The positive Self-Talk in this program is the secret shared by those at the top in sales.
TAPE 411 $12.95

Creative Thinking
Tap into the unused 90% of your creative brain power. Positive self-talk can open your mind to a wealth of new ideas.
TAPE 412 $12.95

"The Pulos system has been invaluable, to myself and to many of our key employees."
Peter H. Thomas, Chairman Century 21 Real Estate

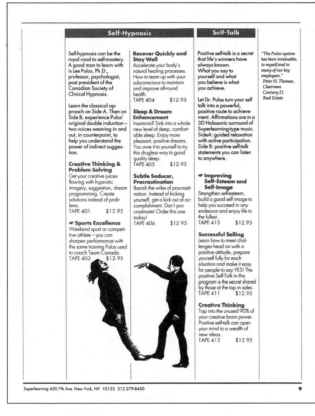

Superlearning 450 7th Ave. New York, NY 10123 212 279-8450 9

The Book that Started It All!

Music & the Art of Learning
Dissolve learning blocks and relax into the optimal state for learning (side A).

The Famous Superlearning music – music to learn faster by – music to reduce stress – beautiful music performed by world class orchestras (side B).
TAPE 101 $13.95

The Beat of Memory
How to put any material you want to learn into the rhythmic Superlearning format. A short demo of Continental menu terms so you know exactly how a lesson should sound (side A). Better than a metronome, this timer tape with four second clicks helps you pace material correctly (side B).
TAPE 102 $13.95

Superlearning
A do-it-yourself book that reads like an adventure story. Reveals the secrets of fast, stress-free learning and ultra performance. More than 800,000 copies sold.

"Superlearning...Super reading" — Gannett

"Highly readable" — Psychology Today

Hardcover 100 $14.95

The All-Music Tape
Find out how good it feels to start tapping unused capabilities with Superlearning music. Heighten learning, relaxation, visualization. Get in an ideal state for mental training for sports and creative performance.
TAPE 103 $13.95

Very Special Limited Offer – Help someone else get started!
Buy any two of the Basic Superlearning Tapes – 101, 102, 103 – and we'll send you the hardcover Superlearning Book free!
A $43.00 value for only $27.95

"Even if you're on the right track, you'll get run over if you just sit there."
Will Rogers

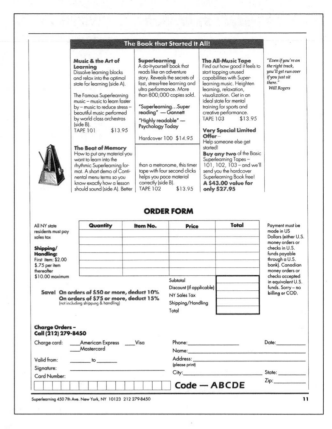

ORDER FORM

All NY state residents must pay sales tax

Shipping/Handling:
First item: $2.00
$.75 per item thereafter
$10.00 maximum

Quantity	Item No.	Price	Total

Subtotal	
Discount (if applicable)	
NY Sales Tax	
Shipping/Handling	
Total	

Payment must be made in US Dollars (either U.S. money orders or checks in U.S. funds payable through a U.S. bank). Canadian money orders or checks accepted in equivalent U.S. funds. Sorry – no billing or COD.

Save! On orders of $50 or more, deduct 10%
On orders of $75 or more, deduct 15%
(not including shipping & handling)

Charge Orders – Call (212) 279-8450

Charge card: ___American Express ___Visa ___Mastercard

Valid from: _______ to _______

Signature: ______________

Card Number: ______________

Phone: ______________ Date: __________

Name: ______________

Address: ______________
(please print)

City: ______________ State: __________

Zip: __________

Code — ABCDE

Superlearning 450 7th Ave. New York, NY 10123 212 279-8450 11

Magic (cont. from p. 2)

will and the imagination are in conflict, the imagination always wins. The task of the will, it seems, is to make a conscious decision. Then, the task of the imagination is to gather all one's forces, conscious and subconscious, physical, emotional, and mental, to bring that goal into reality.

Today, people are proving Coue's law for themselves. They are beginning to know that the pictures we hold inside ourselves, the scenarios we imagine, have a potent influence not just on the functioning of our minds and bodies, but also on the style and nature of our life experience. Imagination is funny, and we bet you'll hear much more about it in the coming decade. We've only begun to understand imagination. But it does appear that almost anyone can learn to use imagination and bring his life closer to the heart's desire. ❋

How to Sharpen Imaginary Senses

"Whatever you do, don't think about a pink elephant!"

Right away, many of us would have trouble keeping visions of pink pachyderms from prancing into mind. That's a reverse way to prove to people that they can visualize. Another, sometimes used by imagery expert Vera Fryling, M.D., is to exclaim, "Oh, someone just threw purple paint on your car!"

As more and more people use imagery rehearsal to improve performance in everything from learning and business to intimate relationships, some are feeling left out because they "can't visualize" or "can't hear a sound in my head." There are remedies.

To begin with, good imagery rehearsal involves all five senses. To improve your imaginative capacity, consider which is your dominant sense. Is your main connection to the world visual? Or audio? Or kinesthetic, through the sense of touch?

When conjuring imaginary experiences, rely first on your dominant sense, just as you do in the outside world. Then start to add the others. If you have difficulty bringing in a sense,try practicing it with the crossover method. If you're an audio type, imagine talking with someone close to you. Listen awhile, then without straining, try to let the image that goes with the voice rise in your mind. Or imagine hearing your special song. Then let the scene that made it special come to you.

If you're the kinesthetic type, imagine running your hands up and down the sides of an oak tree, feeling the rough bark. Then let the image grow between your hands. Or try it with a long, thin icicle sliding between your fingers. Or a heavy ball in one hand.

If you're a visual type, reverse the above exercises. Or conjure any of the myriad things in the world, then add sound, touch – and smell and taste too.

You do have movies in your mind, some experts assert, even if you don't think so. It's just that your images are so fleeting that you're not aware of them. "Such people are turning images into words," says imagery therapist Sally Edwards. The mind labels so quickly that the image goes unperceived. Edwards suggests taking a few minutes a day to practice turning off verbal noise. Just look around, don't name or label. Just see objects, lines, colors, movements.

Learning to sharpen all five of your senses will add power to your imaginary rehearsal. A little practice can also enrich your experience of the outside world. ❋

Super Relief the Natural Way

Head hurt? Let chiropractors Catherine Sweet and Lisa Pete help you keep a clear head. Find out what kind of headache you suffer from. Discover how various body systems are involved. Learn how you can help yourself with nutrition, herbs, reflex points, acupressure, and other easy-to-practice techniques. What to do when you feel pain coming on. How to ease a full blown headache. Best of all, how to prevent many headaches. Includes reflex point chart.
TAPE 740 $11.95

6 Superlearning 450 7th Ave. New York, NY 10123 212 279-8450

New Musical Memory Booster (cont. from p. 4)

received books in French and is featured in such magazines as "Paris Match." He's travelled through Europe, South and North America and the East seeking out new ideas, new techniques. But he's best known for bringing Sophrology into sports, an area where success – or failure, is dramatic and very visible.

Years before mental training was fashionable, Abrezol started coaching tennis players and skiers with Sophrology. Word of some remarkable achievements got around the peaks and valleys of Abrezol's tight-knit land. He was asked to coach four members of the Swiss Olympic team, not a powerhouse at the time. At the 1968 Winter Olympics at Grenoble, three of the four won medals. The sensible Swiss stuck with Sophrology and in the 1972 Sapporo Olympics, three more medals were won.

Abrezol, a mountain climber and swimmer himself, went on from there, coaching professionals and amateurs of every stripe: golfers, skeet shooters, boxers, stunt fliers, canoeists, cyclists. As for the Olympics, by 1987, his trainees had garnered 114 medals.

Still active in mental coaching, still training other medical people, still fulfilling his role as a healer to his patients, Abrezol seems to be increasingly interested in seeking out ways to bring forth the "possible human" now, the human that could be, if we started using not the 90%, but – Abrezol insists – the 99% of our capacity that lies waiting within us.

For more data:

The International Sophrology Institute
381 Park Avenue South
New York, NY 10016
718-849-9335 ❋

Better Than Twenty Winks

What's better than twenty winks? A six-second way to relax called the Quieting Reflex (QR) by its creator, Dr. Charles Stroebel, a Connecticut psychiatrist. QR is simple, deceptively so, says Stroebel who maintains it can take six months' practice before you get it down perfectly and experience the full health benefits. The benefits seem more than worth the minimum effort. Reversing the body's stress reactions as you go through the day can alleviate or ward off many common complaints – hypertension, back trouble, ulcers, migraines and tension headaches. Stroebel himself devised QR almost as a last resort to conquer his excruciating chronic headaches. Stress, of course, is a factor in many, maybe most, physical problems. Beyond that, when you're not uptight, you can perform better during the day – and enjoy the evening. Thanks to QR, Stroebel says he's "involved in lots of things that normally would have pushed me to the exhaustion point."

The six steps of QR:

1. Become aware that you are tense.
2. Say to yourself, "Alert mind, calm body."
3. Sparkle and smile inwardly to relax your face.
4. Relax your jaws and inhale, imagining the air coming up through the soles of your feet, to the count of three.
5. Imagine the air coming up your legs into your belly and stomach.
6. Exhale, letting jaws, tongue, shoulders go limp, feeling heaviness leave the body.

For more information see:
QR: The Quieting Reflex — G.P. Putnam's Sons. ❋

Super Sports

Tennis Flow by Dyveke Spino
Increase enjoyment and performance with mental training. Play centered, stress-free tennis. Imagery rehearsal to enhance concentration and improve your stroke. Part of Spino's top-rated tennis course.
TAPE 321 $12.95

Creative Running by Dyveke Spino
Pointers for stress-free running. Exercises to increase energy and avoid injury. Visualization to attune yourself to motion. For all who like to move in the outdoors.
TAPE 322 $12.95

Creative Running II by Dyveke Spino
"If you're a jogger, you will love it. Imagery experiences for transcending pain and awakening the heroic. I listen at home and afterwards go out and run as smoothly as a deer for as long as I want." – Gene Bruce. East/West Journal.
TAPE 323 $12.95

Superlearning 450 7th Ave. New York, NY 10123 212 279-8450 7

A collage-style approach

Within the basic three-column structure, this format allows the designer to nestle variable-width text blocks around art as needed. The large page size makes it possible to present several items on a single page, which reinforces the thematic organization of material and encourages browsing as well.

For this particular publication, the format solves the problem of placing a great many loose elements on the page—each of the items on the page shown includes the publishing information, the book cover, a brief one-paragraph review, text and art excerpted from the book being reviewed, and captions. The collage-style approach is a visual signature of the magazine from which this book spins off.

The underlying structure for this collage-style page is three 17-pica columns.

A pragmatic use of rules and boxes helps organize the disparate elements and separate one item from another. Boxes and silhouettes that overhang the rules create a dimensionality that lightens up the densely packed pages.

Design decisions are required for almost every text block in a grid used with this much flexibility. While most grids dictate the placement of elements on the page, this grid provides but a subtle understructure for the multitude of elements.

The type is from the Helvetica family, an ideal choice for its efficient word count and its legibility in small sizes as well as for the variety afforded within a single type family. The introduction of a second typeface to such a complex page could easily create chaos.

Design: Kathleen O'Neill

Pages from Signal, *a book created by* Whole Earth Review.
Trim size: 10-1/2 by 12-1/8

Playing with frames

This three + two-column format plays with rules to create frames within frames. The underlying grid is very symmetrical and modular, but the elements break through it and out of it in many different and sometimes subtly humorous ways. The resulting playfulness is especially useful in balancing the medical, scientific, and fundamentally difficult subject of aging.

Three 10-pica columns are used for the short items that make up this news section of a monthly magazine. Items whose headlines run across two or three columns take on more importance than those with single-column heads. The column width of the "featured" stories varies: two or three 10-pica columns, one 20-pica column, and two 14p6 columns are all used.

The narrow outer margins (4 picas from rule to rule) are used exclusively for captions. Brevity is essential in lines that rarely contain more than a single word.

The overall effect, which is very open and accessible, is achieved by sacrificing a considerable amount of text space. A distinct advantage of the format, not seen in the pages reproduced here, is that it creates a strong contrast when editorial and advertising pages face each other on the same spread.

Art almost invariably breaks out of the grid, creating a variety of depth illusions. Type, too, can appear to move through a three-dimensional page: The clipped-off bottoms of the Anti-Aging headline (left) make the type appear to be moving down through the box.

The body text is Helvetica with Futura headlines.

The paper is a heavy, noncoated, gray stock, which adds considerable bulk to a 36-page magazine. Blue and burgundy, used for banners, headlines, and tones behind the featured items, add color and reinforce the modular structure. Another similarly formatted section in the magazine uses green and purple.

Design: Regina Marsh (New York, NY)

Pages from Longevity, *published monthly by Omni International. Trim size: 8-1/4 by 10-3/4*

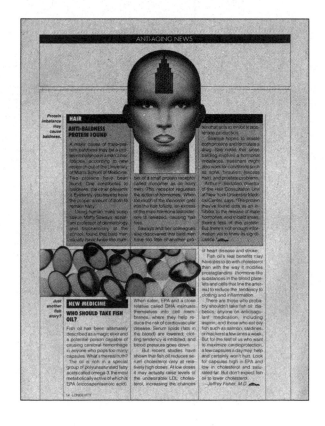

Variable column width

When you have variable-length components and want to contain each one within a single column, you can let the length of each item dictate the column width. Putting together such a page is a little like doing a jigsaw puzzle. This layout would be exceedingly expensive and time-consuming using tradtional typesetting and pasteup. But the ability to stretch or shrink a text block in PageMaker gives you extraordinary on-screen control over the width and depth of each column. You assemble this kind of page from left to right, and then make adjustments as needed.

The key to balancing all the elements on the page is to establish some horizontal constants in either text placement or illustration depth. In addition to unifying the page, these horizontal guidelines will help keep you from getting lost in a sea of choices.

A horizontal grid is used to balance the elements in variable-width columns on the the two pages shown here. The headings for all items sit on a baseline 4p6 from the top of the page. The first line of body text sits on one of three baselines, all measured from the top trim: 11p, 27p6, or 39p.

The margins are 3 picas for the sides and bottom and 4 picas for the top.

The text is 10/12.5, with headlines in Helvetica Condensed Black and body text in Helvetica Condensed. Condensed sans serif faces are a good choice for short copy in narrow columns.

The Allsport title was set in Helvetica Condensed Black in Freehand, further condensed, rotated, and then placed in the PageMaker document.

The rules are 1 point—heavier than usually found—in order to give more structure to the page.

Duis autem vel eum

ALLSPORT

Duis autem vel eum iriure dolor in esse hendrerit in vulputate velit esse molestie consequat, vel illum dolore eu feugiat nulla facilisis at vero eros et accumsan et iusto odio dignissim qui blandit praesent luptatum zzril delenit augue duis dolore te feugait nulla facilisi.
Lorem ipsum dolor sit amet, consectetuer adipiscing elit, sed diam nonummy nibh euismod tincidunt ut laoreet dolore magna aliquam erat volutpat. Ut wisi enim ad minim veniam, quis nostrud exerci tation ullamcorper suscipit lobortis nisl ut aliquip ex ea commodo consequat.
Duis autem vel eum iriure dolor in hendrerit in vulputate velit esse molestie consequat, vel illum dolore eu feugiat nulla facilisis at vero eros et accumsan et iusto odio dignissim qui blandit praesent luptatum zzril delenit augue duis dolore te feugait nulla facilisi. Nam liber tempor cum soluta nobis eleifend option congue nihil imperdiet doming id quod mazim placerat facer possim assum. Lorem ipsum dolor sit amet, consectetuer adipiscing elit, sed diam nonummy nibh euismod tincidunt ut laoreet dolore magna

Lorem ipsum dolor sit amet, consectetuer adipiscing elit, sed diam nonummy nibh euismod tincidunt ut laoreet dolore magna aliquam erat volutpat. Ut wisi enim ad minim veniam, quis nostrud exerci tation ullamcorper suscipit lobortis nisl ut aliquip ex ea commodo consequat.

Lorem ipsum

Aliquam erat esse volutpat. Ut wisi enim ad minim veniam, quis nostrud exerci tation ullamcorper suscipit lobortis nisl ut aliquip ex ea commodo consequat.
Duis autem vel eum iriure dolor in hendrerit in vulputate velit esse molestie consequat, vel illum dolore eu feugiat nulla facilisis at vero eros et accumsan et iusto odio dignissim qui

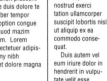

Duis autem vel eum iriure dolor in hendrerit in vulputate velit esse molestie lorem ipsum

Blandit praesent luptatum zzril delenit augue duis dolore te feugait nulla facilisi. Lorem ipsum dolor sit amet, consectetuer adipiscing elit, sed diam nonummy nibh euismod tincidunt ut laoreet dolore magna Lorem ipsum dolor sit amet, consectetuer adipiscing elit, sed diam nonummy nibh euismod tincidunt ut laoreet dolore magna aliquam erat

volutpat. Ut wisi enim ad minim veniam, quis nostrud exerci tation ullamcorper suscipit lobortis nisl ut aliquip ex ea commodo consequat.
Duis autem vel eum iriure dolor in hendrerit in vulputate velit esse molestie consequat, vel illum dolore eu feugiat nulla facilisis at vero eros et accumsan et iusto odio dignissim qui blandit praesent luptatum zzril delenit augue duis dolore te feugait nulla facilisi. Lorem ipsum dolor sit amet, con-

Ut wisi enim ades min ut wisi enim ad min

Sectetuer adipiscing elit, sed diam nonummy nibh euismod tincidunt ut laoreet dolore magna aliquam erat volutpat.
Ut wisi enim ad minim veniam, quis nostrud exerci tation ullamcorper suscipit lobortis nisl ut aliquip ex ea commodo consequat. Duis autem vel eum iriure dolor in hendrerit in.

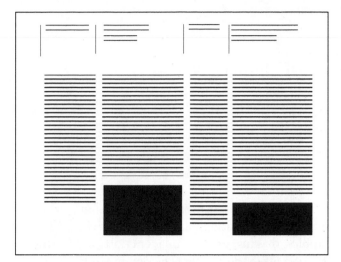

In the schematics above, the approach is to establish a horizon line for the headlines and for body text and then to hang copy from those lines in variable column widths. Art is sized to match the text width in each column, with variable heights but with a common baseline and a fixed amount of space between the bottom of the text and the top of the art.

The left-most schematic shows the same approach in a vertically oriented page. Another approach is to have even bottoms and ragged tops, with art and headlines providing another horizontal constant at the top of the page.

Duis au

Vulputate velit esse molestie consequat, vel illum dolore eu feugiat nulla facilisis at vero eros et accumsan et iusto odio dignissim qui blandit praesent luptatum zzril delenit augue duis dolore te feugait nulla facilisi. Nam liber tempor cum soluta nobis eleifend option congue nihil imperdiet doming id quod mazim placerat facer possim assum.

Lorem ipsum dolor sit amet, consectetuer adipiscing elit, sed diam nonummy nibh euismod tincidunt ut laoreet dolore magna aliquam erat volutpat. Ut wisi enim ad minim veniam, quis nostrud exerci tation ullamcorper suscipit lobortis nisl ut aliquip ex ea commodo consequat. Duis

liriure dolor in hendrerit in vulput

Autem vel eum iriure dolor in hendrerit in vulputate velit esse molestie consequat, vel illum dolore eu feugiat nulla facilisis at vero eros et accumsan et

iusto odio dignissim qui blandit praesent luptatum zzril delenit augue duis dolore te feugait nulla facilisi. Lorem ipsu dolor sit amet con- secteadipis- cing elit, se.

quis nostrud exerci tation ullamcorper suscipit lobortis nisl ut aliquip ex ea c minUt wisi enim

Diam nonummy nibh euismod tincidunt ut laoreet dolore magna. Lorem ipsum dolor sit amet, consectetuer adipiscing elit, sed diam nonummy nibh euismod tincidunt ut laoreet dolore magna aliquam erat volutpat. Ut wisi enim ad minim veniam, quis nostrud exerci tation ullamcorper suscipit lobortis nisl ut aliquip ex ea commodo consequat.

Duis autem vel eum iriure dolor in hendrerit in vulputate velit esse molestie consequat, vel illum dolore eu feugiat nulla facilisis at vero eros et accumsan et iusto odio dignissim qui blandit praesent luptatum zzril delenit augue duis dolore te feugait nulla facilisi.

Lorem ipsum dolor sit amet, consectetuer adipiscing elit, sed diam nonummy nibh euismod tincidunt ut laoreet dolore magna aliquam erat volutpat. Ut wisi enim ad minim veniam, quis nostrud exerci tation ullamcorper suscipit lobortis nisl ut aliquip ex ea commodo consequat.Duis autem vel eum iriure dolor in hendrerit in vulputate velit esse molestie consequat, vel illum dolore eu

Feuga

Feugiat nulla facilisis at vero eros et accumsan et iusto odio dignissim qui blandit praesent.

Lorem ipsum dolor sit amet

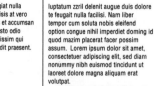

luptatum zzril delenit augue duis dolore te feugait nulla facilisi. Nam liber tempor cum soluta nobis eleifend option congue nihil imperdiet doming id quod mazim placerat facer possim assum. Lorem ipsum dolor sit amet, consectetuer adipiscing elit, sed diam nonummy nibh euismod tincidunt ut laoreet dolore magna aliquam erat volutpat.

Ut wisi enim ad minim veniam, quis nostrud exerci tation ullamcorper suscipit lobortis nisl ut aliquip ex ea commodo consequat. Duis autem vel eum iriure dolor in hendrerit in vulpu- tate velit esse molestie consequat, vel illum dolore eu feugiat nulla facilisis at vero eros et accumsan et iusto odio dignissim qui blandit praesent luptatum zzril delenit augue duis dolore te esse.

CHAPTER 4

THE CIRCULAR NATURE OF PLANNING AND DOING

In describing electronic page composition, many books and manuals depict a neatly linear process of creating master pages, placing edited text and finished graphics, making a few refinements, and then printing out final pages to send off to the printer. The demonstrations of page layout programs are even more misleading. Innocent spectators stand wide-eyed, mouths agape as a demonstrator pours text into pages that seem to compose themselves as if by magic. Everything falls into place without a loose end in sight. How could anyone resist a tool that makes page layout so utterly simple, so fantastically tidy?

The reality of producing almost any publication is considerably different. Rather than being linear, the process is a circular one involving trial and error as well as numerous revisions to make all the elements work together. This case history should give you a better picture of that reality. It shows, for example, that some of the most important design work goes on before you put pencil to paper or turn on the computer and involves simply thinking through the problem of how to get your audience's attention. It looks at the overlapping steps of developing the concept, planning the design, testing the plan with text and graphics in various stages of development, refining the design, altering the text and graphics to fit the refined plan, and then making whatever changes are necessary—in the individual elements as well as the design itself— as all the pieces come together in final form.

Solving a design problem is much like running a maze. The designer selects a line to follow only to learn that the constraints he encounters send him back to probe another direction until he finds a clear path to the solution.

—Allen Hurlburt

The final version of the brochure described in this chapter may look as effortless as the slickest computer-show demonstration, but there was nothing linear about the process of creating it. Unlike a jigsaw puzzle, in which a single fixed piece completes the task, this publication evolved into its final form, and almost everything about it changed at least a little along the way.

The process described in this case history is quite specific to the particular publication. At each stage, our approach grew out of the unique problems and goals of the project and the division of duties among the different people involved. Every project and every team will use a process that is different, sometimes a little different and sometimes dramatically different. The goal of this chapter is simply to reveal the circular and overlapping nature of the two main facets of the work— planning and doing.

**Background:
the need, the purpose,
and the concept**

The New York City Charter Revision Commission was created to study and propose revisions to the city charter. The commission knew that most New Yorkers had never heard of the charter and were not likely to be informed about the proposals that would be on a voter referendum. The purpose of the publication was to increase voter awareness about how the charter affected city government and why it was being changed. Recognizing audience apathy was the first step toward finding an appropriate way to deliver the message.

We were hired as the editorial and design team because of our background in working with interactive techniques—puzzles, games, quizzes, and so on. These activities provide an effective if somewhat subversive way to engage people in a subject they might otherwise not be inclined to read about. Each activity tends to have a different "look," and so in addition to breaking up the text, the activities also vary the texture from one page to the next.

PROJECT AT A GLANCE: THE VOTER'S GUIDEBOOK

Description	An educational brochure produced for The New York City Charter Revision Commission.
Purpose	To increase voter awareness of changes in the city charter that were to be voted on in the coming election.
Specifications	8-1/2 by 11, 16 pages, 2-color, newsprint, suitable for self-mailing. Initial print run: 200,000.
Audience	Citizens in all five boroughs.
Distribution	Bulk distribution through citizen groups, unions, schools, libraries, and civic organizations. "Copies on request" promoted through city payroll, phone bill stuffers, and public service announcements.
Design Objectives	To involve people in a generally tedious subject.
Devices to Achieve Goal	• Puzzles and games as both editorial and design elements. • A modular editorial format to create many entry points for readers. • A strong, tight format to unify disparate elements. • Bold headlines and borders. • A photo of a landmark and a unique headline style to highlight each borough, with a map motif to unify all five of them.
Typeface	Body text: Times Roman. We chose this face because it is serious, sets tightly, and reproduces well in a wide range of situations, making it a safe choice for inexpensive newsprint. Headlines: New Century Schoolbook, condensed in Adobe Illustrator. We chose condensed type because some headlines were fairly long, and we didn't want to sacrifice point size for line length.

Presentation sketch: a miniature booklet

The commission gave us a 3500-word essay on city government and the process of charter revision and a list of concepts and facts that the activities should explain. Every activity had to satisfy two criteria: It had to be fun to do, and it had to deliver information about the charter.

In designing the pages, our first step was to divide the single, continuous narrative into short, self-contained stories. Very few people read a brochure (or any publication other than a book) from cover to cover.

Each story is a potential entry point, each headline an opportunity to hook the audience.

We wanted each spread to carry a small chunk of the text and a related activity. Establishing a relationship between the text and its accompanying activity wasn't always possible, but it was useful to start with that as the organizing principle. Creating a dozen individual stories from the single long one required only a little rewriting because the text had clear and natural divisions. This is not always the case.

Doing early sketches by hand helps you to focus on the big picture, rather than on the mathematical details required in setting up an electronic page.

Although the publication was to be 8-1/2 by 11 inches, we did the presentation sketch at one-fourth that size, with each two-page spread on half of an 8-1/2- by 11-inch page. And we did it by hand rather than on the computer. Computer layouts are unforgiving of imprecision and have a way of looking more cast in stone than is the case at an early stage. Working by hand sometimes helps you to focus on the big picture rather than on the details of spacing and alignment that the computer encourages you to attend to. And working small, when you're working by hand, is simply faster and emphasizes the preliminary nature of the presentation. (Interestingly, people also seem to get a kick out of the tiny pages.)

The pencil sketch (actually, it was done with colored markers) showed the position of each story and activity. It showed the bold borders and the strong headlines surrounded by generous white space as well as the use of red as a second color. Writing and positioning the real headlines at this early stage contributed to everyone's feeling that the concept and design worked. The individual pieces were right, and the pacing was right. Although no real text or art was in place, everyone got a sense of what the publication would look and feel like to the reader. Some stories and placements changed along the way, but this early sketch reflected the tone and structure of the final publication.

A few holes were left in the sketch for activity concepts that hadn't been developed. This was, thankfully, a client with a minimalist attitude toward meetings, and we'd scheduled a brainstorming session immediately following the presentation to fill in those holes.

The manuscript for the original essay had not been created in a word processor, so we keyboarded the text at this stage. We did the first edit in Microsoft Word and printed out galleys with the text in 13-1/2-pica columns for the commission to review along with the sketch.

ANOTHER APPROACH

In the early stages of a project, you'll often want to explore more than one concept. For *The Voter's Guidebook,* we briefly entertained the idea of creating a takeoff on the *New York Post.* Given the number of New Yorkers who follow the infamous Post-style headlines, such a blatant simulation of it, while not a true parody, was sure to get attention.

Several considerations quickly ruled out the idea. The most important was that the design concept would have dictated the contents, rather than the other way around. Much of the information the Charter Revision Commission wanted to convey didn't lend itself to tabloid-style headlines. This meant that we would have had to delete material we wanted to include, write headlines that were inappropriate, or include some headlines that didn't follow through on the concept.

A takeoff on the New York Post *was briefly considered as an alternative approach.*

The *Post* takeoff would also have required writing new copy to carry out the concept and using more photos than the budget allowed. There simply wasn't time or money to execute it.

Further, no one was truly comfortable with the idea. It seemed a little brazen and somehow inappropriate for a city commission to model itself, however tongue in cheek, on a daily tabloid.

We anticipated these problems when we sketched out the idea. But when you edit yourself too much in the early stages of a project, you sacrifice both good ideas and *esprit de corps.* Part of the design process requires striking a balance between anticipating what your client (or boss or editor or communications director) wants and taking some risks. A good working relationship has a free flow of ideas that inspires everyone involved. Daring visuals and bold concepts loosen people up and are catalysts for problem solving. The *New York Post* concept, although discarded, got the project off to a creative, upbeat start. That feeling carried over to the puzzle brainstorming session that followed the design presentation and was largely maintained throughout the project.

The first dummy: copy fitting

After the galleys and presentation sketch were approved, we put each individual essay and activity in its own word-processor file. In a modular publication in which every item is self-contained rather than continuous from one page to the next, fitting the copy into the allotted spaces usually requires cutting or adding text. If the stories had been threaded together in a single document, changes to the line count in one story would have rippled through subsequent stories, requiring much moving back and forth among pages to retrieve errant lines (and risking the kinds of errors that computers should minimize).

While we were still working out some of the design elements, we did a rough electronic dummy to facilitate the copy fitting. It's generally recommended that copy fitting be done in the word-processing program, and when extensive editing is required, we agree. But one of the great advantages of electronic layout is seeing the copy in place. When you cut copy and see the lines on the pasteboard flow up neatly to fill the column, you know that the copy fits and you get a nice feeling of completeness. If the editing and design functions in your office are clearly separated, however, you may not have this choice.

The first electronic dummy substituted readily available PageMaker rules and headline type for the real ones that were to be created in Illustrator. By this time, we had dropped some art shown on the presentation sketch for these pages.

At this point, the master pages had three 13-1/2-pica columns (which later changed to 13 picas to allow for more white space). The text for each story was in place, but other details had to be simulated. The map rules above the headlines and in the box borders hadn't been worked out, so we used PageMaker's bold dashed line to simulate them. The New Century Schoolbook headlines, which were to be condensed in Adobe Illustrator, had not yet been completed, so we used Helvetica.

Simulating the unresolved design elements at this point gave us—and the client—a chance to read the copy in the context of the layout and to evaluate the layout with the copy in place.

The presentation dummy: refining the design

The brochure had been conceived as 24 pages, including a pull-out poster in the center. When the poster idea proved unworkable, we were left with 20 pages. Because publications are generally printed in signatures of 8 or 16 pages, printing 200,000 twenty-page brochures would have wasted an unconscionable amount of paper. After exploring the possibility of expanding or shrinking the brochure, everyone agreed that less was more (this is almost always the case in publication work, as it is in other endeavors), and we dropped down to 16 pages.

Changing the page count midway through a project inevitably solves some problems and creates others. Here, in a nutshell, were the effects that the reduced page count had on *The Voter's Guidebook*:

- We eliminated the weaker activities and were left with the really good, solid, fun stuff.

- We had to juggle the position of some essays and activities. Several crossover spreads had art or stories on facing pages that could not be broken up. When you eliminate one page before a spread that has to stay together, you have to find some other page to fill in. In the course of this juggling, we had to put one puzzle with a lot of specific details about the charter earlier in the brochure than we would have liked, but all decisions have their trade-offs.

- Copy that had been edited to fit in the 24-page dummy had to be edited again to fit the new page count. This kind of reworking is part of the process of publication design, and desktop publishing makes it infinitely easier and cheaper to accomplish than the traditional method, where every change requires that you send out for new type and mechanically paste up the new version.

At this stage, we created the map rules that were to frame the various components. Once we saw them in place, however, we felt they were too bold a device to use throughout, and we decided to substitute a simple double-rule border for the games. The double rule echoed the map rules but was subtler, and so kept the pages from looking too heavy and busy. The two types of borders were exactly the same depth so that they aligned horizontally across the page.

The headline type and initial caps—condensed New Century Schoolbook—were created in Illustrator and placed in PageMaker as Encapsulated PostScript files. (Each headline and each initial cap was a separate file.) These were to be in red, the second color. Again, we felt that having red headlines and initial caps for every item would be too busy, so the games had black headlines and no initial caps.

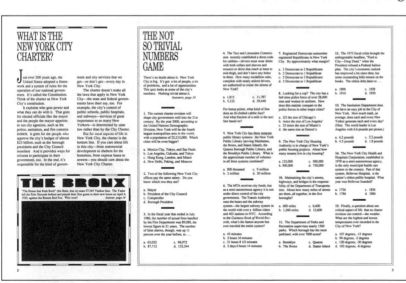

Final page proofs used black boxes to indicate the position of photos that would be stripped in by the printer. The position of the Bronx sidebar changed from the original sketch to the final. And, as a result of deadline pressures, the decorative numbers in the quiz were replaced by rules, which were easier to create.

As a result of these changes, the contrast in rules and color for the two types of material—running text and activities—provided a visual organizing cue for the reader.

Some of the games and puzzles had not yet been completed, so for the presentation dummy we filled in these holes with a pencil sketch of each activity and the working introductory copy. Because the introductions were short, we typed them directly into PageMaker.

The final pages

Desktop publishing enabled us to show the commission more complete proofs for approval earlier in the cycle than would have been possible using traditional typesetting and pasteup methods. This paid off handsomely by minimizing corrections at the final stage. Still, changes were requested, and although they were relatively easy to make on-screen, printing pages was extremely slow. (At the time we were working in PageMaker 2.0 on a Mac Plus with 1 megabyte of internal memory and a slow LaserWriter Plus printer.) Up against the deadline, we printed type patches and pasted in small corrections by hand rather than waiting for a graphics-intensive page to print. (The headlines, initial caps, and borders imported from Illustrator were all graphics; the photographs, however, were stripped in by the printer.)

A strong center axis on the cover makes the offset compass rose, with the commission's logo inside, more prominent. The map and compass rose were created in Adobe Illustrator. The logo was pasted in by hand.

Starting text on the cover, as on the page shown below left, can be an effective way to get the reader's interest. The text must be very strong for this technique to work and must be carefully designed for visual effect.

The back cover is designed as a self-mailer and uses the most universally popular of all puzzles to draw

the reader in. When solved, the crossword reveals a message in the shaded squares that reads: "Vote on charter change in 88." Someone who solves the puzzle but never opens the brochure will still get the most important message of the guidebook. Constructing the grid for the crossword was a snap with the Snap to Guides feature in MacDraw.

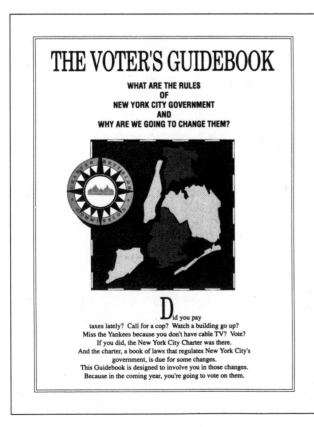

The printed pages for the spread shown throughout this chapter in various stages of its evolution: A trivia quiz reminds readers of the sheer size of city government by supplying such facts as the number of false alarms answered by the fire department and the amount of trash generated, on average, by each citizen every day.

The headlines and initial caps are 36-point New Century Schoolbook, created and condensed to 60% on the horizontal axis in Adobe Illustrator. The heads and caps for primary text print in red to help unify the short essays that run throughout the 16 pages. The activity headlines print in black.

The position of the opening line of text for the essays remains constant throughout the booklet.

The map rules over the essays and around the borough boxes were created in Illustrator from a double hairline rule with black rectangles dropped in. Alignment is critical.

Boxes around the activities use hairline rules. Note that the map rules and the open rules of the boxes align exactly.

Rules crossing the gutter between two pages required manual pasteup for alignment.

The running text for the essays is 11/13 Times Roman set in 13-pica columns. Because they have a map rule above but not around them, these text blocks have a more open look than the activities, which are enclosed in boxes. Eleven-point type was difficult to read on-screen but worked much better in the overall design than 10- or 12-point type.

The text for activities is 10/12 Times Roman. The column width is a half-pica shorter than the width used for the essay text, and the space between columns is also a half-pica shorter, to compensate for the space occupied by the rules around the activity.

Decorative rules, which print in red, separate numbered text blocks in the quiz. For these dividers we copied the rectangle used in the map rule and pasted it repetitively in the quiz.

Borough headlines were created individually in Illustrator to give each borough a different personality. Press type can also be used to create this effect.

WHAT IS THE NEW YORK CITY CHARTER?

Just over 200 years ago, the United States adopted a framework and a system of rules for the operation of our national government. It's called the Constitution. Think of the charter as New York City's constitution.

It explains who gets power and what they can do with it. That goes for elected officials like the mayor and the people the mayor appoints to run city agencies, such as the police, sanitation, and fire commissioners. It goes for the people who approve the city's budget of almost $23 billion, such as the borough presidents and the City Council members. And it provides ways for citizens to participate in their government, too. In the end, it's responsible for the kind of govern-

ment and city services that we get—or don't get—every day in New York City.

The charter doesn't make all the laws that apply in New York City—the state and federal governments have their say, too. For example, the city's control of public schools, public hospitals, and subways—services of great importance to so many New Yorkers—is determined by state law rather than by the City Charter.

But for most aspects of life in New York City, the charter is the bottom line. If you care about life in this city—from commercial development to shelters for the homeless, from express buses to sewers—you should care about the New York City Charter.

THE BRONX

"The House that Ruth Built" (the Babe, that is) seats 57,545 Yankee fans. The Yanks left the Polo Grounds behind and played their first game in their new home on April 4, 1923, against the Boston Red Sox. Who won? *Answer, page 14*

THE NOT SO TRIVIAL NUMBERS GAME

There's no doubt about it: New York City is big. It's got a lot of people, a lot of problems, and a lot of opportunities. This quiz looks at some of the city's numbers. Nothing trivial about it.
Answers, page 14

1. The current charter revision will shape city government well into the 21st century. By the year 2000, according to the United Nations Demographic Division, New York will be the fourth largest metropolitan area in the world, with a population of 22,212,000. Which cities will be even bigger?

a. Mexico City, Tokyo, and Sao Paulo
b. Los Angeles, Calcutta, and Tokyo
c. Hong Kong, London, and Miami
d. New Delhi, Peking, and Moscow

2. Two of the following New York City offices pay the same salary. Do you know which two they are?

a. Mayor
b. President of the City Council
c. Comptroller
d. Borough President

3. In the fiscal year that ended in July 1986, the number of actual fires handled by the Fire Department was 89,088, the lowest figure in 21 years. The number of false alarms, though, was up 11 percent over the year before, to . . .

a. 65,022
c. 96,972
b. 87,712
d. 132,344

4. The Taxi and Limousine Commission recently established a dress code for cabbies—drivers must wear shirts with both collars and sleeves and trousers or skirts that reach at least to mid-thigh, and don't have any holes in them. How many medallion cabs, complete with neatly attired drivers, are authorized to cruise the streets of New York?

a. 1,815
c. 11,787
b. 5,122
d. 29,440

For bonus points, what kind of fine does an ill-clothed cabbie face? And what fraction of a mile is the taxi fare based on?

5. New York City has three separate public library systems: the New York Public Library (serving Manhattan, the Bronx, and Staten Island), the Queens Borough Public Library, and the Brooklyn Public Library. What is the approximate number of volumes in all three systems combined?

a. 800 thousand
c. 9 million
b. 2 million
d. 20 million

6. The MTA receives city funds, but as a semi-autonomous agency it is not under direct control of the city government. The Transit Authority runs the buses and the subway system—the largest subway system in the world with over a billion riders and 463 stations in NYC. According to the *Guinness Book of World Records*, what's the fastest anyone has ever traveled the entire system?

a. 45 minutes
b. 2 hours 16 minutes
c. 21 hours 8 1/2 minutes
d. 2 days 6 hours 14 minutes

7. Registered Democrats outnumber registered Republicans in New York City. By approximately what margin?

a. 3 Democrats to 2 Republicans
b. 2 Democrats to 1 Republican
c. 5 Democrats to 3 Republicans
d. 5 Democrats to 1 Republican

8. Looking for a cop? The city has a full-time police force of over 28,000 men and women in uniform. How does this statistic compare to the police forces in other major cities?

a. 2/3 the size of Chicago's
b. twice the size of Los Angeles'
c. 25 times the size of Miami's
d. the same size as Detroit's

9. The New York City Housing Authority is in charge of New York's public housing projects. About how many tenants live in city housing?

a. 125,000
c. 500,000
b. 300,000
d. 750,000

10. Maintaining the city's streets, highways, and bridges is the responsibility of the Department of Transportation. About how many miles of streets are there, all together, in the five boroughs?

a. 600 miles
c. 6,400
b. 1,260 miles
d. 12,600

11. The Department of Parks and Recreation supervises nearly 1500 parks. Which borough has the most parkland, with over 7000 acres?

a. Brooklyn
c. Queens
b. The Bronx
d. Staten Island

12. The 1975 fiscal crisis brought the unforgettable headline, "Ford to City—Drop Dead," when the President refused a Federal bailout plan. The city's economic outlook has improved a lot since then, but some outstanding bills remain on the books. The oldest debt dates to . . .

a. 1898
c. 1928
b. 1910
d. 1950

13. The Sanitation Department does not have an easy job in the City of New York. How much trash, on average, does each and every New Yorker generate each and every day? (Hint: The world leader is Los Angeles with 6.6 pounds per person.)

a. 6.2 pounds
c. 2.2 pounds
b. 4.5 pounds
d. 1.8 pounds

14. The New York City Health and Hospitals Corporation, established in 1970 as a semi-autonomous agency, is the only municipal health care system in the country. Part of that system, Bellevue Hospital, is the nation's oldest public hospital. What year was Bellevue founded?

a. 1736
c. 1836
b. 1786
d. 1886

15. Finally, a question about one critical aspect of life that no charter revision can control—the weather. What are the highest and lowest temperatures ever recorded in the City of New York?

a. 107 degrees, -15 degrees
b. 99 degrees, -2 degrees
c. 120 degrees, -30 degrees
d. 102 degrees, -6 degrees

Thumbnails: A useful tool

PageMaker has an extremely useful feature that enables you to print miniature pages. In the Print dialog box, simply specify the pages you want printed, click on the Thumbnails option, and indicate how many thumbnails you want printed on each sheet. The size of the thumbnails depends on the trim size of the publication, the number specified, and the size of the paper in your printer. You can print thumbnails only on PostScript printers. On a Macintosh you can print up to 64 thumbnails on a single sheet; on a PC, 16.

The thumbnails on the facing page show the complete *Voter's Guidebook*. Page 16, which actually printed on a second sheet, has been pasted into position facing page 1 so that we can show it here on a single page. Black rectangles indicate frames where halftones were to be stripped in by the printer. The document filename prints in the upper left corner. Adding the date by hand to the printed page provides an invaluable frame of reference.

The ability to view a publication at a glance in this way has many benefits. It gives you a sense of the texture and continuity of the pages and often helps you spot opportunities and problems, both in editorial continuity and format consistency. Thumbnails also serve as a useful tracking and organizational tool. You can note information or material that is still to come (traditional publishing shorthand for that is simply "tk") as well as critical alignments and other details that should be checked on a Linotronic printout or blueline proof.

The thumbnails for this brochure demonstrate the flexibility of the three-column grid for a modular format. You can see how individual elements fill anywhere from one to five columns. But the format does require considerable planning and fine-tuning to make the elements fit within their allotted spaces.

Facing page: The entire 16-page brochure is seen at a glance by using the Thumbnails option in PageMaker's Print dialog box.

If you're wondering how one turns the subject of city government into entertaining activities, here's a description of some of the concepts we included in the booklet:

- Newspaper-style headlines (pages 6-7) asked people to determine whether certain events or situations were possible under the current charter. ("Mayor Names Darryl Strawberry as NYC Comptroller" is impossible, not because of Strawberry's lack of qualifications, but because the comptroller is elected rather than appointed.) Each headline was set in a different typeface and rotated in Illustrator, placed in PageMaker as an Encapsulated PostScript file, and positioned to create a collage effect.

- Photos from around the city involved readers in the city's organization chart (pages 8-9) as they looked for the office responsible for the object or activity shown in each picture (a trash can, a manhole cover, a park lake, and so on).

- A simple board game (page 12) put players at the mayor's desk, divvying up the city's $23 billion budget among the various city agencies on the playing field.

Voter's Guidebook   3/10/88

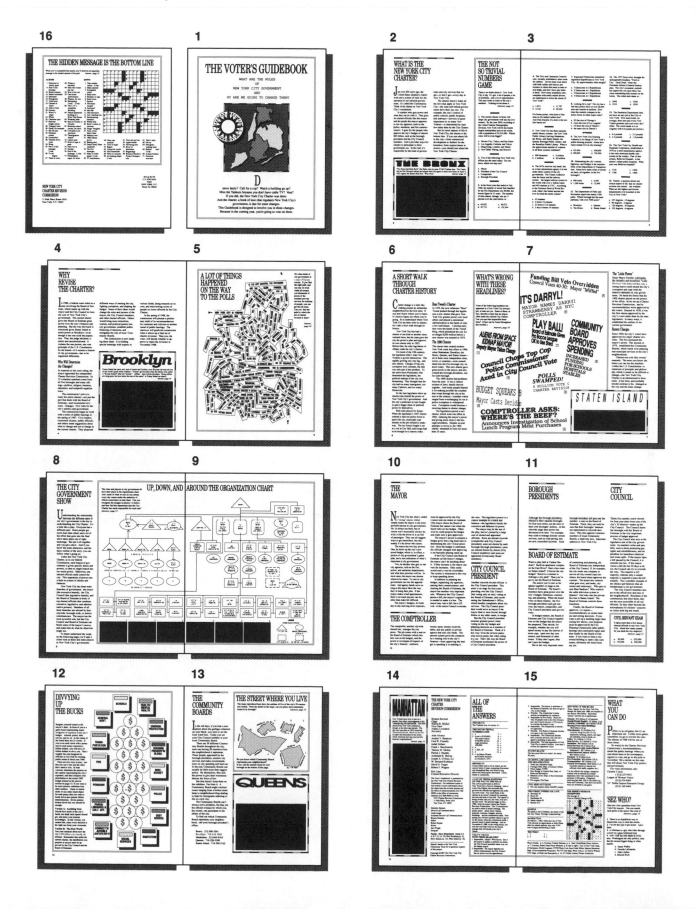

A PAGEMAKER PORTFOLIO

INTRODUCTION TO THE PORTFOLIO

If we are to communicate quickly and clearly (as we must, if we are to retain our audience), then we must accept the fact that WHAT we say is integral with HOW we say it. Visual form and verbal content are inseparable.... Graphic design is not something added to make the pages look lively. It is not an end in itself. It is the means to an end—that of clear, vivid, stirring communication of editorial content.

—Jan White,
Designing for Magazines

You will find in this portfolio a broad selection of publications, from businesses both large and small, with designs that range from simple to complex. The samples were chosen with an eye to variety—different types of messages from many kinds of businesses including those concerned with health, education, manufacturing, sales, service, entertainment, politics, fashion, real estate, law, and art. Some were designed by freelance designers, others by corporate art departments, and still others by top design studios. The level of graphic sophistication varies considerably. A modest layout is often presented side by side with an ambitious one because each represents an appropriate solution to a specific communication need.

This question of appropriateness comes up again and again. Communication is more an art than a science, and the decisions a designer makes are often subjective ones. It is not so much a matter of whether a design is right or wrong, but whether it works for the need at hand.

All of the designers used PageMaker for some part of the design and production process. It can't be said often enough that the technology is only a tool—a remarkable tool to be sure, but still only a tool. If you want to take advantage of the full range of illustration styles, of the best photographic reproduction, of typefaces currently unavailable on the desktop, you will undoubtably combine traditional and desktop approaches, as many of the designers represented here have done.

Behind many of the documents are stories of how organizations and individuals have integrated desktop publishing into their work. Geiger International, for example, is a furniture design firm in Atlanta. In 1985 they were planning a major revision of their product guide and price list. Previously, price lists had been typeset outside and laboriously pasted up by the two-person art and design department. Without really knowing anything about desktop publishing (they hadn't even heard the term), they did know that if they could do the price lists themselves, in-house, they'd have a database that could be updated as needed. Manfred Petri, their new vice president of design, had seen the LaserWriter at an office equipment show in Germany, and he was

Three people [should] be trained to educate and support the others in a work group: a computer-oriented person (to handle hardware and software problems); a designer or graphic artist (to support others in the use of templates and style sheets, among other tools); and a production person (to help manage the document flow). That way, the computer wizard learns about publishing, the publishing people learn about computers, and the rest of the staff has more than one person to go to in times of need.
—Barbara Hawkins,
quoted in Publish!

convinced that it really could produce what was called "near typeset quality." A little research brought PageMaker to their attention, and it looked like it could do the job. Pamela Bryant, an executive assistant in sales, was recruited to translate Petri's paper-and-pencil guidelines into electronic form. She had no graphic design experience and no computer experience beyond word processing on a PC. What she did have was an interest in learning how to use this mouse-driven Macintosh, which she carted home on weekends. The typesetting for the price list redesign would have been $30,000, so the savings on type alone more than covered the purchase of their original Mac Plus and LaserWriter. Three years later, there are still two people in the design department (Bryant being one of them) doing more publication work than they'd previously done plus many thousands of dollars worth of typesetting. In addition, Petri does some of the preliminary work for furniture design and showrooms using MacDraft. (A page from a current Geiger price guide is on the opening spread of Chapter 7.)

Depending on your point of view, it is either easier or more difficult to move into desktop publishing today than it was in 1985. Easier because the tools are more advanced, and there's plenty of evidence that in trained hands those tools can produce high-quality work. But the choices are more various— and hence more complex—and the expectations are so much higher.

Even so, organizations with a definable need and a sensible approach to phasing in the technology tend to realize the benefits they had anticipated. Kathy Tomyris, of the Mill Valley, California gardening emporium Smith & Hawken, writes of 50 percent savings in signage costs and of the ease of producing a wide variety of product information sheets consistent with the high standards of the store's merchandise and the smart image of their mail-order catalog. (The catalog is still produced using traditional typesetting; samples of their product information sheets are in Chapter 7.) Ann Wassmann Gross, a graphic designer at The Art Institute of Chicago, notes that they began using desktop production for gallery labels alone, and within two years were producing half of the museum's printed materials on their Mac, using an outside typesetter's Linotronic 300 for final pages. (A folder and a brochure from the Art Institute are in Chapter 5.)

Jim Parker, the executive director of the Do It Now Foundation in Phoenix, believes desktop publishing literally saved his organization. "We're a not-for-profit educational publisher," Parker writes, "specializing in handout materials on drug and alcohol abuse. We support all our operations from the sales of publications, and dwindling resources and soaring costs in 1984 made our long-term survival seem dubious at best. Desktop publishing (which was little more than smoke and a rumor) was the only thing we could grab at that would float. Things got so bad that we laid off the last of our staff artists and layout people, stripping the foundation to a skeletal staff of four. Then came the Mac, then came PageMaker. Then came our resurgence. Design awards followed. Publication sales have been booming. Now we're in the process of designing and building a new national headquarters. If I sound proud, I guess I am. I'm also grateful that I got the opportunity to develop my publication ideas myself, without the need for costly intermediaries. If I sound like a devotee, I guess I'm that, too. You'd probably sound just the same if you'd come as close as I did to presiding over the demise of a valuable organization because of a simple lack of cost-effective tools to develop, design, and keep current a publication roster of some 120 titles."

Freelance designers and small design studios with a wide variety of clients have a somewhat different experience with desktop publishing than organizations using it for their own publishing and communications needs. One issue for many designers is whether or not they want to become typesetters and, to the degree that they do, how to bill that service back to the client. It's not so much a question of quality anymore but of efficiency.

Tom Suzuki, a former design director of Time-Life Books who has a design studio in Alexandria, Virginia, knows that in comparison to commercial typesetting systems, with their sophisticated hyphenation dictionaries and their algorithms for controlling line length, typesetting on the Mac is extremely labor-intensive. "If you are fussy about typesetting," and Suzuki acknowledges that he is when he says this, "you can spend a large proportion of your time doing typesetting rather than design or layout or production." Keyboarding itself is not the problem; many of his clients provide manuscript on disk, and he has also had considerable success with text scanning. But the need to clean up typewriter conventions (double hyphens for dashes, two spaces after punctuation, and so on) and adjust the rag manually on flush left text is time-consuming, not to mention kerning headlines and making other refinements.

This technology is a force that is going to move everybody up to where we will begin to expect and receive a higher level of sophistication in all areas of our printed communication.

—Roger Black, from an interview in Font & Function

Suzuki's reservations don't undermine his fundamental enthusiasm and belief that the computer will continue to play an important part in his business. Translating tissue layouts to electronic formats, copyfitting early in the production cycle, scanning images for position in order to wrap text around them, doing headlines and logos—these are all areas where he, like many designers, can quantify the hours saved. For one of the monthly publications he designs, the client is on-site during production, able to make copyfitting changes on-screen without even requiring a printout. But fourteen months after bringing the computer into his studio, Suzuki feels his business is still in transition. "It seems to me you have to do one of two things. You either look at the machine and what it's best capable of producing and then go after that work. Or you continue to do the things that you want and like to do, and adapt the machine to that process. And that's where I am. I'm using the computer literally as a very expensive tool, and adapting it where I think it makes sense and experimenting a little." (You'll find a sample of Suzuki's work in Chapter 3.)

There is...an instant...when an idea comes alive! If you freeze it...too soon, it's still unformed and incomplete. Premature. But if you play around too much, you'll wind up with something over-worked.... You lose touch with the vitality of the original impulse, or cover it up so that no one else but you sees it. You have to catch the moment on the wing, so to speak.

—Michael Green,
Zen & the Art of Macintosh

Many of the designers we spoke with acknowledge with good humor their role as pioneers in exploiting the tools of electronic publishing. It's interesting, for example, to compare John McWade's recollections of the commercial work he did with prerelease versions of PageMaker in 1984 with the technological challenges he faced using PageMaker 3.0 in 1988. Of his work prior to the release of version 1.0, when he used a beta version of PageMaker on a 512 Mac with a 400 KB external drive, McWade recalls the difficulty of such a basic procedure as correcting a typo. There were no text-editing functions in PageMaker at that time, and in order to make a correction, he had to go back to his MacWrite file, edit the text there, and then place the entire file over again. If you inadvertently drew a rule off the page, it caused the program to crash. "A great light show," he recalls, "slow but fun." By the middle of 1988, producing a six-color poster on his Mac II, McWade generated positive and negative film from an L300 and puzzled through the problem of color registration with the help of his commercial printer while the page was still on-screen. (The poster is reproduced toward the beginning of Chapter 5.)

To some degree, everyone working with desktop publishing today is a pioneer, puzzling through traditional design considerations one minute and technological challenges the next. This situation will undoubtedly persist as the technology continues to improve, making increasingly sophisticated workstations and programs accessible to more and more people. The end product, the printed page, reflects this increasing sophistication.

In the year that we've been collecting these samples, the level of desktop-published pages has improved dramatically. That's partly a function of the technology, partly a result of the increasing experience of users, and partly a result of the relatively recent attraction of professional designers to electronic tools. It's important, however, not to pass over a simple and modest approach if it is appropriate to your needs and especially if it matches the level of your skill, either as a designer or as a technological pioneer. It's far better to produce a well-executed modest design than to make a mess of a more ambitious one.

In the following pages, the commentary accompanying the sample documents focuses primarily on design elements. But you will also find notes on various software programs and production methods used in some of the publications as well as notes about color, paper stock, and other production values not readily apparent. Each sample is reproduced as large as possible while still allowing room for annotations about the work. Inevitably, both impact and detail are lost in reduction. Of course, color is lost as well. We hope that with a combination of the reproduction, the notes, and your imagination, this section will succeed in representing the graphic style of the wide range of business documents that are being created with PageMaker today.

CHAPTER 5

PROMOTIONS: FLYERS, POSTERS, FOLDERS, AND BROCHURES

Promotional literature is the most image-conscious of all publications. Here, more than anywhere else, the medium really is the message. That doesn't mean that the words don't count, but it does mean that the art, the graphic design, the texture of the paper, the color of the ink, and the overall production values make a first impression that it's difficult for the text to overcome if that impression is off the mark.

Of course, the image and production values that are appropriate vary tremendously. At one end of the spectrum, the category includes simple flyers that grass-roots organizations and small businesses leave under car windshield wipers; at the other end are slick four-color brochures distributed by large corporations to prospective clients. Both extremes, and everything in between, share the need to consider carefully the image they want to convey in order to produce the desired effect.

Promotional literature also presents a conceptual challenge that is rarely found in other kinds of business publications. If you can discover some unique perspective on your event, service, or product, you can turn that into an original and effective promotional idea. This is where catchy slogans, visual metaphors, and all the other tricks of Madison Avenue are used to good advantage. To be sure, if you're promoting a financial service or a funeral home, the style will be decidedly different than for a local eatery or theater group. But regardless of how frivolous or somber the concern, a fresh perspective on it will gain attention and set it apart from the competition.

FLYERS & POSTERS

You can look at flyers as modest posters, and posters as flyers on a grand scale. Though their budgets may differ dramatically, flyers and posters share the challenges inherent in any single-page promotion. To be effective, they have to deliver the strong graphic impression of a well-designed cover and the clear, concise information of a data sheet. Without the graphic appeal, the promotion will get lost amid all the other messages competing for the prospect's time and money; without the clear information, the flyer or poster becomes a piece of art, interesting to look at, perhaps, but probably not very effective.

Flyers and posters in this section

- *California Association of Midwives*—a photographic mandala for a fashion show fund-raiser
- *Student Recital*—the easy appeal of borders
- *Holiday Sale*—well-organized information
- *WGBH Brown Bag Lunches*—a simple format that works
- *A Walk in the Woods*—an illustrated theater announcement
- *AIGA poster*—the drama of life-size bit-mapped art
- *How to Design a Page*—and in doing so take advantage of all the technology

---

For hands-on instructions for creating a flyer with a coupon, see Project 5 in Section 3.

A scanned photo, copied and manipulated to create a mandala-like image, is a dynamic graphic technique for flyers and posters that is relatively easy to create. The digitized image was rotated and flopped in MacPaint to create four versions oriented in different directions. Each version was saved as a separate file and imported into PageMaker, where they were composed into a single image.

The four corners created by the negative space of the art inside the 8-point-rule box provide an effective way to organize the type. The vertical rules add additional structure that keeps the type from floating in space.

The type and art print black against a shocking pink background, enhancing the playful feeling that sets the tone for the fashion show benefit.

The typeface is Garamond with a Futura Extra Bold headline.

Design: John Odam (San Diego, CA)
Flyer for a benefit auction for the California Association of Midwives. Trim size: 8-1/2 by 11

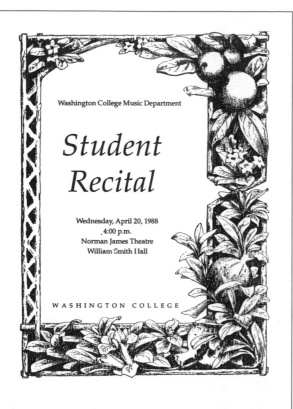

Borders from electronic or traditional clip art provide a quick, easy, and effective way to dress up a simple message. The one here is from *Victorian Pictorial Borders*, a book of public domain art published by Dover Press. The designer simply photocopied the art to the desired size, ran out type on a laser printer, pasted the two together on an 8-1/2-by 11-inch page, and photocopied the result.

The large Palatino headline is easy to read. It combines modern and classical elegance in a style that works well with the floral border and is appropriate for the event.

When considering borders from the ever-expanding clip art universe, keep in mind that you can use and modify segments of them to bracket and separate text.

With desktop publishing, a design studio can take a rough layout provided by a small organization (shown at right) and produce a quick and inexpensive printed page (shown above).

The information is organized with an eye toward line-for-line scanning, and uses horizontal rules to reinforce that approach.

The type is Palatino throughout. Text set in all caps is generally difficult to read, but the choice works here for such a straightforward announcement of what, where, who, and when.

The illustration was drawn by hand and pasted manually onto the electronically-composed page.

Design (above left): Diane Landskroener (Chestertown, MD)

Flyer for a recital at Washington College. Trim size: 8-1/2 by 11

Design (above right): Barbara Trupp; art production: Lisa Marks-Ellis, Synthesis Concepts (Chicago, IL)

Flyer for crafts sale. Trim size: 8-1/2 by 11

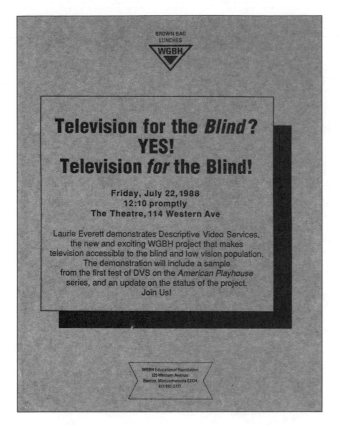

This simple format (above left), printed on brown kraft paper, announces events in a series of "brown bag lunch" lectures and demonstrations. The format establishes a strong identity for the series and is easy to execute for each event.

The shadowed box is a very simple attention-getting graphic. It is left in place on the template for the flyer so that only the type needs to be added for each new event.

The information above and below the boxed copy identifies the series and sponsor and is also a standing item in the template. It prints in red, so it looks stamped on.

The type is all from the Helvetica family.

Design (above left): Andrew Faulkner (Boston, MA)

Flyer for the WGBH brown bag lunches. Trim size: 8-1/2 by 11

A theater announcement (above right) features art based on the title of the play. The art originated as a charcoal drawing on very grainy paper. It was scanned at 72 dots per inch and resized proportionally in PageMaker, creating an image that has the feeling of a lithograph. Framing and centering the art in the formal layout increase its importance on the page.

The hairline border frames the page on three sides only. The dotted border around the coupon (from PageMaker's Lines menu) visually closes the bottom of the page and is an effective way to call attention to the coupon.

The typeface is Palatino, with contrast achieved through size, spacing, and placement. Note that in the two lines at the top of the page, the first line has open spacing and the second line tight spacing so that both are the same width as the art below. Note also the proportions in the treatment of the rule between the title and the author.

Design (above right): John Odam and Doris Bittar (San Diego, CA)

Flyer for a benefit performance for The San Diego Chapter of Freeze/SANE. Trim size: 8-1/2 by 11

This poster for a lecture by two pioneers of electronic art speaks in the language of their subject: the new technology and its impact on graphic design.

A digitized image of the two lecturers is printed almost life-size. The reduction on this page does not do justice to the impact of the 17- by 22-inch poster. This bold enlargement of a digitized image gives the feeling of a glimpse into the future. At a time when we are seeing more and more bit-mapped art (much of it bad), the raw power of the form is particularly evident in this large size.

The art originated as a slide. It was digitized in MacVision, saved as a MacPaint document, and scaled in PageMaker. The oversize page was tiled and pasted together manually.

The text is handled in three panels that jut into the picture plane. A second color (orange) highlights the first name of each speaker and the date and sponsor of the event.

Folded twice, the poster also serves as a self-mailer.

Quoting from the poster: "New electronic formats, including the personal computer, CD's, and video imaging systems, have opened up vast new visual possibilities and have inexorably drawn our profession into a communications environment which is multi-media and interactive. The formerly separate disciplines of writing, visualization, and sound making are joined through these tools. ¶Eric predicts a return to the designer as generalist—fluent in more than one discipline—and feels we need to readjust our notion of what constitutes adequate training for this broader role."

Design: Chris Pullman, WGBH Design (Boston, MA)

Poster for AIGA/Boston lecture by April Greiman and Eric Martin.
Trim size: 17 by 22

Design: John McWade, PageLab
(Sacramento, CA)

Poster produced for Apple Computer as
a takeaway promotion at Apple Business
Forums.
Trim size: 11 by 17

The subject is again technology and design. But while the poster on the opposite page uses dramatic art to get the attention of artists, here an organized, business-like format presents a brief lesson on design for business people being introduced to desktop publishing.

The design successfully incorporates the elements it describes—bold, authoritative headlines, subheads for easy reference, the use of an underlying grid, mug shots cropped and scaled to the same size—both in the poster itself and in the sample page centered under the headline.

Another contrast: Although the poster on the opposite page used a limited number of electronic tools to good effect, this one uses a great many of them. Photographs of live models were taken with an Ikegami CCD (charge-coupled device) camera, transferred via Apple File Exchange to the Macintosh environment, and retouched using Image-Studio. Other software used included, in addition to PageMaker, Microsoft Word, Illustrator 88, and MacPaint. The designer bypassed the traditional mechanical and prepress work by supplying the printer with negative and positive film output from a Linotronic 300 at 1270 dots per inch. (At its maximum resolution of 2540 dots per inch, the L300 currently cannot print a tabloid-size page.)

FOLDERS

Folders provide a convenient format for promoting products, services, and events. The folded piece can be racked or mailed (either in a standard business envelope or as a self-mailer), and the fully open piece can be used as a poster. The folder format also works well for a series—educational literature and programs, for example; once you have a format worked out, you can make a template and reuse it for each piece in the series.

The mechanics of a folded piece present unique conceptual and design opportunities. Try to use the panels to organize and build on a message, to visually lead readers from the cover through the inside flaps to the fully open piece. A folder, especially a large one, requires more effort on the reader's part than a booklet or brochure, so you need to motivate the reader to begin unfolding the piece to get to the message.

The most common sizes for folders are 8-1/2 by 11 (generally folded in half to create four panels or folded twice to create six panels), 8-1/2 by 14 (generally folded into eight panels), and 11 by 17 (generally folded in half twice, or in half and then twice again). When planning the concept and layout, work at full size (you can tape together two or more sheets of paper if necessary) so that you can actually fold the piece and see it as the reader will. Once you have a pencil sketch in this form, you'll need to figure out the most efficient way to assemble the elements in PageMaker. For example, if you are doing an 8-1/2-by-14 folder, you might set it up as four 8-1/2- by 7-inch pages. Keep in mind, also, that flaps that fold in should be a half pica or so narrower than the other panels.

Because the mechanics of certain folds require that some panels be rotated 90 degrees or oriented upside down, and because many folders use larger paper sizes, these publications often require some manual pasteup. (Small amounts of type, such as a return address or postal indicia, can be set and rotated in a drawing program and imported into PageMaker.) You will need, also, to indicate fold marks for the printer; use dotted lines outside the image area on the camera-ready art.

Folders in this section

- *World Trade Institute*—a large-format program announcement
- *Slide Zone*—an accordion fold with a streamlined message
- *Drugs & Alcohol*—a strong, consistent format for a series of educational folders
- *Transpac*—a star unfolds
- *Colligan's Stockton Inn*—warm, friendly, and as suitable for mailing as it is for posting
- *InFractions*—the spotlight on fashion
- *The Man Who Planted Trees*—a program for an in-store event
- *Family Programs*—a poster format for three months of museum events
- *Historic Hudson Valley*—tourist attractions in an 11-by-17 format

World Trade Institute 1988-89 Program

Developing New Markets Through Exporting

This is the first is a series of educational programs organized by the World Trade Institute designed to develop and sharpen the export skills of managers of Atlantic Canadian companies.

The program takes a *highly interactive approach* to the delivery of practical information so that course attendees can put their new skills to work immediately. The program also allows for exporters and those seriously considering export trade to meet and discuss issues of mutual interest.

Each session of the program incorporates case materials from Atlantic Canadian companies whenever possible. Classes will focus on group discussion and group work. Participants will learn directly from guest resource people in various industries, and will make use of computer-assisted instruction, videos, simulations and role playing. This innovative program promises to provide participants with a stimulating and effective method of gaining sound knowledge of the requirements for successful export trade.

Opening Reception
September 11, 1988

1. What you need to know to be a successful exporter
September 12 & 13, 1988
Faculty: Dr. Mary Brooks, Dr. T.S. Chan

This first session of the program will teach you *how to carry out an effective information search.* You will learn what information sources are most useful, their cost, how to access them, and how to decide on your best markets.

2. Creating an Export Strategy
October 17 & 18, 1988
Faculty: Dr. Norman McGuinness,
Dr. Donald J. Patton

Strategic thinking allows you to plan for – and create – export opportunities. This session investigates *exporting as a prime business philosophy* as opposed to an afterthought of domestic operations. Subjects include using exports as a way to grow and spread risk; the issue of long term commitment; and how to develop a practical export game plan.

5. Promoting Your Export Product
February 13, 1989
Faculty: Dr. Donald J. Patton,
Dr. Philip Rosson

In Promoting your Export Product you will learn how effective sales and marketing communications programs are created, what services and materials are required, and how much they will cost. This session will also teach you how to prepare for differing trade customs that affect language, currency, packaging and advertising. *Special emphasis will be placed on using trade fairs and sources of promotional assistance.*

Awards Dinner
February 13, 1989 at the World Trade Club

For further information see the back of this poster, or contact the World Trade Institute for a brochure and registration form.

4. Making the Export Deal
January 9 & 10, 1989
Faculty: Dr. Mary Brooks,
Dr. Norman McGuinness

Making the Export Deal will teach you what you need to know in order to make the export quote. This session defines the fundamentals of exporting: *Pricing, Documentation, Transportation and Foreign Exchange.* Topics to be explored include negotiating tactics, coping with cultural differences when securing an export contract, transportation alternatives, and the effect of efficient distribution on long-term price competitiveness.

3. Decisions, Decisions! Entering and Expanding Export Markets
November 21 & 22, 1988
Faculty: Dr. T.S. Chan, Dr. Philip Rosson

This session looks at the pros and cons of using agents, distributors, and selling direct. The first day highlights *the importance of choosing the right distribution system –and then making it work.* Day two focuses on living with your decisions: establishing, managing and ending the relationship.

World Trade
INSTITUTE

PO Box 955
1800 Argyle Street
Halifax, Nova Scotia
B3J 2V9
Telephone: (902) 428-7233
Fax: (902) 422-2922

The World Trade Institute is a partnership of the World Trade Centre Halifax, Nova Scotia; the Centre for International Business Studies at Dalhousie University; and the Nova Scotia Department of Industry, Trade andTechnology.

Please Post

Design: Paul Hazell,
Communication Design Group Limited
(Halifax, Nova Scotia)

Folder for the World Trade Institute training programs.
Trim Size: 11 by 17, folded in half and then folded twice accordion style

The primary function of the cover of a folder is to get you to unfold it. And art that continues from one panel to another uses the physical properties of the format to achieve that purpose. In this sample, art bleeding off both sides leads the reader to the next panel (not shown) where the loops of the arms are completed. The fully open folder repeats the art.

The art was created in FreeHand and takes advantage of its graduated tones feature, producing an airbrush-like effect.

The logo incorporates a subtly playful effect by transposing the sans serif d in "World" with the serif d in "Trade." Note also the spacing of the word "Institute" to match the length of the words above it.

The type is organized so that each panel contains a different text unit. This works particularly well for a program or series in which each event can be featured, as they are here. Numbering each event reinforces the organization.

The "Please Post" tab in the lower right is also visible in the half-folded position because of the cropped upper-right corner.

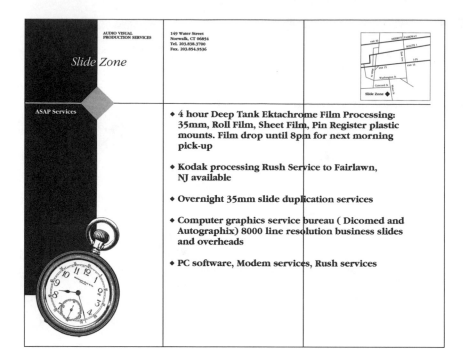

The strong cover of this accordion-fold promotion opens to a single page handsome enough to tack up on the wall for reference.

The butting black-and-white panels, with the word "Slide" reversing out of the black, is the company logo. The negative-positive imagery is delightfully appropriate to the service—film and audio production. The diamond is repeated in the bulleted list and in the map, where it indicates the location of the business.

The clock dramatizes the focus of the folder, entitled ASAP Services. Bulleted copy specifies details for the rush services available.

The typeface is Garamond.

Design (above):
Weisz Yang Dunkelberger Inc.
(Westport, CT)

Folder from Slide Zone.
Trim size: 8-1/2 by 11, folded twice, accordion style

Rules, banners, geometric shapes, and initial caps provide organization and visual continuity for this series of educational pamphlets.

The display type is Avant Garde; the body text is Helvetica. The type prints in purple, and the rules and shapes print in rose. The colors vary from pamphlet to pamphlet.

Design (below): Jim Parker (Phoenix, AZ)
Drugs & Alcohol folder published by the Do It Now Foundation.
Trim size: 14 by 8-1/2, folded in half twice to create four panels

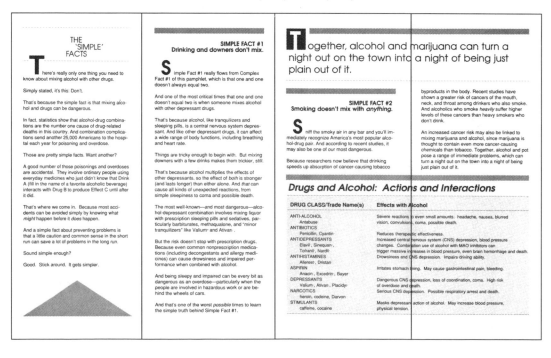

This folder draws on the emotional connotations of the repeating image of the star; the red, white, and blue color scheme; and the corporate headquarters in the center of it all to solicit employee participation in the company's political action committee. The cover (not shown) sets the theme with an American flag in the same mixed-media art style as the panels shown.

The panels are integrated through the unfolding image of the star. When the panel seen on the far right, below, opens, the panel underneath it again completes the star. This is an effective use of the folder format to set a tone in the early panels before delivering specific information.

In the electronic pasteup, each panel was created as a separate 6-1/4- by 9-1/4-inch page and printed with crop marks.

The display text is 30/60 New Century Schoolbook with 72-point initial caps and letterspacing tightened to –8%. The left panel prints in blue, the right one in red.The two unseen panels on the fully open sheet contain running text set 10/12 in a two-column format.

Don't hesitate to combine traditional art with electronic pasteup. The precise, controlled effect of electronic drawing programs, the useful variety of clip art, and the digitized look of art generated in paint programs all provide a wide range of possiblities. But there's a whole world of nonelectronic illustration styles. The art used here has the spontaneous feeling of a colored pencil sketch, an effect we have yet to see produced on a computer.

Design: Partners by Design (N. Hollywood, CA); agency: Jonisch Communications (Los Angeles, CA)

Folder from the Transamerica Corporation Political Action Committee. Trim size: 24-15/16 by 9-1/4, folded three times

W*hen*

people join together,

their power

is fortified,

their message

is clearer,

and their

voices louder.

W*hen*

people join together,

their power

is fortified,

their message

is clearer,

and their

voices louder.

"T*RANSPAC*

is your

opportunity

to join with

other employees

to participate in

our political

process."

Designed for multiple use, this folder can be tacked up on bulletin boards fully open, while the folded piece functions as a self-mailer.

A warm, friendly, cheerful image is conveyed through the art style, typography, and newspaper-like composition. The flavor is just what you'd want from a country inn during the holiday season.

The typeface is New Century Schoolbook. It prints in green on a gray textured paper.

Borders and rules help organize the small items, which are set to different measures.

The art was created by hand and pasted onto camera-ready pages.

Each panel of this accordion-fold design (facing page, bottom) features a different clothes style. The panels were assembed on screen, two to a page, and two pages were pasted together for each four-panel side of the camera-ready art.

Silhouette photos work well for fashion because they highlight the shape of the clothes. The contrast between dark and light, front and back, and large and small adds to the casual liveliness of the composition. Although the larger photos share a common ground, the smaller ones bounce playfully around the page without regard for perspective. The interaction of the image with the background in a context that defies logic brings a fresh spatial energy to the page. Three additional styles, similarly formatted, are printed on the reverse side of the sheet.

The pattern through the center was created in PageMaker and echoes the subtler patten behind the logo. It's a decorative motif especially well suited for fashion literature.

The typeface is Goudy Old Style. Labeling is minimized to keep the spotlight on the clothes. The type and pattern print in teal blue with black accents.

Design (left):
Carla Bond Coutts
(Lahaska, PA)
Folder for
Colligan's
Stockton Inn.
Size: 8-1/2 by 14,
folded in half
twice

Design (facing page, bottom):
Edward Hughes
(Evanston, IL)
Folder from
InFractions, Inc.
Trim size:
17-3/6 by 10-1/8,
folded three times
accordion style

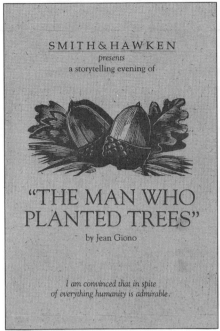

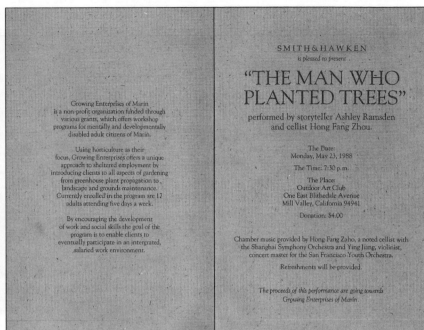

The traditional formality of centered type (above) is balanced by warm brown ink on oatmeal flecked paper.

The woodcut, a piece of art from the book featured at the event, was pasted in by hand.

The type is Goudy Old Style (except for the company logo, which is Palatino). The combination of bold, regular, and italic styles, the varied spacing, and the contrasting silhouettes of the different text blocks keep the centered alignment from becoming stiff or monotonous.

Design: Kathy Tomyris (Mill Valley, CA)
Program/announcement for an in-store performance.
Trim size: 11 by 8-1/2, folded once

A quarterly program of events is designed as a poster, with different styles of art interspersed throughout the listings. Folded, the piece is suitable for self-mailing and is also easily racked in the museum lobby and bookstore.

The headline and names of months are Franklin Gothic Demi. The listings are in the Helvetica family.

The use of color and the space around each listing make it very easy to check out the programs on any given date. The main headline, banners at the top of each column, highlighted events, and dates print in red.

All elements—art, borders, and Macintosh-generated type—were manually pasted onto artboard to create camera-ready pages.

Design: Ann Wassmann Gross (Chicago, IL)

Program from The Art Institute of Chicago. Trim size: 10-7/8 by 22-5/8, folded four times to create five panels

---

Family Programs · Fall '87

September

Sanat Şöleni: A Summer Festival of Turkish Arts
daily through September 7
12:00-3:00 Miniature Painting

Turkish Craft Demonstrations
through September 5
Tuesday, Thursday, Friday, and Saturday
12:30-2:30 Uğur Derman, Calligraphy
F. Çiçek Derman, Embroidery

Gallery Walks and Art Activities

Saturdays and Sundays, 2:00-4:00
Theme: Hispanic Arts in conjunction with the exhibition "Recent Developments in Latin American Drawing"
Saturday, September 12, 19, & 26
Sunday, September 13, 20, & 27

Artist Demonstration

Every Saturday and Sunday from 12:30-2:30
September: Carlos Cortez, Woodcut and linoleum-block printmaking

Arty Animals

Saturday, September 26   Age: 6 and older
Visit the Art Institute's galleries in the morning followed by a lunch break and tour of the Lincoln Park Zoo.

10:30-11:45	Gallery Walk: Animals in Art
11:45-1:00	Lunch on your own Provide your own transportation to zoo
1:00-2:30	Animal Walk: Lincoln Park Zoo
Cost:	$2.00 Member (adult or child) $3.00 Non-member (adult or child)

Name	# of children
Address	# of adults
City State	Zip Code
Telephone number	
Member Non-member	
$	
Amount enclosed	

Send check payable to *Museum Education*
Mail to: The Art Institute of Chicago
       Department of Museum Education
       Family Programs
       Michigan Avenue at Adams Street
       Chicago, IL 60603

October

Saturday, October 3
10:30-11:30   Early Birds: Once Upon a Time
1:00-2:00   Gallery Walk: American Art
2:00-4:00   Family Workshop: A Story in a Picture

Sunday, October 4
12:30-1:30   Early Birds: Once Upon a Time
12:30-1:30   Drawing in the Galleries
2:00-4:00   Family Workshop: A Story in a Picture

Saturday, October 10
10:30-11:30   Early Birds: Over and Under
1:00-2:00   Gallery Walk: That's What They Wore
2:00-4:00   Family Workshop: Weaving

Sunday, October 11
12:30-1:30   Early Birds: Over and Under
12:30-1:30   Drawing in the Galleries
2:00-4:00   Family Workshop: Weaving

Monday, October 12
1:00-3:00   Columbus Day Special: Family Workshop

Saturday, October 17
10:30-11:30   Early Birds: Animal Kingdom
1:00-2:00   Gallery Walk: Vase to Vase
2:00-4:00   Family Workshop: Symbolic Animals

Sunday, October 18
12:30-1:30   Early Birds: Animal Kingdom
12:30-1:30   Drawing in the Galleries
2:00-4:00   Family Workshop: Symbolic Animals

Saturday, October 24
10:30-11:30   Early Birds: Pablo's Palette
1:00-2:00   Gallery Walk: French Art
2:00-4:00   Family Workshop: The Eye of Picasso

Sunday, October 25
12:30-1:30   Early Birds: Pablo's Palette
12:30-1:30   Drawing in the Galleries
2:00-4:00   Family Workshop: The Eye of Picasso

Saturday, October 31
10:30-11:30   Early Birds: Tricks or Treats
1:00-2:00   Gallery Walk: Masks and Cover-ups
2:00-4:00   Family Workshop: 'Day of the Dead' Celebration

Artist Demonstration
Every Saturday and Sunday from 12:30-2:30
October: Noreen Czosnyka, The art of wall stenciling

Storytelling
Every Sunday from 2:00-3:00
October: Carmen Aguilar, Latin American folk tales

November

Sunday, November 1
12:30-1:30   Early Birds: Tricks or Treats
12:30-1:30   Drawing in the Galleries
2:00-4:00   Family Workshop: 'Day of the Dead' Celebration

Saturday, November 7
10:30-11:30   Early Birds: A Taste for Art
1:00-2:00   Gallery Walk: Portraits and Pictures
2:00-4:00   Family Workshop: The Delicious Still Life

Sunday, November 8
12:30-1:30   Early Birds: A Taste for Art
12:30-1:30   Drawing in the Galleries
2:00-4:00   Family Workshop: The Delicious Still Life

Saturday, November 14
10:30-11:30   Early Birds: Funny Food
1:00-2:00   Gallery Walk: Travel Plans
2:00-4:00   Family Workshop: Soft Sculpture

Sunday, November 15
12:30-1:30   Early Birds: Funny Food
12:30-1:30   Drawing in the Galleries
2:00-4:00   Family Workshop: Soft Sculpture

Saturday, November 21
10:30-11:30   Early Birds: Blue Plate Special
1:00-2:00   Gallery Walk: Art of Italy
2:00-4:00   Family Workshop: Designing Dishes

Sunday, November 22
12:30-1:30   Early Birds: Blue Plate Special
12:30-1:30   Drawing in the Galleries
2:00-4:00   Family Workshop: Designing Dishes

Friday, November 27
1:00-3:00   Special: "Day After Thanksgiving" Workshop

Saturday, November 28
10:30-11:30   Early Birds: Incredible Edibles
1:00-2:00   Gallery Walk: Animal Kingdom
2:00-4:00   Family Workshop: Edible Art

Sunday, November 29
12:30-1:30   Early Birds: Incredible Edibles
12:30-1:30   Drawing in the Galleries
2:00-4:00   Family Workshop: Edible Art

Artist Demonstration

Every Saturday and Sunday from 12:30-2:30
November: Lorraine Peltz, Still Life painting

Storytelling

Every Sunday from 2:00-3:00
November: Assorted tales by assorted tellers

Historic Hudson Valley

Kitchen at Van Cortlandt Manor

View of West Point from the Highlands

Miniatures at Montgomery Place

S ettled largely by ambitious and adventuresome immigrants from Europe, the Hudson Valley saw great tracts of land held by single families and cultivated by tenant farmers. Frederick Philipse came to New Amsterdam from Holland as a carpenter and soon owned better than 50,000 acres of land. From the wharf at Philipsburg Manor, Upper Mills, flour and other goods were shipped to ports all over the world. Today, young visitors enjoy the antics of spring lambs on the

Matisse Window, Union Church of Pocantico Hills

farm, while watching early American technology at work in the water-powered grist mill.

Owners of the vast Van Cortlandt Manor were among the most influential families in New York as the new American nation emerged. Pierre Van Cortlandt was the state's first Lieutenant Governor and his son Philip served both as an army officer under General Washington and as a United States Congressman. Visitors to the Manor today find elegant antiques and beautifully restored gardens which capture the spirit of this leading Hudson River Valley family.

Washington Irving, famed author of "Rip Van Winkle" and "The Legend of Sleepy Hollow," often said that in all his European travels he had seen nothing to compare with the view of the Hudson from the porch at Sunnyside. Irving transformed what had been a small, Dutch farm cottage on the Philipse Manor into a picturesque country home he

called his "snuggery." Winding pathways along the river, hillsides of daffodils in the spring and the cozy, hospitable atmosphere of Sunnyside combine to make today's visitors feel they have been the guests of this eminent Hudson Valley squire.

Philipsburg Manor (above)
Christmas at Sunnyside (left)

Albany • • Troy

Kingston •

• Montgomery Place

• Hyde Park

Newburgh •

• Cold Spring

West Point •

Best Mountain • • Van Cortlandt Manor

• Philipsburg Manor

■ Union Church

● Tarrytown

■ Sunnyside

New York City
●

Montgomery Place, one of the ancestral homes of the Hudson Valley's prominent Livingston family, will open to the public in June, 1988. The 23-room mansion was built by Janet Livingston Montgomery, widow of Revolutionary War hero General Richard Montgomery, and later remodeled by America's leading 19th-century architect, Alexander Jackson Davis. Visitors will want to linger on the more than 400 acres of land at Montgomery Place, savoring the beauty of the woods, streams and gardens, taking in the views of the river and the Catskill Mountains, and picking fall apples in the estate's orchards.

Montgomery Place, Annandale-on-Hudson

A unique complement to the other properties of **Historic Hudson Valley** is the Union Church of Pocantico Hills, where light is transformed into vivid color through stained glass windows created by modern masters Henri Matisse and Marc Chagall. The modest stone sanctuary contains the only cycle of church windows by Chagall in the United States.

The collections of **Historic Hudson Valley** represent in every detail the people who have lived on the banks of the river. At each of the four historic properties, original family and authentic period furnishings, objects and works of art are on display. Paintings by many important American artists are apparent, as are children's toys, handwoven textiles and looms, simple kitchen utensils and farm implements, fine porcelains and silver.

Van Cortlandt Manor (right)
Philipsburg Manor (below)

Discover
Historic Hudson Valley

Sunnyside
Philipsburg Manor
Van Cortlandt Manor
Union Church of Pocantico Hills
Montgomery Place

Design: Wadlin & Erber (New Paltz, NY)

Folder published by Historic Hudson Valley.

Trim size: 11 by 17, folded in half and then twice again

The elements needed to promote tourism work well in this 11-by 17-inch sheet, folded first in half and then in thirds.

The front cover, with its oval-shaped detail of an old engraving and centered format, suggests that this is the official guide to the region.

The tall orientation of the fully open sheet works well for a stylized map of the river valley. The river prints in blue, the surrounding valley in green. A detailed road map appears on the back cover (not shown).

A five-column format accommodates photos of different sizes and shapes to break up the text.

The photographs, all in color, were stripped in by the printer. Picture frames were positioned during electronic pasteup to facilitate the text wrap.

For electronic pasteup, the designer set up a file of two 11-by-17 pages, with all of the type right-reading. For the side that would be read partially folded (on which half of the 11-by-17 page prints upside down relative to the other half), the L100 output was cut in half and pasted by hand to create the proper imposition of each panel for folding. (Earlier LaserWriter proofs were tiled and pasted together for client approval.)

BROCHURES

Brochures provide a broader creative challenge than many other kinds of publications. Because they are generally one-shot efforts, intended for use over a relatively long period, more time, effort, planning, and money is often allocated to their development. The challenge, for writers and designers, is to come up with a theme or concept that is unique to the needs of that message for that audience at that particular time. The solution should *look* obvious once it is executed, although of course the conception and development of that absolutely right idea may have taken months of research, analysis, brainstorming, and rethinking of hypotheses, as well as many rounds of rough sketches and format changes along the way.

As the samples in this section demonstrate, there is considerable variety from one brochure to another and even within the pages of a single brochure. The styles are as diverse as the messages they convey; they range from straightforward simplicity to complex persuasion, from the stylishly new wave to the classically elegant, from the quietly dignified to the boisterously bold.

Even the size and shape of the page varies more in brochures than in other kinds of publications. This is partly because brochures are often produced in small press runs where the cost of paper isn't so critical, and partly because brochures often have generous budgets that can absorb the increased cost of a nonstandard paper size. As you'll see in some of the samples, an unusual size or an odd shape feels fresh to the eye just because it's different. Of course nonstandard sizes also give designers an opportunity to create unusual solutions to familiar problems and to play with the shape itself as part of the design motif. But unless the solution is a good one, the shape alone won't carry the message.

Brochures in this section

- *inFidelity: Keith Yates Audio*—stylishly active design
- *Clackamas Community College*—a strong, simple concept
- *Pitney Bowes Mail Management*—a lesson in variety
- *Westchester 2000*—structure and style from vertical headlines
- *Westinghouse Transportation Systems*—highly organized and accessible
- *Why Design?*—a five-column grid with punch
- *European Terracotta Sculpture*—quiet sophistication
- *Syracuse University College of Law*—markedly horizontal
- *Viva Tijuana shopping mall*—a large, bold, double gatefold
- *River Park Cooperative*—quiet quality in the shape of a square
- *Seybold Desktop Publishing Conference*—a stylish conference brochure
- *Subscription Programs*—compact information in an elegant format
- *Islam and the West*—the photographic story of a TV series
- *Sacramento Regional Foundation*—bit-mapped art and mug shots
- *Doane Raymond Accountants*—organized serendipity
- *Extending Desktop Publishing*—A showcase for technology and art

A sales brochure that calls itself a newsletter borrows editorial techniques from the newsletter format.

Each product is treated as a self-contained unit with its own design, and each spread has a different composition. The contrast and varied texture make each spread feel like a collage.

Two unifying elements balance the seemingly dominant diversity: an underlying four-column grid and a stylishly high-tech design that provides its own continuity.

Silhouette photos focus attention on and dramatize the product.

Computer-assembled gray tones of different values, such as the light gray of the first two letters of the logo against the darker gray of the banner, register perfectly. In traditional pasteup it would be virtually impossible to achieve a clean edge with overlapping gray tones.

*Design:
John McWade,
PageLab
(Sacramento, CA)
Brochure published by Keith Yates Audio.
Size: 8-3/8 by 10-3/4*

A simple concept, well executed, makes for a very effective four-color recruitment brochure for a small college.

The cover borrows techniques from advertising design, with large, centered display type expressing a single bold statement. When you use this technique, the statement had better be right on target for your audience.The inside pages answer the question implied on the cover.

Each spread follows an identical layout, creating a strong sense of continuity that orients readers very quickly to the information on the page. This would become monotonous in a longer publication. (Two additional spreads, not shown, do vary from this format, and a bind-in card provides a checklist of additonal information the prospective student can request.)

The strong concept and controlled continuity of the layout require considerable planning. Creating and refining pencil sketches before you begin work on the computer can save a lot of time in this sort of project.

Each spread uses a different color scheme keyed to the box in the upper left corner. (The number in that box prints in reverse type.) The color is used in the banner above the student quote and as a tone behind the boxed copy on the right-hand page.

The bleed photos on the inside spreads heighten the strong horizontal axis created by the rule above them. Actually, there are elements that bleed on all four sides of the spread, setting up a visual tug of war that makes the pages very dynamic.

The principle of contrast is used very effectively here. The angled photos on the right-hand pages contrast with the crisp, clean rectangles that dominate the rest of the layout. These photos are also black and white, whereas the others are in color. And the two small photos play off against the one large one on each spread.

The typeface is Garamond throughout.
Body text:12/20
Captions: 9/11 italic
Numbers: 96 point
Headline: 60 point condensed

Condensed Garamond is currently very "hot" in display typography. Few readers are aware on a conscious level that a particular font is in fashion, but there are subliminal effects to seeing a typeface that has a lot of media penetration. As is true with any kind of fashion, trends in typography change quickly.

Design:
Ralph Rawson
(Oregon City, OR)

A student recruit-ment brochure for Clackamas Community College.
Trim: 8-1/2 by 11

3. A price you can afford.

Chrissy Pagh
Freshman, Gladstone
"I chose Clackamas because I knew the quality of the classes was equal to a four-year school, without having to pay the money. I haven't had a teacher yet who hasn't been great. And because the classes are small, there's a lot more interaction and a lot more learning."

Tuition at CCC is $23 per credit hour, or $230 per term for a full-time student.* That's less than half the cost of tuition at a state university, and a fraction of what you'd pay at many private colleges. It adds up to a sensible, economical solution to the rising cost of a college education.

"Can I get financial aid?"
Last year, nearly half of CCC's full-time students received some kind of financial aid — an average of
...student! The chances are good that...
...work study pro-

...have earned

2. Courses that count.

Neale Frothingham
Sophomore, Oregon City
"Having been here for a year, and realizing how good the instruction is, I realize I made the best choice educationally that I ever could have made. The size of CCC definitely enhances the quality of education. It's very personal."

Planning to transfer to a four-year institution?
All lower division college transfer courses at Clackamas Community College are fully accredited and transferable to any college or university in Oregon, and to public and private institutions throughout the
...country.......can take your freshman and soph-
...a junior to

1. Teachers who care.

*In class and...
students get...
Opportuniti...
theatre, spe...
instrument...
student gov...
student ne...
mural spo...
20 special...
ranging f...
mountain...*

CCC graduate Laura Onstott
(with chemistry instructor Margi Arighi)
"Margi made the class interesting, and fun, and always challenging. She always made me feel that I could succeed. By the end of that year, I knew I wanted to get a degree in chemistry." (Laura, now a senior at Reed College, was recently awarded a scholarship by the American Chemical Society.)

Personal attention to your learning needs comes first at Clackamas Community College. Our classes are small (average size: 21 students). Our teachers can take the time to get to know you, to find out where you're going, and to help you get there. Our total commitment is to make your college experience a success.

At Clackamas, you can explore creative writing with an award-winning novelist, learn algebra with the man who wrote the textbook, or play in the band with some of Oregon's most sought after musicians. CCC's faculty includes nationally recognized experts on subjects ranging from computer-aided drafting to Middle Eastern history.

But our most important recognition comes from former CCC students. In surveys, letters, and interviews, they consistently say that the personal attention they got at Clackamas was a major reason for their success — in college and beyond.

Clackamas Community College is a public two-year college with an annual enrollment of 2400 full-time and 8600 part-time students. The campus is located on 175 acres of forest and farmland in the foothills of the Oregon Cascades, 20 miles southeast of downtown Portland.

Everything you need to succeed.
CCC backs up your classroom experience with first-rate student support services, including:

❑ Program planning with CCC's expert team of counselors and advisors.

❑ Career planning and job placement assistance with the resources of CCC's Career & Job Development Center.

❑ Personal tutoring by CCC instructors and advanced students.

❑ The Computer Lab, with tutors on hand to help you build vital math and computer skills.

❑ And, if you're not yet ready for college level course work, individualized instruction in basic reading, writing, math, and study skills (including high school completion programs).

Clackamas Community College is an equal opportunity, affirmative action institution.

An ambitious, high-budget production gives both the company and the designer an opportunity to dramatize their message. Although the resources to execute a brochure like this may be beyond your budget, the publication has elements you can incorporate in more a modest undertaking.

The story in this brochure is that managing mail is a complex business. The opening page (not shown) contains a single small photo of a row of rural mailboxes and begins, "There was a time when getting the mail out was pretty simple...." When you turn to the page shown below, the helter-skelter array symbolizes the choices, the pace, and the complexities of today's mail.

The words put the pictures into context, and the pictures dramatize the words. The story, as it unfolds on the next spread (not shown), is that increasingly complex mail systems require increasingly complex paperwork. But "Whatever you're sending, no matter where, we can show you how to get it there, how to prepare it for going, how to account for it after it's gone."

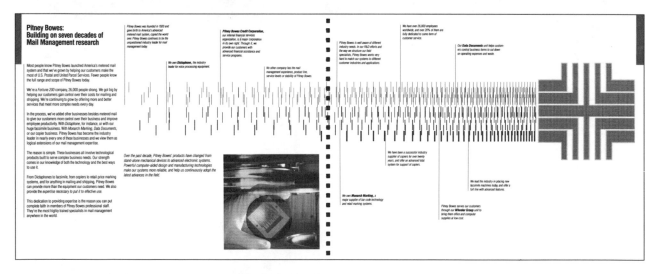

The direct statement of what Pitney Bowes is and what products it offers is presented as time-line-style captions to a piece of art that suggests the speed and intelligence of today's technology. The symbol on the far right is the company logo.

The information is broken down into accessible pieces. The very direct, well-written statement in the left column is only about 250 words long, with very short paragraphs. Each captionlike statement describes a different service or division of the company.

The strong, three-column grid is apparent when you compare the spread shown above to the one at right. The horizontal structure that runs across both is maintained throughout the 34 pages. This grid brings a feeling of order and control to pages that contain a wide variety of photos, charts, diagrams, documents, and other visuals.

The large photo in the spread below introduces a new service and adds yet another texture as you turn the pages.

Subtle graphic humor is seen throughout the brochure. A tortoise-and-hare metaphor is used in the diagram on this spread to compare the old and new meter refill service.

The typeface throughout the brochure is Helvetica Condensed for body text, Helvetica Condensed Black for headlines, and Helvetica Condensed Oblique for captions and for contrast with the opening text. The type treatment is kept simple to balance the diversity of the art and layout, with a crisp, modern, efficient look that is obviously appropriate to the subject.

Design: Weisz Yang Dunkelberger Inc. (Westport, CT)

Pitney Bowes brochure entitled Building on Seven Decades of Mail Management Expertise. *Trim size: 11-1/4 by 8-1/2*

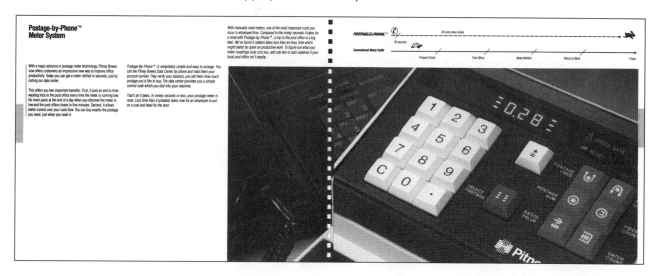

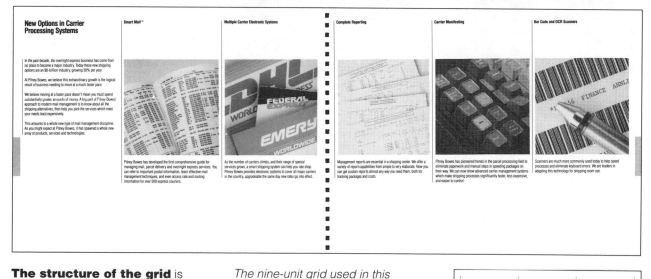

The structure of the grid is most apparent in the spread shown above. The sequence of photos with headings above and text below suggests a series of pigeonholes that echo the partitioning inherent in sorting mail. The grid reinforces an image in which nothing is accidental, everything is tightly choreographed.

The nine-unit grid used in this brochure is diagramed at right. It provides a useful structure for organizing a horizontal page.

The Challenge of Leadership

What will Westchester be like in the year 2000?

by Sidney P. Mudd, Chairman, Westchester 2000 Steering Committee

What will Westchester be like tomorrow and by the year 2000? Putting all guesses aside, we can be certain of our answer: it will be what we want it to be, if that is what we make it to be. There is a vast difference between wanting and making it happen, between just hoping that something will happen and working to make it happen. The degree to which we can shrink that difference will define the future of this lovely but troubled county to the year 2000 and beyond. Perhaps some examples will demonstrate.

Housing

The greatest need we have in Westchester is housing. We want it badly, for our children, our seniors, and for the employees that are sorely needed to keep our service, retail and business economies strong. The way to get it is perfectly clear. We need land, county land, city land, town and village land. We

need lower costs of land per unit; we need rental units. To fill these needs means zoning changes, cluster homes, accessory apartments, the enlightened phase-out of rent control, subsidy where needed—all incentives to housing development.

We may have the means. Do we have the will?

Now the difference between wanting and making. Would we back government leaders, county and local, who seek the changes needed? Would we replace those unwilling to effect them? If we do, we could have the housing. If we won't, we'll never have it. Are there easy decisions to make and will everybody like them? Certainly not. We would all have to give a little. Are we big enough, strong enough, compassionate enough to make it happen? We'll see.

"It will be what we want it to be, if that is what we make it to be. There is a vast difference between wanting and making it happen."

Transportation

Our second greatest need in Westchester is transportation, both private and public. We know right now what the problems are and the solutions. The Hutchinson River Parkway, the Cross Westchester Expressway, the Route 35-202 corridor needs action; buses need lanes and appropriate parkway usage, more routes rather than fewer; commuters need parking, if ride-sharing is to grow and improved rail service is to draw more riders.

But how much do we want better transportation? Do we want it enough to make it happen? Would we support the decision-makers who must make the hard decisions? If we

do, we'll have the transportation. If we don't, we won't have it. That's very clear. Again, we'll see.

A challenge met...A challenge ahead

Few counties, if any, have ever been studied with greater intensity, by a broader range of citizenry than ours has these past four years. Few counties, if any, are as naturally and humanly endowed. Few, if any, have more at stake in planning their future.

These four years have been well spent. They have defined the problems. They have recommended the solutions. The time for implementation is at hand. But, implementation depends on leadership. That is our present and continuing challenge. The challenge of leadership.

The first Westchester 2000 report made 29 general recommendations. Twenty of these 29 recommendations require government action at local, county or state levels and often interaction among these levels. Nine recommendations could be implemented by the private sector alone. So the challenge of leadership falls, if unevenly, on both the public and the private sectors of our citizenry. There is much for all of us to do.

Who will lead us?

Who will provide the essential leadership in the public sector? Here we face an important fact: we have a county government and we have home rule. Westchester is going to go away. Westchester likes it that way. The county executive and board of legislators are responsible for county leadership. Local elected officials are responsible for leadership under home rule. No one else is legally qualified. They either lead or fail to lead. Twenty recommendations challenge that leadership. Will we have it? We'll see.

Who will provide the essential leadership in the private sector? Here we face another important issue: We need more and stronger leadership from the business community of the county. They can make things happen in *Westchester 2000*, for which they generously supplied the original funding. Now is the time for private leadership. Will we have it? We'll see.

What can you do?

What can you a private citizen of Westchester do? Some 800 have already done much these past four years. They have made the broad study, defined the needs and made the recommendations. Now it is the responsibility of each of us, young or old, privileged or not, black, white, hispanic to heed this report, understand it is our future here at stake and resolve to elect, support and exhort the leadership without which this great county of ours can be in serious trouble.

What can business do?

If we are involved in business, regardless of position and certainly if we are among its leaders, we can examine the issues and study the recommendations. We can determine where the strength of our talent, the resources of our corporations can be put to best use for the future of our county. What a great difference that can make when it comes to getting things done. Will we have that private and corporate leadership? We'll see.

Will we meet the challenge?

The future of Westchester is in our hands. We know the problems. We know how to attack them. We know we must give a little to preserve and enhance what we have and hold dear. The challenge now is leadership. ∎

1985 Initial Recommendations

A Blueprint for the Future

The initial *Westchester 2000* report, submitted by over 800 volunteers at a public conference in September 1985, identified the following major recommendations for improving the quality of life here in Westchester County.

1. Increase housing by reducing construction costs and lowering land costs.
2. Establish a non-profit economic development agency to sponsor new housing projects, especially in downtown areas.
3. Establish an organization that will publicize housing needs and the benefits of more housing.
4. Eliminate rent control, except where market rent rates can not be met by tenants.
5. Develop a housing program for people who are hard to house.
6. Create an education consortium that would promote support for schools, museums, and libraries.
7. Support higher state aid for the county's neediest school districts.
8. Use the economic development agency (see recommendation number two) to promote business development in downtown areas.
9. Organize a central contact for families requiring community health and social services.
10. Develop a council of social and health agencies to evaluate new programs pertaining to both areas.

11. Create a human rights commission to help people overcome violations of anti-discrimination laws.
12. Develop a countywide emergency telephone system.
13. Promote good health.
14. Promote ride-sharing.
15. Establish a county authority to provide adequate public parking.
16. Complete a municipal county planning process.
17. Develop a long-range plan to avoid water shortages.
18. Create a geographic information system to help translate data into maps.
19. Establish a council of chief elected officials to promote better regional planning.
20. Develop an intergovernmental relations commission to mediate intergovernmental disputes.
21. Establish a committee from within the intergovernmental commission to consider the reorganization of local government and school district boundaries.
22. Reassess property with protection of residential property as a whole from an increased share of total property taxes.
23. Redistribute some county taxes to impoverished communities.
24. Evaluate open land and take steps to preserve it.
25. Assign responsibility for preserving land to various levels of government.
26. Improve maintenance of our parks and upgrade recreational facilities.
27. Promote financial support for the arts and establish a children's museum.
28. Survey current performing arts facilities and determine whether a newer central facility is needed.
29. Develop a county tourism program.

Both the structure and the personality of this format come from the large vertical headlines and the bold rules with graduated gray tones.

The vertical headlines are New Century Schoolbook italic. They were rotated in Adobe Illustrator and then placed in the PageMaker document. They function as section heads and can be placed in any column except the far right one.

The banners with graduated gray tones were created in Cricket Draw. In the days before desktop technology, this effect had to be rendered by an airbrush artist, and then shot and stripped in as a separate halftone. Today's electronic drawing programs offer a variety of graduated tonal and screen effects that can be employed simply by clicking through a myriad of choices until you get the effect you want.

The headlines within the columns are Helvetica bold italic. The running text is New Century Schoolbook. The quotations inset in the running text are Helvetica italic.

The bottom rule and column rules provide enough structure for the page to allow ragged right and ragged bottom text.

All art and photos have a 1-point rule around them. This is a good technique for unifying photos of varying qualities throughout a publication.

The oversize pages were manually tiled in two sections of 8-1/2- by 11-inch pages printed in the landscape orientation on a LaserWriter. Tiling divides oversize pages into smaller blocks, or tiles, each of which prints on a separate sheet of paper. When tiling manually, you reposition the zero point to specify where each tile starts. In this publication, all of the top sections were printed first, with the zero point in the upper left corner of the page. Then the zero point was moved to the 8-inch point on the vertical ruler to print the bottom half of all the pages. The top and bottom tiles of each page were then manually pasted together at the best breaking point for that page.

Design: Gan Y. Wong (Hoboken, NJ)

Brochure published as a promotional supplement to the Gannett Westchester Newspapers.
Trim size: 11-1/2 by 13-3/4

Westinghouse Transportation
Systems and Support
Division

Overview

Westinghouse Electric Corporation has more than 100 years of transportation experience as a leading supplier of electric propulsion and automatic train control systems for mass transit applications. Westinghouse also pioneered the development and application of automated people mover technology with more operating systems worldwide than any other company.

The purpose here is to organize simple material in a clean, orderly way. Doing that well makes a strong statement about the company's image.

The cover is a quick, businesslike summary of the brochure, an 11- by 17-inch sheet folded once.

The type is Helvetica Light, Helvetica Black, and Helvetica Black Oblique. The light, black, and condensed Helvetica faces provide a range of weights and styles within the same highly legible type family, which is why you see them frequently in this book and elsewhere.

The total measure of the two columns is the same on both pages, but on the left it's a narrow and a wide column, whereas on the right it's two equal columns.

Although this brochure is all text, you could easily introduce photos, charts, and diagrams into this format.

Design:
Agnew, Moyer, Smith
(Pittsburgh, PA)
Brochure for the Westinghouse Transportation Systems and Support Division.
Size: 8-1/2 by 11

Overview

Westinghouse Transportation Locations
The Westinghouse Transportation Systems and Support Division (WTSSD) is headquartered in suburban Pittsburgh, Pennsylvania and operates from two facilities:
• Allegheny County Airport Site (ACAS)
• Lebanon Church Site (LCS)

Total office and manufacturing space is nearly 271,000 square feet.

WTSSD has approximately 25 field locations in the United States, Canada, United Kingdom and Taiwan.

Employes
WTSSD employs about 800 personnel at its two locations near Pittsburgh, and about 125 at its various field sites.

People Mover Test Track
This automated facility, located at the LCS site, is 1570 feet long with a 10 percent grade for testing vehicle acceleration and deceleration, all vehicle operating systems, and includes a hydraulic guideway switch with a turn-out spur. Snow-making equipment enables the simulation of winter climate conditions.

Business Segments and Product Offerings

Original Equipment
AC and DC mass transit propulsion equipment, advanced automatic train controls (ATC), and complete automated people mover systems.

Mass transit propulsion equipment	*ATC system components*	*People mover systems*
• Air-operated cam	• Car-carried	• Airport
• Electrically-operated cam	• Wayside	• Downtown
• Solid-state thyristor chopper	• Station	• Commercial
• AC inverter	• Central	

After-Sales Customer Support
Parts, equipment, and services to operate and maintain mass transit and people mover systems. Designed to manage and maintain system configuration.

Customer support products and services
• Renewal parts and components
• Field engineering services
• Training programs
• Documentation
• Diagnostic services
• Reliability analyses

Mass Transit Contracts

Bay Area Rapid Transit in San Francisco, California
The first automated mass transit system began operation in 1972 with Westinghouse propulsion and ATC. The original 450-carset order represented the world's first production order for chopper control. In 1984, 120 additional carsets were ordered.

São Paulo Metro Transit System
First international application of automatic train control integrated with solid-state chopper-controlled propulsion; began operation in 1975.

Rio de Janeiro Metro Transit System
Microprocessors were applied to chopper propulsion for the first time; began operation in 1979.

Southeastern Pennsylvania Transit Authority System in Philadelphia, Pennsylvania
First chopper application to a light rail vehicle by Westinghouse; began operation in 1981.

Washington Metropolitan Area Transit Authority
Operating 300 cam-controlled cars with Westinghouse equipment since system start-up in 1976; add-on orders for 366 carsets of both cam and chopper propulsion were completed in 1987.

Vancouver Regional Transit System/BC Transit in Vancouver, British Columbia
First application of Westinghouse chopper propulsion to trolley buses. In 1982, 245 new buses began operation using Westinghouse equipment.

New York City Transit Authority
Over 3000 cars of the existing fleet are powered by Westinghouse cam propulsion systems. In 1987, Westinghouse received an order for 200 carsets of cam control equipment for the new R68A fleet.

Baltimore and Miami Metros
The first joint procurement project to obtain Urban Mass Transit Administration funding totalled 208 new cars and began operation in 1983. Baltimore has since ordered 28 additional carsets.

Niagara Frontier Transportation Authority in Buffalo, New York
Ordered 28 carsets of Westinghouse chopper propulsion equipment for its new light rail transit system; operation began in early 1985.

Massachusetts Bay Transportation Authority in Boston, Massachusetts
Awarded a 54-carset order in 1983 for Westinghouse to supply motors and gears with cam-controlled propulsion for the South Shore #2 heavy rail cars. One hundred carsets of light rail vehicle equipment with dual chopper control were also ordered at the same time.

Port Authority Trans Hudson in New York and New Jersey
Westinghouse has supplied PATH propulsion equipment since its inception, twenty-five years ago. A rehabilitation contract and a new car contract totalling 343 carsets of cam propulsion equipment were awarded in 1985.

Municipality of Metropolitan Seattle in Washington
Westinghouse is supplying 236 carsets of AC inverter propulsion for Seattle's new dual-mode trolley buses. This order represents the largest AC propulsion fleet in North America.

The organization of complex, multitiered information is the fundamental challenge in many publications. This tutorial about the effective use of electronic design addresses that very issue and uses the techniques it espouses. Information is broken into manageable "chunks," and the importance of different elements is made readily apparent through the use of head-lines, rules, numbers, and color.

The handwritten annotations are red; the 6-point rules above headlines, the highlighted quote, and the marginal copy are green. Red and green spot color is also used in the diagrams.

The format combines different kinds of editorial material—running text, charts and diagrams, numbered points, quotes offset from the main text, and even handwritten annotations of typeset words. The mix of techniques gives readers different ways to enter the page. It must be carefully organized in order not to backfire.

The five-column grid uses an 8-pica measure with 1 pica between columns. The wider columns in the top spread are 17 picas wide (two of the five-column units plus the space between).

The typography adheres to the principles of simplicity and familiarity—Helvetica and Times Roman are used throughout.

The diagrams were created in Cricket Draw.

Design: Watzman + Keyes (Cambridge, MA)

Brochure entitled Why Design? *published by Watzman + Keyes Information Design. Trim size: 8-1/2 by 11*

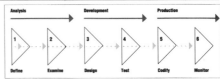

Information Design

The (visual)

Automation and Communication
Most users of electronic publishing focus on automation and assume that communication will take care of itself. They are mismanaging the technology and missing rare opportunities to achieve three things simultaneously:
- **Increase impact and effectiveness** by ensuring that information gets noticed, understood, used and remembered.
- **Develop proprietary, customized systems of graphic standards** to ensure quality and consistency, increase market visibility and streamline the production of communication materials.
- **Leverage the value and competitive advantage that EP technology promises** by encoding standards in software and systems as proprietary templates or style sheets.

Critical Trends
The following trends affect you and your organization's bottom line:

Growing demand for customer services — 1987 / 1990

Diminishing labor supply — 1987 / 1990

Growing demand for publishing services — 1987 / 1990

Information overload — comprehension / amount of information

Growing Demand for Customer Services
The profusion of "smart" products has led to demand for materials which explain them. Clearly, products a customer does not understand, serve neither the customers nor the maker. Careful attention to passive devices (like

Diminishing Labor Supply
The U.S. faces a severe labor shortage at a time when communication skills are at a premium. Since electronic publishing requires skilled professionals, the gap is widening. Design cannot be automated any more than writing can be

Growing Internal Demand for Publishing Services
When customers demand service, managers demand more support – and control and faster turnaround. Electronic publishing creates demand, accelerates production, and decentralizes a process which, because it used to be slow,

Information Overload
There really is such a thing as "too much information." When people are bombarded with more information than they need or can use, their performance actually suffers. Too much information increases error-making, reduces attentiveness, and induces boredom and dissatisfaction. This is a clinical fact

---

The Need for Corporate-Wide Graphic Standards Systems (CoGSS)©

The current emphasis of electronic publishing vendor marketing is on the *freedom and flexi-bility* which their systems provide to individual users. But the "Sorcerer's Apprentice Problem" makes clear that *decentralization* and *loss of corporate control* in the visible area of communications is not good for business. The result is *decreasing quality, decreasing effectiveness, loss of corporate image* and *poor product recognition*.

But electronic publishing technology has another capability which has yet to be developed: it can set consistent, well-defined, customized default standards for published materials (CoGSS). Such standards eliminate much of the time-consuming activity that goes into publishing. At the same time, standards enforce quality and consistency by providing a matrix of solutions to a broad range of communication needs.

The Information Design Perspective: Cognitive Human Factors as a Basis for Design

CoGS Systems produce two outcomes:
First, they provide dramatic managerial control over staff use of money, time and materials. They do this by providing a matrix of predetermined solutions to communication problems. Typical problems are solved in advance, or solved the first time they occur. After that, producers of communication materials are guided by clear procedures which ensure consistency and quality.

Second, CoGS Systems significantly enhance the value of printed materials by using human factors techniques to improve the usefulness of information to readers. With "smart" products which require extensive documentation or complex sales messages, improving reader response has a significant impact on sales, marketing efforts, customer satisfaction, customer service and training costs.

As a growing number of leading companies are discovering, arriving at a performance-oriented CoGS System makes good business sense. Approaching the problem requires skill and knowledge in four areas:

Sensitivity to the importance of careful, informative, writing;

Background in the relatively new field of cognitive human factors;

Education and experience in design and the development of Corporate Graphic Standards Systems;

Familiarity with the proliferating range of EP technologies.

"Information is easier to remember when it is in an orderly state, rich in pattern and structure, highly interconnected, containing a good deal of redundancy. Disordered information that lacks structure is easy to forget."
Jeremy Campbell
Grammatical Man

Developing a CoGS System

Because of the range of disciplines required to develop a CoGS System (and the short-term nature of the projects), companies often turn to outside firms for assistance–and do so before they buy electronic publishing equipment.

Based on experience with Fortune 500 companies, threshold companies and high technology start-ups, Watzman+Keyes has developed a six-stage process for developing a CoGS Systems. The process insures that the system uses *both* capabilities of electronic publishing: it *improves* staff productivity and *enhances* user satisfaction and performance. This six-stage process incorporates research, design, testing and training in an efficient cycle that gives clients cost-effective solutions prior to automation.

The Information Design Process: Six Steps to a Graphic Standards System

Analysis — Development — Production

1 Define — 2 Examine — 3 Design — 4 Test — 5 Codify — 6 Monitor

What Is Information Design?
Information design is a truly professional process which integrates technology, design and cognitive science to achieve three ends:
1 *Streamline* the process of creating documents and communication materials.
2 *Improve* the impact, effectiveness and quality of communication programs and materials.
3 *Manage* the transition to high technology-based print communication programs.

Phase 1: Define
Define the business problem. Who is sending the message? for what purpose? using what technologies? What constraints exist (budgets or staffing, etc.)? What degree of control or decentralization is advisable or realistic? This phase ends in a *compilation and review.*

Phase 2: Examine
Understand the users. Who are they? How do they use information ? What are their backgrounds and educational levels? Do they have unusual constraints? This and Phase 1, are a complete *communication audit.*

Phase 3: Develop
Brief the design team so they can develop design alternatives (several alternatives are necessary for valid testing). This results in a *presentation of alternatives* to the staff who will use the CoGS System.

Phase 4: Test
According to Nobel Laureate and A.I. expert, Herbert Simon, "Design is both the *development* and *testing* of alternatives." In this phase, alternatives are subjected to cognitive testing. The results are used to *refine* the CoGS System.

Phase 5: Codify
Once the CoGS System is developed it can be codified in software or in a manual. These products are used to train staff about the CoGSS System. Electronic publishing *fundamentally alters* the way documents are produced and the way people work, so this phase includes training in teamwork as well as system familiarity.

Phase 6: Monitor
This phase ensures that the system does the two things it is supposed to do: helps *staff* be productive and helps *users* learn complex equipment and tasks easily.

10

11

9

European Terracotta Sculpture
from the Arthur M. Sackler Collections

The Art Institute of Chicago / December 9, 1987 - March 6, 1988

end of the eighteenth century. Clodion's exquisite terracotta statuettes (nos. 19 and 20) captivated Rococo collectors. In his suite, Neoclassical sculptors, such as Simon Louis Boizot (no. 22) and Joseph Chinard (no. 23), perfected his smooth, sensuous surfaces. French artists also adopted the medium for the portrait bust, enlivening this formal type with the vivacity of touch possible in terracotta. Pajou, in his Bust of Corbin de Cordet de Florensac (no. 24), achieves a sense of motion and captures the sitter's alert gaze with the flicker of a modeling tool through the hair and incisions in the pupils. Such Rococo portrait conventions were revived in the nineteenth century by Carrier-Belleuse (no. 29).

Nineteenth- and twentieth-century sculptors flaunted the rugged surfaces of worked clay. The brooding power of Rodin's Titans (no. 31) is emphasized by the retention of the scumbled surfaces and blocky musculature of the figures in their adaptation to the form of a vase. Jagged, seemingly random gouges in Vallmitjana's Wounded Bullfighter (no. 30) underline the violence of the subject. The deliberate roughness of Martini's figural studies expresses barely containable energy (no. 33).

Changing attitudes toward terracotta over the six centuries represented in this exhibition are representative of similar developments throughout the visual arts. One is the shift in attitude toward the medium; it is less important to us today what materials are used by the artist than how they are manipulated. Another is our desire to see the traces of the artist's encounter with the medium—our interest in the process of creation as well as the finished product. These beautiful studies and finished works amply demonstrate the role of terracotta in the development of sculpture from the Renaissance to the twentieth century.

This exhibition has been selected from over one hundred examples in the Arthur M. Sackler collections. In 1981-82 a larger exhibition of these holdings circulated to The National Gallery of Art, Washington, D. C., The Metropolitan Museum of Art, New York, and the Fogg Museum, Boston. It is a great pity that Dr. Sackler's death last May prevented him from the pleasure of seeing his objects in this and other exhibitions from his collections presented this year. We are most grateful to the Sackler Foundation for continuing with plans for this show at such a difficult time and for its generous support for this project. Dr. Lois Katz, Administrator of the Sackler Foundation, has provided invaluable advice and assistance.

Ian Wardropper
Associate Curator
European Decorative Arts and Sculpture

This exhibition was funded by The AMS Foundation for the Arts, Sciences and Humanities, Washington, D.C. and the Arthur M. Sackler Foundation, Washington, D.C.
The Chicago exhibition was partially supported by the John D. and Catherine T. MacArthur Foundation Special Exhibitions Grant.

Jan Baptiste Van der
Haegen
Flemish, 1688-c. 1740
Saint Joseph Holding the
Christ Child, c. 1723
Terracotta statuette

Giuseppe Maria Mazza
Italian, 1653-1741
David Triumphant over
Goliath, c. 1675/1725
Terracotta statuette

The quiet, elegant sophistication of this brochure projects an image that is completely different from any of the other documents in this section. The style is entirely appropriate for the subject of 17th- and 18th-century terracotta sculpture.

The brochure is an 8-1/2- by 25-1/2-inch sheet folded twice to make six 8-1/2- by 11-inch pages. Shown are the cover and the right-hand page of the fully open brochure.

Contrast is an effective element in this design. The saturation of the full bleed, sepia-toned cover plays off against the generous white space of the open text pages as well as the silhouetted shapes inside the brochure. The reverse type in the cover banner is set off like a plaque from the cover art. Note the open letter spacing in the brochure title, which improves legibility of reverse type in relatively small sizes.

The text is 9/14 Times Roman italic in a 14-pica column. The use of italic for running text is unusual because it is generally difficult to read. Here it adds to the traditional elegance; the open leading and surrounding white space compensate to improve readability.

The justified text is in keeping with the formality of the design. The hard edge of the right margin works better with silhouette photos than a ragged right margin would.

The silhouettes are enhanced by other elements in the design. The rules at the top of the page, from which the text seems to hang, create a free but defined space for the shapes. The captions are set on a half-column grid so as not to interrupt that space.

Design: Joseph Cochand,
The Art Institute of Chicago

Brochure for a show of European terracotta sculpture at
The Art Institute of Chicago.
Trim size: 8-1/2 by 25-1/2 folded twice

The unusually long page in the top sample uses rules to emphasize the horizontal format. This motif is established on the cover (not shown), where the four rules are broken only by a single photo that is centered horizontally and bleeds off the top of the page.

The placement of the initial cap and photo over the rules creates a three-dimensional effect, as if these elements float above the page.

The tab-style folio—reverse type in a gray box—is a popular device in today's graphic design.

The initial caps, 96 points, are also printed in gray.

The body text is 10/11 Palatino. That leading is fairly tight, but the 16-pica column width and the generous white space compensate to ensure readability.

The format is repeated on every page of the brochure. Only the depth of the photos varies.

THE FIRST YEAR LAW FIRM

Most American law schools prescribe a curriculum for first year students that has hardly changed at all since it was invented by Christopher Langdell at Harvard in the 1870's. That curriculum utilizes the Socratic teaching method in the traditional private law courses—contracts, torts, procedure, and property. The year is usually rounded out by such courses as constitutional law, criminal law, and legal writing.

Syracuse has not abandoned the features of this traditional curriculum that have rightly proved enduring. It is only that we believe today's beginning law student deserves more than this. Concerned that exclusive reliance on tradition does not provide enough individual attention to the development of basic lawyering skills, the Syracuse faculty has developed a first year program known as "Law Firm."

Organizing into small mock Law Firms, first year Syracuse students begin at once to see the real-world context in which legal problems arise and are resolved. Working together with their Law Firm associates, students develop legal writing, research, problem solving, and client counseling skills. Each Law Firm is directed by a faculty member who guides students through problems drawn from real law practice, integrated with materials covered in the traditional first year courses.

Design (top):
Joanne Lenweaver,
Lenweaver Design
(Syracuse, NY)

Prospectus for
Syracuse University
College of Law.
Trim size:
12-3/16 by 7-5/8

La visita de más de 20 mil personas por día al centro Comercial ¡Viva Tijuana! está garantizada, habida cuenta de que ¡Viva Tijuana! es el paso natural, obligado, desde la Puerta de México hacia el interior de la ciudad. Veinte mil visitantes que ahora utilizan el andador turístico serán, por necesidad geográfica, visitantes del proyecto ¡Viva Tijuana!

Asimismo, es conveniente considerar otros factores a mediano plazo: a) como inversión se alienta todos los días el mejoramiento de la plusvalía, redituando en múltiples beneficios para quienes tengan la visión de ser los primeros en instalarse en ¡Viva Tijuana! b) el número de visitantes a ¡Viva Tijuana! crecerá todos los días por la acción directa del crecimiento explosivo de la zona y c) la realización de diversos programas festivos garantiza la asistencia y permanencia de un público que podrá considerarse cautivo, atraído por los magníficos eventos que en ¡Viva Tijuana! habrán de presentarse.

Este factor es el punto clave que garantiza el éxito, del centro comercial ¡Viva Tijuana!

Su proximidad con la Puerta de México, la de mayor circulación peatonal en toda la frontera de México con Estados Unidos, impone la certidumbre de un incalculable valor a nivel internacional. Todo aquel visitante que desee adquirir alguna mercancía producida en nuestro país, como también ar-

tículos de importación, podrá acudir a ¡Viva Tijuana! en cuestión de minutos, trasladarse desde el sur de California con increíble facilidad.

La instalación de restaurantes de corte nacional e internacional será un atractivo más para la permanencia de visitantes en ¡Viva Tijuana!

Un factor igualmente decisivo, es la facilidad con la que el cliente podrá realizar sus compras en ¡Viva Tijuana! 1) al internarse al país desde Estados Unidos y 2) cuando abandone México, ya que obligadamente habrá de pasar por ¡Viva Tijuana!

En una palabra, ¡Viva Tijuana! ofrece ser el mejor centro comercial situado estratégicamente para recibir al visitante, y el último por el cual el turista saldrá del perímetro de la ciudad.

¡Viva Tijuana! conjuga novedosas técnicas de mercacotecnia con la tradición comercial forjada en la experiencia. ¡Viva Tijuana! es una ventana a dos mundos, un corredor entre la riqueza del Estado de California y la promesa de la Ciudad mexicana más vigorosa y visitada del mundo.

¡VivaTijuana!, por todo lo expuesto, es la realidad comercial esperada tanto tiempo por los inversionistas más exigentes.

¡Viva Tijuana! es la realidad económica de México.

¡Viva! Tijuana!

MAJOR PROGRAM AREAS CURRICULUM

The basic course of advanced law study at Syracuse is an innovative plan called the Major Program Areas Curriculum (MPAC). After the first year, each student selects a major program area that concentrates a portion of his or her study in one of four areas: business organizations and transactions; government and regulation; civil and criminal justice; or international law.

The goal of MPAC is not to force premature career choices or to develop narrow substantive specialties. Rather, its premise is that a good general legal education requires that some area of the law be studied in orderly sequence and in depth.

Rejecting the smorgasboard approach that has characterized much of American legal education in recent times, MPAC offers the Syracuse student an organized, in-depth study of the selected area during the final two years of law school. Integrating materials from disciplines beyond the law, MPAC assures that students not only become well-versed in their areas of current special interest, but that they develop the skills needed to explore the varieties of legal problems they may encounter in the future.

Everything about the design in the bottom sample is bold: the page size, the fold, the type size, and the colors (the background on the pages that unfold is green with orange, red, and magenta accents).

A double gatefold gives new meaning to the landscape-proportioned page. The pages shown below left unfold to a 36-inch-wide sheet (half of the foldout is shown on the right), allowing plenty of room for the artist's rendering of a shopping mall on the Mexican border.

The running text was set at 36 points and output on a LaserWriter. That output was shot down 50%, reducing the type size to 18 points and increasing the resolution from 300 to 600 dots per inch. This is a useful technique for improving the quality of type when you use laser proofs for camera-ready copy.

The display type is Bernhard Antique Bold Condensed. This font is not yet available for desktop computers. The designer pasted it into position on the camera-ready pages.

The photos are a good scale for this design. Because they are relatively small, they make the type seem even larger.

*Design (bottom):
Tom Lewis
(San Diego, CA)*

*Brochure for a shopping mall called ¡Viva Tijuana!
Trim size: 12 by 36 double gatefold*

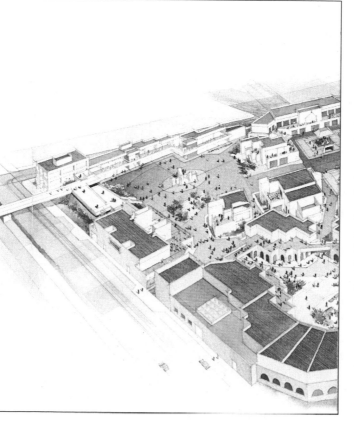

Como una pincelada de increíbles tonalidades. Naranjas, amarillos, verdes, rosas. ¡Viva Tijuana! hace que entre los visitantes renazcan ilusiones y se fortalezcan deseos escondidos. ¡Viva Tijuana! es alegre como el estallido de un cohetón de colores que se abre a la inmensidad de la noche.

Quien piensa en el "Old México", siente que el choque de lo moderno con lo antiguo produce efectos vivificantes, y no desperdicia la oportunidad de disfrutar en ¡Viva Tijuana! de la comodidad de un modernismo arquitectónico en un desarrollo sobre terreno que sabe historias viejas; es la fusión increíble del mañana con el ayer superado por la inteligencia del hombre moderno.

RIVER PARK

Around River Park

Conveniently located in Ulster County, 1-1/2 hours north of New York City, 1/2 hour from Stewart Airport, 15 minutes from the Mid-Hudson Bridge, 5 minutes from the NYS Thruway Exit 18 and the Village of New Paltz with express bus service to NYC and elsewhere.

River Park is just minutes from the Shawangunk Mountains where huge tracts of untouched wilderness include the Mohonk Preserve, a 5,400 acre publicly-accessible land preserve, and Minnewaska State Park covering over 12,000 acres. Numerous hiking trails and over forty miles of carriage roads provide perfect conditions for cross-country skiing, cycling and walking. Public facilities for golf and tennis are located in New Paltz.

New Paltz is famous for Huguenot Street, the oldest street of original homes in the U.S., and for SUNY New Paltz, with its vast educational and cultural facilities. The village boasts unique and interesting shops, diverse night life, and a highly respected public education system.

Area cultural groups and events include the Hudson Valley Philharmonic series, chamber music, concerts, summer theatre, art galleries, museums and open-air concerts.

River Park is surrounded by historic landmarks including the Mohonk Mountain House, West Point, and the Vanderbilt Estate.

The history surrounding River Park is rivaled only by natural and man-made wonders such as the nearby glacial lakes, Mohonk, Min-

newaska and Awosting, with their incredibly clear blue waters and jagged granite-faced shoreline. The cliff faces of the Shawangunk Mountains and old channels and locks from the D & H Canal provide many scenic and recreational possibilities.

The area's growing economic base is led by agriculture, IBM, Stewart Airport, SUNY New Paltz and a host of flourishing smaller businesses. All provide a stable and diverse job market.

An inspiring place, protected and private— River Park offers it all. Enjoy the unparalleled benefits of River Park Cooperative by calling 914-255-7904. Select your homesite and then take a walk in the woods, or meadows , or wander down by the river...

The square shape of the page in the sample above is echoed in the logo, the photos, and the shape of the text block.

High-quality photos of nature set the tone for a real estate development with cooperatively owned wilderness and recreation facilities. The designer chose to let the single photo on the cover sell an image that the inside pages describe.

A coated ivory stock and good printing that holds details in the photos add to the image of quality.

The text is 10/11 Palatino. Again, this is relatively tight leading for body text. Here, the narrow 10-pica column width, the short paragraphs separated by more than a pica of space, and the wide margins ensure readability.

The conference brochure shown below has a highly structured page with banners, rules, boxes, and color tints used to enliven the otherwise straightforward text. The elements are precisely placed in relation to one another. The folio and the rule above it, for example, align with the date to the right and with the black box to the left of the text block.

The single 24-pica column works well on this small page size. On subsequent pages the wide margin is used for bold italic heads set larger than the body text.

The banner to the left of each contents listing is color-coded to the page number. The graduated color tones are picked up as background tints for the respective pages of the brochure; the tints are light enough to ensure legibility of surprinted type.

The Seybold Desktop Publishing Conference is a Seybold Seminars Event

6922 Wildlife Road
Malibu, CA 90265
Telephone: (213) 457-5850
Telex: 6503066263
Fax: 457-4704

SEYBOLD
SEMINARS

Conference Overview

The annual Seybold Desktop Publishing Conference has become the worldwide event-of-record for the burgeoning desktop publishing market, and a "must" occasion for both the publishing and the computer industries.

As the only major computer conference devoted to electronic publishing applications, the Seybold Conference combines a top-level three-day seminar with the world's premier exposition of computer-based publishing solutions. The 1988 Conference takes place September 14 - 17 at the Santa Clara Convention Center in the heart of Silicon Valley. The seminars run Wednesday through Friday, September 14 - 16. The exposition operates Thursday through Saturday, September 15 - 17.

You heard about the 1987 Conference. It brought "PostScript Mania" to the forefront with announcements of Display PostScript and Color PostScript, and the emergence of PostScript printer clones. Other highlights included the launch of desktop presentations, the introduction of "big system" capabilities on the desktop, debates on multi-user networked systems, some lively user sessions on exciting new applications, and a raft of new products.

The 1988 Conference is going to be even better. The market will see many more sophisticated and powerful products, and the collision between Macs, PCs and Unix workstations will be dramatic. Again, the Seybold Conference will be the most exciting (and most valuable) event of the year.

Subscription Series

John Singer Sargent

Kent Lydecker, Executive Director, Department of Museum Education

Tuesday evenings, February 10, 17, 24, and March 3, 6:00-7:00, repeated on Wednesday afternoons, February 11, 18, 25, and March 4, 1:00-2:00

This series complements the *John Singer Sargent* exhibition, on view at the Art Institute February 7 to April 19. Kent Lydecker will present lecture I, II, and IV. Laurel Bradley, Director of Gallery 400, University of Illinois, Chicago, will present lecture III.
I *American Artists Abroad: Sargent in the Expatriate Tradition*
II *The Contemporary Scene: Sargent's Europe*
III *Sargent as a Portraitist*
IV *The Unsung Sargent: The Boston Murals*

John Singer Sargent. *The Fountain, Villa Torlonia, Frascati,* 1907. Oil on canvas. Friends of American Art Collection.

Four 1-hour sessions. Member: $30. Public: $40 Student (with ID) $20. Single tickets sold only at the door on the day of the lecture. Member: $9.50. Public $12. Student (with ID): $5. Meet in Morton Hall.

From Mice to Magic: Film Animation

Moderator: Richard Peña, Director, Film Center, School of the Art Institute

Sunday afternoons, 2:00-3:30, March 15, 22, 29, and April 5

Screen animation is one of the oldest and most popular cinematic traditions — Mickey Mouse is at least as well known internationally as Charlie Chaplin or John Wayne — yet the history and development of the art of animation is usually treated at best as a footnote to film history. In this series, issues in the history of animation, along with exciting new developments in the field,

Betty Boop

will be discussed in lectures featuring the screening of relevant films.

I *Animation in the Silent Cinema: The Pioneers — Emile Cohl, Windsor MacKay, and Lotte Reiniger* Donald Crafton, Professor, University of Wisconsin, Madison, and author of *Before Mickey*
II *Animation in the Studio Era: Mickey Mouse, Betty Boop, and Popeye and Their Creators such as Tex Avery, Chuck Jones, Max Fleischer, and Walt Disney* Maryann Oshana, Northwestern University
III *The Techniques of Screen Animation: cels, pin-screen, sand, clay, puppets, and* "direct animation." Stephanie Maxwell, Visiting Artist, School of the Art Institute, and prize-winning animator
IV *Animation in the Eighties and Future Possibilities* Stephanie Maxwell

Four 1-1/2 hour sessions. Member: $45. Public: $60. Student (with ID) $30. Single tickets sold only at the door on the day of the lecture. Member: $14. Public: $18. Student (with ID): $7.50. Meet in Fullerton Hall.

Baroque and Rococo Art and Architecture in Austria and Bavaria

Robert Eskridge, Lecturer, Department of Museum Education

Monday afternoons, April 6, 13, 20, and 27, 1:00-2:00 repeated on Tuesday evenings, April 7, 14, 21, and 28, 6:00-7:00
Throughout the 18th century a spring-like efflorescence of building and decoration shaped the cities and country villages of Austria and Bavaria. Situated between Italy and France, the region absorbed the best qualities of both to create the distinctive

J.M. Fischer and J.M. Feichtmayr. *Gilded Stucco Cartouche, Priory Church, Diessen, Bavaria.* 1732-34.

monuments of the age. The series traces the Baroque and Rococo from its birth in Rome and Paris to its transformation in Central Europe.

I *The Origins of Baroque and Rococo in Rome and Paris*
II *The Baroque and Rococo in Austria*
III *The Bavarian Rococo Church*
IV *Munich and Würzburg*

Four 1-hour sessions. Member: $30. Public: $40. Student (with ID): $20. Single tickets sold only at the door on the day of the lecture. Member: $9.50 Public: $12. Student (with ID): $5. Meet in Morton Hall.

Johann Bernhard and Joseph Emmanuel Fischer von Erlach. *Karlskirche, Vienna, Austria.* 1716-33.

Design (facing page, top): Wadlin & Erber (New Paltz, NY)

Brochure for the River Park Cooperative. Trim size: 8 by 24 folded twice

Design (facing page, bottom): Weisz, Yang, Dunkelberger, Inc. (Westport, CT)

Brochure for the Seybold Desktop Publishing Conference. Trim size: 6-3/4 by 8-3/8

Design (this page): Mary Grace Quinlan

Subscription programs brochure from The Art Institute of Chicago. Trim size: 4-1/2 by 9

The long, vertical page of the brochure shown above is typical of museum programs. The shape fulfills two very different needs: In its vertical orientation, it is easily racked at information desks and museum stores; in its horizontal orientation, it's a self-mailer.

The two-column grid accommodates several self-contained items on a spread, with headlines in a second color (green here) for easy scanning. Variety on each spread increases the chance of getting the reader's interest.

The body text is 10/11 Garamond. The headlines are 11/13 Garamond bold italic.

Even though the photographs are small, the combination of the narrow page and narrow column width (11 picas) keeps them from looking like postage stamps. Art can also be sized to a two-column width.

This program guide for a TV series, *Islam and the West*, relies heavily on four-color photos to tell its story. The page composition varies considerably from spread to spread, depending on the size and placement of the pictures.

When selecting and placing several photos on a page or spread, keep in mind how they play against one another. When a visually literate eye is at work, as it is here, the photos work together to make a dynamic composition.

Contrast in subject, scale, direction, and color all contribute to the composition. It shows travel by land, travel by sea, and the gold coin that was the very reason for these century-old trade routes. The caravan moves back into the picture plane, the ship moves in a plane perpendicular to the caravan, and the movement of both contrasts with the still life of the coins.The vastness of the mountains makes the caravan seem small, and the coins smaller still. Consider also the visual forms themselves—the jagged mountains, the linear caravan, the circular coins, and the rickety lines of the ship.

The headline treatment at the top of each spread provides a strong unifying element given this varied compositon. The 3-point rule runs from one outer margin to the gutter, bleeding across the gutter (unless there is a full-bleed picture on one page of the spread).

The type is New Baskerville.

Design: Ira Friedlander (New York, NY)

Program guide for Islam and the West, *a television film series.*
Trim Size: 6 by 9

5. TRADE AND COMMERCE

Islam seeks never to separate everyday life from religion. A person's livelihood and his beliefs are linked and he is taught that social and economic justice—and charity—are worthy matters. Thus Islam has always supplied trade and commerce with a formidable religious base.

After the death of the Prophet, both the religion of Islam and Muslim political and economic domination spread with amazing rapidity. So, outward from the heartland of Islam they came—Muslims traders travelling up and down the coast of Africa, across the Sahara, over the Silk Route to China, through the Indian Ocean to the Orient.

The sea routes, which the Muslims controlled, were crucial for the economic life of the Islamic world, as well as for trade between the Far East and Europe. Accounts of travel by sea to distant lands captured the imagination of Islamic peoples and entered into their literature in stories such as 'Sinbad the Sailor' in The Thousand and One Nights.

Over the land routes, traders carried ideas along with spices, silk and paper from the East to the Islamic world and through it to the West. Traders also played a role in the transmission of technology, for example in bringing paper and papermaking from China.

The importance of travel in their lives led Muslims to develop geography on a global scale. Always in their journeys, they relied on a singularly important instrument, the astrolabe. The astrolabe gave these traders their bearings, and gave the West the tool with which to reach the New World. Columbus would have been lost without his astrolabe and maps plotted by Muslim traders. Prince Henry the Navigator depended not only on that device, he also had a Muslim pilot .

Everywhere they went, the Muslim traders brought the Quran, their book of guidance, as well as their science, their art, and their culture.

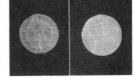

To this day caravans of camels still travel the Silk Route, long the only land link between East and West.
Left, Omani dhow.
Right, Islamic coins.

The cover art was derived from a piece of clip art that was digitized with Thunderscan, saved as a Mac-Paint document, and enlarged in PageMaker. The effective, bit-mapped result bears little resemblance to the fine-line style of the original art. It prints burgundy on a tan background. The same art was reduced for use as a decorative element at the bottom of each page.

The "border within a border" page frame provides a space for the organization's name letterspaced across the top of each page. This open spacing creates an effective and delicate treatment for a running head; you'll see it used in many different ways throughout this book (including our own running heads). Note that the page frame is asymmetrical at the top and bottom, which keeps the page from being too rigid.

The underlying three-column grid used throughout the brochure is carried through on the cover (where one column is used for the title and the other two combine to provide a wide column for art) and on the spread of photos (where the two inner columns on each page have been divided in half to accommodate small mug shots).

The photos were sized and cropped so that all the heads appear approximately the same size and with the same eye level. This technique, which is particularly important when you group mug shots in a linear fashion, gives equal importance to all of the photos and helps minimize their varying reproduction quality. Imagine what a hodgepodge this page would be if all the heads were different sizes.

Design: John McWade, PageLab (Sacramento, CA)

Pages from the Sacramento Regional Foundation Yearbook.
Trim size: 11 by 8-1/2

**Our Professionals
Our Firm**

We measure our competence by your success in adapting to change - and helping you take full advantage of the opportunities change can bring.

At Doane Raymond, we make it our business to keep abreast of current developments. Your success in dealing with change and the opportunities it brings is a measure of our competence. The same philosophy applies to our own business. By using the latest methods and technologies we assure you, our client, of quality service at a fair price.

You need professionals with management knowledge and financial skills. Our investment in training and promoting bright, energetic individuals translates for you into professionals who possess sharp skills and a current, practical knowledge of the business world. Others recognize our leadership. Many of our partners and staff play leading and advisory roles in the accounting profession, business associations, government agencies, and community organizations.

Such involvement and leadership is a great teacher. You, as our client, receive the benefits that a seasoned professional staff can bring to your activities. Solid auditing by our experienced staff yields dependable and practical advice. We respond quickly to your problems, bringing a diversity of experience.

Implementing the latest technologies to assure you of quality service at a fair price.

Giving answers when you need them.

Communication is as crucial to you as it is to us. We talk with our clients. Whether it is a phone call, a meeting, or a report, our professionals know you must have answers. We provide those answers - when you need them.

Partners providing practical advice on your financial activities.

As a Doane Raymond client, you can expect a partner's attention whenever you need it. That same partner is an active member of your community: someone who understands the local business environment and can provide practical advice. In the city or town where you do business, we are there.

An accounting firm presents a clean, organized look in this brochure without being at all stuffy or staid.

The format is built around large photos on the left-hand page and two off-center text columns with smaller photos on the right-hand page. The large photos are nicely framed by a white background and are sized consistently from one spread to the next. The right-hand pages are solid tan, giving the appearance of a different paper stock. The smaller photos are the same size throughout the brochure and their placement bounces about the text columns.

The Bodoni text has very open leading. The italic captions print in blue, as do the subheads, initial caps, and rules that bleed off the top of the left-hand pages.

Captions stating the company's philosophy print in tan banners that match the color of the right-hand pages. The position of this tint block moves around from page to page, but it always overlaps the photo and the white border. This technique is currently a popular graphic device.

Design: Bill Westheuser, Communication Design Group Limited (Halifax, Nova Scotia)

Brochure from Doane Raymond Accountants.
Trim size: 8-1/2 by 11

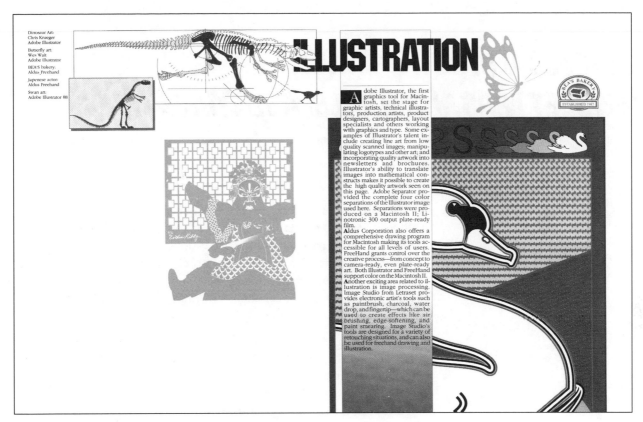

This brochure was produced by a commercial printer to showcase the art and technology of desktop publishing. (It bears mentioning that many printers are less than enthusiastic about desktop technology because it will increasingly move prepress work from the print shop to the publisher.)

The layout is built around columns of type, all the same measure but positioned on the page as free-form art objects. Each type column prints over a different graduated colored tone, which increases in darkness from top to bottom. The tones were created in Cricket Draw.

The art is placed around the type in different ways, depending on the individual pieces. In spite of the absence of a visible grid, the placement is always rectilinear, never haphazard. It takes considerable skill to make each spread function independently and still have a unifying visual style throughout the brochure.

The illustrations on the spread shown were created in Adobe Illustrator (dinosaur and butterfly), Aldus FreeHand (Japanese actor and bakery logo), and Illustrator 88 (the transformation of an S into a swan).

Design: Wes Wait (Portland, OR)

Pages from Extending the Benefits of Desktop Publishing *produced by Dynagraphics.*
Trim size: 8-1/2 by 11

CHAPTER 6

PERIODICALS: NEWSLETTERS, JOURNALS, AND MAGAZINES

Regardless of subject, style, or frequency, the challenge common to all periodicals is to establish a strong identity that remains both familiar and fresh issue after issue. The subject, the tone, and the overall package and format should be unmistakably one's own, clearly established and consistently maintained over time. But within that familiar package it's the fresh ideas, the unexpected images, the new ways of presenting recurring themes that keep readers interested.

Once audience and editorial focus of a periodical is established, the foundation for the balancing act between the familiar and the new is the graphic format. This includes everything from logo and cover design to the treatment of feature stories and housekeeping details (mastheads, letters, calendars, and so on). Items that appear in every issue, such as contents listings, review columns, and news sections, should have a recognizable style and a relatively constant page position from one issue to the next. If there is advertising, the format must take into consideration where in the publication ads will appear, how to handle fractional ads, and how to distinguish clearly between ads and editorial items, especially when they appear on the same spread.

A format that works not only defines your image, it also determines how hard you'll work to produce each issue. A format consistent with your resources spells the difference between efficient and chaotic production. Desktop technology can streamline production tremendously, eliminating the days it used to take to turn manuscript into typeset galleys and to correct galleys as deadlines approached. The technology also gives editors and designers much greater control over the material through every step of the production cycle, allowing more refinement later in the process than was previously possible.

But established periodicals have established production systems. Converting to desktop publishing means that many functions previously performed by outside vendors are brought in-house to staffs that may already feel overworked. The technology is changing the roles of editors, designers, production managers, and layout artists in ways that are too new to be fully understood or predictable and that vary from one organization to another. If you are contemplating or are in the process of making the transition to desktop publishing, expect to spend six to twelve months evolving systems and roles. Talk with other people who have made the transition, and evaluate their experience within the context of your own product and the strengths and weaknesses of your staff. The benefits are ultimately everything they're alleged to be, but the transition can be quite a roller coaster.

NEWSLETTERS

Thousands and thousands of newsletters are published in this country. Whether for internal circulation or public relations, for marketing products or services, for raising money or raising consciousness, most newsletters exist to communicate specialized information to a targeted audience on a regular basis. It's essential to really understand your specialized audience and what you hope to accomplish through the newsletter. You should be able to define not just a general purpose but very specific benefits that your organization can measure as a result of publishing the newsletter.

Unlike magazines, which usually have a staff dedicated to creating and producing the publication, newsletters are often produced by people who perform other functions for an organization. It's very important to match the newsletter format to the time and resources you'll have to produce it. If you're starting a new newsletter or making the transition from traditional to electronic production, you might consider using a free-lance designer, experienced in electronic publishing, to create a format and electronic templates consistent with your needs and resources. This may give you a much smarter look than you could achieve with an in-house design and still yield the cost savings of in-house production.

Newsletters in this section

- *Newservice*—the appeal and accessibility of a modular format
- *Friends of Omega*—on composing photos on the page
- *Apple viewpoints*—a simple wide and narrow column format
- *The Preston Report*—numbers as graphics
- *Nooz*—playfulness in a five-column tabloid
- *The Wire*—newspaper-style flair for a four-color in-house monthly
- *The Freeze Beacon*—magazine-style features in a newsletter format
- *Consumer Markets Abroad*—a format for charts and graphs
- *Perspectives*—a more open version of the two-and-a-half column grid
- *Indications*—marketing analysis with dimensional art
- *O'Connor Quarterly*—a friendly and sophisticated people-publication
- *AmeriNews*—one approach to a tabloid format
- *Re:*—another approach to a tabloid format
- *Litigation News*—typographic variety for all-text pages
- *ThePage*—the impact of strong cover concepts

For hands-on instructions for creating newsletters, see Projects 3 and 4 in Section 3.

A highly organized, modular format takes editorial planning and attention to detail when you assemble the pages but is very appealing and easy to read.

The cover uses multiple "sell" devices to get the reader's attention: a strong bit-mapped photo and caption with boldface leadin, a headline for a related story inset in the cover story, and a contents box.

The bold rules are printed in a second color that changes with each issue. They are 15-point solid boxes, heavier than the rules on PageMaker's Lines menu, which allows ample room for reverse type (Avant Garde, with extra letterspacing).

Art (below) **and pull quotes** (not shown) break the grid at the top of the page. Pull quotes are set short of a two-column measure and are bordered by a vertical rule on the left margin that descends into the text block area. Pull quotes and rules, which print in the second color, are also placed inside columns to break up text in full-page stories.

Design: Jim Parker (Phoenix, AZ)

Pages from Newservice, published bimonthly by the Do It Now Foundation. Size: 8-1/2 by 11

The photographs available for most newsletters lack both the impact and the reproduction quality that would allow them to stand alone on the page. But when you group photos with an eye both to editorial content and the visual relationship that will be created between them, the whole can be greater than the sum of its parts.

Three photos often form an ideal combination. Two alone form only a one-on-one, back-and-forth relationship. Add a third, and you have a new and more dynamic chemistry. Four together will often start to pair off, and you're back with two's again. And visually, three photos can create an interesting triangular path for the reader's eye to follow.

In the example shown here, the photos promote summer workshops at a holistic learning center. The selection balances a single, silhouetted musician, a group seated casually at an outdoor seminar, and a third photo suggesting both the quiet time away from workshops and the recently improved wheelchair access on the campus.

When positioning photos on the page, consider where each picture will take the reader's eye, the relative size of the subjects, the lights and darks, and the horizon lines.

Three strong directions in these photos create visual energy that moves your eye from one picture to another. The silhouetted photo is looking away from the page; the lecturers standing in the group picture are looking into the page; and the figures shown from behind take your eye back into the page.

The people are captured in front views, back views, and profiles, and they are scaled differently in their individual environments. The uniformity of size generally recommended for head-and-shoulder portraits would make a group of casual photos such as this seem too static.

Silhouetting a photo, as in the top picture, can improve it by removing extraneous background images. The original photo in this instance included a group of people seated behind the subject; removing them focuses attention on the subject and also provides an interesting shape to work with. The freeform shape can be considerably larger than the other pictures without being out of balance. And you can rag the copy along the edge of the silhouette, which integrates the type and the photos. In this case, the photo was scanned in to produce a working on-screen image to help define the rag. But for better reproduction in print, a halftone was shot from the original photo and stripped in by the printer.

Visual illusions can be part of the unseen structure in a group of images. In the bottom two pictures, the horizon lines seem to meet, so that for a moment they appear to create a single panorama; the space between them creates the effect of a window on the scene. Opening up the picture plane in this way creates a sense of perspective and gives dimension to the page.

Design: Don Wright (Woodstock, NY)

Pages from Friends of Omega Newsletter, *published by the Omega Institute. Trim size: 8-1/2 by 11*

Apple *viewpoints*

Apple News and Perspectives for the Developer Community

Published weekly by Apple Developer Services   September 12, 1988

Apple Integrated Systems Meets MIS Corporate Needs

Chuck Berger, Vice President, Apple Integrated Systems

In April of 1988, Apple made the decision to form Apple Integrated Systems. As the head of this new group at Apple, I'd like to take a few minutes to tell you about the reasoning behind the creation of Apple Integrated Systems—how we plan to accomplish our mission, and how it will affect you as a developer.

A lot has changed in the Macintosh® world over the past three and a half years. Macintosh has gone from a relatively simple machine to a broad product line including the Mac® II workstation.

"...our customers view Macintosh as the workstation component of their emerging enterprise-wide communications and information systems."

Additionally, we have gone from a handful of applications, peripherals, and virtually no communications capability to literally thousands of application options, complimented by powerful peripherals that have the ability for Macintosh to communicate in virtually any computing or communications environment.

As the capabilities and breadth of solutions that Macintosh offered grew, so did its popularity in the business marketplace. Macintosh has gone from being a relative unknown in the business world to being a strong niche player in the desktop publishing area, to finally being accepted as a general productivity tool throughout the business world.

While that has been great news for all of us, there is even better news ahead. The increased power of Macintosh and the broader range of solutions and applications we can offer, with the help of software and peripherals created by third-party developers, have led our customers to view Macintosh as *the* workstation component of their emerging enterprise-wide communications and information systems.

Continued on next page

NEWSBRIEFS

Special Events at AppleFest

Developer Services Suite
The Developer Services staff will host a hospitality suite at AppleFest® for those of you who would like to come by and talk with us, see demos of *The Information Exchange*, and get answers to your questions. We'll be in Room 106 in the San Francisco Civic Auditorium on Friday, September 16th from 3:00 to 5:00 P.M. Refreshments will be available.

Technical Forum
Bring your Apple® II and IIGS® technical issues with you to the San Francisco AppleFest this month. Apple II engineers, product managers, and writers are gathering each day to "talk tech" with you.
Place: *Brooks Hall, Room 314.*
Time: *Fri.-Sat. 1:30-2:30 P.M.*
    Sun. 1:00-2:00 P.M.
The forum is a special opportunity to discuss your technical questions, suggestions, and needs with the Apple II and IIGS development team. The technical focus will be on programming and hardware

Continued on next page

In this two-column format, the wide column is used for a single essay that continues from the cover to the two inside pages. The narrow column is used for short news items. A simple and effective format editorially and graphically, it is also remarkably easy to execute.

Production takes less than two days. Unformatted word-processor files are sent from Apple to the art production house via AppleLink on Tuesday afternoon. By 10 A.M. Wednesday, copyedited, formatted text has been placed in an electronic dummy and faxed to Apple. Apple phones in corrections by 11, a revised page is faxed to Apple by 1 P.M., and additional corrections are phoned in if necessary. The courier picks up at 4 for delivery to the printer by 5. If you're tempted to say, "Yes, but that's Apple…," consider instead "Yes, keep it simple."

The condensed Garamond text face is made especially for Apple by Adobe. (Well, yes, that *is* Apple….)

Design: The Compage Company (San Francisco, CA)

Cover of Apple viewpoints, *published biweekly by Apple Developer Services.*
Size: 8-1/2 by 11

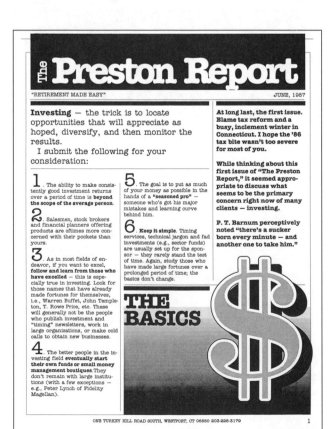

The Preston Report

"RETIREMENT MADE EASY"   JUNE, 1987

Investing — the trick is to locate opportunities that will appreciate as hoped, diversify, and then monitor the results.

I submit the following for your consideration:

1. The ability to make consistently good investment returns over a period of time is **beyond the scope of the average person.**

2. Salesmen, stock brokers and financial planners offering products are oftimes more concerned with their pockets than yours.

3. As in most fields of endeavor, if you want to excel, **follow and learn from those who have excelled** — this is especially true in investing. Look for those names that have already made fortunes for themselves, i.e., Warren Buffet, John Templeton, T. Rowe Price, etc. They will generally not be the people who publish investment and "timing" newsletters, work in large organizations, or make cold calls to obtain new businesses.

4. The better people in the investing field **eventually start their own funds or small money management boutiques.** They don't remain with large institutions (with a few exceptions — e.g., Peter Lynch of Fidelity Magellan).

5. The goal is to put as much of your money as possible in the hands of a **"seasoned pro"** — someone who's got his major mistakes and learning curve behind him.

6. **Keep it simple.** Timing services, technical jargon and fad investments (e.g., sector funds) are usually set up for the sponsor — they rarely stand the test of time. Again, study those who have made large fortunes over a prolonged period of time; the basics don't change.

At long last, the first issue. Blame tax reform and a busy, inclement winter in Connecticut. I hope the '86 tax bite wasn't too severe for most of you.

While thinking about this first issue of "The Preston Report," it seemed appropriate to discuss what seems to be the primary concern right now of many clients — investing.

P. T. Barnum perceptively noted "there's a sucker born every minute — and another one to take him."

THE BASICS

ONE TURKEY HILL ROAD SOUTH, WESTPORT, CT 06880 203-226-3179   1

Bold headlines are assertive, while the American Typewriter face is friendly. The combination is just right for financial advice to retirees.

Introductory copy set to a two-column measure and larger than the body text, helps draw readers into the page and effectively varies the basic three-column grid.

Large numbers (these are 32 point) make lists appealing and function as graphic elements.

The three-layer dollar sign was created in Illustrator and stretched in PageMaker. The font is Bodoni, one of the few with a double downstroke in the dollar sign. The top sign has a 5-point white Stroke and a 30 percent black Fill; the middle one has a 6-point black Stroke to produce the outline; the bottom sign is solid black, set off to create a drop shadow.

The shaded box was created in Cricket Draw. The rotated "The" in the nameplate was imported from Illustrator.

Design: John Odam (San Diego, CA)

Design for The Preston Report *created as a "Page Makeover" for* Publish! *magazine.*
Size: 8-1/2 by 11

Playfulness is the signature of this tabloid monthly newsletter. The typewriter look of Courier sets the casual tone, and every design element follows through in kind.

Mug shots don't have to be boring. The shapes used here only begin to suggest some ingenious ways to treat both casual and posed snapshots. The stars were created in MacDraw, and the other shapes in PageMaker. Photos were stripped in as halftones by the printer.

Letters as visual puns provide more play in the rebus-like graphic. The type was set in PageMaker. The eye was digitized in MacVision from a photo cropped very tight, saved as a MacPaint file, and scaled in PageMaker. The bee was drawn in MacPaint.

The digitized courthouse art is treated as a vignette, with the edges gradually fading into the background of the page. (The effect was created in MacPaint from a MacVision scan.)

The rotated photo provides an opportunity for an unusual caption treatment, with the names of those pictured angled into the photo.

For all the spontaneity in the treatment of graphic elements, the five-column grid provides the necessary understructure.

Design: Paul Souza (Boston, MA)

Pages from Nooz, *published quarterly by WGBH radio.*

Trim size: 11 by 17

The spread from THE WIRE showing the "AROUND CHAMPION" feature page, including photographs, the FORTUNE 100 Paper Companies chart, line art, a LeRoy Neiman print, and the Champion United Way Campaign chart.

This house organ for an international corporation is formatted as a monthly newspaper. The spread shown, a standing feature in every issue, reports "news, events, awards, and issues…from locations throughout North America."

The art is as varied as you'll find in any publication, with charts, photos, paintings, line art, and even a magazine cover contributing to a very spirited page.

The five-column format provides several advantages for a feature with so many pieces. Art can be sized anywhere from one to three columns wide and placed in overlapping columns to make an already lively spread even more dynamic. Narrow columns accommodate the numerous subheads without eating up too much space and give sufficient depth to items that are only 25 to 50 words long. These short text blocks would look like captions in a wider margin.

The cover features a different employee each issue, in the context of his or her committment to some community organization. The typographic treatment of the "Snapshot" text reinforces the informal, personal approach of this cover concept. Depending on the photo, the orientation may be horizontal (as shown here) or vertical.

Design: Weisz Yang Dunkelberger Inc. (Westport, CT)

Pages from THE WIRE, *published monthly by Champion International Corporation. Trim size: 11 by 15*

VOLUME II NO.4 FALL 1987

NAVY WHISTLEBLOWER SPEAKS OUT See Page 6

THE BEACON

Quarterly Newsletter of SANE/FREEZE of San Diego

INF TREATY

An Open Letter to Reagan and Gorbachev

Our organization congratulates both of you for your leadership and courage in bringing about a tentative agreement to eliminate all intermediate nuclear missiles in Europe and Asia. For many years we have been campaigning vigorously to reduce the threat of nuclear war. Now you have heard us!

We look to you, Mr. Reagan, to use your considerable influence with those members of the Senate who oppose arms control to help bring about the ratification of the INF Treaty. We further urge you to do your utmost to oppose any amendments that might defeat its purpose.

We look to you, Mr. Gorbachev, to continue your initiatives to improve the relations between our countries. Allay the fears that your large military forces create in Western Europe by bringing about balanced reductions in offensive conventional weapons. Help to avert a conventional arms buildup to offset the loss of nuclear weapons.

And we ask that neither of you lose sight of the fact that, while an agreement to reduce one particularly provocative and dangerous type of nuclear weapon is greatly welcomed, it will not in itself end the arms race. Nor will it repair the damage done by the scuttling of other arms limitation treaties. Significant though the agreement may be, it will reduce the total world nuclear arsenal only by a slight amount.

Finally, since it is the stated goal of both nations to reduce all nuclear weapons by at least 50%, let us call an **immediate bilateral halt to the testing, production and deployment of any further nuclear weapons systems.** It makes no sense to eliminate some weapons with one hand while creating many more with the other.

Signed, San Diego SANE/FREEZE

MEET THE PRESIDENT

Rev Coffin's Vision for SANE/FREEZE

The following is an edited version of the article by Kathleen Hendrix of the Los Angeles Times which appeared in that paper October 15, 1987. Our Executive Director, David Carpenter, attended the meeting with Rev..Coffin who, when he saw the Beacon, raved about its content and professionalism.

It was a hot night, ending one of several days in which the air refused to budge, and the meeting of the (Southern California regional) chapter of SANE/Freeze was slow to come to order. The 20 or so wilted people gathered in the community room of an apartment building in Hollywood, mixed themselves instant coffee, spread out notices of other meetings ... and waited for the Rev. William Sloane Coffin, Jr., to arrive.

In he came, looking rumpled and slightly paunchy, shirt open at the throat and sleeves rolled up. He appeared undaunted by the heat, ... and with a friendly grin in place, strode across the room relaxed and affable, clapping back at the people who stood to applaud him."It's neat," he told the group, "to get a chance to see what's going on." For many in that room, it was, in return, a chance to meet the legend, and their new national president.

Coffin became a household word during the '60's, when as chaplain at Yale he became a civil rights and anti-Vietnam War activist, joining freedom rides, marching in the South, collecting draft cards with Dr. Benjamin Spock, speaking out and getting arrested over and over again.

Coffin did not start his life this way. Born to wealth, his family founded the W. & J. Sloane furniture business. He first considered a career as a concert pianist, and then a diplomat. He was an Army liaison officer to the French and Soviet armies during World War II, and a CIA officer in West Germany during the Korean War, training anti-communist Russians for work within the Soviet Union. Finally, he said only half-jokingly ..., he lost the battle to stay out of the ministry. World War II had raised too many of the right questions

Last July, saying the timing in history was right, Coffin announced he would step down as senior minister of New York City's Riverside Church at the end of 1987 to become the first president of SANE/Freeze. In creating the position of President, over that of the co-directors of the newly merged groups, the SANE/Freeze ... board announced it was looking for someone to "articulate the vision." If there is one thing Bill Coffin can do, it is articulate the vision. And shape it. It is not without reason that he calls his new job with the secular organization "a full-time peace and justice ministry." . . . As he defines it, the SANE/Freeze (people) join him in a "disarmament and development" organization, concerned with

Continued on page 10

1

A tightly structured nameplate, along with the headline and folio treatments, creates a strong identity for this newsletter. The lighthouse incorporated into the logo is a recognizable local landmark. The banner with reverse type at the top of the cover highlights the feature article shown in the spread below.

A scanned photo on the cover is treated as a posterlike portrait of the subject, producing a more effective result than trying to make a bit-mapped image look like a halftone.

A magazine-style feature provides a change of pace, editorially and visually, from the modular format elsewhere in the newsletter. The bit-mapped art ironically conjures up the image of video games in a story that is all too much anchored in the real world. The art was created in MacPaint and stretched across the two pages in PageMaker.

The typeface is Palatino. Varying the size and measure of individual headlines creates emphasis without the need to change the typeface.

Design:
John Odam
(San Diego, CA)

Pages from The Freeze Beacon, *published quarterly by San Diegans for a Bilateral Nuclear Weapons Freeze. Size: 8-1/2 by 11*

THE BEACON

WASTE & FRAUD

ONE MAN'S NAVY: A CASE STUDY IN DISILLUSIONMENT

By Pat Cegelka

***Editor's Note:** This narrative is based primarily on the written and oral reports of the interviewee. The Beacon interviewed Darrell McGee and reviewed written documents from his service record; it made no independent investigation to verify the facts as reported here.*

Attending our last newsletter team meeting was someone new to our group, an open-faced, eager young man recently discharged from the Navy. He had learned about SANE/FREEZE through his wife's contact with one of our members. He joined us in hopes of finding kindred spirits and sympathetic ears. Dressed in a sports jacket and tie, nervous, unsure about what to expect from us, and eager to tell his story, he shared with us his committment to peaceful resolutions of international conflict. And he told of his disillusionment with the military.

Darrell McGee, from Illinois, joined the Navy in 1976, shortly after high school graduation. He signed up while still a high school senior as part of the delayed entry program. At that time he felt that it was the best thing that ever happened to him. He was pleased with the lifestyle and thrilled with the opportunities that it afforded; and he was proud to be a part of what he believed to be the fine traditions of the military.

From the beginning he was successful, receiving two years of specialized training and then being stationed in San Diego as a Missile Fire Control Technician, Terrier Missile System. During this tour of duty he made two Western Pacific Deployments. Although he loved his work and enjoyed the travel, chronic sea sickness rendered him unable to function at sea and he was reassigned for additional training. Numerous awards and certificates document his subsequent educational and military successes while at NAS, Memphis, preparing to become an Aviation Electronics Technician for S-3A Viking Aircraft. His success in this role led to his transfer to the Quality Assurance Division as a Quality Assurance Inspector. It was in this role that Darrell first began to question the way things were done and the rightness of military ways. It was here that Darrell's disillusionment began.

It soon became clear to him that many of his fellow inspectors, apparently with the blessing of the Command, were cutting corners on established maintenance procedures. These acts jeopardized the safety of aircraft crews and, to Darrell's way of thinking, nullified the reasons for having *quality* control inspectors. Pressure to complete the job faster and to record high percentages of mission-capable aircraft on the daily status reports appeared to take precedence over safety considerations or concerns for personal honesty.

Transferred to Line Division, Darrell's dedication and hard work lead to his promotion to Leading Petty Officer of the Division (i.e., head supervisor for 70 people over four work shifts), where his success in preparing the Division for a major Administrative/Materials Inspection led to his being commended by the Admiral in command. Next he attended advanced electronics training at the Naval Air Technical Training Center, Memphis. Returning once again to San Diego where he was soon promoted to Chief Petty Officer, AirAntiSubmarine Squadron Twenty-One (VS-21), Naval Air Station, North Island, becoming Maintenance Control Chief for the day shift, he was responsible to his superiors for a wide variety of activities. These included such responsibilities as: assigning job control priorities to all supply maintenance and aircraft material supply requisitions; directing and controlling all aircraft cannibalization actions; maintaining current aircraft status on the VIDS boards at all times; assigning all production tasks to the appropriate work centers; submitting configuration, readiness, and flight reports; reviewing all discrepancies; and keeping his superiors advised of all special or unusual requirements or conditions that arose.

Almost immediately Darrell learned that part of his job responsibility was preparing two versions of maintenance reports. One, the *internal* version, accurately reported the maintenance needs of the fleet's equipment, while the *external* version provided a misleadingly optimistic picture of the equipment's condition. The two reports were stapled together, with three copies being forwarded up the chain of command to the Commanding Officer of the squadron. From there, the *external* falsified version was forwarded on to the COM ASW Wing PAC, in this case Admiral Rich (now stationed in Washington D. C.), while the accurate *internal* report was retained at the Command level.

When Darrell approached his supervisor about this, he was told that there was nothing that either of them could do until a new commanding officer took charge. When the subsequent change of command did not address the practice of falsifying documents, Darrell again approached his immediate superior. This time he was told not to worry about things that did not concern him, not to make waves, to do as he was told and to be a

THE BEACON

team player.

He then sought advice from other Chief Petty Officers, hoping to gain assistance from his peers on how to reverse the falsification practices. Instead, they told him that he was being unrealistic and idealistic, that he was not properly attuned to the "real world." His peers explained that lying on official documents, falsifying readiness reports and status reports, and similar dishonesties were not only routine, but viewed as necessary for making rank.

After months of agonizing, Darrell decided that he would have to abandon the military career that he had once wanted so fervently. The price of staying was too high in terms of his personal values.

Darrell's experiences with the Navy did not end with his decision to leave. His immediate superior attempted to persuade Darrell to remain in the Navy; failing that, he warned him not to reveal to the Command his decision to leave at the end of his enlistment period in the summer of 1987. He was told that the Command would not take kindly to having someone at his rank resign. In late December, 1986, he notified the Commanding Officer of his decision to leave the Navy the following July.

Darrell was then relieved of his duties as Maintenance Control Chief and given a make-shift job. Harrassed by his former supervisor and the Command in general, he was finally transferred out of the Command, an action that Darrell maintains was illegal. He spent the remaining two months of his military career at Base General Services and was honorably discharged on July 9, 1987.

Disillusioned though he was, Darrell still believed that good could prevail.

Following his discharge, he met with Congressman Duncan Hunter as well as Congressman Jim Bates. Darrell learned from both Congressmen that his story of wholesale falsification of military documents had been heard before. Congressman Bates reported that he already had initiated a similar investigation through the Inspector General's Office. This encouraged Darrell to approach the Office of the Inspector General, where he talked with Special Agent Kevin A. Keating of the Defense Criminal Investigative Service. Darrell has been told that Keating's two-page report has been sent to the Naval Investigative Service, who should contact him soon. Finally, Darrell has phoned the Defense reporter for the *San Diego Union*. The promised interview has never materialized.

Darrell no longer believes that wars can be won. He knows too much about the military. He knows about its rotation schedule for cannibalizing equipment (moving parts from functioning planes to nonfunctioning ones) in order to report high readiness rates in any given reporting period. He knows about the casual and routine falsification of the documents from which the nation depends for data on its military "readiness." He knows about the career ambitions of officers, about lying and cheating for advancement, about the practices of the "real world" — a world to which Darrell chose not to adapt.

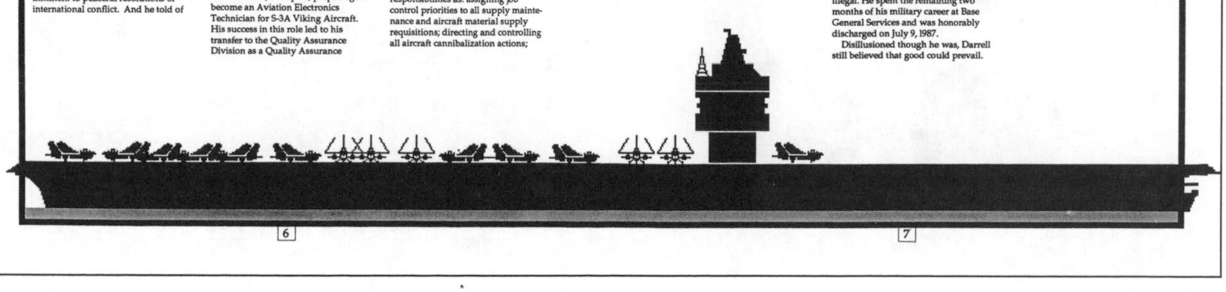

6

7

A two-and-a-half-column format is ideal for accommodating charts, graphs, and tables of different sizes. The narrow column works well for headlines and pull quotes, too. The running text always begins at the top of the page, and the charts are positioned flush with the bottom margin. Occasionally graphics are positioned one on top of another. Given the diversity of the visuals, this consistent placement brings order to pages that might otherwise feel haphazard.

Hairline rules create a half-page frame; a second half-frame brackets the main text block. This motif is adapted for the charts, where the headline and the half-frame are inside a box and alternate from the left to right side. This device might appear contrived in some publications, but it is both functional and subtly decorative here.

Tables are created in Microsoft Word and placed in PageMaker following what the managing editor describes as the Golden Rules of Tabs: Use only one tab for each column of data. (If you need more space between two columns, reset the tabs; do not insert two tabs to increase the space). Do not use the space bar to adjust space between columns. Be sure to specify left, right, or center alignment. And work in the word-processing program at the same column width you will use in your page layout.

Charts are created in Cricket Graph. Maps are drawn by hand and stripped in by the printer.

Design: Carol Terrizzi (Ithaca, NY)

Pages from Consumer Markets Abroad, *published monthly by American Demographics. Trim size: 8-1/2 by 11*

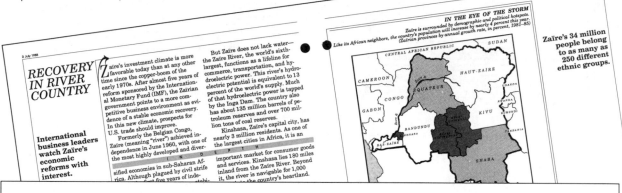

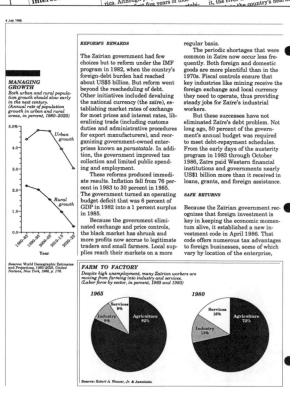

The two-and-a-half-column format has a very different look when it breaks up the text with banners, boxed copy, and illustrations.

Note the absence of rules to separate columns and define the image area. With the wide margin and generous space around headlines, the text block provides sufficient definition. A format with more tightly packed pages would need rules to delineate the elements.

The wide margin is used for quotes, a contents listing, and photos (not shown) that extend an additional 2-1/2 picas into the first text column.

Crimson banners with reverse Garamond type are used for department-style headlines.

The headlines and marginal quotes are Helvetica. The running text is Garamond.

The type prints in blue on bone-colored stock. Boxed copy prints over lavender or light blue tints. A blue tone prints over photos as well.

Design: Partners by Design (N. Hollywood, CA); Agency: Jonisch Communications (Los Angeles, CA)

Pages from Perspectives, published quarterly by the Transamerica Life Companies. Size: 8-1/2 by 11

The reproduced newsletter pages:

IMPACT

Perspectives

Vol. 3 No. 2 Spring, 1988 — Reporting on legislative and political issues

Outlook for AIDS testing looks up, six bills propose eliminating ban

"California now is the only state that forbids AIDS antibody or HIV testing."

The California Legislature's long standing claim to fame is its volume of bills introduced each session. This year is no exception. By the Feb. 19 deadline for new bills, over 7,500 bills were introduced, of which 147 addressed AIDS. These legislative proposals range in subject matter from confidentiality laws, to extensions of HIV testing to provisions for research and education.

Of greatest interest to TLC are six bills that would repeal the prohibition (contained in AB 403, passed in 1985) against antibody testing of insurance applicants for exposure to the AIDS virus. California now is the only state that forbids AIDS antibody or HIV testing. Each measure proposes to authorize health care service plans, nonprofit hospital service plans and/or life and disability insurers to establish mandatory and uniform minimum requirements for assessing AIDS risks for purposes of determining insurability. Specifically, these are: AB 2900 (Johnston, Isenberg); AB 3305 (Johnston); AB 3421 (McClintock); AB 3538 (Johnson; AB 4036 (Mojonnier); and AB 4450 (Peace).

From a political perspective, both AB 2900

Continued on page 2

INSIDE PERSPECTIVES

Political Profile — *Johnston guides Insurance Committee* 3

Who says a vote doesn't count? 3

PAC Talk — *Political pundit offers view on presidential races* 4

Presidential Politics — *Who has what it takes?* 4

June ballot propositions 5

Keeping numbers straight 5

Constituent Action — *TLC to cosponsor AIDS conference* 6

Single premium life:
Congress has mixed view of issue, while industry juggles positions

Threatening serious consequences for the life insurance industry, the confusion continues to grow over the issue of taxation of single premium policies. During March, the House and Senate each held separate subcommittee hearings on single premium and other investment-oriented life insurance products. The general consensus at the conclusion of the hearings was that it seemed unlikely that the current law will be retained without changes.

Due to marketing practices of some companies, many members of Congress view single-premium policies as "tax loopholes." The likelihood of changing the current law is further enhanced by the life insurance industry's disagreement on an accepted industry-wide position. Major life insurance trade associations are advocating different positions or approaches to the problem.

View from the Hill

Continued on page 2

PAC Talk
Political pundit offers view of presidential races

"Despite the fact that Americans are in the mood for a change, there simply isn't enough momentum for the Democrats to get back in the White House."

Described as the "nation's hot new political pundit," political analyst William Schneider set the stage for his observations of the presidential primary campaigns with a few personal definitions before offering any commentary or opinion at the TALCPAC 200 Club breakfast:

"A pundit is someone who comes on to the field of battle after the fighting stops and then shoots the wounded," he explained. "The primary is the 'killing ground' where they try to kill off the candidates. But this year, they all refuse to die!"

Of course, since that Feb. 19 breakfast, the field of presidential candidates has dwindled considerably. In any event, Schneider's perceptions of the 1988 presidential campaigns provided 200 Club members with new and often amusing insights to the primary season.

"For the Democrats to get back to the White House, they must have an issue like the Depression or Watergate," Schneider said. "But so far they only have the stock market crash and 'Iran-gate'. Despite the fact that Americans are in the mood for a change, there simply isn't enough momentum for the Democrats to get back in the White House," he added.

Schneider conceded that all the candidates from both parties were really competent, but pointed out that "there is not a vision between them."

In his comments on various candidates, Schneider quipped that Massachusetts Governor Michael S. Dukakis attracts the "Masterpiece Theatre audience in politics." Dukakis is "addicted to good government" and is "committed to process," he said.

Suggesting that the Massachusetts governor will use Harvard's Kennedy School of Government to fill key management posts, Schneider remarked that with Dukakis in the White House we would have "government by case study."

He described Illinois Senator Paul Simon as the "Orville Redenbacher" of the Democratic party, explaining that Simon "appeals to the constituency that longs for Mario Cuomo to run." Schneider painted a vivid picture of traditional Democratic fundamentalists as those who "cry and cheer when someone gives a revival speech."

As for the Republicans, he called Kansas Sen. Bob Dole a "superb deal maker."

Schneider also accurately predicted that Vice President Bush would nearly capture the GOP nomination on Super Tuesday (March 8). He reasoned that President Reagan had a strong base in the South, which would help Bush. "But Dole lacked the money, the base and the momentum going into the Southern primary to win," Schneider remarked.

Schneider also commented briefly on the vice presidency, calling it "the last cookie on the plate. No one ever wants it, but someone always takes it. If Bush offers George Deukmejian the vice presidency, Duke will take it," stated Schneider.

Presidential Politics
Who has what it takes?

The presidential primary season enters the last stretch of the campaigns with the final primaries in California, New Jersey, Montana, New Mexico and North Dakota.

Vice President George Bush captured enough delegate votes in the Pennsylvania primary to win the Republican nomination. Now, he is watching the Democratic candidates scramble for delegates as he starts to plan strategy for the November election.

Democratic front runner, Massachusetts Governor Michael Dukakis is still short of the 2,081 delegates needed to secure his party's nomination on the first ballot. Even a big win in California or New Jersey on June 7 won't give Dukakis all the delegates he needs. So, he and his staff are busy seeking commitments from delegates from who are uncommitted or whose candidates have withdrawn.

He also must consider the 645 "super delegates." This is a category created by the Democratic Party's new rules. The party awards 15 percent of the convention seats to Democratic officeholders and party leaders.

Although Dukakis has 30 percent more delegates than the Rev. Jesse Jackson, who ranks second in delegate count, he cannot afford to alienate voters committed to other Democratic candidates. Whoever leaves Atlanta with the Democratic nomination will need to unite the party in order to win in November.

June 1988 ballot propositions
Two initiatives call for careful consideration

California voters will be faced with a dozen statewide propositions on their ballots this June. These initiatives cover a broad range of policy issues from earthquake safety and wildlife protection to technical revisions to the state's constitutional spending limits. Of the 12 initiatives, four are bond issues.

Two initiatives, however, are particularly noteworthy on campaign finance reform. The following is a brief description of both.

Between 1976 and 1986, the cost of running for office in California Legislature has skyrocketed. In 1976, 226 candidates ran for 100 seats (80 Assembly; 20 Senate). Each candidate spent an average of $33,933 to run for office. In 1986, the average spent by 192 candidates for the same offices spent an average of $176,195, an increase of 519 percent.

Proposition 68, sponsored by Common Cause and the League of Women Voters, is an attempt to deal with some of the problems of campaign finance. In short, it limits the amount of funds that can be contributed during any one calendar year and election; it prohibits fund raising during nonelection years; it prohibits transfers of campaign money between candidates; and it establishes a limited form of public financing through a voluntary check-off system on the state income tax form. This measure also limits the amount of money legislative candidates can spend, contribute or loan.

Proposition 73, the second campaign funding initiative on the ballot, is not as complicated as Proposition 68. Sponsored by a bipartisan group of legislators, this measure specifically prohibits both public financing for political campaigns and the transfer of funds between candidates. It limits political contributions from individuals, political committees and parties. This measure also limits the honoraria elected officials can accept during a calendar year.

Historical Perspective

Convention Trivia

The Democrats hold the record for the longest nominating convention and most ballots. In 1924, the convention stretched 17 days and 103 ballots before the Democrats selected John W. Davis of West Virginia to run against President Calvin Coolidge.

Keeping numbers straight on initiative process

"Since...1911, 200 initiatives have been up for votes over the past 77 years."

Since California voters approved the initiative and referendum process in 1911, 200 initiatives have been up for votes over the past 77 years. Of these, 54, or 28 percent, have been approved.

The initiative process has proven to be a powerful voice of the public in affecting change throughout the state, and even across the nation. For example, in 1978 the Tax Limitation Measure, commonly known as Proposition 13, put a cap on property taxes. Since then, other states have copied California's lead on this issue.

Until 1982, the slate of ballot measures for each election began numbering with 1. However, this became increasingly confusing with controversial issues. Proposition 13 was a tax-cutting measure in 1978, but a water conservation proposal in 1982 had the same number.

In 1983, the Legislature passed a law requiring ballot measures to be number consecutively beginning with the November 1982 elections and continuing for 20 years.

This year the June ballot measure will begin with number 66. In 2002, initiatives will begin renumbering with number 1.

Ballot Measures 66 77 Through 88 June 7

4 5

A serious, analytical image appropriate for a marketing newsletter is established through the continuous running text and the dimensional, diagramatic art.

The narrow side margins (2 picas 6 points) allow for wide, 14-pica text columns, about the maximum width in a three-column grid. The density of the text is balanced by white space from a deep, 12-pica top margin, the floating art, and the open leading in the breakouts.

The dimensional "Market Power Grid," abstracted from the cover illustration (not shown), is picked up also as a design motif at the start of each section. The tinted square in each icon is keyed either to the larger grid on the page shown or to a similar grid on another page. The grid was created in Illustrator.

A second color is used for the art, headlines, and breakouts. This helps to break up the text and allows for downsized subheads without loss of emphasis.

The leaders and narrow-measure callouts emphasize the vertical structure of the grid and keep the page clean and crisp. The small Helvetica type for the callouts contrasts with the larger Times Roman used for running text and breakouts.

The bold initial cap, floating above a gray tinted box, draws the reader's eye to the beginning of the text. This is particularly effective in a page that lacks any dramatic contrasts.

Design: Marla Schay and Micah Zimring, Watzman + Keyes (Cambridge, MA)

Pages from Indications, *published bimonthly by Index Group, Inc. Trim size: 25-1/2 by 11, folded twice*

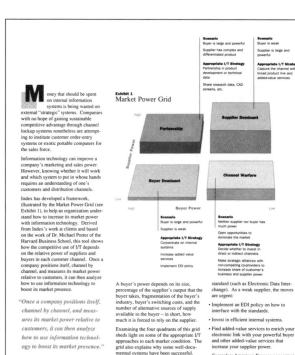

This newsletter achieves a completely different style within the three-column format than does the publication on the facing page. Here, rules and banners separating stories provide a clearly visible page structure, whereas the continuous narrative in the preceding publication is designed with a less apparent, though equally tight, framework. Compare also the justified text of this publication with the ragged right of the preceding one, and the paragraph indents here with the flush left first lines and open paragraph spacing shown on the facing page. Note, too, that the photos here are angled to break out of the grid, while the dimensional art on the facing page is positioned to emphasize the grid.

The angled snapshots over blue shadows loosen up the tightly structured page and also convey a warm, people-oriented image.

Goudy Old Style, used throughout, is a delicate typeface that is handled here with considerable sophistication. Note the open spacing of the all-caps category heads, which set elegantly against the gray banners above each story; the graceful initial caps, which print blue; and the alignment of text in adjacent columns, which adds to the crispness of the justified text. The delicacy of this typeface also makes it relatively forgiving of the uneven spacing often found in justified type.

Design: Kimberly Mancebo, Castro Benson Bryant Mancebo (Campbell, CA)

Pages from the O'Connor Foundation Quarterly. Trim size: 8-1/2 by 11

COMMUNITY OUTREACH

O'Connor Reaches Out to Kids as it Co-Sponsors Children's Discovery Museum Groundbreaking

Why did dozens of O'Connor Hospital employees spend an entire Saturday of their own free time volunteering at the Children's Discovery Museum Groundbreaking?

To help kids learn about health care. They manned interactive learning centers where they showed kids how to splint arms, listen through stethoscopes, navigate wheelchairs, read x-rays, and walk on crutches.

Not only did O'Connor employees participate in the Groundbreaking activities, but they also hope to establish long-term involvement after the Museum opens next year.

ADMINISTRATIVE DIRECTOR of Radiology Carol Yanz explains how x-rays give an "inside out" view of people.

PATIENT CARE

Monte Villa's Self Discovery Helps Troubled Youths

Located in a serene setting in Morgan Hill, O'Connor's Monte Villa Hospital (MVH) offers confidential adolescent psychiatric programs and chemical dependency services.

The Self Discovery program is committed to affirming life and respecting the dignity of adolescents and their families. The program offers troubled youths a chance to feel better about themselves, to understand their feelings and needs, to discover that they are likeable, and to feel accepted.

When a person comes to Monte Villa Hospital for care, he or she undergoes full medical and neuropsychological evaluations. Group and individual counseling promotes healing of specific physical, spiritual, familial, social, educational and emotional problems. Follow-up care is an integral part of the program. Accredited schooling is also available. For details, call Susan Titus at 408/779-4151.

NOBODY SAID ADOLESCENCE WOULD BE EASY, but for some teens it is absolutely overwhelming. Compassionate counselors help these youths find their way. The symbol was created by the teenagers at MVH and is used on T-shirts and binders as a reminder of the importance of their efforts in Self Discovery.

PHYSICIAN PROFILE

Golden Gloves Champion Dr. Calcagno Practices 50 Years at O'Connor

Imagine combining the slam bang vigor of a Golden Gloves boxing champion, the gentle sensitivity of a community volunteer, and the sophisticated intelligence of a physician. Put them all together and you've got the fascinating Dr. Joseph Calcagno, general practitioner at O'Connor for nearly half a century.

From the time Dr. Calcagno was old enough to walk, he gleefully tagged along with his dad to local boxing competitions, dreaming of the day when he, too, would win a title. The day came during pre-med school at Santa Clara University when he "left-and-right-hooked" his way through eliminations to win a 1934 Golden Gloves award in the Lightweight Division. That victory still remains one of the special moments in his life.

When he graduated from medical school in 1939, he joined World War II's War in the Pacific. "I spent the whole six years on the islands in field hospital MASH units," he says. "We were the envy of the soldiers, not only because we got Coca-Cola and fresh milk and meat from Army pilots as fringe benefits, but because we had 30 nurses to work with!"

By 1946, he was home again and opened a medical practice on Race Street. Soon after, his passion for boxing came back into focus, this time not as a participant, but as a licensed ringside physician for the California State Athletic Commission. As such, he has been the attending doctor at boxing and wrestling matches on the average of every other weekend for 46 years, with as many as 3-4 dozen matches in a single weekend. He examines

"In 1946, he opened a medical practice on Race Street, across from the O'Connor Sanitarium. He's been there ever since."

all competing boxers and wrestlers—both amateur and professional—about an hour before each match and treats them immediately after they compete.

"Most injuries are minor face, eye and lip cuts," he explains, "but occasionally the officials or I will stop a fight if we see someone taking a beating, and submit a record to the California Athletic Commission."

As the only boxing/wrestling attending physician in the Santa Clara Valley, he ends up performing annual physicals on at least five professional boxers, wrestlers, officials or judges on any given weekday. They all need Dr. Calcagno's "stamp of approval" to retain their state licences.

A 20-year Volunteer for PAL
As a firm believer in community service, Dr. Calcagno extends his passion for these sports into volunteer work, having regularly donated his time to the boxers and wrestlers of the Police Athletic League (PAL) since the organization was founded in 1968.

Dr. Calcagno is one of those rare individuals who has been able to integrate his professional skills in the healing arts into a hobby which he adores.

"I feel very lucky," he says, "My hobby has become my work. What more could a person ask for!"

DR. CALCAGNO (photo left) now works beneath a wall filled with awards from his four decades of volunteerism. (Right) Barely into his twenties, Santa Clara University student Dr. Calcagno wins a Golden Gloves title.

The two true tabloids on this page use the 11-by-17 page in similar ways but to different effect. Both rely heavily on white space and display type to make the oversize page accessible.

The three + one-column format (above) creates a half-frame of white space around the image area.

Photos, captions, and a statement of goals break into the white space without filling it.

The logo prints in red ("Ameri") and blue ("News"). The red is picked up in the banners with reverse type and in the rule at the bottom of the page. The blue is picked up in the initial cap, the two-column inset text, and the tint in the contents box. Red and blue are crisp, bold colors that liven up a mostly text page.

The two-column format (above right) is unusual for a tabloid, but the wide margin, used only for pull quotes and blurbs, and the space around the bold headlines make it work.

The nameplate banner is repeated in a smaller size on inside pages, providing strong identity.

A second color, crimson, is used for the alternating thick and thin rules, initial caps, display text inset in the running text, and company identification in the lower left.

The type is Helvetica Black for headlines and blurbs inset in running text, and Bookman for running text, captions, and marginal quotes.

Design (above left): Kate Dore, Dore Davis Design (Sacramento, CA)

Cover of AmeriNews, the inhouse newsletter of AmeriGas–Cal Gas. Trim size: 11 by 17

Design (above right): Mary Reed, ImageSet Design (Portland, ME)

Cover of Re:, a commercial/industrial real estate newsletter published by The MacBride Dunham Group. Trim size: 11 by 17

An all-text, newspaper-style page can be made engaging and attractive. Rules, initial caps, white space, and a second color all support the structural device of using story headlines to divide the page into text units with varying sizes and shapes. The effect is infinitely more appealing to readers than columns of type that simply march down the page. The approach here is conservative—and appropriately so for a bar association newsletter; the same devices, however, can be used to create many other styles.

The top of the image area is dropped so as not to crowd the page. The resulting white space creates a strong horizon line.

The body text is Times Roman, and the subheads are Times Roman bold italic.

The headlines and folios are a Caslon Extra Bold display face. The logo and the initial caps are set in Novarese. These faces are not yet available for desktop publishing, but they have been part of the news-letter format for many years and are added to the electronically composed pages by hand.

The headlines are centered between brown rules, with a 2-point rule above and a 1-point rule below.

The initial caps print over a box with a horizontal-line fill and no outside rule (this fill also prints brown). Note the careful alignment of the baseline of the initial cap with the bottom rule in the box and the even spacing between the thin-line rule of the fill with the 1-point rule above. When you rely on typographic devices for the look of a page, these details are critical.

Design: Michael Waitsman, Synthesis Concepts (Chicago, IL)

Pages from Litigation News, *published by the American Bar Association. Trim Size: 10-3/4 by 13-7/8*

The cover-story concept, seen frequently in magazines, has unusual impact when used effectively in a newsletter. At their best, newsletters have an intimacy with their readers (the result of a shared special interest) and a timeliness that even magazines lack in today's fast-paced communications. So a newsletter cover story implicitly announces, "Here's a problem that many of you are grappling with, and here's what we know about it." Anyone who works with PageMaker can see the immediate appeal of the cover stories shown on the facing page, from a newsletter that aptly describes itself as "a visual guide to using the Macintosh and PageMaker in desktop publishing."

The visual continuity in the covers of this newsletter also seems closer to the world of magazines than to that of newsletters. Newsletters typically achieve their cover identity through a familiar grid and typographic treatment. Here, the cover design varies quite a bit from one issue to the next depending on the subject. But the strong nameplate treatment, the unsual shape of the page, and the always-on-target theme provide their own very effective and unmistakable identity.

The grid is basically one wide column with a wide margin used for captions, art, and marginalia. One advantage of this format, especially in a narrow page such as this, is that you can easily break the grid and use the whole page.

Design: David Doty, PageWorks (Chicago, IL)

Pages from ThePage, *published monthly by PageWorks.*
Trim size: 7 by 11

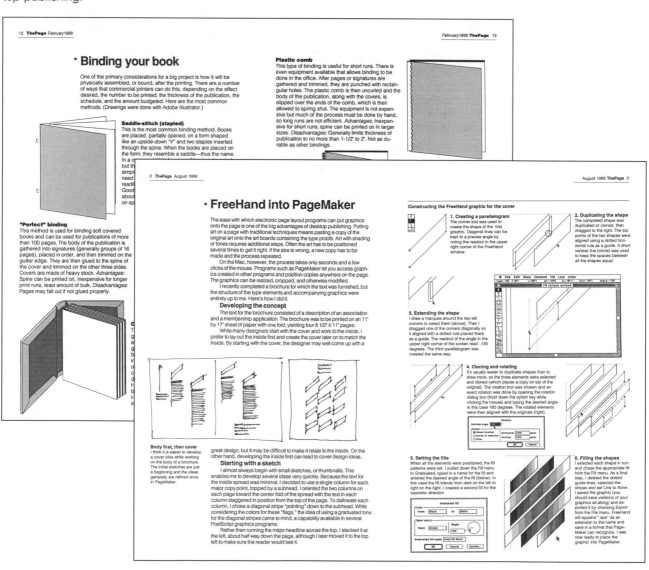

October 1987

A visual guide to
using the Macintosh
in desktop publishing

ThePage10

High resolution reproduction

Which sections of the object below have been reproduced on
a Linotron and which on a LaserWriter?

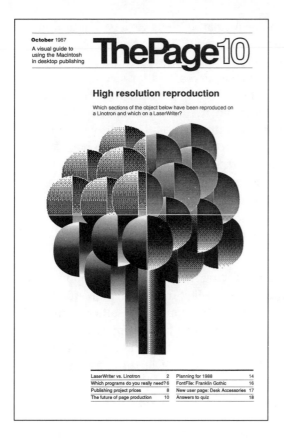

May 1988

A visual guide to
using the Macintosh
in desktop publishing

ThePage17

Design ideas for newsletters

NEWSLETTER DESIGN

EpiGram

Nameplate, flag, banner, logo, or masthead?

What do you call that splash
of type across the top of a
newsletter or magazine? It is
often referred to as the
masthead. That's actually the
one thing it is not. The masthead of a publication is the
listing of the staff, generally
found on the inside pages.

The most appropriate term
is banner, or banner head, but
nameplate is also widely used.
The term logo is less
appropriate unless the design
is also a symbol representing
an organization.

Inside...
Newsletter ideas, publications
of interest, the Bettmann
Archive, putting photos on the
page, ThunderScan into Page-
Maker, more clip art, and
EmDash fonts (this page is set
in ArchiText by EmDash).

Create a unique look for your newsletter

Newsletters are one of the forces
propelling the desktop publishing
revolution. They are seen as a quick way
to gain a foothold in the publishing
business. Design a newsletter for your
client or boss and you're all set, right?
What could be easier?

Newsletters are more complex than
they appear. With choices of type,
numbers of columns, use of photographs
or art, handling of running heads, and all
the little details of design, there is
much to consider before arriving at a
final solution.

More important, however, is that the
above elements combine to form a
unique and unified whole. On the next six
pages are six fictional newsletter
designs. Use them as idea starters to
help structure your own design efforts.

February 1988

A visual guide to
using the Macintosh
in desktop publishing

ThePage14

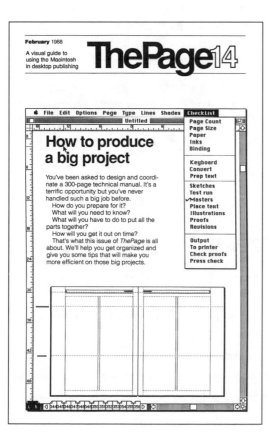

 File Edit Options Page Type Lines Shades **CheckList**

Untitled

How to produce a big project

You've been asked to design and coordinate a 300-page technical manual. It's a
terrific opportunity but you've never
handled such a big job before.

How do you prepare for it?
What will you need to know?
What will you have to do to put all the
parts together?

How will you get it out on time?

That's what this issue of *ThePage* is all
about. We'll help you get organized and
give you some tips that will make you
more efficient on those big projects.

Page Count
Page Size
Paper
Inks
Binding

Keyboard
Convert
Prep text

Sketches
Test run
✓**Masters**
Place text
Illustrations
Proofs
Revisions

Output
To printer
Check proofs
Press check

June 1988

A visual guide to
using the Macintosh
in desktop publishing

ThePage18

The graphics evolution

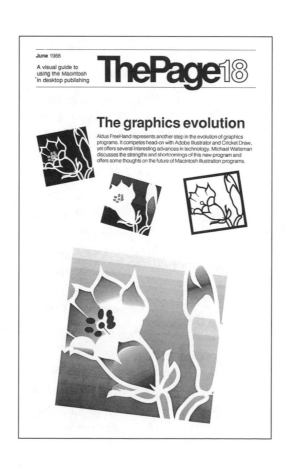

Aldus FreeHand represents another step in the evolution of graphics
programs. It competes head-on with Adobe Illustrator and Cricket Draw,
yet offers several interesting advances in technology. Michael Waitsman
discusses the strengths and shortcomings of this new program and
offers some thoughts on the future of Macintosh illustration programs.

JOURNALS & MAGAZINES

The complexity of the magazine format, with its variety of editorial material in any given issue and the need to juggle several issues at once, makes the collaborative effort between editors and graphic designers one of the key elements of success. Editors who think visually and designers who get involved in the content of the material produce stories that are dynamic and attention-getting, with innovative approaches to even the most familiar ideas. The editor's job isn't over when the manuscript moves from word processor to page layout, and the designer doesn't wait for the manuscript to begin his or her work. Both work together to develop, shape, present, and refine each idea throughout the production cycle. Although desktop publishing is changing the nature of that collaboration, in some ways it presents the greatest opportunities for those editors and designers who don't see their functions as limited to either words or pictures.

Another unique challenge in producing magazines is the opportunity to use the dimension of time that is implicit in the magazine format. Each department and feature story is developed as a self-contained unit, but when you bind them together they become pieces of a whole. Play with that dimension as you make up the order of items in the magazine. Move from a picture story to an article with sustained reading text, from a story with black-and-white photographs to one that uses color illustration, from an idea that is light and accessible to one that is provocative and demanding. Even though few people read magazines from front to back, offering contrast from one story to the next creates an interesting texture and an attention-getting pace. Besides, using that dimension is fun and keeps your job interesting. The more you work with the flow and the pacing, the more they become a useful guide both in early planning and last-minute problem solving.

One of the great dangers in magazine publishing is that your approach will become stale. Don't confuse a consistent format with overreliance on formula. The degree to which you are inspired in producing each issue is probably a good measure of how that issue will be received by readers.

Journals and magazines in this section

- *Washington College Magazine*—a good format for feature articles in an alumni magazine
- *Back Talk Journal*—sophisticated type and photography in a small-format journal
- *American Demographics*—a format designed to introduce data, and some good filler ideas
- *Business North Carolina*—lessons learned from the redesign of a regional business magazine
- *Verbum*—a showcase for electronic art
- *HeartCorps*—a stylish, upbeat design for an audience of heart patients
- *Mother Earth News*—quick, low-resolution scans as a high-efficiency production tool

K arl and Irma Miller nurture the College's students as lovingly as the Hynson-Ringgold gardens. Young adults who know the elderly couple say they have an uncanny ability to bridge the generation gap.

A B O U T   T O W N

Karl And Irma Miller: Tillers Of Good Will

by Sue De Pasquale '87
Photographs by J.M. Fragomeni '88

Karl and Irma Miller are matter-of-fact when it ... about their gardening projects in ...

At 84 and 81, they see nothing unusual about a workload that keeps them bending, hoeing, digging and watering for hours upon hours nearly every day of the week. But ask people half their age—a quarter—who know ...

P I E C E S   O F   T H E   P A S T

Colonel Brown And The Dancing Duo

by P.J. Wingate '33

Although Washington College has been promoting the arts and sciences for over 200 years, it is not well known for its contributions to the performing arts. Nevertheless, a Washington College graduate played a vital role in creating the most celebrated dance team in the history of the theatre—Fred Astaire and Ginger Rogers.

This alumnus was Hiram S. Brown, Class of 1900, and later president of the movie firm RKO, which produced the first Astaire-Rogers film, "Flying Down to Rio," and subsequently made millions of dollars from a series of movies by this most gifted pair of dancers. Colonel Brown, as he was known throughout most of his adult life, was no longer president of RKO when most of those later movies were produced, but it took no great foresight for Brown's successors to see that they had an artistic diamond necklace and a financial gold mine in the dance team of Ginger Rogers and Fred Astaire.

Both Rogers and Astaire had played in Broadway shows before they made their first movie together, and had also played minor roles in the movies, but neither was even close to being called a movie star when Hiram Brown brought them together in 1933. The best that could be said for them then was that they were featured players. The listed stars for "Flying Down to Rio" were Gene Raymond and Dolores Del Rio, both of whom have long since vanished into the mists of obscurity along with the plot of the movie itself.

Not so for Rogers and Astaire. They shot up into the theatrical sky like rockets, propelled by their own incomparable talents and the enchanting tunes by Vincent Youmans who provided the music they danced to: "The Carioca," "Orchids in the Moonlight," "Music Makes Me," and the title song, "Flying Down to Rio." In all subsequent movies which they made together, Ginger Rogers and Fred Astaire were the stars, and their dancing became artistic treasures which will be preserved for centuries to come.

The story of this famous dance team is too well known to be repeated here,

PHOTO: CULVER PICTURES

18   19

21

This alumni publication used to be a tabloid. After converting to desktop production, they saved enough money on typesetting and pasteup to upgrade the tabloid to the glossy magazine format shown on this page.

The style of feature articles defines a magazine's personality as much as any other element. Here, good photos given lots of space, graceful Palatino italic headlines, upsized introductions set on a two-column measure, and plenty of white space define an accessible style that opens every feature article. Subsequent pages of features follow the three-column format with photographs sized one, two, or three columns wide. This consistent style greatly speeds up layout and production time because so many decisions are already made.

The understated style works fine for a captive audience, which an alumni magazine such as this enjoys. A magazine with paid circulation has to work harder at varying its style and using catchy headlines to sell readers on each story.

Design: Meredith Davies (Chestertown, MD)

Pages from Washington College Magazine, *published quarterly. Trim size: 8-1/2 by 11*

A Legal Perspective

SEE YOU IN
COURT

A *BACK TALK* INTERVIEW WITH JOHN E. COLLINS, COUNSEL FOR THE PLAINTIFF.

Back injury accounts for one in five injuries in the workplace. It cripples not only employees, but also corporate profits, as employers are left to carry the burden of low productivity and ever-increasing insurance premiums from workers' compensation carriers.

After injury, it's often left to attorneys to argue accountability. Accordingly, *Back Talk* asked one, "Who's to blame?"

John E. Collins has practiced civil and criminal law in Dallas for more than 20 years. He notes that he is board-certified in the specialty of Personal Injury Trial Law, and is a past president of the Texas Trial Lawyers Association and the Association of Trial Lawyers of America. Currently, 85 percent of his firm's business is in the field of personal injury claims, half of which is back injury.

Collins provides a lawyer's perspective on the problem of back injury — and some free counsel to those employers and insurance companies interested in lowering the cost of back injury permanently:

EDITOR: Each year in the United States, it's believed that back injuries cost $16 billion in disability and lost productivity. Indeed, one-third of all compensation

At odds with back-injured employees? A personal injury attorney tells how to lower a company's risk of litigation.

costs are related to low back pain. Depending on who one talks to, different people are accountable for the problem. Let's address the medical system first. In Texas, for example, an injured worker chooses the health care provider, not the company. Is that a positive or negative aspect of the system?

COLLINS: It's clearly positive. Before the workers' compensation law was amended, workers were very suspicious about going to a doctor of someone else's choosing. That created hostility between the patient and the health care provider.

EDITOR: On the other hand, is there inherent risk that the person will access the health care system through the wrong portal of entry, and thereby lower the chance of recovery?

COLLINS: Free choice will always have risk.

EDITOR: In your experience, how many people get sidetracked with a questionable medical provider?

COLLINS: Not many. Less than 10 percent. Most people will go to great lengths to obtain the best possible medical treatment.

EDITOR: In general, do you think doctors do a good enough job in identifying those people who might be classified as "malingerers," i.e., those trying to fake injury for disability payment.

COLLINS: I don't see many of those people. Most of the time, when I turn down a case, it's often that the injury is not serious enough to warrant my involvement — like a back strain. The employee is off only a couple weeks. These people usually want to consult an attorney just to ensure that, long-term, they'll have access to medical care for their injury.

Unfortunately, some employers and insurance companies make it a habit to harass people with back injuries, and to run them off after they return to work. And that makes for more problems.

EDITOR: What percent of the disability suits brought nationwide have little substance?

COLLINS: Not many. I don't want to take a case to the courthouse that's of doubtful merit. Ninety-nine percent of that type of work

Full-bleed photos, used frequently in this journal, have power and impact that you just don't get with photos that are contained on the page. The cover image provides a silhouette that is enviably appropriate for a clinic specializing in back pain.

Good printing on a heavy, coated paper stock brings out the best in the design and photos. The rich blacks contrast with the warm gray/brown used as a second color in the cover type, running heads, bold rules, pull quotes, and boxes for reverse-type initial caps.

The type selection contrasts the clean lines of Helvetica Black with the tall, thin shape of Garamond. The banner centered under the running head works because the two words above it have the same number of letters. The initial cap/small cap style of the subhead and running foot adds additional detail to the sophisticated typography.

Design: Bob Reznik (Plano, TX)

Pages from Back Talk Journal, published annually by the Texas Back Institute. Trim size: 7-1/2 by 11

WHAT IS A WORKING WOMAN?

If you think only half of women work, think again.

◆

by Horst H. Stipp

Whether a woman works outside the home or not is a vital piece of information for marketers who target women. Most rely on the standard published figures—52 percent of women aged 16 and older were working in 1986, for example.

New research indicates that this figure may be way off the mark. In fact, among a target group dear to the hearts of marketers—women aged 18 to 49—about 90 percent can be considered part of the labor force. The "typical housewife" has become rare indeed.

How can the standard statistics understate women's work patterns so dramatically? They overlook the fact that women enter and exit the labor force frequently. Both men and women occasionally change jobs, get laid off, or go to school. But many women also

Horst H. Stipp is the director of Social Research at NBC.

stop working for a while after they have a baby, when they get married, and for other reasons. Overall, women enter and exit the labor force much more frequently than men. As a result, a large percentage of women are both working and not working over a relatively short period of time. Many of today's nonworking women will be tomorrow's working women and vice versa. Most important, the attitudes of women with discontinuous work patterns are similar to those of women who are in the work force continuously.

THE PATTERN

The frequency with which women exit and reenter the labor force today is much less than it was 10 or 20 years ago. Nevertheless, demographers Suzanne Bianchi and Daphne Spain find that "women's participation in the labor force over the life course still remains more discontinuous than men's as women continue to exit and reenter the

24 AMERICAN DEMOGRAPHICS / JULY 1988

A magazine that is chock-full of charts, graphs, tables, and just about every other form of statistical data works doubly hard to open each story as a general-interest feature. Bold headlines, hand-tinted photographs framed by heavy rules, and lots of white space provide lively hooks and a respite from the data prevalent elsewhere. The upsized introductory blurbs explain or provide context for the headline.

Effective fillers are the hot spots of many magazines. Fillers are simply standing items of varying length that you can plug in wherever space allows (or requires). A good concept for a filler is a fresh, timely, fascinating, or quirky angle on the magazine's subject matter. It's right on target even when it seems to come out of left field. A good filler is generally a quick read and may well be the first thing some readers look for when they pick up the magazine. The Demo Memo filler (above right) runs several times in each issue of *American Demographics*. It's easy to recognize and, for less than a minute of your time, is almost guaranteed to deliver some fascinating fact. The Lincoln Sample (below right) is, by definition, a limited-run filler: It follows a photographer's route from the Atlantic to the Pacific coast, with a picture of the road ahead taken every nine miles, exactly. Editorial techniques such as these keep magazines lively and changing and also provide flexibility in production.

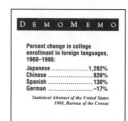

DEMO MEMO

Percent change in college enrollment in foreign languages, 1960–1986:

Japanese 1,282%
Chinese 839%
Spanish 130%
German .... −17%

Statistical Abstract of the United States 1988, Bureau of the Census

26 **THE LINCOLN SAMPLE, STOP NUMBER 26.** 3,060 miles to go. Adams Co., Rt. 30, a few miles past Hubcap City. I am entering Gettysburg, home of The Address, but the sign says we're in Marlboro Country. Beyond the cowboy is the Penn Eagle Motel where I'm spending the night. The owners are from India and it's suppertime—the lobby smells like curry. I made 20 stops today—that's 180 miles. 0 0 2 2 5

Design: Michael Rider (Ithaca, NY)
Pages from American Demographics, published monthly.
Trim size: 8-3/8 by 11

When this regional business magazine approached a redesign, the staff focused on four goals: to capture the contrast of old and new that typified the audience; to sharpen the spotlight on people; to create a simple format that would free the small staff to focus on content rather than layout; and to convert the magazine to desktop publishing.

The audience combined the deep-rooted traditions of the North Carolina mountains and agricultural areas with the high tech innovations of businesses and universities in the state's Golden Triangle. Understanding the unique character of one's audience enables a magazine to use that character as a building block in the publication's design.

The typography in the logo captures the contrast inherent in the audience. The word "Business," set in Futura Extra Bold Oblique, is bold, contemporary, and aggressive. The words "North Carolina," set in the gentile, soft, and almost lyrical Palatino, add a quiet, reserved, and sophisticated counterpoint.

The spotlight on people was part of the magazine's editorial image all along. But the redesign process gives you the opportunity to look with fresh eyes at what you are already doing, as well as the opportunity to redefine your goals and determine how best to reach them. In this case, the new understanding led to a change from covers that varied in their subjects and art styles to photographic covers featuring a single business leader in his or her natural enviroment.

The emphasis on good, interesting photographs continues on the inside pages. Concentrating on a consistent visual approach and finding a small group of photographers who understand and can deliver the magazine's photographic style frees the art director from having to start at square one with every story.

A table of contents should be highly organized, graphically interesting, and uncompromisingly utilitarian—all at the same time.

The numbers in the contents listings are 24-point Futura Extra Bold Oblique. They are graphic as well as functional elements on the page. As is the case with headline type, numbers set in large sizes require careful kerning to achieve the even spacing seen here.

The rules are 18 point with 9-point Futura Extra Bold reverse type in all caps.

The descriptive lines are the 10/13 Palatino used for body text inside the magazine.

Art picked up from inside the magazine makes the contents page visually interesting and is selected both to highlight important stories and to arouse curiosity. If you use the art at the same size as it appears elsewhere in the magazine (even if it's just a detail from a larger picture), you avoid the cost of additional color separations.

FEATURE

BUSINESS IS LOOKING UP FOR GENERAL AVIATION

When it comes to flying for business or pleasure, the sky's not the limit.

By J.A.C. Dunn

Charles (left) and Winfield Causey were farming with their father in 1963. But they got bitten by the flying bug and turned from furrows to runways.

The little plane circles the airport once, a tiny moving X in the cloudless eastern Carolina sky. Its single engine makes a barely audible hum. It disappears briefly beyond the woods, then suddenly reappears just over the trees surrounding the airport and lands on the longer of Warren Field's two runways. Taxiing to the front of the low, brick terminal building, it swings around to face the broad expanse of rough grass between the tarmac. The pilot cuts the engine, steps out of the cockpit and strolls across the apron and through the double glass doors of the terminal lobby.

"Morning," he says, genially, at large. Salesman, you think. He has a little sandy mustache and very alert eyes. Pointing at a tired-looking, twin-engine plane at one side of the apron, he asks, "That airplane out there. What is it? Does it fly?"

"That's an old DC-4," says Joe Leggitt, the airport manager. He's a stocky, muscular young man with a smiling, sunburned face. He used to be a commercial fisherman. He wears a khaki jumpsuit befitting the all-purpose manager of an all-purpose rural airport, but behind the counter he is barefoot: Warren Field is not a stuffy establishment. Authorities, he tells the pilot, impounded the plane after a drug raid last spring. It has been grounded ever since.

"You don't see many of those around any

more," the visitor says reverently. He leans against a counter and lights a cigarette. "I was flying over and noticed it, and I thought, 'I have to find out about *that*.' I'm just flying around, looking at the country. I have an appointment in Baltimore this afternoon. I don't want to get there too soon."

He introduces himself: Richard Leachman of Cessna Finance Corp. in Raleigh. Aircraft finance. It fit with the blue blazer, gray slacks, white button-down shirt, necktie and polished loafers. An airplane nowadays is often a corporate asset, not a Sunday toy, and its pilot, rather than a flying playboy nicknamed Ace, is likely to wear a business suit with a briefcase as his co-pilot. The Aircraft Owners and Pilots Association describes the average general aviator as 44 years old, the owner of a house and two cars, married with two children, a licensed, instrument-rated pilot who flies a single-engine, fixed-gear aircraft 116 hours a year and likes to fish.

Despite its apparent imprecision, the term "general aviation" is very specific. It embraces all flight except commercial airlines and the military. It doesn't grab the headlines, the way Piedmont's recent merger with USAir or the opening of a regional airline hub does, but its statistics are astonishing. The nation's general

---

FEATURE

Phyllis Gallup replaced one plane wrecked by a student, who walked away from the crash. "All she said was, 'Oh, my hair must be a mess,'" Gallup says.

was a licensed pilot before he was 21. In 1921, he flew from London to China solo. The Winston-Salem airport bears his name.

But it was only after World War II that airports, and aircraft to use them, began to take off in North Carolina. The stimulus was a liberal sprinkling of leftover military airfields, most of them in the eastern part of the state. The airports at Wilson, Rocky Mount (now closed), Lumberton, Kinston, New Bern, Beaufort-Morehead City, Washington, Manteo and Edenton were all originally military fields.

Most were used for training. Warren Field had T-6 trainers based on it, and the original runways are still in use, although their 45-year-old concrete pavement is showing signs of wear. The 82nd Airborne Division flew troop-carrying gliders at Maxton, and pilots took basic flight training at Horace Williams Field in Chapel Hill. When the present Raleigh-Durham Airport replaced Raleigh Municipal, it was called Raleigh-Durham Army Air Base until transferred to civilian hands after the war.

Several airports are still used by the military, such as McCall Field in Aberdeen and Oak Grove at New Bern. Thirty miles southeast of Elizabeth City is Harvey's Point, a small airfield deliberately kept small because the Central Intelligence Agency operates it. Some of the participants in the Bay of Pigs invasion were trained there.

During the 1950s, the economic value of general aviation began to take off. In 1958, the Federal Aviation Act provided the first federal funds for airport development. Nearly 20 North Carolina airports received improvement money until 1970.

In 1965, Gov. Dan Moore created the position of aviation specialist in what was then the Department of Conservation and Development to help communities attract

new business by providing a place for companies to park their planes. The state established an airport aid program with $127,000 in 1967, though this money could not be used to improve airports that had scheduled commercial service. The fund was increased to $150,000 a year in 1971.

The airport aid fund was increased to $2 million in 1973, when the reorganization of state government placed the aviation specialist in the Department of Transportation. Half the money went to airports with commercial service. The fund was increased to $3 million in 1974 and the distinction between commercial and general-aviation airports removed.

The federal deregulation of commercial airlines brought about this change. Before deregulation, airlines were subsidized, sometimes by as much as $60 per passenger per stop at an airport, to enable airlines to serve relatively low-traffic places, such as Elizabeth City. Airport managements charged the airlines for airport improvements, which the airlines paid for from their subsidies.

After deregulation, it became harder to maintain and improve airports because airline subsidy money was gone. But most communities found it worth their while to

A plane is a time machine, says the N.C. Division of Aviation's Willard Plentl. He wants every industrial area of the state to have an airport within a half-hour drive.

Design:
R. Kimble Walker
(Charlotte, NC)

Pages from
Business North
Carolina,
published monthly.
Trim size: 8-1/4 by
10-7/8

A strong, simple format enables the small staff to produce a quality magazine that competes for readers' time with big-budget national business magazines. By minimizing the choices for each story, the editor and art director can concentrate on substance rather than form.

The 72-point Futura Extra Bold initial cap with an 18-point bold rule continues the visual motif from the cover. Rules over photos print in a different color for each feature. This bold, crisp look helps tie together editorial pages in a magazine fractured by small-space ads.

The body text, 10/13 Palatino in two 16-pica ragged right columns, sets about one-third fewer words than the more typical 9/10 justified text found in many magazines. The open text was another result of the redesign, and the editors feel that less has proved to be more.

In a showcase for electronic art, the variety of subjects, shapes, colors, styles, and textures puts any grid through its paces.

In the two spreads shown on the facing page, *Verbum* designer John Odam displays and comments on the capabilities of Illustrator 88 and FreeHand. The four-column grid on these pages combines maximum flexibility for sizing art with efficient copy fitting in the narrow, 10-pica columns.

In the spread below, the open type of a wide column provides a good balance against the black panels used to group small pieces of art. Although the size of the panels would work in a four-column grid, the denser type of a narrow measure would make the pages very dark.

Grouped captions in all three spreads are cross-referenced to the art by numbers, the size and placement of which makes them relatively inconspicuous without compromising legibility.

For the first piece of art he created in FreeHand (upper right in the top spread), Odam got film-positive color separations overnight from an L300. Of the implications of this, which registered several weeks after the fact, he writes: "I had produced a $500 airbrush illustration in 20 minutes and paid $20 for a color separation. Not only that, but the blending of two ink colors in graduated steps could not have been accomplished with airbrush without using all four printers' colors, or by using cumbersome overlays in which the exact color scheme could not be previsualized. I felt the same rush of adrenalin that I had experienced when I first saw a Linotronic proof."

Of graphics programs in general, Odam says, "There was a time once when you could tell which Macintosh application had been used to produce a graphic, but many programs on the market now are capable of producing the same end result with varying degrees of ease.... In the end, it is what best suits the individual user that counts."

Design: John Odam (San Diego, CA)

Pages from Verbum, *published quarterly. Trim size: 8-1/2 by 11*

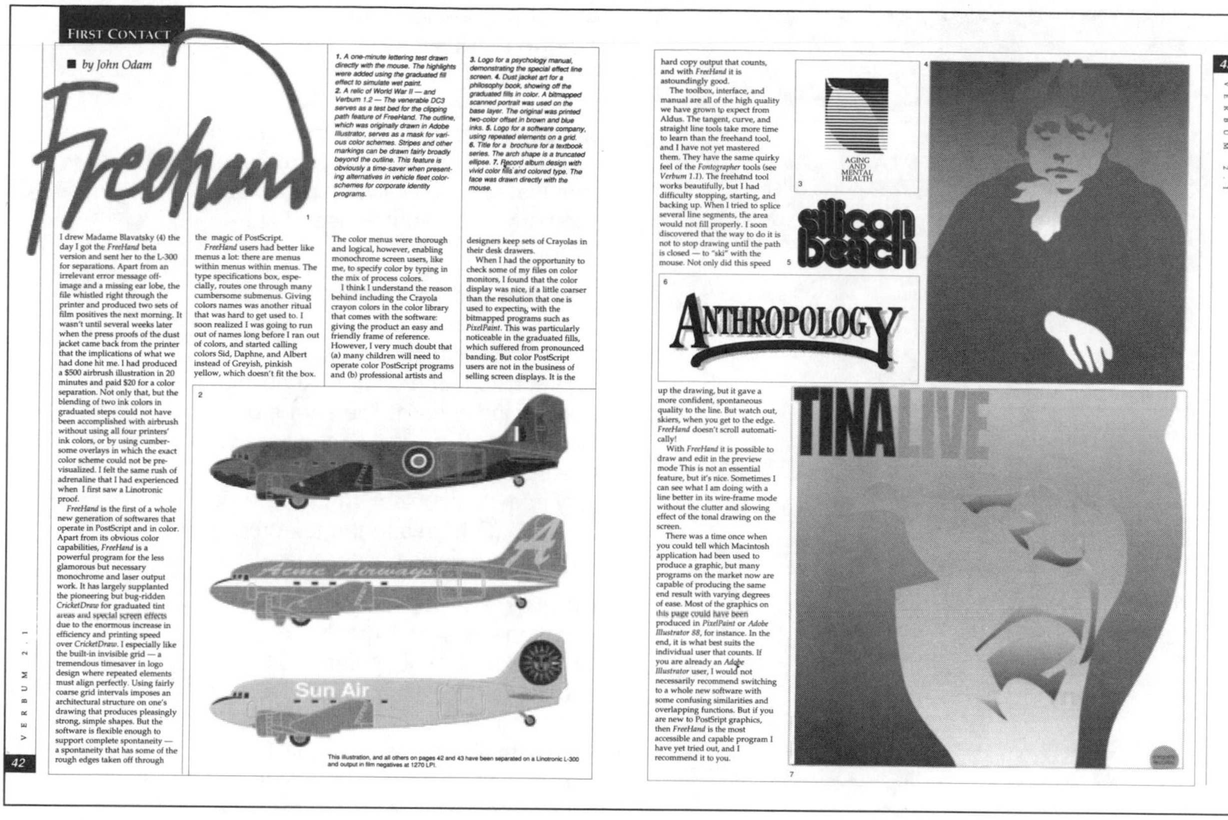

FIRST CONTACT

■ by John Odam

Freehand

I drew Madame Blavatsky (4) the day I got the *FreeHand* beta version and sent her to the L-300 for separations. Apart from an irrelevant error message off-image and a missing ear lobe, the file whistled right through the printer and produced two sets of film positives the next morning. It wasn't until several weeks later when the press proofs of the dust jacket came back from the printer that the implications of what we had done hit me. I had produced a $500 airbrush illustration in 20 minutes and paid $20 for a color separation. Not only that, but the blending of two ink colors in graduated steps could not have been accomplished without using all four printers' ink colors, or by using cumbersome overlays in which the exact color scheme could not be previsualized. I felt the same rush of adrenaline that I had experienced when I first saw a Linotronic proof.

FreeHand is the first of a whole new generation of softwares that operate in PostScript and in color. Apart from its obvious color capabilities, *FreeHand* is a powerful program for the less glamorous but necessary monochrome and laser output work. It has largely supplanted the pioneering but bug-ridden *CricketDraw* for graduated tint areas and special screen effects due to the enormous increase in efficiency and printing speed over *CricketDraw*. I especially like the built-in invisible grid — a tremendous timesaver in logo design where repeated elements must align perfectly. Using fairly coarse grid intervals imposes an architectural structure on one's drawing that produces pleasingly strong, simple shapes. But the software is flexible enough to support complete spontaneity — a spontaneity that has some of the rough edges taken off through the magic of PostScript.

FreeHand users had better like menus a lot: there are menus within menus within menus. The type specifications box, especially, routes one through many cumbersome submenus. Giving colors names was another ritual that was hard to get used to. I soon realized I was going to run out of names long before I ran out of colors, and started calling colors Sid, Daphne, and Albert instead of Greyish, pinkish yellow, which doesn't fit the box.

The color menus were thorough and logical, however, enabling monochrome screen users, like me, to specify color by typing in the mix of process colors.

I think I understand the reason behind including the Crayola crayon colors in the color library that comes with the software: giving the product an easy and friendly frame of reference. However, I very much doubt that (a) many children will need to operate color PostScript programs and (b) professional artists and designers keep sets of Crayolas in their desk drawers.

When I had the opportunity to check some of my files on color monitors, I found that the color display was nice, if a little coarser than the resolution that one is used to expecting, with the bitmapped programs such as *PixelPaint*. This was particularly noticeable in the graduated fills, which suffered from pronounced banding. But color PostScript users are not in the business of selling screen displays. It is the hard copy output that counts, and with *FreeHand* it is astoundingly good.

The toolbox, interface, and manual are all of the high quality we have grown to expect from Aldus. The tangent, curve, and straight line tools take more time to learn than the freehand tool, and I have not yet mastered them. They have the same quirky feel of the *Fontographer* tools (see *Verbum 1.1*). The freehand tool works beautifully, but I had difficulty stopping, starting, and backing up. When I tried to splice several line segments, the area would not fill properly. I soon discovered that the way to do it is not to stop drawing until the path is closed — to "ski" with the mouse. Not only did this speed up the drawing, but it gave a more confident, spontaneous quality to the line. But watch out, skiers, when you get to the edge. *FreeHand* won't scroll automatically!

With *FreeHand* it is possible to draw and edit in the preview mode This is not an essential feature, but it's nice. Sometimes I can see what I am doing with a line better in its wire-frame mode without the clutter and slowing effect of the tonal drawing on the screen.

There was a time once when you could tell which Macintosh application had been used to produce a graphic, but many programs on the market now are capable of producing the same end result with varying degrees of ease. Most of the graphics on this page could have been produced in *PixelPaint* or *Adobe Illustrator 88*, for instance. In the end, it is what best suits the individual user that counts. If you are already an *Adobe Illustrator* user, I would not necessarily recommend switching to a whole new software with some confusing similarities and overlapping functions. But if you are new to PostScript graphics, then *FreeHand* is the most accessible and capable program I have yet tried out, and I recommend it to you.

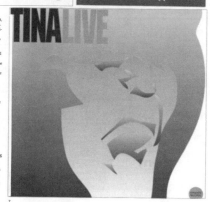

1. A one-minute lettering test drawn directly with the mouse. The highlights were added using the graduated fill effect to simulate wet paint.
2. A relic of World War II — and *Verbum 1.2* — The venerable DC3 serves as a test bed for the clipping path feature of *FreeHand*. The outline, which was originally drawn in *Adobe Illustrator*, serves as a mask for various color schemes. Stripes and other markings can be drawn fairly broadly beyond the outline. This feature is obviously a time-saver when presenting alternatives in vehicle fleet color-schemes for corporate identity programs.

3. Logo for a psychology manual, demonstrating the special effect line screen. 4. Dust jacket art for a philosophy book, showing off the graduated fills in color. A bitmapped scanned portrait was used on the base layer. The original was printed two-color either in brown and blue inks. 5. Logo for a software company, using repeated elements on a grid. 6. Title for a brochure for a textbook series. The arch shape is a truncated ellipse. 7. Record album design with vivid color fills and colored type. The face was drawn directly with the mouse.

This illustration, and all others on pages 42 and 43 have been separated on a Linotronic L-300 and output in film negatives at 1270 LPI.

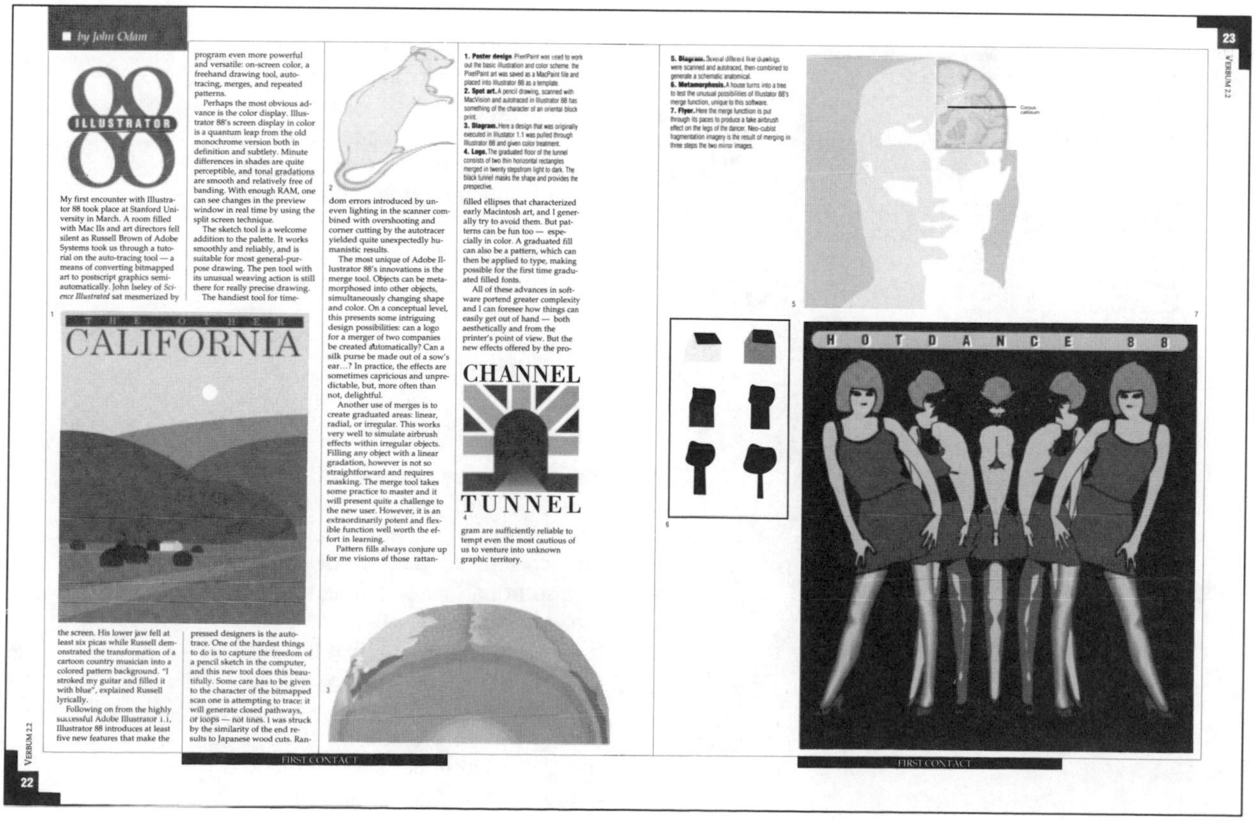

■ by John Odam

ILLUSTRATOR 88

My first encounter with Illustrator 88 took place at Stanford University in March. A room filled with Mac IIs and art directors fell silent as Russell Brown of Adobe Systems took us through a tutorial on the auto-tracing tool — a means of converting bitmapped art to postscript graphics semiautomatically. John Iseley of *Science Illustrated* sat mesmerized by

the screen. His lower jaw fell at least six picas while Russell demonstrated the transformation of a cartoon country musician into a colored pattern background. "I stroked my guitar and filled it with blue", explained Russell lyrically.

Following on from the highly successful Adobe Illustrator 1.1, Illustrator 88 introduces at least five new features that make the program even more powerful and versatile: on-screen color, a freehand drawing tool, auto-tracing, merges, and repeated patterns.

Perhaps the most obvious advance is the color display. Illustrator 88's screen display in color is a quantum leap from the old monochrome version both in definition and subtlety. Minute differences in shades are quite perceptible, and tonal gradations are smooth and relatively free of banding. With enough RAM, one can see changes in the preview window in real time by using the split screen technique.

The sketch tool is a welcome addition to the palette. It works smoothly and reliably, and is suitable for most general-purpose drawing. The pen tool with its unusual weaving action is still there for really precise drawing.

The handiest tool for time-pressed designers is the autotrace. One of the hardest things to do is to capture the freedom of a pencil sketch in the computer, and this new tool does this beautifully. Some care has to be given to the character of the bitmapped scan one is attempting to trace: it will generate closed pathways, or loops — not lines. I was struck by the similarity of the end results to Japanese wood cuts. Random errors introduced by uneven lighting in the scanner combined with overshooting and corner cutting by the autotracer yielded quite unexpectedly humanistic results.

The most unique of Adobe Illustrator 88's innovations is the merge tool. Objects can be metamorphosed into other objects, simultaneously changing shape and color. On a conceptual level, this presents some intriguing design possibilities: can a logo for a merger of two companies be created automatically? Can a silk purse be made out of a sow's ear…? In practice, the effects are sometimes capricious and unpredictable, but, more often than not, delightful.

Another use of merges is to create graduated areas: linear, radial, or irregular. This works very well to simulate airbrush effects within irregular objects. Filling any object with a linear gradation, however, is not so straightforward and requires masking. The merge tool takes some practice to master and it will present quite a challenge to the new user. However, it is an extraordinarily potent and flexible function well worth the effort in learning.

Pattern fills always conjure up for me visions of those rattan-filled ellipses that characterized early Macintosh art, and I generally try to avoid them. But patterns can be fun too — especially in color. A graduated fill can also be a pattern, which can then be applied to type, making possible for the first time graduated filled fonts.

All of these advances in software portend greater complexity and I can foresee how things can easily get out of hand — both aesthetically and from the printer's point of view. But the new effects offered by the program is sufficiently reliable to tempt even the most cautious of us to venture into unknown graphic territory.

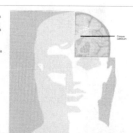

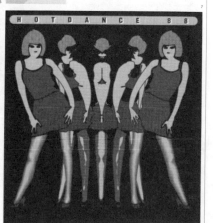

1. Poster design. PixelPaint was used to work out the basic illustration and color scheme: the PixelPaint art was saved as a MacPaint file and placed into Illustrator 88 as a template.
2. Spot art. A pencil drawing, scanned with Macintosh and autotraced in Illustrator 88 has something of the character of an oriental block print.
3. Diagram. Here a design that was originally executed in Illustrator 1.1 was pulled through Illustrator 88 and given color treatment.
4. Logo. The graduated floor of the tunnel consists of two then horizontal rectangles merged in twenty steps from light to dark. The black tunnel masks the shape and provides the perspective.

5. Diagram. Several different liver drawings were scanned and autotraced, then combined to generate a schematic anatomical.
6. Metamorphosis. A house turns into a tree to test the unusual possibilities of Illustrator 88's merge function, unique to this software.
7. Flyer. Here the merge function is put through its paces to produce a fake airbrush effect on the legs of the dancer. Neo-cubist fragmentation imagery is the result of merging in three steps the two mirror images.

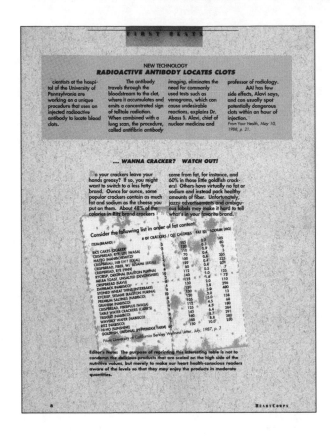

A stylish, varied, and active design gives a very upbeat image to this magazine for heart patients. The pages are full of tips, techniques, charts, and other information highlighted through a visual repertoire that includes initial caps, large numbers, and frequent use of sidebars.

Department pages such as the ones shown at left break from the traditional columnar format by having each item treated almost as if it were an index card. The shape of the text block, as well as the type size, leading, and column width, vary from item to item, but the single typeface (Futura) and the textured background unify these pages.

Dimensionality is another signature of this design. Note the use of the cracker as a self-referential background for a chart, with type surprinting at the top and bottom. And in the page shown below left, the first text block appears to be sandwiched between art in the foreground and background; while in the second item, the art is woven under the headline and over the text.

The headline type for feature stories (shown on the facing page) is Bodoni Poster, condensed to different degrees for each story depending on the length of the headline and the layout of the page. This provides the benefits of a unified typeface with many variations. Bodoni Poster works unusually well with this treatment because it maintains its distinctive relationship of thick and thin strokes. Many typefaces deviate too much from the original design when manipulated in this way.

The text wraparound (facing page, bottom) is one of desktop publishing's much ballyhooed bells and whistles. One of the benefits of a wraparound, seen in this spread, is that it minimizes the text lost to a fairly large illustration. But the time and expense required to execute this technique with commercial typesetting can be prohibitive. (For hands-on instructions for creating a customized text wrap, see Project 6.)

Design: Tom Lewis (San Diego, CA)

Pages from Heartcorps, *published bimonthly. Size: 8-1/4 by 10-3/4*

ROPE JUMPING

TOO GOOD TO PASS UP?

BY KEN SOLIS, MD

An often repeated adage states, "The best exercise is the exercise which you do." There are four essential questions which you must ask yourself to define if an exercise is one that you will likely do *on a regular basis and for an indefinite period of time*: 1) Is it right for your body? 2) Is it easily accessible? 3) Will it give the results you are looking for? and 4) Do you enjoy it?

Perhaps surprisingly, rope jumping is one form of aerobic exercise which nicely fits the bill for many people, even recovered heart patients. Now, even without the help of telepathy, I know that a good number of you readers have already been struck with the "but ... too" disease: "I'd love to try it, *but*

I'm *too* uncoordinated to jump rope" - or - "it sounds like fun, *but* it'd be *too* hard on my knees" - or - "it's *too* hard on my wind, and it's *too* boring." In fact, rope jumping is one of the most user-friendly, safe, versatile and productive exercises available. Unfortunately, it is also one of the most misunderstood. So before we write off rope jumping to highly-tuned pugilists and energetic school children, let's see if rope jumping is an exercise which you just might want to do.

ARE YOU READY FOR IT?

First ask your physician if your heart is ready for moderate to vigorous exercise. Rope jumping is not recommended for the early phases of cardiac rehabilitation since the heart rate response is less predictable

RATED PERCEIVED EXERTION (RPE) SCALE

0	Nothing at all
0.5	Extremely weak
1	Very Weak
2	Weak
3	Moderate
4	Somewhat strong
5	Strong
6	
7	Very strong
8	
9	Extremely strong
10	Maximal

FIGURE 1. On a scale of 1 to 10, exercise intensity is guided by using your own internal "sense" of how hard you are working. Exerting yourself in the range of 3 to 5 correlates well to the "target heart range."

(Reference: Borg, G.V., Medicine and Science in Sports and Exercise, 14:377-87, 1982.)

28   HEARTCORPS

BY LEE LIPSKER, PH.D.

TIPS TO GET YOU THROUGH THE HOLIDAYS

Sugar plum fairies, chestnuts roasting on an open fire, colorful wrapping paper, friends and relatives gathered together, ... the holiday period of November through December evokes images which are nearly universal. It seems that most everyone is caught up in the spirit and mood of the season. Just think of the gusto with which we proclaim, "Happy Thanksgiving! ... Happy Hanukah! ... Merry Christmas! ... Happy New Year!" Unfortunately, this two or three month period of the year is often a time of anxiety, stress, and depression for persons with heart disease and their immediate family members.

Depression is a commonly reported problem for those who have experienced myocardial infarction (MI), coronary bypass surgery, angioplasty, or other heart-related illnesses. In fact, the research literature suggests that between 55% and 90% of all heart attack victims experience significant signs of depression as long as one year after the attack. In most cases, the depression and accompa-

1 TALK ABOUT IT. Part of the nature of depression is the tendency to believe that your difficulties are so unique that no one else could possibly understand. After all, you certainly wouldn't want to "burden" someone else with your problems! Nothing could be further from the truth. The many issues discussed here are so common that they are nearly as universal as are the mistletoe and colored lights. Surely everyone has experienced the disappointment felt when our expectations have not been met. Can any one of us honestly say that we have not been disillusioned by the over-commercialization of the holidays - at least for a little while? More significantly, most of your friends and family have had moments of depression. We all know what it is like to be "down."

Talking to someone about our problems can have many beneficial effects. First, by articulating our feelings we get to hear for ourselves just what is bothering us. Once the issues are on the table, we can call on many of our own resources to deal with them. With our thoughts laid out for us, we can identify the ones that are rational and have some basis in truth. Talking about what is bothering us also opens the door for help. It is often enough just to remind ourselves that someone will listen to us and care about how we feel. When we share our pain, discomfort, fear or sadness, we allow others to demonstrate their love and caring for us. In the sharing process, good ideas for solutions or understanding are generated by the parties involved.

Many of the issues that are involved in depression are of interest to the people that are closest to us. The variety of emotions that often accompany heart disease need attention. Your physician may be interested in your feelings for several reasons, not the least of which is the possibility of side-effects from prescribed medication. The holidays are often a period of increased spirituality - the perfect time to call on your pastor or rabbi. Or as described below, the holiday time might be the right time to get involved in a support group. The hardest part is to reach out initially and get beyond the reluctance that you will be "burdening" someone. It is a necessary step in overcoming depression and, once taken, can lead to happiness and long-lasting rewards.

2 GET INVOLVED. Few things contribute to our psychological well-being as greatly as knowing that we're important and needed. The holiday time presents us with a myriad of opportunities to become active in projects that can add immeasurably to our self-esteem. From volunteering on the children's ward at the local hospital to addressing and stuffing envelopes at the area American Heart Association or American Red Cross office - there are unlimited places and programs in which you can direct some energy.

This form of involvement accomplishes

WALKING...

TAKING YOUR EXERCISE IN STRIDE

BY BILL BLISH, EDITOR-IN-CHIEF

One of the most important steps in restoring heart health can be many steps taken in quick succession -- a brisk walk. The remarkable benefits of regular walking for cardiac rehabilitation have been acknowledged by virtually all cardiologists, who cite their own clinical experience and the growing body of long-term research.

Many heart patients wonder how something as easy as walking can have such a big impact on their physical condition. The simple truth is, a good brisk walk, several times a week can strengthen the heart. Adhering to a regular walking program may also have a favorable effect on blood pressure, serum cholesterol level, weight control, and psychological attitude. You may be thinking, "Can just simple walking regularly do all that?" and the answer is a resounding "Yes!"

While it is known and reported that high-intensity, "power" walking delivers great fitness benefits; low-intensity walking, "a brisk walk around the block" will return substantial health benefits as well, especially if done regularly and frequently. This is especially welcome news for the thousands who have come to believe that heart attack recovery and heart health can only be gained through heavy-duty exercise. The "no pain, no gain" body-building adage simply doesn't hold true for cardiac rehab. Dr. Neil Gordon, at the Institute for Aerobics Research in Dallas, Texas, starts every patient with a walking program. According to Gordon, "Walking is the ideal exercise for heart attack patients." He recommends walking for cardiac patients because it tends not to promote the injuries common to jogging, like shin splints, muscle and tendon pulls and joint inflammation. "Often heart patients are older and ill-prepared to suffer the jarring and compression that go with other types of exercise," says Dr. Gordon. "Walking is a natural movement for the body

and, therefore, it is very low impact but can be very aerobic if done properly."

Patients at Gordon's clinic are tested to determine optimum exertion levels for the course of their cardiac rehabilitation. Using a treadmill, Gordon gradually increases speed and elevation to a point where the patient is substantially taxed and approaching problems -- 70% to 85% of that level of exertion is determined to be the patient's "symptom-limited maximum heart rate." Gordon's exercise prescription, which all patients must have before undertaking any type of strenuous program, is typically a regimen calling for walking sessions lasting 20 to 40 minutes, three to five times a week at

the rate determined by the stress test.

Dr. Gordon, in our interview, emphasized that the "symptom-limited maximum heart rate" is quite different from the "target heart rate" training guidelines that have thousands of fitness-devoted Americans regularly checking their pulses during and after exercise. (See page 24.)

The American Heart Association and American College of Sports Medicine recommend an exertion level measured at 60-75% of the maximum heart rate, sustained for 30 minutes at least three times a week. They assert that exercise above 75% may be too strenuous unless in excellent physical condition; and exercise below 60% gives the heart and lungs little physical conditioning.

A good brisk walk, several times a week, can strengthen the heart.

Brisk walking - - about four to five miles per hour, can elevate heart rates into the ideal conditioning range. But even walking at three and one-half miles per hour may be too taxing for those on the mend from a heart attack.

Fortunately, there is an increasing body of knowledge through research that suggests substantial health benefits can be achieved at exercise levels far below the 60% to 75% target zone. "Walking for 45 minutes a day is wonderful, even without ever reaching your target heart rate zone," says Dr. Bob Hopper of the Cardiac Health & Diagnostic Center in Long Beach, California. Hopper, an exercise physiologist, makes a key distinction between *health* and *fitness* : the data suggests physical activity is related to lower heart disease risk, not necessarily fitness. A good physical fitness program will achieve heart healthy benefits, but walking and never achieving your target heart rate is also very good."

Hopper says moderate activity equal to expending about 2000 calories a week will reduce the risk of heart disease, but not necessarily improve fitness. He admits that his is a minority "but growing" opinion on the value of moderate exercise for heart health. However, he argues that nationally, adherence to more rigorous fitness programs have been dismal, especially in older age groups. "The fitness craze has been a failure," says Hopper. "Only a small percentage of Americans, one study says about 6.5%, reach the American College of Sports Medicine guidelines of 30 minutes at the target heart rate, three times a week."

Hopper strongly believes in the ACSM guidelines, but takes a more pragmatic view when dealing with cardiac rehab patients. "We talk with our cardiac patients and find out that they have not been able to stay with a fitness program. For the long term, its better to get heart patients on a

ILLUSTRATION: JOHN CARLYLE

Generally, the more deeply an exercise makes you breath, the more it burns calories and body fat...

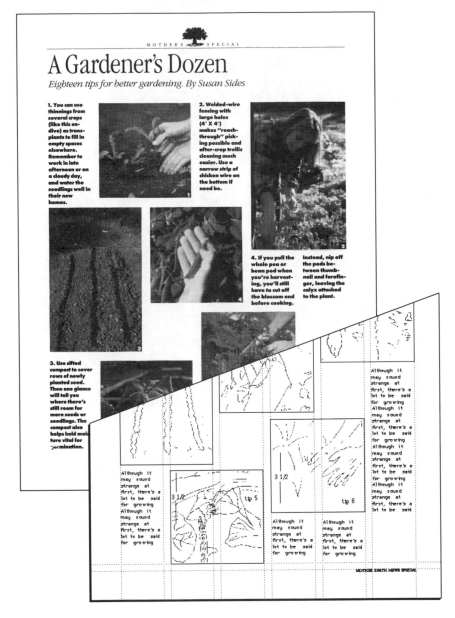

Scanning photographs for reproduction, in both black and white and color, pushes desktop publishing to its outer limits. It can be done, but for most people it requires too much time, skill, and memory to produce a satisfactory result. The cost of converting a photograph to a halftone for black and white reproduction is still one of the best bargains commercial printers offer. And the quality is far superior to what most people can achieve using desktop technology. Color scanning is even more difficult, and of course the hardware required is even more expensive.

Using a scanner as a production tool, on the other hand, provides a great deal of control and flexibility when you design pages that have to accommodate numerous photographs or illustrations. The samples on these two pages show how we used low-resolution scans to do very precise layouts, saving time (and money on photostat bills) for pages that would be commercially typeset and manually pasted up, with color art stripped in by the printer. The on-screen image is shown in front of the printed page.

The page shown at left is the opener for a story that includes 12 color photographs. We received the photos as 35mm transparencies and projected them on a wall to make rough tracings. (We simply put a piece of tracing paper over the projected image and literally traced it.) We scanned each tracing individually, on a Datacopy 730, as simple line art at 150 dots per inch, saved it in MacPaint format, and placed it in the PageMaker document.

Bogus copy, typed in PageMaker in the type style of the article, was sufficient to simulate for layout purposes the caption-style text that accompanied the pictures. With all the elements in electronic form, we could manipulate their sizes and positions to develop the layout.

The laser proof served as the final layout guide for the pasteup artist as well for the printer when stripping in the original art.

If you need more detail in your layout, you can scan black and white photos—or color laser copies—as low-resolution halftones, as we did with the sample shown at left. None of the scans described on this page are memory intensive. The scans of tracings ranged from 9 to 20 KB and took about 18 seconds each; the halftone scans ranged from 12 to 36 KB and took about 40 seconds each.

This poster-style spread was created in a special file so that the pages could be be seen together in a vertical orientation. We created one oversize page and drew a line through the center to mark the gutter between the two real pages.

The artist's rough sketches were faxed to us and then scanned as line art. Each sketch (and scan) had four or five birds on the page, and we needed to position them individually. So we opened each scan in DeskPaint (a desk accessory that you can work in while Page-Maker is active), copied the birds one by one, and pasted them onto the PageMaker page.

The table was typed in PageMaker. Tables are difficult for designers to specify for commercial typesetting, and although creating the one here as a layout guide took some time to get the tabs and vertical spacing right, it eliminated the inevitable galley revisions that tables require.

The captions were received as MCI mail, saved to disk, and then opened in Microsoft Word to create a text file that we could place on the pasteboard in PageMaker. We then cut and pasted each caption so we could manipulate it as an individual, unthreaded text block.

There is no formal grid in this page. Note, in the screen detail, how we used ruler guides to align the elements as the layout evolved.

Having a tight layout (along with oversize printouts of it) enabled the artist to paint all of the birds in relative proportion to one another as a single piece of art. The scans on the layout were checked for accuracy against the final art. (If accurate, scans can be used as FPO guides for the printer when stripping in the art, eliminating the cost of stats.)

The headline is Egyptian Bold Condensed, a font not yet available for desktop publishing. This headline style is used for feature stories in every issue of the magazine, so we've scanned in an alphabet supplied by a commercial typesetter.

The resulting MacPaint file, shown at right, is used like press type only the electronic method is faster: With MacPaint's lasso tool, we select a letter, copy it, then paste in onto a second MacPaint document. (You can have two MacPaint documents open at the same time; on a large monitor they can be side by side.) We continue selecting letters to spell out the headline, save it as a Mac-Paint file, then place and resize it in PageMaker. Again, even though the type is reset commercially, this technique enables you to create tight layouts for pasteup artists to follow.

Design: Don Wright (Woodstock, NY)
Illustration: Kay Holmes Stafford

Pages from Mother Earth News, *published bimonthly.*
Trim size: 8-1/8 by 10-3/4

CHAPTER 7

DATA: CATALOGS, DATA SHEETS, FINANCIALS, AND FORMS

Publications with large amounts of data rely heavily on careful organization and deft styling of typography. Some require clear delineation and consistent handling of repetitive elements, such as product names, prices, and descriptive listings; others require formats that can accommodate different kinds of elements, such as continuous narrative interspersed with tables, charts, and graphs.

Before settling on an approach, you'll need to analyze the material and experiment with different typographic styles. The ability to experiment on the desktop is a decided advantage when you are designing these publications, and you can save time by testing small samples of data before styling the entire document. In testing the type style and tab positions for tables, be sure to include both the maximum and minimum number and length of elements you have to accommodate, so that you can see the balance of the two in any format.

CATALOGS & DATA SHEETS

When you have to pack a lot of text into a small space, you will generally enhance the appeal and overall readability if you choose a small, tightly leaded, condensed type style and maximize the space around the text. Larger sizes surrounded by less white space result in pages that are dark and unrelievedly dense. Use rules and borders to aid organization and to change the color of the page. Even in publications without a second color, rules with contrasting weights can add much-needed graphic variety as well as organizational clarity.

Catalogs and data sheets in this section

- *Tables Specification Guide* —diverse elements in a landscape format
- *Books on Black Culture*—art livens up straightforward catalog listings
- *Beverly Hills Motoring Accessories*—boxes, banners, and more boxes and banners
- *The Concept Technical Manual*—technical illustrations for ski clothes
- *Teaching Tools*—a highly structured catalog of educational software
- *School of Visual Arts*—a little style dresses up straightforward listings
- *Clackamas Community College catalog*—a format that accommodates many different kinds of listings
- *Portland State Quarterly*—adventurous typography in a newspaper format

- *The Huck Lockbolt Fastener Design Guide*—technical illustrations in a utilitarian format
- *Triad Keyboard*—easy-to-scan text and life-sized photos
- *Maxtor Data Sheets*—high-quality, high tech still lifes
- *Infrared Optics Cleaning Kit*—handsome simplicity
- *Smith & Hawken product assembly sheets*—an easily implemented format consistent with the company look
- *Questor Inlets*—leadered callouts and a functional use of color

The horizontal format provides more flexibility than a vertical page in organizing the many options available for items in this catalog.

The master pages include the rules, logo, headlines, and black box on the top page, and the rules and bar coding on the bottom page. In addition to simplifying electronic page assembly, this uniformity brings visual order to a complex document. It also makes it easy for readers to find information about any given product because similar information appears on the same place on every page. If a master item is not used on an actual page, it is masked over with a No Lines-Paper Shade box and that slot appears blank.

The line drawing of each item prints as a white line in a black box. This technique dramatically highlights the subject of each page, making it the dominant item amid the many other kinds of information. The drawings were created in MacDraft, saved as PICT files, and sized proportionately in PageMaker.

For the data on the bottom page, pencil roughs were used to determine the number and depth of items for each table in the catalog. Several templates were then made, with a different configuration of rules on the master page of each one. The text for all pages using the same configuration was created in a single Microsoft Word file and placed in PageMaker. Planning pays off by not having to redraw rules on every page and by being able to refine the tabs in Page-Maker for an entire file, representing many catalog pages at one time.

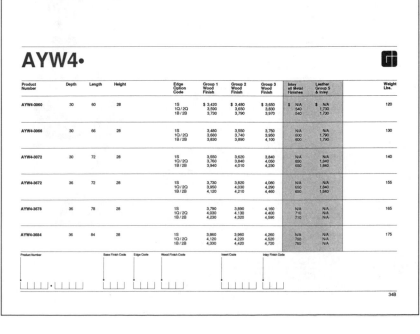

Design: Manfred Petri (Atlanta, GA)

Pages from Tables Specification Guide and Price List, *from Geiger International. Trim size: 11-7/8 by 8-3/8*

The bold banner across the top of each page and the striking silhouettes of the African art give this book catalog a distinctive personality that is obviously appropriate to the theme of black culture.

The two text columns are boxed in with rules. The outer column is consistently used for art, which is photocopied (with permission) from one of the books in the catalog and pasted into position on the camera-ready pages. When a category of books does not require the two text columns on a page, additional art is used as filler.

The typeface for the book listings is Helvetica. The use of boldface caps to set off the titles, regular caps for the authors, and space between this highlighted information and the descriptive listings is handled consistently throughout and makes the catalog easy to use. The type overall is relatively dark, a result of using laser printer output for camera-ready copy. That darkness works here with the art style and format.

The category heads are Times Roman, reversed out of the black banners at the top of each page.

Design: Lisa Menders (Royal Oak, MI)

Pages from Books on Black Culture, *a mail-order catalog published by the* book end *in Southfield, MI.*
Trim size: 8-3/8 by 11

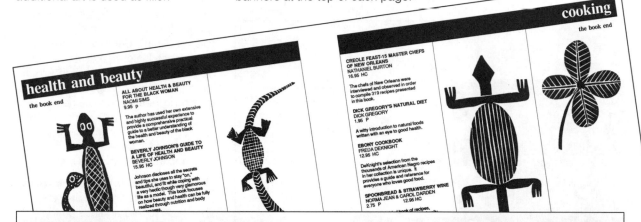

health and beauty
the book end

ALL ABOUT HEALTH & BEAUTY FOR THE BLACK WOMAN
NAOMI SIMS
9.95 P

The author has used her own extensive and highly successful experience to provide a comprehensive practical guide to a better understanding of the health and beauty of the black woman.

BEVERLY JOHNSON'S GUIDE TO A LIFE OF HEALTH AND BEAUTY
BEVERLY JOHNSON
15.95 HC

Johnson discloses all the secrets and tips she uses to stay "on," beautiful, and fit while coping with a very hectic though very glamorous life as a model. This book focuses on how beauty and health can be fully realized through nutrition and body awareness.

cooking
the book end

CREOLE FEAST-15 MASTER CHEFS OF NEW ORLEANS
NATHANIEL BURTON
16.95 HC

The chefs of New Orleans were interviewed and observed in order to compile 319 recipes presented in this book.

DICK GREGORY'S NATURAL DIET
DICK GREGORY
1.95 P

A witty introduction to natural foods written with an eye to good health.

EBONY COOKBOOK
FREDA DEKNIGHT
12.95 HC

DeKnight's selection from the thousands of American Negro recipes in her collection is unique. It provides a guide and reference for everyone who loves good food.

SPOONBREAD & STRAWBERRY WINE
NORMA JEAN & CAROL DARDEN
2.75 P   12.95 HC

biography
the book end

GOOD MORNING BLUES-AUTOBIOGRAPHY OF COUNT BASIE
ALBERT MURRAY
10.95 P

Gives the fascinating life and times of Count Basie, one of the pre-eminent figures in jazz history. Tales of his childhood days to his fame, and his influence on the music world.

GROWING-UP IN A RURAL SETTING
DAVID FIELDS
6.50 P

This book deals with the author's growing up in the rural south, and his leaving the south for the north; and the personal problems he had to overcome in order to maintain his dignity and sanity.

HARRIET TUBMAN-THE MOSES OF HER PEOPLE
SARAH BRADFORD
4.95 P

An exact, unaltered and unabridged, reprint of Bradford's memorable biography of Harriet Tubman.

HARRIET TUBMAN-THE ROAD TO FREEDOM
RAE BAINS
1.95 P

Young person's biography beautifully illustrated telling the tale of Harriet Tubman and her passage to freedom.

HEART OF A WOMAN
MAYA ANGELOU
3.95 P

One of the most remarkable personal narratives of our age. Maya Angelou describes her later years as a singer and dancer, journeys to New York City. Maya speaks with an intimate awareness of the heart within us all. (Fourth of five volumes)

HIT AND RUN-THE JIMI HENDRIX STORY
JERRY HOPKINS
8.95 P

The intimate shocking story of Jimi Hendrix who electrified audiences everywhere. Revealed are his personal battles with sex, drugs and people.

HORNES - AN AMERICAN FAMILY
GAIL LUMET BUCKLEY
18.95 HC

Lena Horne's daughter gives us an intimate look into "America's historic family secret", the black bourgeoisie. In words and pictures kept by family and friends, Buckley brings this fascinating story to life.

I KNOW WHY THE CAGED BIRD SINGS
MAYA ANGELOU
3.95 P

An autobiographical narrative examining black life in a rural community during the 1930's. Her portrait is a Biblical study of life in the midst of death. (first of five volumes)

I WONDER AS I WANDER
LANGSTON HUGHES
9.95 P

The Big Sea was the first volume of Hughes's autobiography. This is the second volume. Personal history intertwined with narratives of his travels. Written with bounce and zest.

I'M GONNA MAKE YOU LOVE ME
JAMES HASKINS
2.75 P

As much as a life story, this is a book about the music business and especially about Motown and the recording industry. A fascinating and dazzling account of Diana Ross's life and rise to stardom.

I, TINA: MY LIFE STORY
TINA TURNER
16.95 HC

One of the most sensational life stories in show business, encompassing the lowest lows and the highest highs. The story of a true survivor, she tells it the way it is.

JACKIE ROBINSON-FIRST OF THE CHOSEN FEW
JOSEPH NAZEL, JR.
2.25 P

The life story of the first black man to play in the major league. Covers his early baseball years to his later career as a successful businessman and civil rights activist.

biography
the book end

JAMES BROWN:GODFATHER OF SOUL
JAMES BROWN
18.95 HC

In his own words, Brown tells of his rise from a world of poverty and segregation to one of wealth, musical pre-eminence, even political influence. More than a revealing celebrity memoir, his autobiography is a spectacular performance.

JAMES VAN DER ZEE-PICTURE TAKIN' MAN
JIM HASKINS
8.95 HC

Based on numerous interviews with James Van DerZee and liberally illustrated with some of his best work, this is an intimate portrait of a gifted artist who recorded more than half century of black history.

JESSE JACKSON AND THE POLITICS OF RACE
THOMAS LANDEES
17.95 HC

Here is Jesse Jackson's life story, from his unusual childhood to his quest for the presidency. Includes the momentous facts of America's civil rights movement and its recent move toward black separatism.

JESSE JACKSON: AMERICA'S DAVID
BARBARA REYNOLDS
11.95 P

One of the most objective, thoroughly researched and documented writings on Jesse Jackson. An important book for everyone.

JOHN COLTRANE
BILL COLE
10.95 P

A biography of the late jazz great John Coltrane, his contribution to American music and some of the forces that shaped his life.

JUST MAHALIA BABY-MAHALIA JACKSON STORY
LAURRAINE GOREAU
13.95 P

A fast-paced and richly detailed biography of the great queen of gospel, Mahalia Jackson. It brings life not only to Mahalia but to an entire ethos for people who will never be able to have any other contact with it.

KAFFIR BOY
MARK MATHABANE
19.95 HC

The true story of a black youth's coming of age under apartheid in South Africa. A descriptive and enlightening story of human struggle in South Africa.

KING REMEMBERED
FLIP SCHULKE
7.95 P

An extraordinary tribute to one of the most influential leaders of our time. Based on exclusive interviews of Dr. King's closest friends and features the most comprehensive single collection of still photographs of King's life and times.

LADY SINGS THE BLUES
BILLIE HOLIDAY
5.95 P

Billie Holiday tells her own story of her turbulent adolescence in Harlem during the 1920s, the excitement of working in New York City's famous jazz clubs with the musicians who brought jazz to the forefront of American culture, and her own dazzling rise to the top.

LANGSTON HUGHES-BEFORE & BEYOND HARLEM
FAITH BERRY
12.95 P

The first full-length portrait of Langston Hughes, one of the finest poets of our times. Berry concentrates on the writer's life and career from his formative years through his involvement in the Harlem Renaissance; she traces his place in the society and in literary and political worlds.

LAY BARE THE HEART
JAMES FARMER
8.95 P

The story of James Farmer's life revealing the mammoth struggle of the civil rights movement. This book captures the inspiring strengths and human weaknesses of the movement.

LEADERSHIP, LOVE & AGGRESSION
ALLISON DAVID
15.95 HC

A brilliant psychobiographical study of the four most important American Negro leaders. Davis brings to this study of the ego-development of four great men both psychological insights and profound knowledge of social anthropology.

6

7

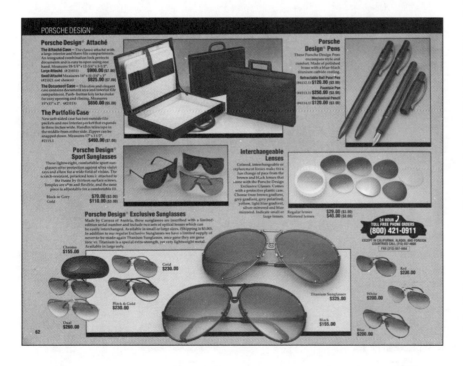

Boxes and banners are used throughout to organize the many elements on each page.

Black banners along the top function as tabs, with product categories in reverse type.

Photos are framed by 0.5-point rules on three sides; the 8-point rule at the bottom of each frame provides a solid base for each photo. This is particularly effective when the product is a car and also gives the catalog a distinctive style. Note the varied directions of the cars in the top row of photos.

Small objects are carefully arranged as still lifes to best display shape, texture, and different views and styles of the same product. The pattern of objects repeated on the page plays with color and shape to provide visual interest. Grouping small objects in one photo saves space as well as photo expenses.

Silhouette photos that extend beyond the picture frames have more dimensionality than photos that are contained. This technique provides variety within the basic format and maximizes the use of space where needed.

Text prints on a gray background. The boldface Helvetica headlines and prices are offset from the descriptive text, which is set smaller in Palatino.

Design: Bob Lee, Lee & Porter Design (Los Angeles, CA)

Pages from a catalog published by Beverly Hills Motoring Accessories. Trim size: 11 by 8-1/2

Simple technical diagrams

with leadered callouts tell the story in this wholesale catalog of ski clothes. Why diagrams? Because here the message is warmth, freedom of movement, and protection from impact and sliding hazards, rather than the fabric and fashion angle typically captured in photographs.

Careful alignment of elements

provides structure within a free-form design. A formal grid would have restricted the size of art and placement of callouts. The distinctive logo treatment, the art and callout style, and the typeface provide visual consistency from page to page.

The typeface is Bodoni, with Helvetica Black used for boldface emphasis in headlines. The ragged right margin suits the casual style and short line length of the callouts. As much as possible, leaders extend from the justified left margin, the top or the bottom, rather than the ragged right.

This highly structured format

positions the product in the same place on every page. The position of the headlines, lists of features, screen details from the programs, system requirements, and other elements also remain constant, making it very easy to find any piece of information for any product.

The headline and other boldface type is American Typewriter and matches the type on the packaging.

The row of triangles under each product name is a right-leadered tab. The leader is customized with a Zapf Dingbat and a character space (the keystroke for the Dingbat is unshifted t). You can define a style for a customized leader; then, each time you want to add it to the document, simply position the cursor, apply the style, and insert the tab.

The triangles in the upper right of each page function as product category tabs. Each category uses a different color for that triangle, for the line of small triangles, and for the quote under each product.

Design (top):
Oscar Anderson,
Weingart/Anderson
(Chicago, IL)

Page from the Concept Technical Manual, *published by Apparel Technology.*
Size: 8-1/2 by 11

Design (bottom):
Partners by Design
(N. Hollywood, CA)

Pages from the Davidson Educational Software *catalog.*
Size: 5-1/2 by 8-1/2

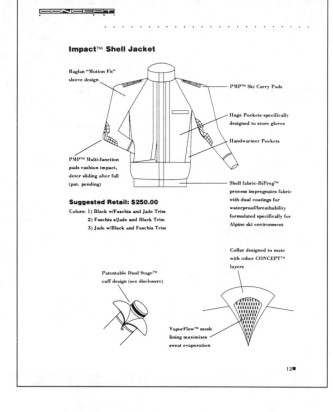

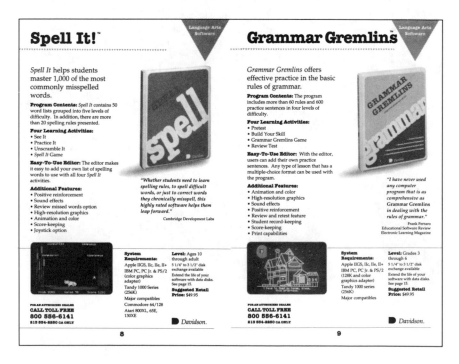

90 JOURNALISM AND PUBLIC RELATIONS

JOURNALISM AND PUBLIC RELATIONS

WRITING AND EDITING are the primary skills needed for a career in journalism and public relations. Learning to think and write clearly are skills that ean be taught. And when the quality of thinking is drawn from intelligence, personal style follows.

Our society becomes increasingly complicated and with that awareness comes the need for skilled professionals who understand how to communicate creatively, to persuade and to present a point of view with clarity.

Journalism today no longer means working only for newspapers. Journalists work on staff and freelance for magazines, radio stations, television local stations, networks and cable stations.

Public relations experts also work on staff and freelance for individual corporations — almost every large company needs a public relations division — educational institutions, in all broadcast media, as well as with specialized public relations firms. As a writer learning or reacquainting yourself with the essentials of style can be the beginning of a new career with a focus. A working knowledge of the press, understanding how to write press releases or copy, and editing can be important regardless of where you focus your writing talent. The more skills and the more flexibility you have as a writer the more valuable you will be in applied writing in journalism and public relations.

Class hours: 7:00 pm to 9:40 pm unless otherwise indicated. Add registration fee (non-refundable) of $20.00 when registering for these courses

TE109A
Freelance Magazine Writing: Making the Right Moves for Success
Mon - 2 Credits - $250.00
Creative careers need professional guidance. This is a course for writers who need to know how the marketplace operates. We will examine how to: query editors, make contacts, exploit research resources, gear an article to the appropriate magazine, negotiate fees and expenses. Drawing on your own editorial interests and enthusiams, you will learn how to produce winning story proposals, getting actual assignments from real magazines. Guest lecturers will include accomplished writers and editors. A certain passion for the printed word, rather than any publishing experience, is the course's only prerequisite.
David Abrahamson, Writer, Journalist. B.A., Johns Hopkins University; M. Journalism, University of California; Oxford University. Formerly, Managing Editor, "Car and Driver." Publications include: "The New York Times Magazine," "Science '86," "New York," "Playboy," "Backpacker."

TE205A
Editing Workshop
Thurs - 2 Credits - $250.00
Copy editors are the unsung heroes of the publishing world. Their work clears what was muddled, simplifies the complex, and imposes stylistic order. Good copy editors are in great demand for newspapers, magazines and book publishers. Learn how to handle the copy - the hard, sweaty part - and write headlines, the fun part.
Jack Robbins, Copy Editor, Business Week. Formerly, Editor, McGraw-Hill; Reporter, "The New York Post."

TE207A
How to Promote Practically Anything — Including Yourself
Thurs - 2 Credits - $250.00
This is a course in personal public relations. You will be shown how to put together your own press package for your company or yourself. Topics will include: working knowledge of the press; release writing; fundamentals of public speaking; projecting your own image.
Marilyn McCrudden, President, McCrudden and Sullivan Communications. B.A., University of Minnesota. Clients include: Grafton Street Irish Imports; Parke Bernet Galleries; Delmonico's Hotel; Carson, Lundin & Thorson, P.C., Architects; Scandinavian Airlines; Hearst Publications. Publications: "Who's Who in American Women."

Open leading and a two-column measure (left) add importance to the introduction for each department without requiring the space of a full page.

Small pieces of art, which print in green, are sprinkled throughout the catalog to help break up the text.

Quotes from instructors and experts in the field (below right) are also used to break up the text. Although the type is smaller than that usually found in blurbs, the open leading, the border, and the green initial cap combine to make this an effective graphic element.

The typography for course listings is simple and effective: a 2-point rule, a Futura Heavy course number, a Futura Bold course title, italic for schedule/credit/fee data, and Century Old Style for running text with the instructor's name in boldface.

The triangle borders use the same Zapf Dingbat technique as the educational catalog on the facing page but without a character space.

Design: School of Visual Arts Press (New York, NY)

Pages from the catalog for The School of Visual Arts. Trim size: 7-1/4 by 10-3/4

68 PHOTOGRAPHY

process their own film outside class.
William L. Broecker, Photographer. B.A., University of Michigan; M.A., Michigan State University. Editor: *ICP Encyclopedia of Photography; Leica Manual 15th ed.*; Associate Technical Director, *Encyclopedia of Practical Photography*. Publications: "Popular Photography," "Invitation To Photography," "35mm Photography," "Color Photography Annual," "Exposure," "Infinity."

PROFESSIONAL

The following courses are offered to advanced students of photography and working photographers who are able to maintain the pace of classes that take for granted basic technical skills and experience. These professional level courses focus on portfolio development in the different photographic specializations. Critical analysis of all aspects of the photograph from concept through to finished prints/chromes is offered. At this stage self-initiated work is essential and the personal aesthetic is further refined.

¶ If you are interested in learning new techniques or exploring unfamiliar advancements in technology, there are a number of courses for you to consider.
¶ If you are dissatisfied with the results your current portfolio is getting, a professional course offering critical analysis may be helpful.

PC300A
Advanced Printing
Tues - 2 Credits - $250.00
Lab Fee, $20.00
A course designed for the intermediate and advanced student who is interested in approaching printing as a fine art. Each print will be tailored to the photograph itself. Students should come to the first class session ready to print. Prerequisites: PC205, Basic Photography II, and PC256, Black and White Printing, or presentation of your portfolio at the first session.
Bob Brooks, Photographer, Printer. Has worked in many studios including those of Irving Penn and Bob Adelman. One-Person Exhibition: Plaza Caribe. Group Exhibitions: Floating Foundation of Photography; The People Yes Show, Central Park. Clients: Xerox Corporation, Playtex, Coca-Cola, Fischbach Gallery. Publications: "U.S. Camera," "The Visual Dialogue," "Art News."

PC307A
Photojournalism
Thurs - 2 Credits - $250.00
A survey of practical photojournalism as it exists at wire services and newspapers. The training of perception and the use of the camera as a reporting tool are stressed. Topics to be discussed include: journalism for the photographer; personal vision vs. professional credibility; new technology and how it will affect you; paying the rent as a freelancer; how words can make your camera lie; the use and abuse of photography in public relations; portfolio critique and preparation. Students must have access to their own or commercial darkroom.
Edward Hart, Picture Editor, United Press International, New York City Bureau. B.A., Long Island University. Formerly, Writer/Producer, UPI Television Service. Member: National Press Photographers Association, Society of Professional Journalists, Reporters Committee for Freedom of the Press.

PC316A
Advanced Studio Photography
Mon - 2 Credits - $250.00
Model and Equipment Fees, $35.00
(Limited to twenty students)
A course designed for the advanced student who has successfully completed PC221, Basic Studio Photography, or equivalent. The first two weeks will be devoted to still-life, shot with the 4" x 5" view camera using Polaroid film. (Students must supply their own Polaroid film Type 52). The remainder of the course will be devoted to 35mm or 2 1/4" x 2 1/4" format. Controlled lighting, using strobe to establish mood rather than just illuminate, will be the theme of all assignments. The student will shoot still-life, fashion, beauty and nudes.
Len DeLessio, Photographer. B.F.A., School of Visual Arts. Publications: "Business Week," "Cosmopolitan," "New York," "Parents," "People," "Penthouse," "Viva," "Time," "Elle," "Working Woman." Clients include: American Optical, Binney & Smith/Crayola, Chesebrough Ponds, Fujinon Optical, Andrew Geller Shoes, General Foods - Gaines Dog Food, Mercedes-Benz, Parke-Davis, Perry Ellis, Pierre Cardin Fragrances, P&G - Cascade, Tide, Highpoint, R.J. Reynolds -

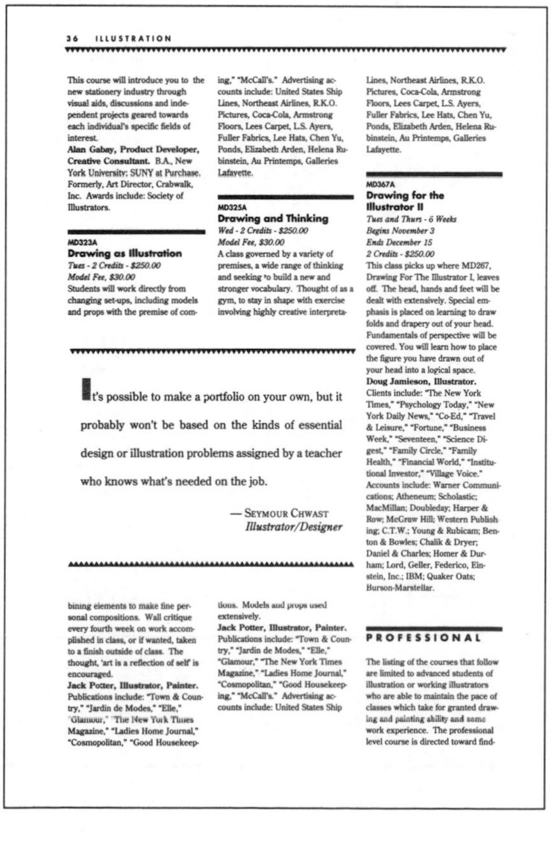

36 ILLUSTRATION

This course will introduce you to the new stationery industry through visual aids, discussions and independent projects geared towards each individual's specific fields of interest.
Alan Gabay, Product Developer, Creative Consultant. B.A., New York University; SUNY at Purchase. Formerly, Art Director, Crabwalk, Inc. Awards include: Society of Illustrators.

MD323A
Drawing as Illustration
Tues - 2 Credits - $250.00
Model Fee, $30.00
Students will work directly from changing set-ups, including models and props with the premise of combining elements to make fine personal compositions. Wall critique every fourth week on work accomplished in class, or if wanted, taken to a finish outside of class. The thought, 'art is a reflection of self' is encouraged.
Jack Potter, Illustrator, Painter. Publications include: "Town & Country," "Jardin de Modes," "Elle," "Glamour," "The New York Times Magazine," "Ladies Home Journal," "Cosmopolitan," "Good Housekeeping," "McCall's." Advertising accounts include: United States Ship Lines, Northeast Airlines, R.K.O. Pictures, Coca-Cola, Armstrong Floors, Lees Carpet, L.S. Ayers, Fuller Fabrics, Lee Hats, Chen Yu, Ponds, Elizabeth Arden, Helena Rubinstein, Au Printemps, Galleries Lafayette.

MD325A
Drawing and Thinking
Wed - 2 Credits - $250.00
Model Fee, $30.00
A class governed by a variety of premises, a wide range of thinking and seeking to build a new and stronger vocabulary. Thought of as a gym, to stay in shape with exercise involving highly creative interpretations. Models and props used extensively.
Jack Potter, Illustrator, Painter. Publications include: "Town & Country," "Jardin de Modes," "Elle," "Glamour," "The New York Times Magazine," "Ladies Home Journal," "Cosmopolitan," "Good Housekeeping," "McCall's." Advertising accounts include: United States Ship Lines, Northeast Airlines, R.K.O. Pictures, Coca-Cola, Armstrong Floors, Lees Carpet, L.S. Ayers, Fuller Fabrics, Lee Hats, Chen Yu, Ponds, Elizabeth Arden, Helena Rubinstein, Au Printemps, Galleries Lafayette.

It's possible to make a portfolio on your own, but it probably won't be based on the kinds of essential design or illustration problems assigned by a teacher who knows what's needed on the job.

— SEYMOUR CHWAST
Illustrator/Designer

MD367A
Drawing for the Illustrator II
Tues and Thurs - 6 Weeks
Begins November 3
Ends December 15
2 Credits - $250.00
This class picks up where MD267, Drawing For The Illustrator I, leaves off. The head, hands and feet will be dealt with extensively. Special emphasis is placed on learning to draw folds and drapery out of your head. Fundamentals of perspective will be covered. You will learn how to place the figure you have drawn out of your head into a logical space.
Doug Jamieson, Illustrator. Clients include: "The New York Times," "Psychology Today," "New York Daily News," "Co-Ed," "Travel & Leisure," "Fortune," "Business Week," "Seventeen," "Science Digest," "Family Circle," "Family Health," "Financial World," "Institutional Investor," "Village Voice." Accounts include: Warner Communications; Atheneum; Scholastic; MacMillan; Doubleday; Harper & Row; McGraw Hill; Western Publishing; C.T.W.; Young & Rubicam; Benton & Bowles; Chalik & Dryer; Daniel & Charles; Homer & Durham; Lord, Geller, Federico, Einstein, Inc.; IBM; Quaker Oats; Burson-Marstellar.

PROFESSIONAL

The listing of the courses that follow are limited to advanced students of illustration or working illustrators who are able to maintain the pace of classes which take for granted drawing and painting ability and some work experience. The professional level course is directed toward find-

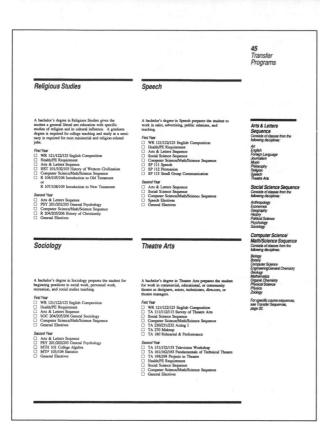

The format for this catalog accommodates several different kinds of listings, three of which are shown here. The distinctive treatment of the top and bottom margins and the consistency of the type style unify the different components of the catalog.

The heavy rules are 4 point.

The typeface makes good use of the contrast between Helvetica Narrow and Times Roman.

Design: Lisa Wilcox and Bill Symes (Oregon City, OR)

Pages from the Clackamas Community College catalog. Trim size: 8-3/8 by 10-3/4

A highly styled newspaper format (below) sets a dynamic tone for the "Course Highlights" section in the opening pages of this continuing education catalog.

The type styling illustrates how you can achieve a great deal of variety through an adventurous use of the two most familiar typefaces. The Helvetica family is used for display and Times Roman for running text. Note, though, the contrasting leading and column widths, the letterspacing, reverse type, wrap-around text, type on tints, dotted rules, initial caps, and boxed copy. Each text block is treated as a pattern of type that is distinct from every other text block on the spread.

The same four-column grid ties together the opening pages and the course information (above right). In the course listings, the outer column is used to list the schedule, credit, and fees for the courses described on that page. Where needed, the outer two columns can be used for this purpose.

Design:
Jonathan Maier
(Portland, OR)

Pages from the Portland State University Quarterly Bulletin for Continuing Education.
Trim size:
11-1/4 by 13-9/16

The Huck Lockbolt Fastening System

The Huck Fastening System consists of three separate components that function as a single operating unit.

1 Fastener: LGP shear-type fasteners and GP tension-type fasteners are available in a wide range of diameters and grip lengths, and a variety of materials and finishes.

2 Nose Assembly: Nose assemblies provide a link between the fastener and the installation tool. Each is designed to install a specific fastener type and diameter. They can be easily attached to and removed from installation tools.

3 Installation Tool: Huck tooling is available in three configurations:

1. Pneumatic hand-held systems which are powered by 90-100 psi air pressure.

2. Hydraulic hand-held systems which are powered by Huck POWERIG® Hydraulic units.

3. Automated Drivmatic drill riveter systems which can be mounted on drill riveter lower rams.

Pin Position and Swage Gage part numbers are listed for each fastener diameter and type. These gages are designed to inspect installed fastener grip and collar swage. For instructions for use, refer to Boeing standard BAC 5004-2.

Head   *Annular Locking Grooves*   *Collar*

Shank   *Breakneck*   *Pintail*

The Lockbolt Pin consists of a head, shank, annular locking grooves, breakneck, and pintail. (note: locking grooves are not helical threads)

The Collar is smooth bore (inside diameter and outside diameter), is symmetrically double-ended, and can be installed in either direction.

The Model 2792 Hydraulic Installation Tool coupled with the Model 940 POWERIG Hydraulic Unit. A combination that's light weight and maneuverable.

A real production workhorse, the Model 225 Pneumatic Installation Tool, like all our tools, is factory tested to offer years of dependable service.

Huck offers a wide variety of nose assemblies to meet the requirements of any application.

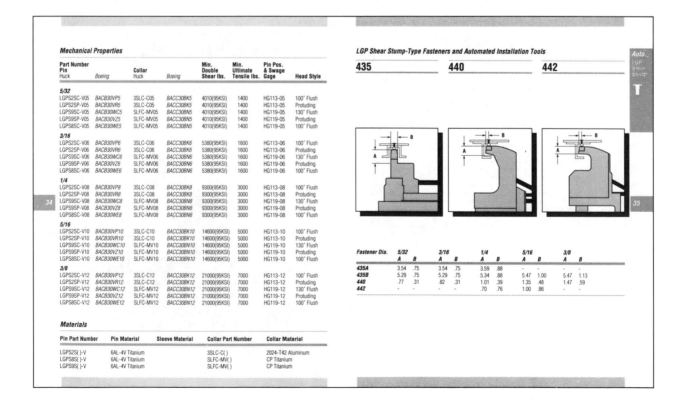

Mechanical Properties

Part Number Pin Huck	Boeing	Collar Huck	Boeing	Min. Double Shear lbs.	Min. Ultimate Tensile lbs.	Pin Pos. & Swage Gage	Head Style
5/32							
LGPS2SC-V05	BACB30VP5	3SLC-C05	BACC30BK5	4010(95KSI)	1400	HG113-05	100° Flush
LGPS2SP-V05	BACB30VR5	3SLC-C05	BACC30BK5	4010(95KSI)	1400	HG113-05	Protruding
LGPS9SC-V05	BACB30WC5	SLFC-MV05	BACC30BN5	4010(95KSI)	1400	HG119-05	130° Flush
LGPS9SP-V05	BACB30VZ5	SLFC-MV05	BACC30BN5	4010(95KSI)	1400	HG119-05	Protruding
LGPS8SC-V05	BACB30WE5	SLFC-MV05	BACC30BN5	4010(95KSI)	1400	HG119-05	100° Flush
3/16							
LGPS2SC-V06	BACB30VP6	3SLC-C06	BACC30BK6	5380(95KSI)	1600	HG113-06	100° Flush
LGPS2SP-V06	BACB30VR6	3SLC-C06	BACC30BK6	5380(95KSI)	1600	HG113-06	Protruding
LGPS9SC-V06	BACB30WC6	SLFC-MV06	BACC30BN6	5380(95KSI)	1600	HG119-06	130° Flush
LGPS9SP-V06	BACB30VZ6	SLFC-MV06	BACC30BN6	5380(95KSI)	1600	HG119-06	Protruding
LGPS8SC-V06	BACB30WE6	SLFC-MV06	BACC30BN6	5380(95KSI)	1600	HG119-06	100° Flush
1/4							
LGPS2SC-V08	BACB30VP8	3SLC-C08	BACC30BK8	9300(95KSI)	3000	HG113-08	100° Flush
LGPS2SP-V08	BACB30VR8	3SLC-C08	BACC30BK8	9300(95KSI)	3000	HG113-08	Protruding
LGPS9SC-V08	BACB30WC8	SLFC-MV08	BACC30BN8	9300(95KSI)	3000	HG119-08	130° Flush
LGPS9SP-V08	BACB30VZ8	SLFC-MV08	BACC30BN8	9300(95KSI)	3000	HG119-08	Protruding
LGPS8SC-V08	BACB30WE8	SLFC-MV08	BACC30BN8	9300(95KSI)	3000	HG119-08	100° Flush
5/16							
LGPS2SC-V10	BACB30VP10	3SLC-C10	BACC30BK10	14600(95KSI)	5000	HG113-10	100° Flush
LGPS2SP-V10	BACB30VR10	3SLC-C10	BACC30BK10	14600(95KSI)	5000	HG113-10	Protruding
LGPS9SC-V10	BACB30WC10	SLFC-MV10	BACC30BN10	14600(95KSI)	5000	HG119-10	130° Flush
LGPS9SP-V10	BACB30VZ10	SLFC-MV10	BACC30BN10	14600(95KSI)	5000	HG119-10	Protruding
LGPS8SC-V10	BACB30WE10	SLFC-MV10	BACC30BN10	14600(95KSI)	5000	HG119-10	100° Flush
3/8							
LGPS2SC-V12	BACB30VP12	3SLC-C12	BACC30BK12	21000(95KSI)	7000	HG113-12	100° Flush
LGPS2SP-V12	BACB30VR12	3SLC-C12	BACC30BK12	21000(95KSI)	7000	HG113-12	Protruding
LGPS9SC-V12	BACB30WC12	SLFC-MV12	BACC30BN12	21000(95KSI)	7000	HG119-12	130° Flush
LGPS9SP-V12	BACB30VZ12	SLFC-MV12	BACC30BN12	21000(95KSI)	7000	HG119-12	Protruding
LGPS8SC-V12	BACB30WE12	SLFC-MV12	BACC30BN12	21000(95KSI)	7000	HG119-12	100° Flush

Materials

Pin Part Number	Pin Material	Sleeve Material	Collar Part Number	Collar Material
LGPS2S( )-V	6AL-4V Titanium		3SLC-C( )	2024-T42 Aluminum
LGPS8S( )-V	6AL-4V Titanium		SLFC-MV( )	CP Titanium
LGPS9S( )-V	6AL-4V Titanium		SLFC-MV( )	CP Titanium

LGP Shear Stump-Type Fasteners and Automated Installation Tools

435   **440**   **442**

Fastener Dia.	5/32		3/16		1/4		5/16		3/8	
	A	B	A	B	A	B	A	B	A	B
435A	3.54	.75	3.54	.75	3.59	.88	-	-	-	-
435B	5.29	.75	5.29	.75	5.34	.88	5.47	1.00	5.47	1.13
440	.77	.31	.82	.31	1.01	.39	1.35	.48	1.47	.59
442	-	-	-	-	.70	.76	1.00	.86	-	-

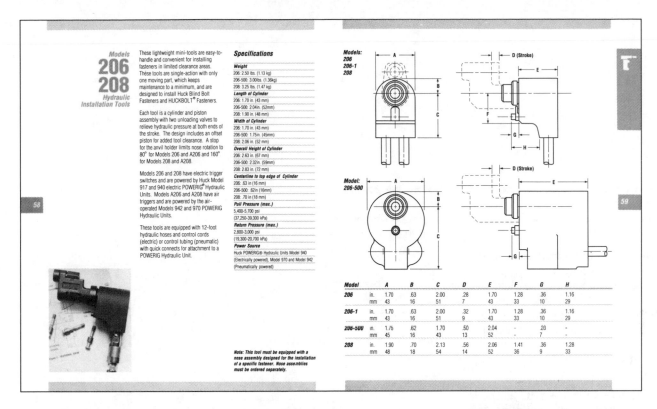

Utility informs every aspect of the design of this technical manual for selecting and using fasteners and fastener installation tools. The manageable size, the spiral binding, the tabbed section dividers, and the careful handling of the many different kinds of material on virtually every spread show consistently high production values.

The three-column format accommodates a wide range of recurring elements—descriptive text, product photos, technical drawings, and specification tables—with generous white space an integral part of the design of most pages.

The introduction to the fastening system (facing page, top) sets the style with dramatically silhouetted product shots complemented by an exceptionally well-rendered technical illustration. The parts on the right-hand page seem to float above the page, a dimensional illusion not often found in technical manuals and specifications. The designer used scanned photos to work out the position of the images on the page and then replaced them with traditional position stats for the camera-ready pages.

The typography throughout is Helvetica Condensed and Helvetica Condensed Bold, both used in roman and oblique for additional contrast where needed. The Helvetica Condensed family (available as downloadable fonts from Adobe Systems) is unequalled for combining economy of space and maximum readability.

Red is used as an accent color throughout—for rules, product headlines, and boxes—to highlight the reverse type of folios and tool silhouettes. The laminated stock used for the tabbed section dividers matches the color of the printed ink exactly.

The black shadows behind boxed illustrations (facing page, bottom) highlight the illustrations and separate them from one another. This device makes it possible to run as many as six of these illustrations on a page with a great deal of text and very little white space.

The technical illustrations were created in Adobe Illustrator.

Design: Steven Bliss (Kingston, NY)

Pages from the Lockbolt Fastener Design Guide, *produced by the Huck Manufacturing Company. Trim size: 7-3/4 by 9-1/8*

Quick and easy scanning is the goal of this format, an 11- by 17- sheet printed on both sides and folded in half.

Bold headlines and subheads, very open leading, and a graphic element to denote itemized text are all designed to move the reader through the copy quickly. This highly utilitarian approach is intended to suggest that the product will be similarly streamlined and easy to use.

The body text is 10/18 Palatino. The headline is 16/18 Helvetica Black, and the subheads are 12/18 Helvetica Black.

Life-size photos deliver impact. Here they create the illusion that there are windows cut into the paper and that you are looking through them to read the keys.

Design: Kimberly Mancebo (Campbell, CA)

Data sheet for Triad Systems Corporation. Trim size: 11 by 17, folded in half

---

Triad's New Easy Keys Are Designed With You In Mind

The keys are grouped the way you'll use them. And each key is labelled with a name that makes sense, so you don't have to memorize abstract "F-key" codes or obscure combinations.

Here Are a Few of The Keys to the Best Point-of-Sale Program In Your Industry

⊕—▼ Our ten-key numerical keypad makes SKU entry quick, easy and accurate for any clerk.

⊕—▼ The CHARGE key automatically sets the correct discounts, pricing and tax for your charge customers. The right price is given to the right customer.

⊕—▼ Clerks can receive payments quickly at Point-of-Sale, just by using the ROA key.

⊕—▼ Clerks can cash checks and process paid-outs quickly

and efficiently, using the PAID OUT and NO SALE keys. And you get a complete report, by clerk and by terminal. So everyone's cash drawer balances at day's end — or you'll know why.

⊕—▼ The VOID key captures information about voids — of single items and of entire

transactions — by clerk and by terminal. You get the register control you need.

⊕—▼ The TOTAL key keeps everything totally up-to-date: inventory quantities, item sales history, customer accounts. Daily reports recap sales and gross profits for the day.

Contractor Point-of-Sale Brings You These Additional Keys To Success

⊕—▼ Clerks can create quotes in minutes — and save them for

later retrieval — just by using the QUOTE key.

⊕—▼ As soon as a customer approves a quote, clerks can retrieve it and create an order from it, using the ORDER key. Without ever re-posting ordered merchandise.

⊕—▼ You can invoice orders automatically, using the INVOICE key. The customer's account balance and available credit are updated instantly. Automatically. Every time.

The New Easy Keys Are Your Key To Back-office Efficiency, Too

⊕—▼ Need help? It's at your fingertips, anytime you need

it, using the HELP key.

⊕—▼ Feeling disoriented? Hit the HOME key. You're instantly back at the top of the screen.

⊕—▼ Want to see it all on paper? The RUN key starts any

report, any time you want a hard copy.

⊕—▼ And the END key takes you back to the hub of your system, the Main Menu.

These two-sided data sheets have the ingredients needed to position an expensive product: a high-quality still life photograph on the front and carefully organized, detailed information on the back.

The tactile quality of the heavy, coated stock used for the data sheets adds measurably to the first impression. Production values are a key element of the image conveyed in sales literature.

The format is maintained for every product in the series: The photo bleeds off the right edge of the paper, the product name prints in reverse type in the banner that bleeds off the top, and the company logo is at the bottom, aligned with the left edge of the photo. Each product is photographed against two sheets of overlapping paper, which add texture and color to the image. The top sheet is gray; the bottom sheet is an accent color that changes from one product sheet to the next, a technique that unifies and distinguishes at the same time.

The layout of the back of the sheet is dictated by the information and changes as needed from one product to another. The margins, typographic style, and logo placement remain consistent throughout the series. Boldface heads, generous space between columns, and bulleted lists with hanging indents all contribute to the clarity of the information and the ease with which it is accessed.

Design: Judy Butler, Barbara Jacobsohn, and Teri Baptiste (San Jose, CA)

Data sheets from the Maxtor Corporation. Trim size: 8-1/2 by 11

THE MAXTOR XT-4000S™

170-, 280- and 380-megabyte 5 1/4-inch Fixed Disk Drives with **Advanced SCSI** Controller.

This high capacity 5 1/4-inch Winchester disk drive has an integral **Advanced SCSI** controller. This provides superior performance, including synchronous data transfers.

Maxtor

THE MAXTOR LXT-200™ FAMILY

KEY FEATURES (DRIVE)

- 200-Megabytes formatted storage capacity (at 512-byte sectors)
- Three recording zones.
- "Dedicated" servo.
- Fits standard 3-1/2-inch mounting locations.
- Rotary Voice-Coil Actuator, with a 16-bit, microprocessor-controlled, closed-loop, track-following servo system.
- No sway space required.
- Available with 5-1/4-inch half high and full high mounting hardware (optional).
- Low 40 dBA audible noise.

KEY FEATURES (EMBEDDED SCSI CONTROLLER)

- ANSI X3.131-1986 SCSI Compatible.
- SCSI Common Command Set (CCS-4B).
- 32K Byte Read-Look-Ahead Cache Buffer (2 tracks).
- Disconnect/Reconnect capability.
- 56-bit ECC.
- SCSI-bus transfer rate of up to 3.0 MBytes per second, asynchronous, and 5.0 MBytes per second, synchronous.

- Disk to head bit transfer rate varies from 8.06 to 13.44 Mbits per second, depending upon recording zone.
- Self-test diagnostics.
- Microcode down-loadable through SCSI or via 2-wire connector.
- On-board synchronized spindle capability.
- Very low (600 microseconds) SCSI command overhead.
- 16-bit microcomputer, to reduce SCSI overhead time.
- Sector sizes of from 1 byte to full-track, with 1-byte granularity.

SPECIFICATIONS

DRIVE AND CONTROLLER PERFORMANCE SPECIFICATIONS

Capacity, formatted (512-byte sectors) - MB/drive	202
Capacity, unformatted - MB/drive	227
Track Seek Time, Typical (ms)	
Average	15
Track-to-track	3
Maximum	30
Command Overhead (microseconds)*	600
SCSI Bus Transfer Rate (MBytes per second)	
Asynchronous	3.0
Synchronous	5.0
Disk Transfer Rate (Mbits per second)	8.06, 10.75 and 13.44 depending on drive recording band.

FUNCTIONAL SPECIFICATIONS

Bit Packing Density (BPI)	24,872
Tracks per Inch (TPI)	1,610
Total Tracks	11,784
Sectors per track	29, 39, and 49
Bytes per sector	512
Cylinders	1,473
Recording Method	1, 7 (3-zone)
Rotational Speed (RPM)	3,600 ± .5%
Average Latency (ms)	8.33

*Includes arbitration, message transfer, command transfer, command interpretation, status interpretation, and the "posting" of status.

SCSI COMMAND SET SUPPORTED

Code	Description
00	Test Unit Ready
01	Rezero Unit
03	Request Sense
04	Format Unit
07	Reassign Blocks
08	Read
0A	Write
0B	Seek
12	Inquiry
15	Mode Select
16	Reserve
17	Release
1A	Mode Sense
1B	Start/Stop Unit
1D	Send Diagnostics
25	Read Capacity
28	Read Extended
2A	Write Extended
2B	Seek Extended
2E	Write and Verify
2F	Verify
37	Read Defect Data
3B	Write Data Buffer
3C	Read Data Buffer
E8	Read Long
EA	Write Long

DRIVE RELIABILITY SPECIFICATIONS

MTBF (hours)	50,000
MTTR (minutes)	20
PM	Not Required

DATA RELIABILITY SPECIFICATIONS

Recoverable Error Rate	10 in 10¹¹
Unrecoverable Error Rate	10 in 10¹⁵
Seek Error Rate	10 in 10⁷

MEDIA AND DRIVE PHYSICAL SPECIFICATIONS

Number of disks	4
Number of Data Heads	7
Dimensions	
Height	1.625 in. (41.3 mm)
Width	4.000 in. (101.6 mm)
Depth	5.750 in. (146 mm)
Shock (G's)	
Non-Operating	50
Operating (No Errors)	3
Operating (Recoverable Errors)	10
Weight	1.8 lbs. (.83 Kg)

ENVIRONMENTAL SPECIFICATIONS

Power Dissipation (Watts)	10
Temperature Limits (Degrees, C)	
Operating	5 to 50
Non-Operating	-40 to 65
Temperature Gradient (Degrees, C, per hr)	20
Relative Humidity Limits (%, Non-Condensing)	
Operating	5 to 95
Non-Operating	5 to 95
Relative Humidity Variance	20%
Audible Noise	Less than 40 dBA

ELECTRICAL SPECIFICATIONS

+12 VDC ± 5%, .75A (typical)	2.0A (instantaneous)
+5 VDC ± 5%, .2A (typical)	

Maxtor

Maxtor Corporation
211 River Oaks Parkway
San Jose, CA 95134
(408) 432-1700
TELEX 171074
FAX (408) 433-0457

This data sheet is not as slick as the one on the preceeding page, but the handsome format, careful product display, and well-organized typography still evoke confidence in the product.

The three-column grid is given a strong horizontal structure through the use of horizontal rules.

The top rule and the company logo print in red, adding a spot of color that contrasts with the overall quietness of the page.

The contents of the kit are itemized in a bulleted list with hanging indents. The typography, Helvetica Black and Helvetica Light, is simple, nicely spaced, and easy to read.

A simple format with well-rendered line drawings (facing page, top left and bottom) is used for all the assembly and care sheets shipped with products from this large mail-order business.

The rules, logo, column guides, and footlines are standing items in the electronic templates, and a text placeholder is left in position for the product name. For each new product, the actual name is typed over the placeholder (maintaining the text specifications and placement), and text is placed in position. Hand-drawn illustrations are pasted manually onto camera-ready pages. The bottom sample is a half-page size, printed two to a sheet and then trimmed.

Before the conversion to desktop publishing, there was no standard format for these information sheets. According to one of the designers, it took only a few hours to go from no standards to an easy-to-implement design that was consistent with the corporate look.

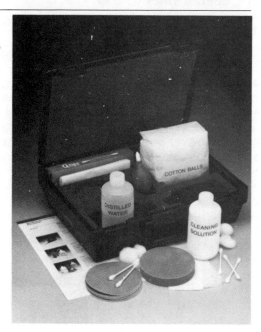

Design (above): Agnew Moyer Smith
(Pittsburgh, PA)

Data sheet for an infrared optics cleaning
kit from Two-Six Incorporated.
Trim size: 8-1/2 by 11

Design (facing page, top left and bottom):
Kathy Tomyris and Deborah Paulson
(Mill Valley, CA)

Product sheets from Smith & Hawken.
Trim size: (top) 8-1/2 by 11; (bottom)
5-1/2 by 8-1/2, printed two to a sheet

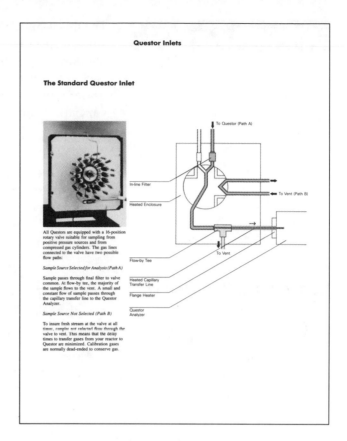

Design (top right):
Agnew Moyer
Smith
(Pittsburgh, PA)

Data sheet for the
Questor Inlet
system from the
Extrel Corporation.
Size: 8-1/2 by 11

A narrow column for the product photo and text (above) leaves plenty of space for the technical illustration and leadered callouts. The illustration was created in MacDraw.

All the leaders are parallel to one another and the callouts align left for a highly organized presentation.

Yellow is used as a functional second color to indicate the flow of gases; the light and bold horizontal rules at the top and bottom of the page also print in yellow.

Three typefaces are used for contrast: Futura Heavy for the boldface, Times Roman for the running text, and Univers Light for the callouts.

FINANCIALS

The financials in this section are from annual reports, where a narrative story, tabular data, and charts and graphs often must coexist between the same covers. In some reports the financials are quarantined in the back. The greater challenge—one that results in a more impressive presentation—is to devise a format that allows you to integrate the financial data into the body of the report.

Annual reports are very image-conscious documents. The style of presentation is obviously related to the size of the organization and the health of the bottom line. But whether yours is a growing company with increased earnings or a modest organization with a not-so-great year, the typographic organization discussed in the introduction to this chapter and in the introduction to the Catalog section is the first building block for financial presentations.

Financials in this section

- *MasterCard*—slick, dramatic photos with a life-sized twist
- *College Auxiliary Service*—mug shots that put a face on numbers
- *Psicor*—tabular data and bar chart highlights
- *Medic Alert*—elegant typography in an integrated format
- *Spencer Foundation*—contrasting type for grant summaries

A lavish annual report such as the one on the facing page reflects the bullishness of a good year. For modest or declining earnings, you'd expect a more conservative presentation.

A photo of the product itself is used to chart growth in comparison to the competition. The life-size photos dramatize the product, especially when juxtaposed against smaller-scale photos of the competition.

The financials in the bottom spread shown give the big picture—cards in circulation, merchant outlets, gross dollar volume—against a dramatic black background in which the earth revolves. The image of the earth reinforces the message of global growth set forth in the table at the top of the page.

Straightforward charts become dramatic when each bar prints in a different color, as they do here, against a black background.

Design: The Will Hopkins Group (New York, NY)

Pages from the annual report of MasterCard International, Inc. Trim size: 8-1/2 by 11

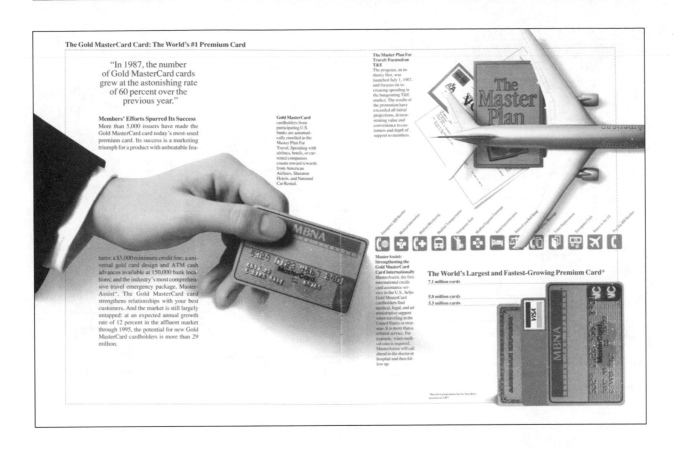

The Gold MasterCard Card: The World's #1 Premium Card

"In 1987, the number of Gold MasterCard cards grew at the astonishing rate of 60 percent over the previous year."

Members' Efforts Spurred Its Success
More than 5,000 issuers have made the Gold MasterCard card today's most-used premium card. Its success is a marketing triumph for a product with unbeatable features: a $5,000 minimum credit line; a universal gold card design and ATM cash advances available at 150,000 bank locations; and the industry's most comprehensive travel emergency package, Master-Assist™. The Gold MasterCard card strengthens relationships with your best customers. And the market is still largely untapped: at an expected annual growth rate of 12 percent in the affluent market through 1995, the potential for new Gold MasterCard cardholders is more than 29 million.

Gold MasterCard cardholders from participating U.S. banks are automatically enrolled in the Master Plan For Travel. Spending with airlines, hotels, or car-rental companies counts toward rewards from American Airlines, Sheraton Hotels, and National Car Rental.

The Master Plan For Travel: Focused on T&E
The program, an industry first, was launched July 1, 1987, and focuses on increasing spending in the burgeoning T&E market. The results of the promotion have exceeded all initial projections, demonstrating value and convenience to customers and depth of support to members.

MasterAssist: Strengthening the Gold MasterCard Card Internationally
MasterAssist, the first international credit card assistance service in the U.S., helps Gold MasterCard cardholders find medical, legal, and administrative support when traveling in the United States or overseas. It is more than a referral service. For example, when medical care is required, MasterAssist will call ahead to the doctor or hospital and then follow up.

The World's Largest and Fastest-Growing Premium Card

7.1 million cards
5.8 million cards
5.5 million cards

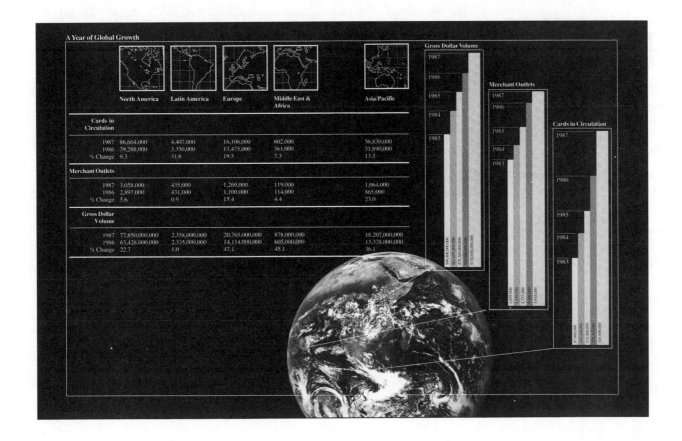

A Year of Global Growth

	North America	Latin America	Europe	Middle East & Africa	Asia/Pacific
Cards in Circulation					
1987	86,664,000	4,407,000	16,106,000	602,000	36,830,000
1986	79,288,000	3,350,000	13,475,000	561,000	31,890,000
% Change	9.3	31.6	19.5	7.3	13.3
Merchant Outlets					
1987	3,058,000	435,000	1,269,000	119,000	1,064,000
1986	2,897,000	431,000	1,100,000	114,000	865,000
% Change	5.6	0.9	15.4	4.4	23.0
Gross Dollar Volume					
1987	77,850,000,000	2,358,000,000	20,765,000,000	878,000,000	18,207,000,000
1986	63,428,000,000	2,335,000,000	14,114,000,000	605,000,000	13,378,000,000
% Change	22.7	1.0	47.1	45.1	36.1

Gross Dollar Volume
1987
1986
1985
1984
1983

Merchant Outlets
1987
1986
1985
1984
1983

Cards in Circulation
1987
1986
1985
1984
1983

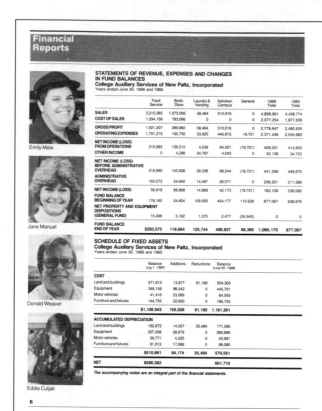

Photos in the narrow outer margins throughout the report above emphasize that this college auxiliary service is a people business. The mug-shot format enables the publication to serve three very different purposes—annual report, morale booster for current employees, and recruiting tool for managerial-level positions.

Contrasting bold and regular Helvetica with light and bold rules helps organize the tables. The tables were set in Microsoft Word and the tabs in PageMaker. The crimson banner at the top of each page provides accent color.

A conservative approach to financial highlights (right) combines straightforward tables and bar charts. Color rules set off the main headline and the income and balance sheet category heads.

The typeface is Futura. The charts print in tones of red and blue.

Design (above): Wadlin & Erber (New Paltz, NY)

Spread from a report for the College Auxiliary Services at The College of New Paltz, State University of New York. Size: 8-1/2 by 11

Design (right): Lisa Menders (Royal Oak, MI)

Page from the Psicor, Inc. Annual Report. Size: 8-1/2 by 11

Financial Highlights

All amounts are in thousands, except per share data.

Income Statement Data:	1982	1983	1984	1985	1986
			Years Ended September 30,		
Revenue	$5,822	$10,151	$13,546	$16,324	$21,162
Expenses:					
Operating supplies	1,442	3,489	4,630	5,113	6,379
Salaries and related expenses	2,232	2,837	4,092	5,829	7,892
General and adminstrative	903	1,151	1,819	2,215	2,746
Depreciation and amortization	696	891	1,003	1,174	1,362
Insurance	94	109	125	98	485
Total expenses	5,367	8,477	11,669	14,429	18,864
Operating income	455	1,674	1,877	1,895	2,298
Other expense—net	615	820	740	520	450
Income (loss) before income taxes	(160)	854	1,137	1,375	1,848
Provision for income taxes	0	62	438	537	665
Net income (loss)	$ (160)	$ 792	$ 699	$ 838	$ 1,183
Earnings (loss) per share (1)	$ (.06)	$ .29	$ .25	$ .30	$ .38
Number of shares used in computation (1)	2,700	2,750	2,779	2,838	3,121

Balance Sheet Data:	1982	1983	1984	1985	1986
			September 30,		
Working capital (deficiency)	$ (834)	$ (378)	$ 80	$ 262	$ 5,428
Total assets	5,838	6,652	6,313	8,402	14,200
Total long-term debt	2,991	2,147	1,570	1,636	355
Shareholders' equity	524	1,316	2,014	2,853	10,690

(1) See "Earnings Per Share" at Note 1 of Notes to Financial Statements.

Revenue | Net Income (Loss) | Earnings (Loss) per share

Years Ended Sept. 30	Revenue	Net Income (Loss)	Earnings (Loss) per share
'86	$21,162	$1,183	$.38
'85	$16,324	$838	$.30
'84	$13,546	$699	$.25
'83	$10,151	$792	$.29
'82	$5,822	$(160)	$(.06)

Financial Highlights . . . The Medic Alert Foundation International accounts for all membership fees, contributions and other revenues with utmost care. These pages were prepared under the direction of Robert C. Johnson, Treasurer, to highlight the financial activity for the twelve month period ended September 30, 1987. A complete, audited financial statement is available on request.

Fund Balance Summary . . . All fund balances for this period increased $1,179,960 because support and revenue exceeded expenditures. All Foundation funds totaled $4,163,018, of which $2,206,916 is invested in the headquarters building. Fund balances are used for working funds and have been designated to cover the cost of updating the Foundation's membership services computer system.

WHAT WE RECEIVED . . .

Total support and revenue for the 12 months was derived from several sources:

Membership Fees - The number of new members was the same as the previous year. However, reorders increased 10% and updates increased by 14%. The volume of gold and silver emblems is also increasing. As a result, membership fees increased 6%.

Contributions - Contributions by our membership for the support of Medic Alert continued to increase. All solicitations were made by mail to members only. Contributions amounted to 42% of the Foundation's total support and revenue.

Other Revenue - Reimbursement from foreign affiliates for support of international membership expansion increased during the year. Earnings on investment increased because the Foundation had larger investment balances.

SUPPORT AND REVENUE

	For Twelve months 9/30/87	Compared to prior 12 month period
Member's Fees	$3,769,278	up 6%
Contributions	3,023,234	up 26%
Other Revenues	379,152	up 60%
Total Support and Revenue	7,171,664	up 13%

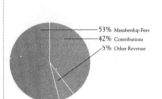

53% Membership Fees
42% Contributions
5% Other Revenue

EXPENSES

	For Twelve months 9/30/87	Percent of Expenditures
Membership Services	$4,096,091	69%
Professional Education Volunteer Training & Public Information	447,860	7%
International Development	221,511	4%
Total Services	$4,765,462	80%
Management & General	546,505	9%
Fund Raising	652,487	11%
TOTAL EXPENSES	$5,964,454	100%

FUND BALANCES

Beginning of Period (10/1/86)	$3,328,254
Support & Revenue	7,171,664
Expenditure and Charges to Funds	<5,991,704>
End of Period (9/30/87)	$4,508,214

69% Member Services
11% Fund Raising
9% Management & General
7% Professional Education & Training; Public Relations
4% International Development

WHAT WE SPENT...

Membership Services - The cost of establishing new members' medical records and maintaining and updating members' records.

Professional Education, Volunteer Training and Public Information - Costs of continuing education of professionals, volunteers and the public to the vital information and lifesaving potential of Medic Alert services.

Fund Raising - Fund raising expenses increased by only 1%, while contributions increased by 26% and substantially increased the number of members and donors to the Foundation.

Management and General - These costs declined slightly, primarily due to one time costs charged in the previous year.

Summary of Grants

Grantee	Unpaid Balance 3/31/86	Authorized During the Fiscal Year	Payments During the Fiscal Year	Unpaid Balance 3/31/87
California State University, Fresno Fresno, California Ernst L. Moerk, language teaching/learning in the home ($49,000 in 1906)	$ 26,000	$	$ 26,000	$
University of California, Berkeley Berkeley, California David L. Kirp, school and community response to children with AIDS	—	102,100	34,600	67,500
University of California, Berkeley Berkeley, California Martin Trow and Sheldon Rothblatt, two centuries of British and American higher education ($195,250 in 1985)	155,750	—	42,500	113,250
University of California, Berkeley Berkeley, California Aaron Wildavsky, cultural theory: foundations, applications, implications	—	146,700	83,100	63,600
University of California, Irvine Irvine, California Ellen Greenberger and Wendy A. Goldberg, impacts of parental employment on the socialization of children	—	7,494	7,494	—
University of California, Irvine Irvine, California Jean Lave, context, cognition, and activity in the lived-in world	—	21,000	21,000	—
University of California, Los Angeles Los Angeles, California Burton R. Clark, research organization and training of advanced scholars	—	340,050	—	340,050
University of California, Los Angeles Los Angeles, California Linda M. Perkins, race, uplift, education, and black women	—	50,700	39,200	11,500
University of California, Los Angeles Los Angeles, California Kathryn Kish Sklar, Florence Kelley and the women's world of reform	—	59,100	—	59,100

44

Design (above):
Tom Lewis
(San Diego, CA)

Pages from the Medic Alert annual report.
Size: 8-1/2 by 11

Design (left):
Edward Hughes
(Evanston, IL)

Pages from The Spencer Foundation Annual Report.
Size: 7-1/4 by 10

Data for revenues and expenses in the report above is accompanied by sidebars with explanatory notes and comparisons to previous years' data.

The format throughout the report combines a single column of running text with one- or two-column text sidebars. On pages without financials, the sidebars focus on human interest stories, such as the volunteer of the year, and special events, such as a video documentary about the foundation.

The elegantly styled typography, with its use of large and small caps, is Goudy Old Style. The running text and financial data print in gray-brown; the sidebar and running head print in black.

Contrasting type makes this summary of grants (left) easy to follow. The boldface is Franklin Gothic Heavy; the regular and italic faces are Goudy Old Style. Italic text and chart headings print in crimson.

FORMS

The goal of a form is decidedly simple: It should be easy to read, easy to complete, and easy to retrieve data from, all of which is easier said than done. Once you think you've got it right, try testing your form on some typical subjects. Chances are they'll question something you thought was obvious or enter information in the wrong place. Of course, there's no way to account for the range of attention, or inattention, respondents will bring to the forms you create. But the goal of designing an effective form is to try to make it is simple as possible.

A company with a long tradition of graphic design excellence turns forms into a minimalist art. Intended for internal use, these forms assume more information on the user's part than would be appropriate in a form to be circulated outside the company.

The black panels with reverse type give the forms a dramatic and sophisticated style. The shadow in the company logo adds to the effect.

An unruled, 10% gray panel sets off the "needed" and "used" dates to be filled in for each item on the billing form. Gray should be used cautiously in spaces where the respondent must write.

Design: Mary Salvadore (Boston, MA)

Forms from WGBH Television.
Trim size: 8-1/2 by 11

Camera Billing Form

Traffic/Archive Recycled Tape Credit Form: 915

Dept./Project

Date Submitted

Intended Date of Recycling

Request Reference Number

Unit Manager

The intended date of recycling asks you to name a date upon which the tape in question may be destroyed.

Credits for recycled tape may be applied to *existing* projects only. Some materials authorized for recycling may not meet even minimum quality standards. In such cases a lesser than standard amount of credit – or none – may be issued. All recycled tape credits must be used during the current fiscal year.

This recycling authorization form must be signed below by an appropriate department head, producer, post-production supervisor, and/or unit manager associated with *the tape to be recycled.*

	Quantity	Archive/Traffic Numbers	Project Code to be Credited
2 Inch Videotape			
1 Inch Videotape			
3/4 Inch Cassette			
Beta/VHS			

The undersigned accepts full responsibility for the destruction/recycling of all materials listed with the understanding that the materials will be destroyed/recycled on or after the indicated intended date of recycling.

Authorized Signature

Forms in this section

- *Billing and Traffic*—an artful style for internal use
- *Employee Information*—a lesson in good spacing
- *Math Learning Center*—the boxed-in approach
- *Proposal Evaluation*—ruled space for narrative responses
- *Subscription Card*—with an electronic picture of the product
- *Application for Admission*—adapting a publication's grid for a form
- *InFractions*—a triplicate sales receipt

Employee Information

Basic Information • *Required for all Actions*							
Action (*circle*) Hire	Separation	Personal	Pay Rate	LOA	Job Change	Other	
Last Name		First Name		Middle Initial			
Effective Date		Employee Number		Dept./Location			

Personal
Street	City
State	Zip Code	Telephone
Birth Date	Social Security No.
Sex (*circle*) Male Female Race (*circle*) White Asian Am. Indian Black Hispanic Other
Salaried Personnel Only • Attach Voided Original Check for Direct Deposit Services

Insurance
Marital Status
Spouse Name	Birth Date
Dependent Name	Birth Date
Dependent Name	Birth Date
Dependent Name	Birth Date
Life Beneficiary	Relation

Leave of Absence
Start Date	Anticipated Return Date
Reason for Leave

Pay Rate • *Do Not Fax Pay Information*
Previous Pay Rate	New Pay Rate	Pay Type (*circle*) Hourly Salary

Job Change
Previous Position/Level	New Position/Level
Previous Department	New Department

Separation of Employment
Type of Separation (*circle*) Resignation Discharge Other
Vacation Pay Due	Severance Pay Due

Explanation • Comments

Authorization / Date
Originator	Senior Management
Human Resources	Payroll

A banner incorporating the company logo, used here and in the forms on the facing page, is a useful device for maintaining a consistent image in forms and other communications.

Ruled gray panels direct the eye to different categories of questions in this employee information form. The distance between the top and bottom of each panel is the same as the distance between all the other rules on the page.

The typeface is Helvetica bold and regular throughout, with italic used to distinguish special instructions (such as the word "circle" when two or more options are given).

Design: Manfred Petri (Atlanta, GA)

Employee Information form from Geiger International.

Trim size: 8-1/2 by 11

Order Form

Math and the **M i n d ' s** Eye

Math Learning Center
P.O. Box 3226, Salem, OR 97302
(503) 370-8130

Bill To _____

Ship To _____

Phone _____

P.O. # _____ Cash Enclosed _____ Charge _____

(Term net 30 days)

Quantity	Catalog #	Description	Unit Price	Total
	ME 1	Unit I **Seeing Mathematical Relationships** available Dec 1, 1987 The Handshake Problem, Cube Patterns, Pattern Block Trains and Perimeters, Diagrams and Sketches	$3.50	
	ME 2	Unit II **Visualizing Number Concepts** available Feb 1, 1988 Basic Operations, Odd and Even Numbers, Factors and Primes, Averaging, Greatest Common Divisors, Least Common Multiples	$5.00	
	ME 3	Unit III **Modeling Whole Numbers** available Oct 1, 1987 Grouping and Numeration, Linear Measure and Dimension, Arithmetic with Number Pieces, Base 10 Numeration, Base 10 Addition and Subtraction, Number Piece Rectangles, Base 10 Multiplication, Base 10 Division	$6.50	
	ME 4	Unit IV **Modeling Rationals** available Apr 1, 1988 Egg Carton Fractions, Fractions on a Line, Fraction Bars, Addition and Subtraction with Fraction Bars, Multiplication and Division with Fraction Bars, Introduction to Decimals, Decimal Addition and Subtraction, Decimal Length and Area, Decimal Multiplication and Division, Fraction Operations Via Area: Addition and Subtraction, Fraction Operations Via Area: Multiplication, Fraction Operations Via Area: Division	$9.75	
	ME 5	Unit V **Looking at Geometry** available Nov 1, 1987 Geoboard Figures, Geoboard Areas, Area of Silhouettes, Geoboard Triangles, Geoboard Squares, Pythagorean Theorem, Geoboard Perimeters, An Introduction to Surface Area and Volume, Shape and Surface Area, Areas of Irregular Shapes	$7.50	

All orders for less than $20, except for school purchase orders, must be prepaid.

All Canadian orders must be paid in U.S. dollars.

Prices are effective October 1, 1987 and subject to change without notice.

We do not accept credit cards

Total for Materials	
No shipping charges to U.S. destinations by Postal Service	
Canadian orders please write for shipping costs	
TOTAL	

☐ Check here if you do not have the 1988 Math Learning Center catalog and want a copy.

THE CENTER FOR FIELD RESEARCH

PROPOSAL EVALUATION

_____ Name of Applicant _____ Title of Proposal

SIGNIFICANCE OF RESEARCH:
To whom, to what, and in what ways, would this research be significant?

CONCEPTUALIZATION:
Are the research objectives well defined with respect to their scholarly, educational, and public contexts?

METHODOLOGY:
Is the methodology appropriate and adequate to the research objectives?

VOLUNTEER ASSIGNMENTS:
Are the assignments for non-specialists useful and valuable, both to the project's objectives and to those participants?

`copyright 1987 Earthwatch`

Boxed information provides a highly organized, easy-to-follow order form.

When a form requires more than a few words for each answer (above right), ruling the space generally improves the legibility of the responses.

The typeface is Times Roman throughout, but the styling of headlines as small and large caps makes it look distinctive and contrasts nicely with the italicized questions below. The type prints in blue on a gray background.

Reproducing a page from a publication is an effective marketing technique for bind-in subscription cards and other circulation and sales promotions.

The page reproduced on the card below is an Encapsulated PostScript file created from the original electronic document of that page; the EPS file was then placed on the order form as a single piece of art. (The EPS option is not currently available in PC PageMaker.)

Design (above left):
Jonathan Maier (Portland, OR)

Order form for educational materials from the Math Learning Center.
Trim size: 8-1/2 by 11

Design (above):
Earthwatch (Watertown, MA)

Form used to evaluate field research proposals by this nonprofit scientific research organization.
Trim size: 8-1/2 by 11

Design (left): Consumer Markets Abroad

Bind-in subscription card from Consumer Markets Abroad.
Trim size: 7-3/4 by 4-1/4

It's time to get your own subscription.

Make sure you see *Consumer Markets Abroad* on time every month. Start your own subscription to *Consumer Markets Abroad*, the newsletter of worldwide consumer trends and lifestyles by returning this postage-free card. **Send no money now.** We will send you a risk-free issue and bill you $189 for a one-year subscription. If you decide not to subscribe, simply write cancel on the invoice, send it back, and keep the free issue. Your subscription includes another eleven issues plus, for your twelfth issue, *Trends and Opportunities Abroad, 1988*, a 200 page softbound reference guide to overseas markets.

Name _____

Company _____

Title _____

Street _____

City/State/Zip _____

Phone _____

CMA/1987

Consumer Markets Abroad is a publication of American Demographics, Inc., a subsidiary of Dow Jones, Inc.

120
Application for Admission

Application for Admission

Date _____ / _____ / _____

Applying for entrance in ☐ Summer ☐ Fall ☐ Winter ☐ Spring 19 _____

Social Security number ☐☐☐ ▨ ☐ ▨ ☐ ☐☐☐☐

Name _____
Last   First   Initial

Date of birth _____ / _____ / _____
Month   Day   Year

Address _____
Street

_____
City   State   Zip

Phone number _____
Day   Evening

State resident ☐ Yes (living in Oregon currently and for preceding 90 days)
☐ No

District resident ☐ Yes (Clackamas County except for Sandy Union High and Lake Oswego School Districts)
☐ No

Course of study _____
Please include program title and code (see back of form).

High school last attended _____
Name   State

Date of high school graduation or GED _____ / _____ / _____
Month   Day   Year

Sex ☐ Male ☐ Female

Ethnic data (optional)
☐ White, non-Hispanic   ☐ Asian or Pacific Islander
☐ Black, non-Hispanic   ☐ American Indian or Alaskan Native
☐ Hispanic   ☐ Handicapped, needing special assistance*

*the Handicap Resource Center coordinates special assistance such as notetakers and sign language interpreters. If you need assistance, check this box and the HRC will contact you. Response is voluntary and will not influence admission to the college.

In case of emergency, please notify _____
Name   Home phone   Work phone

Direct application to
Office of Admissions
Clackamas Community College
19600 South Molalla Avenue
Oregon City, OR 97045

Clackamas Community College supports equal education opportunity regardless of sex, race, national origin, age, marital status, handicap or religion.

---

in

732 West Schubert
Chicago, IL 60614
312.477.5063

Sales Receipt

Sold to:
Name
Address   Apt. No.
City   State   Zip
Day Telephone   Evening Telephone

Ship to:
Name
Address   Apt. No.
City   State   Zip
Day Telephone   Evening Telephone

Office Use Only/Order Number
Date

Style No.	Description	Color Blk	O/W	Blu	Total Quantity	Price Each	Total
101	Long Sleeve Boat Neck Top	☐	☐	☐	_____	$35.00	_____
103	Long Sleeve Cowl Top	☐	☐	☐	_____	45.00	_____
204	Pants	☐	☐	☐	_____	35.00	_____
205	Full Skirt	☐	☐	☐	_____	45.00	_____
206	Straight Skirt	☐	☐	☐	_____	35.00	_____
308	Cowl Dress	☐	☐	☐	_____	80.00	_____
309	Jumper	☐	☐	☐	_____	75.00	_____
410	Jacket	☐	☐	☐	_____	60.00	_____
511	Sash	☐	☐	☐	_____	9.00	_____
	Shoulder Pads	☐	☐		_____	10.00	_____

Signed   Date
Charge to my ☐ MasterCard ☐ Visa Exp. Date _____
☐ a check for the total amount is enclosed. No COD's accepted.

SubTotal _____
Tax _____
Shipping _____
Total _____

Preprinted triplicate sales forms speed up order writing and help ensure completeness and clarity as well. If you compare this form to the sales promotion for the same company (included in the Folders section), you'll see how the combination of a strong logo and consistent type styling create a distinct and consistent image for a company of any size.

Design: Edward Hughes (Evanston, IL)
Order form from InFractions Inc.
Trim size: 5-1/2 by 8-1/2

An application bound into a college catalog uses the catalog grid to create a clear and smart-looking form.

The running head, the 2-point rules at the top and bottom margins, the headline and text style, and the use of the narrow outer column are design elements from the catalog format, shown earlier in this section.

The shadowed ballot boxes for options to be checked by the respondent are Zapf Dingbats (keystroke is unshifted o).

Design: Lisa Wilcox and Bill Symes (Oregon City, OR)
Admission application from the Clackamas Community College catalog.
Trim size: 8-3/8 by 10-3/4

HANDS-ON PROJECTS

SECTION 3

INTRODUCTION TO THE PROJECTS

The projects in this section are structured so that beginners can start right in on Project 1 without any prior experience in creating Page-Maker documents. The instructions do assume, however, that your computer is up and running, that PageMaker is installed and you know how to open it, that you can locate files on your hard disk, and that you know how to print on your workstation.

The purpose of these projects is to provide experience with Page-Maker's tools and techniques in the context of creating real publications. The difference between reading about a technique in a manual and using it in real life provides a stumbling block to many new PageMaker users. Real publications move from one kind of tool or technique to another in a way that is fairly specific to that project. And there's a certain rhythm to using the tools, of PageMaker or any other program, in the context of real work that manuals can't begin to capture. Each job you do with a program not only builds knowledge of specific techniques but, perhaps even more importantly, builds an understanding of the program's internal logic. It's this understanding that enables you, eventually, to figure out why the program responds in certain ways and how to work around apparent limitations.

These projects are therefore intended to supplement the PageMaker manual by applying information covered there to some typical publications. The focus is on building a familiarity with and an understanding of the basic techniques and on developing a certain manual dexterity when you are using those techniques for effects that require some precision.

The layouts of the publications themselves were designed to further this tutorial function. If you find that you can use one of the formats as a prototype for your own publication, that's fine. The point, however, is not so much to say, for example, that you should use racing stripes on a flyer (Project 5) but to take you through the steps involved in creating that kind of graphic effect and incorporating it into a real document. To take another example, you may have an existing format for a newsletter or report that you'd like to convert to desktop production. By working through Project 3 or 4, you should get a good understanding of how to create a template to your own specifications using master pages, spacing guides, placeholders, and standing items on the pasteboard.

One of the wisest and most universally acknowledged pieces of advice in the world of computers is to learn a few programs and to learn them well. With that in mind, we've exploited PageMaker's text and graphic tools as much as possible, more so than one might actually do in real-life work. Certain aspects of the projects could be done faster or more effectively in a graphics program. By doing them in PageMaker, you'll master tools and techniques that will undoubtedly improve your PageMaker skills. So you'll find, for example, instructions for creating a PageMaker truck (Project 6); in the process of creating that truck,

THE PROJECTS AT A GLANCE

The first three projects are arranged in order of difficulty. Each one assumes that you are familiar with techniques used in the previous project. The last three projects are all more complex than the first three, although it's difficult to say that any one of those last three is more complex or difficult than the others. They simply use different techniques. The earlier projects provide more detail about basic techniques; the later projects, while they still take you through each step needed to produce the sample document, assume that you know the basics covered in earlier projects. For example, an early project would tell you where and how to move the zero point, if that was required; a later project would simply tell you where to move it.

If you are a rank beginner, you may want to do the first three projects in sequence. If you have a little experience with PageMaker but don't feel confident of your ability, you might want to start with one of the invitations in Project 2 and then move on to Project 3 to work with master pages and templates. Each project includes a list of techniques you will learn in that project. These lists are intended to help you choose the projects you want to work through.

Project 1: A Simple Certificate for PageMaker Novices

This project guides you through the basic procedures of setting up a new PageMaker document, using the rulers, moving around the publication window, changing the page view, typing text in PageMaker, and using PageMaker's tools to create very simple graphics (circles, rectangles, lines).

Project 2: Two Invitations

There are really two projects in this section. Project 2A, an all-text invitation, takes you through many of the same techniques used in Project 1 but with less detail. Project 2B introduces working with precise increments of space and creating a simple thematic graphic with PageMaker's tools. It also instructs you in how to print multiple copies of an undersized document on a single sheet.

Project 3: A Simple One-Column Format for Newsletters and Reports

This project introduces the use of master pages and templates with a simple format suitable for newsletters and reports. It also introduces placing text in PageMaker that you've created in a word processor; for that purpose you can use the *lorum ipsum* file that came on the PageMaker 3.0 Templates disk—or any text file that you have. The project also includes an exercise using leadered tabs to create a rule; if you have a mental block against tabs (as many people seem to), this may help break through it. Finally, there are sidebars that focus on controlling text in PageMaker.

Project 4: A Two-Column Newsletter

A basic, two-column format is used to create two versions of the newsletter in this project. Different typefaces and headline treatments give each version a unique look. But both use the same basic techniques: working with master pages and templates, defining and applying styles, creating and using a graphic placeholder, and styling hanging indents. The headline treatment used in Project 4B is more demanding than the one in 4A.

Project 5: A Flyer with a Coupon

This project also has two versions using the same format. Here you will work with different column settings within the same page, use tabs in the traditional manner to set columnar material, and set up a coupon. Both versions use Page-Maker graphics that require a certain precision, with Project 5B being more complex than 5A.

Project 6: A Promotional Brochure with Art and Display Typography

This project is divided into modular units so that you can do selected parts of it. The art includes the photo provided on the PageMaker 3.0 Getting Started disk, a truck and map that you can create in PageMaker, and a piece of clip art that you probably won't have. (The clip art exercise is included to show how you can alter clip art to make it work for your layout.) The text gives you experience in refining display type and working with wraparound and justified text.

Ninety-five percent of the people will always use a program at the lowest level. They don't use even 30% of the features, they use 10%; and, next year, when more features come out, they'll use 5% of those.

—Alan Kask,
PC World

you'll become a whiz at using PageMaker's graphics tools, test various fills from the Lines menu, master the program's layering logic, and learn some tricks for centering concentric circles.

The tutorials focus on tasks that beginner and intermediate PageMaker users need in order to utilize the program with some confidence in ongoing document production. Some advanced features, specifically color and Image Control, are not included because we feel their use is still fairly specialized at this point.

Inevitably, projects such as these do not address the very important early stages of publication work—developing the concept, planning the format, and massaging the individual elements to fit the format. For a detailed look at this process in one publication, see the case history in Chapter 4.

The structure of the projects

Each project begins with a brief introduction that describes the format and design elements. The actual document is reproduced full size (or, in the case of documents with a horizontal orientation, as large as is possible on these pages). Within the first few pages of each project, you'll also find a list of the PageMaker techniques you will learn in that project. Use these lists as a guide to help you select which projects you want to work through.

The projects are organized so that numbered, boldface instructions describe the general steps (specify the page setup, define the image area, draw the banner, and so on). Bulleted paragraphs within those numbered instructions detail the specific procedures and techniques required to execute that step. Generally, unbulleted paragraphs explain and amplify the techniques. By organizing the information in this way, we hope you'll be able to move as quickly, or as slowly, through the projects as suits your needs and level of experience.

TIP

Familiarize yourself early on with PageMaker's on-line help. On a Macintosh, you can access this by choosing Guidance from the Apple menu. On a PC, choose Index from the Help menu. In both systems, the on-line help has a branching structure that guides you thorugh a series of lists to a step-by-step procedure for the specific task you need help with.

Marginal tips highlight shortcuts as well as procedures that are important for a fundamental understanding and control of PageMaker's sometimes quirky personality. Most tips are placed adjacent to a step within the project to which that tip can be applied. You'll find additional tips in the margins of the Glossary in the back of the book. The glossary also includes key sequences for many PageMaker commands so you can refer to that section when you can't remember how to bring up the grabber hand, type an em dash, interrupt Autoflow, and so on.

Screen details with captions provide additional tips throughout the project section. Note, however, that the distortion in letter and word spacing that sometimes occurs on-screen in PageMaker is exacerbated when screen images are reduced in size, which they generally are for reproduction in this book.

In addition, throughout the projects you'll find sidebars that focus on PageMaker functions in a context that is both specific to the project at hand and more general as well. You can locate these through the index or by browsing through the project section. These sidebars are highlighted with a gray tint to make them easy to find.

For some projects, we've included variations on the basic design. The purpose of this, as in the grid chapter earlier in the book, is to show how the same underlying page structure can result in publications with rather different "looks," depending on the styling of type and the use of art. If any of the variations meet your own publication needs, you will need to extrapolate some of the details of creating them from the instructions for the basic design.

The projects are self-contained, and all the information you need to complete them is included as part of the instructions. But because the projects build on one another, later projects do not detail certain techniques that have already been covered. Also, some options—such as the page view you work at—vary depending on the size of the monitor you work on, and it would be cumbersome to cover all the possibilities.

To select the tool you need, click on that icon in PageMaker's toolbox. The on-screen pointer turns into different shapes, depending on the tool selected.

▼ ▼ ▼

name	toolbox icon	on-screen icon
pointer tool		
diagonal-line tool		
perpendicular-line tool		
text tool		
square-corner tool		
round-corner tool		
circle tool		
cropping tool		

Macintosh or PC?

The mechanics of working in the PC and Macintosh versions of Page-Maker are virtually identical. For the most part, the differences that do exist have to do with system configuration, font installation, and the need in PC PageMaker to have a working version of Microsoft Windows. The basics of system configuration are beyond the scope of this book; you will need to consult your PageMaker manual, dealer, or whatever technical support is available to you in order to get your system up and running to the point at which you can open PageMaker, begin working in the program, and print.

Once you are up and running, however, you should be able to complete the projects regardless of which computer you use. The projects and instructions were created on a Macintosh and then tested on a PC. With the exception of one procedure (making an Encapsulated Post-Script file in Project 6) and except for the unavailability of outline and shadow-style type on the PC, all procedures work both on the Mac and on the PC. The screen details for menus and dialog boxes were taken from the Mac, but the differences in those screens on a PC are minimal—the text is a little different and occasionally an option is in a different position in the dialog box. Keyboard shortcuts vary from one platform to another. You will generally find the Macintosh shortcut first and the PC alternative immediately following in parentheses.

Capitalization and italics

The names of all menu commands and dialog boxes are capitalized in these instructions, even if part of a name is not capitalized in Page-Maker. For example, whereas the PageMaker menu reads "Page setup," our instructions will tell you to choose the Page Setup command or to specify information in the Page Setup dialog box. On the other hand, if we are speaking generally about page setup, the phrase is not capitalized.

Specific words or values that you are instructed to type in dialog boxes are italicized. If the words should actually be italicized in the publication, that will be stated explicitly.

▲ ▲ ▲
When you want to select a button surrounded by a heavy border, such as the OK button above, simply press the Return or Enter key instead of moving and clicking the mouse. This keyboard shortcut can be used in many PageMaker dialog boxes—including Page Setup, Place, Save As, Type Specs, and Print—so it's a good one to remember.

Menu commands

PageMaker has different kinds of menu commands. Some of them (such as Rulers and Guides) are like toggle switches that you click on and off: A check mark before the command indicates the command is active; no check mark means it is inactive. Similar to these are commands that are on (and checked) until you choose another command in the same category (such as page view and line weights).

Another set of commands (such as Copy and Paste) are either black or gray. When a command is gray, it currently does not apply to anything on the page and cannot be selected. For example, the Copy command will be gray unless some text or a graphic is selected.

Commands that are followed by an ellipsis on the screen, such as Page Setup and Type Specs, display dialog boxes through which you select options and type in specifications.

On the Macintosh, some commands on the Type menu are followed by a solid, right-pointing triangle. Pointing to one of these commands and holding down the mouse button displays a pop-up submenu through which you can change that particular type specification (Font, Size, Leading, and so on).

Defaults

Defaults are preset values or options that PageMaker uses unless you specify otherwise. Like most programs, PageMaker has application defaults and publication defaults. Application defaults apply to all new documents; publication defaults apply only to the current document. You can change and override both kinds of defaults, but it does save time to set them to the choices that you use most frequently.

You can change application defaults *after* you've opened PageMaker but *before* you've opened a document. For example, PageMaker's default unit of measure is inches, so unless you specify otherwise, your ruler increments will be measured in inches. If you work in picas and points more frequently than inches, you'll want to change the application default to picas. Before opening a new document, choose Preferences from the Edit menu and click on Picas in the dialog box. All new documents will then use picas for their unit of measure.

You can change the application default for any menu command that is black, rather than gray, when there is no document open in PageMaker. When you change an application default, the new value will apply to all new publications you open; existing publications will not be affected.

You specify publication defaults after a PageMaker document is open. If, to continue the same example, you have inches as your application default and you open a new document and change the unit of measure to picas, the ruler increments will be picas for that publication but not for subsequent ones. You can change the publication defaults at any time while the document is open.

At those times when PageMaker seems to have a mind of its own, insisting on one typeface or line style when you continue to select another, try changing the publication defaults to the specifications you want. To change a publication default, choose the pointer tool, be sure no text or graphic is selected, and select the specifications you want to set as the current publication defaults. Note that if a tool other than the pointer arrow is active, choosing the arrow will automatically deselect any text or graphics. If the pointer arrow is already active and text or a graphic is selected, click on the selected item to deselect it before resetting the default.

The project instructions generally assume that you are working with PageMaker's original defaults. If you've changed any of the application defaults, your screen may look different from what is described in a particular project. If you want to restore PageMaker's original defaults, simply throw out the default file in your system folder if you have a Macintosh; delete or rename the file named PM.CNF if you are using the IBM version. The next time you open PageMaker, the program will automatically create a new, unaltered default file in your system folder.

Although you can use either inches or picas as the unit of measure in PageMaker, fractions of inches must be specified as decimals. We find the following conversions useful to have on hand.

▼ ▼ ▼

Inches	Decimals	Points	Picas
1/32	0.03125		
1/16	0.625	4.5	
3/32	0.09375	6.75	
1/8	0.125	9	
5/32	0.15625	11.25	
3/16	0.1875	13.5	1p1.5
7/32	0.21875	15.75	1p3.75
1/4	0.250	18	1p6
9/32	0.28125	20.25	1p8.25
5/16	0.3125	22.50	1p10.5
11/32	0.34375	24.75	2p0.75
3/8	0.375	27	2p3
13/32	0.40625	29.25	2p5.25
7/16	0.4375	31.50	2p7.50
15/32	0.46875	33.75	2p9.75
1/2	0.50	36	3p
17/32	0.53125	38.25	3p2.25
9/16	0.5625	40.50	3p4.5
19/32	0.59375	42.75	3p6.75
5/8	0.625	45	3p9
21/32	0.65625	47.25	3p11.25
11/16	0.6875	49.50	4p1.5
23/32	0.71875	51.75	4p3.75
3/4	0.750	54	4p6
25/32	0.78125	56.25	4p8.25
13/16	0.8125	58.50	4p10.5
27/32	0.84375	60.75	5p0.75
7/8	0.875	63	5p3
29/32	0.90625	65.25	5p5.25
15/16	0.9375	67.50	5p7.50
31/32	0.96875	69.75	5p9.75
1	1	72	6p

Measurements

Unit of measure

As was mentioned previously, the Preferences command on PageMaker's Edit menu lets you specify whether you want rulers in inches or picas (or millimeters or ciceros). Most of us think of page size in inches, but picas generally provide a more convenient and flexible measurement system for margins and other page dimensions such as the amount of space between a headline and a rule. Then again, we generally size art in inches, a tradition resulting from the fact that the proportion wheels used to size art give results in inches, not picas.

PageMaker 3.0 has an extremely useful feature that allows you to override the current unit of measure within dialog boxes such as Page Setup or Column Guides. You simply type a one-character abbreviation for the measurement you want to use. This enables you to open a new document with, for example, an 8.5- by 11-inch page size and 3-pica margins all around without converting either measure and also without closing the dialog box to change the Preferences. If the current measure in the Preferences dialog box is set to inches, simply type *8.5* and *11* in the Page Size boxes and *3p* in the Margin boxes.

The abbreviations are logical and easy to remember (do not insert a space before or after the abbreviation):

To change a measurement to	*Type*
inches	*i* after the number
picas	*p* after the number
points	*p* before the number
picas and points	*p* between the numbers
millimeters	*m* after the number

In the project instructions, we freely mix measurement systems, using whichever is most useful for the space or object being measured. This leaves it to you to type the abbreviation or change the Preferences.

▲ ▲ ▲

Here's a quick way to bisect any area of a PageMaker page: With the square-corner tool, draw a rectangle defining the area you want to divide. (In the screen detail above, it's the width of this column.) Then bring in a ruler guide over a center selection handle, which marks the midpoint of each side of the rectangle.

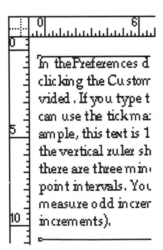

▲ ▲ ▲

If you set the custom vertical ruler to match the leading in your body text, you can use that ruler to count lines on the screen. In the detail shown above, the text is 10/13 and the vertical ruler was customized at 13 points. The major tick marks are at 13-point intervals, with two minor tick marks in between.

Rulers

We almost always work with rulers turned on. To have them appear as a default for all publications, choose Rulers from PageMaker's Options menu when no publication is open on the desktop.

Fractional measurements

In keeping with both traditional usage and PageMaker's menus, fractions of inches are expressed as decimals, fractions of picas are expressed as points, and fractions of points are expressed as decimals. Thus, you'll find measurements such as these:

> 8.5 by 11 inches
> 7 picas 6 points (abbreviated 7p6)
> 9.5 points

Remember that there are 12 points in a pica. When calculating measurements, be careful not to confuse fractions of picas expressed as decimals with points. For the sake of example, if you used a calculator to divide 11 picas in half, you'd get 5.5 picas. Properly translated into points, that's 5 picas 6 points, or 5p6. To convert a fraction of a pica into points, multiply the fraction by 12. Say you want to divide a 7-pica measure into three units: 7 ÷ 3 = 2.33 picas; 0.33 x 12 = 3.96. So one-third of 7 picas is actually 2 picas 3.96 points, or 2p3.96. These fractional differences may seem insignificant, but if they are not accurately worked out, they can throw off your layout as they accumulate and leave you feeling incredibly frustrated.

Counting lines on-screen with the vertical ruler

In the Preferences dialog box, you can customize the vertical ruler by clicking the Custom option and typing a point value in the box provided. If you type the leading value for your type specs in this box, you can use the tick marks on the vertical ruler to count the lines of text. For example, this text is 10/13, and we specified 13 as the custom value for the vertical ruler shown at left. The ruler is shown at Actual Size, and there are two minor tick marks between each of the major tick marks at 13-point intervals. Used in conjunction with Snap to Rulers (described next), the custom vertical ruler can help you align loose text and graphics with your leading grid. And you can use the customized vertical ruler to measure odd spaces (the value you specify can be in 0.5-point increments).

Snap To commands

Snap to Rulers and Snap to Guides are two toggle switches on the Options menu. These commands turn rulers or guides into magnets.

Turn on Snap to Rulers when you

• pull in ruler guides that you want aligned to a specific point in the ruler.

• draw PageMaker graphics (squares and so on) that require precise measurements.

Turn off Snap to Rulers when you
- pull in ruler guides that you want to align with a graphic or text block already on the page.
- want to align text or graphics with an existing guide that may not be on a ruler tick mark.

Turn on Snap to Guides when you
- place text in columns.
- want to align existing graphics with existing guides.

Turn off Snap to Guides when you
- position graphics or text blocks near, but not directly on, the guides.
- use PageMaker's tools to draw graphics, such as squares or rectangles, defined by ruler guides. Theoretically, the graphic should snap to the guides, but we've found that we can align the top or the bottom, the left or the right, but not two opposite sides.

Page view

Five different page views are available on the Page menu. Two additional views not listed on the menu are also available. Larger page views enable you to see less of the page in greater detail than smaller page views. The view you choose depends on what you're doing, the size of your monitor, and the precision (and perfection) you require in your work. Generally, you edit text at Actual Size or 200%, depending on the legibility of the screen font. You check overall page composition at Fit in Window, so you can see the entire page or spread at once. And you check critical alignments at 200% or 400%. Because of the many variables in system configuration, we've generally left it to you to determine the page view as you work on the projects.

We spend a lot of time toggling back and forth between page views and thus find the keyboard shortcuts for doing this among the most frequently used.

Keyboard shortcuts for changing page view

Page view	Macintosh shortcut	PC shortcut	
Actual Size	Command-1	Ctrl-1	(returns center screen to the location last seen at actual size)
Fit in Window	Command-w	Ctrl-w	
50%	Command-5	Ctrl-5	
75%	Command-7	Ctrl-7	
200%	Command-2	Ctrl-2	

To see a specific part of the screen at a different page view:

Actual Size: Command-Option-click mouse button on point you want center screen. (Click the secondary mouse button to do this on a PC.)

200%: Command-Option-Shift-click mouse button on point you want center screen. (Press Shift and click secondary mouse button on a PC.)

To display the next page or spread at Fit in Window:

Press Shift when you click on the page icon.

This is particularly useful when you move through an entire document to check placements and alignments.

To see the entire pasteboard:

Press Shift and then select Fit in Window. (You have to select Fit in Window from the menu; there is no keyboard shortcut.)

This is useful when you want to place a large piece of art or a text block on the pasteboard before moving it onto the page. Also, when you clean up your pages to compress files, use this view to check the pasteboard for items you may have left there. Occasionally one of those items should have been included in the publication, so checking at this view may prevent some omissions.

To magnify the page to 400%:

Press Shift and select 200% from the Page menu. (Again, there is no keyboard shortcut.)

To get the grabber hand:

On the Macintosh press the Option key, then click the mouse button and drag. (On a PC, press the Alt key, then click the main mouse button and drag.)

The grabber hand is used to scroll around the screen at the current page view.

To move to the next page or spread at the view in which it was last seen:

Press Command-Tab (Ctrl-Tab on a PC).

To move to the previous page:

Press Command-Shift-Tab (Ctrl-Shift-Tab on a PC).

Saving your work

A general rule of thumb is to save every 15 to 20 minutes or whenever you've done something you'd really hate to redo. With the exception of a Save and Print instruction at the completion of each project, we've left it to you to save according to your own habit.

The keyboard shortcut for saving—Command-s (Ctrl-s on a PC)—is easy to remember and takes much less time than redoing lost work.

After you've saved a publication for the first time, PageMaker automatically performs a "mini-save" whenever you move to a new page or spread (by clicking on the page icon), insert or delete a page, change the page setup, or click OK in the Define Styles dialog box. You can force a mini-save by clicking on the current page icon, which gives you flexibility when using the Revert command. (See the tip on the following page).

TIP

When editing text in PageMaker, even at Actual Size, there are places where it's difficult to determine on-screen if you have the correct letterspacing and word spacing. Sometimes it looks like there's a space in the middle of a word when in fact there isn't; sometimes it looks like there's no space between two words when in fact there is. A quick way to check is to use the cursor keys (the four keys with arrows pointing up, down, right, and left). With the text tool, set an insertion point in the text in question. Then click the right or left cursor key (depending on the direction in which you're moving for your check). If one click moves the cursor past the next letter, there's no space; if it takes two clicks, there is a space.

The compacting feature of "Save As"

When you save a document with the Save command, changes made since the last save are appended to the end of the file. So even if you delete text or graphics, the document may continue to grow in size.

When you save a document using the Save As command from the File menu, the file is compacted, truly eliminating from memory the discarded elements from previous versions. The difference in file size can be dramatic. To cite just one example, we've seen a file reduced from 810 KB after doing a regular Save to 490 KB after doing a Save As.

So when you've made substantial changes in a complex document, and when you're saving a document before closing it, use the Save As command to compress the file. If you want to keep the same name (we generally do when compressing files), just click OK (or press Return) when the Save As dialog box comes on screen. You'll get another box asking if you want to replace the existing document with that name; click Yes.

You can also use the Save As feature to create a copy of a document while you're working. This is useful when you are experimenting with type specs or layout and want to preserve the existing version before trying another approach.

Master pages

Master pages are a sort of blueprint on which the individual pages of a publication are built. Because they are such a fundamental building block of electronic page assembly, we've collected some information about them here to supplement the specific hands-on techniques described in the projects themselves.

The principle behind master pages is quite simple: Anything you put on a master page will appear on the regular pages of your document, unless you choose to modify or eliminate the master-page elements on individual pages. In Projects 3 and 4, you'll find instructions for creating the following elements on master pages:

- A nonprinting layout grid, which, in addition to the margin guides, includes column guides and vertical and horizontal ruler guides.

- Text and graphics that will appear on most pages of the document. These include page frames, rules between columns, report or issue dates, headline banners, page numbers, and so on.

- Spacing guides, which are rectangles sized to distances you'll need to measure frequently, such as the space between headlines and text or between pictures and captions.

When you use master pages in your own documents, keep these points in mind:

- Master pages are not selected automatically.

  When you open a new document, pages 1 and 2 appear (or only page 1 if the Double-sided option is turned off). If you want to create

PAGEMAKER'S NONPRINTING GUIDES

PageMaker has three types of guides that appear on-screen but do not print, called, logically enough, nonprinting guides. Each of the three looks different on the screen, has slightly different functions, and is set up and manipulated in slightly different ways.

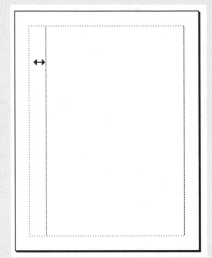

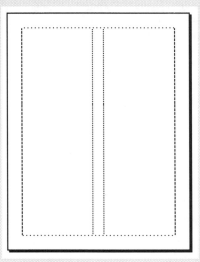

▲ ▲ ▲

Margin guides define the top, bottom, and sides of the image area of the page. Their position is specified in the Page Setup dialog box when you open a new document, and you can change them at any time by returning to that dialog box.

▲ ▲ ▲

Column guides control the alignment of text and graphics. PageMaker's default is one column, defined by the margin guides. The side margins look heavier than the top and bottom ones because they are actually column guides on top of margin guides. When you drag a column guide off the margin guide, the margin guide remains in its original position.

▲ ▲ ▲

To specify two or more columns and the space between them, use the Column Guides command on the Options menu. (See Project 3 for how to create unequal columns.) Note that the column guides do not extend beyond the top and bottom margins.

▶ ▶ ▶

Use the pointer to pull in ruler guides from the vertical and horizontal rulers as needed. In this sample page, ruler guides are used to align elements such as the bottom of the initial cap box and the baseline of adjacent text, and the tops of adjacent picture frames. Ruler guides extend to the page trim; you can use them to align elements that fall outside the margins, such as the folio at right. When a ruler guide is on top of both a margin guide and a column guide, as it is on the far right of this page, it looks on-screen like a solid rule, but it will not print.

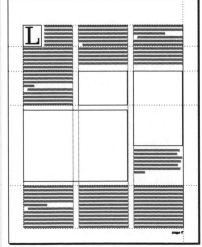

TIPS

To begin with a blank page, specify all margins as 0 in the Page Setup dialog box.

To divide a page into several equal vertical units, you can use the Column Guides command to do the arithmetic and placement. Simply specify the number of units you want as the number of columns and specify 0 as the space in between. Bring in ruler guides over the column guides, and then return to the Column Guides dialog box to specify the number of columns you want for placing text.

TIP

For greatest accuracy when contructing grids, drawing rules at precise locations, and any other procedure that requires precise measurement, turn on Snap To Rulers. As you move the cursor, hairline markers on the rulers corresponding to the cursor's position on the page will then "snap to" the nearest tick mark. We have found that we get greater accuracy at 75% and Actual Size page views using Snap To Rulers than we do at 200% without them.

master pages, you have to remember to click on the L or R icon to the left of the numbered page icons at the bottom of the screen. One of the most frustrating moments in electronic pasteup is when you realize that you've just spent two hours setting up master elements on pages 1 and 2 instead of on the master pages.

Similarly, after you've finished setting up the master pages, don't forget to click on the actual page of the document before proceeding.

- Take time with your master pages. Care and precision there is reflected on every page of your document.

- If your right and left master pages have many of the same printing elements in the same position—page frames, page-number markers, rules between columns, and so forth—create those elements on one page, choose the Select All command, and then copy and paste them onto the other master page. Then add elements that are unique to each page. You will have to create nonprinting ruler guides and customized column guides on each page; they cannot be copied.

- Printing items on the master pages cannot be moved or copied on an individual page.

  If you have a graphic that you will use repeatedly, such as a black banner into which you will drop headlines, put a master on the pasteboard of your master pages. That master will then appear on the pasteboard of all regular pages and can be copied as needed.

- Text-wrap specifications on a master page do not carry over to regular pages. This means you can't use PageMaker's Text Wrap command to keep text from flowing into a certain column or area defined by your grid (such as the narrow left-hand column in the pages of this book).

- You cannot print a master page directly, but if you click on a numbered page icon within the publication, the printing elements from the master page will be displayed there, and you can print that as you would any other page.

Customizing individual pages

To customize nonprinting column and ruler guides on individual pages, display the page you want to customize and use the pointer tool to change the guides on that page manually or change the specifications in the Column Guides dialog box, available from the Options menu. If you change your mind and want to go back to the master guides, choose Copy Master Guides from the Page menu. This command affects only the page or spread currently displayed.

To remove specific printing master items from an individual page, display that page and cover the items you want to eliminate with a white box, which is simply a rectangle with a shade of Paper and a line style of None. When you click on one of these invisible boxes with the pointer, you will see handles around its edges but nothing else. These boxes are also called masks, because they mask the printing items underneath. You will see masks used frequently and in different ways throughout the project section.

If you want to eliminate all of the master-page printing items on a regular page, choose Display Master Items from the Page menu. (Doing this in effect turns off the master items.)

Modifying a master page and reflecting those changes on actual pages

The rules governing the modification of master pages exemplify the trade-offs inherent in many aspects of electronic pasteup, so much so that the following information could be cast as a good news/bad news script. The rules are perfectly logical, if difficult to remember at first, and something that seems a nuisance in one situation can be used to good advantage in another.

- If you return to the master pages and change any printing or nonprinting items there, those changes will be reflected on all of the corresponding regular pages except those that you have customized.

- A customized page is any page on which you have changed the column guides or brought in any ruler guides that aren't on the master pages. If you frequently bring in ruler guides on individual pages, as we do, you'll have a great many customized pages. To have the changes on the master pages appear on those customized pages, you must display those pages and then choose Copy Master Guides from the Page menu.

- When you copy master guides onto a page, however, you lose all of your customized guides. This may not be a problem if your customized guides were temporary ones used to check alignment and to position loose odds and ends. The position of text and graphics already on the page will not change, only the ruler and column guides.

- If your individual pages are a mess of customized ruler guides, you can quickly eliminate them simply by choosing the Copy Master Guides command. This is much faster than dragging every ruler guide off the page. You'll keep all of your master guides and all of the text and graphics added to that individual page, but you won't have a lot of extraneous ruler guides on the screen. If you don't want the master items on your page, you can still use the Copy Master Guides command to get rid of the custom ruler guides, and then turn Display Master Items off.

Copying master pages

You cannot directly copy master-page items from one document to another. But if you do want to reuse the master guides from an existing document, you can open a copy of that document, delete all the regular pages from the file (using the Remove Pages command from the Page menu), and then add new pages (using the Insert Pages command). In this situation, you would probably want to save the new document as a

TIP

Play is generally recognized as an important component of both learning and of creativity. Just "playing around" in PageMaker can accelerate your learning curve and sharpen your graphic eye. When there's no end result at stake, no fear of making a mistake, no deadline to meet, you may find it easier to experiment and become comfortable with certain commands and functions.

template and then open a copy of it before proceding so that you'll have a prototype of that publication for future use. For more information on templates, see Projects 3 and 4.

Numbering pages automatically

If you insert a page-number marker on your master pages, PageMaker will number every page consecutively, beginning with the starting page number specified in the Page Setup dialog box. The page number will be in the same position as the marker.

To create a page-number marker, click the text tool at the desired position on the master page, and then press Command-Option-p (Ctrl-Shift-3 on a PC). For double-sided publications, be sure to create a page-number marker for both master pages.

On the master page, the page-number marker displays as 0; on regular pages, the correct page number will be displayed in the same position. Edit the type specifications for the page-number marker as you would any text. You can also move the page-number marker on the master page as you would any text block.

If your publication is divided into several files, you can still use automatic numbering as long as you insert the marker on the master page. PageMaker begins numbering each file with the starting page number specified in the Page Setup dialog box. So if, for example, you have a 200-page report divided into two files between, say, pages 109 and 110, the Start Page # on the second file would be 110, the first page icon on the bottom of the screen would be 110, and the page-number marker would register as 110.

To create a composite page number, such as "page 1" or "1-1" (for chapter 1, page 1) or "1 of 7," follow a similar procedure, typing the text that remains constant (including hyphens and word spaces) and then pressing Command-Option-p (or Ctrl-Shift-3). If you want, you can apply different type attributes (such as boldface) to part of the composite number.

Position your page numbers where they are easily seen, at the top or bottom outside corners or centered at the bottom of the page. It's best to keep them in the margins so that they won't interfere when you flow text. Be sure, however, that they are within the printer tolerance of your page trim.

For right-aligned page-number markers, be sure to apply the right alignment through the Type menu so that the alignment will be maintained for two-, three-, and four-digit numbers. If you position the page-number marker at the right margin manually with the pointer tool, longer numbers will overhang the margin.

PROJECT 1

A SIMPLE CERTIFICATE FOR PAGEMAKER NOVICES

This project is intended for readers with very little experience using PageMaker. The hands-on instructions will guide you through most of the basic procedures used to create and move around a page, with the exception of importing text and graphics from other applications. Because the document is so simple, it is created entirely in PageMaker. The project also uses of most of the tools in PageMaker's Toolbox.

If you want to produce a quick certificate without so much hands-on instruction, you should be able to move quickly through the boldface and bulleted instructions. Tips and paragraphs without bullets explain the techniques and PageMaker basics in more detail than you will want if you already have a little experience with the program.

A similar diplomalike format could be used for business seminars, training programs, and workshops. It could be adapted to serve as an award—for employee or salesman of the month, for a good safety record, and so on. It could also be more personal—for a boss, a colleague, or an assistant—to recognize a job well done or a gesture appreciated, as a way to say thank you for going beyond the call of duty.

PAGEMAKER TECHNIQUES YOU WILL LEARN

▶ Change the Page Setup specifications

▶ Display the rulers

▶ Bring in ruler guides

▶ Change the page view

▶ Use the Snap to Rulers command

▶ Select and change line weights

▶ Draw lines, rectangles, and circles with PageMaker's graphics tools

▶ Use scroll bars and the grabber hand to move around the screen

▶ Change type specifications

▶ Type text in PageMaker

▶ Move text with the pointer tool

▶ Move PageMaker graphics

▶ Add shades to PageMaker graphics

**A horizontal, or landscape,
page orientation** with equal
margins on all sides is typical of
certificates and diplomas.

ENROLLMENT CERTIFICATE

THE DESKTOP PUBLISHING SCHOOL
ADMITS

TO
THE HANDS-ON DESIGN COURSE

DTP

Times Roman has a utilitarian
elegance appropriate for a design
course.

The triple rule is very assertive
and gives the certificate an official,
bona fide look.

BLUEPRINT FOR THE CERTIFICATE

GETTING SET UP

If you are not already in PageMaker and are using a Macintosh, open the program by double-clicking on its icon.

If you are using an IBM PC or compatible, type *PM* or *WIN PM* at the DOS prompt, depending on your version of Windows.

1. Choose New from the File menu.

- Move the pointer to the File menu, hold down the mouse button, drag to highlight the word "New," and release the mouse button.

  This brings the Page Setup dialog box to the screen.

2. Specify the Page Setup specifications.

- Make any necessary changes in the Page Setup dialog box so that it conforms to the following specifications:

    Page size: Custom (11 by 8.5 inches)

    Orientation: Wide

    Start page #: 1   # of pages: 1

    Options: Click off Double-sided. (The Facing Pages option will automatically turn gray.)

    Margin in inches: Specify 1 for all four margins.

- After you have specified your page setup, click OK.

▶ ▶ ▶

The Page Setup dialog box with the specifications for this project. To change the value in any text box, position the pointer in that box, double-click to highlight the existing value, and then type the new value. To turn an option on or off, click on the appropriate button, box, or name for that option.

Page setup			OK
Page size: ○ Letter ○ Legal ○ Tabloid			Cancel
○ A4 ○ A3 ○ A5 ○ B5			
● Custom: [11] by [8.5] inches			
Orientation: ○ Tall ● Wide			
Start page #: [1] # of pages: [1]			
Options: ☐ Double-sided ☐ Facing pages			
Margin in inches: Left [1] Right [1]			
Top [1] Bottom [1]			

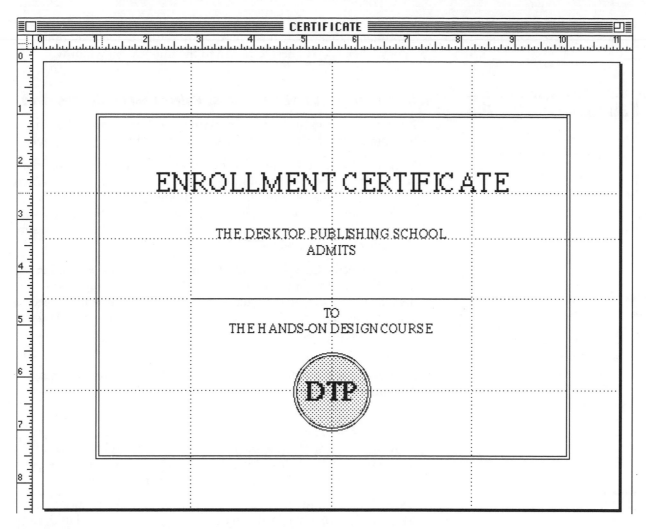

▲ ▲ ▲   *The certificate blueprint with title bar, rulers, and ruler guides.*

3. Check your printer type.

- *If you work on an IBM,* check the printer by choosing the Printer Setup command from the File menu. Select your target printer from the list box and click OK. If you change the printer, Page-Maker will ask if you want to recompose the publication for the new printer. Click OK.

  If the correct printer is not specified, you may encounter difficulties assembling the document, such as the inability to move or place text. And if you change printers after the publication is assembled in PageMaker, you may discover unexpected changes in the page layout when you print.

- *If you work on a Macintosh,* the page makeup and printing functions in PageMaker are isolated from each other, so it is not critical to select the printer before assembling the publication. If you want to check it now, choose Print from the File menu. If the printer type listed at the bottom of the dialog box is not correct, click on the Change button in the lower right to display a dialog box of printer-specific options. Click on the name of the correct printer in that dialog box. Click OK to return to the Print dialog box. Then click Cancel to return to the publication window.

4. If the rulers are not visible, choose *Rulers* from the *Options* menu.

It is almost always useful to work with the rulers visible—they are indispensable for placing items where you want them on the page.

Note that the default setting for the zero point, where the horizontal and vertical rulers meet, is at the upper left corner of the page. When you move the mouse around the publication window, hairline markers move in both rulers to define the position of the cursor on the screen. You can move the zero point by dragging the hairlines in the upper left corner where the rulers intersect.

In this project, all measurements are in inches. This is PageMaker's default setting for measurements, so unless you've changed your defaults you won't need to make any adjustments. If you do need to change from picas to inches, choose Preferences from the Edit menu and click on Inches.

5. Select a page view (from the *Page* menu) that enables you to see the entire document.

The Page menu gives you an option of five different page views. If you are not familiar with these options, take a moment to click on each one and observe how the publication window changes from one view to another. How much of your page you see at each view depends on the size of the page and the size of your monitor.

Because different readers will be working with different monitors, we generally will not specify an optimal page view. You'll undoubtedly need to change views as you work on this and any other document.

When you bring in ruler guides, as you will in the following step, choose a page view that lets you see the entire page at as large a size as possible.

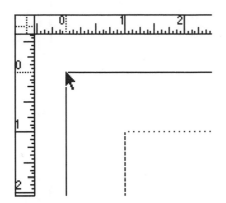

▲ ▲ ▲

Hairline markers on the rulers indicate the position of the mouse on the screen. In this detail, the pointer is at the zero point. You can move the zero point by dragging the intersecting hairlines at the upper left corner of the window.

6. Bring in ruler guides to help position the elements you'll create in later steps.

*   Turn on Snap to Rulers on the Options menu.

*   Position the pointer anywhere on the left ruler, press the mouse button to reveal a double-headed arrow, and drag a dotted vertical guideline to the 5.5-inch mark on the top ruler. This marks the center of the page on a vertical axis.

*   From the top ruler, bring in horizontal ruler guides to the 2-1/2, 3- 3/8, 4-1/2, and 6-1/4 points on the left ruler.

TIP

The Snap to Rulers command pulls ruler guides, text, and graphics to the nearest tick mark on each of the rulers. With Snap to Rulers on, you get the same accuracy at the 50% page view as you do at 200%.

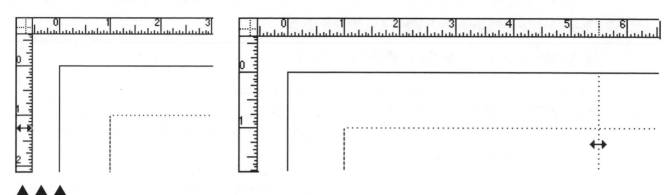

▲ ▲ ▲

Move the pointer into either ruler to drag in ruler guides. These are nonprinting dotted rules used to align text and graphics on the page. To move a ruler guide, point to that guide with the pointer tool and drag the guide to the desired location. To delete a guide, drag it outside the page frame. Any tool turns into the arrow pointer when you move it into one of the rulers, so you don't have to change tools to bring in ruler guides.

TIP

One of the most useful keyboard commands is the one that saves your current document: Command-S (Ctrl-S on a PC).

7. Choose Save from the File menu.

Get in the habit of saving your work every 15 minutes, or sooner if you've just done something to the layout that you'd hate to redo.

The Save and Save As commands in PageMaker are similar to those functions in other applications. Note, however, that in the lower right corner of PageMaker's Save As dialog box you have the option of saving your document as a publication or as a template. For this project, use the default setting of Publication.

CREATING THE CERTIFICATE

1. Create a border.

- Move the pointer to the Lines menu and click on the triple rule to choose it.

- Select the square-corner tool from the Toolbox. Note that the pointer turns into a crossbar.

- Place the crossbar at the upper left corner of the margin guides. Press down the mouse button, drag the crossbar to the lower right margin guide, and release the mouse button.

Note: If you are working at a reduced page view, the border will look like a solid or double line. To see the line as it will print, choose Actual Size from the Page menu. At that size you may need to move around the screen to find the line. (See the box "How to Move Around the PageMaker Screen" on the following page.)

◀ ◀ ◀

You can move the Toolbox away from your work area by pointing to its title bar and dragging it to a new location on the screen. To remove the Toolbox altogether, click on its close box in the upper left corner. To bring it back to the screen, choose Toolbox from the Options menu.

HOW TO MOVE AROUND THE PAGEMAKER SCREEN

Often when you're working in PageMaker, some of your page is hidden from view outside the publication window. There are two ways to move around the screen to display different parts of the page as well as the pasteboard beyond the page.

- **Use the grabber hand.**

  When you hold down the Option key (the Alt key on a PC) and then press the mouse button, the pointer turns into a hand. As you drag the mouse, the hand pushes the page in any direction that you drag, including diagonally. (After you see the hand, you can release the Option or Alt key.)

  If you want to constrain the movement to a horizontal or vertical direction, hold down the Shift key in addition to Option or Alt.

- **Use the scroll bars.**

  Use the gray bar on the right side of the window to move vertically and use the bottom bar to move horizontally around the page.

  Click on the arrows at the ends of the scroll bars to move a short distance; click in the gray bar to move a greater distance. The position of the white box in each scroll bar indicates the position of the screen image relative to the entire page and pasteboard area outside the page; drag the white boxes to approximately where you want to be in the publication window.

  Remember that you can also reveal more of the page by choosing a smaller page view from the Page menu, as described in step 5 of "Getting Set Up," earlier in this project.

▲ ▲ ▲

The text tool cursor is an I-beam with a short horizontal crossbar two-thirds of the way from the top. When you choose an insertion point on the page, position this bar where the baseline of the text should be. (The hairline markers in the rulers will align with this bar.)

2. Add headline type.

- From the Type menu, choose Type Specs. The Type Specifications dialog box appears. Choose these specifications:

      Font: Times Roman

      Size: 36 points

      Leading: 36 points

      Case: All caps

      Position: Normal

      Type Style: Normal

- Specify Align Center. If you are working on a Macintosh, choose Alignment from the Type menu and then choose Align Center from the pop-up menu. If you are working on a PC, you can choose Align Center directly from the Type menu.

- Choose the text tool and click the I-beam on the 2.5-inch horizontal ruler guide. Type *ENROLLMENT CERTIFICATE.*

3. Add the rest of the type.

- Choose Type Specs again from the Type menu. You still want Times Roman, in all caps. Change the size to 18 point and the leading to Auto. Click OK.

- Check to see that center alignment is still in effect.

TIP

You can change the formatting of text at any time. With the text tool active, drag the I-beam across the text you want to reformat and then change the specifications through the Type menu.

• Position the I-beam on the horizontal ruler guide at 3.5 inches, and click. Type

> *THE DESKTOP PUBLISHING SCHOOL* [Return]
>
> *ADMITS* [press Return 4 times for extra line spaces]
>
> *TO* [Return]
>
> *THE HANDS-ON DESIGN COURSE*

Note: If you are working at a small page view, the text may appear on-screen as gray bars. This is called greeked text. To see the real text, choose a larger page view.

4. Add the line for a signature.

You'll want to bring in ruler guides to define the start and end points of the line. In this case, a good balance will be achieved if the line is a little shorter than the headline.

• Move the pointer into the left ruler, and bring in a vertical ruler guide after the second letter in "Enrollment" and before the second-to-last letter in "Certificate."

• Choose the perpendicular line tool, and position the crossbar at the intersection of the third horizontal and first vertical ruler guides. Drag the crossbar along the horizontal guide to the vertical guide that you just brought in to mark the end of the line.

• That's a very thick line. (It's the same triple rule you selected earlier for the border.) While it's still selected, choose .5 pt from the Lines menu.

ABOUT THE TYPE MENU

The Type menus and Type Specifications dialog boxes differ slightly in the Macintosh and PC versions of PageMaker. Take a moment to choose each menu command and familiarize yourself with the options available through the Type menu.

On the Macintosh, Type menu commands followed by arrows display pop-up submenus for font, size, style, and so on, and you scroll the submenu to choose a desired specification. Type menu commands followed by ellipses display dialog boxes through which you can change several specifications. In the Type Specifications dialog box, you can click on text boxes to display pop-up menus and you can also type values for point and leading sizes in the text boxes for those specifications.

On the PC, there are no pop-up menus. You can choose type style and alignment options directly from the Type menu. Menu commands followed by ellipses display dialog boxes, as they do on the Macintosh. In the Type Specifications dialog box, click on the scroll bar to see more font names and sizes if there are too many to be displayed at once. You can also type size and leading values in the text boxes for those specifications. You can specify type style (normal, bold, italic, and so on) in the dialog box as well as on the menu.

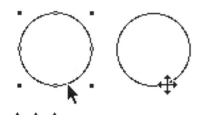

▲ ▲ ▲

When you select a graphic with the pointer, the graphic is surrounded by eight small rectangles, or selection handles. To move a graphic drawn with one of PageMaker's tools, point directly on the outline of the selected graphic; press the mouse button and, when you see a four-headed arrow, drag the graphic to the new position. If you point to a handle and drag, you will resize the graphic. If you mistakenly resize a graphic, choose Undo from the Edit menu or remove the selected graphic (press the Delete or Backspace key) and then redraw it.

▲ ▲ ▲

To move a text unit, click on the text with the pointer tool. Then position the pointer inside the "windowshade" handles and drag the text to the new position.

5. Create a seal.

- Choose the circle tool, and move the crossbar to the zero point on your page frame.

- Hold down the Shift key and drag the crossbar on a diagonal to the 1.5-inch point on either ruler. Release the mouse button before the Shift key. (It's the Shift key that restrains the graphic to a circular rather than an oval shape.) The circle will have the same triple rule as the border.

- Click on the pointer tool and position its tip anywhere directly on the circumference of the circle. Hold down the mouse button, and when you see the four-headed arrow, drag the circle and center it over the intersection of the vertical ruler guide through the center of the page and the horizontal guide at 6.25 inches.

- With the circle still selected, choose 10% from the Shades menu.

- With the text tool, click anywhere next to the circle and type *DTP* in all caps. (Throughout this book we italicize something you type on the page or in a text box. If the type style is also italic, we will state that as part of the type specifications.)

- Drag the I-beam across the type to select it, choose Type Specs, and change the type to 36/36 bold. Check to see that Times Roman is still selected. Click OK.

- Click on the pointer tool and select the DTP initials. You'll see horizontal lines with loops at the top and bottom, called windowshade handles. Position the pointer between the windowshade handles, press the mouse button, and drag the text to center it inside the shaded circle.

When you move text with the pointer tool, press the mouse button until you see a four-headed arrow and the handles defining the text block disappear. If you move text (or graphics) before you see this arrow, the text (or graphic) you've selected will temporarily stay in place while an outline representing it moves. It's easier to position the text itself than the outline.

FINISHING THE JOB

1. Review your work.

Check to make sure everything is centered. Change the page view to Actual Size, and scroll around to check spelling, line weights (the border and the seal should be the same), and placements.

2. Choose Print from the File menu.

- Take a moment to review the options in the Print dialog box. Make sure that you're printing only one copy. Because this is a one-page document, the page range should read From 1 to 1. Scaling should be 100% so that you will print the document at full size. None of the special options are needed for this project.

- Your printer should be listed at the bottom of the dialog box. If it isn't, see step 3 under "Getting Set Up" earlier in this project.

- When all the printer specifications are correct, click OK.

3. Sign your name.

If the printed certificate looks as you expected, congratulations. Sign your name on the line and consider yourself enrolled.

HOW DID YOU DO?

If you had trouble completing this project... We recommend reviewing the tutorials provided with PageMaker to help you become more comfortable with the tools and techniques that you'll use throughout the rest of this book.

If you completed the project but found it difficult... Try Project 2A or 2B. They will give you practice using many of these same tools and will introduce a few new techniques as well.

If you found it easy... You're not a novice after all.

TWO INVITATIONS WITH VARIATIONS ON EACH

Invitations and announcements are so easy to produce with a desktop publishing system that you may look for excuses to create them. Although they are simple, these design tasks still warrant your making a list of the copy points to be included and doing a thumbnail sketch on paper before you sit down at the computer. Once you've determined the basic approach, you can quickly enter and lay out the text directly in PageMaker.

The invitations in this chapter are really two separate projects. One is somewhat formal and straightforward, the other is informal and

The Palatino italic, used for all the type, contrasts subtly with the rectilinearity of the border and rule.

The company name is 14 point with 18-point initial caps, a detail that makes simple typography look smart.

The 10/12 copy is centered using as short a line as possible. The maximum number of lines is 10.

The rule above the date helps the guests see at a glance the date, time, and location.

There is more space above and below the main text block than between the lines.

NORTHERN LIGHT TEXTILES

Invites
you
for
champagne
and
hors d'oeuvres

January 22
5:00 p.m.
La Rondo Room
The Heraldry Hotel

thematic. Both are 5.5 by 4.25 inches. In Project 2A (shown on the opposite page), you'll print one invitation on an 8.5- by 11-inch sheet with cropmarks. In Project 2B (shown on this page), you'll print four copies of the invitation on one sheet. Printing "four up" in this way is very efficient, whether you're doing the printing yourself on a laser printer or using a commercial printer.

If you are printing the invitations yourself, you'll want to a get a 20-pound card stock with matching envelopes. Note that using this stock requires that you select the Manual print option in the Print dialog box; the paper will need to be hand-fed. When printing manually on card stock, we allow for about 15% waste due to poor alignment.

The crisp, structured organization is offset by playful, thematic art.

Avant Garde is a good contemporary face for an informal invitation, and its O's, being perfect circles, echo the sunset theme. The headline is 12/36, all caps. The body type is 10/36.

The text lines must be short enough not to intrude on the art. Maximum line length is about 42 characters.

The sunset motif is created using PageMaker's circle tool with a white rectangle masking the lower part of each circle. See the instructions in Project 2B.

CRUISE ON OVER TO RIVER'S END

The Western Travel Agents Association

invites you to a sunset buffet

on the patio of the River's End Restaurant

Sunday July 24

7:00 p.m.

$10 per person

door prize—Hawaiian vacation

AN EASY FORMAL INVITATION

A formal invitation sets the tone for an elegant event. The basic design for the invitation in this project uses an open banner at the top for the company's name and centered, calligraphic-style type throughout. All of the variations, shown on the pages following the instructions, maintain the formal rules and centered style even when more contemporary decorative elements are added.

As mentioned in the introduction on the previous page, the instructions for this project specify printing one 5.5- by 4.25-inch invitation on a single 8.5- by 11-inch sheet. If you want to print four to a sheet, before beginning this project read the instructions for "How to Print Four Up" at the end of Project 2B and adapt the instructions for a horizontal rather than a vertical orientation.

PAGEMAKER TECHNIQUES YOU WILL LEARN

▶ Override the specified unit of measure

▶ Change the unit of measure

▶ Set the guides in back

▶ Turn off the guides

▶ Change the default setting on the Lines menu

▶ Create initial caps in display text

▶ Select individual letters in italic type

▶ Move a text block in one direction only

▶ Use crop marks

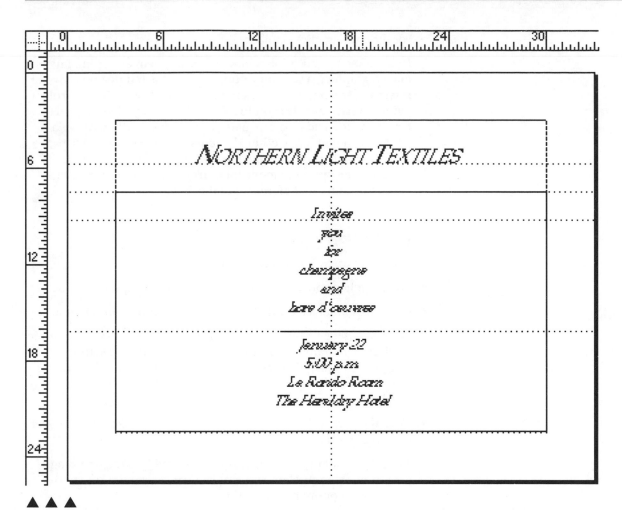

▲ ▲ ▲

The formal invitation is shown with ruler guides in place. Several variations follow the instructions for this basic blueprint.

BLUEPRINT FOR THE FORMAL INVITATION

1. Open a one-page document with the following page setup:

- Size: 5.5 by 4.25 inches (or 33 by 25p6)
- Orientation: Wide
- Margins: 3 picas all around

2. Specify the unit of measure.

- Choose Preferences from the Edit menu. The Preferences dialog box appears.
- For the measurement system, click on Picas. (The vertical ruler option will automatically change to picas.)

• For the Guides, click on Back.

PageMaker's publication window consists of overlapping layers of text, graphics, and nonprinting guides. Each time you move or insert a new item, it becomes the top layer. Positioning the ruler guides in back enables you to select a line that you've drawn on top of a guide and also prevents your inadvertently moving a guide when you move other elements on the page. In later projects we won't specify the position of the guides. Be aware that you have the option to move them from back to front, and vice versa, through the Preferences dialog box.

3. Define the image area.

• Turn on Snap to Rulers on the Options menu.

• Bring in a horizontal guide at 7p6 and a vertical guide at 16p6.

• With the pointer, select the hairline rule from the Lines menu.

When you select a line (or shade) with the pointer and no graphic is selected, that line (or shade) becomes the default setting for that publication. All of the rules in this document are hairlines, so by specifying that as the default you won't have to reselect Hairline each time.

• With the perpendicular tool, draw a hairline horizontal rule over the top margin for the top of the banner.

• With the rectangle tool, draw the text frame by dragging diagonally from its upper left corner at the 7p6 horizontal rule to the lower right bottom margin guide.

4. Add the headline type.

• Bring in a horizontal ruler guide at 5p9.

• With the pointer tool, choose Type Specs from the Type menu. Specify 14/14 Palatino italic. For Case, specify all caps. For Alignment, specify center.

• With the text tool selected, position the bar of the I-beam on the ruler guide at 5p9 and click to select an insertion point.

• Type your company name.

• Change the initial caps to 18 point.

Change the view to 200% to make it easier to select individual letters. Drag the text tool over the first letter of the company name to select that letter. Change the type size to 18 points. Repeat this for the first letter of each word in the company name.

When you change the type size for each initial cap, the top of the cap will appear to be clipped off. This is merely an annoying bug; the type will print correctly. To correct it on-screen, force the screen to "refresh" by clicking in the Size box in the lower right corner of the publication window.

▲ ▲ ▲

Selecting individual letters in italic is a little tricky. An individual letter is selected if, and only if, its lower left corner is highlighted. In the top screen detail shown here, only the L is actually selected; in the bottom detail, both the L and the I are selected .

▲ ▲ ▲

When you want to move a text block in one direction only, hold down the Shift key before you drag the text. When you drag, the four-headed arrow will turn into a double-headed arrow, pointing either vertically or horizontally depending on the direction in which you are dragging.

5. Add the text.

- With the text tool, change the type size to 11/14. Change the case to normal.

- Select an insertion point at the top of the text box for the copy. Type the text line for line as shown on the blueprint, pressing the Return key at the end of each line. Press the Return key twice after "hors d'oeuvres" to leave a space for the rule.

- Bring in a horizontal ruler guide at 9p3.

- With the pointer, select the text so that the windowshade handles appear. Hold down the Shift key and position the pointer inside the windowshade handles. When the four-headed arrow appears, drag the text block so that the baseline of the first line of type sits on the ruler guide you just brought in. (When you drag, the four-headed arrow will turn into a double-headed vertical arrow.)

  Note: If you move the text block before the arrows appear, a box defining the text block will move, rather than the text itself, and you won't be able to see the baseline to position it.

6. Check the alignment.

- Check the center alignment for the headline and the text. If you messed up the horizontal alignment when moving the text vertically, select the text block and reposition it so that the ends of the windowshade handles align with the left and right margins.

TIP

When you need to measure small increments, enlarge your page view to 200%. At that view, the tick marks on the ruler are positioned in 1-point increments.

7. Add the hairline rule above the date.

- Bring in a horizontal ruler guide at 16p2.

- Draw the hairline rule on this guide. The rule should be a little longer than the text above it.

8. Print with crop marks on.

- Choose Print from the File menu.

- In the Print dialog box, click on Crop Marks. (It's listed under Options.)

  When the page size of your document is smaller than the paper in your printer, the document will be centered on the paper when printed. Crop marks are fine lines just outside the image area that mark where the paper should be trimmed to match the page size of your document.

- Review the other printing specifications and check to be sure your target printer is selected.

  You should print one copy to proof. The scaling should be 100%.

TIP

To see the page on-screen as it will print, hide the guides by choosing Guides from the Options menu. The Guides command is one of several toggle switches on Page-Maker's menus: The feature is on when it's checked and off when it's not checked. When you turn the guides on after having hidden them, they reappear in their previous position on the screen.

Turn the page for variations on this invitation.

VARIATIONS

Even within this simple design, you can vary the graphic image considerably. The alternatives shown here use only PageMaker's graphics tools and Zapf Dingbats. The ones on the following spread use borders from various clip art sources. When you use any of these devices to dress up a simple design, be playful but always err on the side of restraint. And be sure to put your result to the test of appropriateness.

For a short company name and for longer lines of text, use the same design in a vertical format, as shown here. The NLT logo is 31 points in a banner that is 4p6 deep, the text is 11/20 Palatino italics, and the design above the date is a 14-point Zapf Dingbat (keystroke is Option-7). The margins are 3 picas all around, as they are in the basic design.

Northern Light Textiles

invites you for

champagne and hors d'oeuvres

when we present

our 1988 fabrics

featuring

new designs by Laurence Ralph

January 22, 5 - 7:30 p.m.

La Rondo Room

The Heraldry Hotel

Zapf Chancery, used here, is often recommended for invitations because it has a personalized, handwritten look. But it can also be a little fussy, especially in all caps, so we've changed the headline here to 14-point upper- and lowercase. The body text is 12/18, the decorative display is a 12-point Zapf Dingbat (keystroke v) with 6 letterspaces between each unit.

The text position and line breaks have been altered from those specified in the blueprint in order to accommodate the decorative elements in this version.

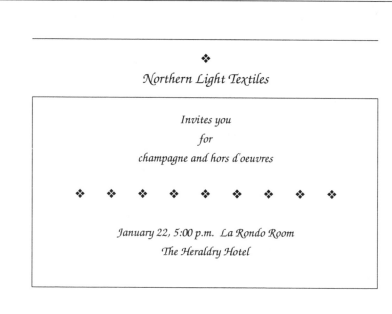

The decorative element here is a 1-pica-deep hairline-rule rectangle with a PageMaker shade as fill. The text is 10/15 Palatino.

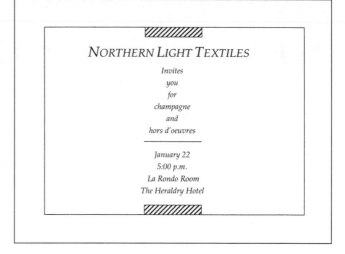

To personalize the invitation, put the invitee's name in the banner and rewrite the text to include the company name. This will take some extra time, of course, but might be a good choice for a limited number of guests and a very important event. Type the guest list one name to a line in your word processor (the example shown is 14-point Palatino italic), place the list on the pasteboard of your PageMaker invitation, and cut and paste each name as you print the cards.

A modern decorative motif contrasts with the formality of the centered type. The corners are built out of rectangular modules with black fill that decrease in width from 4 picas to 1 pica. The stairstepping effect is created with a series of 1-pica hairline-rule squares, masked with a 12-point reverse diagonal line.

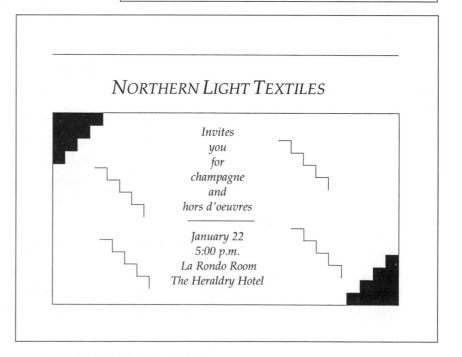

PROJECT 2B

AN INFORMAL INVITATION WITH PAGEMAKER GRAPHICS

This highly structured design could be used for a variety of informal events, with art suggestive of the theme of the party. The crisp organization suggests a shopping-list look, which is offset by playful art. The banner lends itself to different treatments, but the overall format works best with only one line of text occupying each space between the rules. For longer text, create additional spaces, as in the "Silvery Moon" version shown later; for shorter text, have fewer lines with more space between the rules. Several variations are shown following the blueprint instructions.

The invitation is designed so that four cards can be printed on a single 8.5- by 11-inch sheet. See the instructions for "How to Print Four Up," at the end of this project. Of course, you could easily vary the trim size to accommodate more text and print fewer cards on a sheet.

BLUEPRINT FOR THE INFORMAL INVITATION

TIP

Press the Tab key to move from one box to another in the Page Setup dialog box. Press the Return key to OK a dialog box. Both of these keyboard shortcuts can be used so frequently that they are worth remembering early on.

I. Open a 1-page document with the following page setup:

- Size: Letter (8.5 by 11 inches or 51 by 66 picas)
- Orientation: Tall
- Margins: 0 all around

2. Specify the unit of measure.

- Choose Preferences from the Edit menu. When the Preferences dialog box comes on screen, click on Picas.
- Before closing the Preferences dialog box, set the Guides to the back. (See explanation in step 2 of Project 2A.)

3. Divide the page into four quadrants.

- Turn on Snap to Rulers on the Options menu.
- Bring in ruler guides to bisect the page horizontally (at 33p) and vertically (at 25p6), creating a space for four vertical cards of equal size. You'll work in the upper left quadrant to create the master card.

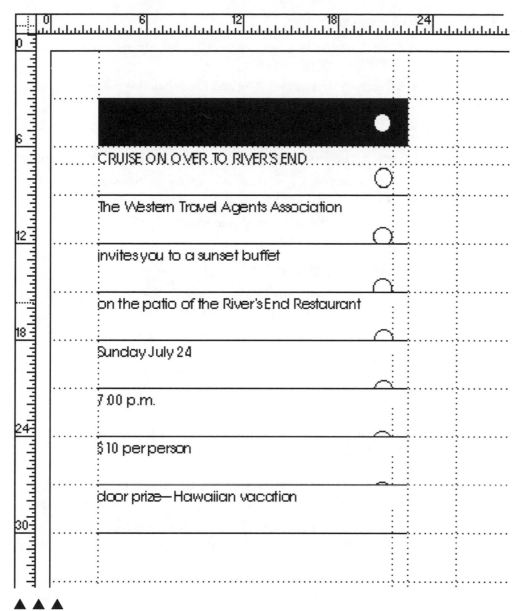

▲ ▲ ▲

The informal invitation is created in the upper left quadrant of an 8.5- by 11-inch sheet, and then copied and pasted three times to print four on a page. The graphics are created with PageMaker's graphics tools.

PAGEMAKER TECHNIQUES YOU WILL LEARN

▶ Define type margins with a bounding box

▶ Create a solid banner

▶ Mask graphics with "invisible" boxes

▶ Copy and paste PageMaker graphics

▶ Use leading to space text between rules

▶ Use PageMaker's Undo command

▶ Use the Select All command

4. Define the image area.

- Bring in horizontal ruler guides at 3p and 30p to define the top and bottom margins.

- Bring in vertical guides at 3p and 22p6 to define the side margins.

5. Create the banner.

- Bring in a horizontal guide at 6p to mark the bottom of the banner.

- With the rectangle tool, draw the box for the banner as defined by the top two ruler guides and side margins.

- Choose Black from the Shades menu.

6. Add the horizontal rules.

- Bring in horizontal ruler guides every 3 picas beginning at 9p and continuing through 27p, for a total of seven.

- With the perpendicular tool selected, choose Hairline from the Lines menu.

- Draw a hairline horizontal rule over the ruler guide at 9p, from the left edge of the image area to the right edge.

  When you draw a line or other graphic in PageMaker, it remains selected until you click elsewhere on the page. When a line is selected, you'll see a little square selection handle at each end. Leave the line selected so that you can copy it in the next step.

- With the line selected, choose Copy from the Edit menu. Then paste the line seven times by choosing Paste from the Edit menu.

  When you paste a graphic, PageMaker centers the graphic in the publication window. When you paste a graphic repeatedly, as instructed here, PageMaker pastes them one on top of another, but you'll be able to move them one by one.

- With the pointer, select the top line, which you just pasted. Drag it into position on the 12p horizontal guide.

  Continue selecting and moving the rules into position on the horizontal ruler guides. The last one should be on the 30p guide.

7. Add the text.

- Bring in a horizontal ruler guide 1p1 below the black banner to align the baseline for the headline.

- With the text tool, select an insertion point on the 3p vertical guide, above the horizontal guide that you just brought in, and draw a "bounding box" by dragging the cursor diagonally to about the 18p point on the horizontal ruler (the depth isn't important). This defines the left and right margins of the text you will type. You'll see the box as you drag, but it will become invisible when you release the mouse.

TIP

When you want to insert a graphic repeatedly in a document, such as the hairline rule in this invitation, it is faster to copy and paste it than to redraw it. Pasting also ensures consistency of size from one graphic to another of the same kind. You have to copy the graphic only once. It will remain on the Clipboard until you replace it with something else. Use the keyboard shortcut for pasting (Command-v on a Macintosh, Ctrl-v on a PC) and you'll find the process very speedy.

TIP

When you type an apostrophe in PageMaker, press Option-Shift-] for the apostrophe designed for that font. Similarly, when you type quotations in PageMaker, press Option-[to open the quotes and Option-Shift-[to close the quotes.

TIP

Use the text tool to select text when you want to edit the text, change the type specifications (font, size, style, and so on), or cut and paste. Use the pointer tool to select text when you want to reposition it on the page. Use either tool to select text when you want to copy it to the Clipboard for insertion on another page or in another document.

- Type the headline and body text in 10/36 Avant Garde. Don't worry about the vertical position of the text block just yet.

- With the text tool, select the headline; change it to 12/36, all caps.

- With the pointer, select the text, hold down the Shift key, and drag the text block vertically so that the baseline of the headline is on the ruler guide just below the black banner. The subsequent lines should fall 13 points below the hairline rules. Check to be sure that the left edge of the type is flush with the 3p vertical guide .

  If some of your hairline rules seem to disappear when you type or move the text, select the text block with the pointer and choose Send to Back from the Edit menu.

8. Add the visual motif for the banner.

You can create the sunset using PageMaker's graphics tools, as described below.

9. Print.

See "How to Print Four Up" following the variations.

HOW TO CREATE A PAGEMAKER SUNSET

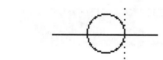

A hairline-rule circle...

partially covered by a rectangle...

with the line set to None and the shade to Paper...

makes a setting sun.

You can create a sunset motif by using a white rectangle to mask more and more of each subsequent circle, thus suggesting the sun sinking below the horizon line.

1. Hold down the Shift key and use the circle tool to create the size sun you want. We wouldn't suggest anything smaller than the one shown in the sample, but you might want a larger one. Set the line weight to Hairline and the shade to None. (For the circle in the black banner, change the shade to White.)

2. Copy the circle once and paste it seven or as many times as you want. Position each copy a little lower on its horizon line than the one before. Use a vertical ruler guide to align the right sides of the setting suns.

3. To cover the part of the circle below the horizontal line, create a hairline-rule rectangle and butt it to the horizontal rule. Then change the line weight of the rectangle to None and the shade to White. You'll have to adjust the position of this "invisible" box through trial and error until the horizon line is unbroken and the portion of the circle below it is completely masked. Use the pointer to select the invisible box and reveal its handles.

If any of the horizontal rules seem to disappear behind the sun, select those rules and choose Bring to Front from the Edit menu.

You can create a moonlight motif with a technique similar to the one used for the sunset. Select White from the Shades menu to reverse the moons out of the black banner. You need five or six moons to convey the feeling of movement across the sky.

This variation has one more line of text than the basic design has, and the text is placed just above the horizontal rules instead of just below them. The space between the rules is 2p9, the baselines for the text are 1p1 above the horizontal rules, and the type specs are 12/33 Avant Garde for the headline and 10/33 for the body text.

A simple, all-text variation for this design uses the banner for the headline type instead of for art. To adapt the blueprint for this treatment, type the headline in reverse 10-point type inside the black banner. Enter the headine as two separate copy blocks so that you can position each block individually in the upper left and lower right corners of the banner.

In the body of the invitation, there are 3 picas between each rule, as there are in the basic design. Bring in a ruler guide 13 points below the first horizontal rule for the baseline of the first line of text. If you type the text in 10/36 Avant Garde, each of the subsequent lines will be 13 points below a horizontal rule.

SWOON BY THE SILVERY MOON

The Western Travel Agents Association

invites you to a moonlight cruise

on the good ship Pacifica

Broadway Pier

Sunday July 24, 9:00 p.m. anchors aweigh

$25 per person

dinner and dancing

Live music by the Streamers

CRUISE ON OVER TO

THE RIVER'S END

The Western Travel Agents Association

invites you to a sunset buffet

on the patio at River's End Restaurant

Sunday July 24

7:00 p.m.

$10 per person

door prize—Hawaiian vacation

Clip art is available to fit almost any party theme you could imagine. Here, the ship is a bit-mapped image from the DeskTop Art Business package; background trees and sky in the original image were erased in DeskPaint to create a silhouette. The palm trees are EPS art created from a single tree in Moonlight Artworks; the original tree was rotated in Adobe Illustrator, and both the original and the rotated image were placed as separate graphics in PageMaker, where they were sized to fit the layout.

The hairline rules are positioned at 4-pica intervals, with the first one drawn 6 picas from the top trim; the line length varies depending on the length of the text and the position of the art.

The type is 10/48 Avant Garde.

CRUISE ON OVER TO RIVER'S END

Western Travel Agents Association

invites you to a sunset buffet

on the good ship Pacifica

Sunday, July 24 at 7 P.M.

door prize—Hawaiian vacation

Typographic details such as initial caps bring a touch of visual interest to an all-text invitation. The cap here is 72-point Zapf Chancery, partially overlapping a 40% black banner.

The specifications for the text and rules are the same as those described in the blueprint, except that the text here is flush right. For right-aligned text, it is very important that you draw a bounding box to define the left and right margins before typing the text. See step 7 of Project 2B.

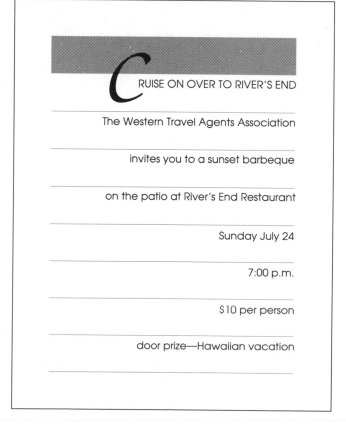

CRUISE ON OVER TO RIVER'S END

The Western Travel Agents Association

invites you to a sunset barbeque

on the patio at River's End Restaurant

Sunday July 24

7:00 p.m.

$10 per person

door prize—Hawaiian vacation

How To Print Four Up

Invitations, business cards, name tags, and other documents with a small trim size can be printed efficiently with multiple copies of the document on one sheet of paper. Simply create a master of the document, copy it, and then repeatedly paste the copy to fill the page, using ruler guides to align the tops and edges of the copies.

The following instructions for printing the invitation in Project 2B four to a page can be adapted easily for other dimensions.

1. Check all the alignments on your master. Print a copy and proofread for spelling, accuracy of information, alignments, and so on.

2. Note that the ruler guides bisecting the page, which you brought in to define the trim of the master, also define the trim for the other three units. If you were printing more copies on a single sheet , you would need to bring in additional ruler guides to divide the page accordingly.

3. Be sure Snap to Guides (on the Options menu) is turned on.

4. With the rectangle tool, draw a temporary page frame around the master, from the zero point in the upper left corner to the midpoint of the 8.5- by 11-inch page (where the 25p6 vertical guide and the 33p horizontal guide intersect).

   When you move the copies of the master in step 7, you'll appreciate the aid of this page frame.

5. Select the entire master, either by choosing Select All from the Edit menu or by using the pointer to draw a marquee around all the elements in the master.

6. Copy and paste the master. PageMaker will paste it in the center of the page, full of handlebars. As long as those handlebars are showing, you know that all the pieces of your copy are selected.

7. With all the pieces of the copy still selected, position the arrow on any side of the temporary page frame and drag the copy into position in the upper right quadrant. Do not point on a handle or you will stretch the frame. (If you inadvertently do stretch that or any other element, choose Undo from the Edit menu; all the pieces of the copy will remain selected after the mistake is undone.)

8. Select All again, copy, and paste. This time you'll have two copies.

9. Move the new copies into position in the bottom half of the page.

10. To remove the temporary page frame around each invitation, select it with the pointer and press the Backspace key.

11. Optional electronic trimming guide: If you plan to print and trim the cards yourself, you may want to add little tick marks to guide your trim. It sounds ridiculous, but we've found that 8-point Helvetica periods, being 1 pixel high, provide a sufficient guide and virtually disappear in trimming. Along the horizontal ruler guide separating the top and bottom cards, place a period at each

▲ ▲ ▲

Copy and paste the master unit to print multiple invitations on the same sheet. Use a temporary page frame (already removed here) to facilitate alignment along the ruler guides that mark the trim for each copy.

corner of the image area. Along the vertical ruler guide separating the right and left cards, place periods to align with the tops of the banners and the last horizontal rules. You should have four periods along each guide.

Old-fashioned trimming guide: Use a ruler and pencil to mark the cuts and erase the pencil marks after trimming.

12. If you are printing the invitations on a laser printer, the 20-pound card stock must be hand-fed. Select the Manual print option in the Print dialog box.

If your cards will be commercially printed, you will need to paste your camera-ready page onto a piece of art board and draw crop marks outside the live area to indicate the inside trim for each card.

PROJECT 3

A SIMPLE ONE-COLUMN FORMAT FOR NEWSLETTERS AND REPORTS

This project introduces three of the most important features of electronic pasteup: creating master pages, designing templates, and placing text created in a word processor. Master pages enable you to create one set of nonprinting guidelines for all the pages in a publication. Templates enable you to have on file an electronic blueprint with master pages, type specifications, headline treatments, and other elements in documents that you produce repeatedly, such as newsletters and reports. Both techniques save you time (you don't have to reinvent the wheel on every page or in every issue) and help you to maintain consistency (you don't have to remember and re-create dozens of different specifications).

If you are unfamiliar with any of these features, this is a good project to do whether or not you need a format such as the one used in this report.

Because this is the first project that involves placing and working with text blocks, we have also included some sidebar information about controlling text in PageMaker.

Although the subhead for *Flash/Memo* labels it a newsletter, the same format could be used for a report. The format is a notch or two more complex and effective than what you could do on a typewriter. In fact, the typewriterlike face (Courier) and wide text column are intended to suggest the spontaneity of a typewritten document. That association may seem ironic given the slickness that desktop publishing offers, but it gives the page a feeling of hot news right off the press. You can't capture that feeling in a more highly formatted design.

The fact that the newsletter looks like it was quickly and easily put together in turn suggests that it can be read quickly and easily. Indeed, the generous white space around the headlines and the boldface leadins facilitate scanning. You would expect the writing style to be fast-paced—informal yet to the point. The format is designed to accommodate short items of about 150 to 200 words. If your editorial material doesn't lend itself to brief stories, this is not the design for you.

You could use this design for a four-, six-, or eight-page document, but anything longer than that would become monotonous and would also undermine the briskness inherent in the design.

We've called this a one-column newsletter because the text is placed in a single column. But in PageMaker, you will set up a two-column document in order to create left and right margins for the headlines.

PAGEMAKER TECHNIQUES

▶ Create and use a template

▶ Set up a master page

▶ Create unequal columns

▶ Change the default typeface

▶ Draw a dotted line using PageMaker's tab leaders

▶ Work on the pasteboard

▶ Make and use a spacing guide

▶ Create a composite page-number marker

▶ Place text

▶ Use the manual text-flow mode

▶ Use a drag-place technique

▶ Thread and unthread text

▶ Manipulate text blocks

▶ Export text to a word-processing application

The Weekly
Newsmemo of
ACE
Marketing Co.

FLASH/Memo

Headline goes here on as many lines as needed

Loren ipsum dolor sit amet, consectetur adipscing elit, sed diam nonnumy eiusmod tempor incidunt ut labore et dolore magna aliquam erat vvolupat. Ut enim ad minimim veniame quis nostrud exercitation ullamcorpor suscipit laboris nisi ut aliquip ex ea commodo consequat. Duis autem vel eum irure dolor in reprehenderit in volupate velit esse molestaie son consequat, vel nostrud exercitation illum dolore exerc

At ve
praes
excep
sunt
rum e
dit d
optio
facer
repel
tum r
et mc

. . . .

Headline goes here on as many lines as needed

Itaqu
prefe
sentr
dare
eam r

Nos a
das d
Et ta
ned l
praid
coerc
igitu
fiden
neg f
et op
velir

. . . .

Headline goes here on as many

Dabut
est a
caus
facil
Loren

---

velit esse molestaie son consequat, vel illum dolore eu fugiat nulla pariatur.

At vero eos et accusam et justo odio dignissim qui blandit praesent lupatum delenit aigue duos dolor et molestais exceptur sint occaecat cupidat non provident, simil tempor sunt in culpa qui officia deserunt mollit anim id est laborum et dolor fugai. Et harumd dereud facilis est er expedit distinct. Nam liber a tempor cum soluta nobis eligend optio comque nihil quod a impedit anim id quod maxim placeat facer possim omnis es voluptas assumenda est, omnis dolor repellend. Temporem autem quinsud et aur office debit aut tum rerum necessit atib saepe eveniet ut er repudiand sint et molestia non este recusand.

. . . .

Headline goes here on as many lines as needed

Itaque earud rerum hic tenetury sapiente delectus au aut prefer andis dolorib asperiore repellat. Hanc ego cum tene sentntiam, quid est cur verear ne ad eam non est cur verear **Loren ipsum dolor** sit amet, consectetur adipscing elit, sed diam nonnumy eiusmod tempor incidunt ut labore et dolore magna aliquam erat vvolupat. Ut enim ad minimim veniame quis nostrud exercitation ullamcorpor suscipit laboris nisi ut aliquip ex ea commodo consequat. Duis autem vel eum irure dolor in reprehenderit est cur verear ne ad eam non possing in volupate velit ess molestaie son consequat, vel illum dolore eu fugiat nulla pariatur.

At vero eos et accusam et justo odio dignissim qui blandit praesent lupatum delenit aigue duos dolor et molestais exceptur sint occaecat cupidat non provident, simil tempor sunt in culpa qui officia deserunt mollit anim id est laborum et dolor fugai. Et harumd dereud facilis est er expedit distinct. Nam liber a tempor cum soluta nobis eligend

. . . .

Headline goes here

Optio comque nihil quod a impedit anim id quod maxim placeat facer possim omnis es voluptas assumenda est, omnis dolor repellend. Temporem autem quinsud et aur office debit aut.

Tum rerum necessit atib saepe eveniet ut er repudiand sint et molestia non este recusand.

Itaque earud rerum hic tenetury sapiente delectus au aut prefer andis dolorib asperiore repellat. Hanc ego cum tene sentntiam, quid est cur verear ne ad eam non possing accomo.

Dare nost ros quos est cur verear ne ad eam non possing tu paulo ante cum memorite it tum etia ergat.

Nos amice et nebevol, olestias access potest fier ad augendas cum conscient to factor tum toen legum odioque civiuda. Et tamen in busdad ne que pecun modut est neque nonor imper.

Ned libiding gen epular religuard on cupiditat, quas nulla praid im umdnat. Improb pary minuiti potius inflammad ut.

Sed diam nonnumy eiusmod tempor incidunt ut labore et dolore magna aliquam erat vvolupat. Ut enim ad minimim veniame quis nostrud exercitation ullamcorpor suscipit laboris nisi Duis autem vel eum irure dolor in reprehenderit in volupate

BLUEPRINT FOR FLASH/MEMO

This newsletter is intended to be printed on both sides of a single sheet of paper. However, by laying it out as if it were a single-sided publication, you'll have to set up only one master page. You will still be able to print on both sides of the paper.

PAGE SETUP

Size: Letter (8.5 by 11 inches or 51 by 66 picas)

Start page #: 1 of 2

Single-sided (click off Double-sided)

Margins:

Left: 5 picas   Top and bottom: 4 picas

Right: 6 picas

Remember that in PageMaker 3.0 you can override the unit of measure by typing abbreviations. Thus, if your preferences are set to inches, type *5p*, *6p*, and *4p* for the margins. The rest of the measurements are given in picas, however, so when you're finished with the page setup, change the unit of measure through the Preferences command on the Edit menu.

MASTER PAGE

1. Click on the icon labeled R at the lower left of the screen.

In single-sided publications, the master page icon is identified as a right-hand page. In double-sided publications there are icons labeled R and L for right and left pages.

2. Create customized column guides.

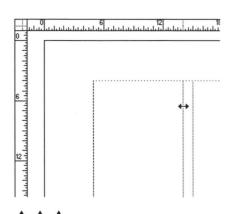

- Choose Column Guides from the Options menu.
- In the Column Guides dialog box, specify 2 columns with a 1p space in between.
- Turn on Snap to Rulers.
- The column guides in the center of the page move as a pair— they're the right margin of the first column and the left margin of the second. Position the pointer on either guide and drag to reposition them at 14p and 15p, respectively. As you drag, the hairline marker in the ruler will move, indicating the position of whichever guide you are pointing to.

▲ ▲ ▲

When you drag the column guides to create columns of unequal widths, the space between columns remains constant. To change that space you must return to the Column Guides dialog box.

▲ ▲ ▲
The cover template contains the nameplate, subhead, and date placeholder as well as nonprinting column guides. Once you've created this template, you can simply open a copy for each issue, change the date, and place the text.

TEXT FORMATTING

Although you can keyboard and edit text in PageMaker, it is not intended as a word processor. In general, if you have more than a paragraph or two of running text you should input, edit, and format it for typeface, size, and style as thoroughly as your word processor and its compatibility with PageMaker allows.

As part of the graduated complexity of the projects in this book, the instructions for controlling typography in *Flash/Memo* focus on changing and using the publication default. If you use this format for a real newsletter or report, you will want to define styles for the headlines and for the space between stories. See Project 4 for using PageMaker's style sheets.

- *The body text* for all the stories should be created as a single file in your word-processing program. (In a modular format, you would want a separate file for each story.) The type specs are 10/Auto Courier with 6 points of space after each paragraph.

If PageMaker does not recognize formatting from your word-processing program, you can format the text after you place it in PageMaker.

- *The space between stories* is 3 picas from the baseline of the last line of one story to the baseline of the first line of the next. To achieve that spacing, select the last paragraph of each story and change the paragraph specification to 24 points after. (One pica of the space from baseline to baseline is taken up by type and leading, because Auto leading for the 10-point body text is 12 points.)

- *The boldface paragraph leadins* can be formatted in the word processor or in PageMaker. These function as subheads, and you might have them for some paragraphs and not for others. The page looks best if you reserve the boldface for the beginnings of paragraphs, but if you can use it more effectively in the middle of paragraphs, do. Be careful, however, of gratuitous emphasis. It's distracting.

- *The headlines* are 12/Auto Courier bold and should be typed directly in PageMaker. If you want to include them in the early drafts of the manuscript, remember to delete them before placing the text in PageMaker.

3. Add ruler guides.

- Bring in a horizontal ruler guide 6 points above the top margin.

- Bring in a vertical ruler guide 6 points to the right of the left margin.

4. Change the default typeface.

Before typing any text in the template, use the pointer to choose the Type Specs command and specify 10/Auto Courier. When you use the pointer tool to change type specifications and no text is selected, those specifications become the default for that document. Any new text you type will have the default specifications. It's more efficient to type all text in the default and then select and change the size and style as needed.

COVER TEMPLATE

1. Click on the page 1 icon at the lower right of the screen.

2. Draw the banner with PageMaker's rectangle tool.

- Line weight: 0.5 point

- Depth: 6 picas from the top margin

- Width: Across both columns

  New users may find it helpful to bring in ruler guides to define rectangles before drawing them and to define the alignment of loose text such as the subhead.

3. Add the newsletter logo or nameplate.

Flash/Memo is 56-point Courier bold outline, flush left with the second column, and centered vertically in the banner.

If you're working on an IBM and don't have outline type available, you can simply use boldface.

4. Add the newsletter subhead.

The four-line subhead in the sample is 12/Auto Courier. It's centered vertically in the banner, 6 points from the left margin of the first column.

5. Add the date placeholder.

- The type specs are the same as those for the subhead.

- The baseline is 6 points above the banner, aligned left with the subhead.

TIP

When you specify single lines of text in large type sizes, make the leading the same size as the type. This keeps the windowshade handles close to the type.

TIP

Text typed outside the margins will not follow the left and right column guides. To avoid having text handles that extend the full width of the page, draw a small "bounding box" before typing the date: Drag the text tool to define an invisible box that is the approximate width and depth of the text you will type.

6. Mark the baseline for the lead story.

- Bring in a horizontal ruler guide 3p below the banner to mark the baseline of the lead story and headline. When you type the headlines, you'll align the bar on the I-beam at this guideline.

- Bring in a second horizontal guide 9 points above the first one. When you place text, you'll align the top of the loaded text icon with this guideline.

7. Draw a dotted line for the rule separating stories.

PageMaker's dotted rule on the Lines menu is too heavy to use for the rule that separates stories. Dotted leaders in various type faces, sizes, and styles provide a large selection of additional rules. The ones in *Flash/Memo* are 14-point Courier bold.

To create this rule, see the instructions on the following two pages.

You will copy and paste this dotted rule between stories after you place the text.

8. Make a 1p6-deep spacing guide.

The rule that separates one story from the next is 1p6 above the baseline of the text that follows it. To ensure that the spacing is consistent throughout the newsletter, make a spacing guide and leave it on the pasteboard with the rule.

- Set the line weight to Hairline.

- Turn off both Snap to Guides.

- Make a 1p6-deep rectangle, label it (just type *1p6* inside the rectangle), and position it on the pasteboard so that its top is flush with the dotted rule.

  When you copy the rule to position it on the actual pages, copy the spacing guide with it; then delete the spacing guide after the rule is in place.

TIP

Turn on Snap to Rulers before you create spacing guides. As you drag the crossbar to draw the rectangle, the tick marks move on the ruler. Watch that movement to measure the depth of the guide. You can also bring in ruler guides to define the spacing guide before you draw it. Ruler guides don't extend to the pasteboard, however, so you would have to work within the page frame and then move the spacing guide.

▶ ▶ ▶ · · · · · · · · · · · · · ▢ 1p6 ▢ · · · · · · · · · · · · ·

A 1p6-deep spacing guide measures the distance from the dotted rule between stories to the baseline of the body text below. Leave the rule and guide on the pasteboard.

Instructions for page 2 of the template continue after the following spread.

HOW TO CREATE A RULE AS A LEADERED TAB IN PAGEMAKER

Tabs can be tricky, and it's tempting to try to work around them. But like so many other aspects of working with computers, it's only through struggling with a difficult feature that it becomes a tool instead of a nemesis. The leadered tab rule in this project is not a typical use for tabs. But precisely because it doesn't involve the familiar alignment of data in columns, some of you who have been avoiding tabs may become more comfortable with them here.

1. **With the text tool, draw a bounding box from the left margin all the way across the page, past the right margin to 47 picas.**

   The ruler in the Indents/Tabs dialog box (which you will bring on-screen in the next step) measures from the left to the right margin of the column in which you've positioned the I-beam. When you want to override the column guides, as you do here in order to set the tab across both columns, drawing a bounding box enables you to do so. (The depth of the bounding box is not relevant here.)

2. **Choose Indents/Tabs from the Type menu.**

   If you haven't worked with PageMaker's tabs, take a minute to orient yourself to the dialog box. Depending on your current page view, you may or may not be able to see all the elements in the screen detail below. If not, click on the arrows on the sides of the dialog box ruler to scroll. Or close the dialog box, choose a reduced page view, and then choose Indents/Tabs again.

   The top row of options defines how text aligns on the tabs; you'll use the Right option here. The second row defines the kind of leader between tab stops; you'll use the dots. (The fifth option in that row is a text box for creating custom leaders. You can type up to two characters, of any font, in that box, which is how we created the triangle border at right.)

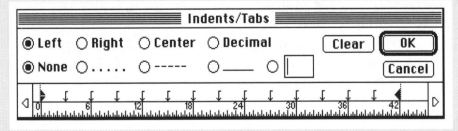

The arrows over the ruler are the default tab stops, which you will clear. You can tell they are left-aligned by their shape.

▲ ▲ ▲

The Indents/Tabs dialog box is shown here with PageMaker's default settings. The right and left margins (dotted lines at 0 and 42 picas) are defined by the bounding box drawn in step 1. When you don't draw a bounding box, the right and left margins are defined by the column guides in which you place the I-beam or, if the pointer tool is active, by the right and left margins of the page.

On the far left above the ruler are two triangular black icons, which control the paragraph indent. The top one is the first-line indent, and the bottom one is the left indent. The triangular black icon above the ruler on the right is the right indent, and the dotted line next to it is the right margin.

It's very useful, when setting tabs, to align the zero point on the Tabs ruler with the left margin of the column you are working in. Do that now by dragging the Tabs dialog box window.

TIP

To get a better feel for the tabs ruler, open a practice document with two or three unequal columns. Place the text I-beam in different columns and choose Indents/Tabs for each position. Move the Tabs window around so that the zero point on its ruler corresponds to the column in which you've set the I-beam. Note the relationship of the left and right margin markers in the tabs ruler to the column guides on the page.

3. **Click on Clear in the Indents/Tabs dialog box to remove the default tab stops.**

4. **Specify the tab settings for the leadered rule.**

   Aldus recommends that you work from the top of the box down:

   • Click on Right.

   • Click on the dotted leader option.

   • Finally, position the tab by clicking at 41p on the ruler.

   A right tab icon will appear on the ruler where you click. The ruler position is also displayed numerically to the left of the Cancel button. If you need to adjust the position of the tab on the ruler, drag the tab icon until the numeric display matches the exact position you want. Then click OK or press the Return key to close the Indents/Tabs dialog box.

▲ ▲ ▲

The tab settings for the Flash/Memo rule.

5. **Insert the Tab stop.**

   The text cursor should still be in position at the left of the bounding box that you drew on the pasteboard.

   • Press the Tab key.

   • Press the Return key.

When you insert leadered tabs, you don't see the leader until you type a character. Pressing Return is, in effect, the character.

6. **Select the dotted rule (click anywhere on it three times), and change the type specs of the rule to 14-point Courier bold.**

   Move the rule on the pasteboard. You'll copy and paste it into position after you place the text.

► ► ►

You can create a wide variety of rules using the technique described on these two pages, thus increasing the lines available within PageMaker.

The dotted leader rule used in Flash/Memo: *14-point Courier bold*

14-point Bookman

The same 14-point Bookman opened up, by specifying a period followed by a space bar in the custom leader box

A custom leader rule created by specifying Zapf Dingbats as the typeface and typing t-space bar *in the custom leader box.*

PageMaker's dotted rule

PAGE 2 TEMPLATE

1. Click on the page 2 icon.

2. Draw the identification banner at the top of the page.

- Line weight: 0.5 point
- Width: Across both columns
- Depth: 2 picas from top margin

3. Type the ID line in the banner.

- The type is 12-point Courier, centered vertically in the banner.
- The date is 6 points from the left margin of the first column. For months with longer names, you will have to abbreviate the date.
- The newsletter title is flush left with the second column.

> **TIP**
>
> To fit a longer title, drop down to 11-point type for the title and date here and on the first page.

4. Add the ruler guides for positioning the text.

- Bring in a horizontal guide 3p below the bottom of the banner.
- Bring in a second guide 9 points above the first one.

5. Add the page number.

The type is 12-point Courier, aligned with the left edge of the date on a baseline 6 points above the top of the banner.

If your newsletter is longer than two pages, create a composite page-number marker on the master page.

> **TIP**
>
> To create a composite page-number marker for a document longer than two pages, type the word *Page* in the desired position, press the space bar, and then press Command-Option-p (Ctrl-Option-p on a PC). On the master page you will see Page 0; Page-Maker will automatically number every page in this position.

6. Save as a template.

In PageMaker 3.0 you can save a file as a publication or as a template. If you choose Template, PageMaker will automatically open a copy of the file in the future, enabling you to reuse the original template each time you lay out the publication.

If you want to make corrections on the original template, be sure to click on Original in the Open dialog box.

USING THE FLASH/MEMO TEMPLATE

1. Open a copy of the template.

When you open a template, PageMaker opens an untitled copy of the original. It's a good habit to save it right away under whatever name you'll be using for the file, such as Flash/Memo 3-89 (or FLSH3-89 if you are using an IBM).

```
Page 2

March 14, 1989   FLASH/Memo The Weekly Newsmemo of ACE Marketing
```

▲ ▲ ▲

The template for page 2 contains the banner, the page-number marker, and the guidelines for placing text.

2. Place the text from your word-processor file in the text column.

If you have formatted the text in your word-processing program without using a style sheet:

Follow the instructions for "How to Place Text in Page-Maker" on the next page.

If you have used a style sheet in your word-processing program:

If you have used the name *body text* for a style defined in your word processor, you must redefine PageMaker's default *body text* style to match the formatting of the text you will place. Otherwise, PageMaker's default will override the formatting defined in your word processor. If you have defined the body text style in your word processor under a name other than *body text*, such as *Normal* or *Flash text*, Page-Maker will import that style and add the name to its style sheet for the publication. An imported style is identified in PageMaker's Styles list by an asterisk following the name.

To redefine a style, choose Define Styles from the Type menu. Click on the name of the style you want to redefine (in this case, *body text*), then click on the Edit button to the right of the Styles list. Click on Type to change the type specifications, click on Para. to change the paragraph specifications, and so on.

If you are placing an unformatted, text-only document:

Place the text as described in "How to Place Text in Page-Maker" on the following spread. Then place the cursor anywhere in the text and choose Select All from the Edit menu to highlight the entire text block on both pages. Using the options on the Type menu, change the type specs to Courier 10/Auto with 0p6 space after each paragraph. Then select the last line of each story and change the spacing after to 2p.

Blueprint instructions continue after the following spread.

HOW TO PLACE TEXT IN PAGEMAKER

PageMaker's Place command enables you to bring text and graphics created in other programs into your PageMaker document. If you have previously defined columns, as you have in this project, the margins will define the shape of the text that you place.

1. **Select the text-flow mode.**

   PageMaker 3.0 has three text-flow modes: automatic, semi-automatic, and manual. In this project you'll use the manual mode, which you select by turning off the Autoflow command on the Options menu.

2. **Choose Place from the File menu to bring the Place dialog box on screen.**

   • Scroll through your file directories until you find the text file for the newsletter.

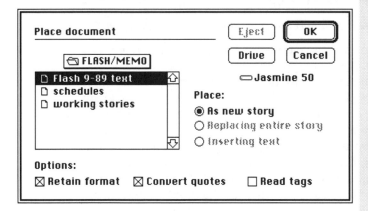

The list in the dialog box includes only those documents that PageMaker can read directly from the folder or directory on the current disk. Because you cannot place one PageMaker document in another, for example, your *Flash/Memo* template will not appear in the list even if it is in the same folder with other files that are listed.

   • Note the options below the directory in the Place dialog box. An x in the box before an option means the option is selected; a blank box means the option is not selected.

   Retain Format: Choose this box when you want PageMaker to retain text formatting

from your word-processing program. If that program supports style sheets, PageMaker also adds any style names defined there to the style sheet in the PageMaker file.

Convert Quotes: Choose this when you want PageMaker to convert straight up-and-down, typewriter-style quotation marks (" ") and apostrophes (') to the characters designed for the typeface you are using (" " and ').

Read Tags: Choose this if, in your word-processing program, you format text with style name tags surrounded by angled brackets (< >). If you've defined style names in your PageMaker publication that match the tag names of the imported document, PageMaker will apply the styles and remove the tags. If a tag does not match a style defined in PageMaker, PageMaker creates a new style with the type specifications of the tag itself.

3. **Select the name of the text file that you want to place.**

   PageMaker automatically highlights the As New Story button.

4. **Click OK.**

   PageMaker loads the pointer with a copy of the text file you've selected. (The original remains unchanged as a word-processing file.) When the dialog box closes, you'll see the loaded text icon, shown below, on the screen.

 The loaded text icon in the manual text-flow mode.

When you move the loaded text icon into the menus, the rulers, the Styles palette, or the page icons at the bottom of the publication window, the pointer temporarily turns into the arrow; it returns as the loaded text icon when you move it back into the publication window.

If you decide you don't want to place the text, click on the pointer in the Toolbox.

5. Select an insertion point for the text.

- First check that the Snap to Guides are on.

- For *Flash/Memo*, align the loaded text icon at the left margin of the wide column and at the 12p horizontal ruler guide.

6. Click the mouse to place the text.

In the manual mode, the text flow stops at the end of each column.

7. Click on the + sign in the bottom handle.

When you click on the + sign, PageMaker reloads the text icon so that you can manually select the next insertion point. Using the

manual text-flow mode lets you leave narrow columns in this format free for headlines. In the autoflow mode, PageMaker would flow text from column to column and from page to page until all the text was placed, filling the narrow columns as well as the wide ones.

8. Click on the page 2 icon at the bottom of the publication window.

9. Place the text on page 2.

- Position the loaded text icon at the intersection of the left margin of the wide column and the 8p horizontal ruler guide.

- Click to place the text.

An open box in the top windowshade handle indicates the beginning of a text file.

Lorem ipsum dolor sit amet, consectetuer adipiscing elit, sed diam nonummy nibh euismod tincidunt ut laoreet dolore erim

A + sign in the bottom handle indicates that there is more text to place.

A + sign in the top handle indicates the continuation of a text block.

minim veniam, quis nostrud exerci tation ullamcorper suscipit lobortis nisl ut aliquip ex ea commodo consequat.

A # sign in the bottom handle indicates the end of that text file (there is no more text to place).

HOW TO "DRAG-PLACE" TEXT WITHOUT FILLING A WHOLE COLUMN

When you are placing text and want to leave room for a graphic, or you have one item across two or three columns on the top half of the page and another item on the bottom, you don't want the text to fill out the entire column.

The most efficient technique in these situations is to "drag-place." Follow the procedure described for placing text through step 5. With the loaded text icon in position, press the mouse button and drag the cursor diagonally to the desired width and depth (as in the first screen detail shown at right). When you release the mouse, the text will pour into the defined area (as in the second screen detail). Of course, you can also fill the column and then adjust the top or bottom windowshade handle to the desired height, but that it is not as efficient as the drag-place technique.

You can use a similar drag-place technique when you type new text in PageMaker. Position the I-beam where you want to begin the new text and then drag on a diagonal to define the line length of the text you will type. This technique is useful when you want to override existing column guides (for a headline that runs across two columns, such as the one above) and when you type loose text on the pasteboard.

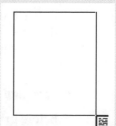

Position the loaded text icon, press the mouse button, and drag the cursor diagonally to the desired width and depth. When you release the mouse, the text will pour into the defined area, called a bounding box.

3. *Before typing the headlines, be sure that they won't fall too close to the bottom of the page.*

You should have at least six lines in a story that begins near the bottom of a page. If you don't, you can cut from and add to stories to adjust the position of headlines; or rearrange the order of stories; or stop the text short of the bottom margin and begin the new story on the next page. (The informal format allows for an uneven bottom.) Whether you make these changes in PageMaker or in your word-processing program depends on the extent of the changes needed. To export changes made in PageMaker back to your original text file, see "Using PageMaker's Export Feature" on the facing page.

4. *Type the headlines in PageMaker.*

Before typing the headlines, use the pointer to choose the Type Specs command from the Type menu and specify 12/Auto Courier bold. These specs will replace the default for the publication. When you move the text cursor from story to story to type the headlines, you won't have to reset the specs each time.

The first line of each headline aligns with the first line of body text for that story. Bring in horizontal ruler guides for each headline to ensure this alignment.

Note: Once you're comfortable with the other basic skills used in this newsletter, you may want to go back to your original template and use the Define Styles command to record the headline style. See Project 4 for an explanation of PageMaker's styles feature.

5. *Type the issue date over the placeholder on the cover and page 2.*

To retain the type specs for the date, use the text tool to select the date in the template, and then type the new date directly over the old one. Do not delete the old date before typing the new one.

6. *Add the dotted rule between stories.*

Copy the rule and spacing guide from the pasteboard and repeatedly paste copies in position between stories. The first dot should align with the left margin, and the rule should extend just to the right margin. The bottom of the spacing guide should align with the baseline of the text that follows the rule.

Delete the spacing guide and label after the rule is aligned and paste the next rule in place. (The rule should still be on the Clipboard unless you have copied something else in the meantime.)

7. *Save and Print.*

Before printing, turn off the Guides to view the document as it will print. Be sure the dotted rules are flush left with the headlines. Alignment is not as critical on the ragged right margin.

TIP

When you change the type specs with the text tool selected, the specs you select are in effect for that text block only. Any time you choose a new insertion point, as you do each time you type a headline, you begin a new text block, and the type specs revert to the default for that publication. Whenever you want to type several small text blocks all with the same specifications, use the pointer tool to select the type specs, thus setting those specs as the current publication default. This distinction is crucial to controlling text in PageMaker rather than having the text seem to control you.

FOR A LONGER FLASH/MEMO

To use this format for a longer document, follow the instructions for the two-page newsletter with these changes and additions:

- While still on the master page, create the identification banner, text baseline, and page number as described for the page 2 template, steps 1 through 4.

- On page 1, mask the ID banner at the top. (Draw a rectangle over it with a line of None and a shade of Paper.) Then create the nameplate, date placeholder, and lead story baseline as described for the cover template, steps 2 through 6.

- The dotted rule and spacing guide (cover template steps 7 and 8) can be created on the master page or on page 1. As long as it is on the pasteboard of any page in the document, it will appear on the pasteboard for every page.

USING PAGEMAKER'S EXPORT FEATURE

When you place a text file in PageMaker, the original document remains intact. Changes, additions, and deletions that you make in Page-Maker are not incorporated into the original file. This can be very useful: If you mess up the text while assembling the pages, you can simply place the text again and start over.

But there are times when you want changes made in PageMaker to be incorporated into the original file or to be saved as a new text file. Perhaps you start editing copy in PageMaker, decide that the work could be done quicker in your word processor, and don't want to lose the changes made so far. Or perhaps you edit some catalog copy that will be further revised in the next edition of the catalog or write captions that you'd like to incorporate into a presentation.

In these and in other situations, you can use the Export command on PageMaker's File menu.

To export an entire story, select an insertion point anywhere in the story, choose Export from the File menu, and when the Export dialog box comes on-screen, click the Entire Story option. (An "entire story" is a series of threaded text blocks, as defined on the next page.)

To export part of a story, select the text with the text tool and click the Selected Text Only option in the Export dialog box.

In the Export dialog box, select the file format you want for the exported text. The name of your word-processing program will be listed if Page-Maker has an export filter for it; or select Text Only to export the text without formatting so that it can be read by most word-processing applications. If you want PageMaker to export style name tags, select the Export Tags option.

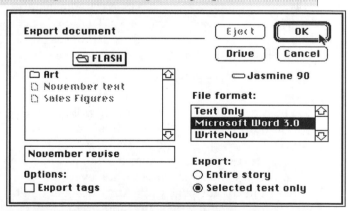

Type the name you want to use for the exported document (to replace an existing document, use the name of that document; to create a new document, type a new name). Then select the drive and folder you want to save to and click OK.

The exported document retains any formatting done in PageMaker that is recognized by your word processor.

A FEW WORDS ABOUT THE MYSTERIES OF THREADED TEXT...

The apparent eccentricities of threaded text are at first both baffling and frustrating. Until you understand the basic mechanics of this feature, text seems to move around a page and within a document as if it had a mind of its own.

What is threaded text?

When you place a single file, inserting various text blocks as you move from one column and page to another, every text block in that file is threaded, or linked, to the one before and the one following it. When you add, delete, or move text within a threaded file, the change "ripples" through to the other text blocks in the file. The concept is best explained by a few examples.

Hypothetical Situation #1 Let's say that in two pages such as those diagrammed here, you place one file in the columns labeled A1, A2, and A3, leaving some space at the bottom of A2 for a photograph. These are three separate text blocks, but they are threaded to one another because

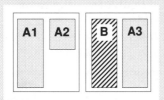

they were part of the same file. Let's say you place a second file in column B as a sidebar to the main story. That text is not threaded to the other columns because it was placed as a separate file.

If you add a paragraph of, say, six lines to column A1, the last six lines in that column will be forced to A2, and six lines in A2 will be forced to A3 (jumping over B because it is not threaded to A). Text blocks A1 and A2 will not change in length; text block A3, because it is the end of that file, will expand by six lines or however many lines fit inside the page trim. Any lines that don't fit within the trim will be invisible; if you select column A3 with the pointer, you'll find a + sign in the bottom windowshade handle, and if you pull the handle below the page, you'll see the additional lines. To continue story A on the next page, you would raise the handle to the bottom margin, click on the + sign, move to the next page, and then click the loaded text icon on the next page.

To reverse the situation, if you cut six lines from A1, lines from A2 and A3 would be pulled up. The lengths of A1 and A2 would remain unchanged, and A3 would become shorter.

Situation #2 You decide to cut a sentence from A1 and use it as a caption for the photo. You select the text, cut it, and then paste it in the bottom of the column under the space reserved for the photo. And you change the type to italic for your caption style. Because this text was pasted outside the threaded file (which stops at the bottom of A2 in that column), the caption will not be affected by changes you make to the threaded text. Obviously, this is desirable; you don't want your caption bouncing around the page.

Situation #3 This time you place all the text in a 12-page document as a single file and you forget to leave the left-hand column on page 2 for the president's message. Thanks to threaded text, all you have to do is select the text in that column with the pointer tool and drag the bottom handle up to the top one; all the text in that column will be forced to the next column, and every subsequent column will be similarly pushed back. (If you only have 12 pages, you'll have to cut somewhere, but that's another problem altogether.)

How to unthread text

Use the text tool to select the text you want to unthread, cut it, then set an insertion point anywhere *outside* the threaded file and paste the text that you cut.

How to thread text

With the text tool, set an insertion point in the threaded file to which you want to add or paste additional text. Then type the new text or paste previously cut text.

To help demystify the behavior of threaded text, open a one-page document with two or three columns, place any file, and then play with the windowshade handles. Raise them, lower them, add text, delete text, break text blocks apart, and watch how the changes ripple through the threaded blocks. You really *will* get the hang of it.

...AND ABOUT CONTROLLING TEXT BLOCKS IN PAGEMAKER

One of the most powerful features in PageMaker is the elasticity of text blocks. You can move them, break them apart, change their shapes, and select them in different ways depending on what you plan to do. Herewith, a few basics.

To select a text block with the text tool

There are several possibilities here similar to the techniques in word-processing programs:

1. To edit or change the type specifications for a short amount of text, drag over the text with the text tool.

2. To select an entire file (all text threaded together), place the I-beam anywhere in the file and choose Select All from the Edit menu (or press Command-A on a Mac, Ctrl-A on a PC). This is useful if you want to change type specs or apply a style to an entire story, or if you want to delete an entire file. Note also that if you have placed part of a file and decide to change the type specs, you can use this Select All feature to change the specs for the unplaced text as well as for the text that is already placed.

3. To select text that breaks across a column or page, set an insertion point at the beginnning of the text that you want to select, then press Shift and click the I-beam at the end of that text. All of the text in between the two insertion points will be highlighted.

To change the shape of the text block

Select the text with the pointer tool. Drag one of the side handles to make the text narrower or wider. (Hold down the Shift key when you drag if you don't want the vertical alignment of the text to change.) Drag the top windowshade handle down to lower the first line of text. Drag the bottom handle up to shorten the text block.

To move a text block with the pointer tool

There are two techniques for moving a text block that you've selected with the pointer:

1. To move the text itself, press the mouse button, wait for the four-headed arrow to appear, and then drag the text to the new position. Use this technique when you want to see the text as you move it, to align it with column or ruler guides, or to position it optically in relation to other elements on the page. In addition to seeing the text, you'll see a dotted line around it that defines the shape of the text block. This line is useful if you have a left or right indent because the dotted rule defines the margin from which the text is indented.

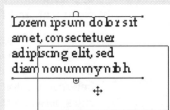

2. To move a bounding box defining the shape of the selected text, press the mouse button and drag immediately, *before* you see the arrow. With this "fast-move" technique, you won't see the text itself. This method is useful for moving text quickly across a spread.

To break apart a text block

Select the text with the pointer tool. Drag the bottom handle up to the point where you want to break the text apart. When you release the mouse, click on the + sign in the handle you just raised; when the loaded text icon appears, click it where you want to insert the text that was below the point to which you raised the handle.

The length of the windowshade handles defines the width of a text block. Drag the handles to stretch or shrink the measure.

A Two-Column Newsletter: Two "Looks" Using the Same Basic Grid

Both newsletters on the facing page are based on a two-column grid that accommodates short and long stories as well as photos, charts, and other artwork. The grid requires more formatting than the single-column *Flash/Memo* in the preceding project, but it is also more flexible. And once you've created the template, the actual newsletter can be put together without a great deal of fuss over details. If you want to practice creating and using a template, you might work through this project even if you don't have a newsletter to design.

Although the grid structure for both newsletters is almost identical, each publication has a distinctly different personality. *Newsline* is informal, friendly, and bulletinlike, whereas *In-House* is more structured and deliberate, with a crisper and more finished look. This apparent difference comes simply from the typeface, the headline treatment, and the style of the rules that frame the text columns.

Of the two designs, *Newsline* will be easier and faster to work with; its headline treatment is simpler than that for *In-House,* and its overall informality is forgiving of inconsistencies such as varying space between photos and text. In both designs, the wide space and vertical rules between the columns eliminate the need to align the text from one column to the next.

The *Newsline* instructions are given in hands-on, step-by-step detail. For *In-House,* you'll find detailed specifications without the step-by-step instructions. The designs are quite parallel, however, so if you're not sure how to execute some element of the *In-House* design, refer to the same element of *Newsline* for more detail.

PAGEMAKER TECHNIQUES YOU WILL LEARN

▶ Create and use a template

▶ Format body text and headlines as a single word-processing file

▶ Create a strong vertical grid on the master page

▶ Create column guides

▶ Create a graphic page frame

▶ Create and use a style sheet

▶ Create headline rules and spacing guides

▶ Create and use continued lines

▶ Mask master page items on individual pages

▶ Create text placeholders

▶ Create graphic placeholders

▶ Use the Text Wrap option

▶ Create different formats within the same document

▶ Use the semi-automatic text-flow mode

What's happening at the Southside Corporation

NEWSLINE

November 1989

Headlines are 14/16 with 14 points before and after

Lorem ipsum dolor sit amet, consectetuer adipiscing elit, sed diam nonummy nibh euismod tincidunt ut laoreet dolore magna aliquam erat volutpat. Ut wisi enim ad minim veniam, quis nostrud exerci tation ullamcorper suscipit lobortis nisl ut aliquip ex ea commodo consequat.

Duis autem vel eum iriure dolor in hendrerit in vulputate velit esse molestie consequat, vel illum dolore eu feugiat nulla facilisis at vero eros et accumsan et iusto odio dignissim qui blandit praesent luptatum zzril delenit augue duis dolore te feugait nulla facilisi.

Ut wisi enim ad minim veniam, quis nostrud exerci tation ullamcorper suscipit lobortis nisl ut aliquip ex ea commodo consequat.

Duis autem vel eum iriure dolor in hendrerit in vulputate velit esse molestie consequat, vel illum dolore eu feugiat nulla facilisis at.

Lorem ipsum dolor sit amet, consectetuer adipiscing elit, sed diam nonummy nibh euismod tincidunt ut laoreet dolore magna aliquam erat nostrud exerci tationuluip.

In this issue

Merger with Odeon announced

Job sharing to begin in September

New safety regulations

Profile: Laurie Bowles, Marketing

Contents type is 10/24 Am. Typ. bold

Ut wisi enim ad minim veniam, quis suscipit lobortis nisl ut aliquip ex ea commodo consequat.

Duis autem vel eum iriure dolor in hendrerit in vulputate velit esse molestie consequat, vel illum dolore eu feugiat nulla facilisis at. Ut wisi enim ad minim veniam, quis nostrud exerci tation ullamcorper suscipit lobortis nisl ut aliquip ex ea commodo consequat.

Duis autem vel eum iriure dolor in hendrerit in vulputate velit esse molestie consequat, vel illum dolore eu feugiat nulla facilisis at vero eros et accumsan et iusto odio dignissim qui blandit praesent luptatum zzril delenit augue duis dolore te feugait nulla facilisi.

Headline goes

Nam liber tempor cum soluta nobis eleifend option congue nihil imperdiet doming id quod mazim placerat facer possim assum.

Lorem ipsum dolor sit amet, consectetuer adipiscing elit, sed diam nonummy euismod tincidunt ut laoreet dolore magna aliquam erat volutpat.

Duis autem vel eum iriure dolor in hendrerit in vulputate velit esse molestie consequat, vel illum dolore eu feugiat nulla facilisis at. Ut wisi enim ad minim veniam, quis nostrud exerci tation ullamcorper suscipit lobortis nisl ut aliquip ex ea commodo consequat.

Vero eros et accumsan et iusto odio dignissim qui blandit praesent luptatum zzril delenit augue duis dolore te feugait nulla facilisi. Lorem ipsum dolor sit amet, consectetuer adipiscing

Continued...

▲ ▲ ▲

American Typewriter is a typewriterlike face that gives *Newsline* a feeling of immediacy.

▶ ▶ ▶

Times Roman, a traditional typeface, gives *In-House* a professional, polished look. It delivers an efficient word count without sacrificing readability, and holds up well under poor printing conditions.

The distinctly different personalities of these two newsletters result from the choice of typeface, headline treatment, and style of rule framing the text columns. *Newsline* is informal, friendly, and bulletinlike, whereas *In-House* has a crisper and more deliberate look.

Issue No. 8 November 1989

The Southside Corporation Employee Newsletter

IN-HOUSE

PRESIDENT'S MESSAGE

Lead Headline Is 18 Helvetica on Two Lines

Loren ipsum dolor sit amet, consectetur adipscing elit, sed diam nonummy eiusmod tempor incidunt ut labore et dolore magna aliquam erat vvolupat. Ut enim ad minimim veniame quis nostrud exercitation ullamcorpor suscipit laboris nisi ut aliquip ex ea commodo consequat. Duis autem vel eum irure dolor in reprehenderit in volupate velit esse molestaie son consequat, vel illum dolore eu fugiat nulla pariatur.

At vero eos et accusam et justo odio dignissim qui blandit praesent lupatum delenit aigue duos dolor et molestais exceptur sint occaecat cupidat non provident, simil tempor sunt in culpa qui officia deserunt mollit anim id est laborum et dolor fugai. Et harumd dereud facilis est er expeddit distinct. Nam liber a tempor cum soluta nobis eligend optio comque nihil quod a impedit anim id quod maxim placeat facer possim omnis es voluptas assumenda est, omnis dolor repellend. Temporem autem quinsud et aur office debit aut tum rerum necessit atib saepe eveniet ut er repudiand sint et molestia non este recusand.

Itaque earud rerum hic tenetury sapiente delectus aut prefer andis dolorib asperiore repellat. Hanc ego cum tene sentntiam, quid est cur verear ne

In this issue

Merger with Odeon announced

Job sharing to begin in September

New safety regulations

Profile: Laurie Bowles, Marketing Director

Type is 10/24 Helvetica bold

ad eam non possing accomodare nost ros quos tu paulo ante cum memorite it tum etia et etia tum ergat.

Nos amice et nebevol, olestias access potest fier ad augendas cum conscient to factor tum toen legum odioque civiuda. Et tamen in busdad ne que pecun modut est neque nonor imper ned libiding gen epular religuard on cupiditat, quas nulla praid im umdnat. Improb pary minuiti potius inflammad ut coercend magist and et dodecendense videantur. Invitat igitur vera ratio bene santos ad justitiame aeuquitated fidem. Neque hominy infant aut inuiste fact est cond que neg facile efficerd possit duo conteud notiner so iffecerit, et opes vel forunag veling en liberalitate magis em conveniunt.

Dabut tutungbene volent sib conciliant et, al is aptissim est ad quiet. Endium caritat preaesert cum omning null siy caus peccand quaerer en imigent cupidat a natura proficis facile explent sine julla inura

HELVETICA 9 POINT

Second Headline Here on Two Lines

Autend unanc sunt isti. Loren ipsum dolor sit amet, Consectetur adipscing elit.Sed diam nonnumy eiusmod tempor incidunt ut labore et dolore magna aliquam erat vvolupat.

Ut enim ad minimim veniame quis nostrud exercitation ullamcorpor suscipit laboris nisi ut aliquip ex ea commodo consequat.

Duis autem vel eum irure dolor in reprehenderit in volupate velit esse molestaie son consequat, vel illum dolore eu fugiat nulla pariatur.

At vero eos et accusam et justo odio dignissim qui blandit praesent lupatum delenit aigue duos dolor et molestais exceptur sint occaecat cupidat non provident, simil tempor sunt in culpa qui officia deserunt

continued on page two

Helvetica is used for the nameplate in both newsletters. The outline style gives this commonly used typeface a more distinctive look.

• • • Continued

nonummy nibh euismod tincidunt ut laoreet dolore magna aliquam erat volutpat.

Ut wisi enim ad minim veniam, quis nostrud exerci tation ullamcorper suscipit lobortis nisl ut aliquip ex ea commodo consequat.

Headlines run on one, two, or three lines, as needed

Duis autem vel eum iriure dolor in hendrerit in vulputate velit esse molestie consequat, vel illum dolore eu feugiat nulla facilisis at vero eros et accumsan et iusto odio dignissim qui blandit praesent luptatum zzril delenit augue duis dolore te feugait nulla facilisi. Lorem ipsum dolor sit amet, consectetuer adipiscing elit, sed diam nonummy nibh euismod tincidunt ut laoreet dolore magna aliquam erat volutpat.

Ut wisi enim ad minim veniam, quis qui blandit praesent luptatum zzril nostrud exerci tation ullamcorper suscipit lobortis nisl ut aliquip ex ea commodo consequat. Duis autem vel eum iriure dolor in hendrerit in vulputate velit esse molestie consequat, vel illum dolore eu feugiat nulla facilisis at vero eros et accumsan et iusto odio dignissim qui blandit praesent luptatum zzril delenit augue.

Caption is set in 10 point Courier bold italic with auto leading on as many lines as needed.

Eu feugiat nulla facilisis at vero eros et accumsan et iusto odio dignissim qui blandit praesent luptatum zzril Autem vel eum iriure dolor in hendrerit in vulputate velit esse molestie consequat, delenit augue duis dolore te feugait nulla facilisi. feugait nulla facilisi.

Lorem ipsum dolor sit amet, consectetuer adipiscing elit, sed eros et accumsan et iusto odio dignissim qui blandit praesent luptatum zzril eros et accumsan et iusto odio dignissim qui blandit praesent luptatum zzrilidam nonummy nibh euismod tincidunt ut laoreet dolore magna aliquam erat volutpat.

Headline goes here

Ut wisi enim ad minim veniam, quis nostrud exerci tation ullamcorper suscipit lobortis nisl ut aliquip ex ea commodo consequat. Duis autem vel eum iriure dolor in hendrerit in vulputate velit esse molestie consequat, vel illum dolore.

Eu feugiat nulla facilisis at vero eros et accumsan et iusto odio dignissim qui blandit praesent luptatum zzril delenit augue duis dolore te feugait nulla facilisi.

Lorem ipsum dolor sit amet, consectetuer adipiscing elit, sed diam nonummy nibh euismod tincidunt ut laoreet dolore magna aliquam erat volutpat. Ut wisi enim ad minim veniam, quis nostrud exerci tation ullamcorper suscipit lobortis nisl ut aliquip ex ea commodo consequat.

Autem vel eum iriure dolor in hendrerit in vulputate velit esse molestie consequat, vel illum dolore eu feugiat nulla facilisis at vero eros et iusto odio dignissim qui blandit praesent luptatum zzril delenit augue duis dolore te feugait nulla facilisi.

Lorem ipsum dolor sit amet, consectetuer adipiscing elit, dignissim qui blandit praesent luptatum zzril delenit augue duis dolore te feugaitsed diam nonummy nibh euismod tincidunt ut laoreet dolore magna aliquam erat volutpat.

NEWSBRIEFS

■ **Et harumd dereud** facilis est er expeddit distinct. Nam liber a tempor cum soluta nobis eligend optio comque nihil quod a impedit anim id quod maxim placeat facer possim omnis es voluptas assumenda est, omnis dolor repellend eveniet ut er repudiand sint et molestia.

■ **Temporem autem quinsud** et aur office debit aut tum rerum neoessit atib saepe eveniet ut er repudiand sint et molestia non este recusand.

■ **Itaque earud rerum hic tenetury** sapiente delectus au aut prefer andis dolorib asperiore repellat. Hanc ego cum tene sententiam, quid est cur verear ne ad eam non possing accomodare nost ros quos tu paulo ante cum memorite it tum etia ergat.

■ **Nos amice** et nebevol, olestias access potest fier potius inflammad ut coercend magist and ad augendas cum conscient to factor tum toen legum odioque civinda.

■ **Et tamen in busdad** ne que pecun modut est neque nonor imper ned libiding gen epular religuard on cupiditat, quas nulla praid im umdnat. Forunag veling en liberalitate magis em Improb pary minuiti potius inflammad ut coercend magist and et dodecendense videantur. Invitat igitur vera ratio bene santos ad justitiame aequitated.

■ **Neque hominy infant aut iniuste** fact est cond que neg facile efficerd possit duo conteud notiner so iffocerit, et opes vel forunag veling en liberalitate magis em conveniunt.

■ **Dabut tutungbene** volent sib conciliant et, al is aptissim est ad quiet.

■ **Endium caritat praesaert cum** omning null siy caus peooand quaerer en imigent cupidat a natura proficis facile explent sine julla inura autend unano sunt isti. Lorem ipsum dolor sit amet, consectetur ad incidunt ut labore et.

■ **Sed diam nonnumy** eiusmod tempor incidunt ut labore et dolore magna aliquam erat vvolupat. Ut enim ad minimim veniame quis nostrud exercitation ullamcorpor suscipit laboris

---

Headline

Ut wisi enim ad minim veniam, quis nostrud exerci tation ullamcorper suscipit lobortis nisl ut aliquip ex ea commodo consequat. Duis autem vel eum iriure dolor in hendrerit in vulputate velit esse molestie consequat, vel illum dolore eu feugiat nulla facilisis.

At vero eros et accumsan et iusto odio dignissim qui blandit praesent luptatum zzril delenit augue duis dolore te feugait nulla facilisi.

Lorem ipsum dolor sit amet, consectetuer adipiscing elit, sed diam nonummy nibh euismod tincidunt ut laoreet dolore magna aliquam erat volutpat. Ut wisi enim ad minim veniam, quis nostrud exerci tation ullamcorper suscipit lobortis nisl ut aliquip ex ea commodo adipiscing elit, sed diam nonummy nibh euismod tincidunt ut laoreet dolore magna consequat.

Headline is 14/16 with 14 points before and after

Lorem ipsum dolor sit amet, consectetuer adipiscing elit, sed diam nonummy nibh euismod tincidunt ut laoreet dolore magna aliquam erat volutpat. Ut wisi enim ad minim veniam, quis nostrud exerci tation ullamcorper suscipit lobortis nisl ut aliquip ex ea commodo consequat.

Duis autem vel eum iriure dolor in hendrerit in vulputate velit esse molestie consequat, vel illum dolore eu feugiat nulla facilisis at vero eros et accumsan et iusto odio dignissim qui blandit praesent luptatum zzril delenit augue duis dolore te feugait nulla facilisi.

Lorem ipsum dolor sit amet, consectetuer adipiscing elit, sed diam nonummy nibh euismod tincidunt ut laoreet dolore magna aliquam erat volutpat. Ut wisi enim ad minim veniam, quis nostrud exerci tation ullamcorper suscipit lobortis nisl ut aliquip ex ea commodo consequat.

Duis autem vel eum iriure dolor in hendrerit in vulputate velit esse molestie consequat, vel illum dolore eu feugiat nulla facilisis at vero eros et accumsan et

Continued • • • • • • • • • • • •

The inside pages of Newsline.

The inside pages of both newsletters show several options for handling different types of material: art (photos, charts, and so on) with captions, as shown on page 2; a "Newsbriefs" column, as shown on page 3; and a "People" column with smaller photos, as shown on page 4 (right). Masthead information can be tucked in the lower right of the last page, set one point size smaller than the body text. The specifications for handling these different formats are included with the blueprint for each newsletter.

You can use this basic grid for a newsletter that's filled with one headline and story after another, but it will not be as visually interesting or appealing as a newsletter with the varied editorial format shown on these pages.

▶ ▶ ▶

The "People" captions are treated differently in the two designs. The spacing in an open typeface such as American Typewriter (near right) would be too uneven in the narrow column used for the Times Roman captions in *In-House* (far right).

PEOPLE

Ame quis nostrud exercitation ullamcorpor suscipit laboris nis nostrud exerci.

Itaque earud rerum hic tenetury sapiente delectus au aut prefer andis dolorib asperiore repellat. Hanc ego cum tene sententiam quid st cur verear ne ad eam.

Non possing accomodare nost ros quos tu paulo et andis dolorib asperiore repellat est cur verear ne ad eam Ut wisi enim ad minim veniam, eu feugiat nulla facilisis

Sotetur adipscing elit, sed diam nonnumy eiusmod tempor incidunt ut labore et dolore magna aliquam erat vvolupat. Ut enim ad minimim veniame quis nostrud exercitation ullamcorpor suscipit laboris nisi.

• • • Continued

iusto odio dignissim qui blandit praesent luptatum zzril delenit augue duis dolore te feugait nulla possim assum. Lorem ipsum dolor sit amet, consectetuer adipiscing elit, sed facilisinostrud exerci tation ullamcorper suscipit lobortis nisl ut aliquip ex ea commodo.

Headline goes here

Nam liber tempor cum soluta nobis eleifend option congue nihil imperdiet doming id quod mazim placerat facer possim assum. Lorem ipsum dolor sit amet, consectetuer adipiscing elit, sed diam nonummy nibh euismod tincidunt ut laoreet dolore magna aliquam erat volutpat.

Ut wisi enim ad minim veniam, quis nostrud exerci tation ullamcorper suscipit lobortis nisl ut aliquip ex ea commodo consequat.

Duis autem vel eum iriure dolor in hendrerit in vulputate velit esse molestie consequat, vel illum dolore eu feugiat nulla facilisis at vero eros et accumsan et iusto odio dignissim qui blandit praesent luptatum zzril delenit augue duis dolore te feugait nulla facilisi.

Lorem ipsum dolor sit amet, consectetuer adipiscing elit, sed diam nonummy nibh euismod tincidunt ut laoreet dolore magna aliquam erat volutpat.

Ut wisi enim ad minim veniam, eu feugiat nulla facilisis at vero molestie consequat, vel hendrerit in vulputate velit esse molestie consequat, vel illum dolore eu feugiat nulla facilisis at vero eros et accumsan et iusto odio dignissim qui blandit praesent luptatum zzril delenit augue duis dolore eu feugiat nulla facilisis at et iusto odio dignissim qui blandit praesent luptatum zzril delenit augue duis eros et accumsan et iusto odio eu feugiat nulla facilisis at vero eros et

Ut aliquip ex ea commodo consequat. Duis autem vel eum iriure dolor in repreHenderit in.

Voluptate velit Esse molestaie.

Con consequat, vel illum dolore eu fugiat.

The inside pages of *In-House*.

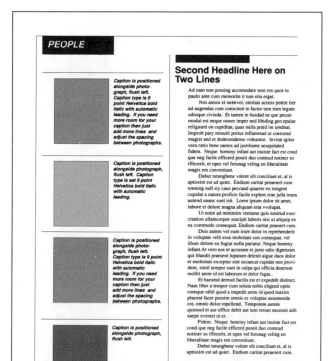

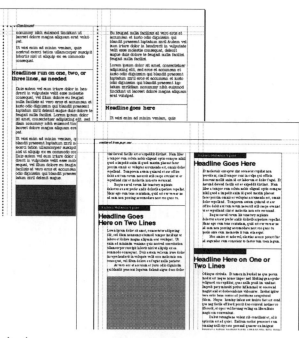

▲▲▲

The grid for both newsletters is based on vertical guides at 1-pica intervals between the rules, headline banners, and running text. This allows headlines and in some cases captions to extend into the margins, adding visual interest to an otherwise straightforward layout.

PROJECT 4A

BLUEPRINT FOR NEWSLINE

PAGE SETUP

Size: Letter (8.5 by 11 inches or 51 by 66 picas)

Start page #: 1 of 4 (or more if your newsletter is more than four pages)

Options: Single-sided (click off Double-sided)

Margins:

Left: 6 picas   Right, top, and bottom: 4 picas

Note: In keeping with the quick-to-produce purpose of these newsletters, we've formatted them as single-sided. You can still print on both sides of the paper, although you won't be able to view and work on facing pages.

Turn page to continue instructions.

TEXT FORMATTING

The key to laying out this newsletter quickly is to format the body text and headlines in your word processor so that you can place all the stories as a single file. (Departments such as "Newsbriefs" should be created as separate files; see the formatting specifications later in the project.)

The body text is indented relative to the headlines; when you place the file, the headlines are aligned at the column guides and the body text is aligned at vertical ruler guides 1 pica to the right of the column guides. The space between the end of a story and the next headline, as well as the space between each headline and the first line of text that follows, can also be formatted in the word processor, as is described below. Only the horizontal rule over each headline must be positioned in PageMaker.

Format the body text and headlines in the word processor as follows. Define these formats as styles if your word processor has that capability.

Body text: 10/12 American Typewriter, 12-point left indent, 6 points space between paragraphs.

Headline: 14/16 American Typewriter bold, flush left, 14 points space before, 14 points space after.

If PageMaker does not recognize formatting from your word processor, you can define the body text and headline styles as part of PageMaker's style sheet (see instructions later in this project) and apply the styles after you place the text.

```
Headline goes here

    Nam liber tempor cum soluta nobis
    eleifend option congue nihil imper-
    diet doming id quod mazim placerat
    facer possim assum.

    Lorem ipsum dolor sit amet, con-
    sectetuer adipiscing elit, sed diam
    nonummy nibh euismod tincidunt ut
    laoreet dolore magna aliquam erat
    volutpat.

    Vero eros et accumsan et iusto odio
    dignissim qui blandit praesent
    luptatum zzril delenit augue duis
```

American Typewriter is a downloadable font; the type in the sample at right is from Adobe Systems. A resident font that you can substitute for a similar newsy and typewriter look is Courier, shown above. Because of Courier's nonvariable spacing (each letter takes up the same amount of horizontal space), it sets more loosely (fewer characters per line) than American Typewriter.

NEWSLINE

November 1989

Headlines are 14/16 with 14 points before and after

Lorem ipsum dolor sit amet, consectetuer adipiscing elit, sed diam nonummy nibh euismod tincidunt ut laoreet dolore magna aliquam erat volutpat. Ut wisi enim ad minim veniam, quis nostrud exerci tation ullamcorper suscipit lobortis nisl ut aliquip ex ea commodo consequat.

Duis autem vel eum iriure dolor in hendrerit in vulputate velit esse molestie consequat, vel illum dolore eu feugiat nulla facilisis at vero eros et accumsan et iusto odio dignissim qui blandit praesent luptatum zzril delenit augue duis dolore te feugait nulla facilisi.

Ut wisi enim ad minim veniam, quis nostrud exerci tation ullamcorper suscipit lobortis nisl ut aliquip ex ea commodo consequat.

Duis autem vel eum iriure dolor in hendrerit in vulputate velit esse molestie consequat, vel illum dolore eu feugiat nulla facilisis at.

Lorem ipsum dolor sit amet, consectetuer adipiscing elit, sed diam nonummy nibh euismod tincidunt ut laoreet dolore magna aliquam erat nostrud exerci tationuluip.

In this issue

Merger with Odeon announced

Job sharing to begin in September

New safety regulations

Profile: Laurie Bowles, Marketing

Contents type is 10/24 Am. Typ. bold

Ut wisi enim ad minim veniam, quis suscipit lobortis nisl ut aliquip ex ea commodo consequat.

Duis autem vel eum iriure dolor in hendrerit in vulputate velit esse molestie consequat, vel illum dolore eu feugiat nulla facilisis at.Ut wisi enim ad minim veniam, quis nostrud exerci tation ullamcorper suscipit lobortis nisl ut aliquip ex ea commodo consequat.

Duis autem vel eum iriure dolor in hendrerit in vulputate velit esse molestie consequat, vel illum dolore eu feugiat nulla facilisis at vero eros et accumsan et iusto odio dignissim qui blandit praesent luptatum zzril delenit augue duis dolore te feugait nulla facilisi.

Headline goes here

Nam liber tempor cum soluta nobis eleifend option congue nihil imperdiet doming id quod mazim placerat facer possim assum.

Lorem ipsum dolor sit amet, consectetuer adipiscing elit, sed diam nonummy nibh euismod tincidunt ut laoreet dolore magna aliquam erat volutpat

Duis autem vel eum iriure dolor in hendrerit in vulputate velit esse molestie consequat, vel illum dolore eu feugiat nulla facilisis at. Ut wisi enim ad minim veniam, quis nostrud exerci tation ullamcorper suscipit lobortis nisl ut aliquip ex ea commodo consequat.

Vero eros et accumsan et iusto odio dignissim qui blandit praesent luptatum zzril delenit augue duis dolore te feugait nulla facilisi. Lorem ipsum dolor sit amet, consectetuer adipiscing elit, sed diam

Continued • • • • • • • • • •

MASTER PAGE

1. Create column guides on the master page.

- Be sure the master page icon is selected.

- In the Column Guides dialog box, specify 2 columns with a 3p space in between.

2. Add the vertical dotted rules to the left of each column.

- Turn Snap to Guides off and Snap to Rulers on.

- Bring in three vertical ruler guides at 4p, 5p, and 7p, and three more at 26p, 27p, and 29p.

- Bring in horizontal ruler guides over the top and bottom margins to define the ends of the rule that sits outside the left margin.

- Choose the dotted rule from the Lines menu.

- Turn both Snap To commands off.

- With the perpendicular line tool, draw a rule from the top margin to the bottom margin, over the leftmost vertical guide. Copy that rule, paste it, and move it into position over the first vertical guide in the alley between the columns.

3. Add ruler guides for text placement.

- Bring in a horizontal ruler guide 6p from the top of the page to mark the baseline for the first line of text.

- Bring in a second horizontal guide 8 points above the first one to mark the top of the text block for body text. When you place text, align the top of the loaded text icon with this guideline.

4. Create the style sheet.

If you are not familiar with PageMaker's style sheets, see the step-by-step instructions on the following spread of this project. Use those instructions to define the styles needed for the newsletter.

If you are familiar with PageMaker's style sheets, redefine PageMaker's default specifications for the *body text* and *headline* styles as follows:

Body text: American Typewriter + size: 10 + leading: 12 + flush left + left indent: 1 + space after: 0p6 + kerning above: 12 + auto hyphenation.

Headline: American Typewriter + bold + size: 14 + leading: 16 + flush left + space before: 1p2 + space after: 1p2 + kerning above: 12.

If your word processor does not have a styles feature and its formatting is recognized by PageMaker, it is not essential (although it is still useful) to redefine any of PageMaker's default styles for this

---

TIP

When you place text, the top of the loaded text icon marks the top of the text block, not the baseline of the first line of text. The top of the text block (determined by the cap height or the top of the ascender, whichever is higher) is two-thirds of the specified leading: For the 14/16 headline, the top of the text block is 10.5 points above the baseline; for the 10/12 body text, the top of the text block is 8 points above the baseline. The text block guideline in step 3 is for placing body text. If a column begins with a headline, after you place the text you should raise that text block 2.5 points so that the baseline of the head is on the 6p rule.

project. As was mentioned previously, if PageMaker does not recognize formatting from your word processor, redefine the default styles in PageMaker as described on the following pages. Then, when you place the text for an issue of the newsletter, select each headline and each story individually and apply the style to it.

5. Create a master headline rule and spacing guide.

- Draw a 0.5-point horizontal rule from 5p to 25p, anywhere in the left column.

- Draw a 1p3-deep hairline-rule box, and position its top flush against the 0.5-point rule. The box is a vertical spacing guide (its width is not important) and will enable you to measure consistently the distance from each headline to the rule above it when you lay out the newsletter.

- Move the rule and spacing guide to the pasteboard. When you lay out the newsletter, after you have placed all the text and made any changes needed for fit, copy this rule and spacing guide and move the unit into position above each headline. (Be sure to leave the original on the pasteboard.) The bottom of the spacing guide should align with the baseline of the first line of the headline. Don't forget to remove the spacing guide after you position each rule.

6. Create the continued lines.

You will need two continued lines:

- *For the bottom of the page* where a story breaks: the word "Continued" (in 10-point American Typewriter italic) followed by an 8p-long dotted rule, which should end at the right margin. The jumpline should sit on or just above the bottom margin, separated from the line of text above it by at least a pica.

- *For the top of the page* on which the story continues: a 4-dot-long dotted rule followed by the word "Continued" in 10-point American Typewriter italic. The dots should make a clean corner with the vertical rule, and the word "Continued" aligns left with the text.

If a story always continues on the page following the one on which it begins, as is the case in the sample, you can omit a page number. Otherwise, add "on page #" and "from page #" to the continued lines and make the dotted rules for both lines four dots long.

- Leave the continued lines on the pasteboard so that you can copy them as needed.

Headline goes here

▲ ▲ ▲

When you position the headline rules, align the bottom of the spacing guide with the baseline of the first line of the headline.

Do not position the headline rules until after you have proofed a copy of your newsletter as laid out in PageMaker. The rules will not be threaded to the text, and if you make any changes in the text you will have to reposition each rule individually.

Vero eros et accumsan et iusto odio dignissim qui blandit praesent luptatum zzril delenit augue duis dolore te feugait nulla facilisi. Lorem ipsum dolor sit amet, consectetuer adipiscing elit, sed diam

Continued ••••••••••••••

• • • •• •*Continued*

nonummy nibh euismod tincidunt ut laoreet dolore magna aliquam erat volutpat.

▲ ▲ ▲

Leave the two different styles of continued lines on the pasteboard and copy, paste, and move them into position as needed. In this format, do not use continued lines in the middle of the page. They will look awful.

Blueprint instructions continue after the following spread.

HOW TO CREATE AND USE A STYLE SHEET IN PAGEMAKER

There are no hard-and-fast rules for using style sheets or for when or how completely you should define them. Generally, however, you will want a style sheet as part of the template for any publication that you create over and over.

1. **Choose Define Styles from the Type menu.**

   The Define Styles dialog box is a sort of home base for defining and editing the style sheet; you move through several layers of dialog boxes as you define or edit the specifications for one style and then return to this dialog box to edit another style or to return to the document.

   The names shown in the Style list box are PageMaker's default styles. The specifications below the list describe whatever style is highlighted on the list. When you edit an existing style, the description changes accordingly. When you add a style with the New option, that style is added to the list. (Styles that you define and apply in your word processor will be added to the list after you place the file in PageMaker; each imported style will have an asterisk after its name. Styles that you define but don't actually apply in your word processor are not imported.)

2. **Redefine any default style that has the same name but different specifications than a style you've defined in your word processor.**

   In the text-formatting instructions earlier in this project, we suggested defining *body text* and *headline* styles in your word processor. These names are descriptive and straightforward and so are a logical choice, but they are also identical to names on PageMaker's default style sheet. This creates a potential conflict because in PageMaker the default definitions are different from the ones for this newsletter, and PageMaker's default styles override imported styles of the same name. So you must redefine the default *body text* and *headline* styles in PageMaker.

Redefine the *body text* style as follows:

- In the Define Styles dialog box, click on *body text* in the Style list box. Then click Edit.

- In the Edit Style dialog box you can access the same Type, Paragraph, and Tabs dialog boxes that you choose through Type menu commands.

  Choose the Type option and specify 10/Auto American Typewriter. Click OK (or press the Return key).

  Choose the Para option and define the left indent as 1p (the first and right indents should be 0) and the spacing after as 0p6. (The spacing before should be 0.) Click OK.

- The description of the *body text* style as edited appears at the bottom of the Edit Style dialog box; this matches the style described earlier in the text-formatting instructions, except that there measurements are expressed as points and PageMaker uses picas. Remember, there are 12 points in a pica, and 0p6 equals 6 points.

- Click OK in the Edit Style dialog box to redefine the *body text* style as edited.

Now redefine the *headline* style:

- In the Define Styles dialog box, click on *headline*. Follow the same procedure you used to redefine the *body text* style.

- In the Type Specifications dialog box, specify 14/16 American Typewriter bold.

- In the Paragraph Specifications dialog box, be sure that auto hyphenation is off. (Headlines should not be hyphenated.) All three indents should be 0. The spacing before and after should both be 1p2. (This is equivalent to the 14 points specified for text formatting.) Click OK in the Paragraph dialog box and in the Edit Style dialog box.

Use the Based On option to redefine the *caption* style:

The caption for column-width photographs is similar to the *body text* style, with a few changes. So in redefining the *caption* style, you can base it on the body text.

- In the Define Styles dialog box, click on *caption*. Then click Edit.

- In the Edit Style dialog box, type *body text* in the Based On text box.

- Click Type and change the specifications to bold italic. Click OK.

- Click Para and change the space after to 0. Turn off auto hyphenation. (Captions are generally not hyphenated.) Click OK.

3. Add new styles to the style sheet.

- To add a new style, click New in the Define Styles dialog box; when the Edit Style dialog box appears, type the name of the new style in the Name box. If a name appears in the Based On box, delete it unless you want to base the new style on that existing one.

- Define a *dept. head* style for the "News-briefs" and "People" columns with these specifications: American Typewriter + bold + italic + size: 24 + leading: 24 + flush left + kerning above: 12.

  Note: You will have to enlarge each initial cap individually. A style applies to an entire paragraph, and you cannot mix styles in the same paragraph. (A headline is considered a paragraph when it is separated from the text that follows by a carriage return.)

4. Remove unneeded styles.

This is more a matter of good housekeeping than necessity. It minimizes the length of the style list when you have the Styles palette on the screen (see step 6).

You remove styles with the Define Styles dialog box. Simply click on the style name in the Styles list box and then click Remove. This removes styles from the current document only. Other documents you create will still list these styles.

In general, be careful when you remove styles. You can't undo actions taken in the Define Styles dialog box.

5. When you are finished defining styles, click OK or Close in the Define Styles dialog box.

A style is not defined until you click OK in the Edit Style dialog box. If you click Cancel after defining a style, that style will not be recorded.

In the Define Styles dialog box, click OK to apply the highlighted style to selected text or to enter styles in the style sheet if no text is selected; click Close to enter styles in the style sheet without applying them; click Cancel to cancel any styles that you have just defined or edited.

6. Use the Styles palette when you assemble the publication.

When you lay out the newsletter, the quickest way to assign a style is to display the Styles palette by choosing it from the Options menu. The Styles palette lists, in alphabetical order, all the styles defined for the publication. It is a window that you can move, resize, or scroll as you would any other window.

To apply a style to any paragraph or group of paragraphs, select the text with the text tool's I-beam pointer and then click on the appropriate style name in the Styles palette.

To select a style before typing new text, click the pointer on the desired style in the Styles palette and then set an insertion point for the new text. (The I-beam automatically turns into the arrow pointer when you move it into the Styles palette.)

COVER TEMPLATE

TIP

The type on the cover template is American Typewriter in different sizes and styles. Use the pointer tool to set the default type specs to 10/Auto American Typewriter with no indents and no paragraph spacing. Type each text unit in this default style, and then select and change it to the correct specs. Remember to draw bounding boxes with the text tool to define margins for loose items of type.

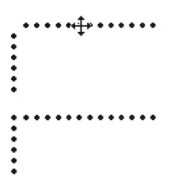

To form a clean corner where the dotted rules meet, place the leftmost dot of the horizontal rule directly over the top dot of the vertical rule until they both disappear. When you release the mouse button, you will see a single dot at the corner.

1. Create the nameplate banner.

- Be sure to click on the page 1 icon before proceeding.

- Bring in a horizontal ruler guide 15p from the top of the page.

- Mask the dotted rules from the top margin to the horizontal ruler guide you just brought in by drawing a rectangle over them with a line of None and a shade of Paper.

- Make a second small mask to cover an additional dot or two in the rule between the columns so that the rule doesn't butt against the horizontal dotted rule you will add in the next step. There should be the equivalent of a one-dot space between the horizontal and vertical rules. (Page layout is full of such details.)

- Draw a horizontal dotted rule at the 15p ruler guide from the leftmost (4p) vertical rule to the right margin. This defines the bottom of the nameplate banner.

  Note: The horizontal rule does not intersect with the dotted rule between the two columns. That little visual space is just enough to unify the two columns and keep the page from appearing rigidly divided. And if you look closely, you'll see that it would be impossible to form a clean corner where the two rules would have intersected.

- Add the subhead box at the top of the page.

  The box extends horizontally from 4p to 47p and vertically from 4p to 6p.

  The line weight is 0.5, the shade is None.

  The subhead is 14/Auto Helvetica bold italic, aligned left at the 5p vertical guide and centered horizontally in the box. Remember that for a correct typeset apostrophe, press Option-Shift-].

- Add the newsletter name.

  In the sample, "Newsline" is 60-point Helvetica bold italic outline, flush right. (There's no outline style on the IBM version. Use bold italic. Or try the stencil variation at the end of Project 4A.)

  It is on a baseline 1p above the horizontal dotted rule.

- Add the date placeholder.

  The date is 10/Auto American Typewriter italic, aligned left at the 5p vertical guide, on the same baseline as the nameplate.

2. Add the baseline for text on the cover.

- Bring in a horizontal ruler guide 17p from the top trim to mark the baseline of the first line of text (headline or body text) on the cover.

- Bring in a second horizontal guide 8 points above the first one to mark the top of the text block.

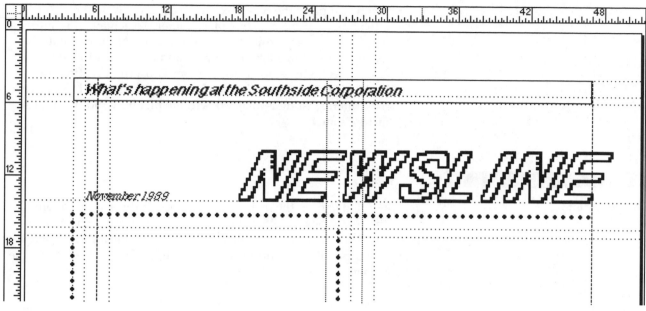

▲ ▲ ▲

Create the nameplate on page 1 of your template. When you assemble each issue of the newsletter, type the new date over the old one. Note that in flush right italic type, the right edge of the baseline (rather than the cap height) is aligned at the margin.

3. Create the contents placeholder.

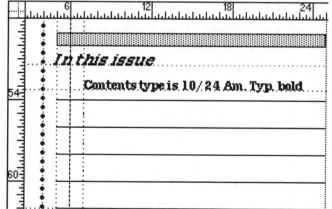

▲ ▲ ▲

Type one line of dummy text 9 points above the first hairline rule in the contents placeholder. When you lay out the newsletter, select that line, type the first real contents line over it, press the Return key, and type the next line. The leading is equal to the distance between the rules, so subsequent lines will fall into place 9 points above each rule.

- The box is 1p deep and extends horizontally from 5p to 25p with a line of 0.5 point and a 20% shade. The placement of the top of the box depends on the number of contents lines. As the sample shows, with five lines, the top of the box is 49p from the top of the page. If you have more or fewer contents lines, adjust the depth of the contents placeholder by 2 picas for each contents line.

- "In this issue" is 14/Auto American Typewriter bold italic, on a baseline 1p6 below the bottom of the box, aligned left with the edge of the box.

- The rules that separate the contents listings are 0.5-point lines, flush with the right and left edges of the box. The first rule is 4p below the bottom of the box. Copy and paste it at 2p intervals. The last rule sits on the bottom margin.

- Bring in a horizontal ruler guide 9 points above the first 0.5-point rule. This is the baseline for the first contents line.

- The contents lines are 10/24 American Typewriter bold, with a 1p left indent.

Page numbers have not been included. In a four-page document, they really aren't necessary.

- When you place the body text in the actual newsletter, you want it to jump over the contents placeholder. To achieve this, create a graphic boundary around the box at the top of the contents listing, with a forced column break and a 0p6 standoff at the top. Use the techniques described in steps 2 to 4 in "Creating the Placeholder" in the sidebar on the facing page. (The box above the contents listing is analogous to the picture window in those instructions.)

INSIDE PAGES

As was noted earlier, the inside pages shown in the sample suggest how different types of editorial material—photographs, short news items, a "People" column—would be handled in this format. There are many other possibilities, of course. See the end of this project for some tips on a few of these.

Column-width art

In this newsletter design, you should position column-width art (photos, charts, tables, illustrations) at the top or bottom of the page, with these guidelines:

- **Art** is 18p wide, from 7p to 25p in the left column, 29p to 47p in the right column. The depth of the art in the sample is also 18p, but this can vary depending on the art.

- **Space from baseline of text to top of photo** is 1p6 (or more).

- **Space from bottom of photo to baseline of caption** is also 1p6.

- **Caption** is 10/Auto American Typewriter bold italic with a 1p left indent. Turn off auto hyphenation for captions.

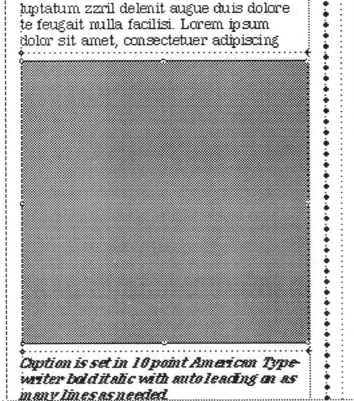

◀ ◀ ◀

There are different approaches to incorporating art into a document. If the placement of art is consistent from one issue to the next, you will find it very efficient to create a graphic placeholder in your template, as shown here. Then, when you place the text in each issue of the newsletter, the text flow will automatically stop at the graphic placeholder. See "How to Create and Use a Graphic Placeholder" on the facing page.

HOW TO CREATE AND USE A GRAPHIC PLACEHOLDER

A graphic placeholder is simply a PageMaker graphic (usually a square or rectangle) that reserves a place for a photo, chart, or illustration to be imported when you lay out the publication (or to be stripped in later by a commercial printer).

Creating the Placeholder

The procedure described here is for creating a graphic placeholder at the bottom of the page, as shown on page 2 of both newsletters. For the contents placeholder on page 1, the gray banner of the contents unit serves the same purpose as the picture window on page 2.

1. Draw a picture window with the rectangle tool. You can adjust the depth of the window later, if you need more space for text or decide you want a taller (or shorter) picture.

2. With the picture window selected, choose Text Wrap from the Options menu. The Text Wrap dialog box appears.

3. From the Wrap options, select the center icon to create a rectangular graphic boundary around the picture window.

4. From the Text Flow options, select the first icon, which forces a column break at the top of the graphic. Type 0 for the left and right standoffs and 0p6 for the top and bottom.

   The standoff of 0p6 at the top is the *closest* text can flow to the graphic. In fact, the text may be farther away. If, for example, the last line of text that can fit in the column without encroaching on the graphic boundary is 6 points from the *boundary*, the distance from the text to the top of the picture would be 1 pica (6 points from the picture to the boundary and another 6 points from the boundary to the text). This newsletter is designed to be forgiving of such imprecision, so you need not worry about it here. In other documents, you may need to adjust the stand-off as described at the end of this sidebar.

Replacing the Placeholder with the Graphic

To import a graphic or a digitized photograph, follow these steps:

1. Select the graphic placeholder with the pointer.

2. Choose Place from the File menu.

3. Click Replacing Entire Graphic on the right side of the Place dialog box.

4. Scroll through your directories to find the name of the graphic, and click twice on it. The graphic will be scaled to fit the size of the placeholder you created for it.

Adjusting the Placeholder

You can make a number of changes in the size and position of the graphic placeholder, as well as in the standoff, when you lay out the publication.

1. If you move the graphic placeholder, the graphic boundary (and the text wrap applied to it) will move also.

2. If you resize the graphic, PageMaker scales the graphic boundary accordingly, but the standoff that you defined between the graphic and boundary remains the same.

3. If you want to adjust the standoff, select the art. Position the pointer on the dotted rule and drag the rule closer to the art (if there is too much space between the text and the art) or farther away (if the space between the art and text is too tight). You can also adjust the standoff by editing the values in the Text Wrap dialog box when the graphic placeholder is selected.

"Newsbriefs" column

When you have a self-contained department such as this, you should create a separate file for it in your word processor so that it won't be threaded to the stories that run continuously on the other pages. Format the text as detailed below.

- **The "Newsbriefs" headline** is 24/24 American Typewriter bold italic, all caps, with a 36-point initial cap. It sits on a baseline 3p below the top margin and is flush with the vertical guide at 7p.

- **News items** are the same as body text: 10/Auto American Typewriter, with a 1p left indent and 0p6 paragraph spacing. The boldface leadins can be formatted in your word processor or in PageMaker.

  If you use styles, remember that you cannot mix styles within a single paragraph, and so you will have to select and change each leadin to boldface. This is called a style override. In the Page-Maker Styles palette, any paragraph with a style override is denoted by a plus sign (+) after the style name.

- **The baseline of the first news item** is 2p below the baseline of the Newsbriefs head. The top of the text block is 8 points above the baseline.

- **Ballot boxes** are 12-point Zapf Dingbats (the keystroke is unshifted n), flush with the left margin and the text baseline.

Position the ballot boxes after the final edit of text. They are not threaded to the text, and so if you make changes after inserting them, you will have to reposition each one individually.

▼ ▼ ▼

Newsbriefs

■ **Et harum d dereud** facilis est er expeddit distinct. Nam liber a tempor cum soluta nobis eligend optio comque nihil quod a impedit anim id quod maxim placeat facer possim omnis es voluptas assumenda est, omnis dolor repellend eveniet ut er repudiand sint et molestia.

■ **Temporem autem quinsud** et aur office debit aut tum rerum necessit atib saepe eveniet ut er repudiand sint et molestia non este recusand.

■ **Itaque earudrerum hic tenetury** sapiente delectus au aut prefer andis dolorib asperiore repellat. Hanc ego cum tene sentntiam, quid est cur verear ne ad eam non possing accomodare nost ros quos tu paulo ante cum memorite it tum etia ergat.

■ **Nosamice** et nebevol, olestias access potest fier potius inflammad ut coercend magist and ad augendas cum conscient to factor tum toen legum odioque civiuda.

Headline

Ut wisi enim ad minim veniam, quis nostrud exerci tation ullamcorper suscipit lobortis nisl ut aliquip ex ea commodo consequat. Duis autem vel eum iriure dolor in hendrerit in vulputate velit esse molestie consequat, vel illum dolore eu feugiat nulla facilisis.

At vero eros et accumsan et iusto odio dignissim qui blandit praesent luptatum zzril delenit augue duis dolore te feugait nulla facilisi.

Lorem ipsum dolor sit amet, consectetuer adipiscing elit, sed diam nonummy nibh euismod tincidunt ut laoreet dolore magna aliquam erat volutpat. Ut wisi enim ad minim veniam, quis nostrud exerci tation ullamcorper suscipit lobortis nisl ut aliquip ex ea commodo adipiscing elit, sed diam nonummy nibh euismod tincidunt ut laoreet dolore magna consequat.

Headline is 14/16 with 14 points before and after

"People" column

- **The headline** has the same specs as the "Newsbriefs" headline.

- **The introduction** is the same style as body text on a baseline 1p6 below the headline and 1p above the top of the first photo.

- **Photos** are 9p by 11p, aligned at the 7p vertical guide.

  Keep photos the same size for even-handed treatment of all people featured.

- **Space from bottom of photo to caption** below is 1p.

- **Space from baseline of caption to top of next photo** is 1p6.

- **Captions** for photos are the same style as body text (10/Auto American Typewriter), with boldface leadins. You might want to type them right into PageMaker.

With an open typewriter face such as American Typewriter, the wider the column the better. That's why the captions run the full width of the column below the photos, instead of alongside the photos, as they do in the *In-House* design.

When you run a continued line at the top of a page with a department head, as in the page detail below, omit the dotted rule over the department head. The two together would be too busy. (You can mask it by drawing a rectangle over it with a shade of Paper and line of None.)

▼ ▼ ▼

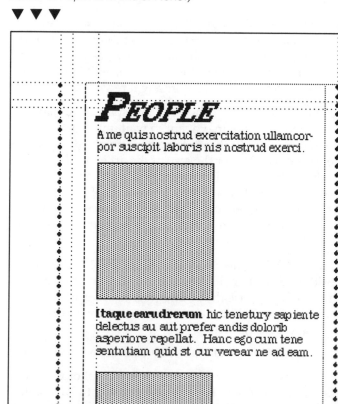

PEOPLE

Ame quis nostrud exercitation ullamcorpor suscipit laboris nis nostrud exerci.

Itaque earudrerum hic tenetury sapiente delectus au aut prefer andis dolorib asperiore repellat. Hanc ego cum tene sentntiam quid st cur verear ne ad eam.

Continued

justo odio dignissim qui blandit praesent luptatum zzril delenit augue duis dolore te feugait nulla possim assum. Lorem ipsum dolor sit amet, consectetuer adipiscing elit, sed facilisinostrud exerci tation ullamcorper suscipit lobortis nisl ut aliquip ex ea commodo consequat.

Headline goes here

Nam liber tempor cum soluta nobis eleifend option congue nihil imperdiet doming id quod mazim placerat facer possim assum. Lorem ipsum dolor sit amet, consectetuer adipiscing elit, sed diam nonummy nibh euismod tincidunt ut laoreet dolore magna aliquam erat volutpat.

Ut wisi enim ad minim veniam, quis nostrud exerci tation ullamcorper suscipit lobortis nisl ut aliquip ex ea commodo consequat.

Duis autem vel eum iriure dolor in hendrerit in vulputate velit esse molestie consequat, vel illum dolore eu feugiat

USING THE NEWSLINE TEMPLATE

The procedure you follow for laying out a publication using an existing template depends on a great many factors, including how carefully you've formatted and proofread the text before placing it, how much and what kind of art is included, and how many different people are working on the publication. Consider the following in the spirit of suggestions and tips rather than hard-and-fast rules.

1. Open a copy of the template and save it under the intended file-name.

2. Change the issue date on the cover. (It's so easy to forget to do this that you should do it immediately!)

3. Use the semi-automatic text-flow mode to place the text for articles, leaving the appropriate columns open for the "Newsbriefs" and "People" items. (See the sidebar on the facing page for how to use the semi-automatic mode.)

4. If you have not left space for art, you can cut in that space after placing the text. To do this, use the pointer to select the column in which the art is to be placed, and then raise or lower the window-shade handles to leave sufficient space for the art.

   If you've placed the text as a single file, when you raise or lower the windowshade handles the text will automatically rewrap. For example, if you raise a windowshade handle 18 picas from the bottom margin, the text that was in those 18 picas will jump to the next column, and each succeeding column will rewrap accordingly.

5. Check to see whether the text fits the available space. You may want to edit to fit now, or you may want to wait until you've placed the art and captions. It depends on how much editing you need to do to fit and on whether the size of the art is flexible. As you consider the need to copy-fit, take into account any continued lines you need (step 6), and also check the position of the head-lines. Are they too close to the top or bottom of the page? Too close to headlines in adjacent columns? Make adjustments as needed as part of the copy-fitting process.

6. Add continued lines where needed. You will probably have to adjust the position of text to make room in any column that has a continued line. To do this, use the pointer tool to select each column that has a continued line, and then raise or lower the windowshade handles as needed.

7. Place the "Newsbriefs" text, and make any changes needed to fit.

8. Add the introduction and captions for the "People" photos. As was suggested earlier, it is easiest to type these directly into PageMaker rather than creating graphic boundaries around all the picture windows. These are the same style as the body text, so click on the *body text* style in the Styles palette, type the text, and then format the boldface leadins through the Type menu.

TIP

Always double-check to be sure that you've placed all your text. Click the pointer tool on the last column of text in the file. If you see a # sign, you know that's the end of the file. If you see a + sign, pull down the windowshade handle to reveal the missing text. Of course, you should check your PageMaker pages against your original manuscript as well.

9. Place the art.

Whether you're placing a digitized photograph, a chart from a spreadsheet program, or a piece of computer-generated art, the process is pretty much the same. If you want PageMaker to scale the graphic to fit the space defined by the graphic placeholder, follow the procedure described in the sidebar "How to Create and Use a Graphic Placeholder" earlier in this project.

If the art does not have the same proportions as the graphic placeholder, you should manually resize and/or crop it rather than having PageMaker scale it. In this case, place the graphic on the pasteboard, size and crop it as desired, and apply the appropriate text wrap and standoff. Delete the graphic placeholder (the text will temporarily rewrap to fill in the hole), and then move the real graphic into place.

10. Add captions for column-width art.

11. Add the contents lines on page 1.

12. Print a copy to proofread.

13. Position the headline rules as described in step 5 for the master page. Remember that the headline rules and "Newsbriefs" bullets are not threaded to the text, so position them last.

14. Place the bullets in the "Newsbriefs" column.

15. Print another copy and and make a final check.

16. If you are having a commercial printer strip in photos or other art, be sure to code each piece of art to the graphic placeholder that marks its place. In addition, it is helpful to paste a "for position only" photocopy or photostat of the art in place on the camera-ready page.

TIP

To see the pages on the screen as they will print, turn off the Guides command on the Options menu. You catch quite a few errors this way, especially problems with alignment. If you need to make adjustments, you can select the command again to restore the guides.

PAGEMAKER'S SEMI-AUTOMATIC TEXT-FLOW MODE

PageMaker 3.0 has three text-flow modes: automatic, semi-automatic, and manual. (The manual mode is equivalent to the text-flow procedure in earlier versions of PageMaker.)

The semi-automatic mode, whose icon is shown here, is a temporary mode; you choose it by holding down the Shift key while you are in either of the other modes, rather than by choosing a menu command.

To use the semi-automatic mode, position the loaded text icon at the cap height guideline in the first column, hold down the Shift key, and click. In this mode, PageMaker stops the text flow at the bottom of each column, but the text icon remains on the screen. To continue flowing text, position the loaded text icon at the next desired place in the document and click.

Semi-automatic text flow eliminates the need to click on the + in the bottom windowshade handle to reload the text icon, as you would in the manual text-flow mode. At the same time, you have control over where the text flow resumes, which is not the case in the autoflow mode.

NAMEPLATE TREATMENTS

Logos, nameplates, and title banners come in all shapes, sizes, and styles. Whether cleverly conceived and carefully rendered or hackneyed and sloppily executed, the title treatment is inextricably linked to the way we perceive the publications we see.

The bold italic outline used for the newsletters in this project is a very simple solution for a nameplate banner, although one that isn't available in PC PageMaker. (The shadow style available on the Macintosh is also not available on the PC.) One alternative is a stencil effect, which has the feeling of immediacy that newsletters often try to convey.

You can buy stencil typefaces, but if you want to use the effect for a single headline or two, you can also create it fairly easily in PageMaker. Because stenciling calls attention to individual letterforms, it requires careful letterspacing and should be used sparingly. Here's one step-by-step example.

NEWSLINE

1. Type the title in 60-point Helvetica bold.

+6	+4	+4	+6	+2	+6	+6

NEWSLINE

2. Adjust the letterspacing by kerning. The keystroke for adding space between letters is Command-Shift-Backspace (Ctrl-Shift-Backspace on a PC). The numbers indicate how many times we pressed the Backspace key to achieve the balance shown. Note that letters with adjoining vertical strokes (NE and IN) require adding more space, because there is less visual space between them to begin with. Letters whose shapes angle away from adjoining shapes (such as the L in the LI letter pair) are visually farther apart and require less additional space.*

3. Select the perpendicular line tool and set the line weight to 4 point. Draw a vertical line through the N, slightly taller than the cap height, so that it butts the right edge of the first downstroke of the letter. Copy the rule and paste a copy into position in each letter that will have a vertical break.

4. Now, with the diagonal line tool, draw a 4-point line parallel to the first downstroke of the W. You may need a second, 1-point rule to get a clean edge on the W without snipping off part of its base. Keep all the lines as short as possible so as not to interfere with other elements on the page.

NEWSLINE

5. With all the "stencil lines" in place, select them all by drawing a marquee around them with the pointer tool. Choose Reverse on the Lines menu and presto, you have a stenciled logo.

AND SOME OTHER PAGEMAKER EFFECTS...

In the first example below, we've evenly spaced eight 1-point horizontal rules through the height of the letters. As with the stencil treatment, we drew the lines in black and then turned them all to reverse. (We also went through a few printouts.) This treatment gives a distinctive news bulletin look to the otherwise plain Helvetica bold type. If you create a logo such as this on a Macintosh, make an Encapsulated PostScript file of it (see Project 6 for instructions) so that you can place the logo as a single object and avoid having the loose lines on the page.

The next treatment, also done in PageMaker, uses the same 60-point Helvetica bold type, this time with a shadow and printed in reverse against a vertical pattern inside a 4-point rule box.

In this last example, the 60-point Helvetica is italic, reversed out of a 6-pica-deep black banner with a 1p3-deep 40% black box through the center. You will need to use the Bring to Front and Send to Back commands when you layer elements in a logo such as this.

PROJECT 4B

IN-HOUSE: A SLICKER VARIATION ON THE SAME THEME

The design of the *In-House* newsletter is more polished than that of *Newsline*, although it is created on the same grid. The headline treatment requires more work and precision than the *Newsline* headlines, and the format requires consistent spacing around photos.

The bold rule, or banner, above each headline can be used to add an overline in reverse type. Overlines—also called eyebrows and kickers—are a very effective way to add emphasis or focus to a story. You can use the overline for a department-style category, such as President's Message, Work Sharing, News from Abroad, and so on and then write a more dramatic or playful headline without sacrificing clarity.

Note that the ragged right text adds a certain informality to an otherwise precise format. And because the top and left edges of the page are well defined by the rules and the position of the text at the top of the two columns, you can have uneven bottoms without undermining the careful look of the page. Uneven, or ragged, bottoms increase your flexibility when you lay out the actual pages, and they also speed up the layout process.

BLUEPRINT FOR IN-HOUSE

PAGE SETUP

Size: Letter (8.5 by 11 inches or 51 by 66 picas)

Start page: 1 of 4 (or more if your newsletter is longer)

Options: Single-sided (click off Double-sided)

Margins:

Left: 5 picas

Top: 7 picas

Right and bottom: 4 picas

Issue No. 8 November 1989

The Southside Corporation Employee Newsletter

IN-HOUSE

PRESIDENT'S MESSAGE

Lead Headline Is 18 Helvetica on Two Lines

Loren ipsum dolor sit amet, consectetur adipscing elit, sed diam nonnumy eiusmod tempor incidunt ut labore et dolore magna aliquam erat vvolupat. Ut enim ad minimim veniame quis nostrud exercitation ullamcorpor suscipit laboris nisi ut aliquip ex ea commodo consequat. Duis autem vel eum irure dolor in reprehenderit in volupate velit esse molestaie son consequat, vel illum dolore eu fugiat nulla pariatur.

At vero eos et accusam et justo odio dignissim qui blandit praesent lupatum delenit aigue duos dolor et molestais exceptur sint occaecat cupidat non provident, simil tempor sunt in culpa qui officia deserunt mollit anim id est laborum et dolor fugai. Et harumd dereud facilis est er expeddit distinct. Nam liber a tempor cum soluta nobis eligend optio comque nihil quod a impedit anim id quod maxim placeat facer possim omnis es voluptas assumcnda cst, omnis dolor repellend. Temporem autem quinsud et aur office debit aut tum rerum necessit atib saepe eveniet ut er repudiand sint et molestia non este recusand.

Itaque earud rerum hic tenetury sapiente delectus au aut prefer andis dolorib asperiore repellat. Hanc ego cum tene sentntiam, quid est cur verear ne

ad eam non possing accomodare nost ros quos tu paulo ante cum memorite it tum etia et etia tum ergat.

Nos amice et nebevol, olestias access potest fier ad augendas cum conscient to factor tum toen legum odioque civiuda. Et tamen in busdad ne que pecun modut est neque nonor imper ned libiding gen epular religuard on cupiditat, quas nulla praid im umdnat. Improb pary minuiti potius inflammad ut coercend magist and et dodecendense videantur. Invitat igitur vera ratio bene santos ad justitiame aeuquitated fidem. Neque hominy infant aut inuiste fact est cond que neg facile efficerd possit duo conteud notiner so iffecerit, et opes vel forunag veling en liberalitate magis em conveniunt.

Dabut tutungbene volent sib conciliant et, al is aptissim est ad quiet. Endium caritat preaesert cum omning null siy caus peccand quaerer en imigent cupidat a natura proficis facile explent sine julla inura

HELVETICA 9 POINT

Second Headline Here on Two Lines

Autend unanc sunt isti. Loren ipsum dolor sit amet, Consectetur adipscing elit.Sed diam nonnumy eiusmod tempor incidunt ut labore et dolore magna aliquam erat vvolupat.

Ut enim ad minimim veniame quis nostrud exercitation ullamcorpor suscipit laboris nisi ut aliquip ex ea commodo consequat.

Duis autem vel eum irure dolor in reprehenderit in volupate velit esse molestaie son consequat, vel illum dolore eu fugiat nulla pariatur.

At vero eos et accusam et justo odio dignissim qui blandit praesent lupatum delenit aigue duos dolor et molestais exceptur sint occaecat cupidat non provident, simil tempor sunt in culpa qui officia deserunt

In this issue

Merger with Odeon announced

Job sharing to begin in September

New safety regulations

Profile: Laurie Bowles, Marketing Director

Type is 10/24 Helvetica bold

continued on page two

MASTER PAGE

Set up the following column and ruler guides:

- 2 columns with a 2p space in between.

- Vertical ruler guides at 4p, 6p, and 7p and at 26p, 28p, and 29p.

- Horizontal ruler guide at 4p to mark the top of the page frame.

- Hairline rules along the 4p vertical and horizontal guides intersect to create a half-page frame.

- Hairline rule between columns runs from the top margin to the bottom margin.

- The top margin marks the top of the text block. When you place text, align the top of the loaded text icon with the top margin.

TEXT FORMATTING

As is the case in the *Newsline* publication, you can save a great deal of time by formatting the headlines and text in your word processor and then placing all the stories as a single file. (Again, the "Newsbriefs" and "People" departments should be treated as separate files.)

Body text: 10/12 Times Roman, 24-point left indent, additional 20-point first-line indent, no paragraph spacing.

Headline: 18/18 Helvetica bold, with 33 points of space before each headline and 4 points after.

The left margin is indented relative to the headlines, and the first line is indented an additional 20 points from the left margin. Note, however, that the first paragraph of each story is flush left, with no first-line indent. You will have to select and format each of these paragraphs individually for a 0 first-line indent.

By formatting the space before and after each headline in your word-processing program, you will ensure consistent spacing between the end of one story and the headline for the next, as well as between each headline and the first line of text that follows. If you need to do any editing after you place the file in PageMaker, either to make small corrections or to adjust the length for fit, the space around the headlines will remain constant because it is threaded to the text.

The only drawback of this technique is that it's cumbersome to adjust the rag of the headlines in PageMaker. For a solution to this problem, see "How to Control Line Breaks in a PageMaker Headline" on the following spread.

If you use a style sheet in your word processor, and use the names *body text* and *headline*, be sure to redefine those default styles in PageMaker before placing the text. For more information on how to do this, see "How to Create and Use a Style Sheet in PageMaker" earlier in this project. Remember, when you define styles in PageMaker, to translate points into picas, so 24 points would be 2 picas, 20 points would be 1p8, and 4 points would be 0p4.

COVER TEMPLATE

Nameplate banner

- **The hairline rule** across the two columns is 19p from the top of the page and runs from the left to the right margin. (Mask the vertical rule between the columns to a depth of 21p from the top of the page.)

- **"In-House"** is 60-point Helvetica bold italic outline, all caps, flush right, on a baseline 1p6 above the hairline rule. (If you don't have outline type in your computer, use bold italic or try a stencil variation like the one shown at the end of Project 4A.)

- **The banner** is a 12p-by-3p solid box, aligned with the left margin; the issue date is 9-point Helvetica reverse, aligned 1p from the left edge of the box, on a baseline about 6 points above the bottom of the box.

- **The subhead** is 12-point Helvetica normal, on a baseline 1p3 above the top of the newsletter title, aligned left with the right edge of the banner above it.

TIP

Leave a copy of the banner on the pasteboard for department heads, such as "Newsbriefs" and "People," on later pages.

▶ ▶ ▶

When you align loose elements, such as the subhead, with other elements on the grid, it gives structure to the page and suggests a planned rather than arbitrary placement.

Contents placeholder

- **The banner** is a 20p-by-1p3 solid box. Note that the depth is the same as that for the headline banners.

- **"In this issue"** is 14-point Helvetica bold on a baseline 1p3 below the bottom of the banner.

- **The first hairline rule** is 4p3 below the bottom of the banner. Copy and paste it at 2p intervals. The last rule should sit on the bottom margin.

- **The contents lines** are 10/24 Helvetica bold on baselines 9 points above the rules, aligned left with the body text at the 7p vertical guide.

TIP

Try to vary the length of headlines to add both visual and verbal variety to the page.

Banners for story headlines

- **The hairline rule** is column width.

- **The banner** is a solid box 12p by 1p3, flush at the top and left with the hairline rule.

- **The space between the hairline rule and the baseline** of the first line of the headline below it is 3p. Make a 3p-deep spacing guide and leave it on the pasteboard with the headline banner.

- **The optional overlines** are 9-point Helvetica bold reverse, all caps, aligned left 1p from the left edge of the banner. Include dummy type in the master unit, and type over or delete it as needed.

▶ ▶ ▶

Note that when headlines fall at the top of a column, you will have to lower the text block 3p below the top margin to accommodate the headline banner.

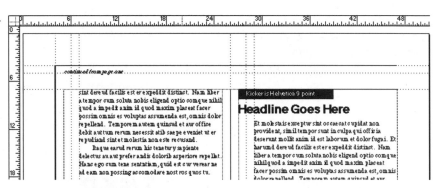

Column-width photos (also charts and other visuals)

- **Art** is 18p wide, aligned left with the left margin of text; depth varies.

- **Space from baseline of text to top of photo** and from bottom of photo to baseline of caption is 1p3.

- **Caption** is 9/Auto Helvetica bold italic, aligned left with the headlines, 2p beyond the left edge of the art.

Continued lines

Note that the continued lines here have page numbers, whereas those in *Newsline* did not. Without the bold structure provided by the short dotted rule in the other design, the continued lines here need length to anchor them to the page. Do not position continued lines in the middle of a page in this format.

- **Type** is 9-point Times Roman italic.

- **"Continued on"** lines are positioned on the bottom margin, flush right, with 2p of space from the baseline of the text to the baseline of the continued line.

- **"Continued from"** lines are on a baseline 1p below the hairline rule at the top of the page, flush left at the left margin. If you need a continued line in the right-hand column, position it flush right at the right margin. The body text for continued stories aligns at the top margin.

consequat, vel illum dolore eu fugiat nulla pariatur. At vero eos et accusam et justo odio dignissim qui blandit praesent lupatum delenit aigue duos dolor

Caption extends 2 picas beyond the photograph, flush left with the headlines. Caption type is 9 point Helvetica bold italic with automatic leading. Try to fill the last line at least halfway to the right margin.

▲ ▲ ▲

The caption is treated as display text to grab the reader's attention.

HOW TO CONTROL LINE BREAKS IN A PAGEMAKER HEADLINE

The rag, or line breaks, in headlines are important, both for editorial impact and visual balance. Note, for example, that the first headline on page 1 of *In-House* has a short first line and a long second line. We didn't want to have the number 18 dangling at the end of the line without the typeface to which it referred.

But in PageMaker, you can't force a line break without creating a paragraph break. And if you have formatted space after your headlines, then creating a paragraph in the middle of a headline will insert that paragraph space in the middle of the headline.

To get around this problem, after you place the text in PageMaker you can manually reformat any headline that requires a forced line break to improve the rag. Select that headline and change the paragraph space after the headline to 0. Force the line breaks as needed by selecting an insertion point and pressing the Return key. Then select the last line of the headline and change the paragraph spacing back to the correct spacing for headlines, in this case 0p4 after.

When you type headlines directly into Page-Maker, simply set the paragraph spacing to 0 so that you will be able to insert carriage returns as needed to control the line breaks.

PRESIDENT'S MESSAGE

Lead Headline Is 18 Helvetica on Two Lines

"Newsbriefs" column

- **"Newsbriefs" department headline** is 18-point Helvetica bold italic reverse, aligned left 1p from the left edge of the banner. (The banner is the same size and position as the issue date banner on the cover.)

- **"Newsbriefs" headlines and text**: Format the type and spacing for this column in your word processor and place it as a single file in PageMaker:

Body text: 10/12 Times Roman, 24-point left indent.

Headline: 12/14 Helvetica bold, flush left, with 6 points of space before.

The baseline for the first head is 3p below the banner. The top of the text block is 9.5 points above the baseline.

Some word-processing programs have a command that lets you repeat the previous action, which greatly speeds up the formatting of a column such as this. (In Microsoft Word, for example, Command-A on the Macintosh or F4 on the IBM repeats the previous action.) With this shortcut, you can type headlines and text in the style for body text, select one headline and apply the correct formatting, and then select subsequent headlines and simply use the keyboard shortcut that repeats the previous action.

NEWSBRIEFS

News heads are 12/14 Helvetica bold

Loren ipsum dolor sit amet, consectetur adipscing elit, sed diam nonnumy eiusmod tempor incidunt ut labore et dolore magna aliquam erat vvolupat. Ut Enim ad minimim veniame quis nostrud exercitation.

News heads are one line

Ullamcorpor suscipit laboris nisi ut aliquip ex ea commodo consequat. Duis autem vel eum irure dolor in reprehenderit in volupate velit esse molestaie son consequat, vel illum dolore eu fugiat nulla pariatur. At vero eos et accusam et justo odio dignissim qui blandit praesent lupatum delenit aigue duos dolor et molestais excepteur sint occaecat cupidat non. Simil tempor sunt in culpa qui officia deserunt mollit.

"People" column

- **The department headline** treatment is the same as that for "Newsbriefs."

- **The first hairline rule** is 3p below the top margin.

- **Photos** are 9p by 10p6, aligned left at the 7p vertical guide.

- **Space from rule to top of photo** is 1p; space from bottom of photo to rule below varies depending on caption length.

- **Space between photo and left margin of caption** is 1p.

- **Captions** are 9/Auto Helvetica bold italic, flush left, on as many lines as needed.

Customize a narrow column for the captions by moving the left column guide so that it aligns with the right edge of the department-head banner. You can move the column guides on one page without affecting the other pages.

Note that the hairline rule aligns with the baseline of the headline in the facing column. This design does not require that you align items in adjacent columns, but when deciding where to place each new element in a format, you should look first for an existing line on the grid.

PEOPLE

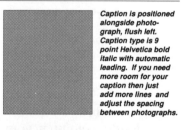

Caption is positioned alongside photo-graph, flush left. Caption type is 9 point Helvetica bold italic with automatic leading. If you need more room for your caption then just add more lines and adjust the spacing between photographs.

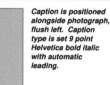

Caption is positioned alongside photograph, flush left. Caption type is set 9 point Helvetica bold italic with automatic leading.

Second Headline Here on Two Lines

Ad eam non possing accomodare nost ros quos tu paulo ante cum memorite it tum etia ergat.

Nos amice et nebevol, olestias access potest fier ad augendas cum conscient to factor tum toen legum odioque civiuda. Et tamen in busdad ne que pecun modut est neque nonor imper ned libiding gen epular religuard on cupiditat, quas nulla praid im umdnat. Improb pary minuiti potius inflammad ut coercend magist and et dodecendense videantur. Invitat igitur vera ratio bene santos ad justitiame aeuquitated fidem. Neque hominy infant aut inuiste fact est cond que neg facile efficerd possit duo conteud notiner so iffecerit, et opes vel forunag veling en liberalitate magis em conveniunt.

Dabut tutungbene volent sib conciliant et, al is aptissim est ad quiet. Endium caritat preaesert cum omning null siy caus peccand quaerer en imigent cupidat a natura proficis facile explent sine julla inura autend unanc sunt isti. Loren ipsum dolor sit amet, labore et dolore magna aliquam erat vvolupat.

Ut enim ad minimim veniame quis nostrud exer-citation ullamcorpor suscipit laboris nisi ut aliquip ex ea commodo consequat. Endium caritat praesert cum.

Duis autem vel eum irure dolor in reprehenderit in volupate velit esse molestaie son consequat, vel

OTHER POSSIBILITIES

Each publication is unique, and it's quite likely that if you use either version of this format for your newsletter you will need to adapt it for your particular situation. In doing so, the most important principles are to keep it simple and to use the vertical grid set up at 1-pica intervals between the dotted rules and column guides. The following tips touch on some likely editorial needs.

Subheads for longer stories

In relatively short stories, like the ones shown in the samples, subheads are neither necessary nor desirable. If you adapt this format for a newsletter with longer stories, however, you might want to incorporate subheads. If so, style the subheads like the "Newsbriefs" headlines.

Bylines

If needed, add each byline on a line by itself following the last line of the story being credited. Use 10/12 Times Roman italic, flush right, with an em dash (keystroke is Option-Shift-hyphen on the Macintosh, Ctrl-Shift-= on the IBM) before the name.

Page numbers

If your newsletter runs longer than four pages, add a page-number marker (keystroke is Command-Option-p on the Macintosh, Crtl-Shift-3 on the IBM) on your master page. PageMaker will number the pages for you. Center the number under the left vertical rule, on a baseline 1p below the bottom margin.

Art and photos

You can run a large photo or chart across two columns.

You can inset small photos, diagrams, or charts into articles and wrap text around them. Keep small photos 9 picas wide, consistent with the width of the "People" photos. The depth can vary depending on the art and the position of other elements on the page relative to the art.

If you have simple pie charts or diagrams, enclose them in hairline-rule boxes.

TWO VERSIONS OF A FLYER WITH A COUPON

This flyer for a corporate fitness program conveys a sporty, stylish, upbeat image. The two designs use an identical grid, but treat rules, headline, and coupon differently. The second version, shown in Project 5B, is more difficult to execute, requiring the use of a graphics program to stretch the headline type and multiple masks to create the diagonal racing stripes.

The typeface for both versions is New Century Schoolbook, which has a friendly, all-American feel. The type is set slightly larger than usual to help convey the open, airy look appropriate for a fitness program. The long line length of the introduction allows for justified type that has fairly even word spacing. Because relatively little text is involved, we typed the copy directly into PageMaker, rather than importing it from a word-processing program.

This project provides some good experience working with tabs, styles, and different kinds of text blocks on the same page. It also exploits PageMaker's graphics tools for effects that are more sophisticated than those seen in earlier projects.

As a blueprint for a flyer of your own, however, the instructions may prove less adaptable than those in the earlier projects. Because the type is so tightly structured, the directions work perfectly if you want to create a flyer with 4 headings over 13 listings that have 3 tabular columns in each listing. More likely than not, you'll have more or fewer items, requiring different tab stops, different vertical guidelines, and perhaps a different type size from the sample.

So in reality, if you're designing a flyer similar to this one, you will probably need to work out the details of your page through trial and error and in a different order from the top-to-bottom-of-the-page sequence in the blueprint. Use these instructions for some hands-on practice with the techniques and see the guidelines at the end of the project for creating your own flyers.

SPRING INTO SHAPE

with the midweek special at The Corporate Health Center

You too can be a mover and a shaker. Just pick the class (or classes) you want. Throughout the month of April our trained instructors want you. Classes are free. All you have to do is be there (with your sweats). You're guaranteed to look better. Feel better. Sleep better. Think better....

Tuesday Evening 6:00

T-1	Beginning Stretches	Room 10
T-2	Beginning Aerobics	Cafeteria
T-3	Intermediate Aerobics	Auditorium
T-4	Low-Impact Aerobics	Annex

Wednesday Evening 5:30

W-1	Beginning Aerobics	Cafeteria
W-2	Jazzercise	Auditorium
W-3	Advanced Aerobics	Annex

Thursday Morning 8:00

| Th-1 | Low-Impact Aerobics | Auditorium |
| Th-2 | Advanced Aerobics | Annex |

Thursday Noon 12:00

Th-3	Yoga (all levels)	Room 5
Th-4	Beginning Aerobics	Auditorium
Th-5	Jazzercise	Annex
Th-6	Advanced Aerobics	Room 12

To register for this one-month introductory on-site health program, fill in the following information and return to Employee Services, Dept. 200.

☐ YES, I do want to spring into shape and this ☐ is the class I want to take.

Name _____ Department _____

Address _____

City _____ State _____ Zip _____

PROJECT 5A

The Simpler Version of the Flyer

BLUEPRINT FOR THE FLYER

PAGE SETUP

Size: Letter (8.5 by 11 inches or 51 by 66 picas)

Start page #: 1 of 1

Options: Single-sided (click off Double-sided)

Margins: 3p6 all around

DEFINING THE IMAGE AREA

1. Bring in a vertical ruler guide at 25p6 to bisect the page.

2. Bring in horizontal ruler guides as follows:

- 16p: bottom of racing stripes under main headline
- 18p: baseline of subhead
- 22p: baseline of introductory copy
- 30p: bottom of first set of racing stripes over program dates
- 31p6: baseline of first program date
- 47p: top of coupon

INTRODUCTORY TEXT

1. Set the type specifications as follows:

Type Specifications: 14/18 New Century Schoolbook.

Paragraph Specifications: Set the first-line indent to 21p to align the initial cap at the center of the page. The left and right indents should be 0. Turn off Auto Hyphenation and specify justified alignment.

2. With the I-beam on the 22p guideline, type the introductory text.

For proper spacing of the ellipsis (dots) at the end of the introduction, type Option-semicolon after each period. If you type three periods without spaces between them, the dots will be too close together; and if you insert spaces between the periods, the dots will be too far apart and perhaps not even on the same line.

Remember, also, when you type an apostrophe in PageMaker to press Option-Shift-] for the apostrophe designed for that font.

TIP

In the Paragraph Specifications dialog box, the values you type for the indents are measured from the column margins, not from the edges of the page.

SPRING INTO SHAPE

with the midweek special at The Corporate Health Center

You too can be a mover and a shaker. Just pick the class (or classes) you want. Throughout the month of April our trained instructors want you. Classes are free. All you have to do is be there (with your sweats). You're guaranteed to look better. Feel better. Sleep better. Think better....

Tuesday Evening 6:00

T-1	Beginning Stretches	Room 10
T-2	Beginning Aerobics	Cafeteria
T-3	Intermediate Aerobics	Auditorium
T-4	Low-Impact Aerobics	Annex

Wednesday Evening 5:30

W-1	Beginning Aerobics	Cafeteria
W-2	Jazzercise	Auditorium
W-3	Advanced Aerobics	Annex

Thursday Morning 8:00

| Th-1 | Low-Impact Aerobics | Auditorium |
| Th-2 | Advanced Aerobics | Annex |

Thursday Noon 12:00

Th-3	Yoga (all levels)	Room 5
Th-4	Beginning Aerobics	Auditorium
Th-5	Jazzercise	Annex
Th-6	Advanced Aerobics	Room 12

To register for this one-month introductory on-site health program, fill in the following information and return to Employee Services, Dept. 200.

☐ YES, I do want to spring into shape and this ☐ is the class I want to take.

Name _____ Department _____

Address _____

City _____ State ____ Zip _____

◀ ◀ ◀

This project provides some experience working with tabs, styles, and different column specifications within a single page. It also exploits Page-Maker's graphics tools for effects that are useful additions to your PageMaker bag of tricks.

PAGEMAKER TECHNIQUES YOU WILL LEARN

▶ Use the Paragraph command to set first-line indent

▶ Create typographic ellipses and apostrophes

▶ Enlarge and kern an initial cap

▶ Magnify the page view to 400%

▶ Change column specifications for different parts of the page

▶ Use the Styles command to define spacing between text items

▶ Type tabular text in PageMaker

▶ Divide a text block

▶ Define and apply a style with the Styles command

▶ Create a coupon

▶ Create a multishade banner and border

▶ Select a graphic that's on top of a ruler guide

▶ Create a special-effects headline

3. Enlarge the initial cap.

- Use the text tool to select the initial cap and change its size to 36 points. Leave the leading at 18. (PageMaker takes the largest leading for any character in a line and applies it to the entire line. So the leading for an enlarged initial cap should be the same as that used for the running text in the rest of the line.)

  Leading that is smaller than the type size is called negative leading. It will cause the top of the letter to be clipped off on the screen. This won't affect the printed page and will be corrected the next time the screen is refreshed. You can force the screen to refresh, or redraw, by changing the page view or (and this varies from one monitor to another) clicking the zoom box in the upper right corner or the size box in the lower right corner of the publication window.)

- Kern the initial cap and first letter if needed.

  The letter pair "Yo" generally requires kerning, a process of adding or removing small amounts of space between two characters so that their spacing is consistent with that of other letter pairs. To achieve the spacing shown in the sample, position the I-beam between the Y and the o, hold down the Command key (the Ctrl key on a PC), and press the Backspace key six times. The cursor may not move on the screen six times, but the information will be recorded and will be sent to the printer when you print.

  Kern at 400% to bring the screen resolution closer to the printer resolution (300 dots per inch on most laser printers). To magnify the image to 400%, press the Shift key before choosing 200% from the Page menu.

The screen detail on the left shows the word before kerning, and the one on the right shows it afterward. To remove extra space, select an insertion point, hold down the Command key (Ctrl on a PC), and press the Backspace key.

THE PROGRAM LISTINGS

TIP

When you design a page that has several components, use PageMaker's style sheets to define spacing attributes. Then, if you need to add or remove a few points or even fractions of points to fit all the elements and balance the white space among them, you can do so by editing the style rather than by selecting and reformatting each component. The short time it takes to define styles gives you the flexibility to experiment and ensures consistency of spacing around similar elements.

1. Use the Column Guides command (on the Options menu) to specify 2 columns with a 2p space between.

You can change the number of columns on the page at any time without affecting previously placed text or graphics.

2. Define the styles for the program listings and program dates.

If you are familiar with PageMaker's styles, define the two new styles listed here and proceed to instruction number 3 on the following spread.

Program Listings: 12/15 New Century Schoolbook, 1p left indent, left tabs at 4p and 15p6.

Program Dates: 14/Auto New Century Schoolbook, flush left, paragraph spacing 2p6 before and 0p6 after.

If you're not familiar with PageMaker's style sheets, follow the step-by-step instructions in the box on the facing page, and then turn the page to continue.

AN EXERCISE WITH STYLES AND TABS

Don't be intimidated by the number of steps in defining these two simple styles. Even though you must go through several dialog boxes and some of them are layered one on top of the other on the screen, defining styles in PageMaker is fairly easy and straightforward.

1. Choose Define Styles from the Type menu.

This brings the Define Styles dialog box on-screen. If you need help orienting yourself to this dialog box, see Project 4, "How to Create and Use a Style Sheet in PageMaker," step 1.

2. Remove unneeded styles.

The styles listed in the dialog box are Page-Maker's default styles. Because you won't be using any of these names or the styles they define, we recommend removing them to simplify what you see in the dialog box.

To remove a style, click on its name in the style list, and then click Remove. That style is deleted for the publication, and the style below it in the list is highlighted. Continue clicking Remove to delete all of PageMaker's styles. This removes the default styles from the current document only. Other documents that you create will still list these styles.

As mentioned previously, be careful when you remove styles. You can't undo actions taken in the Define Styles dialog box.

3. In the Define Styles dialog box, click New. This brings up the Edit Style dialog box.

4. In the Edit Style dialog box, type *Program Listings* in the Name box. Then click Type.

5. In the Type Specifications dialog box, specify New Century Schoolbook. Type *12* in the Size box and *15* in the Leading box. Click OK. This brings back the Edit Style dialog box.

6. In the Edit Style dialog box, click Tabs. When the Indents/Tabs dialog box appears, first click Clear to remove PageMaker's default tab stops.

• Above the ruler in the dialog box are two black triangles; the top one is the first-line indent

marker, and the bottom one is the left indent marker. Drag them both to 1p. (Drag the bottom one into place first, and then position the top one over it; or, if they are already in the same position, simply drag the bottom triangle, and the top one will follow.)

• Check to be sure that the Left button in the top row is selected for a left-aligned tab.

• Click on the ruler tick marks to set tabs at 4p and 15p6. When you click, a left tab arrow appears above the ruler; its position is also displayed numerically below the Clear button. If you need to adjust the position of the tab, drag the arrow until the number you want is displayed.

Note that in formatting the introductory text, you used the Paragraph Specifications dialog box to type in the position of the first-line indent. You can use either the Paragraph command or the Indents/Tabs command to specify indents.

7. Click OK in the Indents/Tabs dialog box. Note that the definition of the style appears at the bottom of the Edit Style dialog box. Click OK.

8. In the Define Styles dialog box, click New.

9. In the Edit Style dialog box, type *Program Dates* in the Name box.

Below the Name box is a Based On box. If any name appears there, delete it. (You can delete and edit style names as you would any other text.)

10. Click on Type.

11. In the Type Specifications dialog box, specify New Century Schoolbook, 14/Auto, and click OK.

12. In the Edit Style dialog box, click Para.

13. In the Spacing options, type *2p6* for Before and *0p6* for After.

The left, first, and right indents should all be 0.

14. Click OK in the Paragraph Specifications dialog box, in the Edit Style dialog box, and again in the Define Styles dialog box.

▲ ▲ ▲

The Styles palette is a window that you can resize (by dragging the size box in the lower right), move (by dragging the title bar), and close (by clicking on the close box in the upper left) as you would any other window.

3. Add the text.

- Choose Styles palette from the Options menu.

- With the text I-beam, click in the left column on the 31p6 guide-line to set an insertion point.

- Click on *Program Listings* in the Styles palette. The text you type will be assigned the *Program Listings* style and will have all the formatting characteristics you defined for that style.

- Type all the text, including the dates, in a single column. Remember to insert tab stops after the identification numbers (T-1, T-2, and so on) and program names (Beginning Stretches and so on).

4. Apply the Program Dates style.

- Select the first date (in the sample, Tuesday Evening), and click on *Program Dates* in the Styles palette. The indent, size, and spacing you defined for *Program Dates* will be applied to the selected text.

- Select each subsequent program date, and then click again on the style name to apply the style.

5. Divide the program listings into two columns.

- With the pointer, select the entire text block for program listings.

- Point to the # sign in the bottom windowshade handle and drag it up until it is just below the last class listed for Wednesday.

- When you release the mouse button, the bottom windowshade handle will have a + sign, indicating that there is more text. Click on the + sign, and then click with the loaded text icon in the second column.

- Adjust the position of the program listings in both columns so that the baseline of the first line of each text block is at 31p6.

THE COUPON

1. Use the Column Guides command to specify 1 column.

2. Define the style for the coupon text.

Follow the procedure described earlier to define *Coupon Text* as a new style with the following specifications:

Type Specifications: 12/Auto New Century Schoolbook.

Paragraph Specifications: Specify both the left and right indents at 2p6. (These indents will allow room for the coupon border.) Specify 1p of space after. The first-line indent and space before should both be 0. Turn off Auto Hyphenation.

Tabs: Clear the existing tabs, and set new left tabs at 5p, 7p9, 30p6, and 36p. You may need to scroll the ruler to set the last two tabs.

TIP

When the Styles palette is on-screen and you want to define a new style, use the keyboard shortcut to display the Edit Style dialog box: Press Command (Ctrl on a PC) and click on *No Style* in the palette. To edit an existing style rather than define a new one, click on that style name while you press Command or Ctrl.

AN EFFICIENT WAY TO WORK WITH TEXT

Although the screen details shown here are specific to this project, the techniques described are time-savers for any document:

1. Type all the text in one style and in a single column.

2. Apply appropriate styles by selecting text with the text tool and clicking on the style name in the Styles palette.

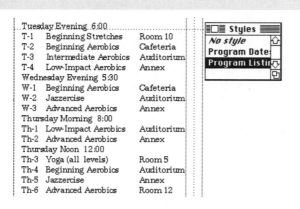

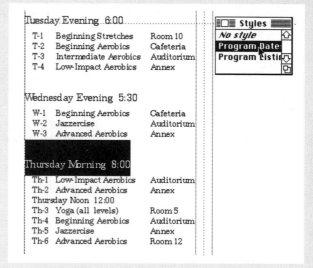

3. Divide the text block by selecting it with the pointer tool and dragging the lower windowshade handle up.

4. Bring in a ruler guide at the top of the text block to mark the alignment for the loaded text icon when you place the second text block. Click on the + sign in the lower windowshade handle to load the text icon, and then click the loaded icon in the second column to position the second half of the text.

3. Type the coupon copy.

- With the text tool selected, set an insertion point below the program listings (the precise vertical alignment is not critical at this point), and select *Coupon Text* from the Styles palette.

- Type the introductory lines with a single carriage return after.

- Insert one tab stop before typing "YES" to begin that line at 5p, and enter one carriage return at the end of that line. You'll add the boxes (and the rules) later.

- Insert two tab stops before typing "Name" to begin that line at 7p9; insert a tab stop after typing "Name" to position "Department" at 30p6. Enter one carriage return at the end of this and each subsequent line.

- Insert two tab stops before typing "Address."

- Insert two tab stops before typing "City," one before typing "State," and another before typing "Zip."

4. Temporarily move the coupon copy to the pasteboard before creating the border.

- Bring in a vertical guideline at the left margin of the coupon text. This will mark the left alignment when you move the text back into position later.

- With the pointer, select the coupon text and drag it off the page to the pasteboard.

5. Draw two rectangles with a 2-point rule between.

- With the pointer tool, set the line weight to Hairline and the shade to None. This setting is temporary and makes constructing the border easier. You'll change the specifications later.

- Turn on Snap to Guides and Snap to Rulers.

- With the rectangle tool, position the crossbar over the left margin at 47p. Drag across and down to the bottom right margin.

- Bring in a ruler guide 1p6 from each edge of the rectangle you just drew. For ease of measuring, you may want to drag the zero point to the corners of the rectangle.

- Draw a second rectangle inside the first one, with corners defined by the intersections of the ruler guides you just brought in.

- Move each of the ruler guides that defined the inner rectangle 9 points toward the outer rectangle, so that they are halfway between the two rectangles. Work at 400% for accuracy (press Shift and select 200% from the Page menu).

- Turn off both Snap To commands.

- Select 2 pt from the Lines menu and, still at 400%, draw a third box, centering its outline over the new set of ruler guides.

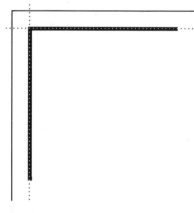

▲ ▲ ▲

When you press the mouse button to drag the 2-point rule, you'll be able to see whether it is centered over the ruler guides. Accurate placement of this rule is essential to the execution of this border.

▲ ▲ ▲

Ruler guides are very useful for defining the size of rectangles before you draw them in PageMaker. But it is difficult to draw rectangles directly over the guides, regardless of whether Snap to Guides is on or off. In many cases, being a raster or two off does not matter so much. But for critical alignments, you should check and adjust your work at a 400% page view.

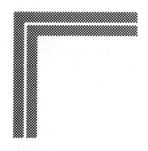

▲ ▲ ▲

The outer rectangle has a 40% shade and a 2-point reverse rule through the center. The inner rectangle has a shade of Paper.

6. Change the line and shade specifications as follows:

- Select the inner rectangle and change the shade to Paper and the line to None.

- Select the outer rectangle and change the shade to 40% and the line to None.

- Select the 2-point rule and change the line to Reverse.

Note: To select a graphic that overlaps a ruler guide, press Command (Ctrl on a PC) and click on the edge of the graphic. Or set the guides to the back through the Preferences command.

7. Move the text back into position.

Drag the coupon text block back into position, aligning it left at the vertical guide 6p from the edge of the page, with the baseline of the first line 50p from the top of the page. (The text is centered inside the border so that there is equal space around it on all sides.)

If you cannot see the ruler guides in the coupon area, set them to the front through the Preferences command.

8. Add the rules and the boxes.

- Before adding the hairline rules and boxes to the coupon, bring in vertical guides to define the beginning and end of each rule. Bring in horizontal guides along the baseline of each of the last four lines of text for the horizontal placement of the rules and boxes. Draw the hairline rules over the guides, and then remove the guides.

- With the rectangle tool selected, hold down the Shift key and draw a small square in front of the word "YES."

- Place the text insertion point after the word "this" and insert 10 to 12 spaces.

- With the pointer tool, copy the square, paste it, and drag it into position in the space you just created. Then drag the right edge so that the box is wide enough to contain the program number. This copy-paste-and-stretch technique ensures that the height of the two response boxes is the same.

BANNERS OVER PROGRAM DATES

Bring in a ruler guide through the center handles to bisect the banner.

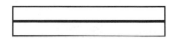

Draw a 2-point rule over the guide.

Change the rectangle's shade to 40%, its line weight to None, and the 2-point rule to Reverse.

Make a spacing guide to measure the distance from the banner to the baseline of the text below.

The technique for creating the banners above the dates is similar to, but simpler than, that used for the coupon border. As you follow the instructions, note the following relationships, which determine the size and placement of the banner:

- The banner is the same 18-point gray panel divided by a 2-point reverse rule that was used in the coupon.

- The space from the bottom of the banner to the baseline of the text below is also 18 points.

- The width of each banner is half the width of the text column.

1. Choose the Column Guides command from the Options menu and specify 2 columns with a 2p space between.

2. With the rectangle tool selected, at 28p6 on the vertical ruler, draw a 1p6-deep hairline-rule box from the left margin to the midpoint of the column (14p). While the box is still selected, bring in a horizontal ruler guide through the center handles.

3. Draw a 2-point horizontal rule through the center of the box. Center the rule over the horizontal guide. Change the line to Reverse.

4. Select the rectangle and specify the shade as 40% and the line as None.

5. Make a 1p6-deep spacing guide to measure the distance from the bottom of each banner to the baseline of the text below it.

6. Use the pointer tool to draw a selection box around the banner and the spacing guide. Copy this unit and paste it three times, moving each copy into position. Remove the spacing guides.

7. Draw a hairline horizontal rule over the vertical guideline that marks the center of the page. The rule extends from the top of the top banner to 1p6 below the baseline of the last line of text in the course listings.

HEADLINE

1. Add the banner.

Paste one more copy of the banner and position it so that its bottom edge is at 16p and it is aligned at the left margin. Use the pointer tool to stretch the banner to the right margin. You will have to stretch the shaded box and the 2-point rule separately.

When you stretch the shaded box, be sure to grab the center handle on the right edge to constrain the stretch to a horizontal axis.

When you stretch the rule, hold down the Shift key to constrain the line to the horizontal axis. (If you stretch a rule without holding down the Shift key, you will get a jagged rule.) You may still have to recenter the 2-point rule after you stretch it. If so, temporarily change the rule to black.

SₚRᵢNG ᴵNᵀᵒ SHAᴾₑ

2. Add the headline type.

The headline is 48/48 New Century Schoolbook, all caps. Each letter is typed as a separate text block and positioned individually. The pattern below the headline is a series of shaded rectangles with hairline rules between them. Creating the headline isn't difficult but does require some care and fuss. Remove ruler guides from the area before you begin in order to provide a clear workspace.

SPRING INTO SHAPE
SₚRᵢNG ᵢNᵀᵒ SHAᴾₑ

▲ ▲ ▲

To guide the horizontal alignment of the letters in the headline, type a temporary headline as a single text block and position it on the page directly above the actual headline area. Use the normal letter-spacing in this temporary headline for the horizontal alignment of each individual letter.

◄ ◄ ◄

Type each letter of the real headline as a separate text block so that you can select and move it into position with the pointer. Be sure to draw a bounding box with the text tool before you type each letter to avoid having a mess of long windowshade handles on your page. You'll find a rhythm of typing a few individual letters, moving each of them into position, and shortening the handles as needed. Sometimes you will need to shorten the handles for one letter before you can draw the bounding box for the next one. You may also have to move a letter to the back (using the Send to Back command on the Edit menu) in order to adjust the position of an adjacent letter. Finally, when letters appear to be clipped off, force the screen to refresh so that you can see the positions of the letters. (As was noted earlier in this project, you can force a screen refresh by changing the page view, by clicking the zoom box, or by clicking the size box, depending on your monitor.)

The vertical positioning of each letter is purely visual. In the sample, the top of the highest letter is at about 5p9, and the baseline of the lowest is at 12p.

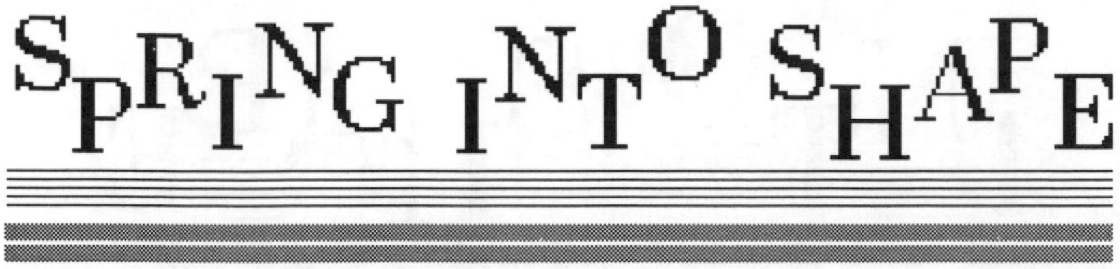
SPRING INTO SHAPE

▲ ▲ ▲

Bring in one horizontal ruler guide about 6 points below the lowest letter and another ruler guide 6 points above the top of the banner. Select a pattern from the Shades menu, set the line to None, and then draw a rectangle the depth of the two horizontal guides under the headline. The rectangle should align left and right with the margins.

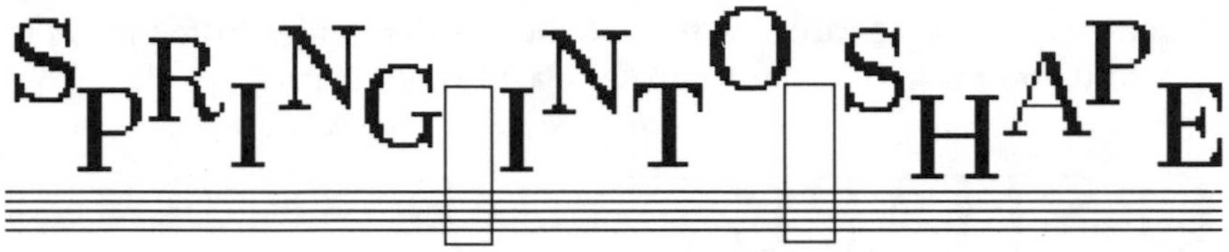
SPRING INTO SHAPE

▲ ▲ ▲

Working at 200%, draw a tall hairline-rule rectangle between the first two words of the headline. Copy, paste, and position a second rectangle between the second and third words.

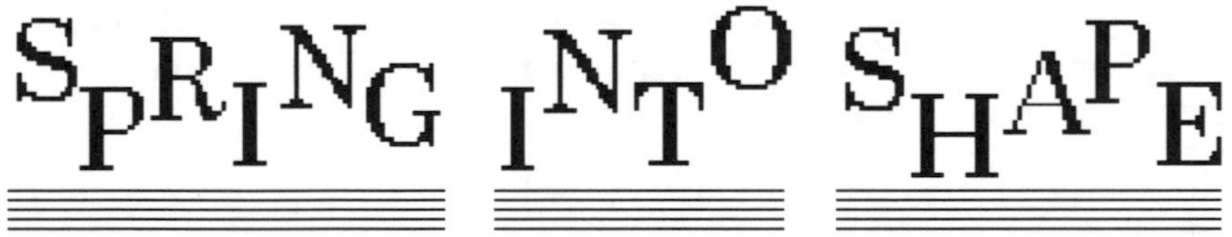
SPRING INTO SHAPE

▲ ▲ ▲

Give both rectangles a line of None and a shade of Paper.

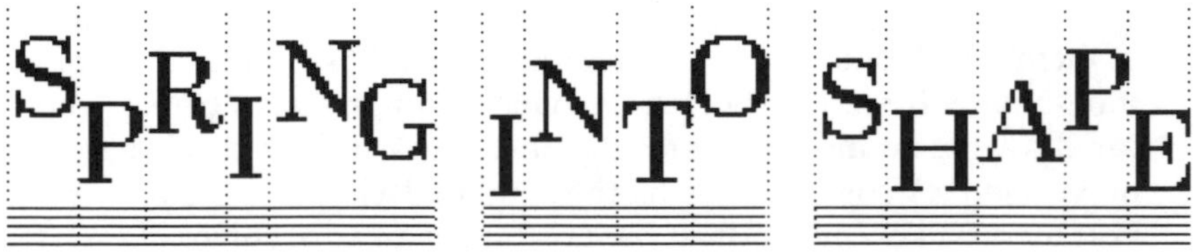
SPRING INTO SHAPE

▲ ▲ ▲

Bring in a vertical guide between each pair of letters and set the guides in front through the Preferences dialog box. If one or two ruler guides stay in back (as ours stubbornly did), just eyeball their position in the following steps.

▲ ▲ ▲

Select the same pattern from the Shades menu as before and draw an additional rectangle under each individual letter.

Each of these rectangles should overlap the long rectangle below the headline. Rectangles under the lower letters should overlap the sides of adjacent rectangles as in the first "I" in the screen detail above. Rectangles under the taller letters should align left and right with the ruler guides between letters as in the "N" in the detail at left.

The computer will align the patterns. Be sure, however, to align the edges of the rectangles under the first and last letters of each word with the right or left edge of the rectangle under the entire word. You might want to check this alignment at 400%.

◀ ◀ ◀

Draw a 2-point reverse rule centered over each vertical guide and extending the full depth of the pattern at that guide. This ensures consistent 2-point spaces between the patterned rectangles under the individual letters.

▲ ▲ ▲

Turn off the Guides option and check your work. Check especially the top line of the pattern under each letter. Depending on where the rectangle ends, the top line of the pattern may be narrower than the other lines in the pattern. If this happens, select that rectangle with the pointer tool and raise or lower the top edge slightly.

3. Add the subhead.

The subhead is 16/Auto New Century Schoolbook, center-aligned. The baseline is 18p from the top trim. Draw a bounding box between the margins so that the type will extend across both columns.

Turn the page for Project 5B, a variation on this flyer.

PROJECT 5B

THE ADVANCED VERSION OF THE FLYER

This version of the fitness flyer uses exactly the same grid and typography (except for the headline) as the simpler version. But the two-tone racing stripes give the page more color and an overall sportier appearance. The flyer has a crisp, smart look, which sets the tone for the program. This version is also more difficult to produce, but if you want to practice some advanced techniques, the banners and coupon in this design give PageMaker's graphics tools a good workout. Keep in mind that the instructions were written with the benefit of hindsight. The real world of creating a PageMaker document is rarely as tidy or efficient.

The page setup and image area are defined using the same specifications as those in the blueprint for the earlier version:

Size: Letter (8.5 by 11 inches or 51 by 66 picas)

Start page #: 1 of 1

Options: Single-sided (click off Double-sided)

Margins: 3p6 all around

Vertical ruler guide at 25p6 to bisect the page

Horizontal ruler guides as follows:

- 16p: bottom of racing stripes under main headline
- 18p: baseline of subhead
- 22p: baseline of introductory copy
- 30p: bottom of first set of racing stripes over program dates
- 31p6: baseline of first program date
- 47p: top of coupon

PAGEMAKER TECHNIQUES YOU WILL LEARN

▶ Draw a gray rule

▶ Use PageMaker rules as spacing guides

▶ Create diagonal edges

▶ Create complex graphics as a series of building blocks

SPRING INTO SHAPE

with the midweek special at The Corporate Health Center

You too can be a mover and a shaker. Just pick the class (or classes) you want. Throughout the month of April our trained instructors want you. All classes are free. All you have to do is be there (with your sweats). You're guaranteed to look better. Feel better. Sleep better. Think better....

Tuesday Evening 6:00

T-1	Beginning Stretches	Room 10
T-2	Beginning Aerobics	Cafeteria
T-3	Intermediate Aerobics	Auditorium
T-4	Low-Impact Aerobics	Annex

Wednesday Evening 5:30

W-1	Beginning Aerobics	Cafeteria
W-2	Jazzercise	Auditorium
W-3	Advanced Aerobics	Annex

Thursday Morning 8:00

Th-1	Low-Impact Aerobics	Auditorium
Th-2	Advanced Aerobics	Annex

Thursday Noon 12:00

Th-3	Yoga (all levels)	Room 5
Th-4	Beginning Aerobics	Auditorium
Th-5	Jazzercise	Annex
Th-6	Advanced Aerobics	Room 12

To register for this one-month introductory on-site health program, fill in the following information and return to Employee Services, Dept. 200.

☐ YES, I do want to spring into shape and this ☐ is the class I want to take.

Name _____ Department _____

Address _____

City _____ State_____ Zip_____

HEADLINE

The type is 36-point New Century Schoolbook with 72-point initial caps for the first and last words. It was typed in Adobe Illustrator, condensed 60 percent on the horizontal axis with the scaling tool, and then imported into PageMaker as a graphic and stretched by the windowshade handles to fit the desired space. The initial cap for the first line of the introduction was created in the same way.

Condensing and stretching type requires a trial-and-error approach to get proportions that work well in the overall design of your page. In comparison with the headline in the simpler version, the type here looks like it's gone on a diet and gotten in shape!

The headline type was condensed in Adobe Illustrator and then stretched in PageMaker. The patterns were added in PageMaker, with ruler guides used to define the spaces between words.

▼ ▼ ▼

The accent patterns add additional movement. They are PageMaker rectangles that use a line of None and different patterns from the Shades menu. Ruler guides were brought in to define the spaces between the words.

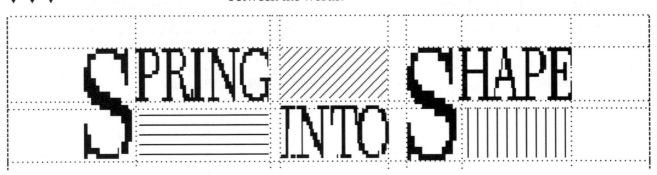

RACING STRIPES: BASIC UNITS

1. With a 4-point line, draw a box 10p6 wide starting at the left margin and compress the sides until the top and bottom touch, as described on the facing page, to make an 8-point compressed box, or rule.

2. Working at 400%, draw a 2-point horizontal rule (a regular rule, not a compressed box) as a spacing guide, and butt its top against the bottom of the 8-point rule. To facilitate moving the guide later, make sure it extends beyond the right edge of the 8-point rule.

3. Copy and paste the 8-point rule. Align the second 8-point rule with the left margin, positioning its top against the bottom of the spacing guide.

▶ ▶ ▶

Temporarily change the line weight of the 8-point compressed boxes to Hairline when you align them against the spacing guide.

4. Remove the spacing guide.

5. Repeat steps 1 through 4 to create two 8-point vertical rules separated by a 2-point space. Make the vertical rules about 10 picas long. (You'll adjust the length later.) Move the vertical rules to the left of the coupon area.

RACING STRIPES: TIPS AND TECHNIQUES

The technique for creating the racing stripes requires understanding several basic principles of PageMaker's graphics tools.

- **You can't draw a gray rule in PageMaker.**

  The technique described here tricks Page-Maker into thinking a rule is a shaded box.

  The principle is simpler to execute than it is to describe: If you set the line weight to 4 pt, draw a rectangle, and then drag the bottom of the rectangle as far as possible toward the top, you will be able to drag only until the inside edges butt one against the other. This gives you a box composed of a 4-point top, a 4-point bottom, and no middle—in other words, an 8-point rule. But because it is actually a box, you can change the line weight to None and the shade to 20%, making it a gray 8-point rule. If you follow the same procedure using a 2-point line weight for the box, you can create a 4-point gray rule; using a 0.5-point line weight, you create a 1-point gray rule, and so on.

  To simplify these instructions, we refer to these rules as compressed boxes and to the technique as compressing a box. You might want to play with this technique a little before continuing with the project.

Draw a rectangle with a 4-point rule...

drag the bottom up to the top so that they butt against each other without any space between...

set the line weight to None and the shade to 20%...

and you'll have an 8-point gray rule.

- **Use rules of different weights to define a fairly small space between two graphics.**

  The fitness flyer uses a 2-point rule as a spacing guide between the two stripes.

- **Create diagonal edges by masking the sides of boxes and rules with reverse diagonal rules.**

  You may need more than one mask for each edge.

- **Don't redraw anything that can be copied and adapted.**

  When you have several similar versions of a complex graphic, create a basic unit, and then copy, paste, and build from it as much as possible, stretching and shrinking where needed. Remember to hold down the Shift key to select several components so that you can copy or move them as a unit.

- **Black rules are easier to align than gray ones.**

  Build the components as black and then change the shades as a finishing touch.

- **On a page with a combination of different text blocks and complex graphics created in PageMaker, finalize the text before you finalize the graphics.**

  After you know that all the text fits and that it is correctly spelled, punctuated, indented, and otherwise styled, move it to the pasteboard as one or several large text blocks. This gives you a blank page (presumably with guidelines in place) and keeps the text from getting in the way when you create the graphics. After the graphics are in place, move the text back onto the page.

- **Before you print, ensure that none of the masks are inadvertently layered on top of the text.**

  Select each individual text block with the pointer tool and then choose the Bring to Front command.

BANNER UNDER HEADLINE

Note: The coupon is created with eight different panels and numerous masks. If you use this graphic device for your own flyer rather than for the hands-on project here, be sure to work out the text and know the correct depth of the coupon before proceeding.

1. Copy the pair of horizontal rules and move the copy into position under the headline.

2. Drag the right edge of each rule to the right margin. You'll add the mask for the diagonal edges later.

   When you stretch the 8-point rules, be sure to click on the center handle and wait to see a double-headed horizontal arrow before you drag. This constrains the stretch to the horizontal axis and ensures that you won't alter the 2-point space between the rules.

COUPON

1. Copy the rules under the headline as a unit; paste two copies, one for the top of the coupon and one for the bottom; and move them into position.

2. Move the 8-point vertical rules into position on the left side of the coupon, with the tops flush against the top margin. (They should fall short of the bottom of the coupon. You'll stretch them in step 3.)

It is essential to get a perfect register, or overlap, of the vertical and horizontal rules. You will know you've achieved this when, as you press the mouse button and drag, you see four white squares where the four corners of the rules overlap.

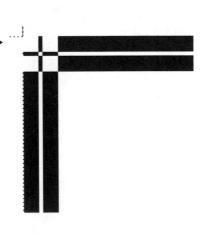

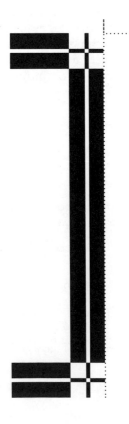

3. With the pointer tool, select the first vertical rule and drag the bottom until it registers with the bottom horizontal rule. Repeat for the second vertical rule.

4. Select the two vertical rules, copy them, and move the copy into position on the right side of the coupon.

5. Working at 400%, drag each edge of each inside rule in until it is flush with the inside edge of the white space between the rules. At this point, you should have two 8-point-rule rectangles, one inside the other, separated all around by 2 points of white space.

▶ ▶ ▶

Drag the edges of the inside rules into position so that their tops are flush with the white space between the two rectangles.

6. Working at a reduced view so that you can see the entire coupon, specify the shades for the borders.

Hold down the Shift key and click on each of the four inside rules. Change their shades to 80% and their line weights to None.

Hold down the Shift key and click on the four outside rules. Change their shades to 20% and their line weights to None.

7. Mask the upper left and lower right corners with 12-point diagonal rules. Be sure to hold down the Shift key to constrain the diagonal rules to 45 degrees for a clean edge. You may need to use two overlapping diagonals and a little square at the tip to create the desired effect.

Work with black rules for ease of placement, and then change the rules to Reverse after the mask for each corner is complete. Don't make the masks any longer than they have to be; you want to minimize the havoc that can be caused by handles around invisible objects.

▶ ▶ ▶

Mask the corners with two 12-point diagonal rules and a small square. Work with black rules for ease of placement and then change the rules to Reverse.

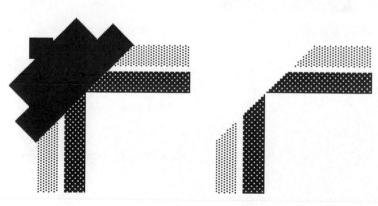

SHORT RACING STRIPES

1. Return to the original pair of horizontal rules. Change the top panel to a line of None and a shade of 20% and the bottom to a line of None and a shade of 80%.

2. Create the diagonal edges, using the same mask technique as that used in the coupon.

   Note that the lower left tip of the bottom rule remains visible against the margin guide. Also, in addition to one 12-point rule, you need a little box to mask the upper left tip of the top rule.

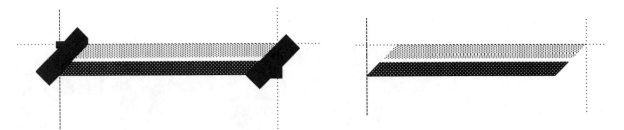

3. Using a 1-point line weight, draw a box from the white space between the upper and lower bars to the column guide. Compress the box to make a 2-point rule. Change the line to None and the Shade to 40%.

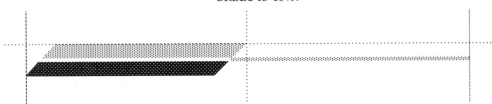

4. Copy the entire unit and paste it three times. (Be sure to include the masks in the selections.) Move each copy into position on the flyer. As a precaution, make an extra copy to leave on the pasteboard in case something gets messed up when you move the type back into place.

FINISHING TOUCHES

1. Change the stripes under the headline to shades of 20% and 80% and mask the edges.

2. Make a vertical, 2-point, 40% gray, compressed box between the program listings.

3. Move the type into place.

4. Print.

Now stretch your bones, rest your eyes, and give yourself a treat.

TIPS FOR CREATING YOUR OWN FLYERS

**Components found
in many flyers**

- Generous space for a thematic headline

- A descriptive subhead

- Brief introductory copy that delivers the basic "what and when" in a writing style consistent with the headline theme

- Tabular listing of the details

- Bold rules or banners to separate parts of the flyer

- A response coupon

Although this flyer was designed for a corporate fitness program, its structure and many of the PageMaker techniques used to produce it can apply to a variety of other flyers.

Of course, it's one thing to follow instructions for a design that has already been worked out and quite another to take raw information and shape it into an effective message. How do you determine the space for the headline? The type specs and tab settings for the listings? The depth of the coupon? Do you work out the graphic elements first and then add the text, or do you work the other way around?

There are few hard-and-fast answers. The approach you take has a great deal to do with your own strengths and involves a fair amount of trial and error.

A person with a strong visual orientation is likely to work out the graphic elements first and fit the text to that design, altering the graphics as needed to make all the elements come together in a balanced, unified page. Someone without a strong design sense is more likely to work out the copy first, using the text blocks to give shape to the page and adding the graphic elements around that. Regardless of which approach you take, you should expect to juggle the elements, adding a little space here, shaving a little there, trying a larger or smaller type size, more or less space between items, and so forth.

As you build your page, keep in mind these general principles:

- Begin with the part of the page that is the least flexible.

In this example, that would be the course listings. You can expand and shrink the headline space, the introduction, and to some extent the coupon, but the text for the program information is fixed.

- Use PageMaker's style sheets to format the spacing for sections of the flyer with multiple components, such as the program listings.

- Remember that you can use the Column Guides command to change the number of columns as you work on different parts of the page without affecting text or graphics already in place.

In this project, the headline, introduction, and coupon are created with the number of columns set to 1; the program listings are created with a 2-column setting.

- Type or place tabular listings as a single long column to evaluate the length and to determine the breaking point between the two columns.

When the program is listed chronologically, as it is in the fitness flyer, you don't have much choice about the breaking point. If listings are thematic, however, you may want to change the sequence of some of them to balance the text in the two columns. In either case, avoid breaking the column in the middle of one group of listings.

A PROMOTIONAL BROCHURE WITH ART AND DISPLAY TYPOGRAPHY

In promotional brochures, the art and display typography are often given more play than the running text, and the design may well evolve from the theme of the art. That's certainly the case with the project reproduced on the next three pages, in which the white space on the cover suggests the wide, open sky above the mountains, and the double rules at the bottom of pages 2 and 4 provide a road for the trucks to ride on.

Because of this thematic approach, the elements in the brochure, with the exception of the basic page grid, really don't lend themselves to easy adaptation. But if you work through the project as a hands-on tutorial, you'll get considerable experience in manipulating graphics and refining typography in PageMaker.

There's no need to re-create the entire brochure, however, if only a few aspects of it interest you. If you want to try your hand at only one or two of the techniques, simply turn to the appropriate section and work through it.

To support the tutorial purpose of the project, we've created the truck with PageMaker's graphics tools and used clip art for the mountains. The rendering doesn't match the quality of photographs or art that you would expect to find in promotional literature. But the techniques used explore some unusual applications for PageMaker's graphics tools, and they're also fun. In addition, Macintosh users will learn to convert

Text continues on the following spread.

PAGEMAKER TECHNIQUES YOU WILL LEARN

▶ Crop and resize line art

▶ Crop and resize scanned photos

▶ Make Encapsulated PostScript files

▶ Work with clip art

▶ Use the Bring to Front/Send to Back command

▶ Wrap text around art

▶ Customize graphic boundaries

▶ Link graphics files

▶ Kern type

▶ Run headlines across the gutter

▶ Center display text

▶ Adjust word-space values

▶ Unthread text

▶ Box an initial cap

**We can
move
mountains…**

The cover is a tease. It doesn't say much and doesn't even identify the company or the product; but the direction of the truck, the ellipsis in the text, and the wide, open white space invite you to turn the page.

The contrast in size between the truck and the mountains accentuates the size of the mountains, which in turn dramatizes the headline. A larger truck would not have the same effect.

The display typeface, ITC Bookman, is a classic, and its sturdiness is quite appropriate for a mountain trucking company. Used in boldface in large type sizes, as it is here, Bookman gives the pages a strong, straightforward look.

The headline is set with negative leading (48/42) and kerned in order to tighten up the spacing between words and letters. This helps hold the type together as a unit, which is especially important when large type is surrounded by so much white space. Note, however, the absence of any letters that hang below the baseline; had there been any descenders, the typography might have required a different treatment.

The headline across the top of these two pages requires careful placement so that it reads seamlessly across the gutter. If you're using a laser printer for final output, you won't be able to print close enough to the edge of the page to simulate normal spacing between the words "bowling" and "balls"; instead, you'll have to print an extra copy of those two words and then mechanically paste them into position on the camera-ready pages.

The shadow behind the initial cap aligns precisely with the baseline of the fifth line of text.

The box and shadow used for the American Crossroads logo are the same size as those used for the initial cap.

The wheels of the truck ride on the top rule, turning a graphic device into a functional element of the design.

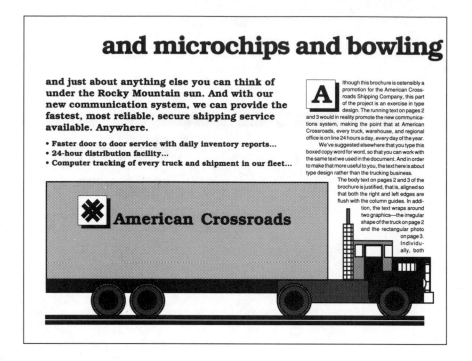

Text continued from the opening page of this project.

PageMaker art into Encapsulated PostScript (EPS) files, which is a useful procedure in itself.

PC users should note that the option to save a document as an EPS file is not available in the IBM version of PageMaker. If you want to reproduce the truck, create it in a graphics program, and then follow the instructions given later in this project for importing and placing the art files.

The photograph on page 3 of the brochure (facing page, top) may look familiar; it's the one provided on PageMaker 3.0's Getting Started disk. Before working through this project, copy the Photo.tif document from that disk to the folder (or directory) for this brochure.

Keyboarding the text for this project is inevitably tedious, but we think that those who persevere will be rewarded. The process of refining the display type includes techniques that distinguish professional from amateur typography. And working with the running text that wraps around the art on pages 2 and 3 should increase your respect for this often-abused technique. If this seems like a great many details for a fairly simple four-page brochure, that just proves another adage: God is in the details.

balls and rocket engines...

justified text and text wraparounds require deft, careful attention. Combined, they are especially demanding. Justified text forces every line to be the same length, and in doing so alters the normal letter and word spacing built into the font by the type designer. This sometimes creates holes, or rivers of white, in the text where additional space has been added to fill out a line. Occasionally, it forces letters closer together than they should be. These inconsistencies make text difficult to read and give type an uneven color on the page. The relatively wide column measure in this brochure minimizes these problems.

When you wrap text around a graphic, you narrow the column measure at certain points, which accentuates the problems inherent in justified type and adds an additional risk of excessive hyphenation. As an extreme, consider the last three lines wrapped around the truck, which are each less than ten characters long.

For wraparound text to be effective, it must have a smooth, even edge that echoes the shape of the graphic. Also, the distance between the text and the graphic should generally be uniform on all sides of the graphic. Something as commonplace as the beginning or end of a paragraph can interrupt the crisp edge of the type.

After you place text around a graphic, check the type carefully. Is the space around the graphic equal on all sides? If not, drag individual lines of

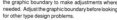

At American Crossroads,
every truck,
warehouse,
and regional office
is on line
24 hours a day.
Every day of the year.

the graphic boundary to make adjustments where needed. Adjust the graphic boundary before looking for other type design problems.

Do paragraph indents break the edge of the text at any point on the wraparound? If you're able to combine or split apart paragraphs without creating grammatical errors, consider yourself blessed with a simple solution. Sometimes you have to rewrite portions of the text to solve the problem. You may end up having to choose between editing text more for visual appearance than for content and going with an imperfect wrap.

Are there lines with too much (or too little) space between words? Changing the Word Space values to 80% generally helps. (See the instructions in the blueprint.) But Page-Maker 3.0 has the severe limitation that spacing values apply to entire text blocks, not just to selected lines or passages. Thus the only way to correct unacceptable spacing in individual lines is to kern letter pairs in those lines.

If this seems like a great deal of trouble, you're absolutely right. Even with the 3.0 release, spacing controls are not PageMaker's strong suit. That's why so many documents created with PageMaker and most other desktop-publishing programs favor ragged right over justified text and use text wraparounds sparingly. Consider yourself forewarned if you use this kind of typography in your own documents.

The body text is Helvetica, probably the most legible of all the sans serif typefaces. It gives the running text an extremely clean look and adds to the crispness of the text wraparounds. The generous leading (the text is 10/13) further increases the legibility.

The justified text is spaced relatively evenly because of the wide column width (18p6).

In the centered type for the pull quote, the line breaks were inserted manually to reinforce the content of the message and to create an interesting shape in the text itself.

The top of the photograph aligns precisely with the top of the truck on the facing page.

The truck and the man at the computer both face into the page, holding the reader's attention to the message at hand.

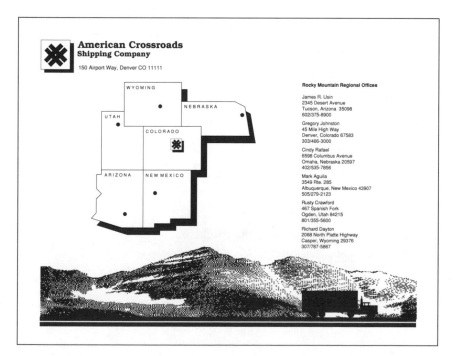

American Crossroads
Shipping Company

150 Airport Way, Denver CO 11111

WYOMING

NEBRASKA

UTAH

COLORADO

ARIZONA   NEW MEXICO

Rocky Mountain Regional Offices

James R. Usin
2345 Desert Avenue
Tucson, Arizona 35098
602/375-8900

Gregory Johnston
45 Mile High Way
Denver, Colorado 67583
303/466-3000

Cindy Rafael
6598 Columbus Avenue
Omaha, Nebraska 20597
402/535-7856

Mark Aguila
3549 Rte. 285
Albuquerque, New Mexico 43907
505/279-2123

Rusty Crawford
467 Spanish Fork
Ogden, Utah 84215
801/355-5600

Richard Dayton
2068 North Platte Highway
Casper, Wyoming 29376
307/787-5867

The back cover appears to have a great many loose elements, but they are all related to the grid and to one another.

The logo and return address anchor the page in the upper left corner, as is traditional.

The map and regional office headline are aligned with the top margin. The map is centered horizontally in the first two columns of the grid.

The truck is aligned left with the column guide. It faces off the page, as if it were delivering in the real world the service that has been promoted in the brochure.

SUMMARY OF PROCEDURES FOR PROJECT 6

Here are the general steps you need to follow to reproduce the entire brochure. Each step is described in detail in the instructions. As was mentioned in the introduction, you may want to select some steps for hands-on experience and skip over others.

1. Create the template.

2. Create the original art.

   Macintosh users: Open a copy of the template. Draw the truck and the map, each on a separate page.

   PC users: Create the truck in a graphics program, as it is not possible to save PC PageMaker documents in EPS format (step 3 below). The map can be created either in a graphics program or in PageMaker.

   Both platforms: The mountain range in the sample is clip art. You can use clip art or create mountains in a graphics program.

3. Mac users only: Save each piece of art as an Encapsulated PostScript (EPS) file.

4. Prepare the text files in your word-processing program.

   • Keyboard the display text as a single file.

   • Keyboard the text for pages 2 and 3.

   • Keyboard the text for the back cover.

5. Assemble the components in PageMaker.

   • Open another copy of the template.

   • Add the double rules on the master pages.

   • Place the art.

   • Create the graphic boundaries around art.

   • Place and kern the display text.

   • Place the running the text on pages 2 and 3, wrapping it around the graphics.

   • Add the pull quote on page 3.

   • Add the logo and name to the truck.

   • Add the text on the back cover.

BLUEPRINT FOR THE BROCHURE

As is the case with some of the other projects in this section, the instructions for re-creating the sample document take you through a slightly different process than the one you would follow if you were designing and producing a document of your own. To take the most obvious example, the creation of art and text files generally takes place simultaneously, rather than one following the other in neat chronological order. Also, we've suggested that you place all of the art and then place all of the text. The ability to work in this fashion assumes that the size and placement of art has previously been worked out and that the text has been edited to fit. In reality, getting to this point in a document generally requires several "passes" in which you fine-tune both the graphic elements and the text.

THE TEMPLATE

PAGE SETUP

Page Size: Letter (11 by 8.5 inches or 66 by 51 picas)

Orientation: Wide

Start Page #: 1 of 4

Options: Double-sided, Facing pages

Margins:

Inside: 3p6

Outside: 3p6

Top: 10p

Bottom: 3p

MASTER PAGES

- Column Guides: 3 columns with a 2p space in between.

  The three-column grid provides a useful guide for positioning graphics, even on pages that don't have three columns of type.

- Ruler Guides: On both pages, bring in a vertical ruler guide over the left margin and bring in a horizontal ruler guide at 6p.

  Note: The guides for the side margins stop at the top and bottom margins. By bringing in a ruler guide over a side margin, you extend that nonprinting guide the full depth of the page.

- Once you've set up the master pages, save the publication as a template. You'll open one copy of the template to create the original art for the truck and the map and a second copy of the template to create the brochure itself.

HOW TO CREATE A PAGEMAKER TRUCK

The truck, built out of squares, rectangles, circles, rounded-corner rectangles, and various shades and patterns, pushes PageMaker's graphics tools nearly to the limit. You can make your truck simpler or more complex than the one shown, but try to keep the outline the same if you plan to follow the text-wrap exercise later in the project.

The page grid for the brochure itself provides useful guidelines for creating the truck, so be sure to create the template (see previous page) before proceeding with the art.

Note to PC users: Because you cannot save a document in EPS format (step 7) in PC Page-Maker, you should, if possible, create the truck in a graphics program and place it in PageMaker as a single piece of art. If you don't have a graphics program, or want to explore PageMaker's graphics tools as part of this project, you can create the truck in PageMaker as described here and then copy it to the Clipboard in order to paste it full size in the brochure. But you won't be able to scale the silhouettes, and wrapping text around the truck will be much more difficult, because you will have many graphic boundaries instead of only one.

Use the following steps to create the truck:

1. Open a copy of the brochure template.

Save the copy under an appropriate name, such as Original Art/Truck Brochure (Macintosh) or TRUCKART (PC).

Create the truck on a page of its own:

2. Set up a grid, following the coordinates on the outline on the facing page.

Draw a horizontal rule as a baseline, and position the zero point on the ruler at the intersection of the baseline and left margin. Bring in ruler guides at the positions shown (coordinate points are in picas.)

3. Begin drawing the truck.

Use a 2-point line weight throughout.

Create the truck, treating shapes you draw with the square, circle, and rectangle tools as building blocks. Draw the big shapes first, shade them, and then add smaller shapes inside the large ones with contrasting shades for detail.

Draw the wheels last. (See step 5.) Use empty circles as temporary wheels, if necessary, as you draw the rest of the truck.

4. Use the Bring to Front/Send to Back feature.

As you work, keep in mind that PageMaker layers text blocks, graphics, and ruler guides. It's as though the objects were stacked one on top of another on the screen. The object you draw first is on the bottom; the object you draw last is on top. When you move a graphic, that graphic moves to the top layer.

You can change the stacking order by selecting an object and choosing Bring to Front or Send to Back from the Edit menu. The keyboard shortcuts for these—Command-F and Command-B (Ctrl-F and Ctrl-B on a PC)—are extremely useful in this project.

As you build the truck, you may lose a piece of it behind a new layer. The Bring to Front/Send to Back keyboard shortcuts should enable you to retrieve pieces that are lower in the stack. If all else fails and you really can't find a piece you know you've drawn, redraw it on top. (We admit to having done this once or twice....)

To select an item lost from view below the top layer, press Command (Ctrl on a PC) and click the pointer on the top layer; click again to select the second layer; click again for the third layer; and so on. You will see only the handles of the lower object (screen detail, above right); when you bring it to the front of the stacking order, you will see the object itself (right).

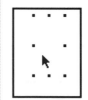

5. Draw the wheels.

Create one wheel, then copy and paste it so that all four wheels will be identical. (Hold down the Shift key to create circles rather than ovals.)

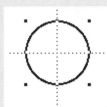

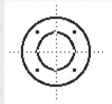

Drawing concentric circles in PageMaker is a little tricky. Draw the largest circle and, while it is selected, bring in ruler guides at the center handles. Draw the next largest circle and move it into place. Unfortunately, when you drag a circle its handles disappear and you can't see if the ruler guides bisect it until you release the mouse button. You may have to move each circle a few times to get it centered inside the larger circles.

When you are satisfied with the shape of the concentric rings of the wheel, add the shades. Again, start from the largest circle, which is on the bottom layer, and move toward the center. If you work in this order, you shouldn't have to fuss with the stacking.

6. Make two silhouettes of the truck.

The brochure uses a full-size truck with all the shades as well as two smaller versions, one white and one black. It's fairly easy to turn the original into a silhouette by choosing Select All and changing the shade to Solid or Paper.

When you're satisfied with the shape of the original truck, use the Select All command and copy the truck. Paste two copies, each on a separate page in the document.

On the first copy, choose the Select All command again. Specify the line weight as Hairline and the shade as Paper.

On the second copy, choose Select All again. For the silhouette, you want to deselect a few details, such as the windows, so that they remain white. To deselect the windows when everything on the page is selected, hold down the Shift key while you click on them. Choose Solid from the Shades menu to turn all but the deselected objects to black.

You'll resize the silhouette when you place the EPS copy of it in the brochure.

7. Make an Encapsulated PostScript file of each of the trucks (Macintosh users only).

Remove the baseline, and then save the trucks in EPS format, following the instructions on the next page. Make a separate file for each of the trucks, and name them EPS Original Truck, EPS White Truck, and EPS Black Truck.

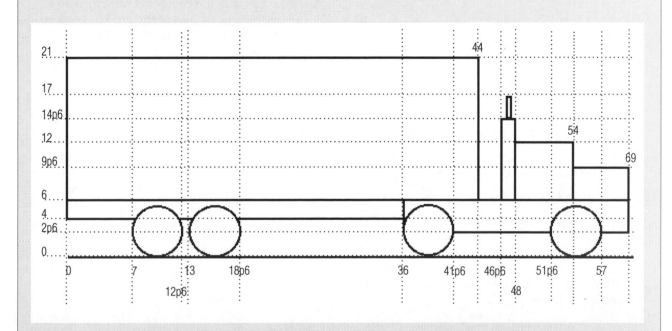

HOW TO MAKE AN ENCAPSULATED POSTSCRIPT FILE

When you use PageMaker's graphics tools to create art such as the truck, you end up with a composite graphic made of many smaller graphics. The truck, for example, has more than 35 shapes, and each shape has 8 handles. All those handles represent potential havoc on a page, and there's no way to resize a composite PageMaker graphic. For these reasons, it is a good idea to save complex art as an EPS file and then import it into your document as a single graphic. Only the Macintosh version of PageMaker offers this feature.

The EPS option prints the page to your hard disk instead of to your printer. The resulting EPS file is, in effect, a picture of the page, which you can then place as a graphic in another PageMaker document. Unlike the original art, with its many pieces and handles, the EPS graphic is a single object with only one set of eight handles. You can copy, stretch, and resize EPS art, wrap type around it, print type over it—in other words, you can manipulate it as you would any draw-type graphic.

Each piece of art should be saved as a separate EPS file, and each EPS file should consist of a single page.

The process is fairly simple:

1. Carefully check the page on which you have created your PageMaker art.

Print a copy of the page and check it as you would any final proof. Be sure there is nothing other than the piece of art on it. Any extraneous type or graphic would become a part of the EPS file.

2. Choose Print from the File menu.

This displays the regular Print dialog box.

Check the page range; be sure it specifies the number of the page that you want to save as an EPS file. Even though your truck may appear on the screen, if it is on page 1 and the page range in the Print dialog box specifies From 2 to 2, you'll make an EPS file of page 2.

Be sure the Driver option is specified as Aldus.

3. Hold down the Option key, and click OK.

This displays the PostScript Print Options dialog box.

4. Select Print PostScript to Disk, and click EPS.

The EPS option creates the PostScript information for the page and also saves a screen image of it so that you can see and manipulate it when you place it in another document. (If you click Normal, you create a PostScript file without the screen image; when you place a PostScript file created with this option in another PageMaker document, all you see on-screen is a box with an ID code.)

5. If your disk has Aldus Prep, turn off the Aldus Prep option in this dialog box.

This will save disk space. If your disk doesn't have Aldus Prep, you must select it here.

6. Deselect the Download Bitmap Fonts and Download PostScript Fonts options.

Since no type is included in the art, these options aren't needed. For the PageMaker-created art in this brochure, we recommend adding the type—such as the name on the truck—after you place the EPS graphic in the brochure, rather than including the type as part of the art. We initially created an EPS file of the truck with the American Crossroads name on it, but when we placed the EPS file in the brochure, the type and pieces of the truck bounced into unexpected positions on the page. These problems can be solved, but you can avoid them by not including type as part of the EPS file.

Note: Many of the problems encountered with EPS files were corrected in PageMaker 3.01. If you intend to use the EPS option in your publication work, be sure to get that upgrade.

7. Select Set File Name.

Type a name in the Name box (be sure to use EPS in the filename so that you can distinguish the EPS truck from the original truck in your directory), and select the folder or disk to which you want to save the EPS file.

If you skip this step, PageMaker will use a default filename, PostScript 01 to 99, and you'll curse yourself trying to identify the correct file when you go to place it.

Note: Unlike documents created and saved in applications such as PageMaker, Adobe Illustrator, Microsoft Word, and so on, EPS documents created in this way are not identified as being in EPS format in the disk directory unless you label them as such as part of the filename.

8. Click OK in the Print PostScript to Disk dialog box and again in the PostScript Print Options dialog box.

If you want to change any of the PostScript options or cancel the operation altogether, click Cancel.

AN IMPORTANT TIP ABOUT PLACING EPS ART

When you place an Encapsulated Postscript file, you place a picture of the page on which that file was created. So the handles take on the shape of that page, rather than the shape of the art itself.

In this project, the truck art was created on an 11- by 8.5-inch landscape page. The EPS file, shown below in a reduced screen detail, has those same proportions.

When you place an EPS file, you should crop the page image to bring the handles as close to the actual art as possible. With the cropping tool active, select the EPS truck art, place the cropping tool over a center handle (below left), and drag that handle to just above the truck (below right). Repeat for each of the other three sides.

HOW TO WORK WITH CLIP ART FOR THE MOUNTAIN RANGE

We used electronic clip art (from WetPaint) for the mountain range on the front and back covers. As is often the case with clip art, the image had to be adapted to suit specific layout needs. For the front cover we wanted a black area on the left side of the mountains against which to place a white truck, and for the back cover we wanted a light area on the right side against which to place a silhouette truck.

The mountain art is fairly independent of other elements in this project, and you'll be able to work with the text and photo portions of the tutorial without placing mountains if you don't have any suitable art.

The original image from a clip art disk often has extraneous visual information, such as the border around the sides and bottom of this picture.

The image was cleaned up in MacPaint by erasing the border. This image was stretched proportionally for the front cover (reproduced on the opening spread of this project), providing a black area on the left side of the image against which to place a white truck.

The cleaned-up image (from above) was flopped horizontally in MacPaint. The flopped image was used on the back cover (see the second spread of this project), cropped and stretched horizontally to produce a flatter range than that on the front cover. When cropping and stretching, we wanted to hold a light area on the lower right against which to place a black truck.

HOW TO CREATE THE MAP ART IN PAGEMAKER

The map shown on the back cover of the brochure was created in Adobe Illustrator in order to get a shadow behind shapes with irregular edges. You can draw a simplified version in PageMaker following one of the options in step 2.

1. Turn to a blank page in your art document.

In a later step you will be placing this art from the Clipboard or Scrapbook exactly as it is drawn in PageMaker. Thus, instead of being a single object, it will be a composite image made up of many different lines or shapes, depending on the technique you choose in the next step. For that reason, you should draw the map at the size it is to be in the brochure.

The map in the sample is 24 picas deep and 26 picas across at its widest point. You may want to bring in ruler guides to define this area before proceeding with step 2.

2. Follow one of these procedures to create a simplified version of the map:

• With a 0.5-point line weight selected, use the diagonal and perpendicular line tools to create the map outline from a series of adjoining lines, working at a large page view to be sure that adjacent lines butt together.

Because the shapes you draw in this way are not solid, you cannot fill them with black to create the shadow. And because an Encapsulated PostScript file is a picture of an entire page, not just the image on it, you can't use that technique to create a shadow either.

• Or, with a 0.5-point line weight selected, use the rectangle tool to draw a map with squared-off borders for all the states. Each state will be a separate solid object, and you can select them all together with either the pointer tool or the Select All command. Copy the map, paste it, fill it with solid black, slide the black map into place over the original, and then send it to the back. Adjust the position of the black map so that it creates a 1-pica shadow behind the original map.

3. Add the state names.

The type for the state names is 8/Auto Helvetica with an extra letterspace between each character. Draw a bounding box with the text tool before typing each name.

The bullets designating the regional office in each state are 10-point bold Zapf Dingbats. (The keystroke is Option-8.)

To place all the names in the same relative position inside their respective borders, draw a square in the upper left corner of the first state. Move the type so that the first letter of the name is tucked into the lower right corner of the square (#1). Then move the square to the upper left corner of the next state and use it as a spacing guide to position that state name (#2).

▼ ▼ ▼

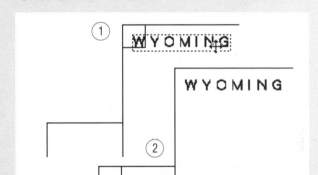

4. Copy the art for the final brochure.

If you are working on a Macintosh, make a copy of the map to leave in your Scrapbook. When you're ready to place the art, open the Scrapbook, find the art, copy it, and paste it on the page. (You could also make an EPS file and place that.)

If you're working on a PC that doesn't have a Scrapbook, you'll have to come back to this original art document when you're ready to place the art, copy the map art to the Clipboard, and paste it onto the back page of the brochure.

HOW TO PREPARE THE TEXT FILES

There are different ways to approach the formatting of text for placement in a PageMaker document. The instructions here, and those given later for placing the text, are simply one relatively efficient method for this document.

1. Type and format the display type on the cover and on pages 2 and 3 as a single file in your word-processing program.

For short manuscripts that will be broken into different text blocks, it is generally more efficient to write, place, and cut apart a single file than it is to place several individual files. After you place the text in your PageMaker document, you can unthread the various components by using the Cut and Paste commands.

The display text includes the cover headline, the headline on pages 2 and 3, the lead paragraph on page 2, and the bulleted text on page 2. For the text, refer to the sample pages reproduced on the opening pages of this project.

Type this text as a single file in your default type style. Make each block a separate paragraph, but don't worry about the line breaks. Do not include the pull quote on page 3 in this file; you will extract it from the running text after you have placed and refined it in PageMaker.

Select the various components and change the type specifications as indicated next. (If Page-Maker does not support formatting from your word-processing program, change the type specs after you place the text in PageMaker.)

    Cover headline: 48/42 Bookman bold, centered

    Headline, pages 2 and 3: 48/42 Bookman bold, aligned left

    Page 2, lead paragraph: 18/Auto Bookman bold, aligned left

    Page 2, bulleted copy: 14/18 Bookman bold, aligned left

2. Type and format the running text on pages 2 and 3.

This text is 10/13 Helvetica, justified, with a 22-point first-line indent.

If you want some hands-on experience with text wraparounds, you'll need to work with the same text used in the sample. Type the text of "A Few Words About Wraparounds and Justified Text," on the facing page, and place that file when you assemble the final document. (Do not include the headline in that text file.)

3. Type and format the list of regional offices on the back cover.

This list is 9/11 Helvetica with a 5-point paragraph space between each listing. The boldface headline is the same size as the listing text.

In many word-processing applications, you can force a line break without creating a new paragraph. For example, in Microsoft Word you can press Shift-Return to enter a newline character that forces the cursor to the next line, generating a line space rather than a paragraph space. Unfortunately, when you place text with this formatting, PageMaker reads the forced line breaks as paragraph breaks.

To get around this problem, specify the paragraph spacing as 0 and type the list line-for-line without any space between items. Then select the last line of each listing and change the paragraph spacing for that line to 5 points.

A FEW WORDS ABOUT TEXT WRAPAROUNDS AND JUSTIFIED TEXT

Although this brochure is ostensibly a promotion for the American Crossroads Shipping Company, this part of the project is an exercise in type design. The running text on pages 2 and 3 would in reality promote the new communications system, making the point that at American Crossroads, every truck, warehouse, and regional office is on line 24 hours a day, every day of the year.

We've suggested elsewhere that you type this boxed copy word for word, so that you can work with the same text we used in the document. And in order to make that more useful to you, the text here is about type design rather than the trucking business.

The body text on pages 2 and 3 of the brochure is justified, that is, aligned so that both the right and left edges are flush with the column guides. In addition, the text wraps around two graphics—the irregular shape of the truck on page 2 and the rectangular photo on page 3.

Individually, both justified text and text wraparounds require deft, careful attention. Combined, they are especially demanding. Justified text forces every line to be the same length, and in doing so alters the normal letter and word spacing built into the font by the type designer. This sometimes creates holes, or rivers of white, in the text where additional space has been added to fill out a line. Occasionally, it forces letters closer together than they should be. These inconsistencies in spacing make text difficult to read and give the type an uneven color on the page. The relatively wide column measure on these two pages minimizes these problems.

When you wrap text around a graphic, you narrow the column measure at certain points, which accentuates the problems inherent in justified type and adds an additional risk of excessive hyphenation. As an extreme, consider the last three lines wrapped around the truck illustration, which are less than ten characters long.

For wraparound text to be effective, it must have a smooth, even edge that echoes the shape of the graphic. (For that reason, you would rarely wrap ragged right text around a graphic.) Also, the distance between the text and the graphic should generally be uniform on all sides of the graphic. Something as seemingly commonplace as the beginning or end of a paragraph can interrupt the crisp edge of the type.

After you place text around a graphic, check the type carefully. Is the space around the graphic equal on all sides? If not, drag individual lines of the graphic boundary to make adjustments where needed. Adjust the graphic boundary before looking for other type design problems.

Do paragraph indents break the edge of the text at any point on the wraparound? If you're able to combine or split apart paragraphs without creating grammatical errors, consider yourself blessed with a simple solution. Sometimes you have to rewrite portions of the text to solve the problem. You may end up having to choose between editing text more for visual appearance than for content and going with an imperfect wrap.

Are there lines with too much (or too little) space between words? Changing the Word Space values to 80% generally helps. (See the instructions in the blueprint.) But PageMaker 3.0 has the severe limitation that spacing values apply to entire text blocks, not just to selected lines or passages. Thus the only way to correct unacceptable spacing in individual lines is to kern letter pairs in those lines.

If this seems like a great deal of trouble, you're absolutely right. Even with the 3.0 release, spacing controls are not PageMaker's strong suit. That's why so many documents created with PageMaker and other desktop-publishing programs favor ragged right over justified text and use text wraparounds sparingly. Be forewarned.

ASSEMBLING THE COMPONENTS OF THE BROCHURE

MASTER PAGES

1. Open a copy of the template

Save the copy as a new file, named American Crossroads Brochure (Macintosh) or CROSSRDS (PC).

2. Add the rules on the master pages.

- The rules are 8-point lines with a 2-point space in between. (Use a 2-point rule as a spacing guide.)

- Create one pair of rules on the left master page, with the base of the lower rule flush against the bottom margin. Copy and paste the same rules on the right master page. Paste a third copy on the pasteboard above the right master page. (You'll use this copy for the rule at the top of page 1 and to create a shorter pair of rules above the pull quote on page 3.)

FRONT COVER ART

1. Place the mountain art.

- If you are using a piece of clip art, place it in the document and move it into position so that its base is flush with the bottom left margin. The mountains should mask the double rules from the master page, which do not print in this position on the cover.

- If you are using the same mountain art on the front and back covers, make a copy of it for the pasteboard before stretching it. (As mentioned in the instructions for preparing the mountain art, we used a flopped version of the original on the back cover.)

- To stretch the art proportionally, hold down the Shift key and drag any handle until the art is flush with the right margin.

TIP

When placing large art on the pasteboard, hold down the Shift key and choose Fit in Window from the Page menu. This gives you a "global view" of the entire pasteboard and a large area to work in.

2. Place the white truck.

- Place the EPS White Truck file (or a truck you created with a graphics program) on the pasteboard.

- Crop the EPS image so that the handles are tight around the truck.

- With the pointer tool, select the art, hold down the Shift key, and drag a corner handle to reduce the size of the truck.

- Move the truck into position in the lower left, with its wheels flush on the bottom margin, and adjust the size if necessary.

TIP

To resize an imported graphic while maintaining its original proportions, hold down the Shift key and drag a corner handle.

3. Position the double rules.

Copy the double rules from the pasteboard. Position the copy on the cover so the base of the bottom rule is 4p9 from the top of the page.

INSIDE ART

1. Place the truck.

- Move to page 2 and place the EPS Original Truck file on the pasteboard (or place a truck created in a graphics program).

- Crop so that the handles are close around the truck.

- Position the truck so that its top is 26p from the top of the page.

2. Add a graphic boundary around the truck.

In order to wrap the text around the truck, you need to add a graphic boundary around it. Note, however, that if your truck is an EPS graphic, the boundary will be the rectangular shape of the page on which it was created. Therefore, you'll have to customize the shape of the graphic boundary, a technique described on the following page. (If you've created the truck in a graphics program, the boundary will be contoured to the shape of the truck itself.)

- Choose Text Wrap from the Options menu.

- Select the center Wrap icon and the third Text Flow icon. For the standoff values, type *1* pica for the top and *0* for the other three sides.

  When you click OK and the screen refreshes, the graphic boundary is displayed as a dotted line with diamond-shaped handles. The square handles inside the boundary define the outline of the art. When you first work with graphic boundaries, it's easy to confuse the two types of handles.

- Customize the graphic boundary, as described next.

The dotted line defines the graphic boundary around the truck.

Square handles inside the boundary define the outline of the Encapsulated PostScript art.

Diamond-shaped handles on the graphic boundary can be added, deleted, and moved to change the shape of the boundary.

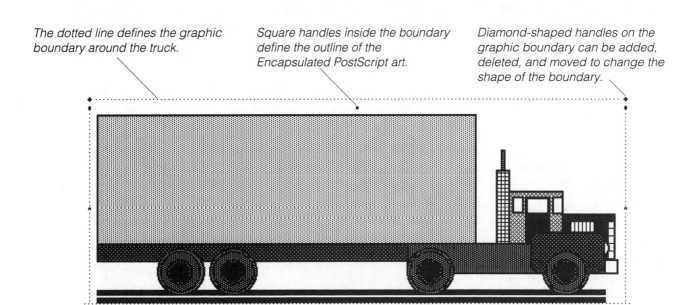

HOW TO CUSTOMIZE A GRAPHIC BOUNDARY

To change the shape of the boundary so that it follows the outline of the truck, divide the boundary into smaller line segments by adding and dragging additional handles. For each line segment you want to create, you add two handles; the distance between the handles defines the length of the new segment.

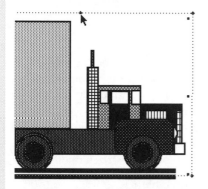 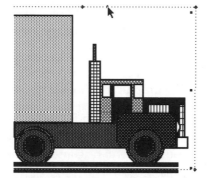 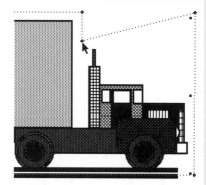

1. Click on the graphic boundary to add the first handle where you want to make the first turn, about two picas in front of the trailer.

2. and 3. Add a second handle and drag it directly below the first one, a pica or two above the exhaust pipe.

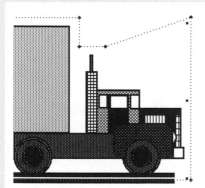 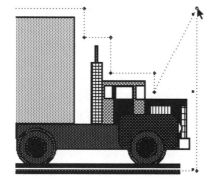 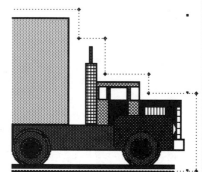

4. Add a third handle and drag it down parallel to the second one.

5. and 6. Continue adding and dragging three more handles to define the shape of the cab and hood, then drag the existing handle from the upper right corner to define the right edge of the line over the hood.

TIPS

Graphic boundaries are extremely elastic. Drag handles to change the direction or length of a line; drag whole lines to change the distance between the boundary and the graphic.

When customizing a graphic boundary, begin by getting the rough shape you want, and then fine-tune the placement of individual handles and lines.

You can edit a graphic boundary after the text wraps around it. Hold down the space bar while you adjust the boundary if you want PageMaker to delay reflowing the text.

To delete a handle on a graphic boundary, drag that handle on top of another handle.

Hold down the Shift key to constrain movement of a handle.

Check to be sure each segment of the boundary is straight.

TIP

Unless you know the proportions of a photo (or any other art) that you're placing, use ruler guides to define its size and position. If, instead, you draw a rectangle and select Replacing Entire Graphic when you place the photo, PageMaker will resize the photo proportionally until its shorter side equals the shorter side of the graphic placeholder. The longer side of the photo will be resized disproportionately, and the art will look distorted.

3. Place the photograph on page 3.

We suggested earlier that you make a copy of the Photo.tif file from PageMaker 3.0's Getting Started disk and place it in the folder or directory for this project. Do that at this point if you haven't already.

- Move the 0 point on the ruler to the upper left corner of page 3. Bring in vertical ruler guides at 18p6 and 47p6 and a horizontal ruler guide at 26p. These ruler guides, along with the bottom margin, define the space the photo will occupy.

- Place the photo and, while it is still selected, drag it into position so that its lower left corner is at the intersection of the bottom margin and the ruler guide at 18p6.

- To resize the photo proportionally, hold down the Shift key and drag the upper right corner of the photo until it is at the 47p6 ruler guide.

- With the cropping tool, select the photo, position the cropping tool over the top center handle, and drag that handle down to the 26p horizontal ruler guide.

- You've probably cut off the top of the man's head, but you can move the photo within the frame of the cropped graphic to reveal portions you've cropped out. Position the cropping tool inside the selected photo, hold down the mouse button, and when the grabber hand appears, drag the photo to reveal the part of it that you want to print.

- Check the photo at a larger page view.

- Add a graphic boundary around the photo. With the photo selected, choose Text Wrap from the Options menu, choose the center Wrap option and the third Text Flow option, and specify a 1-pica standoff for the left, right, and top and 0 for the bottom.

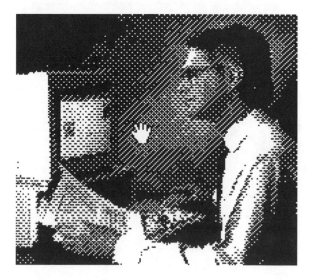

▲ ▲ ▲

To reveal unseen portions of a cropped photo, position the cropping tool inside the selected photo, click, and when the grabber hand appears, scroll the photo in any direction.

Note: Scanned photos are generally memory intensive (the photo in this project is more than 180K). When you place a scanned image larger than 64K in a publication, PageMaker will create a low-resolution screen image of it as part of the file. If you link the original scanned image to the publication file, then when you print the file, Page-Maker will insert the higher-resolution original. Any changes that you've made to the screen version, such as resizing or cropping, are applied to the original when you print. When you see the linking dialog box, if you want PageMaker to print the higher-resolution original, scroll to find Photo.tif in your directory, click on that file, and then click on Link.

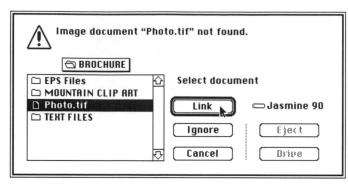

Image document "Photo.tif" not found.

BROCHURE

☐ EPS Files
☐ MOUNTAIN CLIP ART
☐ Photo.tif
☐ TEXT FILES

Select document

[Link] ⊖ Jasmine 90

[Ignore] [Eject]

[Cancel] [Drive]

▲ ▲ ▲

When you incorporate scanned photographs into a PageMaker document, link the file containing the original photograph to the document in which it is placed in order to print the photograph at the highest resolution. If your final output will be from a Linotronic imagesetter, you must supply your service center with the original photo file along with the publication file.

4. Create the short double rules on page 3.

- Make a copy of the double rules on the pasteboard.

- Position the copy flush against the left margin of the center column, with the top of the top rule flush against the top margin at 10p.

- Hold down the Shift key and drag the right handle of the top line to the right margin of the center column. Resize the bottom rule in the same way. By holding down the Shift key and constraining the movement to the horizontal axis, you'll maintain the 2-pica space between the rules.

BACK COVER ART

1. Place the mountain art.

- Place the mountain art on the back cover (in the sample, we placed the flopped clip art) or, if you are using art from the front cover, move it from the pasteboard into position on page 4.

- If you are cropping the art, as we did, crop from the bottom up to the point that you want to align with the double rules.

- Position the base of the mountains flush against the top rule at the bottom of the page. The left side of the mountains should be flush with the left margin.

- Stretch the art so that it extends to the right margin. Note that because of the map and text above the mountains on this page, we stretched the art in a horizontal direction only, rather than holding the Shift key to stretch it proportionally. This produces a flatter range than the mountains on the front cover.

Use column guides and text margins to determine the placement of all art. This gives your page a planned look and holds the elements together with an invisible structure.

2. Place the truck silhouette.

- Place the EPS Black Truck file (or a truck you created with a graphics program) on the pasteboard.

- Crop so that the handles are close around the truck.

- Shrink the truck proportionally by holding down the Shift key and dragging a handle.

- Move the truck into position so that its wheels sit on the top rule that you added on the master page. The back end of the truck is flush against the left margin of the third column. The front of the truck aligns with the right edge of the type in that column. You can resize the art to achieve this planned alignment after you place the text.

3. Position the map art.

If you are working on a Macintosh, the map art should be in the Scrapbook. Open the Scrapbook, copy the map, and then paste it onto page 4.

If you're working on a PC, you'll need to close the brochure, open the art document, copy the map art to the Clipboard, close the original art, open the brochure again, and paste the map from the Clipboard to the brochure.

The top of the map is at the top margin, and the map is centered horizontally within the two left columns.

THE DISPLAY TEXT

1. Place the display text file on the pasteboard.

We suggested earlier that you create all the display type for the cover and pages 2 and 3 as a single text file, even though the manuscript is laid out as four separate copy blocks. Because the text here is relatively short, it's fairly efficient to place it as a single file on the pasteboard and cut apart each of the four components for positioning on the brochure pages.

When you want to unthread individual text blocks from a larger story file, unlink each text block by cutting it from the main story, setting an insertion point outside the main story, and pasting the unlinked text on the page. Changes you make in the unlinked text will not "ripple through" to the rest of the text, and vice versa.

2. Position and kern the cover copy.

- With the text tool, select the cover line and cut it from the rest of the text.

- Draw a bounding box across all three columns. The sides of the box should align precisely with the left and right margins so that the text will be centered within the grid. The depth of the box is not important.

- Paste the text and move it into position so that the top of the cap is flush against the ruler guide at 6p.

- Rebreak the lines as shown in the sample.

- Remove the excess space by kerning the text.

Look closely at the letter and word spacing and note how uneven it is. The reason for this is that as you increase the size of type, the space between letters appears to the eye to grow faster than the letters themselves. The O's especially seem to stand out because of the excess space around them.

To remove excess space, set an insertion point between two letters and press Command-Backspace (Ctrl-Backspace on a PC). Work at 200% or 400% so that your screen resolution will be as close as possible to your printer resolution. Even at that enlarged page view, the insertion point may not move each time you press the Backspace key. Test with your own eye for what looks right, and then compare your result with the sample below. (The numbers indicate the number of times we pressed the Backspace key.)

The cover type before kerning.

We can move mountains...

The cover type after kerning. (The numbers indicate the number of times we pressed the Backspace key to remove space.) If you look at individual letter pairs in the kerned headline, you'll see that some are just barely touching and others are not. The goal is the overall balance of space throughout the headline, which gives the type an even color on the page.

We can move mountains...

The cover type with the line "mountains..." optically centered.

We can move mountains...

- Now look carefully at the word "mountains. " Although it is mathematically centered, the white space around the ellipsis makes it appear visually off center. Bring in a ruler guide to mark the baseline, use the pointer tool to select the text, break the word "mountains" apart from the rest by raising the windowshade handle, and then reposition the line so that it is visually centered.

3. Position and kern the headline on pages 2 and 3.

- With the text tool, select the headline for the top of pages 2 and 3, and cut it from the text block on the pasteboard.

- Draw a bounding box across the two pages, from the left margin on page 2 to the right margin on page 3, and paste the text. The baseline should align with the 6p horizontal ruler guide.

- Kern the line of text to tighten up the spacing. See the annotated line below for guidelines.

-2 -3 -7   -2 -3-2 -2 -2-3 -2-3 -2 -7 -2 -3   -7   -2 -2   -2-2-2 -2 -4   -2 -2-2-2 -7   -2   -3   -7 -2 -2-3 -3-3 -7 -2 -2 -2-2 -3 -2

and microchips and bowling balls and rocket engines...

- Check the alignment of the text across the gutter between the two pages, and reposition it if necessary so that the words break between pages, as shown in the sample at the beginning of the project. It's more important to break the text between the words "bowling" and "balls" than it is to center the line between the left and right edges of the pages.

Note, however, that in order to maintain word spacing consistent with the rest of the headline, you have to position these two words closer to the edge of the paper than most laser printers will print. On a Linotronic imagesetter, your page would be printed on a 12-inch roll of paper, wide enough to print to the edge of paper with an 11-inch trim. But if you are using a laser printer for final output, you have to print a second copy of these two words and mechanically paste them into position on the camera-ready art. The procedure is as follows:

Position the kerned headline so that it is visually correct on screen.

Copy the two words that cross the gutter.

Insert an additional page into the file (using the Insert Pages command on the Page menu), and paste those two words on that page.

When you print the file, the edges of the words at the gutter on pages 2 and 3 will be cut off.

With an X-Acto knife or razor blade, cut each of the words "bowling" and "balls" from the extra page you inserted.

Spray the back of the individual words with an adhesive, such as Spray Mount, and paste each word into position on the camera-ready page, using the type on the original as a guide.

4. Position and tighten the display text on page 2.

- Cut the remaining text from the pasteboard.

- Set an insertion point at the upper left margin of the left column, and paste the text.

- With the pointer tool, drag the windowshade handles to the right so that the text fills two columns. (You could also have drawn a bounding box across the two columns before pasting the text. Both techniques achieve the same purpose of overriding existing column guides.) The tops of the ascenders (letters like t and h that rise above the x-height) should align with the top margin.

  If the bulleted text does not clear the standoff around the truck, select the truck and drag the top of its graphic boundary until it is just above the top of the truck.

- Select the text with the text tool and choose Spacing from the Type menu. Change the values for desired and maximum word spacing to 80%. This will tighten up the text overall and give it a more professional polish.

  The tighter spacing has solved one problem by bringing the word "fleet" up onto the third line of bulleted copy, but there's a new problem with hyphenation. With the text still selected, choose Paragraph from the Type menu and turn off Auto Hyphenation. The text will rewrap without any hyphens.

Spacing attributes				OK
Word space:		**Letter space:**		Cancel
Minimum	50 %	Minimum	-5 %	
Desired	80 %	Desired	0 %	
Maximum	80 %	Maximum	25 %	

▲ ▲ ▲

Use the Spacing command on the Type menu to tighten the normal word spacing to 80% for a more professional look.

- Use the pointer tool to separate the bulleted copy from the text above it so that you can reposition the bulleted copy. Its placement is purely visual: There should be more space after it than before it so that the copy is clearly attached to the text above rather than to the art below. This is a good example of using white space as a structural element of design to define relationships between different elements on the page.

- Select the truck and raise the top line of the graphic boundary until it is about 1 pica from the top of the truck.

THE RUNNING TEXT

1. Place the running text on pages 2 and 3.

This is the file, "A Few Words About Wraparounds and Justified Text," that you were instructed to type in the text-preparation step earlier in this project.

- When you first place the file, don't worry about how the text wraps around the art. On page 3, place the text in the first and third columns only, and raise the windowshade handles so that the text clears the rules at the bottom of the page.

- Remove the paragraph indent on the first line as follows: Select that line, choose Paragraph from the Type menu, and change the first-line indent to 0. Note that this change affects only the selected paragraph.

...brochure is ostensibly a promotion for Crossroads Shipping Company, this project is an exercise in type design. The ...on pages 2 and 3 would in reality promote the new communications system, making the point that at American Crossroads, every truck, warehouse, and regional office is online 24 hours a day, every day of the year.

▲ ▲ ▲

The white square aligns with the top and left margins. The shadow square aligns with the baseline of the fifth line of text.

TIP

While working with the drop-shadow box, you'll inevitably select the text block instead. When that happens, choose the Send to Back command, and deselect the text block by clicking outside the handles. You should then be able to select the box.

2. Add the box for the initial cap on page 2.

- Working right over the text block, hold down the Shift key and with a hairline rule draw a 4p6 square from the upper left margin. Give the square a shade of Paper.

- Copy the square, paste it, and fill the copy with black.

- Move the copy into position over the original so that the black square hangs over about 6 points on the right and is aligned on the bottom with the baseline of the fifth line of text. Then, with the black square still selected, send it to the back by pressing Command-B (Ctrl-B on a PC).

3. Copy the square.

The square that holds the logo on the truck should match the square used for the initial cap. So before proceeding, copy the square and shadow as a unit and paste it onto the truck.

4. Define the graphic boundaries of the box.

- Select the shadow.

- Choose Text Wrap from the Options menu. Select the center Wrap icon and the third Text Flow icon.

- Change the standoff to 0p6 on the right and bottom.

  After you click OK and the screen refreshes, the text will automatically rewrap around the box. Even though the standoffs on the right and bottom are equal, the space below the square will probably be disproportionately large. See the explanation below.

- Visually adjust the graphic boundary by dragging the bottom segment of the dotted line up a few points, so that it clears the sixth line of running text.

- Adjust the right side of the graphic boundary so that the spaces below and to the right of the shadow are visually equal.

Although this brochure is ostensibly a promotion for the American Cross-roads Shipping Company, this part of the project is an exercise in type design. The running text on pages 2 and 3 would in reality promote the new communications system, making the point that at American Crossroads, every truck, warehouse, and regional office is online 24 hours a day, every day of the year.

When you define a standoff, Page-Maker forces the text wrap to the nearest line that will fit without overlapping the standoff. Often, the tip of an ascender or even the space defined by leading will force a line outside the standoff, as it does here.

Although this brochure is ostensibly a promotion for the American Cross-roads Shipping Company, this part of the project is an exercise in type design. The running text on pages 2 and 3 would in reality promote the new communications system, making the point that at American Crossroads, every truck, warehouse, and regional office is online 24 hours a day, every day of the year.

▲ ▲ ▲

Visually adjust the graphic by dragging the bottom segment of the dotted line up a few points so that it clears the sixth line of running text. Remember to point on the line, not on a handle, when you drag.

Although this brochure is ostensibly a promotion for the American Cross-roads Shipping Company, this part of the project is an exercise in type design. The running text on pages 2 and 3 would in reality promote the new communications system, making the point that at American Crossroads, every truck, warehouse, and regional office is online 24 hours a day, every day of the year.

When you release the mouse button, the sixth line should reflow to the left margin. Adjust the right side of the graphic boundary so that the spaces below and to the right of the shadow are visually equal.

5. Add the initial cap.

- Delete the letter "A" from the first line.

- On the pasteboard, type a capital *A* in 48/36 Bookman bold. Drag the handles as tightly around the A as possible.

- With the pointer tool, move the initial cap into position.

6. Refine the text wrap around the truck and photograph.

There are likely to be numerous problems with the justified text that wraps around the art on pages 2 and 3. Making the effort to spot and correct these problems is time-consuming, but if you are going to use sophisticated typography, you are well-advised to apply high standards to your efforts. Note, however, that if your truck and graphic boundary do not exactly match ours, you will find slightly different problems than we did. But our problems—and solutions— should provide guidelines for solving yours.

- First, check the alignment of the text in all three columns. The tops of the ascenders should align with the top margins. Adjustments at this point can affect the text wrap.

- Justified text usually sets better with slightly tighter-than-normal word spacing. Select the entire text block and choose Spacing from the Type menu. In the Word Space options, change both the desired and the maximum word spacing to 80%. Click OK.

- Now check the text wrap around the truck, and adjust the graphic boundary as needed. See the screen details and captions below for explanation.

In the screen detail below, there is too much space between the text and the truck in several places: above the trailer, to the right of the exhaust pipe, and above the hood.

▼ ▼ ▼

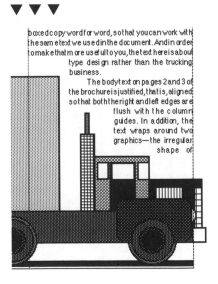

To adjust the text wrap, first select the truck with the pointer tool to reveal the graphic boundary. Then hold down the Shift key, click on the line you want to move, and drag it closer to the truck. When you drag, be sure not to drag a handle, or you will change the angle of the line.

▼ ▼ ▼

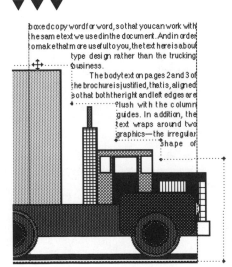

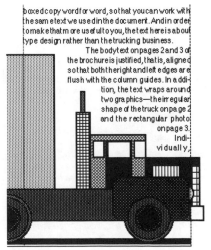

GENERAL PROCEDURE FOR REFINING JUSTIFIED TEXT THAT WRAPS AROUND A GRAPHIC

1. Check the alignment of the text at the top, bottom, and side margins.

2. Tighten up the word spacing if desired.

3. Adjust the graphic boundary if needed.

4. Identify problem areas in text wrap and in word spacing.

5. Make corrections from the beginning to the end of the text. Be sure to watch for new problems that may result from the corrections.

- Check the wrap around the photograph on page 3.

The screen details and captions below describe the problems and solutions.

In this top screen detail, there is too much space between the graphic boundary and the text above it.

To allow an additional line in each column to run the full measure above the photograph, drag the graphic boundary closer to the photo. To delay text flow around a graphic when you adjust the graphic boundary, hold down the space bar while you are dragging a line or handle. PageMaker will not rewrap the text until you release the space bar, saving screen refresh time.

The adjusted graphic boundary has corrected the problem of the text wrap above the photo, but several other problems remain. Turn the page for details.

A paragraph indent at the top of the truck and a four-character indented line just above the hood spoil the effect of the text wraparound (top). After minor adjustments in the copy, the text wrap hugs the graphic without interruption (bottom).

▼ ▼ ▼

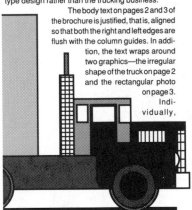

Although this brochure is ostensibly a promotion for the American Cross-roads Shipping Company, this part of the project is an exercise in type design. The running text on pages 2 and 3 would in reality promote the new communications system, making the point that at American Crossroads, every truck, warehouse, and regional office is on line 24 hours a day, every day of the year.

We've suggested elsewhere that you type this boxed copy word for word, so that you can work with the same text we used in the document. And in order to make that more useful to you, the text here is about type design rather than the trucking business.

The body text on pages 2 and 3 of the brochure is justified, that is, aligned so that both the right and left edges are flush with the column guides. In addition, the text wraps around two graphics—the irregular shape of the truck on page 2 and the rectangular photo on page 3. Individually,

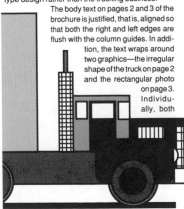

Although this brochure is ostensibly a promotion for the American Cross-roads Shipping Company, this part of the project is an exercise in type design. The running text on pages 2 and 3 would in reality promote the new communications system, making the point that at American Crossroads, every truck, warehouse, and regional office is on line 24 hours a day, every day of the year.

We've suggested elsewhere that you type this boxed copy word for word, so that you can work with the same text we used in the document. And in order to make that more useful to you, the text here is about type design rather than the trucking business.

The body text on pages 2 and 3 of the brochure is justified, that is, aligned so that both the right and left edges are flush with the column guides. In addition, the text wraps around two graphics—the irregular shape of the truck on page 2 and the rectangular photo on page 3. Individually, both

- Check the text on page 2 for spacing problems. The paragraph indent at the top of the truck interrupts the text wrap before it has begun. Because the last line in the preceding paragraph does not fill the column measure, this line will read as the beginning of a new paragraph even without a first-line indent. Select the paragraph, choose Paragraph from the Type menu, and change the first-line indent to 0.

  The next paragraph indent, just above the hood, interrupts the wrap again with a hyphenated four-character line that looks terrible. We have another relatively easy solution in that a paragraph break here isn't essential. So we can run the two paragraphs together by placing the I-beam before "Individually" and pressing the Backspace key to eliminate the carriage return. When you run two paragraphs together in this way, be sure to press the space bar afterward to insert a space between the two sentences.

- Page 2 looks good now.

- There are several problems on page 3, which you can see in the top screen detail on the facing page. With any luck, solving the first couple of problems will help solve some of the others without creating too many new ones.

  In the paragraph at the top of the left column, we pull up the two words at the end of the paragraph by deleting the phrase "in spacing" and the word "the" later in the same sentence and by changing "on these two pages" to "in this brochure."

  In the center paragraph of the same column, we eliminate the gap between the last line and the photo by deleting the word "illustration" and adding the word "each" to the last sentence.

  As a result of these changes, we've cut two lines. We cut two more in the third paragraph in this column by deleting the parenthetical second sentence and the word "seemingly" in the last sentence.

  The deletions have pulled up the widow at the top of the right column; and the second-to-last paragraph now clears the photo.

  The indent for the last paragraph still interrupts the edge of the type around the photo. Here, the content of the text takes precedence over the visual appearance: The concluding paragraph would lose its effectiveness if it ran into the preceding discussion, and so we leave the paragraph indent.

  Only one new problem has been created by the changes: The text is a line short and ends with a widow. We fill out the column by rewriting the last sentence to read "Consider yourself forewarned if you use this kind of typography in your own documents."

  We see that we have a bad line break in this last paragraph, with an end-of-line hyphen in the middle of a hyphenated compound adjective, "desktop-publishing." By adding the word "most," we force "desk-" to the next line.

- We print the pages and check every line for unacceptably loose or tight spacing. It's not as good as commercial typesetting, but it's tidy—and about as good as you can get from PageMaker 3.0.

Subtle problems on this page show the details one must look for in text wraparounds. In the uncorrected screen detail (top), two short lines in the left column create holes on or near the edge of the photo, as do two paragraph indents in the right column. Also, although not directly related to the text wraparound, a widow (or short end-of-paragraph line) at the top of the right column must be eliminated, and the text runs four lines long. The corrected page is seen in the bottom screen detail.

▼ ▼ ▼

justified text and text wraparounds require deft, careful attention. Combined, they are especially demanding. Justified text forces every line to be the same length, and in doing so alters the normal letter and word spacing built into the font by the type designer. This sometimes creates holes, or rivers of white, in the text where additional space has been added to fill out a line. Occasionally, it forces letters closer together than they should be. These inconsistencies in spacing make text difficult to read and give the type an uneven color on the page. The relatively wide column measure on these two pages minimizes these problems.

When you wrap text around a graphic, you narrow the column measure at certain points, which accentuates the problems inherent in justified type and adds an additional risk of excessive hyphenation. As an extreme, consider the last three lines wrapped around the truck illustration, which are less than ten characters long.

For wraparound text to be effective, it must have a smooth, even edge that echoes the shape of the graphic. (For that reason, you would rarely wrap ragged right text around a graphic.) Also, the distance between the text and the graphic should generally be uniform on all sides of the graphic. Something as seemingly commonplace as the beginning or end of a paragraph can interrupt the crisp

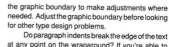

edge of the type.

After you place text around a graphic, check the type carefully. Is the space around the graphic equal on all sides? If not, drag individual lines of the graphic boundary to make adjustments where needed. Adjust the graphic boundary before looking for other type design problems.

Do paragraph indents break the edge of the text at any point on the wraparound? If you're able to combine or split apart paragraphs without creating grammatical errors, consider yourself blessed with a simple solution. Sometimes you have to rewrite portions of the text to solve the problem. You may end up having to choose between editing text more for visual appearance than for content and going with an imperfect wrap.

Are there lines with too much (or too little) space between words? Changing the Word Space values to 80% generally helps. (See the instructions in the blueprint.) But PageMaker 3.0 has the severe limitation that spacing values apply to entire text blocks, not just to selected lines or passages. Thus the only way to correct unacceptable spacing in individual lines is to kern letter pairs in those lines.

If this seems like a great deal of trouble, you're absolutely right. Even with the 3.0 release, spacing controls are not PageMaker's strong suit. That's why so many documents created with PageMaker and other desktop-publishing programs favor ragged

wraparounds sparingly. Be forewarned.

justified text and text wraparounds require deft, careful attention. Combined, they are especially demanding. Justified text forces every line to be the same length, and in doing so alters the normal letter and word spacing built into the font by the type designer. This sometimes creates holes, or rivers of white, in the text where additional space has been added to fill out a line. Occasionally, it forces letters closer together than they should be. These inconsistencies make text difficult to read and give type an uneven color on the page. The relatively wide column measure in this brochure minimizes these problems.

When you wrap text around a graphic, you narrow the column measure at certain points, which accentuates the problems inherent in justified type and adds an additional risk of excessive hyphenation. As an extreme, consider the last three lines wrapped around the truck, which are each less than ten characters long.

For wraparound text to be effective, it must have a smooth, even edge that echoes the shape of the graphic. Also, the distance between the text and the graphic should generally be uniform on all sides of the graphic. Something as commonplace as the beginning or end of a paragraph can interrupt the crisp edge of the type.

After you place text around a graphic, check the type carefully. Is the space around the graphic equal on all sides? If not, drag individual lines of

the graphic boundary to make adjustments where needed. Adjust the graphic boundary before looking for other type design problems.

Do paragraph indents break the edge of the text at any point on the wraparound? If you're able to combine or split apart paragraphs without creating grammatical errors, consider yourself blessed with a simple solution. Sometimes you have to rewrite portions of the text to solve the problem. You may end up having to choose between editing text more for visual appearance than for content and going with an imperfect wrap.

Are there lines with too much (or too little) space between words? Changing the Word Space values to 80% generally helps. (See the instructions in the blueprint.) But PageMaker 3.0 has the severe limitation that spacing values apply to entire text blocks, not just to selected lines or passages. Thus the only way to correct unacceptable spacing in individual lines is to kern letter pairs in those lines.

If this seems like a great deal of trouble, you're absolutely right. Even with the 3.0 release, spacing controls are not PageMaker's strong suit. That's why so many documents created with PageMaker and most other desktop-publishing programs favor ragged right over justified text and use text wraparounds sparingly. Consider yourself forewarned if you use this kind of typography in your own documents.

THE PULL QUOTE

The display copy on page 3 is a pull quote (also called a breakout) excerpted from the running text.

1. Copy and paste the text.

With the text tool, select the last two-and-a-quarter lines in the first paragraph, beginning with the phrase "at American Crossroads." Copy this text, then paste it into the opening in the center column on page 3. Change the type specs to 14/18 Bookman bold. Using the Paragraph command, center the block and turn off Auto Hyphenation. Change the capitalization and punctuation for grammar and emphasis. Then rebreak the lines to create an interesting text shape, keeping the sentence structure of the text in mind as you do.

In the screen detail at right, the text is electronically centered. In the detail at far right, the line breaks have been forced to create an interesting silhouette that reinforces the sentence structure and key points. When forcing line breaks in PageMaker, be sure the spacing for that paragraph is set at 0.

At American Crossroads, every truck, warehouse, and regional office is on line 24 hours a day. Every day of the year.

At American Crossroads, every truck, warehouse, and regional office is on line 24 hours a day. Every day of the year.

2. Adjust the position of the text.

Hold down the Shift key and center the text vertically in the space between the double rules and the photograph.

3. Adjust the position of the double rules above the pull quote.

The top of the top rule should align with the x-height of the first line of running text on either side. (Be sure to select both rules.) If the top rule aligned with the ascenders at the top margin, the rules would appear to sit above the text, because the x-height, not the ascenders, defines the visual height of the text block.

TIP

When ascenders align with the top margin, as they usually do, the x-height provides the strongest visual alignment for graphic elements such as rules.

THE TRUCK LOGO

The logo was created in Adobe Illustrator, but you can make a reasonable facsimile by drawing 8-point rules at a 45-degree angle with a 3-point space between each pair of rules. (You can create a 3-point spacing guide by butting a 2-point rule against a 1-point rule.) It's difficult to draw diagonal lines in PageMaker that are the same length in different directions, so you have to eyeball this as best you can.

Add the logo to the squares you copied to the pasteboard in step 5 of "Place and Refine the Running Text." Select the entire unit, copy it, and then move the copy onto the truck. The left edge of the white square is 5p from the back of the truck, and the bottom of the white square is 6p6 below the top of the truck.

> **TIP**
>
> Hold down the Shift key while you are drawing with the diagonal line tool to maintain a 45-degree angle.

On the pasteboard, type "American Crossroads" in 30/Auto Bookman bold. Tighten up the handles around the type and move it into position on the truck so that the baseline is flush with the bottom of the white square.

If at any point the logo and text disappear behind the truck, select the truck and choose the Send to Back command.

THE TEXT ON THE BACK COVER

Move the logo unit from the pasteboard to the page. The top of the white square is 4p6 from the top of the page, and the left edge is aligned at the left margin.

Add the address in the upper right corner. Type each line as a separate text block and position it inside the vertical space defined by the top and bottom of the squares. The text is Bookman; "American Crossroads" is 18-point boldface, "Shipping Company" is 14-point boldface, and the address is 10-point roman.

Place the list of regional offices. The tops of the caps in the headline are flush with the top margin.

AND A FEW OTHER PAGEMAKER EXERCISES...

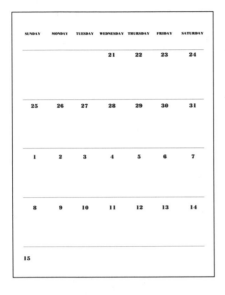

PageMaker calendars are useful for managing work flow, and making them provides practice with the Tabs and Paragraph commands. To set up the tabs, work at a small enough page view so that the ruler in the Indents/Tabs box is wider than the page. That way you'll be able to relate each click in the tabs ruler to its actual position on the page. For the first pass through, position the tabs quickly. You can adjust their placement later.

To create the horizontal spacing, specify a generous value for Space After in the Paragraph Specifications dialog box. And then adjust that value until the weeks you have on your calendar fill out the page.

In the sample shown, the type is Bodoni Poster (10/Auto for the names of days, 16/Auto for the numbers); the Space After is 4p following the names and 11p after the numbers. (Each row is considered a paragraph because it is preceded by a carriage return.) The tabs are center-aligned at 3p, 9p6, 16p, 23p, 29p9, 36p3, and 43p3.

Creating a skyline will give you a good workout with PageMaker's drawing tools and layering logic. You can overlap shapes, change their height or width, play with different shades for the fill, and use reverse diagonal rules to create angular, postmodern lines.

The moving announcement below was created through a playful, trial-and-error approach (and a great many printouts) until a satisfying effect was achieved.

As the skyline developed, we used the Send to Back/Bring to Front commands to create a sense of depth. All the shadows on the sides of the buildings are 80%, and those on the ground are solid black.

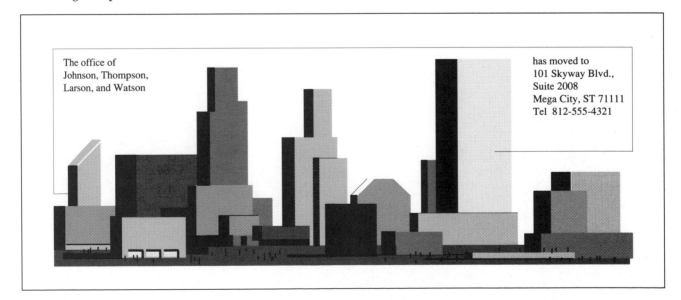

The office of
Johnson, Thompson,
Larson, and Watson

has moved to
101 Skyway Blvd.,
Suite 2008
Mega City, ST 71111
Tel 812-555-4321

Patterns require planning and precision, but the results can be well worth the effort. The basic procedure is fairly straightforward, although there are many different ways to execute the steps:

- Determine the design motif of the pattern.

- Determine the density of the pattern on the page.

- Establish the grid for the pattern by dividing the page size by the number of pattern units.

- Create the grid in PageMaker.

  You can use the Column Guides command to divide a page into equal vertical units (specify 0 as the space between columns) and the custom vertical ruler to measure the horizontal units. (There are three tick marks on the ruler between intervals in whatever measurement you specify.) If you are using a character for your design motif, such as the Zapf Dingbat in the invitation below, you can create the grid using a combination of tabs and paragraph spacing, as described for the calendar.

- Place or create the art for the pattern on the page, then copy, paste, and position it on the grid.

In this invitation, we created the pattern from an 18-point Zapf Dingbat (the keystroke is Shift-9) with nine spaces between each plane.

The page size was 33 picas square, and in order to create 8 equal horizontal units we ended up with the odd measurement of 4p1.5, or 49.5 points. By specifying this value as the custom unit of measure for the vertical ruler, we could easily bring in ruler guides to create the horizontal grid.

After making the first row of planes, we copied and pasted it on the horizontal grid, bringing in vertical ruler guides to align the noses of planes in alternate rows.

THE BACK OF THE BOOK

▼
▼
▼
▼
▼

SOME NOTES ON HOW WE PRODUCED THIS BOOK

"Are you doing it from the desktop?" people would ask. It never occurred to us to do it any other way. We had two agreements with Microsoft Press. One was an author's agreement to write the book. The other was a production agreement to provide electronically composed pages on disk—accompanied by LaserWriter proofs—ready for output on Microsoft's Linotronic 300 imagesetter. That meant that we would serve not only as writers but as designers, typesetters, layout artists, and control central for the book over the course of the year it would take to create it.

In traditional publishing, most books are created in a linear fashion, moving in separate stages from writer to editor to copyeditor to designer to typesetter to proofreader to pasteup artist. At each stage, the content is further transformed from simple manuscript into something that more closely resembles the printed page. This book was created in a much more circular fashion, with most of the production stages existing concurrently.

A single "electronic" copy of this book (excluding the front and back covers) comes to about 18.6 MB of PageMaker files. This includes all the text, screen images, and sample documents that we created, but not, of course, the previously printed documents that were stripped in by the printer.

Before we began writing, we established the 8-1/2- by 11-inch trim size so that we could reproduce sample documents (most of which are also 8-1/2 by 11) as large as possible. But that page size risked being too dense for the instructional material in the project section. So very early on we developed the basic wide-plus-narrow-column grid, which provided the flexibility to move back and forth between a single wide-column format for running text and instructions and a three-column format for art annotations.

We selected the basic type styles—Palatino for body text and the Helvetica family for headlines, captions, and annotations—fairly early as well, although the size and spacing of some elements evolved throughout the entire course of the book's production in a way that would be prohibitively expensive in traditional book publishing. Of course, functioning as typesetters also enabled us to continue adding and editing copy literally through the final weeks of production.

The great advantage of this process was that as creators of the book we could refine the ideas and the presentation simultaneously to an extent that simply isn't possible when a book moves through a linear production process. The disadvantage was that we were juggling so many tasks at once— writing headlines for a sample document one moment, fussing with the alignment of a hanging indent the next, developing the structure of an entire chapter on the heels of that, and, inevitably, solving systems problems whenever they demanded our attention.

Still, having worked in both traditional and desktop publishing, we'll gladly continue to wrestle with the disadvantages of the desktop approach. It's important to keep in mind, also, that a great deal of the

OUR WORKSTATIONS

When we did our very first PageMaker document, we shared a Mac Plus and a LaserWriter Plus. We saw desktop publishing as a grand experiment. Even if the technology couldn't do what the hype promised—well, it was time we had a computer anyway.

After years of traditional publishing, we were giddy when the experiment worked and we produced a sixteen-page brochure, cover to cover, from our home in the mountains two-and-a-half hours away from New York City. But even at the height of our early excitement, we knew that our test system was in no way sufficient for serious production. The shopping list—and the purchases—grew with our enthusiasm; by the time we were gearing up to do this book, bigger and more complex by far than anything we'd done, we joked (having recently read Tom Wolfe's *The Bonfire of the Vanities*) that we were hemorrhaging money.

Here then, are our two workstations:

The hot-rodded Mac Plus: We enhanced our original Mac with a Radius Accelerator Board to increase the speed, a 2 megabyte memory upgrade (for a total of 2.5 MB of RAM) so that we could run MultiFinder, and a Radius Full Page Display to make it a two-monitor system. This station has a Jasmine Direct Drive 50, a DataDesk extended keyboard, a Kensington Turbo Mouse, and a Hayes 2400 modem. We did all of the word processing and administrative work on this system and some page layout and corrections.

The Mac II: Our Mac II has 5 megabytes of internal memory, a Jasmine 90 internal drive, a 13-inch Apple Color Monitor, a 24-inch Moniterm Viking monitor (monochrome), an Apple Extended Keyboard, a Datacopy Proscan 730, and a stylus-driven MacTablet. We created most of the sample documents and page layouts on this system and used it, whenever it was available, for page corrections as well.

The two systems are connected to each other through Tops, and both are connected to an Apple LaserWriter NTX printer via AppleTalk. The NTX makes us realize how slow our original LaserWriter Plus was.

We cannot say enough about the value of large monitors. Trying to design and lay out pages without being able to see the entire canvas is a little like doing manual pasteup with one hand. It's also time-consuming: the process of scrolling around a page on a small monitor and waiting for the screen to redraw at each new position slows page assembly to a degree that is inconsistent with a professional environment. Our 24-inch Moniterm displays two 8-1/2- by 11-inch pages at Actual Size, which brings a real-time/real-space immediacy to electronic page assembly. The small screens that served the desktop pioneers are adequate only for organizations with limited publishing needs. If you have ongoing publishing requirements of any complexity, a large monitor (a full page display, 19-inch or larger) is a must. Otherwise, you may be wasting in time what you're saving in type costs.

The advantages of having a two-monitor system should not be overlooked. Even though you can't have two PageMaker documents open at once, it is extremely convenient to leave a Scrapbook, a style sheet, a spreadsheet, or any number of other things open on the small screen while you compose the page on the large screen.

In addition to our high-tech tools, we have lumbosacral supports in the chairs at both workstations to help prevent the low-back pain that so often results from long hours spent at the computer. (Many chiropractors sell these supports.) And one of us also uses an adjustable footrest (available from mail-order catalogs that feature office products) to encourage healthier sitting posture. Both devices are inexpensive and, in our opinion, invaluable.

work that is done using electronic production involves larger work groups than our own, and thus it has a different production rhythm. Still, many of the techniques we used—and an understanding of some of the problems we encountered—are useful regardless of the configuration of the production team.

Using placeholders

Because of the very different nature of the material in the three sections of the book, each section followed a slightly different course as it was developed and produced.

The project chapters were created in a way that most closely resembles traditional publishing. They were written in Microsoft Word, sent as manuscript (with screen dumps printed as loose art) to Rebecca Pepper, one of our editors, who—in addition to copy editing—also tested all of the Macintosh-generated instructions using the PC version of PageMaker. While she was editing the early projects, we created sample pages in PageMaker, developing type styles that would be applied to the edited manuscript. Editorial changes were made in the word-processing files, some styles were defined and applied there, and then the text and the art were placed in PageMaker.

By the time we were ready to assemble the project pages in PageMaker, we had a project template with a style sheet and numerous place-holders on the pasteboard. Placeholders are an invaluable aspect of working in PageMaker, and a brief description of how they were used in this book may be useful to you in your own publication work.

Consider, for example, tips such as the one at left, with a black box, a reverse type headline, and text inside a frame consisting of two hairline rules. By leaving a master unit on the pasteboard, we were assured that the headline would always be in the same place in the box and that the baseline of the first line of text relative to the box would remain consistent as well. Each time we needed a tip, we drew a marquee around the master on the pasteboard, copied it, and pasted it into position on the page. Then we cut the tip from the main text, thus moving it to the clipboard; dragged over the text in the tip placeholder that had been copied onto the page; and pasted the tip from the clipboard over that. Finally, we selected the vertical hairline rule in the tip frame and, holding down the Shift key to constrain movement, lengthened or shortened the rule so that it would align with the baseline of the last line of the tip.

We found it easier to embed the tips in the running text and then cut and paste them than to create a separate file of tips and try to code them or remember which tip belonged with which instructions. By applying the *Tip* style in the word processor, we could easily spot them in the running text after the file was placed in PageMaker, and the formatting was preserved when the tip text was pasted over the place-holder text. Note also that when you cut material from a text block and paste it outside of the text block, as we did with the tips, that material

---

TIP

When you *paste* text over the text in a placeholder, as we did with many of the tips in this book, the type specs of the pasted text match those of the original text that was cut or copied, but the margins of the pasted text match those of the text in the placeholder. When you *type* new text over text in a placeholder, as we did with many of the captions, the type specs match the style of the placeholder text.

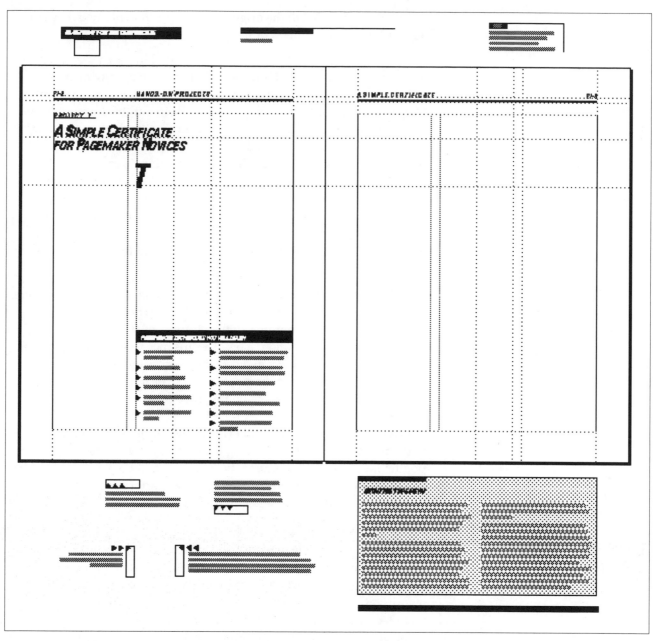

▲ ▲ ▲

The opening spread of the template for the Hands-On Projects shows the basic grid as well as some of the placeholders on the pasteboard. In reality, we had copies of the tip and caption placeholders on different sides of the pasteboard so that they would be easy to get to. (We also had a Scrapbook of all the placeholders so that we'd have quick access to a replacement in case we used or messed up the one on the pasteboard.)

The placeholder for this caption is just below the left-hand page. We copied and pasted it and then positioned the copy so that the top of the box around the arrows aligned with the bottom of the frame around the art. The text in the caption placeholder is a single-column measure; to extend this caption across two columns, we simply selected the text in the placeholder copy, held down the Shift key, stretched the handles to the desired width, and typed the real caption over the one in the placeholder copy. Finally, we selected and deleted the box around the arrows that was used as spacing guide.

is no longer threaded to the original text. For self-contained text, such as tips and captions, this is desirable.

The captions in the project section were treated in much the same way as the tips. But we needed four placeholders: one each with arrows pointing up, down, right, and left. (If we had been able to use Zapf Dingbats for the arrows, they could have been part of the text, simplifying spacing; but in Dingbats there are no right and left arrows in the style we wanted, so we created the arrows in Illustrator and placed them in PageMaker as an EPS file.) Some captions were written in PageMaker, and some of them were cut from the running text. By juggling information among the running text, tips, and captions, we gained considerable control over the relationship of text and visuals and over page breaks as well. This is one aspect of page assembly in which PageMaker provides hands-on control and flexibility that are truly fantastic.

The sidebars in the project section were also created with placeholders. Most of the sidebars have a two-column format; because the text is boxed along the page margins, both columns must be indented from the margins. Having found it a bit of a nuisance to set up new column guides for each sidebar, we avoided the process by using a placeholder: We simply placed the sidebar text over the placeholder text using the Replace Entire Story option in PageMaker's Place dialog box. The new text poured in directly over the placeholder text, maintaining the style of the new text but adhering to the margins that were set up in the placeholder. After replacing the text in this way, we used the pointer tool to adjust the size of the box itself and the length of the text blocks inside it. We added the gray tint (10%) after the text was final. (It is very difficult to read and edit text over a gray tint on-screen.)

Smart scrapbooks and EPS files

The portfolio section was created in a rather different way from the project section. The portfolio template had a three-column measure and many fewer styles than the project template. We did rough pencil layouts on paper to determine the order and size of the samples included in each chapter. Then we created page frames for the art in FreeHand and copied those frames into different Scrapbooks (8-1/2 by 11 vertical, 8-1/2 by 11 landscape, 11 by 17, 7-1/2 by 10, special sizes, and so on). As we assembled the skeleton of each chapter, we called up the appropriate Scrapbook, scrolled to find the reduction we needed (52%, 38%, and so on), and copied and pasted that frame on the page. Once we had all the frames in place, the amount of space for annotations was clearly visible on the page, and we wrote the text for these chapters directly in PageMaker. We felt in some ways that we were breaking the rules—PageMaker is not a word processor—but the ability to see the available space fill up as you write facilitates writing to fit to an almost incredible degree. Of course, there's no spell checker or global search-and-replace option in PageMaker, and editing text at the beginning of a six-paragraph text block can be slow because the

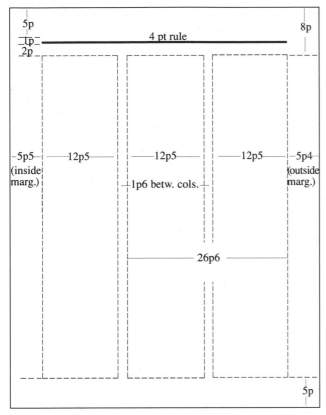

5p

8p

1p

2p

4 pt rule

5p5
(inside
marg.)

12p5

12p5

12p5

5p4
(outside
marg.)

1p6 betw. cols.

26p6

5p

▲ ▲ ▲

The blueprint showing the grid for this book, like the blueprints in the grid chapter, was created as a full-size PageMaker document, saved as an Encapsulated PostScript file, and placed inside a page frame in the actual book pages. We determined that all the blueprints would be reduced to either 38% or 52%. For the 38% reductions, we used 22-point type; for the 52% reductions, 16-point type. This gave the blueprints a consistent look throughout the book.

Styles used in this book

changes have to ripple through the entire block. You can speed this up, though, by dragging the window-shade handles to temporarily hide the copy at the end of the text block while you edit text at the beginning. Then drag the handles back down to reveal subsequent text until you've finished editing. The text remains in PageMaker's memory while you edit, but it doesn't physically have to respond to changes you're making elsewhere as you make them.

It's important to note that the screen legibility of many typefaces in body text sizes is not great in PageMaker, even at Actual Size. We do on-screen writing and editing at 200% on large monitors. At 200% on our 24-inch Moniterm screen, you can see all three columns across half an 8-1/2- by 11-inch page . Working on a small screen, you would spend so much time scrolling and waiting for the screen to redraw that writing more than a few sentences would not be practical.

The grid chapter in Section 1 was handled similarly to the portfolio chapters, although here, of course, we also had to create many of the sample documents and blueprints. The sample documents that are reproduced in a reduced size were saved as Encapsulated PostScript files and then placed electronically in the book pages. The Replacing Entire Graphic Option was a great time-saver with these documents. Using the page-frame Scrapbooks described for the portfolio section, we copied and pasted the desired frames onto the page; but in the grid chapter, we also pasted a second copy of the frame directly over the first. (You know one is directly on top of the other when they both disappear.) Then we selected the top frame, went to the Place dialog box, selected the EPS document we wanted from our directory, and clicked on the Replacing Entire Graphic option. PageMaker automatically reduced the new graphic (in this case, the EPS file) to fit and replace the old (the top copy of the page frame); the bottom copy of the page frame remained to define the page trim.

Whether you define and apply styles in your word processor or in PageMaker depends on a great many variables, including the complexity of the document, the ease of applying styles in your word processor, the structure of your publication team, and the size of your monitor. We used both approaches in the course of preparing this book.

When you're working on a document with a great many styles, it's very helpful to have a printout of the style sheet for reference. You can't print a style sheet in PageMaker 3.0, but we were able to work around this by exporting text from PageMaker to Microsoft Word. PageMaker exports the style sheet along with the text. In Word, if you choose Print while the Define Styles dialog box is open, Word will print the styles list in whatever typeface is defined as Normal for that publication. Text that is not threaded to the main story (such as captions) is not exported, so you might have to add some styles in Word. Also, styles that don't carry over to the word processor (such as reverse type) and style overrides (such as initial caps) will not be included, but these are relatively easy to add by hand.

We've divided the styles listed on these two pages into two groups. In fact, there is some overlap, and the lists do not include every style that we used. But these divisions should help those of you who want to see how we used style sheets or to identify specific type specs in the book.

The wording of each style definition is as it appears in PageMaker's Styles list. Type size and leading are expressed in points; indents and paragraph spacing are in picas. The definition of a style that is based on another style begins with the name of that other style. Information in parentheses indicates a style override, such as an initial cap, which you must format manually.

When you begin adding fonts to your system, the organization of the type menu is confusing. Screen fonts are grouped alphabetically by styles (bold, condensed, italic, and so on) rather than by families. So to select Helvetica Light, the face used in the first style below, you scroll to the L's, not the H's. The first letter of the style (in this case L) precedes the name of the type family. Some oblique fonts are listed under I for italic, others under O for Oblique. You get used to it eventually.

Styles in Sections 1 and 2

Style Name	Definition
art annotations	face: L Helvetica Light + size: 9 + leading: 11 + flush left + space after: 0p5.5 + kerning above: 12 + auto hyphenation (+ Helvetica Black leadins)
caption	face: LI Helvetica Light Oblique + size: 9 + leading: 11 + flush left + kerning above: 12
chapter #	running head
chapter text	project text + leading: 13 + space after: 0p6.5
continued line	caption + flush right
credit-design	credit-samples + space after: 0p3
credit-samples	caption + size: 8 + leading: 10
cross-references	caption + centered
head-bannered	head-chapter + size: 13 + leading: 16 + color: Paper + flush left + space after: 1p7 + kerning above: 12
head-chapter	face: CLBI Helvetica Condensed BlackObl + all caps + size 24 + leading: 26 + flush left + kerning above: 12 (+ 30 point initial cap + kerning as needed)
head-initial cap	head-chapter - all caps + size: 13 + leading: 14
portfolio samples list	chapter text + left indent: 1p2 + first indent: -1p2 + space after: 0p3
running head	face: CLI Helvetica Condensed LightObl + all caps + size: 12 (+ 100% letterspace)

Styles in Section 3

Style Name	Definition
# instructions	face: CLBI Helvetica Condensed BlackObl + size: 11 + Leading: 12 + flush left + left indent: 1 + first indent: -1
# 1 instructions	# instructions + space before: 3
1p hanging indent	project text + left indent: 1 + first indent: -1
1p indent	project text + left indent: 1
1p6 indent	project text + left indent: 1p6
2p indent	project text + left indent: 2
3p indent	project text + left indent: 3
bullets fl left	project text + left indent: 1 + first indent: -1
bullets hang from #	project text + left indent: 2 + first indent: -1
head-bannered	head-chapter + size: 13 + leading: 16 + color: Paper + flush left + space after: 1p7 + kerning above: 12
head-project	face: CLBI Helvetica Condensed BlackObl + all caps + size 24 +leading: 26 + flush left + kerning above: 12 (+ 30 point initial cap + kerning as needed)
head-column	head-project + size: 11 + leading: 12 + space after: 0p6
head-project B	head-project + size: 18 + leading: 18 (+ 24 point initial cap + kerning as needed)
head-sidebar	head-project + size: 13 + leading: 15 + space after: 0p11
head-tips	head-project + size: 9 + leading:9 + color: Paper
head-un#	head-column - all caps + left indent: 1 + first line indent: -1 + space before: 1p6
PM techniques list	face: L Helvetica Light + size: 9 + leading: 11 + space after: 0p9
project text	face: Palatino + size: 10 + leading: 12 + flush left + space after: 0p6 + kerning above: 12 + auto hyphenation
tips	face: L Helvetica Light + size: 9 + leading: 11 + flush left +right indent: 0p6 + space after: 0p6 + kerning above: 12

File size and pagination

Throughout the book, we started with chapter-length files and broke them into even smaller units as needed. The number of pages that constitutes a manageable file depends on the complexity of the pages. Chapters 1 and 4, for example, are mostly running text; at 116 KB and 11 KB respectively, they are quite manageable as single files. The grid chapter, on the other hand, is 60 pages long, and many of these are graphics-intensive. We gradually broke that chapter down into 8 different files, ranging in size from 320 KB to 1.35 MB and adding up to well over 5 MB.

We used composite page-number markers to number pages by chapter. So Chapter 1 was numbered 1-2, 1-3, 1-4, and so on. We had decided with Microsoft that final pagination would be pasted in by hand after the Linotronic pages were printed. This gave us the flexibility of adding pages to any chapter right up to the final weeks of production, which we did.

The cover

A cover such as this, which combines two photographs, a variety of graphic elements, and type, is traditionally created by a combination of calculation, guesswork, and the imprecise art of previsualizing how all the elements and the colors you've chosen will come together. And although we didn't push the technology to its limits in producing what you see on the cover of this book, desktop tools were invaluable in eliminating some of the guesswork involved in developing a tight layout for the commercial separator and printer to follow.

We provided a sketch to photographer Walter Wick, who is a master of special effects. For the shot of the art materials, he glued each object, in-

dividually, to a flexible aluminum wire that was in turn glued to a sheet of four-by-six-foot plexiglass, carefully positioning each object to hide its wire from the camera. Opaque objects overlap transparent ones for the same purpose. He used a lot of light in this shot to bring out the bright colors in the materials. For the shot of the computer, on the other hand, he used less light in order to emphasize the form.

In order to design the type around the graphics, we had color laser copies made from the chromes, which we scanned with a Datacopy 730 as low-resolution MacPaint files. Paint files are transparent, and they enabled us to see the two photos on-screen as a composite. (TIFF and EPS files are opaque.) We then imported the scans into FreeHand, where we sized them, composed the type around them, and selected the colors. The title is Futura Bold Condensed, further condensed in FreeHand; the subtitle and byline are Garamond, also condensed in FreeHand.

Once the layout was finalized electronically, Microsoft used traditional methods for actual production. The black plate from the FreeHand document was printed on their L300 and pasted up as a mechanical. Their color separator combined the two transparencies into one image and manipulated the photo using CEPs and used laser printouts of the cover composite to redraw the graphic elements on a high-resolution, commercial CAD system.

▲ ▲ ▲

The cover layout was created in FreeHand, using low-resolution, bit-mapped scans of the photographs.

Backup strategy

These notes would not be complete without some mention of backup procedures. Using DiskFit, we backed up both hard disks daily. We had a second backup (updated manually once a week) of the book pages in their current PageMaker form. And we believe that this backup strategy was barely adequate to guard against the potential loss of work. We know of one design studio that keeps a backup, updated weekly, off the premises, and we feel somewhat remiss in not adhering to a similarly cautious system.

On one occasion, the DiskFit backup enabled us to restore inadvertently deleted files. On another, the second backup set gave us access to a file that had been corrupted and backed up through DiskFit in its corrupted form. And yes, having a backup did save us on one occasion from losing the entire book. We were a month away from completion, and were it not for our DiskFit backup you would not be holding this book in your hands.

Compatibility with Linotronic imagesetters

Do not assume that whatever can be successfully printed on your desktop printer can be successfully printed on a higher-resolution imagesetter. The compatibility between low- and high-end output devices is sometimes mysteriously imperfect.

We had been concerned early on about printing the EPS files on the L300. The original release of PageMaker 3.0 consistently scrambled type placement when a Linotronic attempted to print pages containing EPS files. This bug was supposedly corrected in version 3.01, and the test pages we sent to Microsoft using 3.01 printed beautifully. But when Microsoft began printing final pages for the book, about half the pages with EPS files had the same problems encountered in 3.0. For many of the pages, Microsoft solved the problem by removing the resident fonts from the PostScript RIP that drives their L300 and downloading them. For some pages, we had to submit new files. (All of the EPS files were made in the same way.)

The typography chapter also presented problems because of its many typeface displays. The pages with those displays were created at a service center in New York City (Microcomputer Publishing Center), where we had access to the entire Adobe type library and some technical assistance in resolving font ID problems.

The problem of conflicting fonts exists because there are more screen fonts than font numbers in the Macintosh environment. When two screen fonts have the same number, you might specify one font on the Type menu but see a different one displayed and printed. Our problem was solved through a two-step process. First, we used Font Harmony (part of Suitcase II). This utility automatically finds and resolves ID problems by renumbering all the specified fonts using the New Font Numbering Table (NFNT), which allows for 1600 fonts. But the computer driving the L300 at Micropublishing does not use the NFNT. So the second part of the solution was to make a PostScript file of each page, thus bypassing the need for information about screen fonts.

We cannot emphasize enough the need to work closely with the service center or publisher who will be doing your high-resolution output. Submit test pages early—and throughout the production process if necessary. Be sure your test documents are representative of the toughest problems you expect to encounter. And then, when all is said and done, leave time in the schedule to solve the problems that will inevitably crop up anyway.

SOFTWARE WE USED A LOT (IN ADDITION, OF COURSE, TO PAGEMAKER)

Applications

Microsoft Word (Microsoft Corporation): For compatibility with PageMaker, Microsoft Word is hard to match. We wrote, edited, spell-checked, and formatted about half the text in Word before placing it in PageMaker.

Illustrator (Adobe): For creating page frames and other precise line art.

FreeHand (Aldus): For setting condensed, expanded, and rotated type and for creating page frames.

MacImage (Datacopy): The scanning software for our Datacopy 730.

ImageStudio (Letraset): For retouching digitized images.

MacPaint (Claris): For cleaning up screen dumps made on the Mac II and for manipulating bit-mapped clip art.

SuperPaint (Silicon Beach): For editing screen dumps made with Capture.

Microsoft Works (Microsoft Corporation): We used the database in Works to keep track of samples, permissions, and copyrights from the many designers and organizations who sent us their work.

Smartcom II (Hayes): Telecommunications software for our Hayes 2400 modem.

DiskExpress (ALSoft, Inc.) As a hard disk becomes full, it may have to store information for a single file in different locations. As a result, when you open or save a file, the drive heads have to search to find not just one file, but various fragments of it. Periodically, we ran DiskExpress to compact these fragmented files and speed up disk performance.

DiskFit (SuperMac Software): The easier it is to back up your files, the more frequently you'll do so. DiskFit is remarkably easy to use, and we used it every day.

Tops (Sun Microsystems): Without a spare computer to use as a file server, we used Tops to network our two workstations.

Desk Accessories, Utilities, and INITs

Capture (Mainstay): Capture enables you to save part of a screen image by dragging a crosshair cursor over the area you want to capture. This eliminates some of the cleaning up necessary with traditional screen dumps. But the crosshair replaces the pointer in the screen you're capturing, so this program doesn't work for screens in which you want the pointer to be included.

DeskPaint (Zedcor): This desk accessory enables you to create and edit Paint and TIFF documents while working in another application. We used DeskPaint to crop screen dumps as we assembled the pages and to manipulate clip art.

DiskTop (CE Software): Invaluable as a file-management desk accessory. We used it constantly to move, rename, and delete files as well as to find them.

LaserStatus (CE Software): A desk accessory packaged with DiskTop, LaserStatus has a wonderful feature that enables you to create sets of downloadable fonts. There are five Helvetica fonts used throughout the book; by configuring them as a set in LaserStatus, we could download them with one simple operation instead of going through the series of Font Downloader dialog boxes for each of the five fonts.

SmartScrap (Solutions International): Thanks to SmartScrap we had a dozen manageable scrapbooks for the book, each named and filed as any other document would be.

WordFinder (Microlytics, Inc.): This on-line thesaurus doesn't deliver a satisfactory synonym as often as our printed Roget's, but it's helpful to have. (And to some extent you can use it as a spell checker in PageMaker.) Then again, we know of nothing as helpful in finding exactly the right word as Webster's Second Unabridged.

Suitcase (Software Supply): This utility let us have automatic access to as many desk accessories and fonts as we had any right to want. The disk includes Pyro, a screen saver that self-installs when the mouse is inactive for a specified period of time.

Typefaces

The typefaces used throughout the book are from Adobe Systems, except as specified in the annotations (and undoubtedly in some samples reproduced from other designers). In addition to the fonts resident in most PostScript printers, the typefaces in the book are from the following families:

Aachen Bold

ITC American Typewriter

Bodoni

Franklin Gothic

Futura

Futura Condensed

ITC Galliard

ITC Garamond

Helvetica Condensed

Helvetica Light/Black

ITC Machine

Clip Art

We used a fair amount of clip art in the sample documents in Chapter 3, "Creating a Grid," for the same reason people often use clip art: it is a fast way to get graphics on a page. As is true for so many publications, we simply didn't have the budget to commission or the time to create much art. Using clip art also gave us the opportunity to display some of what is available, so you can use the samples shown in that chapter to guide you to packages that suit your needs.

The clip art we used came from the following packages:

Artware (Artware Systems)

DeskTop Art Business 1 (Dynamic Graphics)

Draw Art Volume 2 (Desktop Graphics)

Images with Impact (3G Graphics)

Logomaster (Moonlight Artworks)

The Mac Art Dept. (Simon & Schuster)

The MacMemories Catalog (ImageWorld, Inc.)

Moonlight Artworks 1 and 2

NewsletterMaker (Metro ImageBase)

ReportMaker (Metro ImageBase)

WetPaint (Dubl-Click Software)

RESOURCES

Whenever you see an image in a magazine or newspaper or even on a packet of cereal..., cut it out and keep it in a scrapbook. My own method is to put whatever I find into the book in no particular order, just lightly taped so it can be removed if necessary.... When searching for an idea ..., all sorts of images can be viewed that will start the mind working—and perhaps along different lines from the preconceived.... The brain has a great capacity for putting odd images together that it might not have thought up without this visual stimulus.

—Nigel Holmes,
Designer's Guide to Creating
Charts and Diagrams

Charts

Designer's Guide to Creating Charts & Diagrams by Nigel Holmes (1984, Watson-Guptill, 1515 Broadway, New York, NY 10036)

Created by the art director responsible for the charts and diagrams in *Time* magazine, this book provides carefully organized and accessible background on the various types of charts, suggestions on how to analyze information, and numerous examples and common errors. Particularly useful is the chapter on specific assignments, which takes the reader through the analysis of data and creation of charts for nine different problems. (Some problems have multiple audiences and hence multiple solutions.) Although the book predates desktop publishing's time-saving production tools, its conceptual and analytical approach is not the least bit dated.

Using Charts and Graphs: 1000 Ideas for Visual Persuasion by Jan V. White (1984, R.R. Bowker, 245 West 17th St., New York, NY 10011)

We didn't count, but this book probably does have a thousand ideas. And because the emphasis is more on geometrical than conceptual approaches, many of them can be executed with today's electronic drawing tools. (The book itself does not provide that how-to.)

Clip Art

Dover Pictorial Archive Book Catalog (Dover Publications, 31 East 2nd St., Mineola, NY 11501)

Electronic clip art is fairly expensive; traditional clip art is not. For years, Dover Books has been one of the largest suppliers of public domain (copyright-free) art. Their catalog lists over 300 books, with very few costing more than $10; many of them are less than $5. All you need to do is crop and scale the art and manually paste it onto the camera-ready pages.

Electronic Clip Art Collections

For a list of the clip art collections used in this book, see the software sidebar at the end of "Some Notes on How We Produced This Book."

The Electronic Clip Art Digest (1988, The Electronic Clip Art Company, 6376 Quail Run, Kalamazoo, MI 49009)

Volume 1, for the Macintosh, pictures and indexes some 15,000 clip art images from 30 companies in a 600-page looseleaf volume. Reproduction is at about 25 percent of original size. When you send in your registration, you receive a sampler disk with over 30 images. As a purchasing guide to the many clip art packages available, this is a useful, if pricey ($139.95, includes one update) addition to any desktop publishing library.

The Computer Culture and the Future

In addition to being extraordinary tools, computers hold a mirror to some aspects of the culture we live in. As such, they've inspired a number of interesting books by some good and provocative writers.

Computer Lib/Dream Machines by Ted Nelson (revised edition, 1987; Tempus Books, 16011 NE 36th Way, Redmond, WA 98073)

Considered the first cult book of the computer culture, it was first published in 1974, a few months before the announcement of the Altair. The visionary material from the first edition—with its prediction of user-friendly systems, computer-aided instruction, image synthesis, and more—and the new material added to the 1987 edition are served up in small bites in a quirky, nonlinear form that makes a kaleidoscope of the computer and its place in our lives.

The Media Lab: Inventing the Future at MIT by Steward Brand (1987, Viking, 40 West 23rd St., New York, NY 10010)

Apple Fellow Alan Kay has said that "The best way to predict the future is to invent it." And the Media Lab at MIT may well be where the future of publishing, broadcasting, film, and recording is being invented. *Whole Earth Catalog* founder Steward Brand spent several months there, and in addition to providing an in-depth tour of the Media Lab, offers his view of what it means in the larger media lab that we all live in.

The Soul of a New Machine by Tracy Kidder (paperback edition, 1981; Avon Books, 959 Eighth Ave., New York, NY 10019)

The story of the creation of the Eagle computer is told as a technological and human drama. Wonderfully written (the book won a Pulitzer Prize), it's a very enjoyable way to increase your understanding of computers.

Desktop-Published Classics

A great deal has been written about desktop publishing. The two books listed here simply showed what the technology could do and in the process either inspired or convinced a great many people that this particular emperor had clothes after all.

Whale Song: A Pictorial History of Whaling and Hawaii by MacKinnon Simpson and Robert B. Goodman (1986, Beyond Words Publishing, 112 Meleana Place, Honolulu, HI 96817)

This very beautiful history of nineteenth-century whaling does not in itself have anything to do with desktop publishing, except in demonstrating that the technology could be used for the craft of pictorial storytelling. Not only was this the first coffee-table book created with PageMaker, but it was produced from 300-dots-per-inch LaserWriter output on a special paper from S.D. Warren (with color separations done traditionally). A second edition using 600-dpi output will be published in 1989, with a new essay about the technology by photographer, designer, and publisher Bob Goodman.

Zen & The Art of the Macintosh: Discoveries on the Path to Computer Enlightenment by Michael Green (1986, Running Press, 125 South 22nd St., Philadelphia, PA 19103)

A passionately personal exploration of making art on the Macintosh, this book is a crazy quilt of fantastic bit-mapped graphics and 1980s zen musings. It is a testimonial to as well as a reflection on the incredible seductiveness of computers.

When [Media Lab director] Nicholas Negroponte and I originally discussed what this book might be about, he suggested, "It's about quality of life in an electronic age." A few months later he added, "It's a primer for a new life-style." Later still he mentioned, "I was still in my pajamas at ten-thirty this morning after I had been doing Lab work, through e-mail on my computer, for several hours. Maybe what we're talking about is 'The right to stay in your pajamas.'"

—Stewart Brand,
The Media Lab

Desktop Publishing

The Art of Desktop Publishing: Using Personal Computers to Publish It Yourself by Tony Bove, Cheryl Rhodes, and Wes Thomas (second edition, 1988; Bantam Books, 666 Fifth Ave., New York, NY 10103)

This was our introduction to desktop publishing, and its second edition remains an excellent overview of the tools and options of the trade.

DTP Advisor: The Desktop Publishing Tutorial and Project Management System (1988, Brøderbund Software, 17 Paul Drive, San Rafael, CA 94903)

Produced as a HyperCard stack, *DTP Advisor* provides a useful structure for planning and keeping track of publishing projects. You can call up a variety of forms with the click of a mouse: project-definition and cost estimating forms, an interactive scheduling calendar; forms for keeping track of freelance assignments, type specs, and printing specs; and a schematic sketchpad with Paint tools for creating rough dummies. (The Page Size option in the sketchpad lets you choose from one to eight pages.) You can file the forms in the folder for the project at hand and print them out as well. The database provides a structure for keeping track of artists, photographers, writers, printers, and other resources. The graphic design and printing tutorial is necessarily streamlined, but the information provided is good, if very basic. And both the screens and the *User's Guide* are themselves very nicely designed. (The HyperCard application is included in the two-disk set.)

The Electronic Publisher by Diane Burns, S. Venit, and Rebecca Hansen (1988, Brady/Simon & Schuster, 1230 Avenue of the Americas, New York, NY 10020)

Without focusing on any specific software, this book provides an overview of the publishing trade from the perspective of desktop production. Its strength lies in providing a good balance of the general and the specific in the areas of copyrights, design and typography, text processing, illustration, page composition, printing, and binding. Many of the illustrations are chosen with an eye toward demonstrating useful comparisons. For example, the same art is rendered as bit-mapped and object-oriented, and the printing time for each piece is given.

The Illustrated Handbook of Desktop Publishing and Typesetting by Michael L. Kleper (1987, TAB Books, P.O. Box 40, Blue Ridge Summit, PA 17294)

An encyclopedic reference covering both the PC and Macintosh environments, this is the most comprehensive (784 oversize pages) overview we've seen. Its review of hardware and software is already dated but still provides a tremendous amount of information on the options available. It also includes excellent information on typesetting from the perspective of a professional who truly understands the capabilities of desktop typesetting within the context of traditional graphic design and printing. If a second edition is published, don't pass it up.

Graphic Design: Formal and Historical Perspective

Graphic Style from Victorian to Post-Modern by Steven Heller and Seymour Chwast (1988, Harry N. Abrams, 100 Fifth Ave., New York, NY 10011)

A lavishly illustrated review of commercial art (from books to posters to shopping bags), this volume may not relate to your average business publication, but it is glorious to look at and shows how graphic design has interacted with popular tastes ranging from the Victorian to the punk.

There is the jigsaw puzzle aspect of design. The components are put together to tell a story so that the sum is more than its individual parts. In putting the puzzle together, some of the pieces will be changed to improve their fit and some of the pieces will be rejected because they don't contribute enough to the whole.

—DTP Advisor

The designer is confronted, primarily, with three classes of material: a) the given—product, copy, slogan, logotype, format, media, production process; b) the formal—space, contrast, proportion, harmony, rhythm, repetition, line, mass, shape, color, weight, volume, value, texture; c) the psychological—visual perception and optical illusion problems, the spectator's instincts, intuitions, and emotions as well as the designer's own needs.

—Paul Rand,
A Designer's Art

The Grid by Allen Hurlburt (1978, Van Nostrand Reinhold, 115 Fifth Ave., New York, NY 10003)

Allen Hurlburt, who was art director of *Look* magazine for many years, provides a brief and useful introduction to the history of grids along with a collection of grids created by top designers for newspapers, books, and magazines.

How to Understand and Use Design and Layout by Alan Swann (1987, North Light Books, 1507 Dana Ave., Cincinnati, OH 45207)

This book is organized as a three-section design course. The first section has the reader work with simple shapes and lines as a way of exploring proportion before bringing type, color, illustration, and photography onto the evolving page. The second section shows the elements of design applied to a wide variety of products (books, magazines, packaging, and posters). And the final section looks at the evolution of the design for specific products, including a print ad, a newsletter, a direct-mail insert, a full-color brochure, and a poster.

Publication Design: A Guide to Page Layout, Typography, Format and Style by Allen Hurlburt (1976, Van Nostrand Reinhold, 115 Fifth Ave., New York, NY 10003)

An illustrated review of significant developments in magazine design from the 1930s to the 1970s, this book covers a lot of ground briefly and well. Geared to the professional designer, the samples reproduced serve as a gallery of photography and art from a graphic design perspective.

Paul Rand: A Designer's Art (1985, Yale University Press, 302 Temple St., Princeton, NJ 06520)

Paul Rand is one of the giants of contemporary graphic design. This book collects several of his essays on design and displays a wide range of his work, including familiar trademarks (IBM, ABC, and Westinghouse), advertisements, and book and magazine covers.

Thirty Centuries of Graphic Design: An Illustrated Survey by James Craig and Bruce Barton (1987, Watson-Guptill, 1515 Broadway, New York, NY 10036)

Brief commentary and lots of reproductions are accompanied by a chronology of people and events for each era. Available in paperback, this is a useful addition to the library for the desktop designer who wants a sense of the history and traditions of graphic design.

Graphic Design: Tips and How-To Information

Editing by Design: A Guide to Effective Word-and-Picture Communication for Editors and Designers by Jan V. White (1982, R.R. Bowker, 245 West 17th St., New York, NY 10011)

Jan White has written many books about graphic design. The great benefit of this one is that it focuses on the interaction of words and pictures in a way that tries to bridge the gap between the way editors and graphic designers approach publications. In the desktop publishing environment, where traditional roles are being redefined, this perspective is especially useful.

Graphic Idea Notebook: Inventive Techniques for Designing Printed Pages by Jan V. White (1980, Watson-Guptill, 1515 Broadway, New York, NY 10036)

This book is bursting with ideas for how to treat various design components on the printed page. The material is broken out into usefully informal categories such as getting attention, mug shots, boxes, breaking up text, direction, motion and change, and so on. The book is delightfully written as well as playfully

---

In my view a great many well-conceived pieces of design are successful simply because they make full visual and creative use of a limited number of design elements. First, see how well the work develops using one element. Then sparingly introduce the other ingredients, making sure that they do not overwhelm the design. Never use anything for its own sake; always consider and justify its inclusion as a contributor to the overall effect.

　　　　　　　—Alan Swann,
　　　　　　How to Understand and
　　　　　　　Use Design and Layout

A clear area of white space can be as dramatic as a picture (especially if the picture is mediocre, as many often are). It gives the eye a place to rest. It can be a foil to the text: an "empty" contrast to the "full" areas that thereby makes the full areas appear even fuller. It can help to organize the material on the page. It can tie successive pages together by repetition of identifiable areas. White space, if used well, is the cheapest addition to the publication's roster of weapons.

　　　　　　　　　—Jan White,
　　　　　　　　Editing by Design

formatted, with easy-to-find ideas. It is virtually all photos, drawings, and geometric shapes, with very direct annotations on using the visual ideas displayed.

Looking Good in Print: A Guide to Basic Design for Desktop Publishing by Roger C. Parker (1988, Ventana Press, P.O. Box 2468, Chapel Hill, NC 27515)

A good introduction to the general principles of graphic design written for the hands-on desktop publisher who is a novice designer. Particularly useful are the makeover section, showing "before" and "after" versions of a dozen pages, and the sections showing how the same elements—headlines, text, and illustrations—can be designed into very different-looking pages.

Notes on Graphic Design and Visual Communication by Gregg Berryman (revised edition, 1984; William Kaufmann, Inc., 95 First Street, Los Altos, CA 94022)

Slim, inexpensive, and chock-full of useful information, this book is a well-organized collection of notes from the author's 15 years of teaching graphic design. In an age when many books have more white space than substance, this one's a gem.

Inspiration

Design Annuals

Flipping through any of the annual collections of leading work in editorial and advertising graphic design is a good way to stimulate ideas. These books also help you keep a finger on the pulse of the latest trends in typography, layout, illustration, and photography. They include *AIGA Graphic Design, Communication Arts Annual, Art Directors Annual,* and *Graphis Annual.*

The Design Concept : A Guide to Effective Graphic Communication by Allen Hurlburt (1981, Watson-Guptill, 1515 Broadway, New York, NY 10036)

Beginning with an overview of theories on the creative process, this book provides a useful look at the development of an idea. It is illustrated throughout with examples of leading work in advertising, editorial, and information design. The case histories are presented as recollections from a very impressive cast of designers (Paul Rand, Saul Bass, Brad Thompson, George Lois, Milton Glaser, Herb Lubalin, Lou Dorfsman, and Henry Wolf).

Forget All the Rules About Graphic Design (Including the Ones in This Book) by Bob Gill (1981, Watson-Guptill, 1515 Broadway, New York, NY 10036)

Bob Gill is a graphic designer, illustrator, and film-maker who describes his approach to design as taking ordinary boring problems and redefining them so that they are interesting or unique. This book is a collection of such problems and Gill's solutions to them. The title should give you a pretty good sense of his attitude, except that there are no rules in the book to break, just inventive ideas to inspire you.

Ideas on Design by the Pentagram Group (1986, Faber & Faber, Inc., 50 Cross St., Winchester MA 01890)

Through briefly annotated examples of the work of the Pentagram Group, this collection provides a glimpse into how designers come up with some of their ideas. Among the many examples: The colors and typography of a street sign inspire the sign for a boutique called Street Shoes; the relationship of a university health sciences department and the hospital with which it is affiliated is abstracted into a geometric logo, and a collection of found objects triggers the creation of an alphabet.

It is not possible to dig a hole in a different place by digging the same hole deeper and bigger.... If a hole is in the wrong place, then no amount of digging is going to put it in the right place. Vertical thinking is digging the same hole deeper; lateral thinking is trying again somewhere else.

—Edward de Bono,
cited in The Design Concept

Intuition...encourages the mind to jump away from the unexpected, and helps to produce ideas that are surprises as well as solutions....

If good designers have anything in common, it is that they all seem to be equipped with a subconscious sponge, capable of absorbing a wide and unrelated range of stimuli to be tucked away at the back of the mind for future use. A builder's yard or a factory are as likely to provide a fruitful scrap of inspiration as a book on Islamic calligraphy or a visit to the Louvre. But how did that scrap become part of a design solution? Logic? Intuition? Lateral rationalisation? Maybe thinking by jumping is as close a description as we can get.

—Ideas on Design

Newsletters

When we studied our mailing list, we found 158 households that no longer belong. We pay about half a dollar to print, label, and mail one newsletter. The bad addresses represented $79 per issue—$948 per year. That's almost $1,000 per year we were tossing into the wastebasket.

—anecdote from Editing Your Newsletter

Editing Your Newsletter: How to Produce an Effective Publication Using Traditional Tools and Computers by Mark Beach (third edition, 1988; Coast to Coast Books, 1507 Dana Ave., Cincinnati, OH 45207)

This well-balanced guide covers the basic aspects of planning, developing, designing, and producing a newsletter. Chapters on design, typography, and graphics are well illustrated with diverse samples of real and fictional publications, and the chapters on production, printing, and distribution provide useful introductions to these areas. There is very little information about electronic page assembly, which is not a shortcoming in such a useful book, except that the subtitle promises more than it delivers. The Resources section includes lists of newsletter directories, workshops, and awards.

PageMaker

Master Pages (Aldus Corporation, 411 First Avenue South, Seattle, WA 98104)

Free to registered PageMaker users, this bimonthly tabloid-size newsletter shows off PageMaker's capabilities while providing some good information for both novice and more experienced users.

Page Tutor (1988, Personal Training Systems, P.O. Box 54240, San Jose, CA 94154)

This interactive tutorial combines a 90-minute audio tape and a disk with lesson files. Although the narration is gratingly cheerful and the designs of the sample documents are pedestrian at best, the instruction is clear and the development of skills is well paced. A foldout summary card lets you review specific skills and techniques at a later date. Four packages are available: Beginning, Intermediate, Tips & Techniques (even relatively experienced users may learn a few new tricks here), and Advanced Features of PageMaker 3.0 (styles, text wraparound, image control, and color). Available only in the Macintosh format, the packages are not cheap ($49.95 each); but if you're stumbling around after working through the tutorial that came with PageMaker 3.0, this approach will give you some hand-holding experience and help move you toward productivity.

Using Aldus PageMaker 3.0 by Douglas Kramer and Roger C. Parker (second edition,1988; Bantam Books, 666 Fifth Ave., New York, NY 10103)

This revision of one of the early books on PageMaker includes an excellent 50-page chapter that is all tips and techniques, written by Eda Warren. The book covers both the PC and Macintosh versions of PageMaker 3.0.

Paper

Before installing paper into your printer tray, lightly "fan" the paper with your fingers to separate each sheet and to discard any of the cut edges (also known as flashing). The goal is to begin with fresh, flat sheets, free of lint or other small debris that could impair printer performance or lead to premature wear on delicate printer parts.

—Laser Paper Sample Kit

Laser Paper Sample Kit (1988, Portico Press, PO Box 190, New Paltz, NY 12561)

This kit provides five sheets each of 14 different white papers for the user to test in his or her laser printer. An accompanying 12-page report is an accessible introduction to paper in general (brightness, opacity, smoothness and so on) and to its use in laser printers. A chart provides specifications for 49 papers suitable for use in laser printers as well as information about available weights, sizes, and matching stock for envelopes, business cards, and so on. Future kits will be devoted to specialty papers (labels, envelopes, and overhead transparencies) and colored papers. A good value at $21.95.

Production and Printing

Getting It Printed: How to Work with Printers and Graphic Arts Services to Assure Quality, Stay on Schedule, and Control Costs by March Beach, Steve Shepro, and Ken Russon (1986, Coast to Coast Books, 2934 Northeast 16th Ave., Portland, OR 97212)

This book covers much of the same ground that the standard production references, such as *Pocket Pal,* do. But as the subtitle suggests, it also offers advice on how to specify and prepare your work, what you can and cannot expect from printing technologies, and how to work with your printer to get the best possible result. It's practical, technical but accessible, and peppered with anecdotes from publishers and printers.

The Graphic Designer's Handbook by Alastair Campbell (revised edition, 1987; Running Press, 125 South 22nd St., Philadelphia, PA 19103)

Originally published in England, this handbook is a reference to printing options and terms, including paper and binding, page imposition, proof marks, copy-fitting tables, halftone screens, and so on. The color pages, which are numerous, include tint charts. Brief introductory chapters focus on the design process .

Use of the term desktop publishing applied to the graphic arts...can be misleading, for the publishing process encompasses much more than is presently available from desktop publishing systems. In addition to typographic composition, page makeup and laser-printed pages, the process of publishing requires the use of multi-color, high-fidelity halftone reproduction..., large volume, high-speed press runs of multi-page signature forms, ability to print on a variety of different paper stocks, different binding and finishing operations, distribution and many other factors.
—Graphics Master 4

Graphics Master 4 by Dean Phillip Lem (fourth edition, 1988; Dean Lem Associates, Inc., P.O. Box 25920, Los Angeles, CA 90025)

This printing reference is as up to date on desktop publishing as any we've seen. The hardcover, spiral-bound format with heavy card stock makes it a pleasure to use, and it includes two essential tools of the trade: a line gauge (calibrated for the 6-picas-per-inch conversion that has been adopted in electronic page layout programs) and a proportion scale for sizing art. Color tint charts are printed on both coated and uncoated stock, with die-cut tint masks (one black and one white) so that you can isolate any tint from the surrounding colors. The typeface display is extensive for a general reference guide, and the character-count guide includes information for Linotype (and hence Adobe), Bitstream, and Varityper systems. It is not inexpensive ($69.50), but it is a valuable reference aid for the serious desktop designer.

Pasteups & Mechanicals: A Step-by-Step Guide to Preparing Art for Reproduction by Jerry Demoney and Susan E. Meyer (1982, Watson-Guptill, 1515 Broadway, New York, NY 10036)

Close-up photographic sequences take you through the techniques of the traditional art department. And although many of these are replaced by your computer (inking rules and rounded corners, for example), many of them are not (scaling, cropping, and silhouetting photographs—even pasting in type corrections).

Pocket Pal: A Graphic Arts Production Handbook (thirteenth edition, 1983; International Paper Company, 6400 Poplar Ave., Memphis, TN 38197)

An inexpensive and concise guide to the history, process, and language of printing, this has been the standard reference for 50 years. If you have no other reference guide to the world of printing, don't pass up this $4.25 bargain.

Style, Grammar, and Usage

The Chicago Manual of Style (thirteenth edition, 1982; The University of Chicago Press, 5801 Ellis Ave., Chicago, IL 60637)

In addition to setting forth rules for proper punctuation, use of numbers, tables, mathematics, references, notes, and bibliographies, this widely used reference provides an overview of the entire publishing process, from securing rights and permissions through design and typography to printing and binding. The 1982 edition begins to reflect the impact of technology on the editing process, although it stops short of desktop publishing.

The Elements of Style by William Strunk, Jr. and E.B.White (third edition, 1979; Macmillan Publishing Co. Inc., 866 Third Ave., New York, NY 10022)

Of all the many books on style, this is the most universally embraced classic. It is a simple, straightforward model of the lessons it imparts.

The Transitive Vampire: A Handbook of Grammar for the Innocent, the Eager, and the Doomed by Karen Elizabeth Gordon (1984, Times Books, 201 East 50th St., New York NY 10022)

This entertaining and delightfully unorthodox guide uses odd and whimsical words, characters, and illustrations to beguile you into understanding the parts of a sentence and how to put them together properly.

Type

Desktop Publishing Skills : A Primer for Typesetting with Computers and Laser Printers by Jim Felici and Ted Nace (1987, Addison-Wesley, Route 128, Reading, MA 01867)

The authors' understanding of both traditional and computer typesetting makes this a useful guide for readers who want more than a superficial look at the aesthetic and electronic aspects of typography. Its reviews of hardware and software are dated, but it includes much timeless information to recommend it.

Desktop Publishing Type & Graphics by Deke McClelland and Craig Danuloff (1987, Harcourt Brace Jovanovich, 124 Mt. Auburn St., Cambridge, MA 02238)

This volume serves as an annotated type spec book for the faces available for desktop publishing through 1987, and as a visual reference to the appearance of lines, screens, fountains, and patterns at various resolutions in the desktop publishing environment. It includes directories for Symbol, Dingbats, Cairo, Mobile, some foreign-language and notation fonts. Chapters on point size, spacing, leading, and line length provide visual aids to understanding the interaction of these aspects of type.

Font & Function (Adobe Systems, 1585 Charleston Road, P.O. Box 7900, Mountain View, CA 94039)

In addition to displaying the fonts that they sell, Adobe's oversize type catalog is full of information and ideas about using type. And you can get it free by calling 1-800-29-ADOBE.

Herb Lubalin: Art Director, Graphic Designer and Typographer by Gertrude Snyder and Alan Peckolick (1985, American Showcase, 724 5th Ave., New York, NY 10019)

Graphic designer Herb Lubalin brought a new meaning to typographic design. This is a loving tribute and testimonial to his talent by colleagues. It is a book devoted entirely to Lubalin's designs, from logos to typefaces to magazines. If you are the least bit intrigued by letterforms, the life work of this designer will delight and inspire you.

Inversions by Scot Kim (1981, Byte Books, 70 Main St., Peterborough, NH 03458)

Computer programmer and artist Scot Kim has taken ordinary words and

---

Vigorous writing is concise. A sentence should contain no unnecessary words, a paragraph no unnecessary sentences, for the same reason that a drawing should have no unnecessary lines and a machine no unnecessary parts. This requires not that the writer make all his sentences short, or that he avoid all detail and treat his subjects only in outline, but that every word tell.

—The Elements of Style

The principal concept underlying PostScript is that text, graphics, and digitized image handling should all be based on the same model....
One of the main consequences of PostScript's way of handling text, graphics, and images is device independence. Since characters are handled as outlines, the application can ignore the question about whether they will be printed on a 300-dpi laser printer or 2200-dpi phototypesetting machine. The same goes for graphics and halftones, since the graphics primitives and halftone screens that provide the basis for generating line art and halftones are both specified in a manner independent of output resolution.

—Desktop Publishing Skills

rendered them with a magician's sense of visual trickery. Some words read the same right side up and upside down, some words are hidden inside their opposites, some repeat into infinity. Although the book is more likely to be classified as wordplay than typography, it is a delightful way to learn about letterforms, symmetry, and visual perception.

A Manual of Comparative Typography: The Panose System by Benjamin Bauermeister (1988, Van Nostrand Reinhold, 115 Fifth Avenue, New York, NY 10003)

The premise of the PANOSE system is that type, like trees and birds, can be identified by noting special features. The result is a type specimen book in which distinctive features of the letters of each face included are circled. Whether or not you use the system itself, the visual display can be extremely useful for educating your eye to the nuances of type. Although the book is not specific to desktop publishing, it's interesting to note that the author is the technical support manager at Aldus Corporation.

PostScript Type Sampler (1988, MacTography, 702 Twin Brook Parkway, Rockville, MD, 20851)

A DTP type specimen book, this looseleaf volume displays more than 800 PostScript fonts from 17 manufacturers, for Macintosh and IBM-compatible computers. For each typeface, a complete character set is shown in 24-point type followed by a paragraph set 10/12 justified and/or a line of 24- or 36-point display type and a line showing the range from 4 to 36 points. Not a bad value at $49.95.

Typography & Typesetting: Type Design and Manipulation Using Today's Technology by Ronald Labuz (1988, Van Nostrand Reinhold, 115 Fifth Ave., New York, NY 10003)

A very readable and up to date overview of the history, technology, and aesthetics of typography, this book is well illustrated, well designed, and thoughtfully put together. A wide range of sample documents includes pages from newspapers, books, magazines, and advertising.

Magazines and Newsletters

There are a great many magazines covering both the computer field and the field of graphic design—far too many to describe even briefly in these pages. *MacWorld, PC World,* and *MacUser* are among the many that keep technology-hungry users up to date on the latest products. *Art Direction, Communication Arts,* and *Print* display the best editorial and advertising work in this country, and *Graphis* is a source for international coverage. The following publications are of special interest to people working in desktop publishing.

HOW: Ideas and Techniques in Graphic Design (F&W Publications, 1507 Dana Ave., Cincinnati, OH 45207)

If you want to look over the shoulders of artists and designers as they work, this magazine covers a wide range of subjects, including logos, book covers, posters, packaging, sculpture, illustration, corporate identity, and software. It's nicely produced, with lots of color art on coated stock. Bimonthly, $37 per year.

ThePage : A Visual Guide to Using the Macintosh in Desktop Publishing (PageWorks, PO Box 14493, Chicago, IL 60614)

Produced by people who are equally at home in the world of graphic design and computers, this 16-page newsletter is packed with ideas and techniques. And it's very well balanced between information for novices and information of interest to more advanced users. Much of it is PageMaker-specific, although it also has articles on drawing programs, general design problems (logos, covers, newsletter design, typography), and systems management. The material is clearly presented, well illustrated, and highly accessible. For samples from this publication, see the end of the Newsletter section in Chapter 6. Monthly, $55 per year.

Publish! (PCW Communications, 501 Second St., San Francisco, CA 94107)

With its clear focus on desktop publishing tools and process, *Publish!* is a useful source not only for information about the technology but also for insight into how organizations are using it and coping with the good, the bad, and the uncertain. It speaks with equal success to designers making the transition from traditional to desktop production and to businesses of all kinds which, as a result of this technology, find themselves increasingly involved in publishing concerns. In addition to the product evaluations and industry news, useful regular features include "Page Makeover" (showing a business publication before and after a professional redesign), "About Faces" (a relatively in-depth look at a single typeface), and feature stories on issues such as cost effectiveness, networking, and the changing roles brought about by work-group publishing. All of this is sandwiched in between editor Susan Gubernat's hype-debunking column in the front of the issue and managing editor Jim Felici's "End Paper" in the back, which focuses on the magazine's own experience with needs and problems such as color halftones and programs that facilitate automatic kerning. Monthly, $39.90 per year.

Step-by-Step Electronic Design (Dynamic Graphics, 6000 N. Forest Park Drive, Peoria, IL 61614)

A collaboration between *Step-by-Step Graphics* magazine and *Verbum* journal, this new entry in the field promises to be a useful source of information about how different designers use electronic tools in their work. The first issue (January 1989) described in detail the production of a two-color diagram using the combined capabilities of both Illustrator and FreeHand as well as MacVision and MacPaint; the issue included a similarly detailed piece about designing and preparing a slide presentation with PowerPoint and some useful information about Linotronic printing. Monthly, $48 per year.

Verbum: Journal of Personal Computer Aesthetics (Verbum, PO Box 15439, San Diego, CA 92115)

This well-produced gallery of computer art focuses on pushing the limits of the technology, not only in the art it displays but in the production of the magazine as well. For example, in Issue 2.3 (published in December 1988), the cover was developed in FreeHand and proofed on a QMS ColorScript 100 thermal transfer printer, with color separations generated by FreeHand and output on the L300 as 2540-dpi negatives. Other art in the same issue used digital separations of PixelPaint illustrations output to film at 2540 dpi at the proper reduction. Art director John Odam skillfully varies the design every issue—including the logo, folios, and department head treatments—as yet another way of displaying the capabilities of the technology. The journal also includes reviews of art-related hardware and software and a much-needed "Against the Grain" column with articles such as "Oh Wow, Scanners!", which cut through some of the hype surrounding desktop publishing. For sample pages, see the Magazine section of Chapter 6. Quarterly, $28 per year.

Some [Linotronic] serivce bureaus... insist that you send your system file and a collection of the font files you've used, or at least a detailed list of all the font files you've used....You may also have to supply TIFF...files for the graphics included in your pages. That's because the page layout file doesn't include the graphic elements themselves; instead it includes a command to get and print each graphic component at the appropriate point in the printing process. If the TIFF...file isn't on the disk you supply to the service bureau, it won't be available when it's called and...you may end up with a rough bitmap or a blank box in place of your detailed illustration or scanned image.

—Steve Hannaford,
Step-by-Step Electronic Design

GLOSSARY

alignment The placement and shape of type relative to the margins. See also *centered, flush left, flush right, justified, ragged right,* and *wraparound.*

alley The space between two columns of text.

ascender The portion of a lowercase letter, such as b or f, that rises above the x-height.

ASCII An acronym for "American Standard Code for Information Interchange," the form in which text-only files are stored. These files include all characters, tabs, and carriage returns but not character and paragraph formatting such as italic, boldface, hanging indents, and so on.

Autoflow The fastest mode for text placement in PageMaker, in which text flows continuously from column to column and page to page until the entire file has been placed. Select Autoflow from the Options menu. When flowing text in this mode, you can stop the flow at any time by clicking the mouse button. See also *manual text flow* and *semi-automatic text flow.*

Auto leading An amount of space between lines that is always proportional to the type size. The PageMaker default for Auto leading is 120% of the type size. So if your type is 10 point, Auto leading is 12; if the type is 14 point, Auto leading is 17. (PageMaker rounds off to the nearest half point.)

bad break A line break that is visually jarring, such as a page that begins with the suffix "ing" or a column that ends with a single word. See also *orphan* and *widow.*

baseline An imaginary line on which the letters in a line of type sit. The baseline aligns with the bottom of the x-height of the characters, and descenders of letters such as g and p drop below the baseline.

bit-mapped The representation of a character or graphic as a series of square dots or pixels, which sometimes print with jagged edges. See also *paint-type graphics.*

bleed art Any photo, illustration, or tint that runs off the edge of the page.

blurb Text that summarizes an article, usually set smaller than the headline and larger than the running text. Sometimes used interchangeably with "breakout."

body text The main text, also called body copy or running text, usually set in 9- to 12-point type in continuous paragraphs.

border A printing frame around text, graphics, or an entire page. Borders range from simple hairline rules to decorative and thematic graphic elements.

bounding box A rectangular space defined in PageMaker by dragging the mouse diagonally to establish left and right margins between which to place or type text.

breakout A sentence excerpted from the body copy and set in large type, used to break up running text and draw the reader's attention to the page. Also called a pull quote, blurb, or callout.

bullets Dots used to designate items in a list. (Keystroke is Option-8 on the Macintosh, Ctrl-Shift-8 on the PC.)

byline The name of the author of an article.

TIP

If a table has multiple lines for some entries, it is generally better to create it in PageMaker and use column guides to align the text rather than to create it in a word processor and use tabs. Move the insertion point from one column to the next as you create horizontal rows of data so that you will know the depth of each row before typing the text for the next row. When you add a new item to each column, set the insertion point at the end of the previous line and press Return, so that each column can be edited as a single text block.

TIP

If you want baselines of text in adjacent columns to align, any space between paragraphs should be an interval equal to the leading of the text. If subheads have a different size and leading than your body text, calculate the space before and after the subhead to maintain the leading grid.

callout A label that identifies part of an illustration.

camera-ready Photographs, art, and complete pages in a form that the printer can photograph for making printing plates.

cap height The height of a capital letter in a given font and size.

caption The text describing a photograph or illustration.

center axis The imaginary center line through a page, a text block, or a piece of art.

centered Aligned along a center axis.

character An individual letter or symbol.

clip art Public domain art, either in books or on disks, that you can use free of charge and without credit in a publication.

Clipboard An electronic holding place for the most recent cut made from a document. Whatever is on the Clipboard can be pasted into the current document. Note, however, that when you shut down, whatever is on the Clipboard is lost.

column guides Nonprinting vertical rules in a PageMaker document that determine the left and right margins of text that you type or place. You can specify columns through the Column Guides command on the Options menu and reposition them manually with the pointer tool.

column rules Thin vertical rules separating two columns of type.

condensed type Type in which the individual character is narrower than normal, giving you more characters per line.

continued line A line of text indicating the page on which an article continues or the carryover line on the subsequent page that identifies the story being continued. Also called a jumpline.

copy-fitting Editing text to fit a specified space.

copyright Ownership of a work by the writer, artist, photographer, or publisher.

counter The white space inside rounded letters such as a, e, and p.

crop To trim a graphic to fit a space without reducing the size of the graphic.

crop marks Intersecting lines indicating where a page is to be trimmed. When printing pages smaller than the paper size, select the Crop Marks option in the Print dialog box if you want PageMaker to print them. Crop marks are also used to indicate the trim of photos and art that will be stripped in by the printer.

cropping tool The PageMaker tool used to trim graphics.

crossbar The shape of PageMaker's pointer when you select any of the drawing tools.

crossover Type or art that extends across the gutter between two pages. Alignment of crossover elements is critical.

deck A line following the headline that gives more information about a newsletter, magazine, or newspaper story. Also called a tagline.

cursor keys A set of four keys that can move the I-beam in the directions indicated by the arrows on the keys: up, down, right, or left.

default A preset value or option that is used unless you specify otherwise.

TIP

To deselect an individual item from a large group of selected items, hold down the Shift key and click on the item you want to deselect. Similarly, to add an item to a large group of selected items, hold down the Shift key and click on the item you want to add.

TIP

You can trick PageMaker into a spell check of a single word by attempting to insert a discretionary hyphen in it. Type the word at the end of a line on which it won't fit, set an insertion point in between two syllables, and type Command-hyphen (Ctrl-hyphen on a PC). If PageMaker hyphenates the word, it is correctly spelled. If PageMaker doesn't hyphenate the word, either it is spelled incorrectly or it is not included in PageMaker's 110,000-word hyphenation dictionary.

descender The portion of a lowercase letter, such as g or y, that drops below the baseline of the type.

deselect To turn off a command by clicking on it when it is currently selected. Also to cancel the selection of text and graphics in the publication window by clicking elsewhere on the page.

dialog box A box displayed on the screen that enables you to select or specify options and values.

digitize To convert an image into a series of dots stored by the computer so that the image can be manipulated and placed in publications.

dingbat A decorative or symbolic device used to separate items on the page or to denote items on a list.

discretionary hyphen A hyphen inserted manually by typing Command-hyphen (Ctrl-hyphen on a PC). A discretionary hyphen shows on-screen and on the printed page only if it is used to break a word at the end of a line.

display type Large type, often boldface, used for headlines, breakouts, and other attention-getting text.

Double-sided An option in the Page Setup dialog box that tells PageMaker your publication will be printed on both sides of the paper. The inside margin is the right margin of even-numbered pages (the back or left-hand page) and the left margin of odd-numbered pages (the front or right-hand page). See also *single-sided* and *facing pages.*

download To send printer fonts from your computer to your printer. You can let PageMaker automatically download a font each time your use it, or (to save time) you can manually download a font. Fonts that you download manually remain in the printer's memory until you turn off the printer.

downloadable fonts Individual fonts that you can buy and install in your desktop-publishing system.

drag To hold down the mouse button while you move the pointer to a new location on the screen.

drag-place To drag the mouse diagonally, defining the width of a graphic or text block before you place it.

draw-type graphics See *object-oriented graphics.*

drop cap An enlarged initial letter that drops below the first line of body text. See also *stick-up cap.*

dummy A term that means different things in different organizations. It can be a rough preliminary sketch of a publication or story, an early proof with type and rough art in place, or a mock-up of an entire publication.

ellipsis Three dots (...) used to indicate an incomplete thought or that text has been deleted from a quote. To achieve a properly spaced ellipsis, type Option-semicolon in the Macintosh version of PageMaker (and in some word-processing programs). The ASCII value for an ellipsis is 201 in some fonts.

em dash A dash the size of an em space, inserted by pressing Option-Shift-hyphen (Ctrl-Shift-= on a PC).

em space A typographic unit equal to the point size of the type being used. For 10-point type, an em space would be 10 points. To insert an em space in PageMaker, press Command-Shift-m (Ctrl-Shift-m on a PC).

Encapsulated PostScript A file format that enables you to print line art with smooth (rather than jagged) edges and to see and resize the graphic on-screen as it will print. EPS files can be created in graphics programs that produce PostScript code (such as Illustrator or FreeHand) or with the EPS option available in the Macintosh version of PageMaker's Print dialog box. These images can be printed only on PostScript-language printers.

en dash A dash the size of an en space, inserted by pressing Option-hyphen (Ctrl-= on a PC).

en space A space half as wide as an em space, inserted by pressing Command-Shift-n (Ctrl-Shift-n on a PC). In this Glossary, the space between each term and its definition is an en space.

face The name of a typeface, such as Times Roman or Helvetica.

facing pages Two pages that face each other in a printed publication. In PageMaker, you can select the Double-sided and Facing Pages options when you want to view facing pages together on the screen.

fill A pattern or texture inside a rectangle or other closed shape. See the Shades menu for fills available in PageMaker. Other art programs may have additional fills that can be used in imported graphics.

fixed space Space inserted between two characters, specified by font, by pressing Option-space bar (Ctrl-space bar on a PC). Fixed spaces are used frequently in this book to letterspace headlines when the space desired exceeds the 200% maximum available through PageMaker's Spacing command. See also *em space*, *en space*, and *thin space*.

flush Aligned or even with, as in flush left or flush right text.

flush left Aligned along the left edge or margin.

flush right Aligned along the right edge or margin.

fold marks Dotted or dashed lines on camera-ready art that indicate where to fold the printed piece.

folio The page number.

font In desktop publishing, sometimes used interchangeably with "face" to refer to the entire family of letters of a particular shape or design, such as Helvetica. In traditional typesetting, font refers only to one size and style of a given typeface, such as 10-point Helvetica roman or 12-point Helvetica bold.

footer See *running foot*.

format The overall appearance of a publication, including page size, paper, binding, length, and page-design elements such as margins, number of columns, treatment of headlines, and so on.

formatting Type and paragraph specifications that are applied in a word-processing or page layout program.

for position only A photocopy or photostat of a piece of art pasted in place on the camera-ready page to indicate the position of the actual art that is to be stripped in by the printer. Usually written as FPO.

galley Traditionally, proofs of type before it is arranged on the page; used for proofreading and layout. (The term derives from the long, shallow metal trays used to hold metal type after it had been set.) In desktop publishing, you may still want to print galleys to the specified column width in your page layout program for proofreading.

gatefold A paper fold in which one or two sides of an oversize page fold in toward the middle of the sheet.

Gothic-style typefaces Sans serif typefaces.

TIP

If you have altered a graphic that was previously placed, sized, and cropped in a PageMaker file: Select the existing graphic, choose Place from the File menu, select the filename for the edited graphic, click on the Replacing Entire Graphic option, and then click OK. PageMaker will replace the existing graphic with the edited one.

TIP

Sometimes you want to temporarily slide an item or group of items off of the page and onto the pasteboard. If you hold down the Shift key when you drag the items off and then back onto the page, you will be able to easily reposition them with the same horizontal alignment they had before you moved them. The same technique works for vertical movement as well, of course.

TIP

While you reshape a graphic boundary, hold down the space bar to prevent the screen from redrawing the text wrap after each individual adjustment.

grabber hand A PageMaker icon invoked by pressing the Option key (the Alt Key on a PC) and dragging the mouse; used to move around in the publication window.

graphic boundary A nonprinting dotted line around a graphic that determines how close text can come to the graphic. The distance between the graphic boundary and the graphic is called the standoff and is defined through the Text Wrap command on PageMaker's Options menu.

greeking Simulating text as gray bars in order to speed screen display (an option available through PageMaker's Preference's command). Also used to refer to dummy Latin text used to show the look of a document without the actual words.

grid A series of nonprinting vertical and horizontal rules used to determine placement of text and graphics on the page.

guide A nonprinting dotted line on the PageMaker screen used to position text and graphics. See also *column guides, margin guide,* and *ruler guide.*

gutter The space between two facing pages. Sometimes used to refer to the space between two columns of text.

hairline rule A very thin typographic rule. In desktop publishing, the width of a hairline rule varies depending on the resolution of the printer.

halftone The representation of a continuous-tone photograph or illustration as a series of dots that look like gray tones when printed. Also called a screened halftone because traditionally the original image is photographed through a finely ruled screen, the density of which varies depending on the printer's capabilities. In desktop publishing, photographs can be screened during scanning.

handles Used in PageMaker to refer to the eight small solid rectangles that surround a selected graphic. See also *windowshade handles.*

hanging indent A paragraph style in which the left margin of the first line extends beyond the left margin of subsequent lines. To create a hanging indent in PageMaker, define the first-line indent as a negative value relative to the left indent in the Paragraph Specifications dialog box.

header See *running head.*

headline The title of an article or story.

I-beam The shape PageMaker's pointer assumes when you select the text tool.

image area The area inside the page margins. Some page elements, such as page-number markers, are placed outside the image area.

imagesetter An output device, such as the Linotronic, that produces high-resolution pages from desktop-generated files.

initial cap A first letter set in enlarged and sometimes decorative type for graphic emphasis.

insertion point A blinking vertical bar indicating where the next text block will be typed or pasted. The position of the insertion point is set by clicking the I-beam on the page.

inside margin The space between the binding edge of the page and the text. In a double-sided PageMaker publication, the inside margin that you define in the Page Setup dialog box shifts from the left margin of a right-hand page to the right margin of a left-hand page.

italic type Type with letters that slant toward the right, often used for display text and captions. See also *oblique type.*

TIP

When you want to change the specifications for a single paragraph, you don't have to drag to select the entire paragraph. Simply click the text tool anywhere in the paragraph, and PageMaker will apply any changes that you specify through the Paragraph command (indents, spacing, and hyphenation) or the Define Styles command. Alignment and spacing attributes can also be specified in this way, but to change type specifications, you will have to select the entire paragraph.

TIP

To kill a widow when a one-line caption or headline runs over, try changing the alignment to justified. Be sure to check the printout to determine if the justified spacing is acceptable.

TIP

Most service centers that provide Linotronic output base their page rate on a maximum printing time, such as 8 minutes per page. Anything beyond that time is charged as overtime. To minimize overtime charges, keep your pages clean (eliminate items from the pasteboard, avoid unnecessary masks, and so on), and do a Save As to compact the file before you copy it to a floppy disk. For very complex pages, some service centers recommend creating a PostScript file of your document. This sometimes eliminates printing problems as well as problems with conflicting font ID numbers. The procedure for making a PostScript file is the same as that for creating an Encapsulated PostScript file (described in Project 6), except that you do not check the EPS option.

jaggies The stairstepping effect of bit-mapped art and type created by diagonal lines in a technology that is based on square pixels.

jumpline See *continued line*.

justified Type that is flush, or even, on both the right and left margins.

kerning The process of adjusting the space between characters, generally done only in headlines and other display type. To remove space between letters, set an insertion point and press Command-Backspace on a Macintosh, Ctrl-Backspace on a PC. To add space, press Command-Shift-Backspace on a Macintosh, Ctrl-Shift-Backspace on a PC.

kicker A phrase preceding a headline that provides information about the story.

landscape A horizontal page orientation that is wider than it is tall.

layout The arrangement of text and graphics on a page.

leader A rule, often dotted, that moves the eye from a callout or label to the part of the illustration it describes.

leading The distance from the baseline of one line of text to the next, measured in points.

letterspacing The amount of space between letters. In PageMaker, you can control letterspacing through the Spacing dialog box on the Type menu.

Linotronic A high-quality PostScript-compatible output device that can print files created on a desktop system at resolutions up to 2450 dots per inch.

logotype A company, product, or publication name designed as a distinctly recognizable unit.

manual text flow A mode of placing text in PageMaker in which the text flow stops at the end of a column; you must click on the windowshade handle at the bottom of the text block to reload the text icon and continue placing text in the next column or page. To use this mode, turn off the Autoflow command on the Options menu. See also *Autoflow* and *semi-automatic text flow*.

margin guide A nonprinting dotted rule that appears on every page of a PageMaker document as specified in the Page Setup dialog box.

margin The distance from the edge of the paper to the image area occupied by text and graphics.

marquee. See *selection box*.

master page The page, identified by an L (for left) or R (for right) icon in the lower left of PageMaker's publication window, on which you create elements that will appear on all the actual pages of the document. Master-page items can be printing items (such as running heads) or nonprinting items (such as ruler and column guides).

masthead Traditionally, the listing of staff, ownership, and subscription information for a periodical. Masthead is sometimes used to refer to the typographic treatment of the publication name on the cover, although this is more accurately called a nameplate.

measure The length of a line of type, traditionally expressed in picas.

mechanical Traditionally, a piece of artboard with type galleys, line art, and "for-position-only" photostats in place and with tissue overlays marked for color. In electronic publishing, a mechanical is the final camera-ready page, either from a laser printer or an imagesetter, with position-only stats keyed to flat art that is to be stripped in by the printer. Also called a keyline, pasteup, or camera-ready page.

menu A list of commands that appears when you point to any of the items listed just above the publication window (File, Edit, Type, and so on).

menu bar The area at the top of the screen containing menu names.

mini-save An automatic save of a document, which PageMaker generates each time you click a page icon, change the page setup, or insert or delete a page from the publication file. You can revert to the last mini-save by holding down the Shift key when you select the Revert command on the File menu.

modular layout A format in which different elements on a page or spread are designed as self-contained units.

monospacing Letterspacing that is the same for all characters regardless of their shape or width. Traditional typewriter characters are monospaced. See also *proportional spacing*.

nameplate The typographic design of a publication's name as it appears on the cover of the publication.

negative leading A type specification in which there is less space from baseline to baseline than the size of the type itself (for example, 40-point type with 38-point leading). Negative leading is often used with larger type sizes set in all caps in order to tighten up the text unit.

nonbreaking space Space inserted between two words so that they cannot be separated by a line break.

object-oriented graphics Graphics created as a series of mathematically defined curves and lines. They can be resized without causing distortion or moiré patterns. Also called draw-type graphics.

oblique type A slanted style of a roman typeface. The letters, for the most part, maintain their original forms except for the slant, whereas italic letters have a different shape from their roman counterparts. See also *italic type*.

orphan The opening line of a paragraph isolated at the bottom of a column or page, separated from the rest of the paragraph.

outside margin The space between the outside trim and the text.

overline A brief tag, over a headline, that categorizes a story. Also called a kicker or an eyebrow.

page-number marker A key sequence (Command-Option-p on a Macintosh, Ctrl-Shift-3 on a PC), generally typed on the master pages, that instructs PageMaker to insert page numbers in the document.

Page Setup The size, orientation, number of pages, and margins for a document; specified in PageMaker's Page Setup dialog box.

page view The amount of the page and surrounding pasteboard seen on the screen, which varies depending on the size of your monitor and the view selected on PageMaker's Page menu. The choices are Fit in Window, 50%, 75%, Actual size, and 200%. You can also select a global view to reveal the entire pasteboard by pressing Command (or Ctrl)-Shift-Fit in Window, and a 400% view is available by pressing Shift-200%.

paint-type graphics Graphics represented by square dots or pixels, which can be individually manipulated on-screen. These graphics may be distorted or lose resolution when resized. See also *bit-mapped*.

pasteboard The area surrounding the page on-screen in a PageMaker document where you can leave master items, such as standing headline treatments or spacing guides as well as any text or graphics until you are ready to move them into position on the page. Items on the pasteboard appear on the pasteboard of every page of the publication.

TIP

If an item that you place or create on the pasteboard overlaps a page in the document file, PageMaker reads that item as being on the page, and the item will not appear on the pasteboard of other pages in the file.

TIP

Resizing paint-type graphics and scanned images sometimes produces moiré patterns and other distortions. To avoid this problem, hold down the Command key (Ctrl on a PC) as you drag the graphic's handle to resize; this restricts the resizing to a percentage that matches your printer's resolution. If you are resizing proportionally, hold down the Shift key also.

TIP

It is sometimes useful to specify a right-margin indent in your word processor so that you can see your text file at the same column width as you will use in PageMaker. The line breaks will not be entirely accurate, but you can get a sense of approximate length and, if necessary, edit to fit in the text file. But before placing the file in Page-Maker, be sure to remove the right-margin indent. If you don't, Page-Maker will apply that indent to whatever column width you have specified there.

TIP

In PageMaker's Open and Place dialog boxes, you can use the up and down arrow keys to move through a list of filenames; when you reach the file you want, press Return. You can also type the first letter (or first few letters) of the filename and then press Return. (Note, however, that a delay in typing between letters of a name will move the selection to a file-name beginning with the "delayed" letter.)

pasteup Traditionally, the process of assembling mechanicals by pasting galleys and line art in place. In desktop publishing, traditional pasteup has largely been replaced by electronic page assembly in PageMaker and other page layout programs. But if your publication is oversize, or if you have an existing logo or position prints for art to be stripped in by the printer, you may still need to do some pasteup for camera-ready pages.

perpendicular line tool The PageMaker tool used to draw vertical, horizontal, and diagonal lines at 45-degree increments.

perspective The representation of three-dimensional objects on a flat plane as they appear to the eye.

pica A traditional typographic measurement, composed of 12 points. A pica is actually equal to a little less than 1/6 inch, but in desktop publishing you will generally see it expressed as 1/6 inch.

PICT format A Macintosh file format for saving object-oriented graphics.

picture window A rectangle that indicates the position and size of art to be stripped in by the printer.

pixel The smallest dot or unit on a computer screen. The clarity of screen resolution varies depending on the number of pixels per inch on the monitor.

Place A PageMaker command on the File menu that enables you to import text and graphics created and saved in other applications. Note that you cannot place a file in a PageMaker document if that file is currently open.

placeholder Text or graphics that you leave in place in an electronic template so that you can place, paste, or type new items over the placeholder and retain the same spacing relative to other elements on the page.

point The basic measurement of type. There are 12 points to a pica, and 1 point equals about 1/72 inch.

pointer The icon that moves on the screen as you move the mouse. The shape of the pointer depends on which tool is selected.

pointer tool The PageMaker tool, which takes the shape of an arrow on the screen, used for selecting graphics and text blocks. Other PageMaker tools turn into the pointer tool when you move them into the rulers, menu bars, Styles palette, or page icons.

point size The distance from the highest ascender to the lowest descender. See also *point*.

portrait A vertical orientation for pages or photographs. See also *landscape*.

PostScript A page description language developed by Adobe Systems and used by many laser printers and high-resolution typesetters. It is as close to a standard as there is in desktop publishing at this writing.

Preferences A command on PageMaker's Edit menu used to specify the unit of measure (inches, picas, millimeters, and so on) in a publication and to set the ruler guides to the front or back layer on the screen.

printer font A mathematical description of every character in a font, which enables a printer to print characters in any size at the best resolution possible on that printer.

printing rule A rule that traps a screen or surrounds a piece of art.

proofread To check typeset material for spelling, punctuation, alignment of elements, and other details and to be sure that corrections have been made properly. Standard proofreading marks can be found in many printing reference guides, style manuals, and dictionaries.

TIP

To import new text into a story you've already placed: Set the insertion point by clicking the text tool where you want to add the new text, choose Place from the File menu, select the filename for the new text, click on the Inserting Text option, and then click OK. Page-Maker inserts the new text at the insertion point and forces all subsequent text farther down in the existing text block.

TIP

If you distort a graphic while you are resizing it in PageMaker, you can restore the graphic's original proportions by holding down the Shift key and dragging slightly on any handle. This technique enables you to quickly drag-place a graphic to define its approximate size, restore its proportions, and then resize it accurately for the layout and the proportions of the art.

proportional leading A method of leading used in PageMaker that places two-thirds of the specified leading above the text baseline and one-third below it.

proportional spacing Letterspacing that is proportional to the shape of a letter. Computer typefaces are proportional, with the m and the w, for example, taking up more space than the i and the l. See also *monospacing*.

proportion wheel A tool used to calculate the percentage of enlargement or reduction of a piece of art to fit the space specified on a page.

publication window The image that appears on the screen when a document is open, which in PageMaker includes one or two pages, the title bar, page icons, and—if displayed—rulers, scroll bars, toolbox, and palettes.

pull quote See *breakout*.

ragged right Text alignment that is even or flush on the left margin and uneven on the right.

RAM An acronymn for "Random Access Memory." This is where the computer stores information temporarily while you're working with it. If you lose power or shut down before saving to disk, whatever is in RAM at the time is lost.

recto The right-hand page.

registration The alignment of two of more elements, such as a color tone within a box, so that they appear seamless.

resolution The clarity or fineness of detail visible on-screen or in the final printout, expressed as dots per inch. In printed material, the resolution is dependent on the printer's capacity, which in the current desktop technology ranges from 300 dots per inch in most laser printers to 2540 dpi in Linotronic 300 imagesetters.

reverse White letters or rules against a black or color background.

Revert A sort of "multiple undo" command on PageMaker's File menu that lets you return to the last saved version of your document.

Roman-style typefaces Typefaces with serifs.

roman type Vertical-style type, as opposed to italic or oblique. In Page-Maker's type style options, roman type is called Normal; in some word-processing programs, it is called Plain.

rounded-corner tool The PageMaker tool used to draw squares and rectangles with rounded corners. Various corner styles are available through the Rounded Corners command on the Options menu.

ruler guide A nonprinting dotted rule used to determine the alignment of text or graphics on the page. You drag guides in from either the vertical or the horizontal ruler, and they function as extensions of the tick marks on the ruler.

rules Lines in typography, measured in points.

runaround text See *wraparound text*.

running foot A line at the bottom of the page with information similar to that in a running head.

running head A line at the top of the page that helps orient the reader within a document, which may include such information as title, author, chapter, issue date, and page number.

running text See *body text*.

sans serif A typeface without finishing strokes at the ends of the characters. (From the French *sans*, meaning "without.")

scale To calculate the degree of enlargement or reduction of a graphic so that it fits the space allotted for it. A proportion wheel is often used to scale art. You can scale pages when printing by specifying a percentage in the Scaling option in PageMaker's Print dialog box.

scanner A hardware device that reads information from a photograph or other piece of art into a collection of dots that can be stored as a bit-mapped file on a hard disk, manipulated in various software programs, and placed electronically in a page layout program.

Scrapbook A Macintosh desk accessory where you can store text and graphics to be cut and pasted into a document. Unlike the Clipboard, which stores only the most recently cut item and which is in effect erased when you shut down, the Scrapbook stores many items and is saved to disk so that the items are available each time you turn on the computer.

screen A tint, a percentage of either black or a second color, behind text or art. Also called a tone.

screen dump A bit-mapped image of the screen, created on a Macintosh by pressing Command-Shift-3.

screen font The character set that is displayed on-screen as pixels and that calls up the respective printer font when you print a publication.

script Typefaces that simulate handwriting.

scroll bars The gray bars on the right and bottom sides of a publication window used to move horizontally or vertically around the page. PageMaker's Styles and Colors palettes also have scroll bars.

select To indicate where the next action will take place by clicking the pointer on text or graphics or by dragging the cursor across the text..

selection box A box drawn by dragging the pointer tool to enclose and select more than one graphic or text block at a time, so that the material can be copied, cut, or moved as a unit. An item must be completely within the selection box in order to be selected, which for text means that the window-shade handles, not visible when you draw the selection box, must be within the box. Also called a marquee.

self-mailer A printed piece designed to be mailed without an envelope. The area for the mailing label and postal indicia, if there are any, must be designed in accordance with postage regulations.

semi-automatic text flow A mode of placing text in PageMaker in which the text flow stops at the end of a column; the text icon is automatically re-loaded and begins flowing text when you click it into position. You invoke the semi-automatic mode by holding down the Shift key with either the Autoflow or the manual flow selected. See also *Autoflow* and *manual text flow*.

serif A line or curve projecting from the end of a letter form. Typefaces with these additional strokes are called serif faces.

set solid Type set without any leading between lines, specified, for example, as 14/14.

shade In PageMaker, a tone or a pattern chosen from the Shades menu and used to fill a graphic, such as a banner.

show through Printing on one side of the paper that can be seen on the other; commonly found in cheaper quality paper stock.

TIP

To speed up printing when you want to proofread text and don't need to see graphics, click on the Proof Print option in the Print dialog box. PageMaker will print the text as usual and replace each graphic with a large X. (Not available in PC PageMaker.)

TIP

If you have trouble selecting an item on the page or setting an insertion point with the text tool, choose the Select All command. This will reveal the handles around every text block and graphic on the page and enable you to spot where overly long windowshade handles or "invisibles" (such as reverse type and white masking boxes that you've lost) may be creating problems.

sidebar A smaller, self-contained story inside a larger one, usually boxed with its own headline to set it apart from the main text.

silhouette A photograph from which background image has been removed, outlining a subject or group of subjects.

single-sided Refers to publications printed on only one side of the paper. When you click off the Double-sided option in PageMaker's Page Setup dialog box, PageMaker assumes your publication is single-sided and displays only one page at a time and only one master page icon. (The word single-sided does not appear in the dialog box.) See also *Double-sided*.

small caps Capital letters that are smaller than the standard uppercase characters for that typeface and size. In PageMaker, small caps are 70% of the standard cap height and can be specified as the Case in the Type Specifications options.

Snap To Guides A command on PageMaker's Options menu that causes text and graphics being moved or placed to snap to the nearest ruler guide.

Snap To Rulers A command on PageMaker's Options menu that causes ruler guides, text, and graphics being moved or placed to snap to the nearest ruler tick mark.

spacing guide A rectangle sized to match a distance you need to measure frequently in a given publication, such as the space between headlines and text or pictures and captions.

spread Two facing pages in a publication.

square-corner tool The PageMaker tool used to create squares and rectangles.

stacking order The order in which text and graphics overlap on-screen in a PageMaker file. The order can be manipulated through the Bring to Front and Send to Back commands on the Edit menu.

standoff The distance between a graphic and the graphic boundary, defined in PageMaker's Text Wrap dialog box. See also *graphic boundary*.

stick-up cap An enlarged initial letter extending above the body text; used as a graphic element to draw attention to the beginning of a story, chapter, or section.

stripping The assembling of all photographic negatives or positives necessary to create a printing plate of the entire page. Halftones and color separations are often stripped into the film created from an electronically assembled page.

style This word has a multitude of meanings in electronic publishing. On PageMaker's Type menu, style refers to weight, slant, and certain special typographic effects such as outline, shadow, or reverse. It also refers to a group of typographic attributes specified in the Define Styles command that can be applied to selected text by clicking on the appropriate name in the Styles palette. Traditionally, style refers to the broad characteristics of a typeface (such as serif or sans serif.)

Style Palette A list of styles defined for a publication, which you can leave on-screen by selecting the Style Palette command on the Options menu.

surprint To print one image over another, such as type over a graphic.

tabloid A large-format publication, usually half the size of a standard newspaper.

target printer The printer on which the final output will be printed.

TIP

If you frequently turn the Snap To commands on and off, remember these keyboard shortcuts.

Snap to	Macintosh	PC
Guides	Command-U	Ctrl-U
Rulers	Command-Y	Ctrl-Y

TIP

You can copy a style sheet from one PageMaker document to another. Choose Define Styles from the Type menu, click on Copy, and scroll through your directories to find the filename with the styles you want to copy. (You can only copy an entire style sheet, not selected styles from it.) To create a customized style sheet as the application default, follow this same procedure when there is no publication open and PageMaker is active.

TIP

To move to the next page or spread, press Command-Tab (Ctrl-Tab on a PC). To move to the previous page or spread, press Command-Shift-Tab (Ctrl-Shift-Tab on a PC).

template An electronic prototype of a publication that provides the layout grid and style sheets for similar publications. PageMaker 3.0 comes with a library of templates for business documents. You can make your own templates by creating the prototype and selecting the Template option in the Save dialog box.

text block In PageMaker, text (varying in amount) that, when selected, is bound by two windowshade handles with loops at the top and bottom.

text tool The tool used in PageMaker to select text for editing and changing type specifications. When the text tool is selected, the pointer looks like an I-beam.

Text Wrap The command on PageMaker's Options menu that enables you to specify the relationship of text to graphics. Text can wrap around a graphic, flow through a graphic, or jump over a graphic.

thin space A fixed space half the width of an en space, inserted by pressing Command-Shift-T (Ctrl-Shift-T on a PC). See also *em space, en space,* and *fixed space.*

threaded text Text placed or typed as a single file, connected in Page-Maker's memory from one column to the next and from one page to the next. When you cut, add, or move copy in a threaded text file, PageMaker automatically adjusts subsequent text across as many pages as needed to maintain the link between all the text blocks in the threaded file. The beginning of a threaded text file is identified by an open loop in the top windowshade handle; the end is identified by a # symbol in the bottom windowshade handle. All text blocks between the first and the last text blocks in a threaded file are identified by a + symbol in the top and bottom windowshade handles.

thumbnails Rough sketches of a page design. Also miniature pages that you can print by selecting the Thumbnails option in the Print dialog box. (Available only on PostScript printers.)

TIP

To print a page larger than the size of the paper that your printer handles, select the Tile option in the Print dialog box. The page will be printed in sections, or tiles, on individual sheets of paper, which you paste together manually. If you select the manual mode, the tiles are printed one at time; you control the divisions by resetting the zero point to the upper left corner of each tile. In the Auto mode, Page-Maker divides the page with the amount of overlap that you specify. For oversize documents, you can also reduce the page when printing by specifying a value, such as 90% or 75%, through the Scaling option in the Print dialog box.

tick marks Marks on rulers showing the increments of measure. The larger the page view in PageMaker, the finer the increments on the ruler.

TIFF files Short for "Tag Image File Format," a format for electronically storing and transmitting bit-mapped, gray-scale, and color images. Used especially for scanned images.

Tile An option in PageMaker's Print dialog box that enables you to print oversize pages in sections, or tiles. Each section is printed on a single sheet of paper; then the various tiles are pasted together to form a complete page.

tint A percentage of black or a color.

tone See *tint.*

Toolbox A small window containing PageMaker's text and graphic tools.

top of text block The horizontal coordinate at the top of the first line of text in a text block. In PageMaker, when you place text you align the loaded text icon with the horizontal ruler guide that marks the top of the text block.

trim In PageMaker, the page size defined in the Page Setup dialog box. In commercial printing, the size of the page after it is cut during the binding process.

verso The left-hand page.

vignette A graphic in which the background fades gradually until it blends with the unprinted paper.

TIP

If you are unable to move a text block, even though you see the four-way directional arrow when you select and drag, you may have extremely long windowshade handles that are being blocked by the edge of the pasteboard. Similarly, when you use the Select All command and are unable to move selected items as far in one direction as you'd like, there's probably something on the pasteboard blocking the movement. In either case, move to a global view (press the Shift key and select Fit in Window) to see the entire pasteboard so you can shorten the handles or move the obstructing item.

weight The density of letters, traditionally described as light, regular, bold, extra bold, and so on.

white space The areas of the page without text or graphics; used as a deliberate element in good graphic design.

widow A short last line of a paragraph, especially troublesome when it is isolated at the top or bottom of a page or column or when it appears in a caption.

width The horizontal measure of letters, described as condensed, normal, or expanded.

windowshade handles The horizontal lines with loops in the center and square dots on either end that appear at the top and bottom of a selected text block.

word spacing The amount of space between words. In PageMaker, you can control the word spacing through the Spacing command on the Type menu.

wraparound text Text that wraps around a graphic. Also called runaround text. See also *Text Wrap.*

WYSIWYG An acronym for "What You See Is What You Get." Pronounced wizzy-wig, it refers to the representation on a computer screen of text and graphic elements as they will look on the printed page.

x-height The height of the main body of a lowercase letter, excluding ascenders or descenders.

zero point The point at which the 0 on the horizontal ruler intersects with the 0 on the vertical ruler.

INDEX

CREDITS

The sample documents reproduced throughout this book are reprinted by permission.

Chapter 1

No Crack poster, copyright © Do It Now Foundation 1987-88; AIGA Media and Technology insert, copyright © AIGA Boston 1986; *War and Peace in The Nuclear Age*, copyright © WGBH Educational Foundation 1988; *Leadership*, copyright © Weisz Yang Dunkelberger Inc. 1987

Chapter 3

Radon manual, copyright © 1988; GTech brochure, copyright © GTech Corporation 1988; Image Set Services, copyright © Image-Set Design 1988; Giraffe Project acknowledgment, copyright © Scot Louis Gaznier 1988; *The Numbers News*, copyright © American Demographics 1988; *Hardwood Herald*, copyright © Hardwood Manufacturers Association 1988; Kidney Foundation annual report, by permission of The National Kidney Foundation of Maryland; *The Wildman Herald*, copyright © 1988; Solebury School newsletter, copyright © Scot Louis Gaznier 1988; Academic Press listings, copyright © Academic Press, Inc. 1988; Statement of Purpose, copyright © Do It Now Foundation 1987-88; *Newservice*, copyright © Do It Now Foundation 1987; *Dateline!*, copyright © GTech Corporation 1988; *TeleVisual Market Strategies*, copyright © Telecommunications Productivity Center 1986; Medic Alert annual report, copyright © Tom Lewis, Inc. 1988; Roosevelt University annual report, copyright © Roosevelt University 1986; *TeleVisual Market Strategies*, copyright © Telecommunications Productivity Center 1986; *Verbum*, copyright © Donovan Gosney Inc. 87/88; *A Guide to Better Signs*, copyright © Communications Design Group 1986; *Worldnet*, by permission of the United States Information Agency; GTE folder, copyright © Weisz Yang Dunkelberger Inc. 1987-88; *Communique*, copyright © Kate Dore, Dore Davis Design 1987; *FLASH*, copyright © Nautilus Books, Inc. 1988; Superlearning catalog, copyright © Barbara Lee/Folio Consulting 1988; *Signal*, copyright © Point Foundation 1988; *Longevity*, copyright © Omni Publications International Ltd. 1988

Chapter 4

The Voter's Guidebook, copyright © New York City Charter Revision Commission 1988

Chapter 5

Midwives Benefit flyer, copyright © John Odam 1988; Student Recital flyer, copyright © Diane Landskroener 1988; Holiday Sale flyer, copyright © Lisa Marks-Ellis 1988; Brown Bag Lunch flyer, copyright © WGBH Educational Foundation 1986; A Walk In Woods flyer, copyright © John Odam 1988; April–Eric poster, copyright © AIGA/Boston 1988; How to Design A Page, copyright © John M. McWade, PageLab 1988; World Trade Institute program, copyright © Communications Design Group 1988; Slide Zone folder, copyright © Weisz Yang Dunkelberger Inc. 1987-88; Drugs & Alcohol folder, copyright © Do It Now Foundation 1987-88; Transpac folder, copyright © Transamerica Corporation; Colligan's Stocton Inn folder, copyright © Carla Bond Coutts 1987; The Man who Planted Trees program, copyright © SMITH & HAWKEN 1988; Infractions folder, copyright © Infractions 1987; Family Programs, copyright © The Art Institute of Chicago 1987; Historic Hudson Valley folder, copyright © Historic Hudson Valley 1988; *inFidelity*, copyright © Keith Yates Audio 1987-1988; Clackamas College brochure, copyright © Clackamas Community College 1988; Pitney Bowes brochure, copyright © Weisz Yang Dunkelberger Inc. 1987-88; *Westchester 2000*, copyright © Wong, Inc. 1988; Westinghouse brochure, copyright © Westinghouse Electric 1988; *Why Design?*, copyright © Watzman + Keyes Information Design 1987; European Terracotta Sculpture folder, copyright © The Art Institute Of Chicago 1987; Viva Tijuana folder, copyright © Tom

Lewis, Inc. 1988; Syracuse University Law School annual report, copyright © Lenweaver Design 1988; Seybold Exposition brochure, copyright © Weisz Yang Dunkelberger Inc. 1988; River Park folder, copyright © River Park Cooperative 1987; Subscription Programs brochure, copyright © The Art Institute Of Chicago 1988; *Islam and the West*, copyright © Foundation for Traditional Studies 1988; Sacramento Regional Foundation Yearbook, copyright © Sacramento Regional Foundation 1987; Doane Raymond brochure, by permission of Communications Design Group; Dynagraphics brochure, copyright © Dynagraphics 1988

Chapter 6

Newservice, copyright © Do It Now Foundation 1987; *Friends of Omega*, copyright © Omega Institute 1987; *Apple viewpoints*, copyright © Apple viewpoints 1988; *Preston Report*, copyright © John Odam 1988; *NOOZ*, copyright © WGBH Educational Foundation 1986; *The Wire*, copyright © Weisz Yang Dunkelberger Inc. 1988; *The Freeze Beacon*, copyright © John Odam 1987; *Consumer Markets Abroad*, copyright © American Demographics 1988; *Perspectives*, copyright © Transamerica Life Companies 1988; *Indications*, copyright © Index Group, Inc. 1988; *O'Connor Quarterly*, copyright © O'Connor Hospital 1988; *AmeriNews*, copyright © Kate Dore, Dore Davis Design 1987; *Re:*, copyright © ImageSet Design 1988; *Litigation News*, copyright © 1988 American Bar Association; *ThePage*, copyright © Page-Works 1987-88; *Washington College Magazine*, copyright © Washington College 1987-88; *Backtalk*, copyright © Texas Back Institute 1987; *American Demographics*, copyright © American Demographics 1988; *Business North Carolina*, copyright © The News and Observer Publishing Co. 1987-88; *Verbum*, copyright © Donovan Gosney Inc. 87/88; *Heartcorps*, copyright © Heart Corps, Inc. 1988; *Mother Earth News*, copyright © The Mother Earth News Partners 1989

Chapter 7

Table Specification Guide, copyright © Geiger International; the book end catalog, copyright © Lisa Menders 1987; Beverly Hills Auto catalog, copyright © Beverly Hills Motoring Accessories 1988; Concept Technical Manual, copyright © Oscar Anderson 1988; Davidson Software catalog, copyright © Julie Gibbs 1988; School of Visual Arts catalog, copyright © School of Visual Arts Press, Ltd. 1988; Clackamas College catalog, copyright © Clackamas Community College 1988; *Portland State Quarterly*, copyright © 1988; Huck Fastening Design Guide, copyright © Huck Manufacturing Company 1988; Triad Keyboard folder, copyright © Triad Systems Corporation 1987; Maxtor data sheets copyright © Maxtor Corporation 1988; Infrared Optics data sheet, copyright © Two-Six Inc. 1988; Questor Inlets data sheet, copyright © Extrel 1988; product information sheets, copyright © SMITH & HAWKEN 1988; MasterCard International 1988 Annual Report, copyright © MasterCard International 1988; College Auxiliary Services, copyright © College Auxiliary Services, SUNY New Paltz 1987; Psicor annual report, copyright © Lisa Menders 1986; Medic Alert annual report, copyright © Tom Lewis, Inc. 1988; Spencer Foundation annual report, copyright © The Spencer Foundation 1987; Traffic/Archive form, copyright © WGBH Educational Foundation 1986; Camera Billing Form, copyright © WGBH Educational Foundation 1986; Employee Information form, copyright © Geiger International; Math and the Minds Eye order form, copyright © Math Learning Center 1988; Proposal Evaluation form, copyright © Earthwatch 1987; Subscription card, copyright © American Demographics 1988; Admission form, copyright © Clackamas Community College 1988; InFractions order form, copyright © Infractions 1987

Project 6

Photograph of man at the computer, copyright ©1988 Aldus Corporation, all rights reserved. Used with permission. Aldus and PageMaker are registered trademarks of Aldus Corporation.

The manuscript for this book was prepared and submitted to Microsoft Press in electronic form. Text files were processed and formatted using Microsoft Word.

Cover design by Don Wright
Cover photograph by Walter Wick
Interior text design by Don Wright and Ronnie Shushan
Principal production art and coordination by Peggy Herman
Color separations by Wescan Color Corporation, Redmond, WA

Text composition by Don Wright and Ronnie Shushan in Palatino with display in Futura Bold Condensed Italic, using Aldus® Pagemaker® with an Apple® Macintosh® and the Linotronic 300 laser imagesetter.